London in the 1890s:
A Cultural History

ALSO BY KARL BECKSON

Arthur Symons: A Life (1987)
Henry Harland: His Life and Work (1978)

CO-AUTHOR

Arthur Symons: A Bibliography (1990), with Ian Fletcher, Lawrence W. Markert, and John Stokes
Literary Terms: A Dictionary, 3d ed. (1989), with Arthur Ganz

EDITOR

Aesthetes and Decadents of the 1890s, 2d ed. (1981)
The Memoirs of Arthur Symons: Life and Art in the 1890's (1977)
Oscar Wilde: The Critical Heritage (1970)
Great Theories in Literary Criticism (1963)

CO-EDITOR

Arthur Symons: Selected Letters, 1880–1935 (1989), with John M. Munro
Max and Will: Max Beerbohm and William Rothenstein, Their Friendship and Letters, 1893–1945 (1975), with Mary M. Lago

Max Beerbohm, "Some Persons of the 'Nineties' "; front (left to right): Arthur Symons, Henry Harland, Charles Conder, Will Rothenstein, Max Beerbohm, Aubrey Beardsley. Back (left to right): Richard Le Gallienne, Walter Sickert, George Moore, John Davidson, Oscar Wilde, W. B. Yeats, and (barely visible) "Enoch Soames." (Courtesy of Mrs. Eva Reichmann and the Ashmolean Museum, Oxford)

LONDON
in the 1890s

A CULTURAL HISTORY

Karl Beckson

W. W. NORTON & COMPANY

New York   London

The text of this book is composed in Garamond with the display set in
Egmont Bold, Egmont Medium and Florentine Cursive.
Composition and Manufacturing by the Haddon Craftsmen, Inc.
Book design by Susan Hood

Library of Congress Cataloging-in-Publication Data
Beckson, Karl E., 1926—
    London in the 1890s: a cultural history / by Karl Beckson.
       p. cm.
    Includes index.
       1. English literature—19th century—History and criticism.
    2. English literature—England—London—History and criticism.
    3. London (England)—Intellectual life—19th century. 4. Decadence
    (Literary movement)—England—London. 5. Modernism (Literature)—
    England—London. 6. Modernism (Art)—England—London. I. Title.
    PR468.D43B43 1993
    820.9'32421'09034—dc20 92-937

ISBN 0-393-03397-X

W.W. Norton & Company, Inc., 500 Fifth Avenue, New York, N.Y. 10110
W.W. Norton & Company Ltd., 10 Coptic Street, London WC1A 1PU
1 2 3 4 5 6 7 8 9 0

Contents

Illustrations

Prologue

THE ENDS OF centuries have traditionally fascinated and terrified the imagination, for the sense of an ending and an irreversible but inexorable progression to the unknown (or, for Christians, the Last Judgment) have often conjured images of final decay and lingering death. In his diary for 1889, the London publisher Grant Richards recorded that the Reverend Michael Paget Baxter, the author of books of prophecy and editor of the *Christian Herald,* "holds forth that the world comes to an end in 1901 and that in 1896 144,000 devout Christians will be taken up to Heaven." No one can be certain whether such a number of the devout were in fact introduced to Paradise in 1896, but the Reverend Mr. Baxter was not entirely wrong in his other prediction, for Queen Victoria's world did come to an end in 1901, when she expired.

While the demise of a century may encourage such apocalyptic visions, ideological collapses, and exhausted psyches, the human imagination also has the capacity to create images of renewal (based on the perception of nature's rebirth). At the end of the nineteenth century, many intellectuals, having abandoned their religious faith but inspired by utopian dreams, envisioned a new age in the next century, convinced that the past—with its failures and disappointments—was a burden to be abandoned. In 1882, the positivist philosopher and advocate for social and political reform Frederic Harrison wrote: "We *are* on the threshold of a great time, even if our time is not great itself. In science, in religion, in social organisation, we all know what great things are in the air. . . . It is *not* the age of money-bags and cant, soot, hubbub, and ugliness. It is the age of great expectation and unwearied striving after better things." In his introduction to *The New Spirit* (1890), Havelock Ellis also looked forward to a future purged of previous errors: "Certainly old things are passing away; not the old ideals only, but even the regret they leave behind is dead, and we are shaping instinctively our new ideals. . . . The old cycles are for ever renewed, and it is no paradox that he who would advance can never cling too close to the past."

For many, such optimism was fueled by scientific discovery and technological innovation. Hundreds of new inventions, such as faster railroad locomotives, ocean-going steamships, photography, and electric lighting, as well as the rapid growth of such scientific disciplines as physics, astronomy, and chemistry transformed the nineteenth-century view of the world so dramatically that, by the fin de siècle, Victorians referred to their age as "modern." In 1897, J. J. Thompson, of Cambridge University, discovered the electron (the discovery of the atom's nucleus was more than a decade away); by 1900, Gregor Mendel's work in genetics had been rediscovered, and, in the same year, Max Planck theorized that "quanta of energy were involved when light was being absorbed or emitted." In 1905, Einstein's "special theory of relativity" superseded Newton's laws of motion and gravitation as well as James Maxwell's electromagnetic theory of light, thereby making possible new concepts of time, space, and mass. In effect, Einstein established the principle that energy and mass were interconvertible, as indicated in the famous equation $E = mc^2$, the theoretical basis for later nuclear fission.

In *The Idea of Progress* (1920), J. B. Bury observed that, in the nineteenth century, "the achievements of physicial science did more than anything else to convert the imaginations of men to the general doctrine of progress." At the same time, however, many expressed pessimism and doubt, particularly after the publication of Darwin's *Origin of Species* (1859), which followed a series of scientific discoveries and evolutionary theories that undermined orthodox belief in creationism, unsettled religious faith, and ultimately resulted in emotional crises for many Christians. Earlier in the century, the frightening specter of entropy arose from the second law of thermodynamics, which contends that heat from the sun's radiation becomes progressively unusable as it becomes dispersed in the universe (so-called "heat death"). In the 1850s, Sir William Thompson (Lord Kelvin), who was instrumental in formulating the principle, concluded that "the earth must have been, and within a finite period to come, the earth must again be, unfit for the habitation of man as at present constituted."

In his first science fiction novel, *The Time Machine* (1895), H. G. Wells depicts such a bleak future when the Time Traveller travels into the "fourth dimension" and reaches the year 802,701. The humans then living on the earth are the degenerate Eloi, whose gender is indeterminate. Indulging in such trivial pursuits as singing, dancing, and adorning themselves with flowers in their earthly paradise, they exist in a condition of apparent uselessness. However, the "ape-like" Morlocks live in the subterranean depths with the remnants of human technology and feed on the Eloi. Journeying further into the future, the traveler discovers no sign of humanity; instead, the earth is inhabited by giant crabs. Thirty million years later, he finds no traces of any significant life forms; he leaves when darkness descends over the earth after an eclipse of the sun. The second law of thermodynamics has achieved its ultimate triumph.*

A further cause of pessimism in the nineteenth century was the social and psychological effect of the Industrial Revolution, which enslaved millions of workers in gloomy "sweating" industries and created cities of "dreadful night," such as Manchester, Sheffield, and Birmingham. Moreover, the so-called "Great Depression" from the early 1870s to the mid-1890s, resulting from poor harvests, declining arable land, and lower-priced imports, accelerated the migration of almost three million farm workers to the crowded cities or to colonies abroad.† London's East End contained some of the worst slums in England, where disease and despair flourished. Discouraged reformers sought desperate remedies. In his influential survey *In Darkest England and the Way Out* (1890), William Booth, founder and first general of the Salvation Army, rose to exalted rhetoric while describing the degrading living conditions of the London poor: "Talk about Dante's Hell, and all the horrors and cruelties of the torture-chamber of the lost! The man who walks with open eyes and with bleeding heart through the shambles of our civilisation needs no such fantastic images of the poet to teach him horror." Such misery also distressed the socialist and poet William Morris, who yearned for the end of a moribund, corrupt society so that a genuine "barbarism" would return to the world to destroy its false "progress":

> I have [no] more faith than a grain of mustard seed in the future history of "civilization," which I *know* now is doomed to destruction, and probably before very long: what a joy it is to think

---

*In 1904 at Cambridge University, Ernest Rutherford discovered, in such material as radium, the lasting power of radioactivity which creates heat within the earth's rocks. He wrote that "the radioactive elements, which in their disintegration liberate enormous amounts of energy, thus increase the possible limit of the duration of life on this planet. . . ." Rutherford's finding challenged the second law of thermodynamics (quotation from Timothy Ferris, *Coming of Age in the Milky Way* [New York, 1988], 249).

†The economist Alfred Marshall, testifying before the Precious Metals Commission in 1887, asserted that the industrial depression had a greater impact on businessmen than on workers. The result was "a depression of prices, a depression of interest, and a depression of profits" without "any considerable depression in any other respect." Gertrude Himmelfarb has recently written that, "among regularly employed workers, there were depressed seasons and years when unemployment rose and wages fell. . . . But these conditions, however grievous, did not add up, for the working classes as a whole, to a 'Great Depression' " (*Poverty and Compassion: The Moral Imagination of the Late Victorians* [New York, 1991], 70–71).

of! and how often it consoles me to think of barbarism once
more flooding the world, and real feelings and passions, however rudimentary, taking the place of our wretched hypocrisies. . . .

During the final decades of the century, a widespread perception that
Britain and the empire were in a state of decline found expression in the
periodicals, which published articles in profusion with titles announcing
the decline or decay of such phenomena as cricket, genius, war, classical
quotations, romance, marriage, faith, bookselling, and even canine
fidelity. There were also articles on the presumed degeneracy of the race
and the startling increase in insanity and "suicidal mania." Writers
pointed to the decline and fall of the Roman Empire as the analogy of the
anticipated fate of the British Empire, though a writer in *Nineteenth Century* (August 1894) regarded such a view as a "dismal argument," for
though the Romans were a "great nation" and "far ahead of their time,"
they were still "barbarians" compared to the modern British. The sensation of 1895, which appeared just before the even more sensational trials
of Oscar Wilde, was the English translation of Max Nordau's *Degeneration,* which attacked the unorthodox works of such figures as Ibsen, Wagner, Wilde, Nietzsche, and Tolstoy as evidence of cultural decadence.
Bernard Shaw argued that these artists were not suffering from degeneration but were indicative of the spirit of regeneration: "At every new wave
of energy in art the same alarm has been raised, and . . . these alarms
always had their public, like prophecies of the end of the world. . . ."

While many were deploring cultural degeneration and decay, others
were hailing the new, which, like Ellis's New Spirit, was an indication of
presumed liberation from the deadening hand of the past. As soon as late
Victorian cultural developments appeared, they were habitually affixed
with the "new" designation to elevate them to fashionable status and to
ward off the pervasive pessimism of the age. Such were the New Drama,
New Woman, New Journalism, New Imperialism, New Criticism, New
Hedonism, and New Paganism, which appeared in William Sharp's one
and only issue of the *Pagan Review* (August 1892), written under his
various pseudonyms. As the critic H. D. Traill asserted in *The New Fiction and Other Essays* (1897): "Not to be 'new' is, in these days, to be nothing. . . ."

Cultural trends in the final decades of the century were thus moving in
two simultaneously antithetical directions: declining Victorianism (the
synthesis of moral, religious, artistic, political, and social thought that had
produced the wealthiest and most powerful empire on earth) and rising
Modernism (with its challenges by writers and artists to the cultural foundations of Philistine society, which habitually condemned daring innova-

tions in the arts as "immoral" or "degenerate"). Such manifestations of Modernism were frequently described by both sympathetic and hostile critics as characteristic aspects of the fin de siècle. The term, adopted in Britain around 1890 to indicate the end of the century, had such associated meanings as "modern," "advanced," and "decadent." The French themselves had been using the term with increasing looseness: It served, for example, to describe both a shoemaker praised "for being a traditional cobbler rather than fin de siècle" and a blackmailer who lived off his wife's prostitution—"a fin de siècle husband." A verse at the time indicated its imprecision:

> *Fin de siècle! Everywhere*
> *. . . It stands for all that you might care*
> *To name . . .*

Some British writers employed it for its apocalyptic foreboding, as "advanced" writers delighted in uttering oracular premonitions while inspired by an exhausted century. In *The Picture of Dorian Gray* (1890/1891),* Oscar Wilde may have been one of the first in England to make use of such implications. When a dinner guest ponders the current fashion that "all the married men live like bachelors, and all the bachelors like married men," the response is characteristic:

> *"Fin de siècle,"* murmured Lord Henry.
> *"Fin du globe,"* answered his hostess.
> "I wish it were *fin du globe,*" said Dorian with a sigh. "Life is such a great disappointment."

In a letter to a Tory journalist in 1894, Wilde identified the fin de siècle with artistic achievement as opposed to cultural decadence: "All that is known by that term I particularly admire and love. It is the fine flower of our civilisation: the only thing that keeps the world from the commonplace, the coarse, the barbarous."

In John Davidson's comic novel, *A Full and True Account of the Wonderful Mission of Earl Lavender* (1895), a poem precedes the narrative involving Lavender's "mission" to spread the gospel of the "survival of the fittest" in a plot including sexual perversity (a Beardsley drawing for the frontispiece depicts a woman flagellating a figure of indeterminate gender):

---

*Two dates following the title of a work indicate its initial appearance, either in part or whole, in a periodical and its subsequent publication as a book; in the case of a play, the single date indicates its first production or first publication, whichever came first.

Though our thoughts turn ever Doomwards,
Though our sun is well-night set,
Though our Century totters tombwards,
    We may laugh a little yet.

Later in the novel, a matronly Victorian woman evokes, in fractured French, her equivalent of fin de siècle to explain the chaos of modern life: "It's *fang-de-seeaycle* that does it, my dear, and education, and reading French."

The French were indeed the object of suspicion by the British, who regarded their neighbors across the Channel as potential invaders, either by sea or through a proposed tunnel connecting the two. Far worse to those who objected to subversive influences, however, was the invasion of French literature and critical attitudes, especially Zola's Naturalistic novels, often called "decadent" by British critics, as well as the tradition of an amoral *l'art pour l'art* and fin-de-siècle Decadence, which impelled Tennyson to fulminate in verse against the "troughs of Zolaism" and against those Aesthetes who had objected to the moral teaching in the *Idylls of the King* (1869):

Art for Art's sake! Hail, truest Lord of Hell!
Hail Genius, Master of the Moral Will!
"The filthiest all of paintings painted well
Is mightier than the purest painted ill!"

To Tennyson, the doctrine of "art for art's sake" disregarded the "ideal of an integrated culture." The poet and critic Richard Le Gallienne (father of the actress, Eva) also judged the invasion of French Decadence as particularly grave. In the prefatory poem to his *English Poems* (1892), he echoed the title of Tennyson's early poem "The Palace of Art" (1833) in expressing his own anxiety over the fin-de-siècle separation of moral from aesthetic elements in art:

Art was a palace once, things great and fair,
And strong and holy, found a temple there:
Now 'tis a lazar-house of leprous men.
O shall we hear an English song again!

Such anxieties as Tennyson's and Le Gallienne's were widespread at the end of the century, an indication that the earlier cultural synthesis of Victorianism was unraveling as such common beliefs and assumptions concerning social relationships, the nature of reality, and the nature of art were subjected to attack by such groups as the New Women, the New

Dramatists, the New Hedonists, the New Naturalists, as well as the Aesthetes and Decadents.

FOR MANY DECADES, the 1890s have been casually disposed of as the Yellow Nineties, suggestive of decay, principally because of the famous periodical, the *Yellow Book* (1894–1897), and because of a relatively small but articulate band of writers, Wilde included, who proclaimed "art for art's sake." The decade has also been called the "Decadent Nineties" or the "Naughty Nineties." But whatever those terms may mean, the fin de siècle embraced such a wide variety of literary and artistic modes of expression, including Impressionism, Aestheticism, Decadence, Naturalism, and Symbolism, that reducing the late nineteenth century to one of them and branding it "decadent" merely because it was anti-Establishment is to inflict simplicity on complexity. The decade of the nineties was an extraordinary period of artistic activity and energy, many of the greatest figures of the twentieth century, such as Shaw, Yeats, Conrad, and Wells, in their apprenticeship years while older figures, such as Whistler, Wilde, Morris, and Hardy had completed—or were in the process of completing—their major work.

Many moved freely from one mode of expression or group to another as inclination dictated. Wilde wrote an essay still widely read, "The Soul of Man under Socialism" (1891/1895), which fused Aestheticism and anarchist socialism in an attempt to locate beauty and freedom for the artist within a radically new economic and political system. Yeats's aesthetically conceived Celtic poems, such as "A Man Who Dreamed of Fairyland" (the title changed slightly in subsequent printings), were published in W. E. Henley's *National Observer,* a periodical devoted to activist, anti-Decadent causes. Henley nevertheless regarded Yeats the dreamer as one of his "young men." In the late 1880s, Yeats was also a member of Morris's circle at the Socialist League, a short-lived association that ended when the younger man discovered that Morris's literary "dream world . . . knew nothing of intellectual suffering." Shaw, contributed to the first number of the *Savoy* (January 1896), the Symbolist/Decadent periodical that contained much of Beardsley's most daring literary and artistic work, an odd setting for a socialist who publicly expressed scorn for "art for art's sake."

This cultural history focuses on the legendary decade of the 1890s, more a symbol than a mere ten years of the calendar, for an entire age was simultaneously coming to an end as another was in the process of formation. London, also this history's principal focus, is here treated as the heart of the empire as well as the artistic and cultural heart of Britain. Between 1851 and 1901, the area of present-day Greater London had grown from

2.7 million people to 6.6 million, a progressive urbanization that concentrated artistic talent and cultural ferment more densely than in any other British city. As Malcolm Bradbury has shown, London became one of the major "cities of Modernism," closely associated in this international movement with Paris, Berlin, and Vienna. Writers and artists inevitably gravitated to London—as did Yeats, Wilde, and Shaw from Ireland and Henry James, Whistler, and Sargent from America, as well as countless others from provincial British cities. A *Yellow Book* contributor recalled that each was hoping that he might ride "on the crest of the wave that was sweeping away the Victorian tradition" with its undue restrictions in artistic expression based on an outdated conception of the world as one of stable, absolute values. As Modernism developed, the arts sought new forms of personal expression, the new aesthetic values replacing the formerly prescribed moral values of Victorian art.

Pater might have described London as "the focus where the greatest number of vital forces unite[d] in their purest energy." Down from Oxford, the young but "perpetually old" Max Beerbohm luxuriated in such energy despite his dandiacal pose of feigned indifference: "Around me seethed swirls, eddies, torrents, violent cross-currents of human activity. What uproar! Surely I could have no part in modern life." Henry James called London "the biggest aggregation of human life—the most complete compendium of the world." As a constant subject for verse in the nineties, the city assumed the aura of Romantic artifice with its "iron lilies of the Strand" in Richard Le Gallienne's "A Ballad of London": "Ah, London! London! our delight, / Great flower that opens but at night. . . ." The nights of London, when the city became a ghostly apparition in the faint evening light as imagination transformed warehouses into palaces, inspired Whistler's "nocturnes." And Arthur Symons envisioned a magical London in which two lovers, dancer and poet, are entwined in each other's dreams, oblivious to the industrialism, poverty, and despair of the city:

> You the dancer and I the dreamer,
> Children together,
> Wandering lost in the night of London,
> In the miraculous April weather.

Such an aesthetic vision, however, was an escape into romantic fantasy that rejected the world of sordid fact, one that jolted fin-de-siècle reformers and radicals to envision their own dreams of social and political action.

London in the 1890s:

A Cultural History

1

Socialist Utopias and Anarchist Bombs

IN THE LAST decades of the nineteenth century, London abounded with societies and fellowships endlessly debating and planning literary, social, and political change. Utopian schemes flourished, for their idealized visions of perfect worlds provided political goals for those at odds with society's imperfections. During the 1880s and 1890s, many socialists and others with anti-Establishment attitudes urgently felt the need for such utopian alternatives to the status quo, for Britain's economic health was in jeopardy: Its position in world trade, seriously threatened by such competitors as Germany and the United States, was no longer preeminent; industrial decline resulted in large-scale unemployment, particularly in the most populated cities. Moreover, adverse climatic conditions and the importation of inexpensive grain from the United States prolonged an agricultural depression that had begun in the early 1870s.

To make matters worse, William Gladstone, who became the Liberal prime minister in 1880, did little to institute significant economic reforms; instead, he became involved in political and military entanglements in the Middle East, particularly in Afghanistan, where Gladstone reversed the policy of his predecessor, Disraeli, who had divided the country into spheres of influence. In South Africa, Gladstone believed that federation of the colonies was the solution to territorial demands for independence, then changed his mind when the Boers rebelled. In Ireland, he became embroiled in attempts to repress the Irish nationalist movement by stringent police action. Closer to home, one-third of the population in London was living in squalid, unhealthy conditions, sometimes six or more to a room, and women and children were working in "sweating" industries from fourteen to sixteen hours a day for a few shillings.

Though general living and working conditions of the very poor had improved since Queen Victoria's accession to the throne in 1837, the

British were now more aware and consequently more disturbed by the widespread poverty, particularly in the industrialized cities. In his *Problems of Poverty: An Inquiry into the Industrial Condition of the Poor* (1891), the radical economist J. A. Hobson accounted for such an apparently renewed preoccupation:

> If by poverty is meant the difference between felt wants and the power to satisfy them, there is more poverty than ever. The income of the poor has grown, but their desires and needs have grown more rapidly. Hence, the growth of a conscious class hatred, the "growing animosity of the poor against the rich," as [Rev. Samuel] Barnett notes in the slums of Whitechapel. The poor were once too stupid and too sodden for vigorous discontent, now though their poverty may be less intense, it is more alive, and more militant. The rate of improvement in the condition of the poor is not quick enough to stem the current of popular discontent.

With the apparent failure of existing institutions to ameliorate such conditions, many turned to the utopian dream of socialism. In the late nineteenth century, the most significant socialist visionaries were those in the Fabian Society. Intent on bringing about social progress through evolutionary means, the Fabians were not a political party, and since they were not bound by the pressures of political expediency, they incorporated into their ranks the entire spectrum of social reformers determined to keep the spirit of Victorian idealism alive. In the early 1880s, many of those who formed the Fabian Society had been members of the Fellowship of the New Life, a small discussion group founded in Chelsea by the Scottish philosopher Thomas Davidson, "the wandering scholar" who came to London in 1882 after traveling about the world and founding a similar group in New York. The fellowship consisted of bourgeois intellectuals: civil service clerks, disaffected provincials, a medical student (Havelock Ellis), a few "emancipated" women, such as Edith Lees (Ellis's future wife) and Olive Schreiner (the South African author of the widely acclaimed novel *The Story of an African Farm*, 1883), and Edward Carpenter, a socialist who sought to combine the "simplified life" of Thoreau with the homoerotic impulse of Whitman.

The fellowship discussed such topics as radical politics, economic solutions to the problems of an unjust society, and psychic phenomena. They believed that social reforms could be implemented through individual moral perfection. Like many other such groups at the time, the fellowship sought psychological and spiritual sustenance—a faith without a theology—as a bulwark against scientific developments that had progressively destabilized their Christian faith. Wishing to affirm spiritual values, the fellowship emerged with divided aims: Some urged the establishment of a utopian society in southern California or in South America; others supported political beliefs that would transform the world. The fellowship foundered since some of its members, regarded as socialist "agitators," created divisions within the group. Later, Bernard Shaw, who had attended some meetings, recalled: "Certain members of that circle, modestly feeling that the revolution would have to wait an unreasonably long time if postponed until they personally had attained perfection, set up the banner of Socialism militant. . . ."

In January 1884, nine fellowship members agreed to establish the Fabian Society. Frank Podmore, its first secretary, named the society after the Roman general who, he believed, was Hannibal's adversary. The title page of its modest four-page tract, *Why Are the Many Poor?,* provided an alleged historical source of the society's name: "For the right moment you must wait, as Fabius did most patiently when warring against Hannibal, though many censured his delays; but when the time comes you must strike hard, as Fabius did, or your waiting will be in vain, and fruitless."* The society attracted such intellectuals as Ramsay MacDonald (a fellowship member, later prime minister); Annie Besant (successively, an evangelist, atheist, evolutionist, socialist, and finally, as a theosophist, Madame Blavatsky's biographer); Hubert Bland (formerly of the fellowship, a journalist, who was in the chair at the founding meeting of the society); Edith Nesbit (his wife, who achieved fame for her children's stories); Sidney Webb (polemicist and activist in socialist causes); and later, Beatrice Potter.

BEATRICE POTTER, AMONG the most extraordinary women of her time and one who, like other upper middle-class figures, was drawn to the reformist ideals that moved the age, grew up in an affluent home visited by such figures as Herbert Spencer and T. H. Huxley, who were friends of her wealthy capitalist father. Her increasing doubt about her religious faith turned her to the positivism of Auguste Comte, whose Religion of Humanity provided her with a scientific approach to human problems. She subsequently wrote that her spiritual crisis resulted in "the flight of emotion away from the service of God to the service of man." (Indeed, many of the Fabians were deeply affected by the evangelistic fervor that expressed itself in positivistic thinking.) She later wrote that, in the late

---

*It was Scipio Africanus Major, however, not Fabius who defeated Hannibal in the Punic Wars. When no one could identify the source of the quotation, the society was deadlocked in a tie vote to remove the motto, which remained on the pamphlet.

nineteenth century, many "men of intellect and men of property," under-going a crisis of conscience and embarking on sacred missions to save the world, became Marxists, anarchists, or radicals in reaction to "a new consciousness of sin." This new consciousness was not, however, of "personal sin" but of a "collective or class consciousness, a growing uneasiness, amounting to conviction, that the industrial organisation, which had yielded rent, interest and profits on a stupendous scale, had failed to provide a decent livelihood and tolerable conditions for a majority of the inhabitants of Great Britain."

In the mid-1880s, she embarked on an investigation of the deplorable conditions among female workers in the tailoring trade of the East End. The data she gathered while posing as a seamstress became part of a chapter in the first volume of the *Life and Labour of the People in London* (1889) by Charles Booth, whose wife was Beatrice's cousin. Booth, born of a prosperous family, had become rich in a Liverpool shipping concern jointly owned with his brother; in the early 1880s, after he opened a branch of the firm in London, he was impelled by his liberal, Nonconformist background to explore the lives of the poor, using scientific procedures he had learned as a member of the Royal Statistical Society of which he was later president. For the next seventeen years, with the help of many assistants, he published seventeen volumes on the subject.

For the first volume, he focused on the notorious East End of London

Beatrice Potter (Webb)

with its diseased, vermin-infested, and overcrowded tenements, its filthy, unpaved streets with prostitutes openly soliciting and drunkards painfully evident, its criminals waiting for victims in dark courts and alleys. In 1888, the East End was also the setting of five brutal murders, most of the victims prostitutes disembowelled by Jack the Ripper. Earlier, when Booth was planning his survey, he had condemned a report allegedly prepared by the Social Democratic Federation, headed by the wealthy radical socialist Henry Myers Hyndman, as having "grossly overstated the case" that a million Londoners, more than one-fourth of the population, were living in "great poverty."* To his shock, he later discovered that such a figure *underestimated* the number of the poor. In the East End, it was more than one-third. In further studies, Booth found that the poor were by no means concentrated in the East End but were to be found throughout the city, many scattered through middle-class and upper middle-class areas. In the city as a whole in the late 1880s, the number of the poor amounted to nearly two million people, slightly less than one-third of the population.

In addition to providing material on female workers in the tailoring trade for a section of Booth's first volume, Potter contributed an entire chapter on the Jews in the East End, those who had emigrated from Eastern Europe in the 1880s. Their presence had added tension to the area, for they represented further competition for the few jobs and scarce housing; indeed, there were occasional riots against them, and anti-Semitism generated fears that Jack the Ripper was himself a Jew. Potter's chapter reveals a novelist's gift for description and narration, such as her account of the ending of an orthodox synogogue service: "At last you step out, stifled by the heat and dazed by the strange contrast of the old-world memories of a majestic religion and the squalid vulgarity of an East End slum." To give the reader a sense of the immigrant experience, she imagines a ship from Hamburg steaming up the Thames with a crowd of Jews and depicts the chaos when they land at the pier and the victimization, in many instances, that the immigrants face. Clearly, the literary quality of this chapter raises it above that of Booth's and his assistants' generally stolid prose (Booth wrote about half of the seventeen volumes).

Having completed her work for Booth, Potter began a study of the

---

*As Gertrude Himmelfarb has pointed out, Hyndman's *The Record of an Adventurous Life* (1911) has confused historians by its unreliability. The report on the London poor was, in fact, published in a series of articles in February and March of 1886 in the *Pall Mall Gazette,* which undertook to "test" Hyndman's assertion that there was "terrible distress" throughout London (see the introductory article, "The Truth about the Distress," *Pall Mall Gazette,* February 24, 1886, 1). See, also, Himmelfarb's *Poverty and Compassion: The Moral Imagination of the Late Victorians* (New York, 1991) 90–91.

early history of the English cooperatives. For assistance, she sought the advice of a noted authority on the subject, Sidney Webb, who had known of her contributions to Booth's study. Soon after they met in January 1890, he was in love with her (she was thirty-two, he thirty-one). She found in Webb a kindred spirit in his earnest exploration of ideas and in his devotion to details. A clerk in the Colonial Office, he was a startling contrast to the cultured men that Beatrice had known: His cockney speech and manners disconcerted her, but his brilliance in presenting the socialist vision of a more equitable society entranced her. She had found the means of self-fulfillment.

When, however, word of her intended marriage to Webb reached her friends, they were shocked: Herbert Spencer retracted his wish to make her his literary executor, and Charles Booth, antisocialist despite his recognition that social reforms were essential to alleviate the misery of the poor, resolved not to see her. Her marriage in 1892 "to an undersized, underbred, and 'unendowed' little socialist," the "occasion for the final severance," she said, ended her friendship with the Booths, an estrangement that, despite sporadic meetings, lasted for many years. Her only regret was the loss of her name, as she noted in her diary: "Exit Beatrice Potter. Enter Beatrice Webb, or rather (Mrs) Sidney Webb for I lose alas!

Sidney Webb

G. Bernard Shaw

both names." In the 1890s, the Webbs collaborated on such works as *The History of Trade Unionism* (1894) and *Industrial Democracy* (1897).

Unlike Beatrice Webb, Bernard Shaw emerged from a lower middle-class Irish family hovering on the edge of economic disaster. After leaving Dublin for London in 1876, he pursued a course of self-education at the British Museum and attended various meetings devoted to social and political questions. In 1882, having heard the American economist Henry George speak on how idle landlords were profiting from collectively produced wealth, Shaw embraced socialism, then read Marx's *Das Kapital* in French: "Marx was a revelation. . . . He opened my eyes to the facts of history and civilization, gave me an entirely fresh conception of the universe, provided me with a purpose and a mission in life." Inspired also by the art critic John Ruskin and "our one acknowledged Great Man," William Morris—socialist, poet, artist, designer of furniture, wallpaper, and printed books—Shaw became an entertainer with an ulterior purpose: Art, in the service of socialism, could transform the world by eliminating human misery, restoring joy, and making life aesthetically pleasing. He praised Ruskin and Morris as "aristocrats with a developed sense of life" whose aestheticism was socially and morally grounded:

> They are not content with handsome houses: they want handsome cities. They are not content with bediamonded wives and blooming daughters: they complain because the charwoman is badly dressed, because the laundress smells of gin, because the sempstress is anemic. . . . They turn up their noses at their neighbor's drains, and are made ill by the architecture of their neighbor's houses. . . . The very air is not good enough for them; there is too much factory smoke in it. They even demand abstract conditions: justice, honor, a noble moral atmosphere, a mystic nexus to replace the cash nexus.

Morris, who had founded Morris, Marshall, Faulkner & Co. as "Fine Arts Workmen in Painting, Carving, Furniture, and the Metals," and in the early 1870s reincorporated it under his sole ownership as Morris & Co., was a capitalist entrepreneur with socialist convictions. As an enlightened member of a class dependent on the labor of others, he provided his workmen with profit-sharing, flexible hours, and a pleasant environment. In 1881, Morris moved his firm from crowded quarters in Bloomsbury to

William Morris (The Pierpont Morgan Library)

Merton Abbey on the banks of the Wandle River, seven miles south of London, where, in a landscape of willows and poplars, he established an ideal setting for the workplace as described in his essay "A Factory as It Might Be" (1884): "buildings . . . beautiful with their own beauty of simplicity as workshops"; "work . . . useful, and therefore honourable and honoured"; "machines . . . used when necessary . . . to save human labour"; and "no work which would turn men into mere machines."

WHEN HE WAS twenty-seven, Shaw was invited to attend a Fabian meeting by the treasurer, Hubert Bland, who had sent him a copy of the the society's first pamphlet, *Why Are the Many Poor?*. In that year—1884—he was an odd, red-bearded figure whose shabbiness gave him the appearance, an associate said, of a respectable plasterer. The witty Shaw, having overcome his timidity by constant debating at literary and political meetings, regarded himself as "an incorrigible histrionic mountebank, and Webb [as] the simplest of geniuses": "I was often in the centre of the stage whilst he was invisible in the prompter's box." Indeed, in the late 1880s and early 1890s, Webb wrote over twenty pamphlets published by the society in which basic doctrines of progressive municipal socialism were laid out, a piecemeal plan whereby local councils would not only own farms and factories but also provide aid to the unemployed and the aged. In addition, councils would be responsible for all public facilities, including transport and libraries. Early in their association, Shaw encouraged Webb to read Marx's *Das Kapital,* but later Shaw remarked that Webb, already "saturated" with the utilitarian philosophy of John Stuart Mill, was "a ready-made Socialist, and had nothing to learn from Marx theoretically or from me."

The society now consisted of a reasonably homogeneous membership—there was, after all, basic agreement that socialism was the best means of establishing a just society—but disagreements as to a precise agenda were as numerous as they had been in the fellowship. For the first year or two, said Shaw, the Fabians, made up of the "middle-class intelligentsia," were as anarchistic and insurrectionary as those in William Morris's Socialist League and in Henry Hyndman's Social Democratic Federation, two proletarian organizations. Shaw and the Webbs were instrumental in moving the society in the direction of a policy of evolutionary social change. Of such a strategy, Shaw wrote:

> A party informed at all points by men of gentle habits and trained reasoning powers may achieve a complete Revolution without a single act of violence. A mob of desperate sufferers abandoned by the leadership of exasperated sentimentalists and

fanatic theorists may, at vast cost of bloodshed and misery, succeed in removing no single evil, except perhaps the extinction
of the human race.

The insurrectionary Hyndman ("thoroughly bourgeois in manners and
appearance but extreme in his utterances") subscribed to the Marxist
notion of class warfare, and William Morris ("an arresting figure, usually
dressed in a blue serge sailor-cut suit which made him look like the purser
of a Dutch brig"), at first a member of Hyndman's Social Democratic
Federation, had no faith in parliamentary reform and harbored visions of
revolution. Shaw and the Webbs repudiated such impossible dreams.
Wrote Shaw: "Demolishing a Bastille with seven prisoners in it is one
thing: demolishing one with fourteen million prisoners is quite another."
The major social conflict, he said, was not between capitalists and workers, but between all workers and socialists, regardless of class, and the
unproductive idlers, such as those in the aristocracy.

Though many Fabians were also members of the federation and other
socialist groups, membership in the society "was presented as a rare and
difficult privilege of superior persons," the name of the society itself obviously chosen by "classically educated men." Indeed, in 1884, there was
only one worker—a house painter—on its rolls. Nor did the society solicit membership, which in its early years came principally from the ranks
of journalists, clergy, teachers, civil servants, and university dons. The
society's elitism implied a characteristic attitude held by many nineteenth-
century bourgeois intellectuals and artists: an anti-democratic bias
prompted by fears of mob violence on the part of the ignorant, suffering
lower classes. Said Shaw, "We have never advanced the smallest preten-
sion to represent the working classes of this country." Hubert Bland,
however, believed that unity with those classes was essential to the advancement of socialism.

Candidates for election to the society needed two sponsors, and proba-
tionary attendance as guests was required. Though Shaw attended his first
meeting in May 1884, he was not formally enrolled as a member until
September. The prospectuses designed by the artist Walter Crane and the
stylish blood-red invitation cards provoked radicals in the Liberal Party to
call the Fabians "fops and armchair Socialists." Despite such ridicule, H.
G. Wells, who joined in 1902 but later fell out of favor with Shaw and the
Webbs, wrote that in the 1880s the Society, with its fewer than 100
members,* was the predominant dispenser of "Socialist propaganda" in

*By 1891, the Fabian Society had over 300 members, and groups were spreading in
London and in such cities as Manchester, Sheffield, and Birmingham, where the local
society enrolled 100 members within six months. In February 1892, the Fabians held

London. It was, Wells claimed, a society with little ideological coherence: "Some members denounced machinery as the source of all social discomfort, while others built their hopes on mechanisation as the emancipator of labour, some were nationalist and others cosmopolitan . . . some proposing to build up a society out of happy families as units and some wanting to break up the family as completely as did Plato."

In short, the two "distinct" elements in the Fabian Society were the practical and the visionary, Edith Nesbit wrote, "the first being the strongest—but a perpetual warfare goes on between the parties which gives to the Fabian an excitement which it might otherwise lack." By the expediency of establishing a broad general ideal of gradual socialist control of the means of production rather than developing specific strategies for social and political action, the society was able to maintain a reasonable degree of unity between those who accepted its evolutionary method of bringing about change and those who urged radical remedies. Webb and Shaw (as dominant members of the executive committee) were effective in holding the Fabian Society together through the 1880s and 1890s by providing the groundwork for a socialist vision of the future and by effecting conversions to its cause through persuasive argument.

BUT WHEN PERSUASIVE argument proved ineffective against the armed force of the Establishment, the shock had lasting psychological consequences. On November 13, 1887, Bloody Sunday, Shaw and Morris were in Trafalgar Square participating in a potentially dangerous demonstration organized by the Social Democratic Federation. Widespread unemployment had already resulted in violence in various cities. A shocking event had occurred on February 8, 1886, when a large number of federation members assembled in Trafalgar Square to hear inflammatory speeches by Hyndman and others while two other groups, the Labourers' League (meeting on behalf of the unskilled unemployed) and the Free Trade League (supported by protectionists and Tories) were haranguing other crowds. When fighting broke out between the groups, the small number of London police was unable to maintain order among the 15,-000 to 20,000 demonstrators. As reported in the *Times* (February 9), Social Democratic Federation marchers carrying red flags broke through police lines and passed through Pall Mall, lined with private clubs, one of

---

their first annual meeting to which half of the thirty London societies sent delegates. But with the establishment, in 1893, of the Independent Labour Party in Manchester, Fabian membership in the provincial cities (about 1,500 members in seventy-two branches) began to decline when some units of the society reorganized themselves as arms of the new party. Fabianism, however, remained a significant influence.

which had expelled Hyndman for his socialist activities. Soon, stones went flying at their windows, and in Piccadilly and adjacent streets, looting ensued. Queen Victoria reportedly described the "monstrous riot" as "a momentary triumph for socialism and a disgrace to the capital." In the *Pall Mall Gazette* (February 11), Shaw wrote that the unemployed were "as great a nuisance to socialists as to themselves. Angry as they are, they do not want a revolution: they want a job."

By the autumn of 1887, there had been almost weekly demonstrations in Trafalgar Square. On Bloody Sunday, the demonstrators (assembling to protest the arrest and treatment of an Irish M.P., William O'Brien, but also to insist on the right to free speech) approached the square in four converging columns with "drums beating and banners waving, in our tens of thousands," as Shaw later described the scene. But before reaching the square, the marchers were brutally attacked by police swinging batons while fashionable women in nearby hotels applauded and cheered. Despite the chaotic struggle, not a shot was fired by the soldiers, who, having been called in to reinforce the police when the number of demonstrators reaching the square grew alarmingly, retreated to their barracks as the crowds began to disperse by six o'clock. (However, one of the more than 100 injured demonstrators subsequently died.)

Shaw, who had questioned the wisdom of the demonstration and who had left the square in disgust at five o'clock for tea, wrote on the following day to E. T. Cook, the assistant editor of the *Pall Mall Gazette:* "I am happy to say my skull is intact." But he was critical of the demonstrators: ". . . the cowardice of the people was stupendous. Nobody asked them to stand the charges—only to run away down the side streets and get to the square one by one how they could. But ninety percent of them simply turned tail and fled. . . ." Still disturbed by the events, he wrote to Morris a week later:

> Running hardly expresses our collective action. We *skedaddled,* and never drew rein until we were safe on Hampstead Heath or thereabouts. Tarleton [H. B. Tarleton, a member of the Socialist League] found me paralysed with terror and brought me on to the Square, the police kindly letting me through in consideration of my genteel appearance. On the whole, I think it was the most abjectly disgraceful defeat ever suffered by a band of heroes outnumbering their foes a thousand to one.

For Shaw, the debacle confirmed his belief that only rational persuasion, moral regeneration, and the Fabian policy of "permeation" of existing political parties, particularly the radical wing of the Liberal Party, could bring about change. Yet in an essay in *Fabian Essays* (1889), Shaw

Bloody Sunday (*Illustrated London News*, November 19, 1887)

undermined his own position on gradualism in expressing impatience with such a policy, an indication of his humane regard for the millions who "must be left to sweat and suffer in hopeless toil and degradation, whilst parliaments and vestries grudgingly muddle and grope towards paltry instalments of betterment." At one "great stroke," he urged, Justice could be set "on her rightful throne."

As a result of Bloody Sunday, Morris lost much of his own revolutionary fervor; he abandoned public militancy for the converted stable of his house on the Thames, where he later presided over the Hammersmith Socialist Society. Though Shaw and Morris were at opposite poles of the socialist movement, there had been no personal friction. Morris's volatile personality, however, rather baffled Shaw, who sensed a reluctance on his part to agree or disagree on a particular point. In the "early days," Shaw often appeared on street corners with Morris to lecture to passers-by: "We often thought ourselves lucky if we had an audience of 20."

In 1890, Morris landscaped a utopian vision in *News from Nowhere* ("nowhere" a translation of the Greek word for utopia), a prose romance written after he had read *Looking Backward* (1889), a utopian work by the American socialist Edward Bellamy. Opposed to Bellamy's vision of total mechanization and urbanization, *News from Nowhere* takes the form of a dream by its central character who is fifty-six, Morris's own age. The time is the future, sometime in the twenty-first century, but the ideal society, pastoral and free, has the appearance of a fourteenth-century Pre-Raphaelite world of graceful maidens, medieval dress and architecture. The state, as in Marx and Engels's vision of the future in the *Communist Manifesto* (1850), has withered away, and a general benevolence has descended upon its former subjects. Without formal government, a monetary system, private property, or prisons, people are encouraged to engage in handicrafts and participate in a joyous gathering of hay and other necessary communal work, such as weaving and building. Their joy makes them look half their actual ages; indeed, it gives them a "nobility of expression," for they are no longer alienated from the earth by industrialism. Poverty, the result of the oppressive class system, is now extinct, and all enjoy the "Equality of Life."

In pastoral London, Trafalgar Square has been transformed into an orchard of apricot trees; a celebration on May Day commemorates the "Clearing of Misery"—that is, the slums in the East End. The houses of Parliament are now used as a "dung market," and the Thames, once vilely polluted, is now teeming with salmon. In Chapter 17, titled "How the Change Came," the narrator learns how the revolution came about after a disastrous incident in Trafalgar Square (reminiscent of Bloody Sunday). The chapter is a blueprint, presumably inspired by Marx and Engels, outlining the events that could bring about "a new day of fellowship, and rest, and happiness." Indebted to such utopias as W. H. Hudson's *A Crystal Age* (1887), Morris's *News* reveals what Wells later regarded as a sentimental view of human nature, for it was unlikely that humanity would be ennobled merely by a radical transformation of society.

As Lionel Trilling has pointed out, Morris's utopia is disturbingly placid, though instances of violence over love affairs, not unknown, are recognized by the inhabitants as evidence that "love is not a very reasonable thing." No punishment, however, is exacted; instead, a culprit is expected to suffer from remorse. The minor arts and crafts are encouraged instead of the expression of great art. In a traditional humanistic society, Trilling suggests, great art is generally regarded as the triumph of sublimated aggression, involving "goals which are beyond pleasure."

SOCIALIST UTOPIANISM ATTRACTED Oscar Wilde, though he developed a vision radically different from that of the Fabians. He had revealed an intellectual penchant for revolutionary movements in his first play, *Vera; or, The Nihilists* (1880), in which the witty characters are Russian aristocrats and the nihilistic Vera speaks (and dies at her own hand) for the oppressed masses. In 1886, Wilde was the only one to sign a petition circulated by Shaw in support of the anarchists in the Chicago Haymarket riots, and he praised *Chants of Labour: A Song-Book of the People* (1889), edited by Edward Carpenter. At Shaw's invitation, Wilde attended a Fabian Society meeting in 1888, during which Walter Crane discoursed on how socialism would bring about an artistic renaissance. The *Star* (July 7) reported that Wilde expressed the "thought that the art of the future could clothe itself not in works of form and color but in literature," a view with which Shaw agreed. After the meeting, Shaw continued discussing the future of society with Wilde and Sidney Webb as they walked through the dark London streets. It may have been this experience that impelled Wilde to begin writing his essay "The Soul of Man under Socialism," which appeared in the *Fortnightly Review* (February 1891).

The essay—a radical tour de force—is less about socialism than about the privileged status of the artist. Wilde presents an anarchist vision of the artist fulfilling his "Individualism" in a utopian society, one not exercising "that monstrous and ignorant thing that is called Public Opinion, which, bad and well-meaning as it is when it tries to control action, is infamous and of evil meaning when it tries to control Thought or Art." The tyranny of public opinion, indicative of a degraded journalism, challenges and threatens the artist (Keats's death, legend had it, was hastened by hostile reviews of his verse). The artist, Wilde states, "gains something" by being attacked: "His individuality is intensified. He becomes more completely himself." Individualism, then, is the supreme achievement of socialism: "The chief advantage that would result from the establishment of Socialism is, undoubtedly, the fact that Socialism would relieve us from that sordid necessity of living for others which . . . presses so hardly upon almost everybody."

"The Soul of Man" thus advances an idea strikingly different from the traditional collectivism of Socialism, for the artist's individualism is the highest good, and the Renaissance is the model for the good society: ". . . the Renaissance was great . . . because it sought to solve no social problem, and busied itself not about such things, but suffered the individual to develop freely, beautifully, and naturally, and so had great and individual arts, and great and individual men." Wilde's myth of the artist consequently supersedes the historical reality of widespread hunger and misery in the Renaissance. And as for the "People," the artist cannot live with them, Wilde asserts, for they exercise a "blind, deaf, hideous, grotesque, tragic, amusing, serious and obscene" authority. In short, Wilde's utopia is ideally suited for the artist, for "Art is Individualism."

For the Victorians, the concept of individualism was one fraught with apprehension, for it implied private judgment in a society that had traditionally relied on absolute truths. Earlier, such great Romantic individualists as Blake, Shelley, and Byron had rejected traditional authority and had designed the Satanic heroes in their works as challenges to the age. Complicating the cautious Victorian attitude towards the Romantics was the dogma of liberalism, which, in the nineteenth century, advanced the idea that one's individual vision of the truth had positive value. On the threshold of the Victorian age, Thomas Carlyle warned against Romantic self-preoccupation in his *Sartor Resartus* (1833–34/1836) by urging: "Close thy Byron; open thy Goethe." Social responsibility, the final vision of Goethe's heroes Wilhelm Meister and Faust, was essential to maintain a unified culture. However, when tensions between religion and science undermined traditional belief later in the nineteenth century, there was an increasing sense that the conflict between individualism and culture was intensifying.*

By the 1880s, when the doctrine of anarchism emerged in Britain, it was associated with such individualism, and its proponents were widely regarded by the conservative press as threats to the social order. Most anarchists, however, did not advocate violence. In London, terrorist outrages committed by the Fenians, the Irish revolutionaries sometimes referred to as the Irish Republican Brotherhood, were inevitably associated in the public mind with assassinations by the anarchists on the Continent, but the Fenians' principal targets were public buildings, symbols of hated English rule. "The great day of the dynamitards," one that spread panic through London, occurred on January 24, 1885, when the Fenians exploded three bombs simultaneously at Westminster Hall, in the houses of Parliament, and at the Tower of London. Since anarchists and socialists had similar attitudes towards the "evils of capitalism" and the class system, they were often identified by the press and by novelists as two aspects of the same movement. Indeed, reports in the British press of sporadic meetings in Paris and Zurich of socialists, Fenians, anarchists, and nihilists reinforced the impression that such groups were united in an international conspiracy.

---

*As early as the 1830s, John Stuart Mill was writing of the attrition of traditional beliefs and the consequences thereof: "As the old doctrines have gone out, and the new ones have not yet come in, every one must judge for himself as he best may" (*The Spirit of the Age* ed. F. A. von Hayek [Chicago, 1942], 33).

In popular articles, "anarchy" was often associated with anarchism, though social chaos was not the anarchists' goal but the establishment of a new rational order without the intrusion of state control. Nevertheless, the anarchists' wish to destroy parliamentary democracy posed a threat to cherished British institutions and seemed to be further evidence that the Victorian age was in decline. Anarchist-inspired violence on the Continent and in the United States, however, was relatively rare in Britain. In the late nineteenth century, anarchists assassinated such figures as Sadi Carnot, president of France (1894); Antonio Canovas del Castillo, prime minister of Spain (1897); Empress Elizabeth of Austria (1898); King Umberto I of Italy (1900); and President William McKinley of the United States (1901).

Unlike most other European countries, Britain did not outlaw anarchist organizations, nor were anarchists uniformly regarded as dangerous figures. Indeed, the best-known theorist of anarchism, the Russian emigré Prince Kropotkin, whom Shaw described as "amiable to the point of saintliness . . . with his full beard and lovable expression," was a welcome figure in intellectual and social circles and a contributor to such highly regarded publications as the *Fortnightly Review,* the *Nineteenth Century,* and even the *Encyclopaedia Britannica.* In one article, "The Coming Anarchy," a title clearly designed to provoke anxiety, Kropotkin remarks that "we [anarchists] have no objection whatever to the use of the word 'anarchy' as a negation of what has been described as order," which implies "a strong government and a strong police . . . always beneficial." But economic and political freedom, he insists, was only possible "by steadily limiting the functions of government"; observable progress towards such a goal indicated that humanity was "reducing [such functions] finally to *nil.*"

Despite Kropotkin's high seriousness, on occasion an anarchist could be at the center of a comic plot. Before the "great day of the dynamitards," Robert Louis Stevenson and his wife wrote *The Dynamiter* (1885), a whimsical portrayal (chiefly Stevenson's) of an attempt to destroy the statute of Shakespeare in Leicester Square. The inept anarchist, Zero, unable to carry out his mission, eventually flings himself with the bomb harmlessly into the Thames. In *The Princess Casamassima* (1886), however, Henry James expressed in one character's speech the pervasive fear of violent revolution that haunted the Victorians:

> Nothing of it appears above the surface; but there's an immense underworld peopled with a thousand forms of revolutionary passion and devotion. . . . And on top of it all society lives. People go and come, and buy and sell, and drink and dance, and make money and make love, and seem to know nothing and

suspect nothing and think of nothing. . . . All that's one half of it;
the other half is that everything's doomed! In silence, in darkness, but under the feet of each one of us, the revolution lives
and works.

As a result of the anarchist assassinations of governmental leaders on
the Continent, in Britain the stereotype of the anarchist bomb thrower
was firmly established by the early 1890s and scares were often reported
in the press. Indeed, the popular newspapers sensationalized anarchist
plots in order to increase sales by means of anxiety-provoking articles.
The *Evening News* (December 17, 1894), for example, emblazoned its
pages with the headline "8000 Anarchists in London: Where These Enemies of Society Live in This Great Metropolis." A picture of a French
anarchist known for his murders accompanied drawings depicting the
brutal killing of a capitalist. In that year, however, the only death actually
attributed to an anarchist involved a Frenchman who mishandled a home-
made bomb he had carried to Greenwich Park presumably to blow up the
Royal Observatory,* an incident that Conrad drew upon for his novel *The
Secret Agent* (1907). Earlier, Conrad had written two stories of anarchist
machinations in "An Anarchist" (1906) and "The Informer" (1906),
both collected in *A Set of Six* (1908). But by the late nineteenth and early
twentieth century, the bomb thrower, like Zero, the anarchist in Stevenson's *The Dynamiter,* had also become a figure of farce. A classic in the
genre of anarchist fiction, G. K. Chesterton's *The Man Who Was Thurs-
day: A Nightmare* (1908), depicts an assassination plot by the General
Council of the Anarchists of Europe, the members of which turn out to
be—to their mutual astonishment—disguised detectives from Scotland
Yard!

With the earlier background of revolutionary outrages abroad and anxiety over the numerous scares at home, Wilde's "The Soul of Man" was
rather daring since his focus on "Individualism" could be misinterpreted,
in an essay ostensibly on socialism, as covert praise of anarchism.† Shaw

---

*The "Greenwich Bomb Outrage" was reported in the *Morning Leader* (February 16,
1894) in startling headlines:

BLOWN TO PIECES!
Victim an Anarchist (?)
Was he a member of a gang who had
fell designs on London's safety?

A man who carried a terrible explosive blown to pieces at
Greenwich—it is declared that he was the chief of a gang of
anarchists, and was seeking to conceal his bombs. . . .

†In an interview in 1894, Wilde remarked, "We are all of us more or less Socialists
now-a-days. . . . I think I am rather more than a socialist. I am something of an

liked the essay perhaps for its paradoxical style and its subdued ironies. Still, a paper titled "The Difficulties of Anarchism" that Shaw read to the Fabian Society on October 16, 1891, suggests that he, too, may have been troubled by Wilde's "Individualism," for in this piece Shaw attempts to clarify the confusion between socialist collectivism and anarchist individualism—of increasing anxiety to the Fabians, who were concerned over the mistaken notions publicized in the newspapers concerning socialism and anarchism: "In the columns of such papers all revolutionists are Socialists; all Socialists are Anarchists; and all Anarchists are incendiaries, assassins, and thieves. . . . Many persons who are never called Anarchists either by themselves or others take Anarchist ground in their opposition to Social Democracy. . . ." Individualistic anarchism, Shaw believed, did not address itself to the socialist ideal: the public good as opposed to private interest. On the other hand, communistic anarchism, which Kropotkin advocated, was too optimistic—perhaps not even possible—if the success of the new society depended on forced labor: "I submit, then, to our Communist Anarchist friends that Communism requires either external compulsion to labour, or else a social morality which the evils of existing society shew that we have failed as yet to attain."

The general discussion concerning individualism and collectivism remained a preoccupation among the Fabians and other socialists. Shaw agreed with Sidney Webb, who had insisted: "We have no *right* to live our own lives." Yet Shaw believed that in a mediocre, corrupt world his unequaled gifts as artist and polemicist were his best means of advancing socialist goals. On one occasion, he wrote reassuringly to a friend: "Believe me, I always was, & am, an intense Individualist." When Morris invited Shaw to lecture at a meeting of the Hammersmith branch of the Social Democratic Federation, the socialist periodical *Justice* (July 19, 1884) announced the title as "Socialism *versus* Individualism" but on July 26 reported Shaw's denial of the "alleged antagonism" between "Socialism and the Individual."

Like Shaw, Morris wavered on the entire issue of anarchist ideology but recognized the value of individualism in the service of socialist collectivism. After Morris's death, Kropotkin paid tribute to *News from Nowhere* in the anarchist publication *Freedom* (November 1896), perhaps recognizing his own influence on the work, which he described as "perhaps the most thoroughly and deeply Anarchistic conception of future society that has ever been written." Havelock Ellis touched on the continuing debate

---

Anarchist, I believe; but, of course, the dynamite policy is very absurd indeed" (Percival W. H. Almy, "New Views of Mr O. W.," *Theatre* [March 1894]; rpt. in E. H. Mikhail, ed., *Oscar Wilde: Interviews and Recollections* [New York, 1979], 1:232).

in *The Nineteenth Century: A Dialogue in Utopia* (1900) in which one of his speakers, clearly a socialist echoing Wilde's "The Soul of Man under Socialism," remarks that "true individuality, as we know, is impossible until a social state is attained in which the whole of what was called the material side of life—that side on which all have common wants—is automatically supplied."

SHAW'S MAJOR CONTRIBUTION as a propagandist for socialist causes began when he turned his attention to drama after having written five unsuccessful novels. His intellectual energy (or controlled aggression, as Trilling might have called it) resulted in plays that helped transform British drama, for in the early nineties he employed the dramatic form as an expression of social and political views new to the late nineteenth-century London stage. For Shaw, drama was an ideal medium, since its immediacy of confrontation, its rapid play of ideas, its opportunity for irony and paradox were an extension of his own lecturing and debating as proselytizer in the "Fabian vein," which, he wrote, was "largely the vein of comedy and . . . a sense of irony. We laughed at Socialism and laughed at ourselves a good deal." In the theater, his intent was to evoke critical laughter from audiences when presented with social problems and in the process "to make Socialism as possible as Liberalism or Conservatism for the pottering surburban voter who desired to go to church because his neighbours did, and to live always on the side of the police."

In 1884, he began his first play in collaboration with the Scottish drama critic William Archer, who had observed Shaw in the domed reading room of the British Museum alternately poring over Marx's *Das Kapital* and Wagner's *Tristan and Isolde*. The combination of seemingly contradictory works suggests the complexity of his Romantic personality: the rational utopian infused with transcendent eroticism. The collaboration soon foundered, however, when Shaw began the work on his own without consulting Archer and when he seemed to be ignoring the plot provided. Shaw, who regarded it as "twaddling cup-and-saucer comedy," told the angry Archer after he had read the first two acts to him: "You will perceive that my genius has brought the romantic notion which possessed you into vivid contact with real life."

Shaw believed that a play should develop organically though guided by a predetermined social thesis. He abhorred plays that used the well-worn theatrical conventions of the popular "well-made play," involving carefully designed exits and entrances that intensify the drama, in addition to devices, such as incriminating letters or other stage props, that advance the plot to a key climactic scene. Such melodramas, as developed by the French playwrights Eugène Scribe and Victorien Sardou, Shaw later called "Sardoodledom." Archer believed that a play should have a tightly constructed realistic plot but not at the expense of a theatrically compelling development of character.

Despite Shaw's wish to avoid conventional melodrama, what emerged from the aborted collaboration, *Widowers' Houses,* was a well-made play with a difference. The plot concerns Sartorius, a ruthless slum landlord, whose daughter—reminiscent of some of Ibsen's sexually assertive heroines—is determined to marry the aristocratically connected Dr. Trench. The doctor's income from real estate, he discovers to his horror, is from the very property that Sartorius owns. Act III reveals how the Dickensian character Lickcheese, Sartorius's former collector of rents now having unexpectedly become wealthy, brings both Trench and Sartorius together in a mutually profitable conspiracy that will enrich all three. The play ends with the ironic triumph of the villains, who will benefit from a capitalistic system that rewards economic self-interest at the expense of the poor. Shaw's intent was to make the audience question its own participation in such a system while condemning the obvious villainy of the principal characters. By its art of distancing the characters from the audience (thereby preventing its identification with such corrupt figures) and by its use of Act III to express the thesis determining the action, Shaw's dramaturgy later influenced the Marxist playwright Bertolt Brecht, who developed the use of such devices.

Convinced that it was "too experimental" for any of the commercial theaters, Shaw approached J. T. Grein, the Dutch-born naturalized Briton who was a critic, playwright, and founder of the Independent Theatre, which produced avant-garde plays designed for small audiences. Shaw, who had not yet completed the play, managed to convince Grein that his was the English play that the Independent Theatre had been looking for. Produced on December 9, 1892, with only one additional performance, the play created a sensation that delighted Shaw: ". . . the Socialists and Independents applauded me furiously on principle; the ordinary playgoing first-nighters hooted me frantically on the same ground." As was customary in the theater at the time, he appeared before the curtain on opening night, but instead of expressing his gratitude for the reception, he astonished the audience and delighted his friends by delivering an impromptu speech on socialism. Within a fortnight, the play provoked over 130 reviews and articles.

In a letter to the *Star* (December 19, 1892), Shaw responded to the indignant critics who condemned his "distorted and myopic outlook on society" by suggesting that "they do not know life well enough to recognize it in the glare of the footlights" (Shaw had had first-hand experience with the play's thesis, for, when young, he had been a collector of rents in a Dublin slum): "The notion that the people in Widowers' Houses are

J. T. Grein

abnormally vicious or odious could only prevail in a community in which Sartorius is absolutely typical in his unconscious villainy."

WHILE THE RECEPTION of *Widowers' Houses* afforded Shaw the pleasure of shocking the critics, he was experiencing difficulty over an attempt, initiated by Morris, to achieve unity of purpose and action among the three leading socialist groups: the Social Democratic Federation, the Hammersmith Socialist Society (which Morris had founded after the Socialist League dissolved in the late 1880s when extremists dominated it), and the Fabian Society. Urging the drafting of a joint statement, Morris met periodically with Hyndman and Shaw for intense discussions. Shaw and Hyndman (whose "almost legendary conceit and tactlessness" was apparently more than a match for Shaw's) argued constantly over a draft composed by Morris. In May 1893, the Joint Manifesto was finally issued, but it couched the aims of the three organizations in such generalities that few in the constituent bodies were pleased. Forty years later, Shaw recalled that "Morris's draft, horribly eviscerated and patched, was subsequently sold for a penny as the Joint Manifesto of the Socialists of Great Britain. It was the only document any of the three of us had ever signed and published that was honestly not worth a farthing." At the time, however, the attempt at unity provided impetus for the founding of the Independent Labour Party.

LOOKING BACK ON the production of *Widowers' Houses,* Shaw mused: "I had not achieved a success; but I had provoked an uproar; and the sensation was so agreeable that I resolved to try again." In 1893, he wrote a comedy for the Independent Theatre, *The Philanderer,* which focused on the current rage over Ibsen and the New Woman, but because he thought that Grein could not provide the cast needed for such "high comedy," he abandoned it and began writing *Mrs. Warren's Profession,* which treated a "social subject of tremendous force." Its intent, Shaw explained in the preface to the published version, was "to draw attention to the truth that prostitution is caused, not by female depravity and male licentiousness, but simply by underpaying, undervaluing, and overworking women so shamefully that the poorest of them are forced to resort to prostitution to keep body and soul together."

In the play, Mrs. Warren, faced with the prospect of slaving away for sixteen hours a day in a factory and dying before her time, had turned first to prostitution, then established herself as madame and part-owner of several brothels on the Continent. The central irony of the play turns on her daughter Vivie's discovery of the secret that her education at Oxford and her comfortable existence have been funded by the tainted money sent by her mother (once again Shaw employs the devices of the well-made play). Most disturbing to Vivie, however, is that the business is still operating at a considerable profit—in short, capitalism is so versatile that the exploited can convert themselves into exploiters.

When Shaw offered the play to the experimental Independent Theatre, Grein rejected it as too risqué, and the examiner of plays for the Lord Chamberlain (who had absolute power over what appeared on the stage) concurred by refusing to license it. By 1894, Shaw decided to write a play that would place the emphasis on wit rather than socialist propaganda. His chance came when the actress Florence Farr, who, said Shaw, was "in violent reaction against Victorian morals, especially sexual and domestic morals," organized a season of plays at the Avenue Theatre, in Northumberland Avenue, Charing Cross. Farr wanted to produce *Widowers' Houses,* but Shaw persuaded her to stage his new play *Arms and the Man.* Because of his difficulties over *Widowers' Houses* and *Mrs. Warren's Profession,* Shaw turned away from thesis plays preoccupied with ideology to "plays of life, character and human destiny" with no other purpose, he said, than that of "all poets and dramatists."

With such an aesthetic attitude in mind, Shaw shared certain affinities with the Aesthetes, an indication that the fin de siècle was a time of confusing cross-currents when intellectuals embraced seemingly contradictory ideologies. Alienated by society's Philistinism, both Shaw and the Aesthetes insisted on their right to create from personal conviction and vision regardless of society's moral bias as to the function of art (indeed, Shaw believed that art that expressed the prescribed morality of a corrupt society was the worst form of immorality). Furthermore, like the Aesthetes, Shaw regarded aesthetic form in a work of art as essential (though not an end in itself), despite his occasional statements that he had written "propaganda": "Would anyone but a buffleheaded idiot of a university professor, half crazy with correcting examination papers, infer that all my plays were written as economic essays, and not as plays of life, character, and human destiny like those of Shakespear or Euripides?"

Shaw also agreed with Wilde's remark in "The Soul of Man under Socialism" that "Art should never try to be popular. The public should try to make itself artistic." Yet because Shaw also regarded himself as a socialist propagandist and later as a proponent what he called the "Life Force," he rejected the central idea of Aestheticism: that is, that art should be principally concerned with aesthetic perfection, not with morality, religion, politics, or other intrusions that would make art serve "useful" purposes or be judged on any basis other than its artistic achievement. Shaw's most antagonistic statement concerning autonomous art occurred in a speech titled "Literature and Art": ". . . the man who believes in art for art's sake is a fool; that is to say, a man in a state of damnation."

Despite such fulminations, Shaw adopted artistic strategies similar to those of the Aesthetes: shocking the bourgeoisie by advancing unorthodox moral positions and adopting various masks in order to perplex the conventional as to who the real Bernard Shaw was. Clearly, he regarded himself as a serious, though obviously not solemn, artist in the service of moral (and ultimately religious) vision that could be expressed most effectively by artistic means designed to touch and refine mind, feeling, and soul. Unlike the Aesthetes, who withdrew from social concerns and from a hostile audience in order to cultivate their private imaginations, Shaw assumed the public persona of prophet or priest and regarded the theater as his temple, not to advance the cause of art but that of socialism and the Life Force. In this respect, he was the quintessential Victorian despite his subversive drama.

At the premiere performance on April 21, 1894, of Shaw's *Arms and the Man,* a witty, ironic view of war in the farcical setting of Bulgaria (where instead of bullets, the hero prefers chocolate creams),* many of his friends and associates were in the audience, among them Oscar Wilde, George Moore, Sidney Webb, and Yeats, whose one-act play *Land of Heart's Desire* was the curtain-raiser. Later, Yeats wrote: "On the first night the whole pit and gallery, except certain members of the Fabian Society, started to laugh at the author, and then, discovering that they themselves were being laughed at, sat there not converted—their hatred

---

Arms and the Man was adapted by Oscar Straus for his operetta *The Chocolate Soldier* (1908), referred to by Shaw as "that degradation of a decent comedy into a dirty farce" (quoted in Michael Holroyd, *Bernard Shaw* [New York, 1988], 1: 306).

was too bitter for that—but dumbfounded, while the rest of the house cheered and laughed." Much of the satire in the play was directed at the pseudo-idealism of the "higher love" discussed by various utopian groups, including the Fellowship of the New Life. Yeats recalled that he listened to *Arms and the Man* with "admiration and hatred. It seemed inorganic, logical straightness and not the crooked road of life." Soon after, he had a nightmare that he was "haunted by a sewing machine, that clicked and shone, but the incredible thing was that the machine smiled, smiled perpetually."

IN THE LATE summer of 1894, Sidney Webb learned that a supporter of the Fabian Society, Henry Hunt Hutchinson, clerk to the justices of Derby, had committed suicide and had left more than £9,000 to advance the Fabian cause. Webb, designated chairman of the trustees overseeing the fund, immediately laid plans to found an institution for research and teaching. Beatrice recorded in her diary: "His vision is to found, slowly and quietly, a 'London School of Economics and Political Science'—a centre not only of lectures on special subjects, but an association of students who would be directed and supported in doing original work." Some members of the Fabian executive committee, such as Hubert Bland and Sydney Olivier, had misgivings about diverting funds for the establishment of the school without the control of the committee, and Ramsay MacDonald accused the Webbs of not only misusing the Hutchinson funds but also distracting the society from its essential aim, to proselytize for socialism. Shaw convinced the Webbs' opponents, however, that their opposition could possibly endanger the legacy.

In October, 1896, the school took possession of 10 Adelphi Terrace, overlooking the Thames. Among those on its administrative committee were Beatrice Webb, Bland, Olivier, and the young mathematician Bertrand Russell. The occupation of the building was made possible by the financial assistance of the Irish millionaire Charlotte Payne-Townshend, who, weary of her genteel uselessness, had become a member of the society earlier that year. Beatrice Webb described her as "attractive—a large graceful woman with masses of chocolate-brown hair. . . . By temperament she is an anarchist—feeling any regulation or rule intolerable. . . . She is fond of men and impatient of most women, bitterly resents her enforced celibacy but thinks she could not tolerate the matter-of-fact side of marriage."

Payne-Townshend found Shaw a compelling personality, for as he told the actress Ellen Terry, with whom he shared his private fantasies, "after about a year of fascination she [Payne-Townshend] tells me that I am 'the most self-centered man she ever met.' " Their relationship grew increasingly intimate. In August of 1897, Shaw told Ellen Terry that "a sort of earthquake" occurred when Payne-Townshend at last made him "a very generous & romantic proposal—saving it up as a sort of climax to the proofs she was giving me every day of her regard for me. When I received that golden moment with shuddering horror & wildly asked the fare to Australia, she was inexpressibly taken aback, and her pride, which is considerable, was much startled." The "brilliant philanderer," as Beatrice Webb called him, had been taken "in his cold sort of way" with his Irish millionaire, but Beatrice doubted whether Shaw could be induced to marry. In time, his pretended defenses collapsed: They were married on June 1, 1898 (he was forty-two; she, forty-one).

AT THE BEGINNING of the new century, Shaw's *Major Barbara* (1905) reveals a significant development from the earthbound socialism of his earliest drama to a transcendent vision of the Life Force. By this time, Shaw had become increasingly pessimistic about effecting significant changes in society, but he characterized the evolutionary Life Force as "God in the act of creating Himself," manifested in an individual's heroic, creative will. In Andrew Undershaft, Shaw created a brilliant, enlightened capitalist who undermines his daughter's ineffectual efforts as a major in the Salvation Army. Modeled in part, perhaps, after William Morris, who had died in 1896, Undershaft has built a utopian village and armaments foundry at Perivale St. Andrews, lying between two Middlesex hills, "an almost smokeless town of white walls, roofs of narrow green slates or red tiles, tall trees, domes, companiles, and slender chimney shafts, beautifully situated and beautiful in itself."

A witty savior who employs irony as a method of winning adherents to his vision, Undershaft—whose name suggests the symbolic driving force underlying his own apparent immorality—embodies the Life Force, expressing itself paradoxically as "the way of life [that] lies through the factory of death." Undershaft, says Shaw in his preface, "is simply a man who, having grasped the fact that poverty is a crime, knows that when society offered him the alternative of poverty or a lucrative trade in death and destruction, it offered him, not a choice between opulent villainy and humble virtue, but between energetic enterprise and cowardly infamy." In accepting her father's view of the world—that only the strong can create a new order built upon mysterious paradoxes—Barbara has her faith restored but not her faith in Christian self-sacrifice.

The Webbs took Arthur Balfour to the first performance of the play at the Court Theatre on November 28, 1905. In her diary, Beatrice called Shaw's work "a dance of devils—amazingly clever, grimly powerful in the second act, but ending, as all his plays end (or at any rate most of them) in an intellectual and moral morass." Balfour (who was soon to resign as prime minister) was "taken aback," Beatrice noted, "by the triumph of the unmoral purpose."

THE GROWTH OF the Fabian Society in the early years of the twentieth century was stimulated by the victory of the Liberal Party in 1906, when fifty-three members of the newly christened Labour Party, of which some members were Fabians, won parliamentary seats. The pressure on the society to be more vigorous in its proselytizing now became increasingly evident, particularly among the younger members who challenged the society's early founders, the "Old Gang," as they were now called. The best known of the new members was H. G. Wells, a socialist since his student days in the 1880s before he took any interest in the Fabians. At that time, Wells, sporting a red tie, was convinced that some form of socialism would inevitably displace what he perceived as tottering capitalism. By the early years of the new century, Wells had already published more than a dozen books, which, even in his notable science fiction of the 1890s, indicated a central concern with social and political problems; several of his books had been favorably reviewed in the *Fabian News*.

In the autumn of 1902, he was associated with the society, and in 1905, when Wells published *A Modern Utopia,* the Fabians recognized his value to the society in translating socialist doctrine into imaginative, popular fiction. In this work, Wells rejects traditional utopias, with their perfect worlds, as unattainable and impractical:

> Were we free to have our untrammelled desire, I suppose we should follow Morris to his Nowhere, we should change the nature of man and the nature of things together; we should make the whole race wise, tolerant, noble, perfect—wave our hands to a splendid anarchy, every man doing as it pleases him, and none pleased to do evil, in a world as good in its essential nature, as ripe and sunny, as the world before the Fall.

Instead, the "pervading Will to Live sustains for ever more a perpetuity of aggressions." Wells's utopia is, in fact, a mirror image of the world we know except that the social and political conditions are changed in accordance with socialist ideology. In addition, the concept of a world state, scientifically and technologically designed for the welfare of its inhabitants, makes this utopia truly modern in comparison to the many past utopias, usually pastoral and provincial.

Those who govern, the voluntary nobility, are called *samurai,* a term inspired by the recent Japanese victories over the Russians in the war of

1904–1905. The idea of such an elite is drawn from the Fabian belief that a socialist state requires the talents of gifted administrators, reminiscent of Plato's guardians. Of the classes within the state, the highest and most innovative is the "poietic," the creative class consisting of artists and scientists, the merging of both resulting in true philosophers. This imaginatively conceived dynamic new world had wide appeal not only to socialists but also to Henry James, who wrote, "Bravo, bravo, my dear Wells!"

Though Wells had won over the Fabians with *A Modern Utopia,* he grew impatient with Fabian gradualism. Between 1906 and 1908, he led many of the younger members of the society in an attempt to restructure and redirect it. In February 1906, at a meeting "confined strictly" to members, Wells delivered a lecture titled "The Faults of the Fabian." The society, he argued, was, in its financially impoverished state, "extraordinarily inadequate and feeble," an anachronism in a "quite unenlightened and hostile world." It had failed, he said, "to represent the spirit of social reconstruction that is arising all about us, in its failure to use the prestige it has accumulated, to fulfil the promises it once made [to] the world." The society's determination to spread socialist doctrine, Wells asserted, had led only to a "little dribble of activities" and much "wasted time and energy" in taking up "bright, impossible ideas," then abandoning them. He singled out Shaw as "an intensely serious man" who had nevertheless influenced others by his paradoxical wit to perceive "this grave high business of socialism" as "an idiotic middle-class joke." Finally, he suggested that the society had taken its name from the wrong Roman general, for when the time came for Fabius Maximus to act against Hannibal, "he led the party of paralysis."

Shaw and the Webbs, questioning Wells's sincerity, nevertheless attempted conciliation by acceding to his proposals to restructure the society. They also agreed to his nominees to the executive committee, despite his accusation that Sidney Webb and Shaw were "the most intolerable egotists, narrow, suspicious, obstructive" whom he had ever met. Wells believed that the Webbs were excessively concerned with preserving bourgeois values (Beatrice Webb, who had become increasingly irritated by Wells's lower middle-class "insolent bluster" and particularly his table manners, resented his attempt to become the prophet of the society). Shaw frankly advised him:

> You must study people's corns when you go clog dancing. . . .
> You must identify yourself frankly with us, and not play the
> critical outsider and the satirist. We are all very clever; and long
> ago we have come to understand that we must not play our
> cleverness off against one another for the mere fun of it. . . .

there are limits to our powers of enduring humiliations that are totally undeserved. You haven't told us anything yet that we don't know. . . .

The older Fabians, distressed over his views of sexuality (and his adulterous affairs), lost hope that Wells, initially regarded as their "useful missionary," would moderate his position or behavior because of his considerable support from the younger members. The Tories, by their condemnation of his views on sexuality and marriage as a socialist attack on civilization itself, made it clear that Wells was a political liability to the Fabians. Aware that he had contributed little to the advancement of the Fabian Society except internal division, Wells resigned in September 1908.

Recovering from their adventure with Wells, the Fabians consolidated their strength by the time of the First World War, when more Fabians were elected to Parliament. The importance of the society in the development of the Labour movement was incalculable, for the Fabians had demonstrated over the previous thirty years that the presumed ineffectual group of armchair debaters had the capacity to achieve power without firing a shot or throwing a bomb.

2

The Damnation of Decadence

WHEN ERNEST DOWSON died in 1900, the poet and critic Andrew Lang sought to undermine Arthur Symons's appreciative obituary by questioning Dowson's alleged genius. Lang thus satirized the "decadent" who had achieved distinction merely by violating Victorian propriety: "By kicking holes in his boots, crushing in his hat and avoiding soap, any young man may achieve a comfortable degree of sordidness, and then, if his verses are immaterial, and his life suicidal, he may regard himself as a decadent indeed." Lang trivializes what many Decadent writers in the nineties perceived as the serious business of art: to assert its inherent autonomy and to protest against restrictions in subject matter. More important, Lang's use of the term *decadent* to refer to a work of art *and* to the artist's life was confounded in the late nineteenth century not only by critics but also by the public at large.

VOLTAIRE EMPLOYED THE concept of decadence with much the same meaning as it later had in the nineteenth century. In 1770 he wrote that it came "through the ease with which we do things and the sloth that prevents our doing them well, through a surfeit of beauty and a taste for the bizarre. . . . We are in every way in a time of the most horrible decadence." Modern critics associate the term with Théophile Gautier's novel *Mademoiselle de Maupin* (1835), which had a significant impact on later British writers. While the work contains certain elements of Decadence (here capitalized to suggest an aesthetic vision rather than moral, social, or artistic decline), it also contains certain attitudes that the British were later to call "Aestheticism." Indeed, confusion exists to this day concerning the two terms because they shared similar aesthetic attitudes towards art, some of which are expressed in the preface to Gautier's novel: Art cannot serve utilitarian interests, such as social progress; art has it own internal laws; and the artist creates work for its own sake (that is, *l'art pour l'art*). Gautier states in his preface: "Nothing is really beautiful unless it is useless, everything useful is ugly, for it expresses a need and the needs of man are ignoble and disgusting, like his poor weak nature. The most useful place in a house is the lavatory." In 1891 Oscar Wilde, who believed that imitation was the sincerest form of flattery, proclaimed in *his* preface to *The Picture of Dorian Gray* (1891): "All art is quite useless." Decadence, however, went further: It emerged as the dark side of Romanticism in its flaunting of forbidden experiences, and it insisted on the superiority of artifice to nature.

Gautier opposed Victor Hugo's concept of art for progress's sake, an idea he found equally objectionable in such leading French writers as Alfred de Vigny and Alphonse de Lamartine. They were, he insisted, debasing art by devoting their talent to humanitarian causes. To shock his bourgeois audience, Gautier created in *Mademoiselle de Maupin* what has been called an *"apologia* of lesbian love" and "the Bible of the Decadence." Its hero, the Chevalier d'Albert, suffering from spiritual impotence and ennui, craves the impossible—a desire central to the Decadent sensibility. Believing that the ideal human form is the hermaphrodite, he yearns to be a woman in order to savor new sensations. At his mistress's estate, he is enraptured by a "young man," who is, in fact, the disguised Madelaine de Maupin. She, too, has an ideal of human perfection; like the

Ernest Dowson

Chevalier, she is convinced that she can love only a man *and* a woman, who together express the harmony and unity of earthly beauty.

Like other French Romantics of the 1830s, Gautier turned increasingly to the arts as his source of inspiration rather than to the outside world. To limit the presence of evanescent nature, Gautier employed a "transposition of art," which implied a crossing of boundaries from one art to another to emphasize their artifice rather than their moral or social content. Gautier titled one of his poems "Symphony in White Major" to suggest the close relationship of poetry, painting, and music. By the end of the century, Wilde wrote a poem "Symphony in Yellow," and Whistler painted more than one "Symphony in White" as well as "nocturnes" and "harmonies." Decadence, which absorbed such tendencies towards artifice, emerged in the latter half of the nineteenth century, the post-Romantic age, as a subversive gesture designed to undermine the bourgeois conception of art as morally elevating.

The most influential writer associated with such subversion was Baudelaire, who, in 1855, responded to a request for a nature poem by insisting that vegetables did not move him, adding, to indicate his preference for artifice, that he preferred to bathe in a bathtub than in the sea and that a music box was more pleasing than a nightingale. An inspired "imitation" of nature—the classical ideal—should, he implied, be avoided; he also challenged Rousseau's cult of nature, which most Romantics accepted as a primal source of creativity and morality. To counter such a view, Baudelaire wrote in his essay "Praise of Cosmetics" (1863):

> All that is beautiful and noble is the result of reason and calculation. Crime, the taste for which the human animal draws from the womb of his mother, is natural in its origins. Virtue, on the contrary, is *artificial* and supernatural, since gods and prophets were necessary in every epoch and every nation to teach virtue to bestial humanity, and man *alone* would have been powerless to discover it. Evil is done effortlessly and *naturally* by fate; the good is always the product of some art.

Cosmetics, then, were a means of transcending nature, for a woman "performs a kind of duty when she endeavors to appear magical and supernatural. She should therefore borrow from all the arts the means of rising above nature in order to better subjugate all hearts and impress all minds." Indulgence in hashish and an interest in perverse sexuality provided yet other means of enabling the self to transcend its natural state and to enter "artificial paradises."

Baudelaire's vision of the dandy also took on transcendent significance. In his essay "Le Dandy" (1863), Baudelaire modified traditional ideas of the dandy's concern with "an immoderate taste for fine clothes and material elegance." These tastes, for the "perfect dandy," are only a "symbol of the aristocratic superiority of his mind." However, simplicity in dress was the "best way of distinguishing oneself." (Indeed, Baudelaire, in the midst of bohemian artists, usually appeared all in black with only a touch of color in his cravat and gloves.) The dandy, moreover, takes pleasure in astonishing others rather than being astonished. He is cold, self-contained, antidemocratic. Dandyism, touching on spirituality and stoicism, is the "last burst of heroism in a period of decadence"—by which Baudelaire meant, paradoxically, "the rise of democracy."

As Baudelairean dandyism became known to the late Victorians, it shared certain characteristics with Decadence: "worship of the town and the artificial; grace, elegance, the art of the pose; sophistication and the mask. The wit of epigram and paradox was called upon to confound the bourgeois." For the industrious, pious middle classes that increasingly valued social equality, solemn responsibility, and moral energy, the pose of dandyism was patently offensive, for it implied elitest superiority, calculated irresponsibility, and cultivated languor. The image of the dandy, particularly as depicted in Wilde's social comedies, thus embodied the Decadent sensibility in its most subversive form. Wilde also publicized the idea in his "Phrases and Philosophies for the Use of the Young" (1894/1908): "The first duty in life is to be as artificial as possible. What the second duty is no one has as yet discovered. . . . The condition of perfection is idleness. . . . To love oneself is the beginning of a life-long romance" (the latter sentiment is expressed by Lord Goring in Wilde's *An Ideal Husband,* 1895).

In 1868, Gautier's essay on Baudelaire, appearing as the "Notice" to *Les Fleurs du mal,* crystallized current ideas on the stylistic significance of artifice, which Baudelaire had so brilliantly synthesized in his poems and essays. Gautier wrote:

> The style of decadence . . . is nothing else than art arrived at that extreme point of maturity produced by those old civilizations which are growing old with their oblique suns—a style that is ingenious, complicated, learned, full of shades of meaning and research, always pushing further the limits of language, borrowing from all the technical vocabularies, taking colours from all palettes, notes from all keyboards, forcing itself to express in thought that which is most ineffable, and in form the vaguest and most fleeting contours. . . .

This style, says Gautier, is the "last effort of the Word, called upon to express everything, and pushed to the utmost extremity." Here one sees the dawn of Modernism in its preoccupation with new possibilities of language, as in the Symbolists and in the later works of Virginia Woolf, James Joyce, and T. S. Eliot. Gautier also cites Baudelaire's attraction to depravity, which a modern critic has called "an essential part of decadence, a last refinement of artificiality, since it is anti-natural. . . . That taste for sexual perversions, so characteristic of decadent literature, receives theoretic justification in the 'Notice.' . . . To complete the picture, he notes that the setting of Baudelaire's verse is the degenerate capital." One recalls Wilde's *The Importance of Being Earnest* (1895), when Jack Worthing, in revealing the "death" of his imaginary brother, Ernest, says: "He seems to have expressed a desire to be buried in Paris." Exclaims Reverend Chasuble: "In Paris! [*Shakes his head.*] I fear that hardly points to any very serious state of mind at the last."

MANY OF THE themes, images, and attitudes of writers associated with Decadence, from Gautier to Baudelaire, are embodied in Joris-Karl Huysmans's novel *A Rebours* (1884), usually translated as *Against the Grain* or *Against Nature*. Mario Praz has called this key work the "pivot upon which the whole psychology of the Decadent Movement turns." Like many fictional Decadents, Huysmans's bisexual aristocratic hero, Des Esseintes, is the last of his tainted line. In Des Esseintes's philosophy, "artifice was the distinctive mark of human genius": ". . . Nature has had her day; she has definitely and finally tired out by the sickening monotony of her landscapes and skyscapes the patience of refined temperaments." Out of boredom and despair, he secludes himself in his bizarre house outside of Paris to escape from the hateful world of the bourgeoisie. There he cultivates diseased and monstrous orchids that appear artificial,* collects exotic gems that he mounts on the shell of a living tortoise, installs an aquarium with mechanical fish, and, in his quest for new sensations that are *à rebours,* he constructs a "mouth organ" that releases liqueurs in symphonic arrangements conducive to his moods, an ingenious method of synesthesia by which taste and sound are equivalent; thus, crème de menthe and anisette, for example, suggest the sounds of flutes.

Yet to read the novel as a morbid history of a Decadent is to overlook

---

*Gautier's story "Fortunio" (1837) had stimulated an interest in exotic, artificially grown flowers. Its hero, who resembles Huysmans's Des Esseintes, has a greenhouse of tropical plants in the courtyard of a windowless house. Maurice Maeterlinck's *Les Serres chaudes* (1890), or *Hothouses,* continues the tradition, and in the 1890s, Theodore Wratislaw's derivative poems have such titles as "Orchids" and "Hothouse Flowers." In *London Nights* (1895), Arthur Symons affirms that the violet, when cultivated in a hothouse, is "The artificial flower of my ideal."

the satirical touches that abound in the work. Most obvious is the lengthy passage in which the narrator, denigrating nature, asserts that there is "not one of her inventions, deemed so subtle and so wonderful, which the ingenuity of mankind cannot create." Even a woman, held to be nature's "most exquisite" product, has been surpassed by "a being . . . more dazzlingly, more superbly beautiful"—that is, "the two locomotives lately adopted for service on the Northern Railroad of France." A distinctive characteristic of Decadence is its capacity for self-deprecating humor, satire, and parody—an indication that some writers, at least, were acutely aware of the absurdity of an extreme Decadent ideology.

IN 1862, DECADENCE made its first obvious appearance in England in the writings of Algernon Swinburne. At the age of twenty-five, he reviewed Baudelaire's *Les Fleurs du mal,* which, he said, had a "heavy, heated temperature, with dangerous hothouse scents in it." Despite its "strange disease and sin," Swinburne saw "not one poem of the *Fleurs du mal* which has not a distinct and vivid background of morality to it." Furthermore, he argued that "a poet's business is presumably to write good verse, and by no means to redeem the age and remould society." In *William Blake* (1866), Swinburne developed this notion of the autonomy of art derived from Gautier and Baudelaire: "Handmaid of religion, exponent of duty, servant of fact, pioneer of morality, she cannot in any way become. . . . Her business is not to do good on other grounds, but to be good on her own. . . . Art for art's sake first of all, and afterwards we may suppose all the rest shall be added to her. . . ."

Before the publication of his own notorious *Poems and Ballads* (1866), Swinburne had attracted a devoted circle of admirers. On one occasion, according to his biographer Edmund Gosse, "an audience of the elect to whom Swinburne recited the yet unpublished 'Dolores' had been moved to such incredible ecstasy by it that several of them had sunk to their knees then and there, and admired him as a god." Aroused by the rebellious Swinburne, Oxford undergraduates chanted lines from "Dolores" as they strolled, arms linked, down the High Street. The verbal fleshliness of Swinburne's *Poems and Ballads,* however, outraged almost everyone else. Still, though prosecution was mentioned, it was not pressed as it had been against Baudelaire's *Les Fleurs du mal* in France. Nevertheless, the critical onslaught was such that Swinburne's publisher dropped the work, which another publisher (noted for his books on flagellation) took on in the same year.

The reviewer for the *Athenaeum* (August 4, 1866)—later identified as Robert Buchanan, a popular playwright and poet—accused Swinburne of being "unclean for the sake of uncleanness." In the *Pall Mall Gazette*

(August 20), another reviewer regarded Swinburne as "publicly obscene," adding, "There are many passages . . . which bring before the mind the image of a mere madman, one who has got maudlin drunk on lewd ideas and lascivious thoughts." Such a poem as "Anactoria," with its startling lines, displeased most of the critics:

> That I could drink thy veins as wine, and eat
> Thy breasts like honey!

The fusion of sadomasochism with religious allusions in "Dolores" prompted charges of blasphemy:

> By the ravenous teeth that have smitten
>   Through the kisses that blossom and bud,
> By the lips intertwisted and bitten
>   Till the foam has a savour of blood. . . .
> I adjure thee, respond from thine altars,
>   Our Lady of Pain.

In the influential *Saturday Review* (August 4), the critic John Morley raised the question whether there was "really nothing in women worth singing about except 'quivering flanks' and 'splendid supple thighs' ": "Is purity to be expunged from the catalogue of desirable qualities?" Morley wondered whether Swinburne was posing as "the libidinous laureate of a pack of satyrs."

Responding to his critics in an essay titled "Notes on Poems and Reviews" (1866), Swinburne averred that "their verdict is a matter of infinite indifference." *Poems and Ballads,* he insisted, was dramatic, hence "no utterance of enjoyment or despair, belief or unbelief, can properly be assumed as the assertion of its author's personal feeling or faith." In the late 1860s and through the 1870s, however, Swinburne's behavior seemed to reflect the odd predilections of his verse—his life could indeed be charged with decadence. In addition to chronic alcoholism, he frequented a brothel in St. John's Wood in order to be whipped; he also had a well-publicized affair with an American circus performer, who later revealed that "she hadn't been able to get him up to the scratch, and couldn't make him understand that biting's no use." Swinburne's art and life, then, were not as distinct as he had alleged.

Eventually, Buchanan had had enough of Swinburne and his friend Dante Gabriel Rossetti. In an essay in the *Contemporary Review* (October 1871), titled "The Fleshly School of Poetry," he attacked, under the pseudonym of Thomas Maitland, the Pre-Raphaelite poets whom he called the "Mutual Admiration School." In characterizing Rossetti's verse and painting, Buchanan comes close to a definition of Decadence, though he condemns what its adherents later praised: ". . . the same combination of the simple and the grotesque, the same morbid deviation from healthy forms of life, the same sense of weary, wasting, yet exquisite sensuality; nothing virile, nothing tender, nothing completely sane; a superfluity of extreme sensibility, of delight in beautiful forms, hues, and tints. . . ." Buchanan censured Rossetti's and Swinburne's verse for its "nasty animalism": "We get very weary of this protracted hankering after a person of the other sex; it seems meat, drink, thought, sinew, religion for the fleshly school." Buchanan and numerous other critics also objected to the Pre-Raphaelite predilection, particularly in Rossetti's painting and poetry, to combine religious and erotic imagery in a vaguely medieval setting.

Having heard that Buchanan confessed to being the author of "The Fleshly School of Poetry," Swinburne wrote to William Rossetti, Dante Gabriel's brother: "I believe it is a habit with the verminous little cur to sneak into some other hide as mangy as his own. . . ." When Buchanan expanded his diatribe into a pamphlet titled *The Fleshly School of Poetry and Other Phenomena of the Day* (1872), Swinburne was furious at Buchanan's raging against Baudelaire as "a fifth-rate *littérateur*" and "the godfather of the modern Fleshly School." Because of Buchanan's misreading of Baudelaire and of Swinburne's presumed indebtedness, the later association of Decadence with Swinburne, who also wrote fervent patriotic poetry on behalf of Mazzini's struggle to liberate Italy, tended to confuse readers. For example, a modern critic has called Swinburne "the first Decadent in England." Such designations obscure the fact that, at times, some writers adopted the images, motifs, and attitudes associated with Decadence, but at other times insisted on the morality of art.

AS YEATS SAID in his memoirs, "If Rossetti was a subconscious influence [on members of the Rhymers' Club because of his devotion to beauty], and perhaps the most powerful of all, we looked consciously to Pater for our philosophy." *Studies in the History of the Renaissance* (1873), with its hortatory "Conclusion," had such an extraordinary impact on the young fin-de-siècle writers that T. S. Eliot later attributed a number of "untidy lives" to Pater's influence. The "Conclusion," with its sense of urgency concerning the passing of one's life in a universe of death, rejects abstract philosophical systems that deny the uniqueness of an individual's subjective impressions "in his isolation, each mind keeping as a solitary prisoner its own dream of a world":

Not the fruit of experience, but experience itself, is the end. . . . With this sense of the splendour of our experience and of its awful brevity, gathering all we are into one desperate effort to see and touch, we shall hardly have time to make theories about the things we see and touch. What we have to do is to be forever curiously testing new opinions and courting new impressions. . . .

To maintain "ecstasy" while burning with a "hard gemlike flame" was "success in life"—the Paterian formula for a "quickened, multiplied consciousness" to enable the self to transcend the deadening flux of daily existence in an industrial society. The cultivation of intense sensations thus served to unify personality, the means of achieving moral vision. Art, Pater proclaimed, was uniquely endowed with the capacity to provide such vital experiences, indeed to provide "the highest quality to your moments as they pass":

> While all melts under our feet, we may well grasp at any exquisite passion, or any contribution to knowledge that seems by a lifted horizon to set the spirit free for a moment, or any stirring of the senses, strange dyes, strange colours, and curious odours, or work of the artist's hands, or the face of one's friend.

"Strange dyes, strange colours, and curious odours"—here were implications of the Decadent quest, the dark side of Romanticism, derived from Poe and other writers who defined it as strangeness united with beauty. In discussing Leonardo da Vinci, Pater evokes these elements in the portrait of Beatrice d'Este, which reveals Leonardo's "presentiment of early death" and "the refinement of the dead": "Sometimes this curiosity came in conflict with the desire of beauty; it tended to make him go too far below that outside of things in which art begins and ends." "Curiosity"—involving a quest for the unutterable that offended polite society—was thus associated with Decadence by Arthur Symons, Aubrey Beardsley, and others.

Pater wrote of the "touch of something sinister" that plays over all of Leonardo's work, most evident in the Mona Lisa (known also as La Gioconda). His famous passage describing Leonardo's painting is itself disturbing and subversive, for it depicts a corrupt but beautiful ancient reality having evolved through centuries of surfeit and sin (implying Pater's rejection of the Victorian dogma of material and moral progress):

> Hers is the head upon which all "the ends of the world are come," and the eyelids are a little weary. It is a beauty wrought out from within upon the flesh, the deposit, little cell by cell, of strange thoughts and fantastic reveries and exquisite passions. . . . She is older than the rocks among which she sits; like the

vampire she has been dead many times, and learned the secrets of the grave.

Calling this celebrated passage one of "revolutionary importance," Yeats arranged it in the form of free verse and placed it first in his anthology, *The Oxford Book of Modern Verse* (1936). The icon of the femme fatale haunted the late nineteenth century, though one sees it earlier, for example, in Keats's "La Belle Dame sans Merci." As women achieved greater independence and challenged male authority in the fin de siècle, images of seductive fatal women became widespread in literature and art, as though men sensed the possibility of their own marginalization. In Shaw's *Man and Superman* (1905), John Tanner, who discovers that he is "in the grip of the Life Force," calls its embodiment, Ann Whitefield, "a vampire."

Long before *Studies in the History of the Renaissance* appeared, rumors had been circulating among undergraduates at Brasenose College, Oxford, that Pater had "a new and daring philosophy of his own." The impact of the "Conclusion" on the young prompted Pater's colleagues to urge its omission in the second edition, when the title was changed to *The Renaissance: Studies in Art and Poetry* (1877). Acceding to their wishes, he removed it: "I conceived it might possibly mislead some of those young men into whose hands it might fall."

The reputation of *The Renaissance* throughout the remainder of the century was striking: Symons wrote that, from the time of its publication, it was taken as "the manifesto of the so-called 'aesthetic' school." By the late 1880s and 1890s, however, the Decadent elements of the *The Renaissance* were regarded by many as preeminent. Wilde, for example, told Yeats, perhaps facetiously: "It is my golden book; I never travel anywhere without it; but it is the very flower of decadence: the last trumpet should have sounded the moment it was written." The more muted Symons regarded it as "the most beautiful book of prose in our language," the product of an intellect aesthetically refined to the point of Decadence: "Nothing is left to inspiration; like Baudelaire, he would better nature." Employing the familiar hothouse image, Symons characterized Pater's imaginative world: "An almost oppressive quiet—a quietness which seems to breathe of an atmosphere heavy with tropical flowers broods over these pages. . . ."

WITH THE PUBLICATION of his philosophical novel *Marius the Epicurean* (1885), Pater articulated with greater clarity what he had briefly suggested in his "Conclusion" to *The Renaissance.* As a result, when the third edition of *The Renaissance* appeared in 1888, he restored the "Conclusion," slightly revised. In the novel, Marius's increasing responsiveness to ritual is a major aspect of his spiritual development from the pagan religion of his boyhood to a vision of Christianity when he dies in ancient Rome. As Marius matures and discovers his vocation as poet, his aestheticism is reinforced by his friendship with Flavian, a poet determined to experience sensations for their own sake, who sees in literature a "deliverance from mortality." But Marius's development proceeds beyond his friend's; his quest for moral perfection emerges as a corollary to his increasing regard for ritual. He eventually discovers in Christianity the "beauty of holiness" and the "elegance of sanctity": The "ritual system" of the Church is thus regarded as one of the "great . . . and *necessary* products of the human mind." Though Marius dies before he can embrace the Church, Christianity holds out the hope of an eternal order in a transitory universe.

While the novel presents some elements associated with late nineteenth-century Aestheticism, particularly in Marius's attraction to the beauty of ritual, the stylistic features of Pater's work approximate those of Decadence in their deliberate avoidance of the grand literary style familiar to Victorian readers and in the focus on the strange and bizarre. In describing the "Golden Book" (Apuleius's *Golden Ass*) that delights both Marius and Flavian, Pater seems to be describing his own artificial prose style:

> . . . full of archaisms and curious felicities in which that generation delighted, quaint terms and images picked fresh from the early dramatists, the life-like phrases of some lost poet preserved by an old grammarian, racy morsels of the vernacular and studied prettinesses:—all alike, mere playthings for the genuine power and natural eloquence of the erudite artist, unsuppressed by his erudition.

Indeed, such eclectic elements, consisting of numerous quotations in Greek and Latin, a convoluted, hesitant sentence structure, and a tendency to invent new forms of expression, suggest a newly devised literary language designed for learned readers with cultivated aesthetic tastes. A recent critic has remarked that Pater wrote English as though it were "an artificial dialect, a petrifaction, a dead tongue"—indeed, as though it were decadent Latin. Such a subversion of an established traditional style implied that Victorian England was undergoing a cultural crisis, for pride in the achievements of the English language and in the civilizing ideals of the British Empire were ineluctably fused.

THE DESTINY OF the Roman Empire held more than passing interest for the Victorians, who, as the century progressed, suffered increasing anxiety over the the future of their own empire. Not only did many Roman writers themselves provide evidence of the moral corruptions that brought about the destruction of their empire, but Edward Gibbon's six-volume *History of the Decline and Fall of the Roman Empire* (1776–88) also established an awesome model and warning that Victorian historians and moralists cited as their authority. In 1891, for example, T. H. Huxley granted that, though some misery was beyond human control, that which was the result of human failure could destroy England. The analogy between the British Empire and Roman Empire was abundantly clear:

> It is certain that there is an immense amount of remediable misery among us; that, in addition to the poverty, disease and degradation, which are the consequences of causes beyond human control, there is a vast, probably a very much larger, quantity of misery which is the result of individual ignorance, or misconduct, and of faulty social arrangements. Further, I think it is not to be doubted that, unless this remediable misery is effectually dealt with, the hordes of vice and pauperism will destroy modern civilization as effectually as uncivilized tribes of another kind destroyed the great social organization which preceded ours.

In the mid-nineteenth century, the figure of Nero engaged the attention of historians who seized upon him as characteristic of Roman decadence. Charles Merivale, for example, was convinced that while the world endured, "the iniquities of Nero will retain their pre-eminence in infamy. . . ." An often-cited example of Nero's depravity was his method of amusing his guests: He lighted his gardens by having live Christian captives covered with wax and set afire. By the end of the century, the Aesthetes and Decadents, rejecting the moral judgments of the historians, perceived Nero as a cultural hero, an Aesthete (or, some might say, a Decadent) who had brought a new, curious sensibility to a declining world. In imitation, Wilde, on his return from his lecture tour of America in 1882, had his hair curled in Paris after the fashion of the bust of Nero in the Louvre. London, he boasted, was "amazed" by it. In his essay "Pen, Pencil and Poison: A Study in Green" (1889/1891), Wilde anticipated the cultural relativism of our own time by contending that there were many historians "who still think it necessary to apply moral judgments to history, and who distribute their praise or blame with the solemn complacency of a successful schoolmaster. This, however, is a foolish habit. . . .

Nobody with the true historical sense ever dreams of blaming Nero, or scolding Tiberius or censuring Caesar Borgia."

Huysmans's *A Rebours* had provided a suitable chapter on Rome to fire the Decadent imagination. In the third chapter, Des Esseintes prefers the writers of the Latin decadence, particularly Petronius, known as the elegant arbiter of taste in Nero's court. Depicting the "vices of a decrepit civilization" in his *Satyricon,* Petronius portrayed "an empire falling to ruin." For Decadent writers seeking a means of contending with a culture in decline, Petronius provided a stylistic model. As one critic has written: "The decadent style, then, is the agonizingly beautiful lament of the dying civilization. It portrays the civilized man, with exquisite though involuted taste, expiring like a perfect gentleman—the archetypal Petronius banqueting with choice friends before slowly opening his veins, a deliberate smile playing upon his lips, while he utters a final epigram."

THE DECLINING ROMAN world of *Marius the Epicurean* attracted one of Pater's unwelcome disciples, the Irish novelist George Moore, who declared *Marius* "a book to which I owe the last temple in my soul." After a brief period in London, he had gone to Paris in the 1870s to study painting and write poetry. Much of his time, however, was spent in music halls and cafés. In 1878, he published, at his own expense, *Flowers of Passion.* An obvious attempt at Baudelairean imitation, the volume includes among its "pale passion flowers" the "Ode to a Dead Body" with its deathless line: "Poor breasts! whose nipples sins alone have fed." When the volume was declared indecent, Moore withdrew it. Despite an inauspicious beginning, Moore published his second and final effort at verse, *Pagan Poems* (1881), which contained "The Hermaphrodite" (modeled after Gautier and Swinburne, whose "Hermaphroditus" had appeared in *Songs and Ballads*). The volume, according to Moore's biographer, "failed to attract even hostile attention, and the printer soon sold all the copies as waste paper."

Though his early verse had few readers, Moore maintained his sense of integrity in the face of public resistance, a defiant stance that he sustained throughout his career. In a letter to a friend, Moore wrote late in his life: ". . . whosoever follows the fashion loses all individuality—it is necessary to be stiff-necked and obdurate and to treat one's contemporaries with contumely. In the great periods the artist took strength from his environment; he was concentric, but in periods of decadence like the present, the artist must be eccentric, stand aloof and disdainfully." This had been established doctrine among the London avant-garde from Swinburne onwards; its corollary was that periods of social decadence give rise to artistic Decadence. Many nineteenth-century bourgeois critics, however, assumed that both terms were synonomous and hence condemned writers accordingly for suspect aesthetic attitudes or subject matter. In the midst of such perplexity, writers proceeded to add irony and additional confusion to the meaning of "decadence." Symons, for example, shortly before his disastrous mental breakdown in 1908, used the term in his morose struggle to maintain his integrity in a materialistic world seemingly bent on its own destruction:

> There has been great talk of late of degeneracy, decadence, and what are supposed to be perversities: such as religion, art, genius, and individuality. But it is the millionaire, the merchant, the money-maker, the sweater [one who demands hard work for very low wages], who are the degenerates of civilisation, and as the power comes into their hands all noble and beautiful things are being crushed out one after another, by some mechanical device for multiplying inferiority.

Richard Ellmann has written that Yeats spoke derisively of "that decadence we call progress" and that the avant-garde of the fin de siècle regarded the true decadents as those stolid Victorians who accepted the "acquisitive, insensitive, unimaginative world, with all its morality, sincerity and seriousness." In such a culture, the serious artist felt increasingly alienated, his rebelliousness intensifying as the nineteenth century came to an end, and with the early twentieth-century rechristening of Aestheticism and Decadence as "Modernism," the artist's rejection of the bourgeois audience led to an increasingly difficult, obscure art.

Moore had sensed such cultural changes in the late nineteenth century as a result of his early exposure to French literature; in turn, he adopted the poseur's wish to startle his readers. Indeed, in his entertaining autobiographical novel *Confessions of a Young Man* (1887/1888), he simultaneously wished to shock his English readers and amuse himself by creating Edward Dayne, a Decadent and dandy, whom Moore depicts as a farcical figure. Having read Gautier's *Mademoiselle de Maupin,* Dayne undergoes a "conversion": He now leads a life "on a purely pagan basis" with a new creed proclaiming the "divinity of the body." He feeds on "mad and morbid literature" for months, and the apartment that he shares with an artist friend in Paris reflects his newly adopted aesthetic tastes and his need to experience curious sensations from odd juxtapositions of the sacred and the profane: In one room, "you faced an altar, a Buddhist temple, a statue of the Apollo, and a bust of Shelley." Moore, who had read *A Rebours* in 1886, echoes descriptions of Des Esseintes's house outside of Paris, but he prefers a hero who postures more emphatically before the reader: "I am feminine, morbid, perverse. But above all perverse, almost everything perverse interests, fascinates me."

Like Moore, Dayne strives for survival in a world increasingly devoted to respectability and universal education. Like Baudelaire and succeeding Decadents and Symbolists who cultivated a sense of their superiority amidst the growing mediocrity, Dayne expounds late nineteenth-century dogma calculated to infuriate the bourgeoisie:

> We are now in a period of decadence growing steadily more and more acute. The old gods are falling about us, there is little left to raise our hearts and minds to, and amid the wreck and ruin of things only a snobbery is left to us, thank heaven, deeply graven in the English heart; the snob is now the ark that floats triumphant over the democratic wave.

Such antidemocratic attitudes—widespread among intellectuals and artists, whether Fabians, Aesthetes, or Decadents—were shared by such early and later Modernists as Yeats, Ezra Pound, D. H. Lawrence, T. S. Eliot, and Shaw, who were drawn to totalitarian politics in the 1920s and 1930s as strong leaders arose from the debris and disillusionment of the First World War.*

Moore sent his *Confessions* to Pater, who addressed him in a letter as "audacious Moore" in admiration of his "Aristophanic joy, or at least enjoyment, in life—your unfailing liveliness." But Moore's "satiric" work also prompted Pater to quote Hamlet: " 'Thou com'st in such a questionable shape!'—I feel inclined to say, on finishing your book: 'shape'—morally, I mean; not in reference to style." *Confessions,* he believed, had a "cynical, and therefore exclusive, way of looking at the world. You call it only 'realistic.' Still—!"

OSCAR WILDE REPORTEDLY said, with a touch of malice, that George Moore had "conducted his whole education in public." Indeed, *Confessions,* in its quest for "sacred books," was itself an attempt to create one, and somewhat facetiously Moore said that he had succeeded. For Wilde, the "sacred book" was Pater's *The Renaissance,* though he too attempted to create one in his only novel, *The Picture of Dorian Gray* (1890/1891).

*Michael Holroyd concedes that Shaw had "certainly written some silly and insensitive things about Stalin and Hitler when attempting to influence British foreign policy and bring maturity to our democracy," but Shaw was convinced, remarks Holroyd, that "the world would be a better place" without dictators. In 1938, Shaw wrote: "I am tired of the way in which newspapers . . . continue to make it appear that I am an admirer of dictatorship. All my work shows the truth to be otherwise" ("Bernard Shaw," *Times Literary Supplement* [London], September 20, 1991: 15).

As the most famous Decadent novel of the British 1890s, it sums up—and radicalizes—much that Wilde had read in Pater and in French literature, particularly Huysmans's *A Rebours*. Like Moore, Wilde was conducting *his* education in public. Indeed, the reviewer for the *St. James's Gazette* (June 20, 1890) accused Wilde of airing "his cheap research among the garbage of the French *Décadents* like any drivelling pedant."

In Wilde's novel, the dandiacal Lord Henry Wotton presents Dorian with a yellow-backed novel that transfigures his life. This "poisonous book," Wilde said, was "partly suggested" by *A Rebours*, though his was a "fantastic variation" on Huysmans's "study of the artistic temperament in our inartistic age." However, Dorian, the "young Adonis . . . made out of ivory and rose leaves," lacks Des Esseintes's psychological complexity and aesthetic ingenuity. Huysmans's hero is a Decadent who suffers from *ennui* and alienation; Wilde's, on the other hand, is a narcissist who trifles with art initially, then turns to "evil" by distorting Lord Henry's urgent advice: "Live! Live the wonderful life that is in you! Let nothing be lost upon you. Be always searching for new sensations. . . . A new Hedonism—that is what our century wants. You might be its visible symbol." Dorian transforms these distant echoes of Pater's "Conclusion" to *The Renaissance* into a self-destructive vision: "There were moments when he looked on evil simply as a mode through which he could realize his conception of the beautiful."

At the heart of the novel is the magical picture that bears the burden of Dorian's conscience and guilt (the fallen soul), while he retains his seemingly undefiled body. As he leaves a number of destroyed lives behind him, the divided Dorian periodically examines his portrait, the symbolic mirror of his psyche, to see the corrosive effects of his evil. In the 1880s, Wilde had numerous models from which to draw: "magic-picture mania" produced such now-forgotten popular novels as *The Picture's Secret, The Portrait and the Ghost, The Veiled Picture,* and *His Other Self.* In Henry James's *The Tragic Muse* (1889/1890), the idle aesthete Gabriel Nash, having sat only once for his portrait, vanishes from the novel as his portrait magically fades, suggesting a lack of substance in both sitter and picture ("I rove, drift, float," he remarks). Nash is thus denied the narcissistic pleasure of contemplating his own image. In George Moore's *Mike Fletcher* (1889), the hero, also having lived a life of self-indulgence, examines himself in a mirror (the symbolic equivalent of the portrait) before his suicide. As a modern critic has stated: "For the writers of the nineties—as for the Romantics—introspection, mirror-gazing, is a sanctioned activity. For the world, wear your mask; for a true glimpse of yourself, consult your mirror."

Max Beerbohm's "The Happy Hypocrite," which appeared in the *Yellow Book* (October 1896), parodied Wilde's novel in its depiction of the wicked Lord George Hell, who assumes the identity of George Heaven by donning a literal mask of saintliness. When, after George has been married a month, a former lover tears the mask from his face, he is revealed as having been transformed by love from Hell to Heaven (rather than, as in the destruction of Dorian's "mask" of innocent youth, transformed by evil from Heaven to Hell). As a recent critic has observed, "Lord George is saved by a mask, while Dorian is destroyed by one." Wilde's novel—with its observation that "Each of us has Heaven and Hell in him" and with the unmasking of Dorian Gray—no doubt suggested the means by which Beerbohm structured his allegory of good and evil.

Wilde was thoroughly aware that his novel mirrored aspects of himself, despite his remark in the "Preface": "To reveal art and conceal the artist is art's aim." In 1894, he told a correspondent: "Basil Hallward [the painter of Dorian's portrait] is what I think I am: Lord Henry what the world thinks me: Dorian what I would like to be—in other ages, perhaps." When Hallward confronts Dorian with the crucial question, "why is your friendship so fatal to young men?" Wilde circumvents the intriguing query just as he does Hallward's homoerotic impulse, for he was willing to abide by Victorian propriety for the sake of literary fame. Thus, the novel has much about suggestive "secrets" as well as a conventionally moral ending (in which Dorian stabs the painting in a rage, thereby magically restoring the painting to its original condition and transforming himself in death into a hideous old man). Nevertheless, Wilde insisted in the "Preface" that "There is no such thing as a moral or an immoral book."

Wilde probably thought that the ending would satisfy the most demanding guardians of public morals and insure his success. Many critics, however, perceiving homoeroticism, condemned the novel. The reviewer in the *Daily Chronicle* (June 30, 1890) described the novel as "a tale spawned from the leprous literature of the French *Décadents*—a poisonous book, the atmosphere of which is heavy with the mephitic odours of moral and spiritual putrefaction. . . ." And while the reviewer alludes to Dorian's "unbridled indulgence in every form of secret and unspeakable vice," he is clearly reluctant to be specific. In the *Athenaeum* (June 27, 1891), the reviewer called the novel "unmanly, sickening, vicious." (*Secret vice* and *unmanly* were Victorian code words usually implying homosexuality.) Wilde created some confusion by first denying that his novel had a "moral," then revealing what its moral was in response to adverse reviews. To the *St. James's Gazette,* he wrote that the "moral" of the novel was that "All excess, as well as all renunciation, brings its own punishment," but then added facetiously that this "terrible moral" was the only artistic "error" in the book.

IN FEBRUARY 1890, the poet Lionel Johnson, while an undergraduate at New College, Oxford, met Wilde, who was visiting Pater at Brasenose College. In a letter to a friend, Johnson described Wilde as "delightful. . . . He discoursed, with infinite flippancy, of everyone . . . laughed at Pater: and consumed all my cigarettes. I am in love with him." When *The Picture of Dorian Gray* appeared, Johnson wrote a poem of praise in Latin, "In Honorem Doriani Creatorisque Eius" ("In Honour of Dorian and His Creator"), never published in his lifetime: "Avidly he loves strange loves, / Savage with beauty / Plucks strange flowers." With additional allusions to the "apples of Sodom" and "sweet sins," Johnson, who, some modern critics believe, was probably homoerotic, clearly grasped the novel's underlying implications.

Yet in the following year, he published an anonymous satire titled "The Cultured Faun," which appears to be directed at Wilde's novel as an expression of Decadence: "Take a young man, who had brains as a boy and teach him to disbelieve everything that his elders believe in matters of thought, and to reject everything that seems true to himself in matter of sentiment." Bored, the young man must be provided with "a graceful affection" and "a surprising paradox": "Externally, our hero should culti-vate a reassuring sobriety of habit, with just a dash of the dandy . . . a precise appearance, internally, a catholic sympathy with all that exists, and 'therefore' suffers, for art's sake. . . . That is the point: exquisite apprecia-tion of pain, exquisite thrills of anguish, exquisite adoration of suffering."

Johnson satirizes those passages in *Dorian Gray* that are concerned with the aesthetic experience of religious ritual. It is rumored that Dorian "was about to join the Roman Catholic communion; and certainly the Roman ritual had always a great attraction for him," as it had for many in the 1890s. Besides Wilde (who underwent conversion on his death bed), such figures as Lord Alfred Douglas, Lionel Johnson, Ernest Dowson, Aubrey Beardsley, and John Gray also turned to Rome. The paradox of rebellious Decadent writers rejecting the stifling Victorian world of bour-geois morality and the liberal theology of the Church of England in order to embrace the binding dogmas of Roman Catholicism can be explained, in part, by the crisis over faith that had intensified with Darwin's *Origin of Species* (1859) and by the consequent need for ancient, universal author-ity. The aesthetic experience of Roman ritualism was undoubtedly a fur-ther attraction, as Wilde suggests in his novel and as Johnson parodies in "The Cultured Faun." In the former, Dorian loves "to kneel down on the cold marble pavement, and watch the priest, in his stiff flowered dalmatic, slowly and with white hands moving aside the veil of the tabernacle, or raising aloft the jewelled lantern-shaped monstrance with that pallid wafer . . . the bread of angels. . . ." In "The Cultured Faun," Johnson depicts a shallow Aesthete, who, like Dorian Gray, enjoys the sensuous experience of ritual without religious commitment:

> Here comes in a tender patronage of Catholicism: white tapers upon the high altar, an ascetic and beautiful young priest, the great gilt monstrance, the subtle-scented and mystical incense . . . the splendor of the sacred vestments. We kneel at some hour, not too early for our convenience, repeating that solemn Latin, drinking in those Gregorian tones, with plenty of modern French sonnets in memory, should the sermon be dull. But to join the Church! Ah, no! better to dally with the enchanting mysteries. . . .

The satire ends with the Decadent preoccupation with the sins of previous cultures, now resident in London: "And who shall assail us?—what stupid and uncultured critic, what coarse and narrow Philistine? We are the Elect of Beauty: saints and sinners, devils and devotees, Athenians and Parisians, Romans of the Empire and Italians of the Renaissance. *Fin de siècle! Fin de siècle!* Literature is a thing of beauty, blood, and nerves."

The "Elect of Beauty," a concept common to nineteenth-century Aestheticism, was publicized by Wilde, who, in the preface to *Dorian Gray,* announced: "Those who find beautiful meanings in beautiful things are the cultivated. . . . They are the elect to whom beautiful things mean only beauty." For those not of the elect, namely the uneducated and uncultured masses in Victorian society, there could be no hope; they were doomed to the ugliness of the industrial age and the mediocrity of their own narrow minds. Such was the mythology of Aestheticism, which became central to Modernism.

IN LATE JUNE 1892, the French actress Sarah Bernhardt was rehearsing Wilde's one-act play *Salomé* at the Palace Theatre. Following customary procedure, the theater manager had submitted a copy of the play to the Lord Chamberlain's office for official licensing of its production. The examiner of plays, Edward Pigott, notified the manager that licensing the play would be problematic because it contained Biblical characters, a prohibition that had existed since the Reformation in order to discourage Roman Catholic writers from propagandizing in the theater. But undoubtedly the perversity of Salome's desires was the principal reason for Pigott's hesitation. In an interview in the *Pall Mall Budget* (June 30, 1892), conducted before Pigott's decision to ban the play, Wilde remarked: "I care very little about the refusal of the Lord Chamberlain to allow my play to be produced. What I do care about is this—that the Censorship apparently regards the stage as the lowest of all the arts, and looks on acting as a vulgar thing." Furthermore, if *Salomé* were banned, he would leave England and settle in France: ". . . I will take out letters of naturalization. I will not consent to call myself a citizen of a country that shows such narrowness in its artistic judgment. I am not English; I'm Irish—which is quite another thing."

The London press responded with glee: The *Pall Mall Budget* (June 30), in which the interview had appeared, published a cartoon titled "Monsieur Vilde," showing him as a French abbé; *Punch* (July 9) published a cartoon of Wilde as a French conscript with the title "A Wilde Idea. Or, More Injustice to Ireland!"; and William Watson composed "Lines to our new Censor" for the *Spectator* (July 9):

> *And wilt thou, Oscar, from us flee,*
>   *And must we, henceforth, wholly sever?*
> *Shall thy laborious jeux-d'esprit*
>   *Sadden our lives no more for ever?*

To this, Wilde sighed: "There is not enough fire in William Watson's poetry to boil a tea-kettle." Writing from Germany, Wilde told the painter Will Rothenstein that Pigott was "really a commonplace official . . . who panders to the vulgarity and hypocrisy of the English people, by licensing every low farce and vulgar melodrama."

Though Pigott refused to license *Salomé* for the stage, there was no prohibition against its publication: In February 1893, it appeared in its original French version simultaneously in London and Paris. The impact on the critics pleased Wilde, who wrote to the actor Oswald Yorke from Babbacombe Cliff: "I hear London [is] like some grey monster raging over the publication of *Salome,* but I am at peace for the moment." On the day following its appearance, the reviewer for the *Times* (February 23) called it "morbid, *bizarre,* repulsive, and very offensive in its adaptation of scriptural phraseology to situations the reverse of sacred." However, the fusion of erotic Decadence and Christian myth accounts for much of *Salomé*'s power. The "unnatural" incantatory style, which Wilde had modeled after the Symbolist dramatist Maurice Maeterlinck, heightens the Biblical setting and the impression of Decadent artifice.

Though Salome's obsessive desire for the body of Jokanaan, and particularly for his lips, is initially thwarted, she achieves transcendent consummation of her perverse, frighteningly aggressive desire to kiss the mouth of his decapitated head: "I will bite it with my teeth as one bites a ripe fruit." Salome's final line, "I have kissed thy mouth, Jokanaan"—a moment of extraordinary power in its quiet triumph—is followed by

Herod's theatrically compelling final line: "Kill that woman!" Salome is a castrating figure of destruction, whereas Jokanaan, the prophet who had baptized Jesus and had envisioned his saving mission, is associated with his forthcoming martyrdom. Thus, castration and crucifixion are united in Wilde's imagination as symbolic forms of mutilation associated with masochistic debasement and narcissistic elevation—a pattern enacted by Wilde himself in the tragic year of 1895. That Wilde identified himself with Salomé is apparent in a revealing photograph published in Richard Ellmann's biography depicting Wilde as Salome in drag and wig, reaching for the head of Jokanaan on a silver shield.

The focus on the central images of moon, blood, and Salome's dance of the seven veils—embodying the characters' states of mind and suggesting transcendental realities—reveals Wilde's intention to write a Symbolist play; indeed, critics have declared *Salome* as the only truly English Symbolist work of the 1890s. In the play, Herod warns: "It is not wise to find symbols in everything that one sees. It makes life too full of terrors," implying possibilities of forbidden knowledge and dire consequences. In the "Preface" to *The Picture of Dorian Gray,* Wilde had previously written: "All art is at once surface and symbol. Those who go beneath the surface do so at their peril. Those who read the symbol do so at their peril."

The French Symbolists, the major influence on Wilde in the writing of the play, were antirationalists convinced that occult correspondences between the phenomenal and transcendental worlds could be evoked by symbols. It was possible, then, for "each mind keeping as a solitary prisoner in its own dream of a world"—as Pater had said—to escape to other worlds. The Symbolists also understood that symbols concealed as well as revealed the inner world of the symbol maker and symbol interpreter: In the prepsychoanalytic world of the early 1890s, Wilde intuitively grasped the power of symbols and their subterranean existence. In *Sartor Resartus* (1833–34), Thomas Carlyle had already pointed out their characteristics and their capacity to shape and affect human consciousness: "It is in and through Symbols that man, consciously or unconsciously, lives, works, and has his being." Since symbol and "mask" are aesthetically related, each providing a means by which the imagination shapes our most profound conceptions of self, Wilde proposed in his essay "The Critic as Artist" (1890/1891): "Man is least himself when he talks in his own person. Give him a mask, and he will tell you the truth."

In February 1894, Wilde's *Salome* was published in an English translation by Lord Alfred Douglas with Wilde's revisions. The brilliant twenty-one-year-old artist Aubrey Beardsley contributed eleven illustrations, his most enduringly popular work, a form of Decadent art influenced by the Japanese print. However, Beardsley experienced considerable stress over his pictures when the publisher John Lane of the Bodley Head and Wilde objected to some of the more outrageous illustrations that depicted male

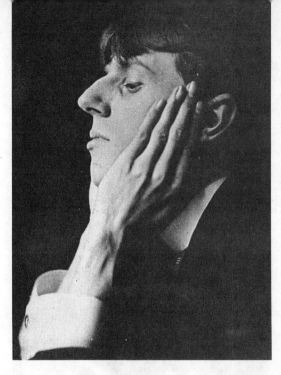

Aubrey Beardsley

and female nudes, some of them obvious hermaphrodites, others clearly androgynous. To Robert Ross, Wilde's intimate friend and later literary executor, Beardsley wrote in November 1893: "I suppose you've heard all about the *Salomé* row. I can tell you I had a warm time of it between Lane and Oscar and Co. For one week the numbers of telegraph and messenger boys who came to the door was simply scandalous. . . . I have withdrawn three of the illustrations and supplied their places with three new ones (simply beautiful and quite irrelevant)."

Though some depict scenes that seem to have no relevance to the play, they often reveal a parallel vision of erotic Decadence. The first version of the title page, for example, depicts an obscenely leering priapus,* here a hermaphrodite with eyes for nipples and and navel, anticipating Surrealism in the next century. (In the final version, Beardsley removed the genitals from the priapus and from the kneeling angelic figure.) Further anticipations of Surrealism occur in "The Woman in the Moon" (its original title: "The Man in the Moon"); the "woman," of course, is Wilde in his bloated sensuality. The void in which the two figures stand is a dream world of indeterminate time and space. The single flower (as opposed to clusters of what are probably roses in some other drawings) suggests the

---

*In many ancient cultures, the priapus was a stylized statue of the phallic god Priapus, the alleged offspring of Dionysus and Aphrodite (gods of love and regeneration). Usually without arms or legs, sometimes with exposed genitals, sometimes horned— suggesting an identification with Pan, the pastoral god of fertility—priapuses were often placed in gardens to stimulate regeneration and to act as scarecrows.

Beardsley's "Herodias and Page" in *Salome*

Suppressed title page for *Salome*

green carnation, the unnatural flower of Decadence that Wilde wore publicly at the premiere of *Lady Windermere's Fan* (1892) and *The Importance of Being Earnest* (1895) and that in Paris was worn as a symbol of homosexuality. The sinister implications of the color green had already been suggested by Wilde in his biographical study "Pen, Pencil, and Poison" (1889/1891) of the poisoner Thomas Giffiths Wainewright, who had "that curious love of green, which in individuals is always the sign of a subtle artistic temperament, and in nations is said to denote a laxity, if not a decadence, of morals."

In the play, Salome promises that if the Young Syrian permits her to see Jokanaan, she will "let fall . . . a little flower, a little green flower"—her own symbol of perverse, forbidden desire. On at least one occasion, Beardsley wore the flower in Wilde's company, but in "The Woman in the Moon," he now mocked its significance by including a stylized version, not green but ashen white. Perhaps the most remarkable of the illustrations anticipating Surrealism is "The Climax," its narcissistic dream flight achieved in literal and symbolic imagery as Salome floats in space with the severed, snakelike head of Jokanaan, the object of her lust held before her as though suggesting the familiar icon of Narcissus gazing at his own image, an emblem of self-destructiveness (perhaps Beardsley's veiled prophecy of Wilde's tragic end).

IN 1889, WILDE had met John Gray, a handsome twenty-three-year-old civil servant of Scots background, at a dinner party in London. An aspiring poet interested in the French Symbolists, Gray had educated himself in the arts and had learned to speak French. In the early nineties, he emerged in literary circles as a dandy and wit. Having achieved small

"The Woman in the Moon" in *Salome*

notoriety as the possible model for Dorian Gray, Gray gathered a sufficient number of poems for his first volume, *Silverpoints* (1893), a title
suggesting the interrelationship of poetry and the visual arts (a silverpoint
being a stylus that leaves an indelible trace of silver-gray on paper coated
with opaque white). The volume, designed by the noted artist Charles
Ricketts, is one of the most distinctive aesthetic volumes of the decade: A
slender, elongated book of only thirty-eight pages, its green boards bear a
flame motif stamped in gold over undulating gold lines running the
length of the volume, and on its expensive handmade paper, the poems
are printed in italics.

Silverpoints has intimations of Decadence in its characteristic fin-de-siècle daintiness of expression and occasionally startling violence. Moreover, versions (rather than translations) of poems by such poets as
Verlaine, Mallarmé, Baudelaire, Laforgue, and Rimbaud provide evidence of the volume's French Symbolist influences. A leading motif of
Gray's poems is the familiar theme of nature transformed by the unnatural, the Decadent ideal. In "Poem," a flower bed is infested by "the
daisies' leprous stain," which mysteriously regenerates itself each day:
"Each night the daisies burst again, / Though every day the gardener

"The Climax" in *Sa-
lome*

crops their heads." In "Summer Past," dedicated to Wilde, suggestive eroticism suffuses nature's familiar forms: "There / Warm hours of leaf-lipped song, / And dripping amber sweat." The "proud leaves curl / In ecstasy."

"The Barber" and "Mishka," two remarkable poems in the volume, contain sexual dreams that anticipate Surrealism by their depiction of the aggressive nature of the unconscious and of the creative process. In "The Barber," the barber as artist attempts to transcend nature by applying pigments to "many a pleasant girl" and by employing the Decadent convention of adding decorative gems:

> *The dream grew vague. I moulded with my hands*
> *The mobile breasts, the valley; and the waist*
> *I touched; and pigments reverently placed*
> *Upon their thighs in sapient spots and stains,*
> *Beryls and crysolites and diaphanes,*
> *And gems whose hot harsh names are never said.*
> *I was a masseur; and my fingers bled*
> *With wonder as I touched their awful limbs.*

Nature, however, has its triumph as Decadence fails:

> *The breasts rose up and offered each a mouth.*
> *And on the belly pallid blushes crept,*
> *That maddened me, until I laughed and wept.*

Mishka, a bear, is a "poet among the beasts" whose imaginative world comes alive when he is "at play in the land of sleep." In his dream, Mishka is lured into the lair of a female, "Dragged in the net of her yellow hair," an omnivorous femme fatale who winds the "triple coil of her hair" round his throat and strokes his limbs with "a humming sound." While the experience is seemingly unbearable, Mishka, as poet of the dream world, imagines his honey bear dissolving into exquisitely natural forms, such as an olive tree, "the voice of birds and the voice of flowers," and a "winged-bee." The final ecstasy of the dream involves the flowing music of nocturnal emission: "Her touch is a perfume, a melody."

Silverpoints was simultaneously Gray's bid for status as an avant-garde poet and his farewell, for his poems in the remaining years of the nineties were principally religious. Later, as a priest in Edinburgh, Gray searched for extant copies of *Silverpoints* in order to obliterate any lingering connection between him and Decadence. Understandably, he never permitted the volume to be reprinted in his lifetime.

―――

TRANSPLANTED TO ENGLAND from France, Decadence did not thrive in Victorian soil. It was regarded as a deviant literary idea, incompatible with the prevailing notions of the function of literature; worse, it was foreign. Furthermore, it lacked the coherence of a movement that the French appeared to give it. By the mid-1880s, *les décadents* in Paris were a recognizable, if ambiguous, group of writers who regarded the term as their badge of honor and whose principal journal, *Le Décadent,* appeared between 1886 and 1889. In England, the term "Decadence" was usually avoided by writers who presumably had affinities with the French, though the epithet was invoked by critics and reviewers when they recognized certain of its alleged qualities in works under review. In 1892, Richard Le Gallienne, who looked like an Aesthete from Gilbert and Sullivan's *Patience,* nevertheless waged a minor campaign against French Decadence in "To the Reader," in *English Poems,* contending that the English nightingale was no longer heard in poetry; the "new voice" was

> *Music of France that once was of the spheres;*
> *And not of thee [the English nightingale] these*
> *   strange green flowers that spring*
> *From daisy roots and seem to bear a sting.*

The "strange green flowers" are again the green carnations that Wilde and his friends wore in public as emblems of Decadence, following Des Esseintes's preference for artifice. A shop in the Burlington Arcade, it was said, provided dyed carnations daily. For Le Gallienne, the color green, in its "more complex forms," implied something "not quite good, something almost sinister . . . though in its simple form, as we find it in outdoor nature, it is innocent enough." But, he contends, the green of the Aesthete (he should have said "Decadent") "does not suggest innocence": "There will always be wearers of the green carnation; but the popular vogue which green has enjoyed for the last ten or fifteen years is probably passing. Even the aesthete himself would seem to be growing a little weary of its infinitely divided tones." In the "so-called aesthetic renaissance the sunflower went before the green carnation—which is, indeed, the badge of but a small schism of aesthetes, and not worn by the great body of the more catholic lovers of beauty." Now the color yellow has made its return and is "becoming more and more dominant in decoration." This "Boom in Yellow," Le Gallienne suggests, is casting its hue on the entire decade of the nineties.*

---

*Besides the famed *Yellow Book* (1894–97), Arthur Benson's privately printed volume of poems was identically titled: *Le Cahier Jaune* (1892); *The Yellow Aster* (1894) was a novel by Kathleen Caffyn, whose pseudonym was "Iota"; Andrew Lang fol-

Richard Le Gallienne

Le Gallienne's best-known assault on Decadence occurred in a review in which he raised the question of proportion: "In all great vital literature, the theme, great or small, is considered in all its relations near and far, and above all in relation to the sum-total of things, to the Infinite, as we phrase it; in decadent literature the relations, the due proportions, are ignored." Le Gallienne may have borrowed this idea from the French critic and novelist Paul Bourget, who had written: "A style of decadence is one in which the unity of the book is decomposed to give place to the independence of the page, in which the page is decomposed to give place to the independence of the phrase, and the phrase to give place to the independence of the word." If such was the case, said Le Gallienne, disease, the "favourite theme of *décadents,*" was not in itself an indication of Decadence:

> . . . it is only when, as often, it is studied apart from its relations
> to health, to the great vital centre of things, that it does so. Any
> point of view, seriously taken, which ignores the complete view,
> approaches decadence. To notice only the picturesque effect of

---

lowed fashion with his *Yellow Fairy Book* (1894), though he employed ten other colors, both before and after 1894, for other volumes of fairy tales.

a beggar's rags, like Gautier; the colour-scheme of a tippler's nose, like M. Huysmans; to consider one's mother merely prismatically, like Mr. Whistler—these are examples of the decadent attitude. At the bottom, decadence is merely limited thinking, often insane thinking.

In *The Religion of a Literary Man* (1893), Le Gallienne continued his campaign: As an "expression of moral, mental, and spiritual disease," Decadence ignores "the higher sensibilities of heart and spirit." Regarding this view as erroneous, Arthur Symons offered a corrective interpretation in an essay published in November 1893. "The Decadent Movement in Literature," the most notable attempt of the decade to define the new phenomenon, is an indication that early Modernism had established a local habitation and a name. Symons's publicizing of the avant-garde at the same time that he became involved in arranging Verlaine's lecture visit to London reinforced the impression that Symons was the major spokesman in England for Decadence.

Symons's strategy was to transform Le Gallienne's condemnation into praise and, in the process, to shock readers accustomed to the conventional Victorian conception of art as moral enlightenment. Decadence, Symons says, has "all the qualities that mark the end of great periods, the qualities that we find in the Greek, the Latin, decadence: an intense self-consciousness, a restless curiosity in research, an over-subtilizing refinement upon refinement, a spiritual and moral perversity." Symons also insists on a startling transvaluation: ". . . this representative literature of to-day, interesting, beautiful, novel as it is, is really a new and beautiful and interesting disease. Healthy we cannot call it, and healthy it does not wish to be considered." In citing the French writer Ernest Hello, Symons points to Hello's worship of a "God of darkness": "And this unreason of the soul—of which Hello himself is so curious a victim—this unstable equilibrium which has overbalanced so many brilliant intelligences into one form or another of spiritual confusion, is but another form of the *maladie fin de siècle.*" (Here is a striking anticipation of Yeats's later mythologizing of the "Tragic Generation" in London.)

As an imaginative response to the end of the nineteenth century, Decadence, Symons states, embraces "two main branches of the movement": Impressionism and Symbolism. Both work in different directions, both seek *la vérité vraie:* "the very essence of truth—the truth of appearances to the senses, of the visible world to the eyes that see it; and the truth of spiritual things to the spiritual vision." (By the end of the decade, Symons was convinced that Symbolism was not an aspect of Decadence but a unique means of summoning unseen earthly and transcendental realities; here, however, was the germ of the idea.) In characterizing the effect of Impressionism and Symbolism on the reader, Symons employs a meta-

Arthur Symons (Princeton University Library)

phor derived from his interpretation of Browning's method by which a moment of tension revealed the essence of character or situation: "The Impressionist, in literature as in painting, would flash upon you in a new, sudden way so exact an image of what you have just seen, just as you have seen it. . . . The Symbolist, in this new sudden way, would flash upon you the 'soul' of that which can be apprehended only by the soul—the finer sense of things unseen, the deeper meaning of things evident." In *An Introduction to the Study of Browning* (1886), Symons had asserted that the poet's practice was "to reveal the soul to itself" by a sudden test, which shall "condense the long trial of years into a single moment, and so 'flash the truth out by one blow.' " In the following century, the device of the symbolic moment (anticipated by Wordsworth in his phrase "spots of time") is evident in Joyce's "epiphany" and in Virginia Woolf's "moments of being."

Symons, whose constant visits to France brought him into contact with virtually every important writer, had met Mallarmé, whom he now called in "The Decadent Movement in Literature" the "prophet and pontiff of the movement, the mystical and theoretical leader of the great emancipation." Symons had also met Huysmans, whose *A Rebours* contained "all that is delicately depraved, all that is beautifully, curiously poisonous, in modern art" with a central character who was "effeminate, over-civilized, [a] deliberately abnormal creature who is the last product of our society . . . exhausted by spiritual and sensory debauches in the delights of the artificial. . . ." Verlaine, the French poet Symons most admired, had achieved the "ideal of Decadence: to be a disembodied voice, and yet the voice of a human soul."

When writing the essay, Symons was convinced that Pater and W. E.

Henley, the poet and journalist, had affinities with the "Decadent Movement." Pater's "morbid curiosity," which attracted him to strangeness in beauty, seemed to suggest correspondences with the French *décadents*. Henley's verse, particularly "In Hospital," was "a poetry of the disagreeable" whose stark impressionism could go "no further." Apparently Symons was willing to ignore the obvious fact that Henley, the editor of the *National Observer*, was the most ardent of the anti-Decadents of the nineties; indeed, his aggressive personality had attracted to the periodical a group of writers (most of them now unknown) who shared his characteristically Victorian assumptions that the age required manliness and determination to sustain Britain's industrial progress, its programs of reform, and the expansion of its empire. Henley's volume, *Song of the Sword and Other Verses* (1892), suggested such imperial aspirations. Indeed, Max Beerbohm facetiously dubbed the writers associated with Henley as "the Henley Regatta," implying a vigorous activism as opposed to a febrile Decadence.

ATTACKS ON DECADENCE came not only from such hostile "outsiders" as Henley but also, as we have seen, from within the circle of writers associated with the style. In 1894, Robert Hichens's brilliant satire, *The Green Carnation*, captured with uncanny accuracy the mannerisms of Wilde, called "Esme Amarinth," and of Lord Alfred Douglas, called "Lord Reggie," presumably to include their mutual friend Reggie Turner, later a novelist, in a composite portrait. Homosexual himself, Hichens had socialized with Wilde, Douglas, and Turner; possibly he had even heard Wilde utter such witticisms as those assigned to Amarinth: "How splendid to die with a paradox upon one's lips!" At the opening of the novel, Lord Reggie is seen in a moment of narcissistic self-admiration in a passage parodying *The Picture of Dorian Gray:* "He slipped a green carnation into his evening coat, fixed it in its place with a pin, and looked at himself in the glass, the long glass that stood near the window of his London bedroom. The summer evening was so bright that he could see his double clearly. . . ." Lord Reggie, we are told, looks "astonishingly young," for "his sins keep him fresh."

Wilde's name appears as a pun when Lord Reggie is appropriately referred to as "one of the wildest young men in London."* Lady Locke,

---

*For many years, *Punch* had used and abused Wilde's name for comic purposes. In *The Picture of Dorian Gray*, Wilde employed his own name as a pun in "wild," "wilder," "wildest," and "wildly," some thirty-four times throughout the novel. See Karl Beckson, "Wilde's Autobiographical Signature in "The Picture of Dorian Gray," *Victorian Newsletter* 69 (Spring 1986): 30–32.

prepared to abandon her interest in Lord Reggie, tells him: ". . . if you could be like a man, instead of like nothing at all in heaven or earth except that dyed flower, I might perhaps care for you in the right way. But your mind is artificially coloured: it comes from the dyer's. It is a green carnation; and I want a natural blossom to wear in my heart." While amused by the novel, Wilde apparently felt some anxiety over the exposure of his relationship with Douglas, telling a friend that Hichens, "the doubting disciple," had written "a false gospel." When rumors circulated that Wilde himself had written *The Green Carnation,* he informed the editor of the *Pall Mall Gazette* (October 1): "I invented that magnificent flower. . . . The flower is a work of art. The book is not."*

As Wilde's fame grew in the nineties and as Decadence achieved notoriety, Henley regarded the Decadents as an obvious challenge to Tory sentiments, to the ideal of manliness, and to standards of common decency. As his biographer has stated, Henley fervently believed that "Nature was now and always man's gallant protest against Art." In the pages of Henley's *National Observer,* attacks on Decadence escalated, a notable instance occurring in the issue of February 23, 1895, in which the anonymous writer thundered in "The Damnation of Decadence":

> And what are these who now whine and write their sickly stuff about *décadence,* and pretend to gird at *décadence,* hoping all the while to gain the crapulous glory of being classed themselves among the *décadents* whom, with their puling whimper, they pretend to decry? The answer is simple. Such creatures are the most despicable excrescences that can grow upon literature. They have not the daring for immorality, and they hug themselves upon being above or beneath morality. They hang helpless, fatuous, incapable of any true thought or action, scorned of all. . . . They have been tolerated, why one does not know, and

---

*Other satires of Decadence are worth noting: G. S. Street's *The Autobiography of a Boy* (1894), for example, has a central character who is described as "a severe ritualist [in his first year at Oxford], in his second year an anarchist and an atheist, in his third wearily indifferent to all things. . . ." Owen Seaman, well known for his satires and parodies, often addressed himself to Decadence, most notably in "To a Boy-Poet of the Decadence" in *The Battle of the Bays* (1896):

> *The erotic affairs that you fiddle aloud*
> *Are as vulgar as coin of the mint;*
> *And you merely distinguish yourself from the crowd*
> *By the fact that you put 'em in print.*

Max Beerbohm's classic short story "Enoch Soames" (1912), reprinted in *Seven Men* (1919), depicts the eponymous hero, a morose Decadent poet desperate for fame whose volume of incomprehensible verse, titled *Fungoids,* sells only three copies.

have presumed on toleration. The time has surely come when
there should be an end of this, and when every man who cares
for the manhood of literature should lift his pen against so dis-
gustful a crew.

Within a month, Henley saw the "damnation of Decadence" in a startlingly unexpected manner with the publication of the most famous—
surely infamous—attack of the decade: Max Nordau's *Degeneration* (a
translation of the original German edition of 1892).

A physician, novelist, and social critic, Nordau admired the work of the
Italian criminologist and physician Cesare Lombroso, who had developed
theories concerning the relationship between genius and insanity in *The
Man of Genius* (English trans., 1891, of *L'Uomo di Genio,* the fifth edition
1888). Lombroso's reductionistic views look forward to Nordau's, as in
the following characteristic observation: "We have seen that a love of
symbolism is one of the characteristics of monomaniacs." Lombroso described the French *décadent* poets as the "new variety of literary mad-
men." The concern with degeneration, not only in artists but also in the
general population, provoked numerous studies in the nineteenth century, an indication of the age's anxiety that "a rising tide of crime and a
surge of unassimilable misfits threatened (as Lombroso put it) to submerge civilization."

During the last third of the century, an increasing preoccupation with
such fears resulted in the doctrine of "race improvement," or "eugenics," the term coined in 1883 by the scientist Francis Galton, Darwin's
cousin. Though he presented convincing evidence that certain traits were
hereditary, a program of selective breeding, such as Galton advocated,
could not guarantee that superior intelligence would be consistently inherited; as a modern writer on the subject has observed: ". . . there are
many instances of men of great genius being born to the most improbable
parents." The English psychologist Henry Maudsley, a follower of the
positivist Auguste Comte, studied pathological states of mind in his major
work, *Body and Will, Being an Essay Concerning Will in its Metaphysical,
Physiological, and Pathological Aspects* (1884), and concluded that humanity
was doomed: ". . . we fix attention too much perhaps on the process of
evolution, to the overlooking of the correlative process of degeneration
that is going on, not only in low but in high organisms . . . not only in
body but in mind; not only in individuals but in societies. . . ." Though
there will be "further great gains in evolution . . . its range on earth is
limited . . . foredoomed in the future": "What an awful contemplation,
that of the human race bereft of its evolutional energy, disillusioned,
without enthusiasm, without hope, without aspiration, without an ideal."

While such late nineteenth-century scientists were charting either the
hope or the doom of humanity with respect to evolutionary theory, non-

scientists argued what its application was with respect to the artist's creative genius. Huysmans regarded the artist's illness as a creative expression of modernity: In *A Rebours,* he refers to Gustave Moreau's Salomé paintings as a "morbid perspicuity of an entirely modern sensibility," and to Odilon Redon's drawings as "a new type of fantasy, born of sickness and delirium." Havelock Ellis, who translated Lombroso's *The Man of Genius,* mused in *The New Spirit* (1890) that "it may be that what we call 'genius' is something abnormal and distorted," and in *The Insanity of Genius* (1891), J. F. Nisbet concluded that "all the available evidence . . . points clearly to the existence of nerve-disorder as a fundamental element of genius in relation to colour and form." As Symons implied in his 1893 essay on Decadence, such views justified the avant-garde artist's sense of superiority to and alienation from the common man.

In *Degeneration,* which Nordau dedicated to Lombroso, his "Dear and Honoured Master," there are unmistakable traces of *The Man of Genius:* Both works discuss a number of the same figures, such as Mallarmé, Verlaine, Baudelaire, Whitman, and Poe, and their central thesis has numerous similarities. Nordau announced that the most widely acclaimed artists, such as William Morris, Ibsen, Tolstoy, Wagner, Huysmans, Manet, Wilde,* Rodin, the Impressionists, the Pre-Raphaelites, and Symbolists were "degenerates," the result of various forms of excessive emotionality. The disease, he said, was not new, but its modern manifestations had reached epidemic proportions (indeed, long before Lombroso and other nineteenth-century theorists, the presumed madness of the poet had been asserted by Plato, versified by Shakespeare, and exploited by the Romantics). In using the terms *degeneration* and *decadence* indiscriminately to suggest racial and artistic decline, Nordau warned that a threat existed to the moral and cultural advances achieved by mankind through evolution. If degeneration was "the dark side of progress," its reversal, Nordau suggested, was essential to restore health to "a dying world." The sensationalism and vibrant style of *Degeneration,* which obviously confirmed Philistine opinion concerning those rejecting conventional standards in art and life, resulted in seven printings within six months.

What infuriated the more discerning readers was the simple-mindedness of the argument. In Nordau's vision of the world, deviations from the ordinary forms of art or expressions of such emotions as melancholy

*Writing from Reading Prison in July 1896, Wilde petitioned the Home Secretary for early release, pleading that he was "rightly found guilty . . . [of] forms of sexual madness . . . diseases to be cured by a physician, rather than crimes to be punished by a judge. In the works of eminent men of science such as Lombroso and Nordau . . . this is specially insisted on with reference to the intimate connection between madness and the literary and artistic temperament. . . ." Wilde cited Nordau's chapter on him "as a specially typical example of this fatal law" (*Letters of Oscar Wilde,* ed. Rupert Hart-Davis [New York, 1962], 402).

or pessimism were indications of the artist's pathology. By extension, departures from social custom or the acceptance of art for art's sake ("ego-mania," he called it) were indications of the artist's immorality. Nordau adopts Lombroso's theory of the organic nature of criminality in his Philistine view that an artist depicting immorality must himself be guilty of it (this view, an astonishing misreading of the creative imagination, is odd, for Nordau was also a novelist):

> It never occurs to us to permit the criminal by organic disposi-
> tion to expand his individuality in crime and just as little can it
> be expected of us to permit the degenerate artist to expand his
> individuality in immoral works of art. The artist who compla-
> cently represents what is reprehensible, vicious, criminal, ap-
> proves of it, perhaps glorifies it, differs not in kind but only in
> degree, from the criminal who actually commits it.

Obviously, Nordau found many supporters for such an assertion. In New York, for example, the *Critic* (January 2, 1897) commented that the recent suicide of Hubert Crackanthorpe, a contributor to the *Yellow Book*, was no surprise: "No young man, or old one, for that matter, could write such morbid, loathsome stories as he wrote and have a sane mind. He was the most pronounced type of the decadent. . . . There is, after all, a good deal of truth in some of Nordau's theories. A man must have a diseased mind who finds pleasure in writing of diseased morals."

Distressed by such "manifest nonsense," Benjamin Tucker, the American editor of the anarchist publication *Liberty* (New York) asked Shaw, "the only man in the world capable of tackling Nordau," to write a response. In his open letter to Tucker, who published it on July 27, 1895 with the title "A Degenerate's View of Nordau," Shaw undermined *Degeneration* at every point by hailing those whom Nordau had attacked; to Shaw, they were the cultural heroes of the age: "There is no need for me to go at any great length into the grounds on which any development in our moral views must at first appear insane and blasphemous to people who are satisfied, or more than satisfied, with the current morality." Nordau, he suggested facetiously, was "shrewd enough to see that there is a good opening for a big reactionary book as a relief to the Wagner and Ibsen booms. . . ." In the preface to his revised version, *The Sanity of Art* (1908), Shaw recalled that Tucker sent a copy of *Liberty* containing the open letter to every American newspaper: "There was a brisk and quick sale of copies in London among the cognoscenti. And *Degeneration* was never heard of again."*

---

*Nevertheless, Nordau continued to be published in Britain. In 1896, Nordau's novel, *The Malady of the Century*, appeared, as did various other books during the following decade, including *On Art and Artists* (1907), which praised many

THOUGH IT WAS doubtful that Decadence was sufficiently widespread in London literary circles to constitute a "movement," Symons's volume of poetry *London Nights* (1895) aroused such anxiety that its presumed Decadence implied a continuing cultural crisis. The virulent abuse by reviewers, directed towards both book and author, had not been seen in Britain since the publication of Swinburne's *Poems and Ballads*. Often regarded as Symons's most Decadent work, *London Nights* was issued by Leonard Smithers, who, already known as a publisher of erotica, was determined to challenge the Establishment. To the American writer Vincent O'Sullivan, he declared: "I'll publish anything that the others are afraid of." Symons, however, characterized him as "my cynical publisher, Smithers, with the diabolical monocle."

London Nights could not have appeared at a more unfavorable time, for its publication in June, a month after Wilde's conviction for sexual indecency, intensified the adverse reaction: "I had expected opposition," Symons later wrote, ". . . but I must confess to some surprise at the nature of the opposition, the extent of the prejudice, which it was my fortune to encounter." The critics, he maintained, had confused art and morality, for they had condemned the book "not because it is bad art, but because they think it bad morality. . . ." And affirming his discipleship to Pater, Symons reiterated the central creed of late nineteenth-century Aestheticism, which developed into twentieth-century Modernism: "I contend on behalf of the liberty of art, and I deny that morals have any right of jurisdiction over it. Art may be served by morality; it can never be its servant. For the principles of art are eternal, while the principles of morality fluctuate with the spiritual ebb and flow of the ages. . . ."

Many of the poems in *London Nights* celebrate human flesh not only in the innocence of love but also in the context of harlotry. In "Idealism," a title perhaps calculated to startle the average Victorian reader, Symons writes: "It is her flesh that I adore . . . / Her perfect body, Earth's most eloquent / Music, divinest human harmony," and in "To One in Alienation": ". . . I lay on the stranger's bed, / And clasped the stranger-woman I had hired." But the poem that particularly offended the critics was "Stella Maris," with its religious associations, in which Symons depicts a chance meeting with a prostitute:

Why is it I remember yet
You, of all women one has met

---

artists, such as Monet, Degas, and Pissarro, whom Nordau had damned in *Degeneration*.

In random wayfare, as one meets
The chance romances of the streets,
The Juliet of a night?

The memory of their love-making evokes daring explicit imagery that recalls Swinburne:

I feel your breast that heaves and dips,
Desiring my desirous lips
And that ineffable delight
When souls turn bodies, and unite
In the intolerable, the whole
Rapture of the embodied soul.

The "singular unanimity of abuse," which Symons deplored, was nowhere more apparent than in an anonymous review in the *Pall Mall Gazette* (September 2, 1895), entitled "Pah!":

> Mr. Arthur Symons is a dirty-minded man, and his mind is reflected in the puddle of his bad verses. It may be that there are other dirty-minded men who will rejoice in the jungle that records the squalid and inexpensive amours of Mr. Symons, but our faith jumps to our hope that such men are not. He informs us in his prologue that his life is like a music-hall,* which should bring him a joint-action for libel from every decent institution of the kind in London. By his own showing, his life's more like a pig-sty, and one dull below the ordinary at that. Every women he pays to meet him, he tells us, is desirous to kiss his lips; our boots too are desirous, but of quite another part of him, for quite another purpose.

Yet the volume contains other poems that express Romantic attitudes towards nature as though Symons sensed that the erotic and the artificial required the ideal balance of Victorian wholesomeness of mind and spirit, an indication that the Decadent wish to shock the bourgeoisie was itself, as Symons himself had observed, a bourgeois impulse. In one of his na-

---

*"Prologue: In the Stalls":

My life is like a music-hall,
Where, in the impotence of rage,
Chained by enchantment to my stall,
I see myself upon the stage
Dance to amuse a music-hall.

ture poems written while in Italy, Symons evokes a contemplative mood
involving a contrast between the artifice of London and the redemptive
meadows at Mantua:

> *But to have lain upon the grass*
> *One perfect day, one perfect hour,*
> *Beholding all things mortal pass*
> *Into the quiet of green grass . . .*
>
> *Ah, in these flaring London nights,*
> *Where midnight withers into morn,*
> *How blissful a rebuke it writes*
> *Across the sky of London nights!*

IT HAS OFTEN been said that Wilde's imprisonment marked the end of
Decadence, but it is now clear that the phenomenon was a significant
manifestation of early Modernism in its demand for greater freedom in
exploring hitherto forbidden subjects, in its insistence on the autonomy
of art, and in its contention that art owed less to nature than to the imagination of the artist. As we have seen, Swinburne had encountered widespread abuse directed against him and his *Poems and Ballads* for his
challenge to Victorian restrictions. Those writers inspired by Swinburne
often met similar fates. Decadence, in one form or another, continued not
only through the remainder of the nineties (as Andrew Lang's facetious
remarks at the beginning of this chapter indicate) but also into the main-
stream of high Modernism in the following century.

In 1908, when Ezra Pound arrived in London dressed in what he obviously regarded as Aesthetic dress, including a velvet cloak and later a
turquoise earring, he brought with him "a set of poetic enthusiasms some
ten or fifteen years out of date." His poem "The Decadence" (1908), by
its identification with such figures as Hubert Crackenthorpe, Ernest Dowson, Lionel Johnson, Aubrey Beardsley, and Oscar Wilde, reveals a wish
to reenact the aborted lives of those "Bearers of beauty [who] flame and
wane":

> *Tarnished we! Tarnished! Wastrals all!*
> *And yet the art goes on, goes on.*
> *Broken our strength, yea as crushed reeds we fall,*
> *And yet the art, the art goes on.*
>
> *Broken our manhood for the wrack and strain;*
> *Drink of our hearts the sunset and the cry*

"Io Triumphe!" Tho our lips be slain
We see Art vivant, and exult to die.

Pound thus provided part of the groundwork for the later myth of the "Tragic Generation," celebrated by Yeats in prose and verse, a myth endowing Modernism with images of Romantic self-destructiveness, artistic martyrdom, and the Religion of Art.

But at the time of the First World War, the spectacle of fin-de-siecle Decadence remained a source of merriment, as, indeed, it still does, though combined with a distant admiration for even flawed creative genius. Robert Service, for example, wrote in his amusing "Gods in the Gutter" (1914):

Oh Wilde, Verlaine and Baudelaire, their lips were wet with wine;
Oh poseur, pimp, and libertine! Oh cynic, sot and swine!
Oh voteries of velvet vice! . . . Oh gods of light divine!

Oh Baudelaire, Verlaine and Wilde, they knew the sinks of shame;
Their sun-aspiring wings they scorched at passion's altar flame;
Yet lo! enthroned, enskied they stand, Immortal Sons of Fame.

3

Tragic Rhymers and Mythic Celts

A PERSISTENT CLICHÉ about the Rhymers' Club, the most celebrated group of poets in the 1890s, is that they were Decadents who came to bad ends by "falling off stools, collapsing in gutters, jumping off cliffs, or going mad." However, this facetious version of the Romantic icon of the suffering, alienated artist reveals only partial truth. Yeats, the principal source for this view, identified those associated with the club as the "Tragic Generation," for in the quest for inviolable truth and artistic fulfillment, their destiny was self-destructiveness. Their emblematic lives, Yeats implied, revealed the artist's struggle to achieve unity of being in a fragmented world.

Though religion and art provided refuge to such poets as Lionel Johnson and Ernest Dowson—figures central to Yeats's grand myth of the cursed poet—these Rhymers had failed to unify the corrosive divisions of flesh and spirit that destroyed them while still in their early thirties:

> Some friends of mine [Yeats later recalled] saw them one moon-light night returning from the "Crown" public-house which had just closed, their zig-zagging feet requiring the whole width of Oxford Street, Lionel Johnson talking. My friend stood still eavesdropping; Lionel Johnson was expounding a Father of the Church. Their piety, in Dowson a penitential sadness, in Lionel Johnson more often a noble ecstasy, was, I think, illuminated and intensified by their contrasting puppet-shows, those elegant, tragic penitents, those great men in their triumph.

Yet these "great men" were minor poets. By inventing a usable past that endowed them with transcendent meaning, Yeats invested the Rhymers with tragic grandeur to dramatize the stifling, destructive Victo-

W. B. Yeats

rian world as well as his own capacity for survival. By sacrificing mere fact
to idealized vision, Yeats transformed the remnants of history into an
aesthetic design and created the Tragic Generation. The Rhymers' Club
thus provided Yeats with a myth that made his early years in London
comprehensible, one that reinforced his Romantic vision of the aspiring
artist. When, in 1910, he lectured on contemporary poetry, he alluded to
the poets of the 1890s as a "doomed generation, and there is hardly one
of them still alive." Ernest Rhys, a founding member of the club, wrote to
Yeats protesting that he was still breathing—or at least believed he was.
Apologizing, Yeats replied: "One begins to think of 'The Rhymers' as
those who sang of wine and women—I no more than you am typical"—a
revealing statement that suggests Yeat's mythic intent. The irony of
Rhys's objection and Yeats's response is that most of the Rhymers were
not at all typical of the Rhymers: few sang of wine and women, and most
lived long, respectable lives. As poets, the Rhymers represented a significant attempt to form an organized group in the early 1890s to advance
their own poetic agenda by attacking the sentimentality and didacticism in
Victorian verse. Of equal importance to the cultural history of the time,
the Rhymers' Club was actively involved in the London manifestations of
the Irish literary renaissance.

DURING THE LATE 1880s, the Rhymers' Club developed out of an intricate series of associations between poets who, in various ways, were alienated from the prevailing bourgeois Victorian culture and who wished to establish a cultivated island of their own. From the time of Yeats's birth in Dublin, his father, an artist, had moved his family periodically between Ireland and England. Now separated from his friends in Ireland, Yeats felt like "Robinson Crusoe in this dreadful London." His sense of isolation was soon overcome when he met some clever "literary men," but he was disturbed by the "absence of convictions that characterize their tribe." "London litterary folk," he wrote with his scandalous spelling to the Irish poet Katharine Tynan,

> seem to divide into two classes—the stupid men with brains and the clever ones without any. . . . The latter is the most numerous—young men possesing only an indolent and restless talent that warms nothing and lights nothing. Indeed I find little good, with scarcely an exception, in any of these young litterary men. . . .

One whom he liked, however, was Rhys, a man he thought, punning weakly, "not brilliant but very earnest." Born in London of Welsh parents, Rhys had abandoned his vocation as a mining engineer in the north for the literary life. On a rainy evening in the mid-1880s, he found himself alone in the "richest city of the world": " 'O London,' I thought, 'thou that killest the prophets, that let Blake get poorer and poorer, and Chatterton starve, what will you do with me, a waverer, who have not the money-sense, the gift of tongues, nor even an umbrella?' " Eventually providing himself with protection against the London rain, he became acquainted with various writers and intellectuals, some of them associated with the Fellowship of the New Life. Rhys took Yeats to one of its meetings.

Yeats and Rhys also joined William Morris for suppers at his home in Hammersmith, where the Socialist League met on Sunday evenings: Yeats recalled "pictures by Rossetti all round the room and in the middle much socialistic conversation." Such talk prompted Rhys to join the march to Trafalgar Square on Bloody Sunday. Excited by "the fierce young adherents of the [Socialist] League, [who] went about declaring that it was the real beginning of a revolution which would shake London and the British Isles, and spread them to the cities and countries abroad," Rhys followed Morris and other league members but was soon separated from the group in the ensuing melee; like Morris, Rhys lost his zeal for open revolution.

Yeats, less revolutionary, declined an invitation from Morris to write on the Irish question for his periodical, *Commonweal:* "However though I think socialism good work," Yeats told Katharine Tynan, "I am not sure that it is my work." Indeed, despite the pleasure of Morris's company, he found "his philosophy of life altogather [*sic*] alien." Morris the poet interested him, however, because of his narratives drawn from Icelandic sagas and classical legend. When Yeats published a long narrative poem based on Irish myth, *The Wanderings of Oisin* (1889), Morris, perhaps sensing influence, told him: "It is my kind of poetry."

Meanwhile, Yeats was reestablishing friendships in London with some older writers and artists he had known in Dublin, such as John Todhunter, a physician and professor of English literature at Alexandra College, Dublin, who had abandoned both academe and medicine; Thomas William Rolleston, editor of the *Dublin University Review* in the mid-1880s and translator of Whitman into German; and Edwin J. Ellis, a Welsh painter, poet, and friend of Yeats's father, who had just arrived in London after having lived for several years in Italy. By 1888, Yeats had also met, among the younger writers, the brilliant Herbert Horne, who, at the age of twenty-three, was an architect, poet, and editor of the *Century Guild Hobby Horse,* the aesthetic publication of the Century Guild of Artists. At 20 Fitzroy Street, Horne shared the house with Selwyn Image, a former clergyman, who was a poet and designer of stained glass. In the summer of 1890, Horne rented two spacious rooms at the top of the house to Lionel Johnson, just down from Oxford, who had been a contributor to the *Hobby Horse.*

The Century Guild, organized in 1882 by Arthur Mackmurdo, an architect who designed the Savoy Theatre for Richard D'Oyly Carte, was inspired by Morris & Co. Like Morris, Mackmurdo was concerned with the increasing isolation of the artist and craftsman in a machine-made culture. What was needed in such an age, he insisted, was a reuniting of the arts, such as existed in the Middle Ages. In addition to offices and living quarters, the Fitzroy house had a concert room built for the performance of Renaissance music. The Belgian-born Arnold Dolmetsch, stimulating a renewal of interest in such music, performed there on the clavichord and other early instruments on "Hobby Horse evenings," where Rhys recalls having seen Bernard Shaw. In the late 1880s and early 1890s, "Fitzroy" was a "movement, an influence, a glory"—a leading artistic center in London—indeed, a refuge for the Hobby Horsemen from the Victorian world of industrialism and material progress presided over by a shopkeeper mentality.

FROM THIS SETTING emerged the nucleus of the Rhymers' Club, for Horne had probably invited Yeats and other poets to meet at Fitzroy to read and discuss their verse. In his memoirs, Yeats recalled that he said to Rhys: "I am growing jealous of other poets and we shall all grow jealous of each other unless we know each other and so feel a share in each other's triumph. . . ." Such a proposed association of poets, moreover, would help overcome his persistent sense of isolation in "hateful London." With Rhys and Rolleston, he founded the Rhymers' Club (in its first few months often called the "Rhymsters' Club" by some of its members) at the Old Cheshire Cheese pub off Fleet Street in Wine Office Court.* Not since the Pre-Raphaelite Brotherhood in the 1860s had artists united out of a sense of isolation from the dominant culture. Though the Pre-Raphaelite painters were determined to reject the traditional art of the Royal Academy, the Rhymers had no precise orientation other than a dissatisfaction with the state of current Victorian poetry. Yeats later insisted that the Rhymers wished to disengage themselves from nonliterary considerations in their verse: ". . . Swinburne in one way, Browning in another, and Tennyson in a third, had filled their work with what I called 'impurities,' curiosities about politics, science, about history, about religion; and that we must create once more the pure work." But few of the Rhymers subscribed to art for art's sake; indeed, Yeats in the 1890s was himself unable to sustain "pure work" when his Irish nationalism was in the ascendancy. In his "Dedication of 'Irish Tales' " (1891), included in the first Rhymers' Club anthology, he expressed admiration for "Exiles wandering over many seas" and for "men who loved the cause that never dies," an allusion to the Fenian revolutionaries.

In May 1890, the probable month when the club was founded,† Yeats told Katharine Tynan: "We meet once a week there & smoke & talk & hope to get all the yonger [sic] writers of verse in to it in time. . . . [John] O'Leary has been there for the last two evenings. Those of us who are in funds dine there at seven & those of us that are not turn up later." After dining on church-pew benches with tankards of ale, the Rhymers retreated to the small room on the second floor and lighted old-fashioned long clays, or churchwarden pipes, as though to harmonize with their setting.

---

*In addition to the Rhymers' Club, other literary groups flourished in fin-de-siècle London, though they were principally interested in antiquarian, bibliographical, and scholarly concerns. Many Rhymers were members or guests of such organizations as the Sette of Odd Volumes, the Omar Khayyam Club, the Browning Society, and the Shelley Society.

†T. W. Rolleston's "Ballade of Ye Olde Cheshire Cheese" (reprinted in the Rhymers' first anthology as "Ballade of the 'Cheshire Cheese' ") appeared in the the *Academy*, 37 (May 17, 1890): 337, confirming the likelihood that the Rhymers' Club was founded in May of that year. In an unpublished letter to G. A. Greene on October 18, 1891, Rolleston remarked that his ballade had helped to inaugurate the Rhymers' meetings at the Cheshire Cheese, that "sacred spot" (G. C. R. Greene Collection).

The roster of members who met at the Cheshire Cheese or on occasion at members' homes remains problematic. Yeats later wrote: "Lionel Johnson, Ernest Dowson, Victor Plarr, Ernest Radford, John Davidson, Richard Le Gallienne, T. W. Rolleston, Selwyn Image, Edwin Ellis, and John Todhunter came constantly for a time, Arthur Symons and Herbert Horne, less constantly, while William Watson joined but never came and Francis Thompson came once but never joined." How William Watson (an "accomplished" rather than inspired poet, said Yeats) and the self-destructive Francis Thompson could have "joined" remains mystifying, for there were no established rules governing membership. On occasion, though, poets were voted out at informal meetings. Those who attended occasionally were called guests and sometimes referred to as new Rhymers. In the four years that the club flourished, many writers and many invited guests who were not writers sporadically attended meetings. But only a dozen or so poets, most of whom contributed to the club's two anthologies published by the Bodley Head, were regarded as members. The honorary secretary—the Club's only officer—was George A. Greene, formerly a professor of English at Alexandra College, Dublin.

The presence at the club's early meetings of John O'Leary, appearing like a bearded Old Testament prophet, is revealing. He was not a poet but an Irish revolutionary who had spent twenty years in English prisons and in exile in France, returning to Ireland in 1885. Yeats and Rolleston may have invited O'Leary as a reciprocal gesture, for they had attended meetings in Dublin of the Young Ireland Society over which O'Leary had presided. He had urged that a nationalistic impulse need not result in mediocre poetry, such as that in the widely read volume of Young Ireland poets, *The Spirit of the Nation* (1843), which contained such patriotic verse as the following:

> How thrive we by the Union?
> Look round our native land;
> In ruined trade and wealth decayed
> See slavery's surest brand;
> Our glory as a nation gone,
> Our substance drained away.

Yeats's decision to become an *Irish* writer was principally influenced by O'Leary's contention that "there is no fine nationality without literature . . . no fine literature without nationality." It was this "old Fenian leader," Yeats later said, through whom he found his "theme" in verse. With O'Leary's help, Yeats edited *Poems and Ballads of Young Ireland* (1888), which included not only his own poems but also those by Todhunter and Rolleston, whose dedicatory poem celebrated O'Leary as one who had "suffered for the cause."

In addition to the Irish Rhymers, others such as the Welshman Ernest Rhys, the Scotsman John Davidson, the Cornishman Arthur Symons, and the Englishman Lionel Johnson (who nonetheless claimed Irish relatives) declared themselves Celts. Indeed, pan-Celtic enthusiasm so amused the writer Edgar Jepson, who occasionally attended meetings, that he described its influence on the group with more levity than accuracy:

> They were all very Celtic too, for it was the days of the Celtic Fringe. John Todhunter . . . was a Celt; and Plarr, whose father was an Alsation, was a Celt; and Johnson . . . was a Celt—at one time he assumed a brogue and addressed me as "me dearr"; and Mr. Symons, a Druidian Welshman, was a Celt; and Dowson, who was probably of as pure Norman London descent as you can find, was inclined to believe that there was a Celtic strain in him, and Yeats, who was plainly a Firbolg [a member of a legendary colonizing tribe in Ireland, apparently an allusion to Yeats's Anglican forebears], was the most Celtic of all, and they all declared that there was a Celtic renaissance.

For the Rhymers, the term *Celtic* was ideological rather than racial, for many of the Rhymers, like Yeats, had English forebears or were born into the Anglo-Irish Protestant ascendancy. Celtic identification was a means of divorcing themselves from traditional English poetry, but except for Yeats, the avowed Celts included few traces of Celtic subject matter in their verse.

The Rhymers, Rhys recalled, were expected "to bring rhymes in their pockets, to be read aloud and left to the tender mercies of the club for criticism." When, at meetings, Yeats theorized about poetry, a gloomy silence ensued. The Rhymers opposed "ideas, all generalizations that can be explained or debated," said Yeats. When Symons, having returned from Paris, announced, "We are concerned with nothing but impressions," that also met with "stony silence." Yeats attributes the survival of the club during its first "difficult months" to the Irish members, "who said whatever came into their heads." Meetings were also occasionally enlivened by the benign presence of Oscar Wilde, who attended on rare occasions when the club met in private homes. At one notable meeting, a Rhymer recalled, Wilde's presence was riveting:

> Mr. Walter Crane [the Fabian artist and writer] stood with his back to the mantelpiece, deciding very kindly, on the merits of our effusions. And round Oscar Wilde, not then under a cloud, hovered reverently Lionel Johnson and Ernest Dowson with others. . . . I marvelled at the time to notice the fascination which poor Wilde exercised over the otherwise rational. He sat

as it were enthroned and surrounded by a deferential circle.
. . . Wilde wore a black shirt front and . . . Dowson and Johnson,
small fairy creatures in white, climbed about upon it.

Since many of the Rhymers were writing for various newspapers in
order to survive, maintaining useful friendly relations with members of
the club could be beneficial to one's career. Like the hero of George
Gissing's *New Grub Street* (1891), John Davidson went to the world of
Fleet Street, which he described in a newspaper piece: "The ever-increas-
ing numbers, ambitious of literary distinction, who flock to London
yearly, to become hacks and journalists, regard the work by which they
gain a livelihood as a mere industry, a stepping-stone to higher things—
alas! a stepping-stone on which the great majority of them have to maintain a precarious footing all their lives. . . . ." When Davidson submitted
the manuscript of his *Fleet Street Ecloques* to the Bodley Head, the chief
reader was fellow Rhymer Richard Le Gallienne, who urged publication.
When it appeared in 1893, Davidson wrote to John Lane at the Bodley
Head: "Is Le Gallienne responsible for both these exceedingly generous
reviews in *Star* and *Chronicle?*" In 1891, Le Gallienne had succeeded
Davidson as the literary critic for the popular newspaper, the *Star,* signing his name to columns appropriately as "Log-roller." On occasion, logrolling in the 1890s (involving writers who reviewed each other's books
favorably) provoked acrimonious discussions in the press. The practice
was made possible, however, by the widespread policy of anonymous
reviewing.

Yeats told Katharine Tynan that his own friendships were enabling him
to make his way in the literary world. Indeed, the Rhymers had infiltrated
the very heart of journalistic London, perhaps one reason why they found
the location of the Cheshire Cheese so convenient. A journalist and critic
in the 1890s, Arthur Waugh (father of Evelyn and Alec), recalls that the
Rhymers had captured page 3 of the *Daily Chronicle,* "the most attractive
and entertaining of all these literary bulletins." As might be expected,
"those critics who did not happen to belong to the club might be over-
heard from time to time, grumbling that the book-page of the *Daily
Chronicle* had become the private preserve of the Bodley Head."

DURING THE FIRST two years of the Rhymers' Club, Yeats, Rolleston,
and Todhunter had also been attending meetings of the Southwark Irish
Literary Club. In 1888, Yeats's first appearance there was noted by one of
its members, W. P. Ryan: "In appearance he was tall, slight, and mystic of
the mystical. His face was not so much dreamy as haunting: a little weird
even. . . . He spoke in a hushed, musical, eerie tone: a tone which had

constant suggestions of the faery world." But Ryan's impression revealed only one side of the complex Yeats, whose activism in the world of fact complemented rather than clashed with his world of imagination. By late 1891, Yeats had decided to reorganize the Southwark club into a more meaningful society that would "create a standard of criticism" to denounce propagandist verse and prose, de-Anglicize poetry written by Irishmen, and in general revive Irish literature, which had fallen into contempt. Indeed, the club had ceased meeting because, as Yeats noted, "the girls got the giggles when any member of the Committee got up to speak," and every member "had said all he had to say many times over."

The immediate impetus for Yeats's decision was the fall of Charles Stewart Parnell, the leader of the Irish Parliamentary party who had been involved in an adulterous relationship with the wife of Captain William O'Shea, an associate of Parnell. O'Shea had probably known of the affair from the beginning: In the early 1880s, he had been separated from his wife at the time that three children were born of the affair. Throughout this time, Cabinet ministers, including Gladstone, knew that Mrs. O'Shea was Parnell's mistress. O'Shea pretended ignorance, apparently in the hope of political advancement and in the expectation of inheriting part of a fortune from his wife's aunt (who would have disinherited them if the Parnell liaison had been made public).

When both hopes were dashed, O'Shea turned on his wife and sued for a divorce in December 1889, naming Parnell as co-respondent. When the suit came to trial in November 1890, O'Shea won the case. Many in Ireland initially supported their uncrowned king, but soon anti-Parnellite factions developed. Bitter debates over Parnell's status in the party and the future of Home Rule for Ireland divided not only politicians but also families. Because the Liberals in London were also split by Parnell's continuation as leader of the Irish Parliamentary party, Gladstone refused to support the Home Rule Bill if Parnell did not retire. Without Parnell's departure from politics, the forthcoming election would result in the defeat of the Liberal party. Complicating an already complicated situation in Ireland, outraged Catholic bishops called for Parnell's repudiation.* The Parnellite *Freeman's Journal* (November 18, 1890) defended the leader by evoking Biblical imagery: "Let him who is without stain among you cast the first stone. . . . He has brought [Ireland] out of bondage. He

---

*Shaw registered his own outrage in a letter to the editor of the *Star* (November 20, 1890): ". . . the relation between Mr Parnell and Mrs O'Shea was a perfectly natural and right one; and the whole mischief in the matter lay in the law that tied the husband and wife together and forced Mr Parnell to play the part of clandestine intriguer, instead of enabling them to dissolve the marriage by mutual consent, without disgrace to either party" (reprinted in Shaw, *The Trouble with Ireland,* eds. Dan H. Laurence and David H. Greene [New York, 1962], 25).

has led her within sight of the Promised Land." Before a vote was taken on the party chairmanship, John O'Leary insisted in a letter to the *Irish Times* (December 1, 1890) that Parnell should not be discarded simply because "the whole howling voice of prurient British hypocrisy has been heard." When Parnell refused to resign, the Irish members proceeded to vote him out, faithfully following his advice that the interests of the party superseded those of any individual member. In an attempt to regain his former status, Parnell married Katharine O'Shea, but the emotional strain of his disgrace and rejection brought about his end in October 1891. The black-bordered pages of *United Ireland* (October 10) lamented the treachery involved in Parnell's death by evoking the image of a betrayed Caesar, the myth of martyrdom prominent in subsequent prose and verse:

> Slain, sacrificed by Irishmen on the alter of English Liberalism he, the greatest Chief that this land has known in the struggle of centuries against English domination, has been murdered by the men whom he dragged from obscurity and who hated him, even whilst they fawned upon him, because they could never repay all that he had done for them personally. Murdered he has been as certainly as if the gang of conspirators had surrounded him and hacked him to pieces.

In the same issue, Yeats published "Mourn—And Then Onward!" in an apparent attempt to effect reconciliation between the warring factions:

> *Mourn—and then onward, there is no returning*
> *He guides ye from the tomb;*
> *His memory now is a tall pillar, burning*
> *Before us in the gloom!*

Before the crisis within the Irish Parliamentary party, Yeats had shown little interest in Parnell. With the leader's fall and death, however, the image of the martyred hero attracted Yeats, whose aristocratic sensibility increasingly found inspiration in Parnell's career. Yeats's stories, such as "The Crucifixion of the Outcast" (1894), often depict the failure of heroism in a hostile world. (As late as 1922, Yeats wrote: "The Irish seem to me like a pack of hounds, always dragging down some noble stag.") Within three months of Parnell's death, Yeats was prepared to enter the world of action as though a new hero were about to emerge from the shambles. He now saw that what he had prophesied in his introduction to *Representative Irish Tales* (1891) had come to pass: that "a new Irish literary movement" would—or, at least, could—occur "at the first lull in this storm of politics."

Determined to fulfill his own prophecy, Yeats invited Rolleston, Todhunter, and prominent members of the Southwark club to his home in Bedford Park on December 28 to discuss a new society that would stimulate creative effort, inaugurate lectures, and publish Irish books. Those who arrived at Yeats's home on that wet and windy night talked about Rolleston's probable role in the new Irish Literary Society before he arrived late in the evening. When he and Todhunter joined the group, they agreed to ask Sir Charles Gavan Duffy to be the society's president (he had been the founder of the Dublin newspaper the *Nation* in 1842 and had emigrated to Australia, where he remained until 1880, becoming Speaker of the Australian House of Assembly); Stopford Brooke was chosen as the first vice-president (he was an Anglo-Irish writer and former clergyman who had left the Church of England). Rolleston accepted the post of second vice-president, and Greene was elected vice-chairman of the society's committee.

Before the inaugural general meeting was held at the Caledonian Hotel in May 1892, there had been smaller informal meetings held at members' homes and at the Cheshire Cheese, where the Rhymers' Club acted as host. On March 4, Johnson informed Rhys: "You have shamefully abandoned the Rhymers of late. . . . The Celts were in force last night: inaugural meeting of the 'Irish Literary.' "* Rolleston invited Johnson to join the Irish Literary Society, presumably on the strength of his distant Irish relatives. Responding with delight, Johnson wrote: "My people lived in Ireland for about two centuries, and became as usual Hibernis Hiberniores: I have endless swarms of Irish relatives; and I am connected with Yeats, which ought to be enough of itself to make me Irish." Johnson, who had converted to Roman Catholicism in the preceding year, could provide support as critic and "theologian," thought Yeats, to counter opposition to the new literary movement from the Church in Ireland. Among other charter members of the society were Oscar Wilde, his elder brother Willie (a journalist and poet), and their mother, Lady Wilde (a prominent nationalist poet who had published verse under the name "Speranza").

Shortly before the inaugural meeting of the society on May 12, Yeats informed Rolleston that he was leaving for Dublin "to found there a society of like purpose and nature":

We cannot carry out our programe [*sic*] with full success—at least in the matter of Irish books—unless we persuade Ireland to

---

*A previous Celtic evening for the Rhymers had been a special meeting in early November 1891 at Edwin J. Ellis's home for Maud Gonne, the Irish activist, who was departing for France. In 1889, she had met Yeats, whose unrequited love and rejected marriage proposals provided the inspiration for many of his poems.

take part with us. A society in Dublin could help our London organization to focuss [*sic*] the scattered energies of lovers of Irish literature, & they & we together would be able to do much for the cause of Irish letters.

Yeats succeeded in finding support for a national literary society, but his hope that the Dublin and London societies would cooperate was soon thwarted. He encountered much dissension within each society and much conflict between them. The founders of the Dublin group were determined to maintain a distance from the older Young Ireland Societies, which were more politically oriented, but some members of the National Literary Society objected to its own nonpolitical direction. A major controversy erupted over a joint proposal to publish a series of inexpensive Irish books and establish lending libraries, the London and Dublin societies attempting to advance their own preferences. Finally, disputes arose between the two groups concerning the National Literary Society's wish to regard itself as the natural focal point for the Irish literary renaissance.

WHILE MANY OF the Rhymers had been involved in the organization and development of the Irish Literary Society, they had also looked forward to the publication of *The Book of the Rhymers' Club*. In his memoirs, Yeats again envisions himself as the inspiration: Because he wished to hold both Dowson's "O Mors" and "Villanelle of Sunset" in his hand, he suggested the publication of an anthology. By early June 1891, the Rhymers agreed to finance publication of the book, each poet to be represented by between three and six poems to be selected by a committee from a group of poems submitted. With premature enthusiasm, Yeats told Katharine Tynan, " 'The Rhymers Club' will publish a book of verse almost at once."

When the book finally appeared in February 1892, the 350 copies sold out within a month, but it was only sporadically reviewed. In general, reviewers were indulgent, on occasion faintly amused, as was the critic in the *Academy* (March 26, 1892), who called the book "the first joint output of our young English 'Parnassians,' " unaware, apparently, that most of them preferred to be called Celts. In the *Daily News* (February 20, 1892), Andrew Lang's review offended the Rhymers, Yeats later calling it "very uncivil indeed." Lang, who thought "a ransom of five shillings seems rather exorbitant for their combined effort," regarded the small number of copies printed as a indication of the public's unsympathetic view of poetry. The Rhymers, in Lang's view clearly minor poets, would be unable to win over the Philistines, but, Lang added, they were to be commended for disregarding public indifference. Lionel Johnson, who believed that responding to such reviews served no purpose, told Greene: "For my own part, I should never answer anything in a newspaper, short of bringing an action for libel. Mere controversy with this sort of scum does no good."

The club's anthology—often discussed but little read—contains a diversity of forms and themes. The striking impression is their traditionalism; indeed, there is little in the volume to suggest that the club thought of itself as an avant-garde group. The varied selection, moreover, demonstrates the Rhymers' independence of any one school of verse. Rhys's opening poem—"At the Rhymers' Club: The Toast"—presumably suggests the volume's tone and direction:

> *Set fools unto their folly!*
> *Our folly is pure wit,*
> *As 'twere the Muse turned jolly:*
> *For poets' melancholy,—*
> *We will not think of it.*

But clearly the toast does not describe the Rhymers' verse, which is rarely jolly or witty; indeed, much is rather solemn and melancholy befitting minor poets, some of them reflecting the anxiety-ridden fin de siècle.

Though, as a group, the Rhymers were not generally called Aesthetes or Decadents by contemporary critics, several poems depict the alienated poet retreating to the private world of his imagination, expressed in several poems as a death wish. Thus, Greene's "Drifting":

> *Such is my song. Borne downward on the tide,*
> *I cannot tell what echoes of my breath*
> *Are caught by listeners on the riverside:*
> *I and my song glide onward unto death.*

Greene's "Song of the Songsmiths" concludes the volume with an apparent statement of the Rhymers' intention "To hammer the golden rhyme, / Hammer the ringing rhyme / Till the mad world hears." The familiar ambivalence informs Romantic attitudes: Ignored, the artist welcomes self-oblivion; indifferent, the world cannot long ignore the artist's voice. Greene's "Keats' Grave," which recalls Wilde's "The Grave of Keats," deplores the "world's indifference to souls sublime."*

---

*Wilde had embraced the myth of the victimized artist as martyr, central to the Religion of Art, as early as 1877, when, as he stood at the gravesite of John Keats in the Protestant Cemetery, "the holiest place in Rome," his thoughts of "this divine boy" shaped themselves into rhyme in "The Grave of Keats": "The youngest of the

Rhys's "Chatterton in Holborn," evoking the poet's suicide in his lonely room, also suggests the familiar theme of the world's indifference:

> *The windows saw him come and pass,*
> *And come and go again;*
> *And still the throng swept by—alas!*
> *The barren face of men.*

Retreat from the world, predominant in Dowson's "Carmelite Nuns of the Perpetual Adoration," is the symbolic counterpart of Greene's "Drifting," in which art provides refuge:

> *Outside, the world is wild and passionate;*
> *Man's weary laughter, and his sick despair*
> *Entreat at their impenetrable gate:*
> *They heed no voices in their dream of prayer.*

And Dowson's "Villanelle of Sunset," which initially attracted Yeats, is a variation of such yearning:

> *Come hither, child! and rest:*
> *This is the end of day,*
> *Behold the weary West!*

Despite such yearning, Greene's "The Pathfinder" expresses conventional Victorian attitudes associated with the activism that emerged from evangelical sentiments in a religiously inspired industrial world:

> *Because to aspire is better than to attain:*
> *Because the will is nobler than the deed,*
> *The blossom glorious more than is the fruit;*
> *The worker knows he hath not striven in vain.*

Except for Yeats, there is little Celtic subject matter used by the Rhymers—"The Song of Tristram" by Todhunter a notable exception. Despite his assertions, Johnson included no poems confirming his "swarms of Irish relatives." His religiously inspired "A Burden of Easter Vigil" dramatizes the widespread doubt among Victorian intellectuals, as revealed in the climactic line fearfully questioning Jesus's resurrection:

---

martyrs here is lain, / Fair as Sebastian, and as foully slain." Wilde adopted "Sebastian" as his Christian name on his release from prison in 1897.

> *But if He rise not? Over the far main,*
> *The sun of glory falls indeed: the stars are plain.*

"God hath died," spake Nietzsche in *Thus Spake Zarathustra* (1892), an announcement that for many confirmed the long-held suspicion that God had been ailing. Wilde, however, offered comfort in *The Picture of Dorian Gray* (1891) with the paradoxical observation that "Scepticism is the beginning of Faith," a variant of Tennyson's famous lines in *In Memoriam* (1850): "There lives more faith in honest doubt, / Believe me, than in half the creeds." Yet when Dowson lost both parents as the result of their suicide a few months apart, he suffered from a spiritual void, as his "Song of the XIXth Century" (a poem unpublished in his lifetime) reveals:

> *O give us faith—*
> *In God, Man, anything to rise and break*
> *The mist of doubt, we cry, but like a wraith*
> *It still eludes our grasp and no rays streak*
>   *The dark of Death.*

Of Symons's contributions to the Rhymers' anthology, the striking "Javanese Dancers" is one of many dance poems that he wrote in the nineties that would increasingly attract Yeats by their nondiscursive symbolic possibilities:

> *Still with fixed eyes, monotonously still,*
>   *Mysteriously, with smiles inanimate,*
>   *With lingering feet that undulate,*
> *With sinuous fingers, spectral hands that thrill . . .*

Symons had written that the "test of poetry which professes to be modern" was "its capacity for dealing with London." For many in the avant-garde, the city was the supreme work of artifice and, as Baudelaire revealed, the symbolic embodiment of the soul. In the late nineteenth century, the city emerged as a central image in verse, often suggesting the mutilated creature of industrialism, a symbolic Hell. A modern critic has called James Thomson's "The City of Dreadful Night" (1874/1880) "a symbolic vision of the city as *the* condition of human life." Later, T. S. Eliot's *The Waste Land* (1922) would envision the modern city in similar terms.

In the Rhymers' anthology, such poems as Johnson's "Plato in London" and "By the Statue of King Charles the First at Charing Cross," Rhys's "Chatterton in Holborn," Rolleston's "Ballade of the 'Cheshire Cheese,'" and Le Gallienne's "Sunset in the City" reveal the many faces

of London. Le Gallienne's striking image of sunset is associated imagisti-
cally with the city's industrialism, but the Romantic vision of the moon,
anticipating later Imagist poems, is transcendent:

> *Above the town a monstrous wheel is turning,*
> *   With glowing spokes of red,*
> *Low in the west its fiery axle burning;*
> *   And, lost amid the spaces overhead,*
> *A vague white moth, the moon, is fluttering.*

Le Gallienne then achieves a Whistlerian effect, that of nocturnal transformation by the poet's imaginative vision:

> *Within the town the streets grow strange and haunted,*
> *   And, dark against the western lakes of green,*
> *The buildings change to temples. . . .*

Yeats's distaste for London is apparent by its exclusion from his verse. In
his two most famous poems in the anthology, the source of his art is the
melancholy world of the Celtic twilight,* which he fused with his current
interest in occult symbolism: "The Lake Isle of Innisfree," a poem of
imagined retreat from the city, not to self-annihilation but to a setting
reminiscent of Thoreau's ("I will arise and go now, and go to Innisfree, /
And a small cabin build there"); and "The Man Who Dreamed of Fairyland," where the Celtic soul finds its ancient spiritual realities.

THE INTIMATE ASSOCIATION of the Irish Literary Society with the
Rhymers began to affect Yeats's view of the club and its ultimate direc-
tion. In April 1892, he published an article on the Rhymers in the Irish-
American newspaper, the *Boston Pilot*. O'Leary had recommended Yeats
to the editor as able to acquaint its audience with new developments in
Irish literature. Describing England as "a land of literary Ishmaels,"
Yeats remarks that "it is only among the sociable Celtic nations that men
draw nearer to each other when they want to think and dream and work.
All this makes the existence of the Rhymers' Club the more remarkable a
thing." With the exception of Le Gallienne, only "Celts" are mentioned,
Yeats even referring to a poem by Johnson as "full of Catholic theology"
to suggest the un-English nature of the club. Significantly, Yeats ends the
piece with a discussion of Todhunter's Irish subject matter in *The Banshee
and Other Poems* (1888), concluding:

---

*In the dream-world of *Finnegans Wake* (1939), Joyce called Yeats's symbolic world
the "cultic twalette."

May many follow the road Dr. Todhunter has chosen. It leads where there is no lack of subjects, for the literature of Ireland is still young, and on all sides of this road is Celtic tradition, and Celtic passion crying for singers to give them voice. England is old and her poets must scrape up the crumbs of an almost finished banquet, but Ireland has still full tables.

The heading, "The Celt in London," implied that the Rhymers were at the forefront of new artistic developments at the nerve center of the imperialistic British Empire.

However, Yeats was uncertain not only of his own artistic attitudes but also of those of the Rhymers (a confusion compounded later by his transforming mythic vision of the past). His article on the club states that the Rhymers "resemble each other in but one thing: they all believe that the deluge of triolets and rondeaus has passed away, that we must look once more upon the world with serious eyes and set to music—each according to his lights—the deep soul of humanity." Early in his career, Yeats was concerned about his own disengagement from the common concerns of humanity and indeed faced the same problem that Tennyson had had to resolve: how to reach an audience despite the use of poetic expression that focuses upon itself. In 1888, Yeats confessed to Katharine Tynan: "I have noticed some things about my poetry, I did not know before, . . . for instance, that it is almost all a flight into fairy land from the real world, and a summons to that flight. . . . I hope some day to alter that and write poetry of insight and knowledge."

In October 1892, he attacked the idea of art for art's sake, perhaps because his own nationalistic impulses had come to the fore and perhaps because the new French literature, with its strong tradition of *l'art pour l'art,* had attracted his close friend Lionel Johnson:

> In England amongst the best minds art and poetry are becoming every day more entirely ends in themselves, and all life is more and more but so much fuel to feed their fire. It is partly the influence of France that is bringing this about. . . . The influence of that school which calls itself, in the words of its leader, Verlaine, a school of the sunset, or by the term which was flung at it "as a reproach, and caught up as a battle cry," Decadence is now the dominating thing in many lives. Poetry is an end in itself; it has nothing to do with thought, nothing to do with philosophy, nothing to do with life, nothing to do with anything but the music of cadence, and beauty of phrase. . . . It is not possible to call a literature produced in this way the literature of energy and youth.

Yet Yeats later recalled that the weary sentiment of Dowson's "Villanelle of Sunset," with its exclusive concern for music and form, was the principal reason for his suggestion that the Rhymers publish an anthology.

IN NOVEMBER 1893, the Rhymers were stirred by the news that Paul Verlaine had agreed to give lectures in England. Pleased by the prospect of revisiting England after twenty years, Verlaine "talked again of the days spent at Brighton, where he had been a schoolmaster, and of visits to London with Rimbaud." In Belgium, Verlaine, who had had a turbulent homosexual relationship with the younger poet, had been imprisoned from August 1873 to January 1875 for shooting him in the wrist. Thus, his reputation as a Decadent poet was attributable as much to his notorious life as to his art. An admirer of Verlaine's poetry since the late 1880s, Symons had not only published reviews and essays celebrating its modernity but had also begun to imitate it in his own verse. Symons regarded Verlaine's art

> as lyrical as Shelley's, as fluid, as magical—though the magic is a new one. It is a twilight art, full of reticence, of perfumed shadows, of hushed melodies. It suggests, it gives impressions, with a subtle avoidance of any too definite or precise effect of line or colour. The words are now *récherché,* now confidently commonplace—words of the boudoir, words of the street!

Verlaine was an inspiration, said Symons, for he had "given equally exact expression to flesh and spirit," and out of a life of disorder had come a "final harmony" in his art.

On November 20, Symons brought Verlaine to Barnard's Inn in Holborn for the first lecture. Arthur Waugh later described the "strange little crowd of critics and poets, artists and musicians" who were in the audience: "M. Verlaine entered, rather lame, impeded by an extreme lameness, on the arm of Mr. Arthur Symons, his most active supporter in this country." At a great oak table, Verlaine, reading his lecture in French, objected to the use of free verse and rhyme by the younger poets. He urged poets to be "absolutely sincere but absolutely conscientious." Then, he read and briefly commented on several of his own poems, concluding with an expression of gratitude for the "delicious hour in which I have felt your sympathy about me, as I have spoken of my own country in a country I so greatly love and admire. . . ."

When Verlaine returned to London from Manchester on Christmas Day, Dowson wrote to Plarr that he was dining with Verlaine and Horne; he would, if courage prevailed, invite the "Master" to honor his "disciples" with a visit to the Cheshire Cheese. Whether Verlaine accepted the invitation—or whether Dowson extended it—is not known. Most of the Rhymers would have objected to Dowson's assumption that they were Verlaine's devoted followers. Indeed, Lionel Johnson, whose poetry often depicted religious and psychological conflict, had little tolerance for Verlaine's impressionistic verse. He was also critical of Symons's "Parisian impressionism," which was associated, in its use of artifice and depiction of squalor, with Decadence: ". . . a London fog, the blurred, tawny lamplight, the red omnibus, the dreary rain, the depressing mud, the glaring gin shop, the slatternly shivering women, three dexterous stanzas telling you that and nothing more." Though Johnson acknowledged that Symons had written "things of power and things of charm," he was convinced that Symons was "a slave to impressionism," but "if he would wash and be clean, he might be of the elect." Obviously facetious, Johnson's remarks reveal the common association at the time of Impressionism, Decadence, and Zola's Naturalism, which depicted the sordid realities of city life. Yet Verlaine had employed the imagery of common life as the symbolic correspondence of his own emotional state, and Symons, who had studied Baudelaire, discovered the means by which a new literature could be created and by which a new symbolism of the city was possible.

AT THE TIME of Verlaine's appearance in London, the Rhymers were in the process of selecting poems for *The Second Book of the Rhymers' Club,* which would run to 136 pages as opposed to the 94 pages in the first anthology, an indication that the club was confident of its reception. In distinct contrast with the optimistic account of the Celtic Rhymers in his 1892 essay, when the anthology appeared in June 1894, Yeats expressed his distaste for many of the poems in a letter to O'Leary: "I send you 'The Second Book of the Rhymers' Club' in which everybody is tolerably good except the Trinity College men, Rolleston, Hillier, Todhunter & Greene who are intollerably [*sic*] bad as was to be expected . . . & some are exceeding good notably, Plar [*sic*], Dowson, Johnson & Le Galliene [*sic*]." Like the first anthology, *The Second Book of the Rhymers' Club* reveals no commonly agreed-upon attitudes. The commonplace shared by some modern critics that the Rhymers were "highly polished craftsmen with little interest in anything but literature, particularly melancholy lyrical poetry" reveals another half-truth. In the second anthology, the most startling and seemingly anomalous poem (if one recalls Yeats's remark that the Rhymers were interested in "pure poetry") is "Song in the Labour Movement" by Ernest Radford, a lawyer and Fabian socialist whose poem consists of rhythmically arranged Hyde Park oratory:

Oh, you whose sluggard hours are spent
  The rule of Mammon to prolong,
What know you of the stern intent
  Of hosted labour marching song?
When we have righted what is wrong,
  Great singing shall your ears entreat . . .

Apparently, Radford was concerned about the club's exclusion of women; there is no evidence that the subject ever arose at meetings, an indication that such a topic required no discussion. Aware of his own slender poetic gifts and those of his colleagues, he wrote a tribute to his more gifted wife, the poet Dollie Radford, in a brief poem titled "The Book of the Rhymers' Club, Vol. II," which appeared in his volume of verse *Old and New* (1895):

Had you increased our number,
What sweetness might have been
Uprising as from slumber
We bards, in all thirteen,
Amassed this muck and lumber
Sad work without a Queen!

The most famous poem in the second anthology is Dowson's "Non sum qualis eram bonae sub regno Cynarae" ("I am not what once I was in kind Cynara's day"), which contains the phrase "gone with the wind" (to be raised to even greater fame in novel and film). The narrator in the poem recalls his experience with a prostitute ("I have forgot much, Cynara! . . . Flung roses, roses riotously with the throng; / Dancing to put thy pale, lost lilies out of mind"), and "desolate and sick of an old passion," he concludes his memories of quests for "madder music and for stronger wine" with the refrain: "I have been faithful to thee, Cynara! in my fashion." T. S. Eliot later observed that "by a slight shift of rhythm," Dowson freed himself from the poetic practice of his time. Dowson may have derived the idea for "Cynara" from Baudelaire's "Une nuit que j'étais près d'une affreuse Juive" ("One night as I lay near a frightful Jewess") in *Les Fleurs du mal,* but the major difference between the two poems is that Baudelaire's speaker is filled with horror and awe.

Among the poems with discernible Celtic subject matter are Rhys's "Howel the Tall," Plarr's "To a Breton Beggar," Todhunter's "The Song of Tristram," Johnson's "Celtic Speech," and Yeats's six contributions. Johnson's "The Dark Angel," cited by Harold Bloom as "the representative poem of its decade," reveals the poet's psychic divisions and moral dilemmas in his intense struggle with self-destructive drives, the

Dark Angel his adversary as well as second self. Johnson's equally effective "Mystic and Cavalier" contains dark prophecy: "Go from me: I am one of those, who fall." Indeed, he did fall, not from grace but from a bar stool to his death in 1902, the result of a cerebral hemmorhage. Dowson's "Extreme Unction," like Johnson's "The Dark Angel," depicts a ritualized experience of yearning for "lost innocence."

In the autumn of 1894, the Club was planning to issue a third anthology, Greene to act again as general editor. How much of the manuscript was assembled is unknown. What is clear, however, is that the Rhymers were faced with the problem of selecting as their publisher either Elkin Mathews or John Lane, for Mathews and Lane were in the process of dissolving their partnership in the Bodley Head. On September 20, 1894, Mathews wrote to Herbert Horne:

> Writers in the *Second Book of the Rhymers' Club* have to decide whether Lane or myself is to be the publisher. G. A. Greene who edited the volume is now asking the twelve with whom they wish it to go, and as Lane is doing his best to get everything over for himself it behooves me to do my utmost to retain some of my old authors.

Allegiances and friendships with Mathews and Lane inevitably divided the Rhymers. Many followed Lane across Vigo Street, where he opened his own firm under the name of the Bodley Head.

Yet dissolution did not immediately end the club, though it obviously prevented publication of the third anthology. In May 1895, Greene informed Mathews of a Rhymers' dinner and invited him to attend with a guest, an indication that negotiations may not have ended and that perhaps Mathews was to be their publisher, as well as a clear sign that the club was not yet dead. But there is no evidence of any other meetings of the club in that year. In the following year, Yeats convened a meeting, but whether he was attempting to resuscitate the club or whether there were any other meetings also remains unknown.

Several factors brought about the demise of the club. The growing involvement of the Irish Rhymers in the Irish Literary Society progressively shifted their interest from the informally structured, undoctrinaire club to the ideologically determined society. Indeed, as W. P. Ryan, the historian of the Irish literary revival, noted in 1894:

> In addition to Rolleston, Yeats, Dr. Todhunter, and Lionel Johnson, The "Rhymers' Club" gave the Society some promising poets. . . . Amongst them was G. A. Greene. . . . Victor Plarr and A. C. Hillier were also attracted from the little Parnassus of

the "Rhymers," and mean, I hope, to "hammer the ringing rhyme" on a Celtic anvil henceforward.

There were other factors contributing to the end of the club. Yeats and Rolleston were making frequent trips to Dublin to coordinate the activities of the two branches of the Irish Literary Society, Johnson was lecturing before various Irish groups in England and Ireland, while Dowson was spending most of his time in France. As many of the Rhymers were rarely in London, Rhymers' Club meetings grew progressively more infrequent. Moreover, by 1895, many of the Rhymers were well enough known, having published books individually, to abandon the casual meetings at the Cheshire Cheese. Perhaps such a club had not found the right soil. Symons, whose attendance slackened with time, regarded the Rhymers' Club as "a desperate and ineffectual attempt to get into key with the Latin Quarter. Though few of us were, as a matter of fact, Anglo-Saxon, we could not help feeling that we were in London, and the atmosphere of London is not the atmosphere of movements or of societies."

Thus, the Rhymers passed into history to be transformed by Yeats into the most celebrated tragic *cénacle* of the century. Despite the few important achievements by the Rhymers, the myth prevailed for Yeats, who memorialized his "tavern comrades" in "The Grey Rock," the opening poem of his *Responsibilities* (1914):

> *You kept the Muses' sterner laws,*
> *And unrepenting faced your ends,*
> *And therefore earned the right—and yet*
> *Dowson and Johnson most I praise—*
> *To troop with those the world's forgot,*
> *And copy their proud steady gaze.*

At this time, both Dowson and Johnson were dead; Symons had suffered a mental breakdown in 1908, and Davidson had committed suicide in 1909 out of despair over cancer and public neglect. As the greatest of the Rhymers, Yeats, who evolved into a lyric and dramatic poet of dazzling versatility, managed to escape from the "rhythm of heroic failure." However, he ineluctably identified himself with some of his friends, for he saw his own achievement as the product of the same intense struggle that had destroyed them. In "The Choice" (1932), he expressed what was, in fact, the basic paradigm of the Tragic Generation:

> *The intellect of man is forced to choose*
> *The perfection of the life, or of the work,*
> *And if it take the second must refuse*
> *A heavenly mansion, raging in the dark.*

But the disasters that overtook some of the Rhymers continued to be the central enigma of his mythic view: "Why should men, who spoke their opinions in low voices, . . . live lives of such disorder and seek to rediscover in verse the syntax of impulsive common life? Was it that we lived in what is called 'an age of transition' and so lacked coherence, or did we but pursue antithesis?" He recalled that Pater's philosophy involved "the wish to express life at its intense moments and at those moments alone." Such a view, Yeats said, "taught us to walk upon a rope, tightly stretched through serene air, and we were left to keep our feet upon a swaying rope in a storm." When he wrote an introduction to his *Oxford Book of Modern Verse* (1936), however, he seemed to have conveniently forgotten the very myth that he had created in the "Tragic Generation" section of *The Trembling of the Veil* (1922): ". . . in 1900 everybody got down off his stilts; henceforth nobody drank absinthe with his black coffee; nobody went mad; nobody committed suicide; nobody joined the Catholic Church. . . . Victorianism had been defeated."

IN 1908, THE poet and critic T. E. Hulme, who later expounded on Imagism as the basis of a new poetics, was a founder, with Edmund Gosse and others, of the Poets' Club, which met once a month for dinner at Rumpelmayer's in St. James's Street. Above the restaurant, at the United Arts Club, they read their unpublished poems and critical papers as a basis for discussion. Clearly, it sought to be the spiritual successor to the Rhymers' Club, for such Rhymers as Victor Plarr, Ernest Rhys, John Todhunter, Selwyn Image, and G. A. Greene were among those present. Moreover, the Poets' Club published three volumes of its verse, its first and second volumes titled *The Book of the Poets' Club* (1909) and *The Second Book of the Poets' Club* (1911), echoing the Rhymers' titles.

By March 1909, Hulme and F. S. Flint (now a follower of Hulme), the "little Secessionist" group, left the Poets' Club, the members of which were still writing poems in the long-exhausted Victorian style of lofty declamation and allegorical tropes rather than the hard, clear Imagist verse that Hulme had espoused—that is, a means of eliminating sentimentality by employing an objective image to embody the poet's psychic state. Early Imagist meetings were held in Hulme's rooms as well as at the Irish Literary Society in Hanover Square. Leading discussions within the new group—which now included Ernest Rhys, Ernest Radford, and, by late April, Ezra Pound—at the Tour d'Eiffel restaurant near Soho, Hulme insisted that in poetry the "great aim is accurate, precise, and definite description. It is essential to prove that beauty may be in small, dry things." In short, the Imagists preferred direct presentation of the image as opposed to the Symbolists, who suggested the existence of unseen realities by indirect presentation. Pound defined the image as "an emotional and intellectual complex in an instant of time"—thus, says René Taupin, "between the 'image' of the Imagists and the 'symbol' of the Symbolists, there is a difference only of precision."

In December 1909, Rhys invited Pound, Yeats, Radford, Ford Madox Hueffer (later Ford), who brought D. H. Lawrence, to a dinner followed by readings and discussions, resuming, he later wrote, "the nights at the Old Cheshire Cheese of the Rhymers' Club." Yeats "held forth at length on [the] new art of bringing music and poetry together," an allusion to his many years of experimentation with the actress Florence Farr of chanting to the psaltery. After the recitations of verse by the guests, Farr chanted Yeats's "The Man Who Dreamed of Faeryland" in a "haunting wail . . . rather suggestive of a priestess intoning a litany." A modern critic has written that, as Imagism developed, "Yeats, Farr, and a growing number of allies kept the pressure on the imagists, determined never to let them substitute a visual for an aural paradigm."

Disinclined to follow anyone, Pound announced in his *Ripostes* (1912) the existence of *"Les Imagistes,* the decendants of the forgotten school of 1909." Like the Rhymers, Pound's *Imagistes* had a brief existence: He edited *Des Imagistes: An Anthology* (1914), containing poems by such figures as H. D., Richard Aldington, John Gould Fletcher, James Joyce, and Pound himself. When it "fell dead" in London, Pound promptly disavowed Imagism and joined Wyndham Lewis and the Vorticists, who promised more aggressive artistic expression to overcome their sense of cultural isolation in an increasingly inhospitable world.

4

The Quest for a
Poet Laureate

At 1:35 A.M. on October 6, 1892, Alfred Lord Tennyson, poet laureate for an unprecedented forty-two years, died in his Sussex home after suffering for a week from influenza and gout "in a ritualized hush that seem[ed] more like an elaborate death-bed scene from a Victorian novel than the end of an actual man's life." Three days before, he had asked for a volume of Shakespeare's *Cymbeline* to be placed in his hands, but almost immediately he laid it aside, saying to his doctor that he believed the end was near. For the next two days, the volume was taken from him but restored when he insisted on it. At his death, with the moonlight streaming in from the oriel window, he lay with his hand on the cracked spine of the book open to the page that contained lines, spoken by Posthumus to Imogen, that had always moved him: "Hang there like fruit, my soul, / Till the tree die." The death of Tennyson, as his doctor described it, brought to the minds of those witnessing it "The Passing of Arthur," the final section of the laureate's noble epic, *The Idylls of the King* (1869), the glory of Britain's past and present united in death.

On October 12, virtually every poet of any significance in England attended the funeral at Westminster Abbey. The notable exception was Swinburne, widely regarded as the principal candidate for the laureateship. The groundswell of sentiment over Tennyson's death seemed to be confirmation that the Victorian era itself was coming to an end (the Queen was now 73). From numerous pulpits, there was lamentation that "one of the immortals" had departed, for he was the conscience and prophet of the age, one who had provided guidance to Victorians perplexed by such problems as that of religious belief in the face of scientific discovery and the difficulty of maintaining moral and spiritual integrity in a culture devoted to material progress. He himself had struggled with such dilemmas and thus gave personal meaning to public utterance, as in his reassuring lines from *Idylls of the King,* which readers seized upon:

"More things are wrought by prayer / Than this world dreams of." Poetic eulogies poured from innumerable pens into newspapers and periodicals over the next few months as poets sought to voice the grief of a nation—not one of the poems, however, meriting any claim to distinction.

Several days after Tennyson had been laid to rest in the Poets' Corner at the abbey near such figures as Dryden and Browning, Swinburne wrote to the Pre-Raphaelite painter Edward Burne-Jones from The Pines, Putney, that he had declined to attend the ceremonies because he hated "all crowds and all functions, but especially the funereal kind beyond all decent expression." He wrote an uninspired elegy, a tribute to Tennyson's stature depicted by the poet's "proud head pillowed on Shakespeare's breast / Hand in hand with him, soon to stand where shine the glories that death loves best. . . ."

Though Yeats later often disparaged Tennyson and attributed his own views to his fellow Rhymers (namely, that the laureate had sullied his work with religion and other "impurities," and that they "must create once more the pure work"), several of the club members nevertheless composed tributes to him. John Todhunter's "In Westminster Abbey: October 12, 1892" later appeared as the opening poem of *The Second Book of the Rhymers' Club* (1894):

> *We saw him stand, a lordly forest tree,*
> *His branches filled with music, all the air*
> *Glad for his presence, fallen at last is he,*
> *   And all the land is bare.*

Shortly after hearing the news of Tennyson's death, Ernest Dowson, writing to his fellow Rhymer Victor Plarr, praised the poet's artistic integrity and dreaded the next poet laureate:

> I am sorry that Tennyson has crossed the bar: if only, that it leaves us so much at the mercy of Sir Edwin [Arnold],* L[ewis] Morris, Austin et Cie. But he was un grand poète, tout de même. Above all I love him because he did sacredly hate the

---

*A leading contender among the minor poets, Sir Edwin Arnold was best known for his popular work, *The Light of Asia; or, the Great Renunciation* (1879), which contains such titles as "Samodadamodaro" and "Kleshakeshavo." His exoticism and his favorable attitude towards Buddhism may have disqualified Arnold from the laureateship, which he had expected to attain. Owen Seaman's parody "For the Albums of Crowned Heads Only" imagines a jubilee poem written by Arnold: "Yá Yá! Best Belovéd! I look to thy dimples and drink; / Tiddlihî! to thy cheek-pits and chin-pit, my Tulip, my Pink!" (*The Battle of the Bays* [London, 1896], 5).

mob—which whether it be the well dressed mob whom Browning pandered to, or the evil smelling mob to which William Morris does now, to the detriment of his art and of his own dignity still pander, I hold alike to be damnable, unwholesome and obscene.

In "The Passing of Tennyson," (echoing Tennyson's "The Passing of Arthur," Dowson draws parallels between the noble king and the noble laureate, now inseparable in the nation's sensibility:

> *As his own Arthur fared across the mere,*
> *With the grave Queen, past knowledge of the throng,*
> *Serene and calm, rebuking grief and tear,*
> *Departs this prince of song.*

Richard Le Gallienne, who had attended the funeral service and who never forgot its "solemn grandeur, its symbolic impressiveness . . . less like an ending of mortal greatness than a triumphal entry into immortality," composed "Alfred Tennyson: (Westminster, October 12, 1892)," a grave but spiritless elegy:

> *Great man of song, whose glorious laurelled head*
> *Within the lap of death sleeps well at last,*
> *Down the dark road, seeking the deathless dead,*
> *Thy faithful, fearless, shining soul hath passed.*

INEVITABLY, THE DEATH of Tennyson provoked extensive private and public debates concerning the next poet laureate, filling the columns of newspapers and periodicals for more than three years. The fear most frequently expressed was that a minor talent might succeed Wordsworth and Tennyson, two of the greatest laureates since Dryden became the first official poet laureate in 1670. Such a calamity would reduce the significance and prestige of the office; worse, it would place the aging Queen, charged with conferring the honor, in an embarrassing position, for she had named Wordsworth in 1843 and Tennyson in 1850 as laureates. Since British culture itself was symbolized by the artistic eminence and universal voice of its most honored poet, an egregious blunder on the part of her advisors would suggest a lack of confidence and direction in the last years of the Queen's reign. In short, the naming of a laureate involved complex social and political considerations not to be ignored.

Though the question of Tennyson's successor was raised while eulogies continued to appear through the remainder of 1892, speculation concern-

ing a new laureate had previously been widespread after Tennyson's re-
covery from an illness early in 1890, when he was eighty-one. In the
Fortnightly Review (May 1890), an anonymous article reviewed the status
of various poets, bearing in mind that "the laureateship, if preserved at
all, must continue to be the titular symbol of a real and just poetical
primacy." And since the appointment had a "bearing on the imperial and
representative character of the English monarchy," the question of Tennyson's successor was not "to be deemed a trifle." The laureate, the
writer concludes, must then be "not only a poet of real distinction, but a
scholar and a man of letters; and moreover his poetry should have a
certain catholic extension." Also, the laureate should "accept with loyalty
or self-respect the personal relation to the Crown." With such criteria,
one of the "foremost living poets," William Morris, "appears to have
wholly excluded himself . . . from the field of choice," though ten or
twelve years ago he would have been a strong candidate. Lately, he had
become "a preacher of Socialist homilies, not even particularly good of
their kind."

As for Swinburne, controversies swirling around *Poems and Ballads* had
long since past; more important was his attitude toward the Crown, particularly his staunch republican views expressed in *Songs before Sunrise*
(1871)—implying, said the writer in the *Fortnightly Review,* that "the English monarchy was only a little more tolerable than other monarchies
and empires." But, he concludes, when one considers that such poets as
Alfred Austin and Lewis Morris may be considered for the office, "next to
Tennyson, the primacy belongs to Mr. Swinburne" as the man of letters
with the greatest stature. If he is not chosen, "then let the name and office
of Laureate be done away rather than sink below the level at which we
and our fathers have seen them maintained." Later discussions of Tennyson's successor often conclude on this note: Better to eliminate the office
than to permit it to fall into the hands of a poetaster rather than a true
poet.

AFTER TENNYSON'S INTERMENT in the abbey, one of the first articles on
the appointment appeared in the *Saturday Review* (October 15, 1892), a
facetious lament that there have been "infinitely worse laureates than any
one who is likely to be chosen." Even so, "the best laureate, alas! must
die; the worst, thank Heaven! will." The *Bookman* (November 1892)
invited four writers to ponder the question of whether to continue the
laureateship and, if so, to suggest a successor. Two of the anonymous
respondents favoring Swinburne as the likely successor refer to him as
"the greatest lyrical writer of our generation" who has the "pre-eminent
right to the honour." The respondent signing himself "R. B.," probably

Robert Bridges, believes that William Morris is the worthiest candidate, but because he is a militant socialist, "surely a Radical Poet Laureate would be an anomaly." Swinburne, then, "the greatest lyrical writer of our generation," is R. B.'s choice.

Yeats's letter to the editor (who published it anonymously) insisted that the "only two men fitted" to be the laureate—Swinburne and William Morris—would be reluctant to accept the office if they were required to compose songs about royal marriages. If the duties of the laureate are not substantially changed (from its obligations to the Court to a closer connection with the people), only an "unreadable mediocrity or fluent monger of platitudes" is likely to be appointed. In the month before, however, an anonymous writer in the *Spectator* (October 15, 1892) insisted that the laureate was not obligated to serve the Crown, nor was he expected "to exercise his art against his will, either for the laudation of the Sovereign, or the exaltation of the ceremonials she may from time to time be called on to perform."

Brooding on the question of Tennyson's successor, Edmund Gosse, in a notable essay in the *New Review* (November 1892), recalled his observation of the "unparalleled masses of the curious" outside the abbey and the hawkers moving through the crowd selling broadside copies of Tennyson's "Crossing the Bar." The contrast between the solemnity of the interment and the mood of those outside led him to believe that that "poetry, authority, the grace and dignity of life, seemed to have been left behind us for ever in that twilight where Tennyson was sleeping with Chaucer and with Dryden." He wondered whether the "prestige of verse" had also been left behind, and he questioned the expression of grief by those who were denied access to the services. Since the noblest verse appealed to the few, he found himself "depressed and terrified" at such an open display of feeling by those unlikely to have read a word of Tennyson: "The democracy doth protest too much, and there is danger in this hollow reverence."* The danger lay in the crowd's concern with the poet rather than his poems (in short, with what we now recognize as the modern obsession with fame and personality rather than with achievement). Since Wordsworth's death, such a focus on the poet, he states,

> has taken colossal proportions, without, so far as can be observed, any parallel quickening of the taste for poetry itself. The

*The novelist George Gissing, after reading Gosse's article, wrote to him on November 20: "After fifteen years' observation of the poorer classes of English folk, chiefly in London and the south, I am pretty well assured that, whatever civilizing agencies may be at work among the democracy, poetry is not one of them" (Gissing's letter is printed in Gosse's *Questions at Issue* [London, 1893] with the article titled "Tennyson—and After").

result is that a very interesting or picturesque figure, if identified with poetry, may attract an amount of attention and admiration which is spurious as regards the poetry, and of no real significance. . . . The world now expects its poets to be as picturesque, as aged, and as individual as [Tennyson] was, or else it will pay poetry no attention.

Gosse expressed a common fear among the privileged classes in the nineteenth century that English society might one day fall victim to the undisciplined, uneducated, and uncultured mob and that the chaos of the French Revolution could also occur on British soil. For many, Carlyle's widely read *History of the French Revolution* (1847) served as a warning that social upheavals were inevitable if reforms were ignored. More recently, the Paris Commune of 1871 had been a further example of such potential chaos. (After the Franco-Prussian War, radical republicans, reenacting the days of the revolution, seized control of the city, an action resulting in widespread death and destruction.) By exaggerated analogy (indicating the depth of his anxiety), Gosse suggested the dreaded possibility of "the eruption of a sort of Commune in literature" once the remarkable phenomenon of Tennyson's popularity is over: "At no period could the danger of such an outbreak of rebellion against tradition be so great as during the reaction which must follow the death of our most illustrious writer. Then, if ever, I should expect to see a determined resistance made to the pretensions of whatever is rare, or delicate, or abstruse."

Currently, Gosse insisted, "our living poets present a variety and amplitude of talent, a fulness of tone, an accomplishment in art, such as few other generations in England, and still fewer elsewhere, have been in a position to exult in." He cites Swinburne (significantly, first), then Christina Rossetti (the first article after Tennyson's death in which a woman was proposed as a possible laureate), William Morris, Coventry Patmore, Austin Dobson, and Robert Bridges. Whoever is chosen, Gosse urges "those who are our recognised judges of literary merit to resist more strenuously than ever the inroads of mere commercial success into the Temple of Fame."

THE POSSIBILITY OF Swinburne's appointment was complicated by factors other than his artistic preeminence. Besides the republican spirit of his *Songs before Sunrise* (1871), in 1885 he expressed his hostility in verse for the prime minister's inability or unwillingness to send a rescue force to save the heroic General Gordon at Kartoum during a siege of the city (the Queen, to whom Swinburne remained devoted, joined in the general outburst of indignation directed at Gladstone):

Forsaken, silent, Gordon dies and gives
Example: loud and shameless Gladstone lives,
No faction unembraced or unbetrayed,
No chance unwelcomed and no vote unweighed. . . .

Gladstone, who probably never saw these unpublished lines, had begun to solicit opinions concerning a new laureate even before Tennyson was lowered into his tomb. Swinburne's was the first name to appear in his queries, an indication of the poet's undisputed stature. Gosse, who was later the librarian of the House of Lords and who had probably heard much of what transpired behind the scenes, reported that the Queen had said to Gladstone: "I am told that Mr. Swinburne is the best poet in my dominions." But Swinburne's name provoked anxiety in Gladstone, who had been raised in a strict evangelical Scots household and who had once intended to become a clergyman. In a letter dated October 7 to the historian Lord Acton, a close friend and advisor, Gladstone revealed his disquiet over the laureateship: "The question of the succession comes before me with very ugly features. I have, as it happens, the old *Poems and Ballads* 1866. They are both bad and terrible. Have they been dropped? If they have is it a reparation? Wordsworth and Tennyson have made the place great. They have also made it extremely clean. . . . I do not like the look of the affair."

On October 10, Gladstone told Acton that Swinburne was "impossible" for the office, but a week later he asked him "whether Swinburne by withdrawl or otherwise brings himself within the range of possibility." *Poems and Ballads,* Acton assured him, had never been withdrawn, and he warned that Swinburne's appointment "would stimulate the circulation of the offending volume (and condone it)." Swinburne's extreme republicanism, moreover, would be an offense to the Queen. He had published "Russia: An Ode" in the *Fortnightly Review* (August 1890), which, Acton told Gladstone, revealed "an unbroken consistency in evil in the mind and career of the man." Swinburne's appointment to the laureateship would also be an "offence to Her Majesty's Imperial Brother and ally, to place in office involving appearance at Court, a man who clamours to have him murdered, and whose plea for Tyrannicide is not remote, or obscure, or unnoticed. . . ."* By October 20, Gladstone, though convinced of

---

*Swinburne had written the poem after reading of the deplorable conditions in Russian prisons. On August 5, 1890, a member of the House of Commons asked the first lord of the treasury "whether Her Majesty's Government intend to prosecute Mr. A. C. Swinburne or the publisher or printer of the *Fortnightly Review* for this gross incitement to assassination of the Sovereign of a friendly nation." He read the most offensive line in the poem: "Night hath none but one red star—Tyrannicide." The Speaker responded: "Order, order! This House has no control over a poet's opinions." The

Swinburne's *"pre-*eminence as a poet,"* regretfully concluded in a letter to
Sir Henry Ponsonby, the Queen's secretary, that the appointment was
"absolutely impossible": "It is a sad pity; I have always been deeply impressed by his genius."

Acton suggested another possibility—John Ruskin—but the objection
might be raised that he was principally a writer of prose. Since Ruskin had
recently been ill with a manic-depressive psychosis, Gladstone wrote to
Sir Henry Acland, Regius Professor of Medicine at Oxford: "It is most
desirable to keep [the laureateship] on the high moral plane where
Wordsworth and Tennyson placed it. Is Ruskin impossible?" Acland,
who had not seen Ruskin for some years, consulted a local physician
acquainted with the illness. The result was that Ruskin was ruled out.
Finally, Gladstone, doubtful of William Morris, wrote to Acton on October 17: "I understand Mr. W. Morris is an out and out socialist." Acton
replied that Morris was "quite a flaring Communist, with unpleasant associations," though James Bryce, a member of the Cabinet, informed Gladstone that he saw no incitements to violence in Morris's socialism. Bryce
received a letter from Morris, who, having been sounded out on the
laureateship, wrote: "I am a sincere republican, and therefore could not
accept a post which would give me even the appearance of serving a court
for complaisance sake."

Of the lesser poets, none was given sufficient support within court
circles to convince Gladstone that a choice could be made without widespread objection. On November 4, Gladstone informed the Queen that
he could not "at present see his way to making an unexceptionable
recommendation." Two days later, in a memorandum prepared for the
Queen, Bryce summarized views on some minor poets (such as Coventry
Patmore, Robert Bridges, and William Watson) and concluded: "Any
selection from among these might probably excite hostile criticism more
profuse than any satisfaction it could evoke." There was, however, a way
out of the dilemma: ". . . there is precedent for declining to abolish [the
laureateship], but letting it remain vacant until there arises a poet conspicuously worthy to fill it." The Queen agreed.

On February 2, 1893, Gladstone was queried by a member of the
House of Commons whether any recommendation to the office of the
poet laureate had been made to Her Majesty. None had been made, he
said, nor was there any "immediate intention" to do so.* On July 21,

---

same M.P. raised the question again on August 11 and 12. On both occasions, the
Speaker again shouted: "Order, order!" See *Hansard Parliamentary Debates,* 3d ser.,
(London, 1890) 347: 1921; 348: 526, 721.
Punch (February 11, 1893) responded with "A Plaint from Parnassus": "Glorious
Apollo! This is wondrous hard, / Fancy John Bull without Official Bard!"

another member of the Commons raised the question, to which Gladstone responded: "There is no intention at present of making the appointment." With Gladstone's retirement in March 1894, the Earl of Rosebery, who was the foreign secretary, became the new prime minister. In his brief tenure in office, he apparently devoted little attention to the question of a new laureate.

As the delay continued without public explanation into the following year, members of the House of Commons raised the question anew. On July 17, 1894, the chancellor of the exchequer, Sir William Harcourt, was asked to account for the "delay in filling up the post of poet laureate; and when it is likely to be filled up?" But before he could respond, another M.P. raised an extraordinary question: ". . . may I ask will the Government test the soundness of the hereditary principle by recommending the appointment of the present Lord Tennyson in succession to his father?" Sir William declined to test the "principle": "This is rather a delicate question, and amid conflicting claims I must shelter myself in the decent obscurity of a learned language and reply, *Poeta nascitur, non fit* [A poet is born, not made]."

Another member inquired whether, in view of the two-year delay in filling up the "ancient office" and the "injustice to possible candidates of further delay," Sir William would inform the prime minister of "the general feeling in favour of an early decision." Sir William responded: "My hon. Friend must remember what happened to the shepherd Paris when he had to award the apple, and the misfortunes which befell him and his partner. . . ." In a final question, a member of the House asked whether Sir William would propose "to hold a limited competition, and ask the poets to send in their specimens." Sir William declined to answer. The fear of an unwise choice appears to have had its impact on the Rosebery ministry; in any event, he fell from power in July 1895. Lord Salisbury, who succeeded him, finally responded to the increasing pressure to recommend a laureate to the Queen.

The widespread interest in the laureateship was clearly stimulating a new interest in the symbolic—if not the inherent—importance of poetry, as indicated by the queries in the House of Commons. With the likely exclusion of Swinburne and Morris from serious consideration as laureates, dozens of lesser poets were suddenly thrust into brief prominence, for now one of them could hope to receive the honor. At the same time, an additional factor may have been responsible for the delay in the appointment. Three years after the choice was made, a writer discussing William Watson in the *Conservative Review* (May 1899) recalled the "logrolling" that occurred on behalf of prospective candidates: It was, he wrote, "like a disgraceful funeral game around Tennyson's solemn pyre." Such partisan politics had the "effect of exciting to an unwonted degree the curiosity of the public regarding the new and, for the most part, unknown poets of the day."

Meanwhile, the discussions continued unabated in the press, and as one might expect, there was much levity over the matter in such publications as *Punch* and *Judy.* Owen Seaman, a contributor to the former, regularly published parodies of poems by the major and minor poets comically contending for the laureateship. (They appeared in his collection, *The Battle of the Bays,* alluding to the bay leaf, or laurel, traditionally used in crowning laureates.) In "A Song of Renunciation," a parody of Swinburne's rollicking rhythms, the speaker—Swinburne himself—concludes with the wish that his youthful *Poems and Ballads* would fade away:

> *When the trill of my juvenile trumpet*
>   *Is dead and its echoes are dead;*
> *Then the laurel shall lie on the crumpet*
>   *And crown of my head!*

Seaman, not a parodist of the first rank, also takes aim at such poets as Kipling ("The Rhyme of the Kipperling"), Sir Edwin Arnold, and various members of the Rhymers' Club, including Le Gallienne, Symons, and John Davidson, never serious contenders for the laureateship but suitable for laughter precisely because, as minor figures scornful of Victorian respectability, they were puffed by Seaman as possible candidates.

In April 1895, the *Idler Magazine* asked twenty-two writers to respond to the question "Who Should be Laureate?" Sir Edwin Arnold, obviously reluctant to publicize one of his competitors, replied tersely: "The man whom Her Majesty chooses." Most of those responding named Swinburne. Wilde announced, however, that "Mr. Swinburne is already the Poet Laureate of England. The fact that his appointment to this high post has not been degraded by official confirmation renders his position all the more unassailable. He whom all poets love is the Laureate Poet always." Bernard Shaw declined to name the next laureate, though he conceded that Swinburne was a "born Poet Laureate: he has always been worshipping somebody." The drama critic William Archer, after naming Swinburne and William Morris as the only possible choices, concludes with a now familiar view: "Better let [the laureateship] end in a blaze of glory with Tennyson, than flicker out, as a rank anachronism, in a blast of ridicule."

A notable exception to the majority view was the novelist Israel Zangwill's choice of Kipling, who "has sung the song of the British flag in verses of unsurpassed imaginative vigour." And in a remark that invites an ambiguous reading, Zangwill states that Kipling's mind has that "narrowness that makes a national bard and that breadth which is indispensable for a British national bard, whose strains must echo the morning-roll of the drum that follows the sunrise round the world." Though Kipling was only thirty, "the only impediment against him," he was already "practically the Laureate of the British Empire." Edith Nesbit, like Zangwill, favored Kipling since the laureate was required by his very office to be loyal to the monarch and to sing of glorious battles past. Swinburne, though the preeminent poet, could not thus be considered.

The most facetious response was given by "John Strange Winter," the pseudonym of the popular novelist Henrietta Vaughan Stannard, who announced: "Truth to tell, I can only think of one person really suitable for the office of Poet Laureate. That person is not a man, but a woman— that person is myself." She urges this choice for the "general public good and for the promotion of peace in this our native land." Since, she insists, she is totally without qualifications for the office, every major and minor poet would feel equally dissatisfied and "each would be able to rest assured that he had been passed over for one whom no person, in the full possession of his or her senses, could believe to be a better poet than himself."

By late 1895, the press had all but exhausted the topic of Tennyson's successor, and no one in the House of Commons raised further queries. In October, however, Coventry Patmore wrote to the *Saturday Review* to propose a candidate hitherto unmentioned in the various discussions and debates—his close friend, Alice Meynell. He had heard a rumor that Lord Salisbury had expressed his intention of "complimenting journalism" by selecting the next laureate from its ranks. Patmore suggested that a "double compliment" (to poetry as well as to journalism) could be achieved if the appointment went to Mrs. Meynell, at once a distinguished poet and a practicing journalist who regularly contributed a column to the *Pall Mall Gazette* and who wrote articles for a variety of periodicals, including the *National Review* and *Fortnightly Review.* As for her political position, she was "well known, to perhaps the largest and most influential circle of literary men and women in London, to combine strong Radical principles with equally vigorous Tory tastes. . . ." Patmore warned that, if the appointment were made to someone other than Mrs. Meynell, Lord Salisbury would "bring a fine nest of hornets about his head." And in an age in which "woman's claims occupy the world's attention as they never did before," her appointment would be "expedient and popular as it would be just."

LORD SALISBURY WAS prepared to risk the nest of hornets. He had been a close friend and associate of Alfred Austin, who, since the 1860s, had been editing the Conservative *National Review.* The prime minister's daughter recalled that Austin "was a whole-hearted supporter of Lord Salisbury's policy both at home and abroad, was personally attached to him, and a frequent visitor at Hatfield. Their intercourse enabled him to forward the Minister's policy by calling anonymous attention to aspects of it upon which Lord Salisbury could not himself dwell publicly, and this assistance was certainly welcomed. . . ." Moreover, Austin was widely known for his ability to turn out the appropriate patriotic poem when the occasion demanded it, and he shared a fondness for nature that nineteenth-century poets, Tennyson included, regarded as a characteristic English trait. If he lacked distinction as a poet, he was, at the very least, a staunch upholder of the empire and of the monarchy. In effect, Austin's appointment would amount to a political reward.

On October 26, 1895, the *Critic* (New York) published Arthur Waugh's weekly "London Letter," which reported that "the air is full of rumors of the laureateship" and that it was "secretly whispered that Her Majesty was engaged in a study of Mr. ———'s poems, which she confessed herself unable to understand." The new laureate, Waugh wrote, will most likely be either Sir Edwin Arnold or Alfred Austin. In the following month, the *Illustrated London News* (November 9) revealed what apparently was widely known: "It may be assumed the appointment of Alfred Austin as Poet Laureate will be announced in a few days. Now that the thing is definitely settled, it is perhaps to find out wherein the selection is satisfactory rather than where it is not. . . ."

As Robert Graves later wrote with a touch of malice:

> Morris was a Socialist, Swinburne a drunkard, Hardy an Atheist, Watson had, it was said, once assaulted the Prince of Wales in a park, and Kipling had earned Queen Victoria's anger by disrespectfully terming her "the Widow of Windsor."* So the Queen was asked to settle for Alfred Austin—a loyal, literary Conservative journalist, presentable at Court though very small beer as a poet.

Austin was also very small in height (he was barely five feet tall), a fact that delighted satirists. *Punch* (January 11, 1896) hailed him as "Alfred

---

*"The Widow at Windsor," with its original title "The Sons of the Widow," first appeared in the *Scots Observer* (April 26, 1890), reprinted in *Barrack-Room Ballads* (1892), the speaker a Cockney soldier in India:

> 'Ave you 'eard o' the Widow at Windsor
> With a hairy gold crown on 'er 'ead?
> She 'as ships on the foam—she 'as millions at 'ome,
>   An' she pays us poor beggars in red.

Punch on Alfred Austin
(*Punch*, January 11, 1896)

ALFRED THE LITTLE.

Sir Edwin Arn-ld (bitterly). "'Fortunate!' Ha! ha!" *Sir Lew s Mrr s (moodily).* "'England's darling!' He! he!"

"The Queen has been pleased to appoint Alfred Austin, Esq., to be Poet Laureate to Her Majesty."—*Daily Papers, January 1, 1896.*

the Little" (as opposed to Tennyson, "Alfred the Great"), and Gosse delighted in a story told by Browning concerning a dinner party he once attended. When the butler opened a door and announced Alfred Austin, Browning said: "And I give you my word of honour, *nothing whatever* came into the room. . . ."

On January 1, 1896, the miniscule Austin was officially named as the poet laureate in the New Year's honors list. By disposing of Swinburne and Morris as candidates, the Queen's advisors had preserved the laureateship as an office safe from poets potentially disturbing to the Crown and to the general public. Though Austin told Austin Dobson that the "distinction assigned to me was none of my own seeking and that it came to me by *surprise,* on the last day of the year," he was known to have said to others that his appointment was merely the recognition of his being "at the head of English literature." As his biographer had written, "Such egotism perhaps deserved the fierce lampoons and frenzied parody which marked his laureateship more than that of any other of England's appointed bards."*

---

*A notable exception to widespread denigration of Austin as laureate occurred in D. F. Hannigan's "The New Poet Laureate" in the *Westminster Review* (March 1896), which devalued Tennyson's Arthurian epic as "a dreary and unenjoyable experience" and *In Memoriam* as "a feeble effort" because of its didacticism. "Not so Mr. Austin.

Ten days after his appointment to the laureateship, Austin published a poem in the *Times* (January 11) named for the Jameson raid, which had occurred on December 29, 1895, when Dr. L. Storr Jameson, an administrator in the British South Africa Company, rode with 470 men into the Transvaal to join non-Boer European workers, mostly British, in an attempt to overthrow President Paul Kruger's Boer government. The conspiracy failed, and Jameson's party was captured within four days. The political repercussions led eventually to the Boer War in 1899.

In a monologue, Austin's poem depicts one of Jameson's followers on the eve of the raid and in the aftermath, a jingoist view that revealed to the world Lord Salisbury's error in recommending his friend as the poet laureate:

> *Wrong! Is it wrong? Well, may be*
> *But I'm going, boys, all the same.*
> *Do they think me a Burgher's baby,*
> *To be scared by a scolding name?*
> *They may argue, and prate, and order;*
> *Go, tell them to save their breath:*
> *Then, over the Transvaal border,*
> *And gallop for life or death!*
>
> . . . .
>
> *I suppose we were wrong, were madmen,*
> *Still I think at the Judgment Day,*
> *When God sifts the good from the bad men,*
> *There'll be something more to say,*
> *We were wrong, but we aren't half sorry. . . .*

Satires of the poem flooded newspapers and periodicals as every would-be parodist tried his hand at derision. In *Punch* (January 18, 1896), "The Laureate's First Ride" was one of the most trenchant:

> *Say, is it song? Well—blow it!*
> *But I'll sing it, boys, all the same*
> *Because I'm the Laureate Poet,*
> *That's the worst of having a name!*
> *I must be inspired to order,*
> *'Go, tell 'em, to save their breath:'*

His lyrical poems are essentially spontaneous, and have a freshness and tenderness which is unsurpassed by the work of any other living English writer of verse." Hannigan's view was, to say the least, an uncommon one.

> *I can rhyme to 'order' with 'border,'*
> *And jingle to 'breath' and 'death.'*

A few days after Austin's poem appeared, the Queen wrote in distress to Lord Salisbury, who responded that he had "missed Mr. Austin's poem, but he has heard it condemned by many persons, both from a political and literary point of view. It is a pity that this effusion was his first performance. Unluckily it is to the taste of the galleries in the lower class of theatres, and they sing it with vehemence."* Sir William Harcourt was less restrained in his reaction: He told his son that it was a "monstrous poem" and that Austin "ought to be cashiered." Though, by March, the furor over the poem had subsided, the poet Francis Thompson told Coventry Patmore: "What a pity that you could not have upheld the dignity of the Laureateship in the eyes of Europe! This absurd appointment might have been pointedly contrived to give the office its death-blow."

Austin's "Jameson's Raid," though the first, was not the last of his unfortunate productions as poet laureate. In 1900, William Archer raised a question in the New York *Critic:* "Is it not time . . . that someone should gently but firmly remonstrate with Mr. Alfred Austin . . . whose indiscreet utterances in the newspapers are becoming a national scandal? . . . How long are we fated to grin and bear it?" Despite such hostility, Austin maintained an imperturbable serenity, though he responded to Archer in a letter to the *Critic* that the Queen had appointed him as poet laureate on the "recommendation of her chief minister, who doubtless acted in conformity with what he believed to be the preponderant genuine literary opinion of his fellow countrymen."

In his later years, Austin lived at Swinford Old Manor in Kent, occupying his time with gardening, writing, and entertaining. Dinner guests were occasionally startled but amused when a servant announced their hosts' grand entrance: "The Poet Laureate and Mrs. Austin." With Austin's death on June 2, 1913, lengthy obituaries and public reactions had little trace of the grief that had accompanied Tennyson's passing. On July 15, the laureateship recovered something of its former stature and dignity with the appointment of Robert Bridges.

---

*Though Austin's poem received its deserved ridicule, there was considerable support for Jameson's impetuous heroism, despite its political consequences. In a letter to the editor of the *Times* (January 13, 1896), one C. R. Low, concerned with the image of the empire, states: "At a time when foreigners speak of the decadence of the old British spirit, the devoted valour of Jameson's horsemen gives a lie to the slander. Like the charge of the 'Six Hundred' [immortalized in Tennyson's "Charge of the Light Brigade"] at Balaclava, it may be said, though their audacious attack was contrary to the rules of war, it was 'magnificent. . . .'" In another letter in the same issue, the novelist H. Rider Haggard defended Jameson for his bravery in attempting to prevent a massacre of the Uitlanders at the hands of the Boers.

5

Prostitutes on the Promenade

IN THE LATE nineteenth century, estimates varied radically on the number of prostitutes plying their trade in London from the fashionable brothels in the West End to those "low women, who under cover of darkness, make use of back streets and open spaces, and whose unprotected state gave rise to the horrible tragedies of a few years back," an allusion to Jack the Ripper's victims in the East End. In the mid-nineteenth century, the bishop of London had estimated that there were 80,000 prostitutes in the metropolis, a figure also given by Henry Mayhew in his *London Labour and the London Poor* (1851). In the 1860s, the London police had records of only about 6,000 prostitutes, but given the clandestine nature of prostitution, such a figure was obviously unreliable. In 1890, the estimate of between 60,000 and 80,000 prostitutes in London was attacked by General William Booth of the Salvation Army, who called such a figure "a monstrous exaggeration if it meant to apply to those who make their living solely and habitually by prostitution." Of such prostitutes, he said, there were probably over 30,000 in London and over 100,000 in Great Britain (not including an additional 100,000 who secretly increased their earnings by occasional prostitution). Clearly, neither the police nor the various rescue groups, such as the Salvation Army, had precise methods of compiling statistics, but for reformers and antivice crusaders, the higher the estimates, the greater was the justification for their existence.

In the final volume of his *Life and Labour of the People in London* (1902), Charles Booth remarked that though "Law and Gospel are unhesitating in their condemnation of prostitution . . . yet the practice continues unchecked, and in some of its manifestations is a positive scandal." Attempts to suppress this "Great Social Evil" or to rescue the women had been of no avail, he insisted, since most prostitutes were "strictly professional," their passions "hardly involved at all . . . moved neither by excitement nor by pleasure . . . induced to follow this course of life by the desire for fine clothes and luxuries not otherwise attainable." Some women, Booth observed, became prostitutes only occasionally when circumstances compelled:

> . . . tailoresses or dressmakers, for example, who return to their trade in busy times; girls from low neighborhoods who eke out a living in this way; or poor women, neglected wives, or widows, under pressure of poverty; or worst of all, such as are driven to this course by a bad husband or a bad father. Some jealousy is felt by those, who are more strictly professional, of incursions into the field occupied.

Booth reported that from the "high-class houses" of prostitution some women frequented the music halls to extend the range of their contacts. According to a contemporary account of the variety stage, the new music halls of the 1880s, beginning with the elegant Pavilion, attracted a superior class of patrons to these "handsome 'Palaces' of amusement, and in the grand saloons of the West End halls the most prominent and distinguished representatives of art, literature, and the law mingled nightly with city financiers, lights of the sporting and dramatic world, and a very liberal sprinkling of the 'upper crust'. . . . " A suggestion of such quality occurs in Act I of Wilde's *The Importance of Being Earnest* when Algernon suggests to Jack that they "trot round to the Empire." In a retrospective BBC radio talk, Max Beerbohm recalled his initial experience at the Pavilion:

> I was filled with an awful, but pleasant, sense of audacity in venturing into such a place, so plebeian and unhallowed a den, as a Music Hall; and I was relieved, though slightly disappointed also, at finding that the Pavilion seemed very like a theatre, except that the men around us were mostly smoking, and not in evening clothes, and there was alongside of the stalls an extensive drinking-bar, of which the barmaids were the only—or almost the only—ladies present. . . .

In such theaters as the Tivoli in the Strand, the Palace in Cambridge Circus, and the Empire in Leicester Square, where ballets were an integral part of the program, patrons could walk about on the promenade (located at the rear of the dress circle on the second level) when a "turn" was dull and encounter a different class of prostitute from that of the common streetwalker.

———

INFLUENCED BY such French artists as Toulouse-Lautrec and Degas, the imagery of the British music halls in essays, poems, and paintings suggested all that was flamboyant and daring—singers, dancers, and other performers often challenging Victorian standards of respectability. For avant-garde artists and writers avidly searching for new subject matter, the music hall was an absorbing subject for artistic expression and aesthetic discussion. Noting this abandonment of nature in the quest for artifice and the reaction from "the super-refinement of much recent life and poetry," Yeats wrote in in 1892: "The cultivated man has begun a somewhat hectic search for the common pleasures of common men and for the rough accidents of life. The typical young poet of our day is an aesthete with a surfeit, searching sadly for his lost Philistinism, his heart full of an unsatisfied hunger for the commonplace" (the prologue, clearly, to such later works as Joyce's *Ulysses,* T. S. Eliot's *The Waste Land,*

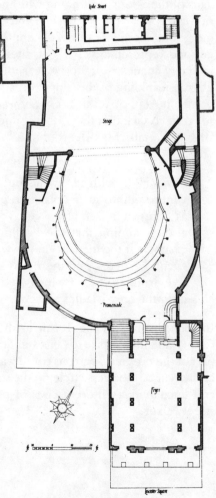

Floor plan of the Empire Theatre

and Beckett's *Waiting for Godot,* which employ music hall motifs and
routines in the Modernist mode of ironically juxtaposing popular and
exalted modes of expression). Beerbohm recalled the pleasure of the
halls when he wearied of the "demands of an intellectual life":

> . . . I stray into the Tivoli, and would fain soothe my nerves with
> folly, I find an entertainment that is not only worthy of atten-
> tion, but is even most exigent of all my aesthetic faculties. There
> is a swift succession of strongly, variously defined personalities
> . . . all imitating this or that phase of modern life within the
> limits of their new art.

Arthur Symons, whom Yeats called "a scholar in music halls," was
more accurately a lyric poet of the sexually provocative dance. Indeed,
Beerbohm conceded that Symons had "secured the Laureateship" of the
halls. In many poems, Symons recorded his impressions of dancers and of
casual encounters with "light loves" in the music halls, deliberate attempts to startle or even outrage his bourgeois readers. Baudelaire's essay
in praise of cosmetics had concluded that "rouge adds to the face of a
beautiful woman the mysterious passion of the priestess." In writing
about the dancers at the Alhambra Theatre, Symons went further by
suggesting a connection between the theatrical performer and the prostitute in the effect produced by make-up, thereby offering limitless possibilities of fantasy, particularly to one who, like Symons, had been raised in a
strict Nonconformist home:

> In a plain girl, make-up only seems to intensify her plainness; for
> make-up does but give colour and piquancy to what is already in
> a face, it adds nothing new. But in a pretty girl how exquisitely
> becoming all this is, what a new kind of exciting savour it gives
> to her real charm! It has, to the remnant of Puritan conscience
> or consciousness that is the heritage of us all, a certain sense of
> dangerous wickedness, the delight of forbidden fruit. The very
> phrase, painted women, has come to have an association of sin;
> and to have put paint on her cheeks, though for the innocent
> necessities of her profession, gives to a woman a sort of sym-
> bolic corruption.

In "Maquillage" (1891), Symons writes of an encounter with a prostitute
on the promenade with an implication of such "symbolic corruption":

> *The charm of rouge on fragile cheeks,*
> *Pearl-powder, and, about the eyes,*

The dark and lustrous eastern dyes;
A voice of violets that speaks
Of perfumed hours of day, and doubtful night
Of alcoves curtained close against the light.

Such responses to "painted women," whether on stage or on the promenade, shaped many of Symons's poems. "To a Dancer" (1892) embodies one of his characteristic visions of an alluring dancer with a painted face and an indiscreet costume, both providing fantasies of sexual encounter:

Intoxicatingly
Her eyes across the footlights gleam,
(The wine of love, the wine of dream)
Her eyes, that gleam for me!

And in "At the Stage-Door" (1893), the speaker awaits the appearance of a performer still in make-up among the "thin, bright faces of girls" as they leave the theater:

Steadily, face after face,
Cheeks with the blush of the paint yet lingering, eyes
Still with their circle of black . . .

Other avant-garde writers attracted to the subject matter of the music halls depicted the vitality, even vulgarity, of the performers and audience, as in John Davidson's *In a Music Hall and Other Poems* (1891), or the experience of the "low and soft luxurious promenade" in Theodore Wratislaw's "At the Empire" (1896):

The calm and brilliant Circes who retard
Your passage with the skirts and rouge that spice
The changeless programme of insipid vice
And stun you with a languid strange regard.

Wratislaw's other music hall poems included "A Ballet Dancer" and "The Music-Hall" in *Caprices* (1893); and—in addition to "At the Empire"—"A Dancer" and "At the Stage-Door" in *Orchids* (1896).

Walter Sickert, the prominent British artist of the 1890s who had been Whistler's pupil, painted scenes of such music halls as Collins', Gatti's, the Middlesex, and his favorite, the Old Bedford Music Hall—several of which appeared in the *Yellow Book*. Sickert's biographer interprets the attraction to such subject matter as "a symptom of his determination to emancipate himself from Whistler's paternalistic domination over his artistic life." Shunning realism, Sickert painted in the post-impressionist style: Figures are usually firmly modeled but seen from a great distance, their features lost in the theatrical setting. He preferred to emphasize the theater's architectural charm with an audience absorbed by the performers on the illuminated stage. In the Edwardian years, Spencer Gore established a reputation as Sickert's disciple in his paintings of scenes from the Alhambra Theatre.

IN MANY OF the music halls, the presence of prostitutes on the promenade added a sense of adventure to the setting of theatrical artifice. Such women were heavily made-up, an emblem of their availability, as noted by Charles Booth in his survey: "It is said that the ladies' public lavatories and dress-rooms in Central London are used for putting on and (before going home) washing off, the customary paint." In the minds of proper Victorians, theater people were believed to be no different from common prostitutes because of their provocative make-up, free and easy manner, self-sufficiency, and notorious reputation for moral laxity. Indeed, a rumor circulated that a "secret underground passageway" connected the Lyceum Theatre in Wellington Street with a brothel. George Moore's *A Mummer's Wife* (1884) portrays the bourgeois attitude towards actresses in a conversation between Ralph Ede, the invalid owner of the house where a theater manager-actor has rented rooms; Ralph's wife, Kate; and his mother, Mrs. Ede, concerning late-night visits:

> "... I should like to know [says Ralph] who these women are he has dared to bring into— People he has met in Piccadilly, I suppose!"
> "Oh no!" interrupted Kate, "I'm sure that they are the ladies of the theatre."
> "And where's the difference?" Mrs. Ede asked fiercely. Sectarian hatred of worldly amusement flamed in her eyes, and made common cause with the ordinary prejudice of the British landlady.

Kate runs off with the manager to act on the stage; later, in despair and in poverty because of his desertion, she turns to prostitution, as though Moore were confirming the inevitable association. The link between prostitution and the theater also occurs in a suggestive cartoon in the popular paper *To-Day* (November 18, 1893), which depicts a top-hatted, monocled patron in a theater talking to a ballet dancer in costume:

> *He:* "When is an actress not an actress?"
> *She:* "When—when she's a 'star'?"

He: "Guess again?"
She: "When she—no, I give it up."
He: "Nine times out of ten."

Yet the evidence of police records and other sources indicates that among prostitutes the number of women who were also employed as actresses or dancers was very small. The associations between the two groups resulted in part from their presence in the same theaters and, in part, from the fact that such women were outside the standard "professions." Few occupations could be so financially rewarding as acting and prostitution for "single, independent Victorian women of outgoing character, fine build, and attractive features." However, the general public's disapproval of theatrical folk—particularly of the less illustrious actresses and music hall performers—continued throughout the nineteenth century. The notable exception occurred when great beauty and talent were present, as in such actresses as Mrs. Patrick Campbell, Lillie Langtry, and Ellen Terry, who met with little condemnation despite her two illegitimate children and her bohemian existence. Lady Salisbury's remark concerning Terry—"never immoral, only rather illegal"—reveals a respectable Victorian's reluctance to condemn such an acclaimed figure.

The attempt to remedy common bourgeois attitudes towards theatrical performers was the mission of the Reverend Stewart Headlam, an early Fabian socialist whose writings about the aesthetic beauty of ballet led to the end of his curacy at St. Mathews, Bethnal Green, in 1878. He had challenged the clergy "to face the fact, whether they think the human body an evil thing or the temple of the Holy Ghost." In 1879, he founded the Church and Stage Guild, which often met in the foyer of the Drury Lane Theatre and included church members as well as dancers from the Empire and Alhambra. In outlining the purpose of the guild, he later stated:

> The objects of the Guild were to break down the prejudice against theatres, actors, music-hall artists, stage-singers, and dancers, in those days only too common among Churchmen; to promote social and religious sympathy between Church and Stage; to vindicate the worthiness of acting and dancing as arts, no less capable of being dedicated to God's service than any other work of man conscientiously pursued. . . .

One of Headlam's socialist preoccupations was the effect of the Industrial Revolution on Victorian cities and on the human soul. The theater was the means of restoring to the spirit what industrialism had deadened: "Our surroundings are so ugly—gloom, dirt, mud-coloured streets—our very work, which should be to us a source of joy, is made by its monotony and its many sub-divisions often little better than a mere grind. . . . Counteracting all this the Theatre has been at work with its heavenly mission; there the contemplation of beauty has been made possible for the people."

At work on his novel *Immaturity* in 1879, Bernard Shaw depicted a character who is enthralled by a dancer at the Alhambra and who condemns "the indifference of the herd to refined art." The influence of Headlam is apparent, for the character talks of "the poetry of motion"— the phrase that Headlam had always used to describe the ballet. Later, when Shaw was preparing his novel for publication, he told Headlam: "You were making efforts in the Church and Stage Guild and at every other opportunity to make people understand that this kind of dancing is a fine art; but until the Russian ballet arrived . . . , there were practically no converts; and the Alhambra ballets ranked with the other Leicester Square entertainments as pornographic and outside criticism."

Though Headlam was inspired by an exalted vision of how the theater could reveal God's beauty to those laboring long hours in gloomy factories, Arthur Symons, a seasoned prowler of the promenades, had a more intimate knowledge than Headlam of ballet girls and performers in the music halls. Though Symons may have been influenced by Headlam's aesthetic vision of the dance as an autonomous art, he could not take the guild seriously. To an unidentified correspondent, he wrote facetiously: "On Sunday I am going to a ballet-girls' picnic which promises great fun: it is one of the little jokes of the Church and Stage Guild." On occasion, the guild gave parties for ballet girls that lasted until 4:30 A.M.—no doubt alarming to those concerned for Headlam's reputation. An early supporter of Headlam, the respectable actress Mrs. Madge Kendal, lost interest in the guild perhaps because of the presence of music hall performers, from whom actresses in the legitimate theater were trying to dissociate themselves.

In the forefront of the avant-garde, Symons nevertheless held a conventional view of theater people and freely acknowledged their sexual looseness. Moreover, the presence of prostitutes on the promenade must have seemed to him as an ironic counterpoint to Headlam's devotion to the "heavenly mission" of the theater. In a letter to Katherine Willard, the niece of the founder of the Woman's Christian Temperance Union, Symons dissuaded her from pursuing a career in the theater, which would disappoint her expectations: "I used to think at one time that it was merely a Puritan prejudice to look on actors and actresses as specially immoral people. But now that I have so many opportunities of seeing for myself, I find it is only the truth. They *are,* as a class, more uniformly immoral than any other class of people." He urged her to avoid theater performers, for she would react with "a feeling of considerable discomfort and even disgust."

IN OCTOBER OF 1894, a challenge to an entire way of life produced a cause célèbre when social reformers launched an attack on the Empire Theatre in order to eliminate the promenade, where prostitutes were accosting patrons. This famous episode involved several writers who regarded the music halls as relatively innocent, indeed even beneficial to patrons who enjoyed everything from dog acts to ballets. Moreover, the reaction to the campaign against the Empire reveals the ferocity with which the presumably staid Victorians often resisted the attempts of the anti-vice reformers to regulate places of public amusement. On another level of understanding, the episode reveals Victorian anxieties concerning prostitution and drinking as well as suggestive dancers and costumes—perhaps, as Peter Gay has stated, an indication of the "buried wishes" and "unsatisfied erotic needs" in those who were outraged at what they saw.

Theaters that were flagrantly permissive in allowing reputedly corrupt-

Facade of the Empire Theatre

ing influences to flourish were in need, said the reformers, of corrective action by the London authorities charged with regulation. Inevitably, many disparate issues came together in a welter of charges and counter-charges by reformers and officials, each of whom miscalculated the devotion of the diverse audiences to the music halls under attack. In the final analysis, none of the reformers could provide evidence of moral contamination from the activities either on stage or on the promenade. The puritan's commonplace—then as now—contended that mere exposure to the unconventional constituted a danger to one's moral fiber, always frail when exposed to temptation.

Throughout Victoria's reign, various vigilance organizations were formed to curb or to eliminate the most offensive manifestations of indecency and vice. One of the most active was the National Vigilance Association, whose members were sometimes referred to as "Purity Crusaders" by hostile journalists. On October 10, 1894, a representative of the association, Mrs. Sheldon Amos, appeared before the Licensing Committee of the London County Council (charged with relicensing music halls and theaters each year) to complain that "the dancing [at the Empire Theatre] was designed to excite impure thought and passion." Though the ballet, with its revealing costumes, was a major objection among the reformers, other aspects of the theater's operation, such as the promenade and the sale of intoxicating drinks, were equally objectionable. The major focus that emerged, however, was the promenade, where prostitutes were charged with open solicitation. (In a recent study of the promenade, John Stokes remarks that it was a "convention of the Empire that women never approached potential customers but simply placed themselves at conspicuous points." Apparently, though, there were breaches of such decorum.)

In the *Daily Telegraph* (October 11, 1894), Mrs. Laura Ormiston Chant, a suffragist, novelist, poet, and nurse who was a prominent member of the association, stated that her attention was first directed to the Empire earlier in the year by two American gentlemen who were solicited on the promenade:

> They were so shocked that she was determined to visit the theater, but did not until July, when the Living Pictures had made so much stir.* Early in the evening there were comparatively few

*In a review of the popular Living Pictures (in which live figures on stage posed to recreate famous works of art) at the Palace Theatre, Shaw noted of the performers: "I need hardly say that the ladies who impersonated the figures in these pictures were not actually braving our climate without any protection. . . . what was presented as flesh was really spun silk. . . . The living pictures are not only works of art: they are excellent practical sermons; and I urge every father of a family who cannot afford to

people in the promenade, but after nine o'clock the number increased. She noticed young women enter alone, more or less painted, and gorgeously dressed. They accosted young gentlemen who were strangers to them, and paid little attention to the performance.

In describing these events later, Mrs. Chant envisioned her mission in religiously inspired global terms: ". . . the Love that overcame negro slavery in the United States shall overcome the white slavery of London, of England." But as a recent historian has noted, the circumstance of the typical prostitute "challenges a whole series of conventional assumptions about prostitutes handed down to us from the Victorian period. She was not the innocent victim of middle-class seduction and betrayal; nor was she a mere child drugged and entrapped into prostitution by white slavers. Instead her entry into prostitution seems to have been voluntary and gradual."

Having heard initial evidence from various speakers on the Empire, the Licensing Committee of the London County Council recommended renewing the theater's license with the proviso that the promenade be abolished (by adding new seats in its space) and that the sale of intoxicating drinks be eliminated. For the next two weeks, hearings were held before the entire council to argue the committee's recommendation of October 10. Testifying before the council, one director of the Empire stated that he knew the "face of every street-walker in London and that street-walkers [were] not allowed admission to the Empire" (in fact, the policy at the Empire was to permit "respectable" prostitutes to enter, sometimes without an admission charge). Another director averred that if a woman was seen *"markedly* soliciting," she was touched on the shoulder *"by an official appointed for the purpose,* and cautioned, if need be turned out." Such a disclosure, Mrs. Chant insisted, was sufficient evidence that prostitution was such a problem that an official had to be appointed to warn the more aggressive women. The less aggressive prostitutes were presumably permitted to remain on the promenade.

In a letter to the *Pall Mall Gazette* (October 15, 1894), Symons described the Empire "as a place of entertainment, the most genuinely artistic and the most absolutely unobjectionable that I know in any country." Moreover, it was managed "with a discretion which compares very favourably indeed with the policy generally pursued on the Continent." At the

---

send his daughters the round of the picture galleries . . . to take them all (with their brothers) to the Palace Theatre" (first published in the *Saturday Review* [April 6, 1895]; rpt. in *Our Theatres in the Nineties* [London, 1932], 1: 80).

Casino de Paris, the most popular music hall in Paris, women were admitted without payment "expressly for the purpose of plying their trade and drawing visitors to the place; and both they, and some of the performers in the dances, accost visitors who have come merely to see the performance." As for women at the Empire accosting men, Symons states, ". . . my own experience assures me that this is extremely improbable":

> I have visited the Empire on an average about once a week for the last year or two in my function as critic for several newspapers, and I must say that whenever I have had occasion to stand in the promenade I have never in a single instance been accosted by a woman. That women come to the Empire for the purpose of meeting men, and men for the purpose of meeting women is, of course, obvious. They also go to every other music-hall in London for precisely the same reason. . . . Vice, unfortunately, cannot be suppressed; it can only be regulated.

But Symons was disingenuous, for while it may have been true that prostitutes did not always aggressively accost potential clients, their make-up and demeanor clearly indicated their intentions. Symons himself often approached such unescorted women.

He further argued that if these women were turned out of the Empire within three weeks "a new rendezvous will have been made at another music-hall." He could not see "the wisdom of driving these poor women into the open streets," and "to single out the Empire, and the Empire only—that seems to me a grave injustice." Symons's letter, in its curious admission that there were prostitutes at the Empire, pleads for tolerance. Mrs. Chant, however, was unconcerned whether or not prostitutes accosted men on the promenade; she insisted on the suppression, not the regulation, of vice.

Bernard Shaw entered the fray with his own letter to the *Pall Mall Gazette* (October 16, 1894), quoting Mrs. Chant in an interview that had appeared in that newspaper. She reportedly remarked: "Why, I had a girl here from the Empire lounge—a girl earning her £20 and 30 a week from the lounge habitués"—to which Shaw ironically responded:

> That single utterance of Mrs. Chant's is calculated to make more prostitutes in a week than the "Living Pictures" will in ten years. The impression it produces is that a girl has only to resort to the Empire lounge to make an income of £1,000 a year, exactly what every procuress assures the girls whom she is tempting into prostitution. Mrs. Chant says, "I am not a woman who is easily deceived." Now, I am a man who is very easily

deceived; but if I were to invite a prostitute to come and look at my house, as Mrs. Ormiston Chant very kindly did, I should forgive the girl for trying to represent her income to me as between £1,000 and £1,500 a year; but I should not believe her.

Shaw, who had just completed writing *Mrs. Warren's Profession,* echoed the theme of his play by his insistence that an unjust economic system did more damage to exploited women than the "foolishly openhanded young gentlemen of the Empire lounge": "It is our pious shareholders who use them up by the thousand, and who make them into most ugly living pictures of premature old age, clad in miserable garments that have an indecency far more disgraceful to us than the rosy nothings worn by the more fortunate living pictures at the music-halls." Clearly, advised Shaw, Mrs. Chant and those who wished to abolish prostitution would accomplish more by making it "better worth an attractive girl's while to be a respectable worker than to be a prostitute."

On the following day, more letters to the editor of the *Pall Mall Gazette* appeared, one by Theodore Wratislaw, who branded statements before the council by Mrs. Amos and Mrs. Chant as "wilfully false": "Though the letter of Mr. Arthur Symons which you have published seems to me to be lukewarm in his defense of the Empire, I can corroborate him in saying that never have I been accosted in that promenade by women." (His poem "At the Empire," with its lines "The calm and brilliant Circes who retard / Your passage. . . . / And stun you with a languid strange regard," suggests otherwise.) As for Mrs. Amos's reaction to the ballet at the Empire, Wratislaw responds: "The music-hall performance is so modest and prudish that it may even appear insipid by the side of a theatrical burlesque." In general, he believed that the Empire was "a paradise of order and propriety when contrasted with other London halls. . . ." (Indeed, the Alhambra was notorious for its more open toleration of prostitutes.)

An anonymous article in the *Saturday Review* (October 13, 1894) revealed that Mrs. Chant had twice visited the Empire—"this improper scene"—to see for herself the inproprieties of the tableaux vivants and the promenade. On her first visit, the writer states, she wore "the quiet dress of the elect":

> . . . her garb betrayed her, modesty fell over the spectators of the *tableaux vivants* like a pall, and the case against the Empire was in danger of collapsing. Whereupon Mrs. Chant resolved to conform to the usages of a world living in wickedness. She put on her beautiful garments and visited the Empire yet again. The

result surpassed her fondest expectations; she was herself accosted by a gentleman.

Mrs. Chant's own account reveals her sensible response to her own self-consciousness on the promenade: "Much capital has been made out of the fact that I went to the Empire in evening dress, but surely I only did what was dictated by common sense when I found that when I went in ordinary walking dress I was a marked woman and was followed about by those whose attention was thus directed to me." She was convinced that "poor souls" fall at such places as the Empire and then "parade the streets afterwards"—an apparent reversal of cause and effect. Her awareness of the social evils that contributed to the misery of such women is nevertheless acute: "Unfair wages, overtasked strength, inadequate preparation for the duties of life, unhappy home-life, betrayed love, amusements that corrupt, the many snares set for inexperience by cunning hands, and a low estimate of women on the part of men,—these are some of the sources from which the dark stream of human ruin on the streets is supplied. . . ."

A letter to the *Times* (October 13, 1894) from "An Old Woman" proposed that Mrs. Chant and others would find "really moral work to do" outside of the music halls and theaters—at railway station waiting rooms: ". . . the material for reform is there in abundance—vice, open, flagrant, under the eyes and in the path of all, young and old." In music halls, vice had to be sought for, "but in the streets and around our railway stations vice lies in wait for everybody." Since Mrs. Chant was now the object of attack from various quarters, she wrote to the editor of the *Daily Telegraph* (October 18, 1894) to clarify her position. Her intent was to "clear certain of the music halls of the unclean features which debar decent folks from attending and enjoying the performances." She had visited the Palace Theatre of Varieties and was "charmed and delighted." The Living Pictures were, with the exception of two or three, "beautiful." She had no objection to the ballet, though at times the "obvious suggestiveness" of the dance "makes the thing evil."

In the hearings before the entire council, which took place between October 11 and 26, the counsel for the Empire argued that management had, in fact, maintained "order and decorum." An editorial in the *Times* (October 30, 1894) contended that there was "no proof, and no allegation, that the managers of the Empire Theatre did anything to encourage or facilitate the presence of women of bad character." Another argument—an indication of the close relationship between economics and sexual impropriety—was that seven hundred jobs were at stake, for imposing the Licensing Committee's recommendations would mean the closing of the theater. "Will the number of loose women be reduced thereby?" the counsel inquired. To impress the council, dismissal notices were prepared for distribution by management—"an unsuccessful farce," Mrs. Chant contended. In another letter to the *Pall Mall Gazette* (October 25, 1894), Symons argued that the closing of the promenade would reduce the Empire "to the level of constraint and discomfort of an ordinary theater," for "you are not obliged to sit solemnly through a whole evening's performance, but can take your pick of the programme, filling up the dull moments by walking about." This was "the great secret of music-hall success." By ignoring the position of the "crusaders," Symons' letter reveals how arguments over the Empire were at times irrelevant, at other times indicative of confusion between moral and aesthetic values.

On October 26, the council met at Spring Gardens to consider the recommendations of the Licensing Committee. (The British Women's Temperance Association, with which Mrs. Chant was also associated, held a four-hour prayer meeting concurrently with the council's sitting.) In describing the scene, Mrs. Chant remarked that the "women's voice" had pleaded to the council: "You will this day sign the Magna Charta of Public Amusements." And raising the feminist issue of just representation, she commented on her detractors: ". . . they asked in passionate tones if London was to be governed by women, and yet clamoured about an irresponsible body of men like the London County Council having the power to grant licenses, forgetting that there is not one woman on the County Council." She praised the council for its "hearty, untiring, and liberal" sympathy with amusements and recreation of every kind, particularly in its "splendid service to out-door sports, games, music, music-hall, and theatre-going," which, despite her "Non-Conformist conscience," she wished to preserve.

After final arguments were heard by the council, the vote was taken. Those in favor of eliminating the promenade and drinking in the theater were victorious: seventy-five for, thirty-two against, with eight abstentions and twenty absentees (the latter figure rather startling for such an important issue). Mrs. Chant later remarked that October 26 was "a memorable day in the history of London." The radical *Pall Mall Gazette* (October 27, 1894), staunchly opposed to the "Purity Crusaders," lamented the Council's decision: "We regret it in the name of our national reputation, which threatens to become a byword for cant and hypocrisy." It was, the paper stated, an action instigated by "a few irresponsible busybodies actuated doubtless by excellent intentions," but in their focusing on 1 place of amusement out of 245, the crusaders "will not rescue one single 'poor Magdalen,' and may not inconceivably contribute to swell the ranks of prostitution."

In the evening following the council's vote, the Empire was crowded, particularly on the promenade, in anticipation of a demonstration. Among those present were several titled patrons, including Sir Augustus

Harris, the well-known impresario who "strolled about with a cheerful countenance." When the curtain fell on the last ballet, George Edwardes, the managing director, received an ovation when he appeared on stage to announce that, owing to the decision of the council, the theater would be closed, prompting "prolonged hoots and hisses, and cries of 'Out with them!' " and "Shame!" Edwardes continued:

> Believe me, I say this more in sorrow than in anger. We have not had an opportunity of replying to all the unfounded charges which were made against the Empire at the Council meeting today. Thank you all for the patronage you have extended to that which has been the most successful theatre in this country. The directors feel that they have the sympathy of you and of the London public.

The band struck up "Rule Britannia," and "for ten minutes there ensued a scene of the greatest turbulence. Everyone in the place seemed to be shouting, cheering, or hooting, with the exception of the pressmen, who were there in great strength." Since no one was leaving the theater, the curtain went up and down more than once, the performers, some still in costume, waved to the audience with their fans, boas, and handkerchiefs, and the stage manager said a few words. "Three hearty groans for the London County Council" were called for, and a woman in the audience called for three additional groans for Mrs. Chant. Singing "Auld Lang Syne," the audience slowly emptied the theater.

THE IMMEDIATE RESULT of its temporary closing was that such rival theaters as the Pavilion, Oxford, and Alhambra were now "almost inconveniently crowded," an indication, said the *Pall Mall Gazette* (November 1, 1894), of the "monumental folly and injustice" of the council: "Whether the Empire be reopened or not, the Chant party, for all its prayer-meetings, cannot claim the slightest victory. What was to be seen on the north side of Leicester Square is now transferred to the east side: the shares of one company have gone down, and the shares of a company less deserving, in that its show has not proved so much to the public taste, have gone up."

On Saturday evening, November 3, the partially renovated Empire reopened with a huge audience that had filled the theater fifteen minutes after the doors were opened. As the *Pall Mall Gazette* (November 5, 1894) reported the event: "A wild burst of applause" greeted the conductor of the orchestra at the opening of the ballet *La Frolique,* and at its conclusion the premier dancer, Madame Katti Lanner, had two curtain calls. Cries for the manager, George Edwardes, went unheeded, for he was apparently unavailable for an appearance on stage. After the ballet, "varieties" followed: the Living Pictures, operatic duets, acrobats, performing dogs, and sentimental solos, all of them appreciated by "an audience which had apparently come only to cheer itself hoarse."

The promenade, still in the process of reconstruction, was "packed with well-dressed men" (apparently no women were permitted access), and the bars in the auditorium were all dismantled, including one at the back of the promenade. At one point in the evening, several of the well-dressed men—"some of them almost middle-aged"—began kicking holes in the canvas screen on the promenade that separated the area in the back where the bar had once stood; eventually, the wooden frame was also demolished, to the delight of the crowd, which "began to go out into London brandishing fragments of the screen." One of those who participated in the demonstration by mounting the debris and haranguing the crowd was the young Winston Churchill, then a cadet at Sandhurst. Churchill later remarked that he had been "scandalized" by Mrs. Chant's "charges and insinuations" concerning the promenade at the Empire Theatre since he had never seen anything occur that was offensive.

In the *Saturday Review* (November 10), Symons raised the question of human nature, arguing that since sexual drives were natural, they could not be suppressed by law or morality:

> Does any one really think that by closing, not the Empire alone,
> but every music-hall in London, there will be a single virtuous
> man the more? Is not human nature human nature, and are not
> the streets the streets, and is not Piccadilly as convenient a
> rendez-vous as the Empire? . . . In the normal man and woman
> there are certain instincts which demand satisfaction, and which,
> if merely restrained and fettered by law, are certain by some
> means or other to find that satisfaction.

Though the license of the Empire, Symons states, had been confirmed "year after year by the County Council" (indeed, since 1887), suddenly, on the complaint of "several persons known to hold extreme views on all questions of morality and social order," prohibitions had been singularly imposed on the Empire.

The elimination of the promenade remained in force until the following October, when the Licensing Committee again reviewed the licensing of music halls; this time, however, it recommended the removal of restrictions imposed in 1894 on the Empire. The action evoked a protest from many clergymen and lay people, who urged the continuation of the policy adopted in the previous year. When in October of 1896, the Licensing

Committee again reviewed arguments concerning licensing, a major objection to the Empire (and to the Oxford) was again raised by the Social Purity branch of the British Women's Temperance Association, which protested against "the kind of women who frequented the promenade." Interestingly, in this history of the attack on the Empire, the focus was principally on prostitutes who were defiling the music hall, rarely on men who sought out and attracted these "fallen" women. Nevertheless, the council granted the Empire its license.

SIR COMPTON MACKENZIE recalls how, in the Edwardian period, the music halls began to change with respect to their promenades and to their entertainment (the "revue" replacing "varieties"):

> The promenade was still full enough; but the hobbled skirts of 1910 had cramped the style of peripatetic harlotry. Large hats, long trains, ample busts, sequins and silk petticoats gave the women of the Alhambra and . . . Empire promenades that five-pound look which for thirty years had been accepted as the standard of a luxury article. . . . Full-rigged whores were going the way of full-rigged ships: the promenade . . . was not what it was.

During the First World War, however, the question of the music halls and immorality again arose when it was noted that the "physical collapse through sexual sin of an extraordinary number of men" was preventing them from serving in the armed forces. Now that national security was at stake, the traditional opponents of the music halls had a compelling argument at their command. On March 1, 1916, the bishop of London charged before the London County Council that certain music halls were tolerating solicitation on the promenades. Letters to various publications on the subject inevitably followed. In the *Times* (July 10), a reader protested the moral laxity of the halls where many soldiers and sailors were patrons: "One had hoped that the terrible lessons of this great national struggle, in which the youth of the nation has displayed noble qualities of character, would have prevented the managers of these so-called theatres from increasing the temptations to vice and debauchery which at all times have been bad enough. . . ."

With such a public response, the bishop restated his charge in the *Times* (July 18) that certain theaters, licensed to provide entertainment, were a "constant danger and temptation to the young men." An incident that apparently prompted the bishop to renew his attack on the music halls involved a Canadian officer in England who, when many young officers and men had been incapacited by venereal disease, traced much of it to one or two London music halls. The Canadian reportedly brought his fist down upon an unspecified table with "fiery indignation" and charged an unnamed listener: "I tell you, Sir, the mothers of Canada will hold *you* [the people of England] responsible for this!" From another part of the empire, a medical correspondent in the *British Australasian* (August 17) wrote of

> . . . fine, tall, athletic boys, with their splendid military bearing, leaving their Antipodean homes, amid the blessings of relative and friends, full of hope and ambition, and eager to strike a blow for humanity, coming to the Empire's metropolis—for what? To go to hospital, suffering from a deadly disease. . . .

The clergy, especially those in whose jurisdictions the offending music halls were located, voiced support for the bishop's position. The vicar of St. Martin's-in-the-Fields, Trafalgar Square, whose parish embraced a part of Leicester Square, received more than a thousand letters from parishioners in a single month concerning the "immoral conditions prevailing in the district, especially the temptations and incitements offered in music halls."

As a result of such a concerted effort on the part of the "new moral crusade," the London County Council issued a statement that in the future the granting of licenses would be "subject to a condition to the effect that prostitutes shall not habitually use any part of the premises for the purposes of prostitution." Though an ambiguous statement at best, it prompted music hall managers—faced also with the public outcry—to bring "the open scandal of the London music hall promenades" to an end. In 1894, Mrs. Chant and the Purity Crusaders had achieved only a momentary success for their cause principally because they lacked the public support that accompanied the renewed crusade in 1916. By emphasizing the danger of the promenades to the nation's young wartime defenders, the foes of the music halls finally achieved victory but, ironically, not over the vice that eluded them.

6

The New Woman

As THOUGH WRITTEN by Gilbert for Sullivan, the following satirical lines won a prize for the "best epigrammatic definition of the expression, the 'New Woman' " in the popular one-penny paper *Woman* (September 26, 1894), whose assistant editor was Arnold Bennett and whose motto was "Forward but not too fast":

> *She flouts Love's caresses,*
> *Reforms ladies' dresses,*
> *And scorns the Man-Monster's tirades;*
> *She seems scarcely human,*
> *This mannish "New Woman,"*
> *This "Queen of the Blushless Brigade."*

In the nineties, such views ridiculed the New Woman who aggressively rejected the prescribed sacred function of angelic wife and bearer of children. However, actual women of "advanced" views, while agitating for suffrage, were often quite conservative in their attitudes towards marriage and motherhood, reluctant to redefine women's sexuality or their place in society. Though the image of the New Woman was beset by such inconsistencies and contradictions when applied to individual women, it was artistically and politically useful to those who were either attracted to or alienated from the strident radicalism of the new feminists.

In art and in life, the New Woman insisted on alternatives to the traditional roles for women. Her smoking in public, riding bicycles without escorts, or wearing "rational dress" (that is, the divided skirt) was not the result of mere whim or self-indulgence but of principle, for she was determined to oppose restrictions and injustices in the political, educational, economic, and sexual realms in order to achieve equality with men. In a story, for example, by George Egerton (the pseudonym of Mrs. George

Egerton Clairmonte), the attitude of the unhappy New Woman towards sexuality is concisely stated: ". . . marriage becomes for many women a legal prostitution, a nightly degradation, a hateful yoke under which they age, mere bearers of children conceived in a sense of duty, not love." Because the reinterpretation of sexual relationships was perhaps the most provocative of the issues, the New Woman seemed "to have ranged herself perversely with the forces of cultural anarchism and decay."

As noted by a recent historian, the tensions between the traditional conception of women and the emerging New Woman were confined principally to the middle and wealthy classes: "Working-class women, while no longer hauling coal in mines eleven hours a day, still led lives so totally remote from the cosy domesticity and shining feminine ideal against which the New Woman was reacting that this kind of revolt could do nothing for them." Earlier in the century, however, no such class distinctions were made by English socialists and Saint-Simonians, followers of the French social philosopher Comte de Saint-Simon, who had advocated a radical reorganization of society. For these thinkers, the emancipation of all women was essential to an effective division of labor in a new industrial state. In the *Westminster Review* (January–April 1832), a writer on the question concluded: "There can be no doubt that the political inequality of woman is a remnant of the barbarous state, which will be removed exactly as that is receded from, and that a time will come when the equal rights of women will be made a powerful lever. . . ."

The conventional view of woman's place in Victorian society, however, remained untouched by such utopian thought; if anything, it gathered strength in the nineteenth century, as expressed by the prince's conservative father in Tennyson's long, enormously popular narrative poem *The Princess* (1847):

> *"Man for the field, and woman for the hearth;*
> *Man for the sword, and for the needle she;*
> *Man with the head, and woman with the heart;*
> *Man to command, and woman to obey;*
> *All else confusion."*

Anticipating the New Woman of the nineties, Princess Ida reacts to such a demeaning view by establishing a university from which men are excluded. When it fails, the prince, who courts her, offers comfortless words concerning the ideal marriage:

> *". . . seeing either sex alone*
> *Is half itself, and in true marriage lies*
> *Nor equal, nor unequal: each fulfils*

Defect in each, and always thought in thought,
Purpose in purpose, will in will, they grow,
The single pure and perfect animal. . . ."
        And again sighing she spoke: "A dream
That once was mine! what woman taught you this?"

That the ideal had remained only an ideal in the unequal world of the sexes is Tennyson's view of the disparity that had driven the princess to her radical adventure.

In the equally popular poem by Coventry Patmore, *Angel in the House* (1854–56), the less troubled—indeed, sublimely acquiescent—married woman accepts her principal duty as presider over the sacred hearth, the refuge where she acts as her husband's comforter on his return from the vulgar and corrupt world of commerce. Ruskin's famous essay "Of Queens' Gardens" (1865) expresses similar attitudes towards the middle-class woman's place in the world:

> The man, in his rough work in open world, must encounter all peril and trial. . . . But he guards the woman from all this; within his house, as ruled by her, unless she herself has sought it, need enter no danger, no temptation, no cause of error or offence. This is the true nature of home—it is the place of Peace; the shelter, not only from all injury, but from all terror, doubt and division.

Such stifling views of the ideal marriage, in which the wife has no other destiny than to provide marital bliss and improve her husband's moral state, prompted new calls for female emancipation. In 1865, T. H. Huxley regarded such liberation as touching all classes, which would be "relieved from restrictions imposed by the artifice of man and not by the necessities of Nature." The most influential thinker at the time on the Woman Question, John Stuart Mill, issued what was, in effect, a manifesto justifying a new sense of self and direction for women rejecting conventional—and enslaving—notions of womanhood. As the feminists' sacred text in the fin de siècle, *The Subjection of Women* (1869) delineated the condition and cause of women's unhappy state:

> All women are brought up from the very earliest years in the belief that their ideal of character is the very opposite to that of men; not self-will, and government by self-control, but submission, and yielding to the control of others. All the moralities tell them that it is the duty of women, and all the current sentimentalities that it is their nature, to live for others; to make complete

abnegation of themselves, and to have no life but in their affections.

Queen Victoria herself struggled with divided feelings concerning woman's proper function as wife and mother. "For all her simplicities," remarks a recent historian, Victoria "is representative of the conflictive era named after her." A striking passage illustrating her views occurs in a letter written to her recently married eldest daughter:

> There is great happiness and great blessedness in devoting oneself to another who is worthy of one's affection; still, men are very selfish and the woman's devotion is always one of submission which makes our poor sex so very unenviable. This you will feel hereafter—I know; though it cannot be otherwise as God has willed it so.

By and large, the Queen's female subjects accepted the view—though perhaps with similar ambivalence—that their duties as wives and mothers were divinely ordained.

Understandably, then, Victoria opposed "Woman's Rights," as she told Sir Theodore Martin, chosen to write her dead husband's biography. Yet her passion on the subject suggests deep-seated conflicts over her own position:

> The Queen is most anxious to enlist every one who can speak or write to join in checking this mad, wicked folly of "Woman's Rights," with all its attendant horrors, on which her poor feeble sex is bent, forgetting every sense of womanly feeling and propriety. . . .
>
> It is a subject which makes the Queen so furious that she cannot contain herself. God created men and women different—then let them remain each in their own position. Tennyson has some beautiful lines on the difference of men and women in *The Princess.* Woman would become the most hateful, heathen, and disgusting of human beings were she allowed to unsex herself; and where would be the protection which man was intended to give the weaker sex?

Not unexpectedly, she also believed that women were unsuited to handling the reins of government, yet she qualified her remarks to imply her own capacity as a ruler: "We women are not *made* for governing—and if we are good women, we must *dislike* these masculine occupations; but there are times which force one to take *interest* in them . . . and I do, of course, *intensely.*"

IN THE NINETEENTH century, cultural developments enabling the New Woman to emerge in the fin de siècle involved the establishment of new educational institutions for women and reforms in marital laws, the result of extensive social transformations. The Victorian age witnessed a remarkable transition from a traditional society controlled by a patriarchal landed gentry to a modern democratic, industrial state in which outmoded laws and customs required changes to accommodate new social structures, particularly those affecting women. By the 1860s, for example, more than one-third of the country's workers, principally among the lower classes, consisted of women, of whom nearly one-fourth were married. Greater access to education at all levels was therefore necessary to increase efficiency in the thriving industrial economy, and greater protection for women in property laws was deemed crucial in view of their earning ability. As more middle-class women joined the work force, frequently as teachers and governesses, increasingly as civil servants, and by the nineties as professionals, reforms were progressively instituted as the result of extensive petitioning by feminist organizations.

In higher education, slow but substantial advances occurred in the founding of Queen's College (1848) and Bedford College (1849) in London, thereby resulting in the first generation of college-educated women teachers. At Cambridge University, Girton College (1869) and Newnham College (1873) were founded as women's colleges, but instead of receiving degrees on completion of their studies, women were awarded "certificates of degrees"—"often to meet with mistrust and misunderstanding from a suspicious world." Nevertheless, such developments provided more extensive occupational opportunities and marked the first incursions into the two most prestigious British universities.*

With respect to reforms in marital laws, eighteen Married Women's Property Bills were introduced into Parliament between 1857 and 1882 of which five were passed. The most important of these was the last, which gave women a right to their own property after marriage; in the event of divorce (particularly difficult for women as a result of the Divorce Act of 1857) or widowhood, the wife's property rights were protected; as a result, women acquired a new sense of self-determination. As one writer observed in 1883: "The difference caused by mental change is

---

*By 1901, the end of Victoria's reign, there were twelve universities and colleges that enabled women to earn their degrees. Cambridge and Oxford withheld the granting of degrees to women until the 1920s; full university status was not granted to Girton and Newnham until 1948. At Oxford, four women's colleges founded in the nineteenth century—beginning with Lady Margaret Hall (1878)—did not achieve full university status until 1959.

much greater than the difference caused by material change, and the mental change will be very great. . . . This increase of individuality is about to accrue, moreover . . . when women are seeking individuality with a sort of passion. . . ."

The quest by the emerging New Woman for "individuality with a sort of passion" inevitably produced challenges to the inequities within marriage. The Marriage Question suddenly erupted in the press when the novelist Mona Caird published an article titled "Marriage" in the *Westminster Review* (August 1888). Referring to the institution as "a vexatious failure," Caird insisted that it had evolved into a relationship of lord and servant "without the cook's privilege of being able to give warning." Sensing the possibility of a public reaction, the *Daily Telegraph* posed the question "Is Marriage a Failure?" Within two months, this device of the New Journalism had provoked a controversy resulting in an avalanche of 27,000 letters to the editor, who announced on September 29 that no further correspondence on the question would be published.

Later that year, Harry Quilter, the well-known barrister, critic, and editor of the *Universal Review,* published a selection of these letters on "the greatest newspaper controversy of modern times" in *Is Marriage a Failure?* (1888), which revealed much marital unhappiness as well as reasonable contentment. A letter from the wife of a working man (one of the few from that class) said no to the question, revealing her acceptance of current cultural norms: "Why are we made men and women? Clearly to be partners one to the other, and to fulfill the divine mandate, 'Increase and multiply.' We are not put on this earth by God merely to amuse ourselves, but to do a work. Women's work is to be a mother and form her children's minds and educate their hearts." But those who said yes to the question often responded with the familiar rhetoric of the later New Woman fiction, as in the following from a woman: "[Mona Caird] is not afraid to expose the wretched marriage tie in all its mockery. . . . She speaks the truth in every line, and there is not a woman in England or Ireland who will not secretly own to that fact." Another letter from a woman who found marriage "a most dismal failure" gave a particularly gruesome account of her husband's cruelty:

> Married when only a girl, after a few years I am practically only
> a widow, having been obliged, from my husband's brutality, to
> seek a separation. This was not until, through his brutality, I lost
> an eye, principally owing to the very merciful law which com-
> pelled me to live with a man until I was maimed for life.

In addition to the quest for "individuality," which often meant freedom from the marriage bond as then legally established, the New Woman was identifiable by her determination to acquire suffrage. (In the Victorian period, the term *suffragist* was used for members of either sex seeking the vote through legal means, whereas in the Edwardian period, *suffragette* was often used to identify militant women willing to break the law to achieve this end.) The suffragists were met with increasing resistance not only from Liberal and Conservative leaders in Parliament but also from unsympathetic prime ministers, such as Gladstone, who held the common belief that women were unsuited to politics and that, by entering such a turbulent world, they would abdicate their sacred mission as wives and mothers. Furthermore, suffragists met considerable opposition from conservative women who regarded the franchise as a threat to their traditional roles.

When in 1889, for example, a proposal came before the House of Commons to permit women to vote for members of Parliament, more than one hundred women issued "An Appeal against Female Suffrage" in the *Nineteenth Century* (June 1889). Despite the fact that the signatories were forward-looking women (and some may even have seen themselves as New Women willing to compromise on suffrage), they nevertheless insisted that governing the empire required the special abilities of men:

> While desiring the fullest possible development of the powers, energies, and education of women, we believe that their work for the State, and their responsibilities towards it, must always differ essentially from those of men, and that therefore their share in the working of the State machinery should be different from that assigned to men.

Women's "disabilities of sex" and men's "physical difference" were determining factors, the signatories stated, when it came to such matters as "the struggle of debate and legislation in Parliament" and "the hard and exhausting labour implied in the administration of the national resources and power." The acquisition of the vote "would tend to blunt the special moral qualities of women, and so to lessen the national reserves of moral force." (This point was dominant in the period: Woman possessed a "natural superiority" with respect to morality, a view disputed by radical feminists who deplored the "angel in the house" image.) As the education of women advanced, the signatories argued, they would increasingly exert moral influence on politicians. Though some women had insisted that the franchise would result in the elimination of "certain injustices of the law," the signatories responded that "during the past half century all the principal injustices of the law towards women have been amended by means of the existing constitutional machinery" and that "a new spirit of justice and sympathy" had arisen in men.

Among those who signed this appeal were Lady Randolph Churchill (mother of Winston), Mrs. Matthew Arnold, Mrs. Leslie Stephen (mother of Virginia Woolf), Mrs. H. H. Asquith (wife of the future prime minister), Mrs. Humphry Ward (the prominent novelist who was among those responsible for initiating the appeal), and Beatrice Potter (later Webb). In her autobiography, Potter conceded that she took what afterwards seemed "a false step" in signing the "notorious manifesto," for it aroused hostility among women and undermined her reputation as an "impartial investigator of women's questions." Characterizing herself as "conservative by temperament and anti-democratic through social environment," she had never suffered any disabilities "assumed to arise from my sex."

Despite her conservative view of suffrage, Potter was a New Woman in her transgression of traditional barriers against women and in her view of motherhood. In her diary in 1887, she wrote: ". . . it will be needful for women with strong natures to remain celibate; so that the special force of womanhood—motherly feeling—may be forced into public work." She also described an incident at a conference of a cooperative production society that she had attended in which such "special force" was given expression: "After dinner, in spite of the chairman's disapproval, we smoke cigarettes and our conversation becomes more that of business *camaraderie.* I am a general favourite with these stout, hard-hearted but true-hearted men and they look upon me as a strange apparition in their midst. . . ." Twenty years later, however, she joined the suffrage movement, convinced that the time had come.

In July 1889, *Nineteenth Century* published two replies from women in favor of the vote, but in August the periodical published a further "Appeal against Female Suffrage" signed by more than 1,800 women who believed that if the measure before Parliament were passed, it would be "distasteful to the great majority of the women of the country—unnecessary—and mischievous both to themselves and to the State." Among the signatories were many titled women, a dozen students each from Girton College, Cambridge, and from Lady Margaret Hall, Oxford, as well as the poet Christina Rossetti.

Through the nineties, suffragists continued their efforts through various organizations, such as the Women's Franchise League and the Women's Emancipation Union, but with limited results. Clearly, though, support for the cause among women increased after the defeat of the suffrage bill in 1892 (undoubtedly, the stimulus for a stronger effort by suffrage groups and unaffiliated women). By May 1896, an "Appeal from Women of All Parties and All Classes," signed by 270,000 supporters, was presented to Parliament. Throughout the decade, however, suffragists met with continued resistance from both Liberal and Conservative members of Parliament, but in local elections there was a progressive advance for many women. By 1897, women "rate-payers," consisting principally of widows and single women, comprised about 15 percent of the local government electorate. For the suffragists, however, participation in parliamentary elections remained the ultimate goal.

DESPITE THE FAILURE to obtain the crucial parliamentary vote, the fin-de-siècle New Woman pursued professional interests with a new awareness of financial and sexual independence. Much writing—some of it satirical—emphasized the New Woman's individuality and her slow but progressive increase in power and influence within a masculine-dominated society. In his sympathetic *Women and Marriage* (1888), Havelock Ellis contended that "sexual relationships, so long as they do not result in the production of children, are matters in which the community has, as a community, little or no concern." His most recent biographer has stated that throughout his career Ellis wrote "rapturously about the joys of motherhood, which he viewed as the chief fulfilling purpose for women on this earth," though when he married a New Woman (the writer Edith Lees), "there was a very clear understanding that there were to be no children." In his "Introduction" to *The New Spirit* (1890), Ellis prophesied that

> the rise of women—who form the majority of the race in most civilized countries—to their fair share of power, is certain. Whether one looks at it with hope or with despair one has to recognize it. . . . Our most strenuous efforts will be needed to see to it that women gain the wider experience of life, the larger education in the full sense of the word, the entire freedom of development, without which their vast power of interference in social organization might have disastrous as well as happy results.

Ellis's intimate relationship with Olive Schreiner reinforced his attitude towards a freer sexuality, and her popular novel *The Story of an African Farm* (1883) convinced him that growing up female was a "curse," with its rigid restrictions, and that marriage could be a form of entrapment rather than, as Schreiner said, the "perfect mental and physical life-long union of one man with one woman." In addition to her novel, Schreiner's letters reveal why she was later regarded as a significant forerunner of the New Woman. To one female correspondent, she wrote:

> Our first duty is to develop ourselves. Then you are ready for any kind of work that comes. The woman who does this is doing more to do away with prostitution and the inequalities between

man and woman, and to make possible a nobler race of human beings, than by all the talking and vituperation possible. It is not against men we have to fight but against *ourselves* within ourselves.

When editing the Camelot series in 1886 for the Walter Scott Publishing Company, Ernest Rhys invited Schreiner to write an introduction to the feminist classic *A Vindication of the Rights of Woman* (1792) by Mary Wollstonecraft. Though enthusiastic over the prospect, Schreiner never completed it. Her biographers contend that the manuscript indicates Schreiner's disillusionment with the *Vindication:* "... that [it] appeared to have had little influence on the women's movement, that it lacked genius, that it would convince no one." In one of her letters, Schreiner nevertheless informed a correspondent that she intended to discuss Wollstonecraft's "greatness" with respect to her view of marriage: "... she is the greatest of English women because she saw a hundred years ago with regard to sex and sex relationships what a few see today, and what the world will see in three hundred years' time."

With such incendiary issues as marriage and sexuality increasingly before the public, productions of Ibsen's *A Doll's House, Hedda Gabler,* and *Ghosts* between 1889 and 1891 provoked a storm of abuse in the press by their depictions of strong-willed, sensual women who violate Victorian standards of female decorum. Clement Scott, the editor of *Theatre* (July 1, 1889), called *A Doll's House* "a congregation of men and women without one spark of nobility in their nature." But Ibsen (whose plays *Punch* alluded to as "Ibscenity") loomed large as the most significant playwright to help shape the provocative image of the New Woman.* Recalling the first production of *A Doll's House,* particularly Nora's celebrated slamming of the door at the end when she leaves husband and children, Edith Lees vividly described its impact on her and her friends:

> How well I remember, after the first performance of Ibsen's drama in London ... when a few of us collected outside the theatre breathless with excitement. Olive Schreiner was there and Dolly [*sic*] Radford the poetess. ... We were restive and impetuous and almost savage in our arguments. This was either

---

*In May 1898, Ibsen disclaimed "the honor of having consciously worked for the women's rights movement" at a banquet celebrating his seventieth birthday by the Norwegian Women's Rights League: "True enough, it is desirable to solve the woman problem, along with all the others; but that has not been the whole purpose. My task has been the description of humanity" (*Letters and Speeches,* ed. and trans. Evert Sprinchorn [New York, 1964], 337).

the end of the world or the beginning of a new world for
women. . . . I remember that I was literally prostrate with excitement because of the new revelation.

The impact of Edith Lees on Ernest Rhys, who met her at a picnic of the
Fellowship of the New Life, was even more shattering, for the "vehe-
ment" Lees left him thinking of an "imminent new race of women whom
I, as a decadent Victorian male, might well have reason to fear."

Rhys's apprehension, probably shared widely by other men at the time,
emerges in the late nineteenth century in a variety of disguised and not-
so-disguised forms. The image of the aggressive female, intent on emas-
culating the "decadent Victorian male"—transposed to a biblical
setting—achieved its most strident expression in Wilde's *Salomé* (1893)
and in Beardsley's illustrations for the English translation. As a recent
critic has suggested, Wilde and Beardsley, "through a notable representation of perverse sexuality in their work, participate in a devastating *fin-de-
siècle* attack on the conventions of patriarchal culture even as they express
their horror at the threatening female energy which is the instrument of
that attack." Indeed, the image of the pathological species of the New
Woman associated with Ibsen prompted William Archer to call the fatal
Salomé "an oriental Hedda Gabler."

George Gissing (Beinecke Rare Book
and Manuscript Library, Yale University)

THE NUMEROUS DEBATES on and satires of the New Woman in the early nineties had their impact on George Gissing, whose novel *The Odd Women* (1893) reveals a complex, ambivalent vision of women who are simultaneously attracted by the possibility of independence and of marriage. An indication of Gissing's sympathetic view is expressed by Miss Mary Barfoot, who trains young women at her school in clerical skills to compete with men. She tells her students that they should *"earn money, but that women in general shall become rational and responsible human beings"*—the fundamental work ethic of the age as espoused by such figures as Carlyle and Ruskin. But with the startling rhetoric of the New Woman, she also inspires students with her subversive militancy:

> "I am a troublesome, aggressive, revolutionary person. I want to do away with that common confusion of the words womanly and womanish, and I see very clearly that this can only be affected by an armed movement, an invasion by women of the spheres which men have always forbidden us to enter. . . . We are educating ourselves. There must be a new type of woman, active in every sphere of life: a new worker out in the world, a new ruler of the home. . . . Let a woman be gentle, but at the same time let her be strong. . . . The mass of women have always been paltry creatures, and their paltriness has proved a curse to men. . . ."

But in his next novel, *In the Year of Jubilee* (1894), Gissing presents an alternative to his image of the New Woman. The quest for a "sham education" is useless at best, dangerous at worst. His persona, the father of the heroine, speaks to the point with the characteristic antifeminist rhetoric of the time:

> "Wherever you look now-a-days there's sham and rottenness; but the most worthless creature living is one of these trashy, flashy, girls,—the kind of girl you see everywhere, high and low,—calling themselves 'ladies,'—thinking themselves too good for any honest, womanly work. . . . They're educated; oh yes, they're educated! What sort of wives do they make, with their education? What sort of mothers are they?"

The two sisters, Beatrice and Fanny French, reveal themselves as "the product of sham education and mock refinement grafted upon a stock of robust vulgarity" by their ferocious struggle on the floor: "Now indeed the last trace of veneer was gone, the last rag of pseudo-civilisation was rent off these young women; . . . they revealed themselves as born—raw material which the mill of education is supposed to convert into middle-class ladyhood." Gissing's ambivalence towards the Woman Question undoubtedly arose from his two disastrous marriages—his first wife a prostitute and alcoholic, his second an uneducated, disturbed servant girl. Such liaisons, his biographer suggests, were possibly unconscious "acts of self-mortification."

Among the popular works written by women who advanced "New Woman fiction," *The Heavenly Twins* (1893) by Sarah Grand (the pseudonym of Mrs. Frances Elizabeth McFall) created something of a sensation by its depictions of transvestism, venereal illness, and psychotic breakdown. She is generally credited with first using the term "new woman," in "The New Aspect of the Woman Question," *North American Review* (March 1894). In the May issue, the novelist "Ouida" (Marie de la Ramée) capitalized the phrase in a hostile article titled "The New Woman." Other notable New Woman works are George Egerton's *Keynotes* (1893) and *A Yellow Aster* (1894) by "Iota" (Mrs. Mannington Caffyn), which dramatize the struggle by heroines against rigid social restrictions and the seemingly condoned double-standard of morality enjoyed by men. In the latter novel, the heroine deplores those men who regarded her merely as an object: "My lovers? They weren't lovers at all, they were explorers, experimental philosophers. They had the same strong yearning for me that a botanist has for a blue crysanthemum, or a yellow aster." Though such issues are cited as direct causes of dissatisfaction, marriage itself was not usually condemned. Indeed, Sarah Grand, who had left her husband in 1890 and subsequently became mayor of Bath six times, told an interviewer: "Women will always be women, and men always men, and marriage, in my opinion, must always be the ideal state." Yet these popular novels, undermining basic assumptions about the "angel in the house," prompted a reviewer in the *Bookman* (November 1894) to write of the heroine of *A Yellow Aster:*

> She is icily pure in her dislike of the marriage bond. She despises the world, and men, and herself, and is superbly unhappy. In spite of her purity, she is not very wholesome; she generally has a mission to solve the problems of existence, and on her erratic path through life she is helped by no sense of humour.

Other critical reactions to New Woman novelists were equally condemnatory. In *Woman* (May 2, 1894), they were declared "petticoat anarchists who put a blazing torch to the shrine of self-respect and feminine shame." And a writer in *All the Year Round* (December 8, 1894) evoked the image of the conventional Victorian woman as the counter-point to the New Woman novelists who

> appear to have cultivated the intellect at the expense of all wom-anly feeling and instinctive delicacy, and to have cast aside all reticence in the mad desire to make others eat as freely as them-selves of the forbidden fruit of the tree of knowledge. . . . if the New Woman elects to be judged by the fiction she writes, reads, and applauds, nay—may we not justly add—inspires, then she must . . . accept the position of the bitterest foe to the cherished modesty of our sex that the century has known.

The idea of the "cherished modesty of our sex"—the antifeminist posi-tion—was advanced by the popular writer Eliza Lynn Linton, who dedi-cated her novel *The One Too Many* (1894) to the "sweet girls still left among us, who have no part in the new revolt, but are content to be dutiful, innocent, and sheltered." Elsewhere, she wrote of the eman-cipated woman as "aggressive, disturbing, officious, unquiet, rebellious to authority and tyrannous . . . the most unlovely specimen the sex has yet produced."

Though often condemned by critics, New Woman novels certainly had admirers. In his *Review of Reviews* (July 1894), W. T. Stead hailed the "Modern Woman" who flees from the "monogamic prostitution of love-less marriage and the hideous outrage of enforced maternity. . . ." Stead commiserates with the modern woman's "deep conviction": "Better law-less love than loveless marriage." The cultural reverberations of these novels, Stead insists, will be vast: "All social conventions, all religious teachings, and all moral conceptions will have to be reconsidered and readjusted in harmony with this new central factor in the problem. . . ." He quotes Ella Hepworth Dixon, who, after the publication of her novel *The Story of a Modern Woman* (1894), remarked: "The keynote of the book is the phrase: 'All we modern women mean to help each other now. If we were united, we could lead the world.' "

Such a messianic vision increasingly developed among women writers in the fin de siècle. In an address at the Women Writers Dinner in 1894, Mary Haweis (the author of *The Art of Decoration* and *The Art of Housekeep-ing,* which seems to have influenced her choice of metaphors) reminded her listeners: "In women's hands—in women writers' hands—lies the regeneration of the world. Let us go on with our tongues of fire, conse-crated to an entirely holy work, cleaning, repairing, beautifying as we go, the page of the world's history which lies before us now." And Katherine Bradley (who, with her niece Edith Cooper, published poetry and drama as Michael Field) recorded in her diary what in effect was the Victorian feminine ideal transposed to an aesthetic realm: "We hold ourselves bound in life and in literature to reveal—as far as may be—the beauty of the high feminine standard of *the ought to be.*" But as the "Appeal against Female Suffrage" had revealed in 1889, the attempt to unite all women under one banner—no matter how inspiring or noble—resulted in internal divisions with respect to their sense of cultural destiny.

WHILE SOLEMN CRITICS were castigating New Woman novelists in the press, a satirical view of the New Woman reached the stage of the Comedy Theatre on September 1, 1894. Sydney Grundy's *The New Woman,* containing four of the species, touches lightly on such inevitable topics as the "Advancement of Woman" and the "Decay of Man" while developing the slender plot about the writing of a book titled *The Ethics of Marriage.* The Marriage Question undergoes expected treatment, as when a harried husband remarks: "I belong to my wife, but my wife doesn't belong to me. . . . Mrs. Sylvester is not my wife; I am her husband." His friend, the colonel, concludes: "That is what comes of educating women. We have created a Frankenstein."

Grundy also satirizes the ideal of equality between the sexes when Sylvester remarks of one of the New Women, "Her theory is that boys ought to be girls, and young men should be maids," and of another New Woman: "She's also for equality. Her theory is that girls should be boys, and maids should be young men."* Responding to these theories, the colonel blusters:

> These people [the New Wo-
> men] are a sex of their own.
> . . . They have invented a

---

*With characteristic levity, Max Beerbohm warned in the *Yellow Book* (April 1894) that if men used cosmetics it would "tend to promote that amalgamation of the sexes which is one of the chief planks in the decadent platform. . . ." In *Punch* (April 27, 1895), the "Angry Old Buffer" ponders the transformations that could result from the New Woman's masculinity and the Decadent's effeminacy:

> . . . *a new fear my bosom vexes;*
> *To-morrow there may be* no *sexes!*
> *Unless, as end to all pother,*
> *Each one in fact becomes the other.*
> *E'en* then *perhaps they'll start amain*
> *A-trying to change back again!*
> *Woman* was *woman, man* was *man,*
> *When Adam delved and Eve span.*
> *Now he can't dig and she won't spin,*
> *Unless 'tis tales all slang and sin!*

new gender. . . . Every-
thing's New nowadays! We
have a New Art—

Enid [a New Woman]: A New Journalism—
Victoria [another New Woman]: A New Political Economy—
Doctor [the third New Woman]: A New Morality—
Colonel: A New Sex!

But the play itself was not new. Designed according to formula, it ends with the long-expected confrontation between Margery, the innocent-but-wise farmer's daughter who remains loyal to her husband, and her rival, Mrs. Sylvester, whom she assails: "You call yourself a New Woman—you're not New at all. You're just as old as Eve. You only want one thing—the one thing every woman wants—the one thing that no woman's life's worth living without! A true man's love!" Thus, the voice of convention triumphs in the play, which had a successful run of 173 performances, indicating that even pallid satire could amuse a predominantly conservative audience eager for retribution.

While Grundy could achieve a respectable success on the topic of the New Woman, Shaw could only fume at the examiner of plays for refusing to license his recently completed play, *Mrs. Warren's Profession.* Grundy satirized what he perceived as the New Woman's pretentiousness and intellectual dishonesty; Shaw recognized the necessity of her development in late nineteenth-century culture, for, as he said, the "horrible artificiality of that impudent sham the Victorian womanly woman, a sham manufactured by men for men," perpetuated the inequities between the sexes. A strong supporter of women's rights, Richard Le Gallienne described the "impudent sham": "To be truly womanly you must be shrinking and clinging in manner and trivial in conversation; you must have no ideas, and rejoice that you wish for none; you must thank Heaven that you have never ridden a bicycle or smoked a cigarette; and you must be prepared to do a thousand other absurd and ridiculous things."

In Shaw's play, the Cambridge-educated Vivie Warren intends to work in London and read law "with an eye on the Stock Exchange." On discovering that her mother has transformed herself from victim to victimizer, Vivie rejects her "few cheap tears" and a daughter's "duty," the Victorian talisman: "We must part. It will not make much difference to us: instead of meeting one another for perhaps a few months in twenty years, we shall never meet: that's all." In one stroke, Shaw rejected the sentimentality of the Victorian theater and its sacred devotion to the family—the need, in melodrama, for reconcilation before the final curtain. The stage direction that describes Mrs. Warren's departure after refusing to shake hands with her daughter echoes the final moment in *A Doll's House:* "Mrs. Warren goes out slamming the door behind her"—not a New

Woman like Ibsen's Nora but, as Vivie ironically calls her, "a conventional woman at heart." Now possessed of new independence, Vivie turns contentedly to her work on actuarial calculations.

WHILE MANY fin-de-siècle New Woman novels were written by women, several of the most acclaimed male writers of the late nineteenth and early twentieth century (including, as we have seen, George Gissing), turned their attention to the Woman Question. George Meredith, for example, was particularly noted for his feminist sympathies and his consistent view that education was essential to women's emancipation. In 1888, Meredith wrote to a correspondent: "I can foresee great and blessed changes for the race when they have achieved independence; for that must come of the exercise of their minds." In *Beauchamp's Career* (1875), Meredith's Cecilia Halkett is the conventional Victorian woman who is described as "one of the artificial creatures called women . . . who dare not be spontaneous, and cannot act independently if they would continue to be admirable in the world's eye. . . ."

In the 1890s, the women in Meredith's novels reveal his increasing interest in the nature of the New Woman, though he wished her to retain certain traditional feminine qualities. In *Lord Ormont and His Aminta* (1894), Meredith discloses the impact of the anti-marriage novels when he takes up the central question: "That Institution of Marriage was eyed. Is it not a halting step to happiness? Our cry is rather for circumstance and occasion to use our functions, and the conditions are denied to women by Marriage." Despite her relative freedom (Lord Ormont is frequently away on the continent), Aminta feels the constraints of a traditional marriage: ". . . her title was Lady Ormont: her condition actually slave." Shaking loose the "bonds in revolt from marriage" and foregoing a life of comfort, she goes off with a lover to found a coeducational school in Switzerland.

Such New Woman novels, with their startling insistence on independence at the expense of social propriety, were suddenly confronted by Grant Allen's *The Woman Who Did* (1895), which, a modern critic has remarked, "was often taken to be the most shocking, dangerous and revolutionary of all the New Woman novels." It outsold all of those written by women and within a few months went through twenty printings. But if the many reviews were any indication, the reading public was deeply divided over the ironic, melodramatic story of an "advanced" woman, Herminia, who redeems herself by her steadfast love for her illegitimate daughter, Dolores. Clearly, the ambiguities in the story suggest Allen's own ambivalence towards both marriage and the New Woman.

Though Herminia views marriage as a "malignant thing . . . a system of slavery," she welcomes the child from her love affair—a new burden to be endured alone: "Herminia was far removed indeed from that blatant and decadent sect of 'advanced women' who talk as though motherhood were a disgrace and a burden, instead of being, as it is, the full realization of woman's faculties. . . ." When Dolores later discovers her illegitimacy, she is devastated; as a result, Herminia commits suicide in a sacrificial act so that her daughter may be free to marry—an ironic, seemingly contradictory gesture from a New Woman who had opposed the principle of marriage. Is Allen suggesting that sorrow (the meaning of Dolores's name) is the inevitable consequence of the New Woman's rebellion against convention? If so, the novel conforms to the nineteenth-century myth of the fallen woman, designed in novels and plays as a warning that misery and isolation follow moral transgression. Allen's wish to confer the nobility of martyrdom on Herminia is undermined by his uncertainty concerning her independence—hence the sentimentality of Herminia's end "with hands folded on her breast, like some saint of the middle ages."

Central to the novel is Herminia's conviction that her education at Girton College had been a fraud: "The whole object of the training was to see just how far you could manage to push a woman's education without the faintest danger of her emancipation." For Herminia, emancipation meant freedom from the "perpetual pressure of social and ethical restrictions"—freedom she could never achieve. Wells called the novel a "hasty, headlong, incompetent book [that] seemed like treason to a great cause" and Herminia "a kind of plaster cast of 'Pure Womanhood' in a halo, with a soul of abstractions, a machine to carry out a purely sentimental principle to its logical conclusion." The heroine as "a kind of plaster cast of 'Pure Womanhood' " also appears in Victoria Crosse's *The Woman Who Didn't* (1895), a conservative response to Allen's more daring "woman who did" in its depiction of marriage as a state of misery endured by a "martyr and a saint."

Also appearing in 1895, Hardy's *Jude the Obscure* was the greatest of the fin-de-siècle works attacking the institution of marriage while presenting a pathological version of the New Woman. In Hardy's previous novels, women's instability caused men grief, though in *Tess of the D'Urbervilles* (1891), Tess is a victim not only of male cruelty but also of the hypocritical double-standard in male sexual behavior. By adding the subtitle *A Pure Woman,* Hardy insisted on Tess's moral integrity despite her fate as a deceived "fallen woman." While an enlightened view of sexuality and marriage is central to the novel, Tess is clearly not the New Woman that Sue Bridehead is in *Jude the Obscure.* Sue's remark—"I shall do just as I choose!"—guides her throughout her life. Her seeming sexual frigidity (her name "Bridehead" suggesting a virginal maidenhead) and her ambivalence towards marriage result from her belief that freedom cannot be achieved so long as passion and male domination prevail. When Hardy thought of dramatizing the novel, he contemplated using the title *The New Woman* or *A Woman with Ideas.*

In a postscript to the Wessex Edition (1912), Hardy recalled—with apparent approval—what a German critic had told him when *Jude the Obscure* first appeared as a serial: ". . . Sue Bridehead, the heroine, was the first delineation in fiction of the woman who was coming into notice in her thousands every year—the woman of the feminist movement—the slight, pale 'bachelor' girl—the intellectualized, emancipated bundle of nerves that modern conditions were producing, mainly in cities. . . ." When the novel appeared in book form, Hardy remained silent on his heroine's unorthodox views and behavior, but ten years later he revealed:

> I have for a long time been in favour of woman-suffrage. . . . I am in favour of it because I think the tendency of the woman's vote will be to break up the present pernicious conventions in respect of manners, customs, religion, illegitimacy, the stereotyped household (that it must be the unit of society), the father of a woman's child (that it is anybody's business but the woman's own, except in cases of disease or insanity) . . . and other matters which I got into hot water for touching on many years ago.

Reviewers generally associated *Jude the Obscure* with such popular New Woman novels as Grant Allen's. The well-known novelist and critic Mrs. Margaret Oliphant attacked the novel's "grossness, indecency, and horror" in her essay "The Anti-Marriage League," insisting that *Jude* was "intended as an assault on the stronghold of marriage, which is now beleaguered on every side." Hardy had first denied that the Marriage Question was central to the novel, but in the preface to the Wessex Edition, he remarked: "My opinion at that time [1895] was what it is now, that a marriage should be dissolved as soon as it becomes a cruelty to either of the partners . . . and it seemed a good foundation for the fable of tragedy." Though there were many vitriolic reviews (one reviewer referred to the work as *Jude the Obscene*), such writers as Edmund Gosse, Richard Le Gallienne, and Havelock Ellis praised it as a major achievement. Nevertheless, Hardy was so distressed by his attackers that he never wrote another novel.

EARLY IN 1895, Richard Le Gallienne took to the lecture circuit in England and Scotland to speak on "The Revolt of the Daughters," which hailed the New Woman as opposed to the Old Male: "Talk of revolt! Why, it is already victory, and why, because man has had nothing to fight with but silly, worn-out platitudes. Woman has had commonsense and the Time-Spirit." In *Fortnightly Review* (June 1895), Harry Quilter raised questions concerning the plethora of books and articles written in such "praise of revolt" and their ultimate effect on culture:

> And strangely enough, the foremost in the assault, the most eager in the work of destruction, are—women; and, with characteristic impulsiveness, they have decided that now is the moment when every mystery connected with life and thought must be laid bare, every problem solved, every restriction removed, every belief be challenged or destroyed.

Quilter, to be sure, was principally concerned with and clearly distressed by the progressive advance of women: "One by one the inner citadels of man's supremacy are stormed and taken." In the previous twenty years, he notes, women had moved into such formerly exclusive male occupations as medical doctor and factory inspector; indeed, "the captain of the *Pinafore* will be attended by his sisters, and his cousins, and his aunts, in an official instead of a private capacity." However, advanced women exhibited a "determination, as settled as it is illogical and futile, to retain both the old privileges and the new concessions, to claim at once the rights of an equal, the immunities of a dependent and the respect due to a superior." Women, he insists, will have to pay a "price" for their new social status by relinquishing once-cherished privileges.

Concern over the significance of the New Woman's progress within Victorian culture is implicit in Alice Meynell's satire in her column, "The Wares of Autolycus," in the *Pall Mall Gazette* (January 2, 1896). A New Woman, contemplating "the various little triumphs she had won in the struggle with her oppressor, Man," cites smoking and wearing knickerbockers instead of the hated petticoats. Despite such "little triumphs," she believes that her university education is a decided advance over former expectations for a young lady:

> To hammer out an air with variations on the piano, paint hideous caricatures of flowers and know a sentence or two of French and German was all that was allowed her by way of culture for the mind, and lessons in deportment and dancing was all that was permitted her in the way of athletics for the development of her body. But she had changed all that.

Yet there was "still much to gain before she would have attained to perfect equality with man. There was that vote she was always bothering about. She must have it eventually, she knew, but were there not other things she wanted more?" Politics bored her, and she was sleepy. What she wanted first was to discard "that odious system of men proposing." Yes, that also must be changed.* In this amusing and revealing sketch, Meynell has only satiric scorn for this New Woman's limited aspirations.

By the mid-1890s, the radical New Woman often incurred the resentment of conservative women who deplored the "insurrection" of the "wild women," or the "shrieking sisterhood," and of men who reacted to such perceived aggressiveness with anxiety. When, in 1896, the publisher Leonard Smithers commissioned Aubrey Beardsley to illustrate Aristophanes's antiwar feminist play *Lysistrata* (411 B.C.), the artist undertook a series of satiric tableaux involving a struggle for supremacy by Lysistrata and her followers to correspond with the phenomenon of the New Woman in London. The inspiration to publish an illustrated *Lysistrata* may have come to Smithers or Beardsley from *The Strike of a Sex* (1890), a novel by the American writer George Noyes Miller, who depicted the refusal of the women in a small town to submit to men's wishes with respect to sex and maternity. In the early nineties, the novel appeared in London in at least two editions.

The central metaphor of the play as well as the illustrations is the equivalence of war and sexuality, both involving attack and retreat. In Beardsley's startling illustrations, the aggressive women, who withhold sexual favors unless their husbands abandon the long war against Sparta, suffer deprivation equally and turn to open masturbation and lesbianism. The male figures' enormous, rigid phalluses, which threaten to topple their owners, are doomed to perpetual unfulfilled tumescence unless the war is terminated. The only remaining expression of male supremacy occurs in a drawing in which, as Ian Fletcher has pointed out, a statuesque phallus "emits a gloria, like those on the heads of saints."

Bordering on the pornographic, Beardsley's depictions of sexual angst are some of his most powerful. His black lines and white voids recall the brilliant style of his illustrations for *Salome,* but the aggressive designs for *Lysistrata* express a new energy to underscore female power. Indeed, when Lysistrata and her followers capture the citadel on the Acropolis, their action prompts women in the other warring city-states to join in the cause. As a result, peace is finally restored. Yet female power in Beardsley's designs is accompanied by comic bathos, a vision of the New

---

*Olive Schreiner, whom W. T. Stead called the "founder and high priestess of the school" of "Modern Women" novelists, had already shown how her heroine in *The Story of an African Farm* (1883), pregnant by one man, proposed to another: "If you are willing to give me your name within three weeks' time, I am willing to marry you; if not, well. . . . That is a clear proposal, is it not?"

Beardsley's Frontispiece for *Lysistrata*

"Lysistrata Haranguing the Athenian Women"

"Lysistrata Defending the Acropolis"

"Examining the Spartan Herald" in *Lysistrata*

"The Spartan Ambassadors" in *Lysistrata*

Woman's descent into vulgarity. Since Smithers would have risked immediate arrest had he published the edition, it was printed for private distribution; hence, there were no reviews and no responses from feminists.

   In the late nineteenth century, female aggressiveness, often associated
with unrestrained sexuality, manifested itself in the anxiety-provoking
image of the femme fatale and the female vampire in the imagination of
men, unconsciously yearning, perhaps, for encounters with such alluring
evil. At the same time, these myths—in part, a reaction to the "angel in
the house" image of women—suggest fears that the male will be "mar-
ginalized" by "an explosively mobile, magic woman, who breaks the
boundaries of family within which her society restricts her." Such anxiety
occurs in Arthur Symons's "The Dance of the Daughters of Herodias"
(1897), a version of the Salome story that acquires a deadly transcendent
significance:

> *They dance, the daughters of Herodias,*
> *With their eternal, white, unfaltering feet,*
> *And always, when they dance, for their delight,*
> *Always a man's head falls because of them.*

In "Nineteen Hundred and Nineteen" (1919), Yeats echoed the image
in his famous line suggesting the imminence of universal anarchy in the
aftermath of the First World War: "Herodias' daughters have returned
again."

Amused by the phenomenon of the New Woman, Max Beerbohm began writing a "comic epic in prose" in 1898, completing it in 1910, and publishing it as *Zuleika Dobson; or, an Oxford Love Story* in 1911. The plot, as one critic has called it, is "deliberately preposterous": Zuleika, a performer of magic tricks, visits her grandfather, the warden of Judas College at Oxford. On her arrival, the charming but aggressive Zuleika causes the busts of the Roman emperors on the gate surrounding the Sheldonian Theatre to glisten with perspiration, an omen of things to come. Having fallen in love with her and having been rejected, the dandiacal Duke of Dorset resolves to die for her. As a New Woman, Zuleika remarks: "I could no more marry a man about whom I could not make a fool of myself than I could marry one who made a fool of himself about me." Once the duke has fulfilled his intention, all of the other undergraduates, also hopelessly in love with Zuleika, follow the duke by drowning themselves in the river. Informed of the disaster, the warden urges Zuleika to leave. The next day she takes a special train to Cambridge, where presumably she will again decimate the undergraduate population.* Surely, such fatality in a woman had never before been responsible, even in the realm of fantasy, for so many suicides. In the mannered prose of caricature and parody, Beerbohm approximates that of Beardsley's *Venus and Tannhäuser* in presenting a comic variant of the late Victorian myth of the demonic woman.

Like the femme fatale, the icon of the female vampire represented another threat to the male imagination. In Symons's "The Vampire" (1896), a "white bloodless creature of the night, / Whose lust of blood has blanched her chill veins white" drains the man's life-blood as he "swoons ecstatically on death." Less lugubrious, Rudyard Kipling's "The Vampire" (1897) opens with the famous lines: "A fool there was and he made his prayer. . . . / To a rag and a bone and a hank of hair. . . . / But the fool he called her his lady fair." The unsuspecting male falls prey to the allure of the vampirish New Woman:

> *The fool was stripped to his foolish hide*
> *(Even as you and I!)*
> *Which she might have seen when she threw him aside—*
> *(But it isn't on record the lady tried)*
> *So some of him lived but the most of him died—*

In Bram Stoker's *Dracula* (1897), Lucy and Mina are, in fact, transformed into vampires, revealing apprehensions concerning female sexuality and

---

*In his comic sequel, *Zuleika in Cambridge* (1941), S. C. Roberts preferred a different outcome: "Cambridge men gave no sign of wanting to lie down and die for love of her. Instead, they stood about and made harmless jokes."

the New Woman. In her journal, Mina records her satiric opinions as she thinks of Lucy, the dangerous nocturnal predator whose "sweetness was turned to . . . cruelty, and the purity to voluptuous wantonness"—sexuality itself constituting, as it does in Salome, the ultimate agent of social disorder: "Some of the 'New Women' writers will someday start an idea that men and women should be allowed to see each other asleep before proposing or accepting. But I suppose the New Woman won't condescend in future to accept; she will do the proposing herself."

As the 1890s neared their end, the image of the New Woman in its various forms lost its radical capacity to provoke controversy. Popular culture and serious authors had exploited the fashion during the relatively few years of its notoriety, and in the world of New Journalism and circulating libraries, whatever was "New" soon grew old. Moreover, the reform-minded Victorians had the capacity to absorb and assuage the anguish of their ostensible opponents. Designed for a popular audience, Mary Beaumont's *Two New Women* (1899) was one of the last New Woman novels of the decade (a recent critic estimates that more than one hundred novels about the New Woman appeared between 1883 and 1900). The heroines of *Two New Women,* a doctor and a landscape gardener, wonder at their muscles, symbols of achievement and power ("Feel that arm!"), and boast of their sporting abilities. The male characters are duly impressed but also subdued: ". . . quite the newest women! So emancipated that emancipation is a matter of ancient history, and they say nothing about it." For all its importance in the history of the feminist movement, the time had come for activists to dispose of the New Woman as a cultural icon, perhaps because it alienated more women than it attracted, and to resume the struggle in earnest for the long-delayed right to vote. In the following century, the New Woman reemerged as a transformed feminist turned militant whose aggressiveness reached unforeseen extremes of violence.

IN THE BOSTON *Arena* (April 1902), a writer (possibly male) hailed the successes of the New Woman, but conventional Victorian views persisted in the evaluation: "In few respects has mankind made a greater advance than in the position of women—legal, social and educational. From the darkness of ignorance and servitude women have passed into the open light of equal freedom." Despite such achievements, the writer cautions the New Woman to retain her feminine qualities in a passage expressing common anxieties over the nature of the "advanced" woman, who should now

bear in mind that in becoming a brilliant mathematician, a sharp critic, a faultless grammarian, she may do so at the expense of that ready sympathy, modesty, noble self-control, gentleness, personal tact and temper, so essential for the best type of womanhood and the most exalted standards of female excellence.

Such views of women were soon subjected to strenuous attack as a new phase of the feminist movement called for more radical methods to win the franchise. In 1903, Mrs. Emmeline Pankhurst and her two daughters founded the Women's Social and Political Union, the most significant organization devoted to suffrage in the Edwardian period. Compared to the new suffragette, the fin-de-siècle New Woman now seemed tame and ineffectual. In its attempt to generate as much publicity as possible by embarrassing the government, the union staged clashes with the police as members attempted to march on Parliament or to present petitions to the prime minister in Downing Street, broke windows in public buildings as well as in private property, slashed paintings at the Royal Academy and the National Gallery (including Velasquez's masterpiece, the *Rokeby Venus,* then valued at the enormous sum of £45,000), conducted hunger strikes by jailed feminists until they were force-fed, and committed acts of arson as violence escalated in the years before the First World War.

"Why," asks a recent historian, "did these suffragists feel it necessary to struggle, and suffer even to the point of torture or self-destruction, in a twentieth-century parliamentary democracy, ruled by a Liberal government, in pursuit of a reform which has, arguably, directly affected

Mrs. Pankhurst's arrest (Museum of London)

women's lives very little? What gave such actions their legitimacy among followers of the Women's Social and Political Union?" The answers to such questions lie partly in the disillusionment among the more militant feminists in the Union with the parliamentary methods of the rival organization, the National Union of Women Suffrage Societies, led by Millicent Garrett Fawcett, who believed in "the rule of law, the exercise of reason, and evolutionary progress . . . through representative parliamentary government." Unlike Fawcett, Mrs. Pankhurst was a devoted social revolutionary determined to change the world by force, if need be. In *My Own Story* (1914), Pankhurst expressed the belief that future generations of women "may sometimes wish that they could have lived in the heroic days of stress and struggle and have shared with us the joy of battle, the exultation that comes of sacrifice of self for a great object." Her motto—"Deeds, not words," those that would be "woven into the fabric of human civilization"—inspired the members of her union to commit what the press called "outrages." Such actions alienated many of the moderate supporters of suffrage as well as members of Parliament, who now pointed to evidence that women, by their antisocial acts, had disqualified themselves from the vote!* At the height of the violence, the attitude of the *Daily Chronicle* (March 5, 1912) was typical: "All sensible people are being forced to the conclusion that there can be no women's franchise legislation under the present conditions."

On February 13, 1907, a widely publicized incident occurred when the union held its own Women's Parliament at Caxton Hall in Caxton Street on the day following the King's speech, which had made no mention of votes for women. Resolving to deliver a petition to the prime minister, the Women's Parliament responded to Mrs. Pankhurst's cry, "Rise up, women!" by marching 400 strong to the House of Commons. But the police, already prepared, barred them at Westminster Abbey. Struggles ensued, the mounted police directing their horses into the surging women carrying placards and wearing banners while police on foot diverted other demonstrators into side streets. Hours later, fifteen of the marchers managed to reach the lobby, where they were arrested (in all, fifty-nine arrests were made).

The incident prompted Arthur Symons to write "On Reading of Women Rioting for Their Rights" (February 15, 1907), which reveals

---

*In Wales, crowd reaction to the suffragettes was less tolerant than in England. On two occasions in September 1912, crowds attacked female militants heckling Lloyd George and ripped their clothing, one of them stripped to the waist before the constabulary could intervene: ". . . two women's shirts were cut up and pieces were distributed amongst the crowd as souvenirs of the occasion" (Andrew Rosen, *Rise up, Women!: The Militant Campaign of the Women's Social and Political Union, 1903–1914* [London, 1974], 171).

his orthodox view of women's moral purity and superiority, traditionally an argument against woman suffrage:

> *What is this unimaginable desire*
> *In women's heads? Would you come down again*
> *From where you are, to be no more than men?*
> *Why is it that you call it getting higher*
> *To slip with each step deeper into the mire?*

Symons soon began writing a satirical play titled *The Superwomen: A Farce,* which revealed his increasing fears over the power of women, who, in the play, rule Britain. A leading figure in the avant-garde with sympathy for such outcasts as Gypsies and prostitutes, Symons was now ridiculing militant women and thereby defending his supposed privileged position as if he were a member of the Establishment—a telling example of how the issue of suffrage produced odd contradictions among intellectuals.

THOUGH, IN LATER years, Sidney Webb stated that the Fabians "had persistently demanded equal adult suffrage in our lectures and manifestoes," the evidence indicates that "the male direction of the Society was uninterested in the subject, and regarded it, like Home Rule, as something on which Fabians did not need to make pronouncements." Beatrice Webb, we recall, had signed the "Appeal against Woman Suffrage" (1889), and in a letter to the Boston *Woman's Journal* (September 1, 1906), Shaw also revealed a lack of enthusiasm for the issue:

> Personally I care very little for giving women the vote, except as
> a means of getting women on public bodies. . . . If you had sat, as
> I have, for years, on a health committee, trying to persuade a
> parcel of men who regarded women as angels and subjects for
> loose jests, and who burst into shouts of laughter when the
> doctor mentioned a maternity case . . . you would not press me
> for my reasons.

By this time, however, the Fabian Society had a large contingent of women who insisted on the adoption of the following as one of the "Objects of the Society": "The establishment of equal citizenship between men and women." To avert rebellion by the feminists, the society conceded.

In November 1906, Beatrice Webb informed Millicent Fawcett that the time had arrived for her to support the franchise for women. Having been content to leave the "rough and tumble of party politics" to men, she now believed that women needed the vote because "the rearing of children, the advancement of learning, and the promotion of the spiritual life," which she regarded as the "particular obligations of women," had become the "main preoccupations of the community as a whole." The Fabian Women's Group, now frequently reported in the press as participants in suffragette demonstrations, abandoned the Fabian principle of "permeation" on this volatile issue.

Shaw also came forward in support of universal suffrage in a speech printed in the *New York American* (April 21, 1907), in which he jocularly announced his support of the franchise:

> England has a Liberal party; it has a Conservative party; it has a Labor party; it has an Irish party. Unfortunately it has not yet got a Shaw party. If it had, that party would be uncompromisingly on the side of giving the suffrage to women, and I can promise that should they get it the House of Commons will be quite the most amusing Legislature on the face of the globe.

Shaw contended that, by giving women the vote, England would "set free an immense and beneficial flood of political and social energy which is now being taken up by this question." On another occasion, he signed a petition favoring suffrage—along with hundreds of other male advocates, such as Thomas Hardy, William Archer, Arthur Wing Pinero, and James M. Barrie—which was published in the *Times* (March 23, 1909).

Despite such expressions of support, Shaw harbored a lingering ambivalence toward the suffrage question. In his one-act farce *Press Cuttings* (1909), he dramatized suffragette aggressiveness by revealing its effect on absurd government officials (Prime Minister Balsquith, the name fusing Balfour and Asquith, dresses in women's clothing to escape from the militants). In view of the increasing seriousness of female militancy as reported in the daily press, Shaw's seemingly inappropriate farcical treatment may indicate a fear that the suffragettes had chosen inappropriate means to achieve worthy ends. To compound the plot and add contrast, Shaw introduces offensive female antisuffragettes, more unbearable than the suffragettes, who are heard at the beginning of the play outside the War Office but who never appear:

A VOICE FROM THE STREET. Votes for Women!
   The General starts convulsively; snatches a revolver from a drawer; and listens in an agony of apprehension.

Mrs. Banger, the virago who is organizing secretary of the Anti-Suffraget League, is so determined to take charge of the British Army that the general, in despair, says: "If this is the alternative to votes for women, I shall advocate giving every woman in the country six votes." Yet he tells Balsquith, "What I can't stand is giving in to that Pankhurst lot." An elitist, Shaw also found it difficult to give in. In nine years, Britain could no longer withhold the franchise when three million previously unemployed women entered the work force during the First World War and acquitted themselves well in such demanding occupations as those in the armaments factories. Women over thirty were thus given the vote.

THOUGH THE EDWARDIANS regarded themselves as more enlightened on the Woman Question than the Victorians, many of the old social problems affecting women remained as though engraved in stone. An indication that the problems of the past were merely transposed to the new age is obvious in the reception of Wells's novel *Ann Veronica* (1909). Reviewers condemned its sexual immorality, *The Spectator* (November 20) calling it "a poisonous book" because of Wells's apparent approval of the heroine's illicit sexual behavior and her abandonment of "self-sacrifice." Wells responded by suggesting that Ann reflected rather than challenged the cultural values of the time: "The Family *does not work* as it used to do, and we do not know why, and we have to look into it."

The reviewer in *T. P.'s Weekly* (October 22, 1909) likewise condemned *Ann Veronica* as a "dangerous novel" because the heroine regards her defiance of the "old morality" as "glorious": "To condemn her at all will seem to many a young reader like depreciating love, courage, and emancipation." But, the reviewer states, "the best woman is still the good woman, who maintains her culture by imparting it to her children ... and who makes her own home a microcosm of Utopia. ... She will be lovely and lovable in her life, and in her coffin more beautiful than she whose beauty launched a thousand ships and burned the topless towers of Ilium." The review—with its respectably gruesome image of the good woman in her coffin—reads as though written in the mid-Victorian years.

To the reviewers of *Ann Veronica,* Wells posed a threat to Edwardian stability by depicting an unstable heroine. Having surpassed the nineties' New Woman, Ann Veronica enters the Imperial College to study for a degree in biology, joins a group of suffragettes, lays seige to Parliament in a characteristic act by the new militants, and endures self-martyrdom in prison. Nevertheless, such liberating experiences leave her as perplexed as the "advanced" woman of the previous age, partly because Wells created a feminist who likes men as opposed to some militant separatists who sought to eliminate them.* In prison with other women, she muses:

---

*Samuel Hynes alludes to letters to the *Times* at the time of suffragette militancy from women who "argued the eventual superfluity of man (as the race evolves) and the

"The reason why I am out of place here," she said, "is because I like men. I can talk with them. I've never found them hostile. I've got no feminine class feeling. . . .

A woman wants a proper alliance with a man, a man who is better stuff than herself. She wants that and needs it more than anything else in the world. It may not be just, it may not be fair; but things are so. . . . She wants to be free—she wants to be legally and economically free, so as not to be made subject to the wrong man; but only God, who made the world, can alter things to prevent her being a slave to the right one."

Though Ann leads a sexually free life with a married man, this is prelude to marriage and domesticity. Her father lays the blame for his daughter's unorthodox behavior on "these damned novels. . . . These sham ideals and advanced notions, Women Who Dids, and all that kind of thing." But the happy ending to the novel—a major reason for the *Spectator*'s outrage—departs from the misery endured by women in the New Woman fiction of the fin de siècle. As a modern critic states: "The recognition of female sexuality, which had seemed such a central part of the New Woman's struggle for emancipation, can now be easily assimilated into the old values."

The frank acknowledgment of sexuality in New Woman fiction, particularly in Hardy's *Jude the Obscure*—the greatest and most complex of them all—led to the extensive exploration of female psychology in such modernist writers as D. H. Lawrence, Dorothy Richardson, Virginia Woolf, and James Joyce. Clearly, there had been a parallel development between the significant step towards emancipation in the emergence of the New Woman and the progressive freeing of the English novel from restrictions in subject matter, particularly in sexual relationships, between the fin de siècle and the early twentieth century.

---

superiority of women, a view summed up in one brief slogan: 'Life is feminine.' One suffragette argued that in the original text of the book of Genesis, where we now read 'male and female created He them,' the pronoun should in fact be feminine" (*The Edwardian Turn of Mind* [Princeton, 1968], 205).

7

The New Drama

On June 9, 1889, two days following the first London performance of Henrik Ibsen's *A Doll's House* at the Novelty Theatre, the *Star*'s drama critic, A. B. Walkley, hailed it as "the beginning of a dramatic revolution": "After *A Doll's House,* we may be of good cheer. The great intellectual movement of the day has at length reached the theatre. There is a future for the stage, after all." After decades of sentimental comedies, melodramas, farces, spectacles, and musical plays, enlightened theatergoers could now encounter drama capable of making them question their basic ideals regarding human relationships. Though Nora's slamming of the door on her husband and children as she leaves their home was heard by exultant audiences around the world (beginning in various Scandinavian cities in 1880), many of Walkley's fellow reviewers condemned the play as an attack on decency and morality. The noted conservative critic Clement Scott, then editor of *Theatre,* published a lengthy review in July 1889 that upheld the widespread conception of the ideal woman, clearly the "angel in the house" that Ibsen had repudiated. Of Nora in *A Doll's House,* Scott wrote sullenly: "It is all self, self, self! This is the ideal woman of the new creed; not a woman who is the fountain of love and forgiveness and charity, not the pattern woman we have admired in our mothers and our sisters. . . ."

Like Walkley, Shaw regarded Ibsen's play as not only the herald of a new era in drama but, more importantly, the means by which the unquestioned assumptions of an entire age could be openly and startlingly challenged. In a letter to the *Pall Mall Gazette* (June 13, 1889), Shaw described his experience at the production of *A Doll's House:* "[I] see a vital truth searched out and held up in a light intense enough to dispel all the mists and shadows that obscure it in actual life. I see people silent, attentive, thoughtful, startled—struck to the heart, some of them." Despite the outraged reactions of hostile critics, *A Doll's House* ran for twenty-four days to crowded houses (performances had been scheduled for only a week), closing only because the leading actors, Janet Achurch and her husband Charles Charrington, had made previous arrangements to perform the play again as part of their Australian tour.

The intense antagonism towards the succès d'estime of *A Doll's House* inevitably led to extended articles that took up the challenge of Ibsenism (the Ibsen phenomenon now elevated to the status of a cultural ideology of revolt against Victorian pieties). With the departure of the play from London and in apparent reaction to Shaw's letter in the *Pall Mall Gazette,* Robert Buchanan (who had attacked Swinburne and Rossetti as "The Fleshly School of Poetry") expressed his moral displeasure with Ibsen by focusing in the *Contemporary Review* (December 1889) on the significance of his success: "It means that the stage is better employed in the washing of dirty linen than in the presentation of great thoughts, great ideas, great characters"—the Victorian injunction that the theater (indeed, art in general) should be inspiring and instructive; anything less would demean the most advanced nation on earth. Buchanan praised the playwright Tom Robertson as "the most modern of the moderns," for his " 'cup-and-saucer pieces' " of the 1860s were "exquisitely true to Nature" (William Archer had suggested that Robertson's socially conscious plays with their realistic staging may have been the harbinger of the New Drama). Robertson, said Buchanan, was "earnest and virile . . . imaginative and optimistic, not pessimistic and cynical."

In his innovative dramaturgy, Ibsen rejected the conventional ending of the popular "well-made play," in which a secret once exposed leads inevitably to a satisfying denouement. Instead, he designed the final scene of *A Doll's House* as a problematic beginning rather than a reassuring ending. In the *English Illustrated Magazine* (January 1890), the best-selling novelist Walter Besant dutifully provided morally outraged readers with a sequel to the play—"The Doll's House—and After," a short story that outlines the disastrous effects of Nora's desertion of her family. Twenty years later, her husband and son are alcoholics, the second son is a thief, and the daughter commits suicide: All suffer the shame of the mother's abandonment. Unlike those in her family, Nora is financially comfortable as a successful novelist, and her indifference to husband, sons, and daughter is chilling.

In a facetious letter to Charles Charrington, still in Australia, Shaw acknowledged Besant's story as a significant indication of current attitudes towards Ibsen:

> The Ibsenites here turned up their noses & said it was beneath notice; but it struck me as being of enormous importance as a representative middle class evangelical verdict on the play. Besides which, the ball must be kept rolling on every possible pretext, so that by the time you come back, everybody who has

not seen the Doll's House will feel quite out of it, especially in the provinces.

To keep the Ibsen ball rolling, Shaw wrote a sequel to Besant's sequel for *Time* (February 1890): "The worst of it is that my sequel is declared [by friends who had seen the proofs] to be beneath the level even of Besant's—to be slosh, rubbish, dull dreary Philistine stuff. . . . It is 'not even comic' they say. They are all wrong: it is first rate."

Though "Still after the Doll's House" may not be "first rate," Shaw's story, an Ibsen-inspired vision of human relationships, surpasses Besant's narrowly bourgeois view of Nora. During a lengthy dialogue between her and Krogstad (in Ibsen's play, the moneylender who had threatened to expose Nora's forgery; in the story, the mayor of the town), Shaw reveals the secret liaisons between various members of Nora's salon. Charging that Krogstad's own marriage is based on the dubious morality of master and slave, Nora tells him: "Twenty years ago, when I walked out of the doll's house, I saw only my own side of the question. . . . I did not see that the man must walk out of the doll's house as well as the woman." Before Krogstad storms out, Nora utters the central theme of their encounter: "Mastery is the worst slavery of all." Ironically, Krogstad slams the door as he leaves.

INSPIRED BY THE acclaimed and condemned London production of *A Doll's House* as well as performances given by the visiting Théâtre Libre early in 1889, George Moore published an attack in the *Fortnightly Review* (November 1889) on such popular playwrights as Henry Arthur Jones, Arthur Wing Pinero, Sydney Grundy, and W. S. Gilbert—none of whom, he claimed, had written a play of any literary distinction. The assault on such revered men of the theater drew blood from a variety of newspaper critics, to whom Moore replied in the *Hawk* (November 12): "Mr. Swinburne says that as the intelligence of Elizabethan England was poured into the drama, so the intelligence of today is poured into the novel and the poem. This is my article in essence." Moore resumed his campaign against the London theater by publishing a four-part article in the same periodical (June 17 to July 8, 1890), which called for a British equivalent of the successful Théâtre Libre. In the *Pall Mall Gazette* (June 5, 1890), Arthur Symons, who had been in Paris with Moore to see a performance of Ibsen's *Ghosts,* had anticipated his friend's position, perhaps by prearranged strategy:

We have not yet a Théâtre Libre and it is possible that the Lord Chamberlain might have but little desire to license a play which is not even an adaptation from the French. But a Théâtre Libre could be improvised for the occasion, and *Ghosts* in this way at least, performed—privately, if the guardians of our morality forbid the production of a play which contains so much that is "properer for a sermon."

In 1887, André Antoine (an amateur actor, formerly an employee in a gas company) had founded the Théâtre Libre in Paris. When, in 1889, his company agreed to perform in London, the journalistic response in the *Times* (February 5) focused on his alleged taste for the outrageous: ". . . the Théâtre Libre [is] the happy hunting ground of the ultra-realistic or fin-de-siècle dramatist who specially affects the horrible and the revolting." Commenting on the first production, an adaptation of Zola's novel *Jacques Damour,* the *Morning Post* (February 5) doubted whether the art of the "realistic school" would "commend itself to the English public, or indeed to the French public. . . . Last night's entertainment, though well received in the main, provoked as least as much astonishment as interest." In the *Era* (February 9), the reviewer concluded: "What naturalism on the stage means, in theory, is the throwing overboard of the conventions—no 'points,' no 'curtains,' no 'crisis,' very often no 'denouement,' simply a page cut, without erasure or addition from the book of life."

In Paris, the company had staged plays by hitherto unproduced playwrights as well as by those well known, such as Ibsen, Tolstoy, Strindberg, the Goncourt brothers, and Zola, whose insistence on absolute fidelity to the minutiae of reality in staging, dialogue, and characterization concurred with Antoine's opposition to romantic melodrama. A major impulse for the founding of the Théâtre Libre was that on the Parisian stage many writers had been producing well-made plays "tolerably alike," each playwright rewriting the "same play a little worse every time, for age intervenes, and the hand grows heavier." The result, George Moore concluded, was that the public had grown "indifferent" to recycled drama. Moreover, the decline in the quality of commercial drama resulted from the dissolution of acting companies and their replacement with the "star system" that exploited the unique talents of such a figure as Sarah Bernhardt. Finally, admission prices at the commercial theaters had risen to prohibitive levels.

The situation in the London theater, Moore insisted, was analogous to that in Paris. Since theater managers needed long runs to produce profits, they catered to the largely lower-class audience's preference for sentimental plays. Only a new infusion of serious drama would attract enlightened middle- and upper-class theatergoers. Moore's avant-garde position implied the elitist notion that a revolutionary new theater was needed for the three or four thousand people "who are more or less directly interested in literature and new artistic manifestations." Essential to the success of the new theater was the rejection of "good conventional plays" as well as "bad ones." A British equivalent of the Théâtre Libre would stage plays usually rejected by the commercial theaters, "plays that deal with religious and moral problems in such ways as would not command the instantaneous and unanimous approval of a large audience drawn from all classes of society." As a literary and artistic theater, it "must offer a supremacy of sensation—the strange, the unknown, the unexpected," including a certain proportion of the *"bizarre."* In short, Moore seems to have envisioned an avant-garde theater with Decadent elements that would challenge the popular theater in its reliance on well-made melodramas and farces. The reassuring conventions of the London stage would thus be undermined.

Such popular playwrights as Jones, Arthur Wing Pinero, and Sydney Grundy had been pleasing audiences with "intellectual" drama that confirmed Victorian ideals of morality, a compromise resulting in extraordinary successes but hindering what Jones hoped for, a "renascence of the English drama" that would deal with "religion, politics, science, education, philosophy . . . on the English stage during the next generation." Such a renascence, he implied, would involve drama's new role, for "the more and more the Church becomes a museum of fossil dogmas, the less hold and command will it have over the religion and morality of the nation. If the Pulpit loses its power, will the Drama take its place?" As a recent theater historian has remarked, Jones was "far more progressive in his propaganda than in his plays."

Though Moore later claimed that he had initiated the suggestion for the establishment of a British theater equivalent to the Théâtre Libre, J. T. Grein had anticipated Moore in an editorial he wrote with C. W. Jarvis in their periodical, *Weekly Comedy: A Review of the Drama, Music and Literature* (November 30, 1889). They urged the establishment of "a theatre free from the shackles of the censor, free from the fetters of convention, unhampered by financial considerations," its "aim neither at fostering play-writing of a merely didactic kind, nor at introducing subjects of an immoral, or even unwholesomely realistic nature." Within two years of this proposal, Grein joined with Moore and others to found the Independent Theatre Society, among whose 175 members were Meredith, Hardy, Jones, and Pinero (the presence of the latter two playwrights suggesting, perhaps, their willingness to support privately produced experimental drama that would not compete commercially with their own successful plays).

Ibsen's *Ghosts,* the initial production of the Independent Theatre, opened on March 13, 1891. On the following day in the illustrated periodical *Black and White,* Grein called the selection a "manifesto—a demonstration of my plan of campaign." In fact, his choice echoed that of the Théâtre Libre, whose first production was also *Ghosts:*

> In nearly every centre of civilisation—in Berlin, in Paris, in Christiania [later, Oslo], in Copenhagen, in Amsterdam, in Brussels—the earnest students of the advancing drama have had an opportunity to see this work, read and discussed as it is by everyone, and have applauded it. The London stage alone, ruled by an iron rod of medieval narrowness and dictatorship . . . dared not produce the most modern, the most classical drama of the age. Thus the Independent Theatre Society, where art, not money or long runs, is the cry, has stepped in to free the London stage from the taunt of artistic orthodoxy.

Grein recalled that the production resulted in no less than five hundred articles and reviews "mostly vituperating Ibsen . . . and obtained for me the honorary, if somewhat unflattering, title of the 'best-abused man in London.' . . . It cost me practically ten years of my life to overcome the prejudice created by an undertaking which, even the enemy must admit, has left its mark upon the history of our stage."

In "Ghosts and Gibberings," published in the *Pall Mall Gazette* (April 8, 1891), Archer quoted from many of the most outrageous reviews (a device that amused both Shaw and Henry James):

> "An open drain: a loathsome sore unbandaged; a dirty act done publicly" *(Daily Telegraph);* "Morbid, unhealthy, unwholesome and disgusting story. . . . A piece to bring the stage into disrepute and dishonour with every right-thinking man and woman" *(Lloyd's);* "Most loathsome of all Ibsen's plays. . . . Garbage and offal" *(Truth);* "Ninety-seven per cent of the people who go to see *Ghosts* are nasty-minded people who find the discussion of nasty subjects to their taste, in exact proportion to their nastiness" *(Sporting News)*.

In a letter to the *Times* (October 13, 1891), Moore was pleased that the "savagery of the attack, full of howls for the [Lord] Chamberlain and the police, served at least one good purpose—it called attention to the Independent Theatre . . . and eventually brought us a good many subscribers." The press, he said, "strove to force us into public avowal that we were wrong, and that if a play did not appeal to the general public it was a quite inconceivably useless thing."

Following *Ghosts,* the Independent Theatre produced *Hedda Gabler* in a memorable matinee performance on April 20, 1891, with the actress

Elizabeth Robins in the leading role. The essentially modern note, as expressed by Hedda's startling instability, marked the play as a frightening vision for the critic in the *Hawk* (April 28, 1891): "I know of no play in the whole range of modern comedy, or tragedy, which presents so true and so terrible a picture of certain phases of human life familiar to all who observe." As might be expected, the sensation created by *Ghosts* and *Hedda Gabler* aroused *Punch* to parody the "Ibscenity" in the theater, and James M. Barrie (later of *Peter Pan* fame) wrote a one-act burlesque and sequel to *Hedda Gabler* titled *Ibsen's Ghost.* Staged anonymously on May 31, 1891, at Toole's Theatre in William IV Street, the play featured the character Thea Tesman's grandfather, who was made up to resemble Ibsen; the program noted that the grandfather used "Mr. Gosse's translation, and the other characters Mr. Archer's." In the play, George Tesman keeps confusing his second wife, Thea, with Hedda, his first wife, uttering endlessly, "Fancy that!" At the end, Thea kills herself with a child's popgun (in Ibsen's play, Hedda slays herself with her father's pistol).

IN OCTOBER 1891, the appearance of *The Quintessence of Ibsenism* established Shaw as one of Ibsen's foremost advocates. In providing an ideological framework of moral revolt as his fundamental approach to Ibsen's plays, Shaw reminded his readers in the preface that he had not written "a critical essay on the poetic beauties of Ibsen, but simply an exposition of Ibsenism." Its genesis began in the spring of 1890 when Shaw agreed to address the Fabian Society on Ibsen at St. James's Restaurant, Piccadilly, on July 18. To the crowded audience on that evening, Shaw delivered a lengthy lecture, the opening salvo of which revealed Shaw as an agent provocateur in confronting his Fabian colleagues with an ideology radically different from their evolutionary socialism:

> Ibsen's message to you is—If you are a member of a society, defy it; if you have a duty, violate it; if you have a sacred tie, break it; if you have a religion, stand on it instead of crouching under it; if you have bound yourself by a promise or an oath, cast them to the winds; if the lust of self-sacrifice seize you, wrestle with it as with the devil; and if, in spite of all, you cannot resist the temptation to be virtuous, go drown yourself before you have time to waste the lives of all about you with the infection of that disease. Here at last is a call to arms that has some hope in it.

Sidney Webb, who was at the lecture, told Beatrice: "It is very clever, and not so bad as I feared. . . . But his glorification of the Individual Will distresses me."

Shaw warned his Fabian colleagues of the debilitating effect of idealism
on socialists, especially those in Hyndman's Social Democratic Federation.* Socialism undermined its own goals by clinging to abstractions
rather than by finding pragmatic solutions to social problems. Ibsen's
significance was that he was the exemplary dramatist of failed idealists:
"The dual aspects of his idealist figures, who are at once higher and more
mischievous than the ordinary Philistines, puzzles the conventional actor,
who persists in assuming that if he is to be selfish on the stage he must be
villainous; that if he is to be self-sacrificing and scrupulous he must be a
hero. . . ." Ibsen insisted on "the need for constantly renewing our ideals,
throwing out the stale as we take in the fresh; recognizing that the truth of
yesterday is the superstition of to-day; and above all, never indulging in
the dream that it is possible to go back to old ideals. . . ."

The Quintessence of Ibsenism embodies and develops such ideas in Shaw's
discussion of specific plays: ". . . a typical Ibsen play is one in which the
leading lady is an unwomanly woman, and the villain an idealist." But
what is missing in Shaw's discussion of Ibsenism is a vision of the anguished inner worlds of characters haunted by the ghosts of the past and a
discussion of how Ibsen manages symbolism within the framework of
realistic drama—in short, what Shaw dismissed as "the poetic beauties of
Ibsen." In an open letter to Shaw in the *New Review* (November 1891),
Archer recalled the lecture on Ibsen that Shaw had given to the Fabian
Society in July 1890. He had already become accustomed to Shaw's
"freakish irrationalism" and "perverse Schopenhauerism," presumably
referring to an assertion of individual will rather than Schopenhauer's
renunciation of will in order to avoid pain and suffering. Shaw's transformation of such a philosophical view, Archer said, was "Shawpenhauer-
ism," but he was himself "gradually becoming a convert." While
preferring Ibsen as poet and Symbolist, Archer nevertheless praised *The
Quintessence,* but as the decade progressed, his view of Shaw's service to
Ibsen underwent considerable change.

Though *The Quintessence* propelled Shaw to the forefront of the "Ibsen
campaign" to transform English drama, the leading Ibsenites were, in
fact, William Archer and Edmund Gosse. As the "prophet" of the New
Drama, Archer was Ibsen's principal translator; the author of dozens of
critical articles, reviews, and books wholly or partially on Ibsen between
1878 and 1923; the editor of numerous editions of his collected works;

---

*The oft-repeated suggestion that Shaw turned Ibsen into a socialist is refuted by his
lecture at the Fabian Society meeting despite the title of the announced series, "Socialism in Contemporary Literature": "I now come to the bearing of Ibsen's thesis on
ourselves as Socialists. Ibsen himself has made no such application; for he is not a
Socialist." Shaw saw only certain parallels in the social attitudes of Ibsenism and
socialism ("Fragments of a Fabian Lecture 1890," *Shaw and Ibsen: Bernard Shaw's "The
Quintessence of Ibsenism" and Related Writings,* ed. J. L. Wisenthal [Toronto, 1979], 87).

and the overseer of most of the twenty-three London productions of Ibsen's plays. In the *Clarion* (June 1, 1906), Shaw acknowledged that it was Archer's "devotion to the task of translating Ibsen's plays that made the whole movement possible, and actually secured recognition for Ibsen's greatness in England."

Edmund Gosse claimed that he was the first to introduce Ibsen to English readers, including Archer. He had reviewed Ibsen's poems in the *Spectator* (March 16, 1872) and subsequently wrote on *Peer Gynt* and *The Pretenders* in the same year. (The bilingual Archer, however, said that he had discovered Ibsen independently at about the same time while visiting relatives in Norway, where he had spent many of his boyhood years.) Gosse continued his advocacy of Ibsen in books and articles well into the next century, even collaborating with Archer on several translations of Ibsen's plays. Moreover, Gosse wrote long articles on Ibsen for the 1902 and 1911 editions of the *Encyclopaedia Britannica,* and on Ibsen's death in 1906, the *Times* chose Gosse to compose its lengthy obituary. In the introduction to his *Ibsen* (1907), Gosse revised the significance of his own role by generously citing Archer as "the introducer of Ibsen to English readers" and as the "protagonist in the fight" to secure for Ibsen "the recognition due to his genius."

Shaw's attraction to Ibsen inevitably resulted in his own satiric view of the fin-de-siècle understanding (or, perhaps, misunderstanding) of Ibsenism. In the topical comedy *The Philanderer* (written in 1893, published in 1898, and produced in 1905), New Women and Ibsenites come together at the Ibsen Club, where a bust of the playwright observes the events taking place in the library. Grace Tranfield, a New Woman who succeeds in dominating Leonard Charteris, "the famous Ibsenist philosopher," strikes a familiar, ironic note early in the play: "No woman is the property of a man. A woman belongs to herself and to nobody else." Finding this view congenial, Charteris the philanderer naively concurs: "Quite right. Ibsen for ever!" (Shaw confessed that he himself served as the model for this Ibsenite philanderer.)

Among the characters is the drama critic Jo Cuthbertson, modeled after the well-known antagonist of Ibsen, Clement Scott, who had condemned *Ghosts* in the *Daily Telegraph* as "an open drain." (Shaw told Charrington that Scott was "much agitated" when he learned that "a man named Bernard Shaw had got up in the Playgoers' Club and thanked his almighty God that Ibsen would be the end of Scott and all his works.") Shaking his fist at the bust of Ibsen as though blaming him for transforming personal relationships, presumably from the ideal to the real, Cuthbertson tells a friend that the "whole modern movement" was "abhorrent" to him as a drama critic because his "life had been passed in witnessing scenes of suffering nobly endured and sacrifice willingly rendered by womanly women and manly men. . . ." Charteris reminds everyone that the rules of the club require that "every candidate for membership must be nomi- nated by a man and a woman, who both guarantee that the candidate, if female, is not womanly, and if male, not manly." Clearly, Cuthbertson is hopelessly out of place at the Ibsen Club, Shaw's elaborate jest presum- ably intended to discomfort Clement Scott.

Both Gosse and Archer came to deplore what they perceived as Shaw's transformation of Ibsen into a social prophet and his plays into dramas of ideas, Archer contending that Ibsen had "no gospel whatever, in the sense of a systematic body of doctrine." In 1898, Gosse complained that Shaw had been fuming in the *Saturday Review* (March 26) at the bungling among Ibsenites who had sent a "paltry present" to Ibsen on his seven- tieth birthday. Shaw also chided Archer for his poem in the *Daily Chroni- cle,* which expressed the view that Ibsen "will go the way that Shakespear went, which may mean no more than the way of all flesh." Annoyed, Archer wrote to Gosse:

> . . . I have long ago given up reading Shaw, more especially on
> . . . Ibsen—for I quite agree with you as to the harm he does to
> Ibsen and the higher drama in general, while at the same time I
> am unwilling to be perpetually at loggerheads with him. . . .
>
> I quite agree with you that it doesn't matter a jot what Shaw
> or anyone else says—the Old Man has been gratified [by the
> reception of his work in Britain]. . . ."

WITH THE PREMIERE performance of *Lady Windermere's Fan* at the St. James's Theatre on February 20, 1892, Oscar Wilde revealed how the well-made play, which had influenced Ibsen and an entire generation of playwrights, could be revitalized. Wilde used the familiar elements made popular by Scribe and Sardou: the character with a secret past, the crucial theatrical prop (a fan, a letter, a glove), the *scene à faire* (the "obligatory scene" that propels the action to a climax), and the denouement that satisfies moral sensibilities. The Victorian convention of the fallen woman—in Wilde's play, Mrs. Erlynne—continued to be used widely in fin-de-siècle drama, the designation of "Mrs." conferring the appearance of respectability upon a woman with a questionable past who attempts to reenter fashionable society. Other such women in plays of the nineties were Wilde's Mrs. Arbuthnot in *A Woman of No Importance* (originally titled *Mrs. Arbuthnot*), and those named in such titles as Shaw's *Mrs. Warren's Profession,* Jones's *Mrs. Dane's Defence,* and Pinero's *The Second Mrs. Tanqueray* and *The Notorious Mrs. Ebbsmith.*

In addition to the conventions of the well-made play, Wilde also introduced an epigrammatic, dandiacal style of dialogue that denigrates widely accepted cultural attitudes and undermines the moral earnestness of the main plot. In *Lady Windermere's Fan,* "All the men talk like Mr. Oscar Wilde," said A. B. Walkley in the *Spectator* (February 27, 1892):

> Everything is discussed paradoxically, from the connection between London fogs and seriousness—"whether London fogs produce the serious people or serious people the London fogs"—to the connection between feminine frivolity and feminine charms—"nothing is so unbecoming to a woman as a Nonconformist conscience."

The principal dandy in the play, Lord Darlington, like Lord Illingworth in Wilde's *A Woman of No Importance* (1893) and Lord Goring in *An Ideal Husband* (1895), regards himself as beyond the realm of commonplace morality: "It is absurd to divide people into good and bad. People are either charming or tedious." The more likeable Lord Goring insists that "to love oneself is the beginning of a life-long romance." Enamored of his presumed wicked qualities, he remarks: "When I think of them at night, I go to sleep at once."

The ostensibly amoral dandies in Wilde's plays—often aristocrats, whose social status symbolizes their distance from the common man mired in paralyzing morality and thought—express the attitude of many Victorian intellectuals and artists concerned with the growing egalitarianism of the age: namely, that democracy was a political ideology celebrating mediocrity. In *A Woman of No Importance,* Lord Illingworth implies such a view in a conversation with his illegitimate son, Gerald (reminiscent of the dialogues between Dorian Gray and Lord Henry Wotton):

> *Lord Illingworth:* I suppose your mother is very religious, and that sort of thing.
> *Gerald:* Oh, yes, she's always going to church.
> *Lord Illingworth:* Ah! She is not modern, and to be modern is the only thing worth being nowadays. You want to be modern, don't you, Gerald? You want to know life as it really is. Not be put off with any old-fashioned theories about life. Well, what you have to do at present is simply to fit yourself for the best society. A man who can dominate a London dinner-table can dominate the world. The future belongs to the dandy. It is the exquisites who are going to rule.

Wilde developed his dandiacal attitudes into the extraordinary utopian world of *The Importance of Being Earnest* (1895), in which all the characters speak as though they are dandies—indeed, as though they are all facets of Wilde's own personality. Despite its uniqueness in the history of English drama, the play utilizes the worn conventions of the well-made play, though brilliantly transformed: Jack Worthing's secret past and secret identity as "Ernest," the handbag as crucial theatrical prop,* the *scene à faire* involving the unmasking of pretended identities, and the humorous denouement of romantic comedy. In the process, the familiar elements are themselves satirized as dandyism triumphs over the conventional and the commonplace by employing aesthetic rather than moral judgments of characters and events. As one character remarks: "In matters of grave importance, style, not sincerity is the vital thing."

Hamilton Fyfe, the drama critic of the *Times* sent a brief account to the *New York Times* (February 17, 1895) of the opening night, indicating that a London audience did not always consist of the hopeless dullards depicted by some disaffected critics: "Since *Charley's Aunt* was first brought from the provinces to London I have not heard such unrestrained, incessant laughter from all parts of the theatre, and those laughed the loudest whose approved mission it is to read Oscar long lectures in the press on his dramatic and ethical shortcomings." Archer regarded *Earnest* as "nothing but an absolutely wilful expression of an irrepressibly witty personality," but Shaw could not approve of a comedy of manners— however amusing—that remained aloof from society's social and political ills: "I cannot say that I greatly cared for *The Importance of Being Earnest.* It amused me, of course; but unless comedy touches me as well as amuses me, it leaves me with a sense of having wasted my evening. I go to the theatre to be moved to laughter, not be tickled or bustled into it." It may be argued, however, that Wilde's play of masks and seemingly irrational dialogue found their logical conclusion in the Theater of the Absurd, the

---

*Wilde's initial outline of the play (as indicated in a recently discovered transcript letter, to the actor-manager George Alexander, undated, at the William Andrews Clark Memorial Library, Los Angeles) is basically that of the final version of *The Importance of Being Earnest* except for the handbag episode, which was added later. Also, Miss Prism (the only character whose name was retained from the initial outline) is quite unlike the Miss Prism of *Earnest,* for she "has [matrimonial] designs on the guardian"—that is, Jack Worthing in the final version (see the letter published by Peter Raby, "The Making of *The Importance of Being Earnest,"* *Times Literary Supplement* [London], December 20, 1991: 13). Kerry Powell contends that Wilde borrowed the foundling portion of the plot from W. Lestocq and E. M. Robson's play *The Foundling,* which premiered on August 30, 1894, at Terry's Theatre when Wilde was writing *Earnest.* Small portions of the plot and dialogue—though without Wilde's wit—are remarkably close to the later *Earnest* (*Oscar Wilde and the Theatre of the 1890s* [Cambridge, Eng., 1990], 108–23).

plays of such writers as Beckett and Pinter providing a new sense of aesthetic order in a chaotic world.

Just as Wilde invented a new type of the well-made play, Shaw inaugurated a new type of the problem play with the production of *Widowers' Houses* by the Independent Theatre Society in December 1892. Though the earlier dramatist Tom Robertson had touched on social issues, Shaw made them the central focus of several plays, introduced the "discussion" in the concluding act (a device derived from Ibsen), and thereby developed a drama of ideas. While regarding the conventions of the well-made play to be a hindrance to the New Drama, Shaw nevertheless made use of them in *Widowers' Houses*—that is, by employing the exposed secret and the incriminating document that reveal the scandal of slum-landlordism. Shaw denied that Ibsen had influenced his play, but *Widowers' Houses* was, to some degree, designed for the recently founded Independent Theatre Society, which Shaw claimed in the preface to his *Plays Unpleasant* (1898) "would never have come into existence but for the plays of Ibsen." As a modern critic has remarked on Shaw's inevitable revision of history: "Shaw saw his own plays as the heralds of a new dramatic age, for, as it turned out, *he* was the messiah he had long been awaiting."

Shaw's problem plays are predicated on the fact that in the audience, as Hamlet said, there are "guilty creatures sitting at a play." The spectators proclaim their "malefactions" by being jolted into a painful self-awareness of the social problems they had sought to escape in the theater. In the preface of the appropriately titled *Plays Unpleasant,* Shaw remarked that "their dramatic power is used to force the spectator to face unpleasant facts." Following Ibsen, Shaw also cunningly manipulated the stereotypical heroes and villains of melodrama to suggest how such roles were interchangeable—or, at least, difficult to identify—as the result of corrupt values and social injustices. In discussing *Widowers' Houses,* which he described as "An Original Didactic Realistic Play," he remarks: "I have shewn middle class respectability and younger son gentility fattening on the poverty of the slum as flies fatten on filth." Also published in the same volume, his next two plays, *The Philanderer* and *Mrs. Warren's Profession,* dwell, as we have seen, on the problems of sexual domination and prostitution, but other plays in the decade, such as *Arms and the Man* and *Candida,* which appeared in *Plays Pleasant* (1898), shift the dramatic focus from unpleasant social problems to comedies of "youthful romance and disillusion."

Because of the daring subject matter and iconoclastic vision in his plays (or, perhaps, his reluctance to expose some of them to unreceptive audiences), Shaw had few productions in the West End theaters of the nineties. Indeed, only three plays were produced between 1890 and 1899 (*Widowers' Houses, Arms and the Man,* and *You Never Can Tell*). Shaw's

role in the development of the New Drama, reinforced by his proselytizing as drama critic of the *Saturday Review* (1895–1898), is thus all the
more remarkable when one considers that, excluding single copyright
performances,* the three productions of his plays in West End theaters
resulted in only seventy-eight performances, as compared to the number
of productions, including revivals, of three of the most popular playwrights of the decade: Pinero (thirty), Jones (thirty-two), and Grundy
(thirty-six), each playwright enjoying a total of over 2,000 performances
of his plays.

Clearly, then, Shaw's early career as a rarely produced playwright was
principally determined by theater managers who presumed that audiences preferred less challenging fare than his problem plays. The situation in the late Victorian theater is amply illustrated by the fact that in
December 1892 *Widowers' Houses* was given only two matinee performances; in the same month, Brandon Thomas's farce *Charley's Aunt* began
its marathon run of 1,469 performances. When the Independent Theatre
Society rejected *Mrs. Warren's Profession* as too risky even for an unlicensed private performance, Shaw exclaimed: "The Independent
Theatre is becoming wretchedly respectable"—or more accurately, perhaps, interested in its own survival.

The staging of foreign plays—by such writers as Ibsen, Zola, Banville,
Coppée, and Brieux—was a significant achievement of the Independent
Theatre Society despite the fact that it did not immediately fulfill Grein's
expectation, as expressed in *Black and White* (March 14, 1891), that it
would ". . . stimulate the production of a native unconventional drama."
In various articles, Moore had urged Hardy, Stevenson, and Meredith to
devote their talents to the theater, but nothing came of his proposal. With
the exception of Shaw and Wilde, British drama in the nineties remained
conventional: The triumph of the New Drama would have to wait until
later in the decade and in the Edwardian period.

IN HIS 1886 survey of English drama, Archer had contended that contemporary plays seemed to be approaching an Ibsenite realism: "I cannot

---

*Such performances were, in fact, mere readings, as in the case of Ibsen's *The Master
Builder,* described by Edmund Gosse in a letter to a friend: ". . . Heinemann [the
publisher] rented the Haymarket Theatre, put a bill outside, and inside, with an
audience of 4 persons, we read the play in Norwegian. I send you the bill (of which 12
copies only were printed); it marks my solitary appearance as an actor! [Gosse took
the role of Dr. Herdal.] It was odd to think that all this could go on in the very heart of
London, where everybody thirsts for something new, and yet totally escape the newspapers" (Letter dated December 8, 1892, in Evan Charteris, *The Life and Letters of Sir
Edmund Gosse* [London, 1931], 226).

quite lose faith in the ultimate evolution of a form of drama which shall soberly and simply reproduce the everyday aspects of modern life, without having recourse to lost wills and mysterious murders. . . ." Of the popular playwrights of the time, Pinero was the most promising to fulfill Archer's hope. The other leading dramatist, Henry Arthur Jones, resisted Ibsen's growing influence despite his rather daring play—*Saints and Sinners* (1884)—about seduction in a parson's family. Jones regarded the New Drama as "a school of modern realism which founded dramas on disease, ugliness and vice." He also asserted that he had "fought for sanity and wholesomeness, for largeness and breadth of view . . . against the cramping and deadening influences of modern pessimistic realism, its bitterness, its ugliness, its narrowness, its parochial aims." Objecting to Jones's own narrowness, A. B. Walkley recommended that he study the Théâtre Libre: "It would, I trust, convince him that the hope of a great future for the stage lies in perfect freedom; freedom to try every kind of experiment; freedom to be realistic or idealist, prosaic or futuristic, 'well-made' or plotless, 'healthy' or pathological. . . ."

The more gifted Pinero (whose farces *Dandy Dick* and *Trelawny of the "Wells"* continue to be revived) was progressively developing convincing characters and plots by trying to free them from the rigidities of the well-made play. In *The Profligate* (1889), sometimes called his "first true problem play," Pinero condemned the male privilege of the double standard in sexuality, a widely discussed issue of the time in relation to the Marriage Question. In the original version, the repentant profligate takes poison moments before his forgiving wife appears; but in the weakened stage version (urged upon Pinero by the theater manager), he flings the poison from his lips. Pinero defended his happy ending in a letter to Clement Scott by insisting that the issue of suicide would have resulted in the loss of sympathy for the character, an indication that, in the 1880s, suicide on stage remained problematic: "Could not the moral I had set myself to illustrate be enforced without distressing the audience by sacrificing the life of a character whose sufferings were intended to win sympathy? Reflection convinced me that such a course was not only possible but was one which in no way tended to weaken the termination of my story. . . ." Moore commented that if Pinero had had the "strength" to let his hero remain a profligate, the play would have been the best since Sheridan's *The School for Scandal* (1777).

However, the boldness that Pinero had attempted in the original version of *The Profligate* was achieved four years later on May 27, 1893, at the St. James's Theatre with the production of his twenty-eighth play, *The Second Mrs. Tanqueray*. Here, the "fallen woman" emerges as a tragic heroine driven to suicide once her secret life is revealed—an affront to the conventional demand for punishment rather than sympathy. A theater

Arthur Wing Pinero

Scene from *The Second Mrs Tanqueray*, featuring Mrs. Patrick Campbell and George Alexander

historian recalled "one of the most sensational first nights within living memory":

> The daring of the play, the extraordinary powers revealed by Mrs. Patrick Campbell, who, until then, had been regarded as a competent actress, literally electrified the audience and critics. "The greatest play of the century" was the artistic verdict. "The most immoral production that has ever disgraced the English stage" was the whine of the Philistines. Controversy raged between the two parties, clergymen made Mrs. Tanqueray their text; but the work was so great, the acting so striking, curiosity so eager, that the public filled the theatre to overflowing.

Overwhelmingly, the critics hailed Pinero as the foremost playwright of the English theater.

Though Pinero was widely praised for his mastery of stagecraft, Shaw regarded it as one of his weaknesses: "the naïve machinery of the exposition in the first act, in which two whole actors are wasted on sham parts," the clumsy use of the confidant, "the number of doors which Mr. Pinero needs to get his characters on and off the stage," and "recklessness in the substitution of dead machinery and lay figures for vital action and real characters." Shaw concluded that

> Mr. Pinero is no interpreter of character, but simply an adroit describer of people as the ordinary man sees and judges them. Add to this a clear head, a love of the stage, and a fair talent for fiction, all highly cultivated by hard and honorable work as a writer of effective stage plays for the modern commercial theatre; and you have him on his real level.

The Second Mrs. Tanqueray succeeded, Shaw was convinced, because the "commonplace playgoer . . . believed that he was one of the select few for whom 'the literary drama' exists, and thus combined the delights of an evening at a play . . . with a sense of being immensely in the modern movement." In this way, Pinero "conquered the public by the exquisite flattery of giving them plays that they really liked, whilst persuading them that such appreciation was only possible from persons of great culture and intellectual acuteness." After reading *The Second Mrs. Tanqueray,* Shaw remarked that Pinero had "never written a line from which it could be guessed that he is a contemporary of Ibsen, Tolstoi, Meredith, or Sarah Grand."

The success of *The Second Mrs. Tanqueray* encouraged Pinero to write another play about a fallen woman, *The Notorious Mrs. Ebbsmith* (1895), again starring Mrs. Patrick Campbell. He now depicted an intellectual

New Woman, the activist daughter of a revolutionary socialist and atheist, who prefers chastity while living with a promising political figure in a
"free union." Though looking forward to a life of lecturing and writing,
she progressively discovers that her femininity cannot be denied. Disillusionment leads to a renewal of her religious impulses. Characteristically,
Shaw condemned Mrs. Ebbsmith as a stage character, "fully as artificial as
Mrs. Tanqueray herself": "Although educated, well conducted, beautiful, and a sufficiently powerful speaker to produce a great effect in Trafalgar Square, she loses her voice from starvation, and has to fall back on
nursing—a piece of fiction which shews that Mr. Pinero has not the faintest idea of what such a woman's career is in reality."

Shaw's merciless dissection of this play (which he called "The Obnox-
ious Mrs. Ebbsmith") includes the famous scene in which the heroine
flings a Bible into the fire, only to rescue it amidst her screams of pain. But
since she had been raised as a secularist, Shaw condemns this stage business as "claptrap": "As in *The Profligate* and in *The Second Mrs. Tanqueray,*
[Pinero] has had no idea beyond that of doing something daring and
bringing down the house by running away from the consequences."

Though Henry Arthur Jones, like Pinero, was convinced that he understood what his audiences wanted—drama that would be inspirational and
morally elevating—he miscalculated in his favorite play, *Michael and His
Lost Angel.* Produced in January 1896 at the Lyceum Theatre, it closed
after only ten performances. Clearly, the predominantly middle-class audience was unprepared for such an uncharacteristic Jones drama, the plot
of which involves a clergyman's affair with a young woman, his struggle
with conscience, her unrepentant end when she dies in his arms, and his
incapacity to part with her: "I'll believe all, do all, suffer all—only—only
persuade me that I shall meet her again!"

In rehearsal, Mrs. Patrick Campbell had misgivings about the role.
Required to be dressed in jewels and evening cloak in a scene laid in
church and to speak lines that she regarded as blasphemous, she resigned
from the production just days before the opening, creating a sensation in
the press and undoubtedly contributing to its brief run. The affair reinforced the contention of the theater's traditional enemies that the stage
was inherently immoral after all. Clearly, audiences were reluctant to
expose themselves to an experience beyond the conventionally moral.
Shaw remarked that, without Mrs. Campbell, the performance had taken
"all the heart" out of his hope of "gaining general assent to my high
estimate of Michael and his Lost Angel."

BY THE END of the nineties, the modest success of the Independent
Theatre Society resulted in the founding of two more experimental
groups that advanced the development of the New Drama. In 1897,

William Archer, the playwright Alfred Sutro, and the actress Elizabeth Robins founded the New Century Theatre Company, proclaiming that "with the new century a new departure may be looked for in English theatrical life." Archer regarded the company as a significant step in the development of a national repertory theater, an idea that he had been advancing since 1877, when he published his first book, *The Fashionable Tragedian,* concerned principally with the theatrical mannerisms of Henry Irving's acting at the expense of other aspects of play production. Archer (and his coauthor, the theater historian and biographer R. W. Lowe) concluded that "the only remedy lies in a National Theatre, with good endowment, good traditions, good government."

As its first production, the New Century Theatre Company presented Ibsen's *John Gabriel Borkman* in Archer's translation at the Strand Theatre on May 3, 1897. Though disappointed by the staging, Shaw called the play the "the latest masterpiece of the acknowledged chief of European dramatic art," whereas Clement Scott, maintaining his role as Ibsen's foremost antagonist, began his review in the *Daily Telegraph* (May 4, 1897) in his characteristically Philistine manner:

> It was a relief to get out of the gloomy atmosphere of Ibsen, charged to the full with the Scandinavian spirit of sublimated selfishness, and moans and groans and wrecked lives and defiant egotism! It was a treat to leave a grim and darkened theatre and to meet healthy, cheery, buoyant life again in the Strand, where it was all bustle and activity, and boys were shouting about cricket and exhibiting placards. . . . But the Ibsenites issuing forth in a mournful throng were not to be influenced by light or life, or air or nature.

Other than some productions of Ibsen and a few new plays, including *Admiral Guinea* (1897) by Robert Louis Stevenson and W. E. Henley, the New Century Theatre Company led a precarious existence, though in 1904 it sponsored productions of Gilbert Murray's translations of Euripides's *Hippolytus, The Trojan Women,* and *Electra,* which resulted in a significant revival of interest in ancient Greek drama.

In staging its last production in 1898, the Independent Theatre Society concluded after seven years with a record of twenty-six new plays. More importantly, it provided the model for other theatrical societies in London and in the provinces. The most significant of these was the Stage Society, founded in 1899 by such figures as Janet Achurch, Charles Charrington, the Fabian artist Walter Crane, the novelist William Sharp, and the publisher Grant Richards. In 1904, it was restructured as the Incorporated Stage Society. Its chief function was "the search for new playwrights," though it was also committed to producing classical and contemporary plays by foreign authors. Beyond these theatrical goals, the Stage Society, like those before and after it, regarded itself as "an Experimental Theatre unhampered by the crippling influence of the Censor."

Its first production, Shaw's *You Never Can Tell* on November 26, 1899, resulted in a police raid on the Royalty Theatre in order to prevent an illegal Sunday night performance (the society had employed professional actors who were available on Sundays when the West End theaters were closed). The society's contention that the theater was being used privately and hence not subject to the ban was successfully argued in court with the result that in 1902 the first production of *Mrs. Warren's Profession* established the society's right to stage unlicensed plays. In the forty years of its existence, the Stage Society was at the forefront of the New Drama, producing over two hundred plays, including those by Ibsen, Hauptmann, Somerset Maugham, Maeterlinck, Conrad, Turgenev, Hardy, and Yeats. In the 1920s, the society staged Pirandello's *Six Characters in Search of an Author* and Joyce's *Exiles*. *

The impulse to establish a theater group that would circumvent popular commercial drama with its trivial amusements prompted Yeats, Lady Gregory, George Moore, and Edward Martyn to establish the Irish Literary Theatre in Dublin in 1899, a brief excursion into Symbolist drama by Yeats and Ibsenite drama by Martyn. Within three years, the experiment involving such diverse aesthetic aims left Yeats dissatisfied. Back in London, he was determined to establish a theater of romantic drama that would include the occult, formal ritualism, and chanted speech. Previously, he and the actress Florence Farr had experimented with "dreamy and strange" chanting by the fairy child in Yeats's *The Land of Heart's Desire* at the Avenue Theatre in 1894. In 1896, he and Symons had attended a performance of Alfred Jarry's *Ubu Roi* in Paris, the "first Symbolist farce," said Symons. In 1897, Robert Bridges's *The Return of Ulysses* convinced Yeats that this "kind of our new drama of wisdom," with its "classical gravity of speech," would surpass Ibsenite social realism.

In 1901, he joined such figures as the scene designer Gordon Craig, whose designs startled him with their originality; Charles Ricketts, the artist and book designer who now turned to scene and costume design; and T. Sturge Moore, the playwright, in the founding of the Literary

---

Exiles, written in 1915, testifies to Joyce's long-held admiration of Ibsen. When he was eighteen, Joyce published his first prose piece, "Ibsen's New Drama," in the *Fortnightly Review* (April 1, 1900), a review of *When We Dead Awaken*. Ibsen, Joyce wrote, was one of the "world's great men before whom criticism can make but feeble show." Having read the review, Ibsen asked Archer to send his thanks to the "very benevolent" Joyce. In a reply to Archer, Joyce wrote that "the words of Ibsen I shall keep in my heart all my life" (Richard Ellmann, *James Joyce* [Oxford, 1983], 74).

Theatre Club (later, the Literary Theatre Society). The organizational difficulties of getting his plays staged by the club prompted Yeats to found yet another new theatrical group. On March 17, 1903, he wrote to Gilbert Murray, the Oxford professor of classics and distinguished translator of ancient Greek drama, asking him to join "Arthur Symons, Sturge Moore, Edith Craig [Gordon's sister, now also a scene designer], myself, and others who agree in wanting plays that have some beauty" to form a committee of "a new sort of Stage Society." Problem plays would be avoided; instead, such works as Marlowe's *Dr. Faustus,* Murray's translation of *Hippolytus,* and contemporary works like Bridges's *The Return of Ulysses* as well as masques and ballets would be staged.

Yeats proposed that the new society be called "The Theatre of Beauty," which infuriated Murray: "A preposterous name. . . . I shall decline to be on the Committee," he told his wife. Yeats agreed to change the name to "The Masquers," which, he told Murray, "is at any rate harmless." In less than a year, however, the Masquers Society found itself unable to proceed with its plan to produce Yeats's *The King's Threshold* since many on the committee were involved in their own careers or were abroad on personal business. The disappointing number of subscribers was an additional discouraging factor. Again, organizational difficulties resulted in the doom of an independent theater group. Many in the Masquers Society and the Literary Theatre Society eventually joined the more successful Stage Society, which was presenting a varied program of plays and attracting many subscribers. The history of such independent theaters revealed the need, as Archer had long advocated, for a national repertory theater to stage noncommercial drama.

SUMMING UP IBSEN'S significance for English drama in *Literature* (August 17, 1901), A. B. Walkley noted the decline in productions of Ibsen since *John Gabriel Borkman* in 1897: "Is there a single theatre in London which includes a single Ibsen play in its repertory? And has not Mr. William Archer recently had to admit that 'Pillars of Society' has been acted in Germany over twelve hundred times and in England exactly twice?" Yet Ibsen *was* read, clearly evident from the new, revised five-volume edition of his prose plays, edited by Archer, and if "you do not see him 'materialized' on the stage," Walkley remarked, "his spirit is felt to be hovering in the air." Though "Women's Righters" and socialists were "under the quaint delusion that they had found a new prophet," Ibsen made his greatest impact on the continuing development of English drama: "Our serious playwrights must, willy-nilly, go to him to learn their business." There may be, Walkley contended, "no future for him as an acted dramatist in this country," but Ibsen remains "incontestably the greatest" of the "dramatists' dramatists." But Walkley's contention that there was "no future" for Ibsen in England was unduly pessimistic, for in the new decade at least ten of his plays were staged (*Hebba Gabler,* for example, revived in three different years), and productions of Ibsen's plays continued unabated into the 1920s.

Still "hovering in the air," Ibsen remained an inspiration to the development of the New Drama in the Edwardian period. The cumulative effect of Ibsenism had its impact on such an unlikely playwright as Yeats, who had always harbored reservations about Ibsen's theatrical style, one too often rooted in the commonplace. Yet he admired his daring and sensed his preoccupation with symbolism, as indicated in a 1902 article:

> Drama describes the adventures of men's souls among the thoughts that are most interesting to the dramatist. . . . Shakespeare's age was interested in questions of policy and kingcraft. . . . We are interested in religion and in private morals and personal emotion, and so it is precisely out of the rushing journey of the soul through these things that Ibsen and Wagner get the tumult that is drama.

Yeats, who had seen the first performances of *A Doll's House* and *Ghosts* in London, objected to the Philistine attacks on the plays, aware that both he and Ibsen had "the same enemies"—that is, a bourgeois public resistant to artistic innovation and fearful of challenging subject matter. When Yeats wrote *Where There is Nothing* (1903), he adopted some of the conventions of Ibsenite drama: a contemporary setting, colloquial dialogue instead of his customary use of verse, and a hero who, like Nora, rejects a stifling middle-class existence by "plucking off the rags and tatters of the world." Yeats suggested that his play, if produced in Dublin, might even provoke something of the "indignant noise when Ibsen's 'Ghosts' was played in London." He was spared the ordeal, for it was never produced.

Ibsenism, which had had a major impact on the Independent Theatre Society and the Stage Society as a revolt against commercial entertainment, continued to influence other such theatrical groups in Edwardian London. In April and May 1904, John E. Vedrenne, manager of the Court Theatre (later, the Royal Court) in Sloan Square, far from the fashionable West End theaters, staged Shaw's *Candida* in six matinees. Its success encouraged Vedrenne to join with the actor and playwright Harley Granville Barker in a partnership that in four years resulted in thirty-two productions by seventeen playwrights, such as Ibsen, Hauptmann, Maeterlinck, Somerset Maugham, Harley Granville Barker, Laurence Housman, W. B. Yeats, Arthur Schnitzler, and John Masefield.

In the few years of the Vedrenne-Barker partnership, the Court be-

came the mecca of modern theatrical art for an educated audience enthralled by the New Drama, whereas the West End theaters continued to
present well-made plays of intrigue and romance in fashionable society.
Ibsenite innovations in dramaturgy involving new pacing as opposed to
the frenzied style of farce and melodrama and a more naturalistic style of
acting to replace the traditional histrionics of the Victorian stage marked
the Court offerings, which attracted new playwrights intent on avoiding
West End commercialism. Writing later, Archer regarded the years of the
Vedrenne-Barker management as a period of "almost miraculous renascence."

Despite the number of playwrights produced, Shaw dominated the
Court stage: eleven of his plays appeared, the most notable of which were
John Bull's Other Island (1904), *Major Barbara* (1905), and *Man and Superman* (1905). Shaw controlled all aspects in the production of his own
plays: In addition to directing, rehearsing, and choosing performers, he
advised on the sets, music, and props. When Beatrice Webb brought the
prime minister, Arthur Balfour, to a performance of Shaw's comedy of
manners, *John Bull's Other Island,* Balfour was so delighted that he returned for a second viewing with a leader of the opposition and a third
time with the other leader, Herbert Asquith. When King Edward VII
wished to see it, a command performance was arranged for March 11,
1905. Sitting on elegant furniture rented by Vedrenne, the King laughed

"The Dramatists" (Barrie, Galsworthy, Shaw, Barker) (International Museum of
Photography at George Eastman House)

so uproariously that he reportedly broke his chair.

The command performance and the King's response confirmed Shaw's status as England's foremost playwright—an ironic, almost Aristotelean reversal from his status as a playwright ignored by the West End theaters of the nineties. With such acclaim, Shaw was increasingly annoyed by theater managers seeking his plays, as he wrote to his agent: "These idiots leave me in peace for ten years and then rush for me because the King orders a performance at the Court Theatre. They will make just as great a mess of producing me as they did before of *not* producing me. Put them out. Order them off. Call the police if necessary."

With the production of *Man and Superman* (without Act III, "Don Juan in Hell," which was first performed separately in 1907 at the Court), Shaw "entered upon his greatness." He had published the play in August 1903; earlier that year, he had spent three evenings reading it to his Fabian friends: Beatrice Webb noted in her diary that it was "a great work, quite the biggest thing he has done. He has found his *form,* a play which is not a play; but only a combination of essay treaties [*sic*], interlude, lyric—all the different forms illustrating the same central idea. . . ." Combining elements of old-fashioned melodrama with those of romantic comedy, the play involves brigands, rescuers, and the happy joining of the young lovers. Nevertheless, Shaw's brilliant manipulation of the conventional elements of traditional drama and the innovations mentioned by Beatrice Webb indicate the advent of Modernism.

Appended to the play as the epilogue is "The Revolutionist's Handbook," written by John Tanner, Shaw's hero, in the form of maxims after Nietzsche's *Thus Spake Zarathustra* despite Shaw's insistence that he was not Nietzsche's disciple. Nevertheless, Shaw later regarded the "handbook" and Act III as "the new religion at the centre of the intellectual whirlpool": Tanner cannot change the world until he acknowledges the nature of his biological destiny and his participation in it. Revolutionists need a necessary grounding, Shaw suggests, in mystical vision. In time, Tanner will evolve into a figure of domestic bliss, assure the continuation of the evolutionary scheme of nature and society, and abandon revolution. Ann Whitefield, who embodies the Life Force, reverses bourgeois expectations by her aggressive pursuit of the quarry, Tanner, who is unaware that he has been chosen. When Ann learns that the superman has not yet been created, she exclaims, "Not yet created! Then my work is not yet done. I believe in the Life to Come. A father! a father for the Superman!"

In Act III, a depiction of Tanner's dream world, he is transformed into the mythical Don Juan, the philanderer, from whom Tanner has evolved (as had Shaw: like *The Philanderer, Man and Superman* has been called "both autobiographical and apologetic"). In Hell, the superman is a subject for discussion, and Nietzsche is facetiously identified as though he were *Shaw's* disciple:

> *The Statue:* And who the deuce is the Superman?
> *The Devil:* Oh, the latest fashion among the Life Force fanatics. Did you not meet in Heaven, among the new arrivals, that German Polish madman? What was his name? Nietzsche?
> *The Statue:* Never heard of him.
> *The Devil:* Well, he came here first, before he recovered his wits. I had some hopes for him; but he was a confirmed Life Force worshipper. It was he who raked up the Superman, who is as old as Prometheus.

For Nietzsche, the *Übermensch* (or "Overman") embodied a noble, life-affirming morality beyond the decadent "slave morality" of Christianity. His creative passion and "will to power," striving against the restrictions of conventional good and evil, would distinguish him from bourgeois mediocrity. Some of these ideals touched Shaw, who transformed Nietzsche's *Übermensch* into a Shavian superman: ". . . the need for the Superman is, in its most imperative aspect, a political one" since democracy, by its very nature, is incapable of rising above its own level. With suggestions of Galton's eugenics and his own elitist attitudes, Shaw concludes: "The only fundamental and possible Socialism is the socialization of the selective breeding of Man: in other terms, of human evolution. We must eliminate the Yahoo or his vote will wreck the commonwealth."

Aside from Shaw, the most promising of the new playwrights at the Court was John Galsworthy, who, having just revised proofs of his novel *A Man of Property,* wrote his first play, *The Silver Box,* within six weeks. It was accepted by Barker and Shaw almost immediately for eight matinee performances (the usual run at the Court) beginning in late September 1906. The plot of *The Silver Box* is simple and direct, the scenes alternating between the upper-class home of a Liberal M.P. and the bare room of an unemployed laborer, a device that Galsworthy would use in many other plays. The central focus is on the silver box (a vestigial device from the well-made play), which is stolen by a laborer as a purse is stolen by the M.P.'s son. Social injustice—the play's central theme—evolves as the protesting laborer is sent to jail while the son manages, through his father's cunning attorney, to escape being charged. Galsworthy's major achievements are naturalistic dialogue, complexity of characterization, and trenchant dramatic ironies. The reviewers hailed the play as "a triumph of realism," and audience reaction required that the production be given in the evening for an additional twenty-nine performances, unusual for the Court.

By 1907, success ruined the Vedrenne-Barker experiment, which ended in bankruptcy within the year of their optimistic move to the Savoy Theatre and their use of other theaters for various other productions. The smaller Court Theatre was more suitable to the nature of experimental theater than the large commercial Savoy since expenses could be held in check with modest productions. Among its accomplishments, the Court had made it possible for the New Drama to invade the West End theaters, for Shaw was now acknowledged to be eminently entertaining, having abandoned the problem play, and the new native playwrights were prepared to challenge their Continental counterparts. Of particular significance was that the Vedrenne-Barker venture was yet another step towards the fulfillment of a national repertory theater.

With the production of his successful play *Justice* (1910), a realistic depiction of the trial and imprisonment of a young man who has forged a check in order to rescue an abused young married woman whom he loves, Galsworthy was now a box office success in the commercial theater and his play an indication of how far the New Drama had come from the first productions of Ibsen. Max Beerbohm, having assumed Shaw's position as drama critic of the *Saturday Review* in 1898, noted the transformation of drama since the Victorian well-made play:

> We are getting on. Time was when our drama was so utterly divorced from life that the critics never dreamed of condemning a play for artificiality. It is but a few years since they acquired the habit of judging plays in relation to life. And now (so fast has our drama been moving) they are beginning to decry plays on the ground that they are indistinguishable from life.

The New Drama, as pioneered by Ibsen and Shaw, had made it possible for Edwardian plays to appear as though they were indistinguishable from life, for their intent was to depict the real world of human relationships rather than an imaginary one. But as realism inevitably exhausted itself, playwrights sought new means of presentation. The New Drama eventually gave way to even newer drama as such later Modernist playwrights as T. S. Eliot, Beckett, and Pinter regenerated the theater once again with their individual visions of reality, often startlingly problematic, by dramatizing the forces below the level of consciousness in a new mode of theatrical expression.

8

Love in Earnest:
The Importance of
Being Uranian

WHEN WILDE'S *The Importance of Being Earnest* opened at the St. James's Theatre on February 14, 1895, its use of "earnest" as a pun on the central character's name, Ernest, was only part of its intent to satirize Victorian moral earnestness. For the leading female characters, the importance of being loved in earnest by someone named Ernest is essential to their happiness. Homosexual members of the audience probably grasped the pun's other significance in the subculture of the nineties, for Uranian "love in earnest" was love of the same sex.* The term *Uranian* was derived from the name of the Greek god Uranus ("Heaven"), whose genitals were severed by his son, Chronus, and cast into the sea, the bubbling foam around them generating the birth of Aphrodite. The focus in the myth is on the male's creative capacity without the female. In fin-de-siècle London, a Uranian (or the less widely used "Urning") was a male homosexual; as an adjective, the term referred to both adult homosexuality and "boy love." The German lawyer Karl Heinrich Ulrichs, who devised such terms, was himself a Uranian. In twelve works published between 1864 and 1879, he argued that homosexuality was congenital, hence natural.

On the surface, *Earnest* presents culturally approved heterosexual love in a farcical web of intrigue disclosing double lives and the recurrent theme in Wilde's social comedies of an obscure or secret past (a wide-

---

*In Wilde's initial outline of *Earnest* in the previously mentioned typescript letter at the William Andrews Clark Memorial Library (Los Angeles), the character later called "Algernon Moncrieff" is named Lord Alfred Rufford (approximating "Douglas"), no doubt changed to avoid the obvious identification.

spread convention of the well-made play). *Earnest* involves the love of two men for two women, all of whom speak with the artful strategems of dandyism. The play also has subtle indications of Wilde's own sexual preoccupations. For example, in Act II, Gwendolyn tells Cecily: "The home seems to me to be the proper sphere for the man. And certainly once a man begins to neglect his domestic duties he becomes painfully effeminate, does he not? And I don't like that. It makes men so very attractive." This revealing passage echoes Wilde's increasing attention in the late 1880s and early 1890s to intimate friends and male prostitutes, his dining with them at fashionable Willis's and bedding them at the Savoy Hotel while his wife, Constance, was at home with the children. (In *The Picture of Dorian Gray,* Lord Henry remarks that "the one charm of marriage is that it makes a life of deception absolutely necessary for both parties.")

By including numerous references in *Earnest* to "bunburying," Algernon's means of evading social obligations by inventing an ill friend named Bunbury, whom he pretends to visit, Wilde employed a farcical device that paralleled his own secret life. A recent critic has gone further by asserting, without citing a source, that in the 1890s "perhaps the most widely circulated private joke perpetrated openly on a largely unknowing audience was Wilde's frequent use of the term for a homosexual pickup, 'bunbury.' " But the term apparently acquired such Uranian implications *after* production of the play.* Auden, for example, wrote of bunburying: "Whenever I see or read the play, I always wish I did not know what I do about Wilde's life at the the time he was writing it."

In 1892, an open expression of Uranian love with a pun on the name of Ernest had appeared in *Love in Earnest,* a volume of poems by John Gambril Nicholson, a young schoolmaster in his mid-twenties. The first poem, "Dedication: To W.E.M." (the fourteen-year-old William Ernest Mather), contains the opening line: "Some lightly love, but mine is Love in Earnest." A sequence of fifty sonnets traces the poet's love for Ernest, followed by a *ballade* titled "Of Boys' Names: To W.E.M.," in which Nicholson reveals the identity of the unnamed person in the sonnets. After mentioning several names that stir the imagination, he concludes each stanza with a slightly varied refrain: "But Ernest sets my heart

---

*An anonymous reviewer in *Time* (February 2, 1970, page 73) alleged that "Bunburying was shorthand for a visit to a fashionable London male whorehouse," but this assigned meaning to bunburying also seems to be post-*Earnest*. See William Green, "Oscar Wilde and the Bunburys," *Modern Drama* 21 (1978): 67–80. The Uranian meaning of bunburying next appeared in Joel Fineman's "The Significance of Literature: *The Importance of Being Earnest, October* 15 (Winter, 1980), which asserts that bunburying was "British slang for a male brothel" (89), once again with no source cited but probably derived from the *Time* reviewer.

a-flame." (Ironically, a copy at Columbia University, inscribed to Ernest by the devoted Nicholson—"his affectionate friend"—and presumably presented to him, contains many uncut pages.)

Nicholson's pun on the name is a perverse jest on evangelical preoccupations with the concept of moral earnestness. In the dialogue "The Critic as Artist" (1890/1891), Wilde had employed the name of Ernest for the speaker whose earnest views of art reflect current bourgeois concerns. Earlier, in *The Way of All Flesh* (written between 1872 and 1884, published posthumously in 1903), Samuel Butler had anticipated both Nicholson and Wilde with something of the latter's satiric intent. In the novel, the name of the future hero was to be decided upon by his grandfather, Mr. Pontifex, who, in the 1830s,* clearly recognizes the importance of being Ernest: "The word 'earnest' was just beginning to come into fashion, and he thought the possession of such a name might, like his having been baptised in water from the Jordan, have a permanent effect upon the boy's character, and influence him for good during the more critical periods of his life."

Though no evidence exists that Wilde and Nicholson were friends, it is likely that, as one moving in clandestine Uranian circles, Wilde knew what was being published on the forbidden subject. Even in far-off Davos Platz, Switzerland, John Addington Symonds, one of the leading Uranian men of letters, noted historian of the Renaissance, and first English translator of Michelangelo's sonnets, kept abreast of Uranian publications. In a letter to a close friend, he wrote on July 2, 1892: "Have you read a volume of Sonnets called 'Love in Earnest'? It is written by a Schoolmaster in love with a boy called Ernest." On a trip to England later that year, he met Nicholson, whom he liked, but Symonds thought it advisable for the young man to cease being a schoolmaster, perhaps because of pederastic temptation.

The Uranian subculture extended in various directions: For example, Symonds, Wilde, and Lord Alfred Douglas were contributors to the *Spirit Lamp,* an Oxford undergraduate publication, for a short time edited by Douglas. Nicholson and Douglas contributed to the *Artist and Journal of Home Culture,* a publication for the amateur and professional artist that had a Uranian editor, Charles Kains Jackson, a friend of Symonds. When the *Spirit Lamp* expired in 1893, Douglas urged Wilde to contribute to another Oxford undergraduate periodical with a title suggesting a cun-

---

*Walter Houghton has written of the challenges of the Evangelical Movement: "In the 1830s the most sensitive minds became aware that England was faced by a profound crisis. The intellectual world, the Christian Church, and the social order were all in grave peril, to be averted only by the most earnest search for saving ideas and the most earnest life of moral dedication" (*The Victorian Frame of Mind, 1830–1870* [New Haven, 1957], 222).

(above) John Addington Symonds
(University of Bristol)

(right) Oscar Wilde and Lord Alfred
Douglas

ning disguise, the *Chameleon,* which did not survive its first issue in December 1894. Wilde submitted "Phrases and Philosophies for the Use of the Young," epigrams that subvert Victorian proprieties. In the same issue, Nicholson's "The Shadow of the End," a prose poem written in pseudo-Biblical style, depicts the speaker's loss of his sixteen-year-old Uranian love, and Douglas contributed two dream poems (the dream providing a discreet distance from forbidden reality): "In Praise of Shame" and "Two Loves," which ends with the most widely quoted line in Uranian literature—"I am the love that dare not speak its name."

The editor of the *Chameleon* contributed a long story, "The Priest and the Acolyte," signed "X," in reality written by John Francis Bloxom, whom Wilde described as "an undergraduate of strange beauty" (in *Earnest,* the allusion to a "Lady Bloxham" suggests another Uranian joke). The story is derived from a type of nineteenth-century French pornographic fiction involving a priest's pederastic interest in altar boys and choirboys (a traditional anti–Roman Catholic accusation).* Echoes of *The*

---

*Bloxom's story, which Timothy d'Arch Smith regards as perhaps "the first piece of English fiction to echo the firmly-founded French syndrome of the 'naughty' priest," stimulated Uranian variations, such as Montague Summers's *Antinous and Other Poems*

Picture of Dorian Gray abound: For example, the priest tells his superior, who has discovered the erotic relationship, that "there are sins more beautiful than anything else in the world." In deciding on a double suicide, the priest conducts a private mass with the altar boy, which concludes with the drinking of a poisoned chalice: "Never had the priest's voice trembled with such wonderful earnestness. . . ." In "one last kiss of perfect love," they lie embracing before the altar in death. After reading the story, Wilde thought that it was "too direct: there is no nuance: it profanes a little by revelation: God and other artists are always a little obscure."* In short, Uranian impulses required suitable artistic disguise, as in *The Importance of Being Earnest*. Thus, Wilde was most subversive when seeming to conform to Victorian conventions.

In the popular periodical *To-Day* (December 29, 1894), the humorist and journalist Jerome K. Jerome attacked the *Chameleon* for the "undesirable nature of some of its contents." Making a distinction between public and private dissemination of printed matter, Jerome conceded that

> A hundred gentleman or so have as much right to circulate indecency among themselves, by means of the printing press, as they have to tell each other dirty stories in the club smoking-room. Each to his taste. But if the *Chameleon* is issued broadcast, and any immature youth, or foolish New Young Woman, can obtain it, then it is certainly a case for the police. The publication appears to be nothing more nor less than an advocacy for indulgence in the cravings of an unnatural disease. . . .

Jerome's allusion to the right of a "hundred gentleman . . . to circulate indecency among themselves" suggests that he may have known of the homosexual novel *Teleny; or the Reverse of the Medal* (1893), in which Wilde possibly had a hand. Before it was privately printed by Leonard Smithers, who added the sexually suggestive subtitle, the novel seems to have developed in a clandestine manner around 1890, when, according to a former London bookseller in Coventry Street, Wilde brought the manuscript to him with instructions to give it to a friend who would call

---

(1907), John Gambril Nicholson's *The Romance of a Choir-Boy* (1916), and Ronald Firbank's *Concerning the Eccentricities of Cardinal Pirelli* (1926). See *Love in Earnest: Some Notes on the Lives and Writings of English 'Uranian' Poets from 1889–1930* (London, 1970), 56, 119.

*When Wilde was later questioned about the story in his libel case against the Marquess of Queensberry, he was understandably more biting: "I thought it bad and indecent, and I strongly disapproved of it" (quoted in H. Montgomery Hyde, *The Three Trials of Oscar Wilde* [1962; New York, 1973], 104).

for it. In this way, it circulated within a group of several "friends" who may have added portions to it until Wilde finally retrieved it. Whether, in fact, Wilde was involved in such a bizarre undertaking or whether he contributed anything substantive to the manuscript remains uncertain, but the novel contains a revealing passage—odd for a blatantly pornographic work—that underscores Uranian fears concerning exposure, particularly since the passage of the Criminal Law Amendment Act in 1885. Despite his seeming disregard for public opinion, sometimes amounting to recklessness, Wilde shared such fears, particularly after achieving his brilliant success as a dramatist. In *Teleny,* when the narrator, a "sodomite," is threatened with an exposé, he reacts remarkably like Wilde at the time of his own personal crisis: "Today you are a man of a spotless reputation; tomorrow, a single word uttered against you in the street by a hired ruffian, a paragraph in a ranting paper by one of the *bravi* of the press, and your fair name is blasted forevermore."

BEFORE THE CRIMINAL Law Amendment Act, "the abominable crime" of buggery (the legal term for sodomy since the sixteenth century) had carried the death penalty from the time of Henry VIII. During Victoria's reign, however, until 1861, when the law was changed, no one was executed for the crime. In the new law of 1885, with its notorious Section XI, any homosexual act between males, whether in public or private, could lead to imprisonment. The law by-passed the Offenses against the Person Act of 1861, which, though rarely invoked, provided penalties ranging from ten years to life imprisonment for anal intercourse or for the sexual exploitation of those under the legal age.

The original intent of the Criminal Law Amendment Act was "to make further provision for the protection of women and girls, the suppression of brothels and other purposes." By his own investigations into the problem, W. T. Stead, the liberal editor of the *Pall Mall Gazette,* had brought public pressure to bear upon the government to end juvenile prostitution and white slavery. Initially, he made no mention of homosexuality. However, before the bill was scheduled to be considered in the House of Commons on the night of August 6, 1885, he informed Henry Labouchere, the Liberal-Radical member of Parliament and proprietor-editor of the popular periodical *Truth,* that male prostitution was widespread in London. Thereupon, at the eleventh hour in the meagerly attended House meeting, Labouchere proposed an amendment making "any act of gross indecency" by a male "with another male person" subject to one year in prison with or without hard labor. In open committee, however, the term was extended to two years. The far-reaching consequences of this hasty, ill-advised action are summarized by a recent historian: *"All* male homosexual activities were illegal between 1885 and 1967 (when the law was finally rescinded by the Sex Offenses Act), and this fact largely shaped the nature of the homosexual underworld in the period 'between the Acts.' "

Despite the 1885 law, those charged with enforcing it preferred caution. In 1889, the director of public prosecutions believed it expedient not to give "unnecessary publicity" to cases of "gross indecency." The better course was to allow "private persons—being full grown men—to indulge their unnatural tastes in private." But male prostitutes ("poufs" or "Mary-Annes,"* as they were often called) were another matter, for the law, covering any homosexual act, now gave them extended opportunities to blackmail their clients. Indeed, the act was soon dubbed "The Blackmailers' Charter." Oscar Wilde was to be a notable victim.

Before the Wilde affair, the new act plunged several aristocrats into serious trouble. In July 1889, the police uncovered a male prostitution ring at 19 Cleveland Street in the West End, involving some telegraph delivery boys. Among the frequenters of the brothel was Sir Arthur Somerset, then thirty-eight, the superintendent of the Prince of Wales's stables. The prince and Lord Salisbury, the prime minister, permitted Somerset to escape to the Continent, where he lived until his death in 1926. Other clients of the brothel, including some members of Parliament and the aristocracy (associated with the Prince of Wales's son) were also protected from exposure in order to shield the royal family. Those directly involved in the operation of the brothel were tried quietly without implicating its habitués. The press gave virtually no publicity to the affair.

There was, however, a brief but veiled allusion to the scandal in W. T. Stead's *Pall Mall Gazette.* But on September 28, 1889, Ernest Parke, the young proprietor and editor of the radical weekly *North London Press,* gave extensive details of the event from police reports, though without naming the brothel's clients. As the story unfolded, Parke (erroneously) reported in November that Lord Euston had fled to Peru as a result of the exposure. Known as a man-about-town, Euston insisted that he had been handed a card in Piccadilly announcing a performance in Cleveland Street of *poses plastiques,* presumably a more daring form of Living Pictures, and that he left immediately on hearing of the true nature of the establishment (he was later implicated by one of the male prostitutes).

---

*The term was apparently derived from the privately printed anonymous work *The Sins of the Cities of the Plain; or, The Recollections of a Mary-Anne* (1881), which depicts the male homosexual underworld of London. At one point, the narrator remarks: "The extent to which pederasty is carried on in London between gentlemen and young fellows is little dreamed of by the outside public."

According to Frank Harris, then editor of the *Fortnightly Review,* Euston was "the last person in the world to be suspected of abnormal propensities." Euston charged Parke with criminal libel, resulting in Parke's imprisonment for one year.

At the time of the trial, Bernard Shaw wrote to *Truth* on the sensitive subject of homosexuality and the new act with enlightenment and forthrightness rare at the time. Alluding to the subject of both male and female homosexuality in history, literature, and Greek philosophy, Shaw protested

> against any journalist writing, as nine out of ten are at this moment dipping their pens to write, as if he had never heard of such things except as vague and sinister rumours concerning the most corrupt phases in the decadence of Babylon, Greece and Rome. All men of the world know that they are constantly carried on by a small minority of people, just as morphine injecting or opium smoking are constantly carried on; and that wherever the passions are denied their natural satisfaction . . . the alternative will become correspondingly general unless it is prevented by stringent surveillance.

He urged Herbert Spencer and other "champions of individual rights" to join him in opposing "a law by which two adult men can be sentenced to twenty years penal servitude for a private act, freely consented to and desired by both, which concerns themselves alone. There is absolutely no justification for the law except the old theological one of making the secular arm the instrument of God's vengeance." Parke, said Shaw, was being "menaced with proceedings which would never have been dreamt of had he advanced charges—socially much more serious—of polluting rivers with factory refuse, or paying women wages that needed to be eked out to subsistence point by prostitution." Labouchere refused to print the letter.

When the first version of *The Picture of Dorian Gray* appeared on June 20, 1890, in the July issue of *Lippincott's Monthly Magazine,* the Cleveland Street scandal was still fresh in the mind of the *Scots Observer* reviewer: "Why go grubbing in muck-heaps? . . . Mr. Oscar Wilde has again been writing stuff that were better unwritten. . . . Mr. Wilde has brains, and art, and style; but if he can write for none but outlawed noblemen and perverted telegraph boys, the sooner he takes to tailoring (or some other decent trade) the better for his own reputation and the public morals." Wilde responded to the review and to letters from one of the paper's staff in three lengthy letters to W. E. Henley, the editor. The opportunity to advertise his own novel was tempting, to be sure, but the charge that

Wilde could write only for "outlawed noblemen and perverted telegraph boys" apparently signaled in him the anxiety of exposure. The passage of the Criminal Law Amendment Act, just five years before, no doubt contributed to Wilde's attempt to neutralize the effect of the review. In the *Scots Observer* letters, he attempted to reorient the discussion in the direction of several aesthetic principles later embodied in the preface to the 1891 edition of *The Picture of Dorian Gray*—for example, "An artist, sir, has no ethical sympathies at all," and "It is the spectator, and not life, that art really mirrors."

THE CRIMINAL LAW Amendment Act particularly incensed John Addington Symonds. Over the years, Symonds's own Uranian attachments had included schoolboys, young soldiers, Swiss peasants, and Venetian gondoliers. Such choices were characteristic of middle and upper-class Uranians who often felt that "sex could not be spontaneous or 'natural' within the framework of one's one class." Thus, typical partners, besides the usual telegraph boys, were stable boys and clerks. Wilde told Lord Alfred Douglas that courting such young men, some of whom were prostitutes from the lower classes, was like "feasting with panthers," adding that the "danger was half the excitement."

Sexual egalitarianism was central to two other Uranians, Edward Carpenter and E. M. Forster. Carpenter, a socialist, envisioned in his lengthy Whitmanesque poem *Towards Democracy* (1883–1902) members of a new society in erotic terms—for example, "the thick-thighed, hot, coarse-fleshed young bricklayer with the strap around his waist." For some thirty years, he lived with a much younger man from the Sheffield slums. In fiction, E. M. Forster expressed his own yearning "to love a strong young man of the lower classes and be loved by him." Following an inspiring visit to Edward Carpenter in 1913, Forster began writing a homosexual novel titled *Maurice* (posthumously published in 1971), in which he pondered the relationship between spiritual and physical manifestations of Uranian love between different classes. A recent critic has remarked that for Carpenter, marriage was "linked to property, whereas homosexuality exists outside of class and ownership." Similarly, Forster's Maurice and his lover would have "to live outside class, without relations or money; they must work and stick to each other till death." Such talk was "pure Carpenter" and "pure Whitman," recalling the latter's closing stanza of "Song of the Open Road":

> *Camerado, I give you my hand!*
> *I give you my love more precious than money,*
> *I give you myself before preaching or law;*

Will you give me yourself? will you come travel with me?
Shall we stick by each other as long as we live?

Like many other nineteenth-century Uranians, John Addington Symonds felt, as his most recent biographer states, that "one of the great miseries he endured throughout his life was the conviction that he was a pariah, a creature unlike other men." Guarding his own chastity after he arrived at Harrow in 1854 at the age of fourteen, Symonds became increasingly aware of his fellow students' lust. What he witnessed filled him with "disgust and loathing." To his distress, his closest friend informed him of a love affair he was having with the married headmaster, Dr. Charles John Vaughan, widely regarded as one of the most distinguished educators of the century. Soon, Symonds also found himself the object of Vaughan's attentions, which he later reported to his father, a prominent Bristol physician. Dr. Symonds threatened to reveal the truth unless the headmaster resigned and never assumed any significant ecclesiastical post. When he later discovered that Vaughan had been offered a bishopric by the prime minister, he dispatched a telegram warning the hapless Vaughan not to accept the appointment. As a result, Vaughan declined not only one but two other high church appointments.* Thus, a respected member of the upper classes engaged in blackmail, the very crime associated with male prostitutes.

Cultural historians have traditionally blamed the initiation into (or perhaps reinforcement of) homosexual practices at the English public schools on the rigid separation of the sexes and the system of "fagging," which allowed older boys to prey on the younger ones. In the nineteenth century, such privileged institutions as Eton and Harrow were described as hotbeds of "vice" (for which, read "homosexuality"), and scandals periodically required the hasty departure of a master or student or both. In an address to the Education Society on "Immorality in Public Schools and its Relation to Religion" in the *Journal of Education* (November 1, 1881), J. M. Wilson, later headmaster of Clifton College, expressed his anxiety over increasing "immorality," a term he was confident would be understood by his audience as an allusion to homosexuality:

> It must I believe be admitted as a fact that immorality, used in a special sense, which I need not define, has been of late increasing among the upper classes in England, and specially in the great cities. Those who have the best opportunities of knowing,

---

*After Dr. Symonds's death in 1871, Vaughan accepted the lesser post of dean of Llandaff and master of the Temple, thereafter remaining discreetly out of the public eye.

who can from personal knowledge compare the tone of society with that of twenty, thirty, forty years ago, speak most positively of this deterioration. This is not the place to present details of evidence. There is amply sufficient ground for alarm that the nation may be on the eve of an age of voluptuousness and reckless immorality.

Yet there was splendid irony, presumably unintended, in Wilson's assurance that the very boys who had indulged in "immorality" in their public schools had become happy and successful men—cabinet ministers, army officers, clergymen, and respected men of other professions, and nearly all of them "fathers of thriving families." Others were less circumspect than Wilson in alluding to "immorality." Jerome K. Jerome, for example, openly damned the Uranian contents of the *Chameleon* by relating them to life in the public schools: "That young men are here and there cursed with these unnatural cravings, no one acquainted with our public school life can deny. It is for such to wrestle with the devil within them; and many a long and agonized struggle is fought, unseen and unknown, within the heart of a young man." The poet Robert Graves, who had attended Charterhouse, took an extreme view of sexual experiences in the public schools, where, he said, "romance is necessarily homosexual. The opposite sex is despised and treated as something obscene. Many boys never recover from this perversion. For every one born homosexual, at least ten permanent pseudo-homosexuals are made by the public school system. . . ."

To many, the public school curriculum also contributed significantly to homosexuality. As a result of the Victorian revival of interest in Plato, students studied such dialogues as the *Symposium* and *Phaedrus,* both of which expound on ideal love between men and between men and boys. Whereas earlier in the century Plato had seemed an inappropriate subject for study in an age of materialistic progress and utilitarian morality, his philosophical idealism was admired by later Victorians perplexed by religious skepticism, which left them groping for alternatives to Christianity. However, the widespread concern among churchmen, who were often headmasters of public schools, was not with Plato's paganism but with the possible effect of the *Symposium* and *Phaedrus* on impressionable young minds that might be drawn to "unnatural vice." Addressing himself to the issue, the prominent radical utilitarian George Grote argued that the "theory of Eros" in the *Phaedrus* and *Symposium* was a "stimulus to philosophy": "The spectacle of a beautiful youth is considered necessary to set light to various elements in the mind, which would otherwise remain dormant and never burn; it enables the pregnant and capable mind to bring forth what it has within and to put out its hidden strength."

If Grote wrote candidly of Plato's doctrine of male love, others like the Oxford classicist and translator of Plato Benjamin Jowett wrote apologetically to tranquilize Victorian sensibilities. Of *Phaedrus,* he remarked: ". . . what Plato says of the loves of men must be transferred to the loves of women before we can attach any serious meaning to his words. Had he lived in our times, he would have made the transposition himself." In 1888, when Jowett was translating the *Symposium,* John Addington Symonds played devil's advocate by warning him of the danger of putting Plato in the hands of young men. Privately, Symonds objected to Jowett and other interpreters who habitually wrote of Plato's vision of male love as merely metaphorical.

Symonds said later in life that, despite the considerable body of work that he had accomplished, he would have done more if "he had not been blighted by the strain of accommodating himself to conventional morality." His marriage, in particular, intensified rather than diminished his conflicts when his wife suffered from depression after the births of their four children. Edmund Gosse informed Henry James, both repressed Uranians,* of Symonds's private life, particularly his wife's negative attitude towards his writings—a view, however, not entirely in accord with the facts. According to James's notebook entry, Gosse told him of Symonds's "extreme and somewhat hysterical aestheticism, etc: the sad conditions of his life, exiled to Davos by the state of his lungs. . . . Then he said that, to crown his unhappiness, poor S.'s wife was in no sort of sympathy with what he wrote; disapproving of its tone, thinking his books immoral, pagan. . . ."

Gosse's information provided James with the basis for his tale "The Author of Beltraffio" (1884). Whether James knew of Symonds's overt homosexuality at this time remains uncertain, but James informed Gosse: "Perhaps I *have* divined the innermost cause of J. A. S.'s discomfort," and citing a passage in his story that seems to have evoked a response from

---

*Years after Gosse's death, Rupert Hart-Davis reported what Siegfried Sassoon had told him in conversation: "Gosse, though perfectly normal in every other way, had what can only be described as a passion for Siegfried Sassoon's uncle, Hamo Thornycroft, the sculptor." This confirmed Lytton Strachey's jest when asked whether Gosse was a homosexual: "No, but he's Hamo-sexual" (quotations from Ann Thwaite, *Edmund Gosse: A Literary Landscape, 1849–1928* [Chicago, 1984], 194). Leon Edel has written that James's tale "A Light Man" (1869/1884) "brings us into the deeper realm of the homoerotic feeling that Henry must have had for his brother William and which William sensed and feared." Some of Henry's novels, such as *The Princess Casamassima,* depict suggestive homoerotic relationships between characters, but since he had a "highly puritanical upbringing, . . . today we might wonder whether James acted out his capacity for tenderness towards men—but in his catalogue of life homosexuality could be as frightening as women" (*Henry James: A Life* [New York, 1985], 82, 166–67).

Gosse, James entreated him to "relieve the suspense of the perhaps-al-ready-too-indiscreet—H.J." James's intuitive awareness of Symonds's difficulty over his homoerotic impulses may be seen in the story when the young narrator says of the author, Mark Ambient: "I saw that in his books he had only said half of his thoughts. . . . [He] had an extreme dread of scandal." James told his brother, William, that he had heard, "on all sides," that his tale was "a living and scandalous portrait of J. A. Symonds and his wife, whom I have never seen."

To relieve his continuing distress, Symonds sought understanding and catharsis in the writings on "inverts" by such figures as Krafft-Ebing, the Viennese professor of psychiatry who regarded homosexuality as a patho-logical condition. Symonds also read the work of Karl Heinrich Ulrichs, who believed that the Uranian's instincts, in most instances, were inborn but healthy, that in the majority of cases such instincts could not be con-verted into "normal channels," and that such men were not inferior, intellectually or morally, to "normally constituted individuals." Sy-monds's plea in *Studies of the Greek Poets* (1876) for a sympathetic under-standing of pederasty was, he believed, the reason why he failed to obtain the chair of poetry at Oxford University. The offending final chapter was a reply to the Establishment view expressed in the *History of European Morals from Augustus to Charlemagne* (1869) by the distinguished historian W. E. H. Lecky, who referred to homosexuality as "the lowest abyss of unnatural love," the "strongest taint" of Greek culture.

Cautiously, Symonds later disseminated his views in privately printed pamphlets. Sending a friend one of the ten copies of *A Problem in Greek Ethics, Being an Inquiry into the Phenomenon of Sexual Inversion Addressed Especially to Medical Psychologists and Jurists* (1883), he warned: "please be discreet about it." The pamphlet focuses on the "spiritual value" of "ho-mosexual passions" and their benefits to society—as the ancient Greeks understood them—and in the relationship between pederasty and the Greeks' aesthetic conception of religion. Influenced by Ulrichs, Symonds emphasized the healthy and natural aspects of Uranian passion.

Oscar Wilde, who had read *Studies of the Greek Poets* and initiated a correspondence with Symonds, sent him a copy of the first version of *The Picture of Dorian Gray* (1890). Symonds's reaction in a letter to Horatio Brown, later his literary executor, was ironically no different from that of the conservative critics: "It is an odd and very audacious production, unwholesome in tone, but artistically and psychologically interesting. If the British public will stand this, they can stand anything. However, I resent the unhealthy, scented, mystic, congested touch which a man of this sort has on moral problems." Certain passages in Chapter VII of the novel no doubt provoked Symonds by their frenetic, verbal excesses, as when the painter Basil Hallward expresses his passion for Dorian (the subsequently excised passages in the expanded book version of 1891 are here italicized):

> *It is quite true that I have worshipped you with far more romance of feeling than a man usually gives to a friend. Somehow, I had never loved a woman.* . . . Well, from the moment I met you, your personality had the most extraordinary influence over me. *I quite admit that I adored you madly, extravagantly, absurdly.* I was jealous of every one to whom you spoke. I wanted to have you all to myself. I was only happy when I was with you.

Intent upon disseminating his views on "inversion," Symonds had another pamphlet privately printed, *A Problem in Modern Ethics* (1891), which cites the passion found in civilized and savage societies determining the Uranian's clandestine life: "Sometimes it skulks in holes and corners, hiding an abashed head and shrinking from the light of day, as in the capitals of modern Europe. . . . Yet no one dares to speak of it . . ." (could this be the source of Douglas's "Love that dare not speak its name"?). Uranians who could not read German found a useful summary of Ulrichs's untranslated works in Chapter VII. Since, as a follower of Ulrichs, Symonds believed that the inclusion of inversion in the Criminal Law Amendment Act was unjust, "a disgrace to legislation by its vagueness of diction and the obvious incitement to false accusation," he concludes: "The problem ought to be left to the physician, the moralist, the educator, and finally to the operation of social opinion."

THE DISCREET EVASIONS in Symonds's verse, such as references to "comradeship" and "soul-commingling friendship passion-fraught," became code words among the Uranians for homosexual relationships or fantasies. In this, Symonds believed that he had grasped Whitman's intent in the "Calamus" section of *Leaves of Grass* (1855). In "The Song of Love and Death" (1875), honoring Whitman, Symonds associates "comrades thick as flowers" with the concept of chivalry that had emerged from the earlier Romantic Movement:

> *By the sole law of love their will obey,*
> *Shall make the world one fellowship, and plant*
> *New Paradise for nations yet to be.*
> *O nobler peerage than that ancient vaunt*
> *Of Arthur or of Roland! Chivalry*
> *Long sought, last found! Knights of the Holy Ghost!*

The Uranian Edward FitzGerald, later the translator of *The Rubaiyat of Omar Khayyam,* had suggested in his anonymous *Euphranor, A Dialogue on Youth* (1851) the possibility of joining young male friendship to the Romantic concept of chivalry, the spirit of which "keeps men and nations most conversant with what is beautiful and sublime in the moral and intellectual world." When Charles Kains Jackson concluded his editorship of the *Artist and Journal of Home Culture,* he wrote for his last issue (April 2, 1894) an essay titled "The New Chivalry," in all probability influenced by FitzGerald's work (Jackson even alludes to Omar Khayyam): ". . . just as the flower of the early and imperfect civilization was in what we may call the Old Chivalry, or the exaltation of the youthful feminine ideal, so the flower of the adult and perfect civilization will be found in the New Chivalry or the exaltation of the youthful masculine ideal." To justify this new ideal, Jackson combines Malthusian and evolutionary theories:

> The direction in which it is to be found is indicated by the natural tendencies which secure the survival of the fittest. . . . Wherefore the human animal to which the spiritual has been added, will eventually find the line of proper and ultimate evolution is emphasizing that which has been added. The men of most influence on their fellows will be those who are the most spiritual, not those who are the most animal. . . .
>
> The New Chivalry then is also the new necessity. Happily it is already with us. The advanced—the more spiritual types of English manhood—already look to beauty first. In the past the beauty has been conditioned and confined to such beauty as could be found in some fair being *capable of increasing the population.* The condition italicized is now for the intelligent, removed.

With its aristocratic and medieval implications of male privilege, the New Chivalry was antithetical to the liberal views of Edward Carpenter. In 1894, Carpenter gave a lecture in Manchester on "comradeship" between men and between women, a paean to its "intensity (and let us say *healthiness*)," and he subsequently published his views in a pamphlet, *Homogenic Love and Its Place in a Free Society* (1895). One who objected to Carpenter's socialism and paganism, the painter, novelist, and author of "Ballade of Boys Bathing," Frederick Rolfe ("Baron Corvo"), had been discharged in 1890 from the Scots College in Rome, thereby ending his hoped-for career in the church. A fellow student, later a priest, regarded Rolfe as "a liar, an ingrate, a *poseur,* a man without piety and affection, and a sufferer from 'a sort of spiritual myopia.' " In Rolfe's extraordinary novel of Venetian pederasty, punningly titled *The Desire and Pursuit of the Whole* (written in 1909, published in 1934), the autobiographical character contemplates writing a long poem titled *Towards Aristocracy* as a "counterblast" to Carpenter's *Towards Democracy.* In 1918, the prolific but dull Edwin Bradford, like many Uranian poets an Anglican clergyman, responded to Jackson's call for the new masculine ideal with *The New Chivalry and Other Poems* (1918), which contains such stirring lines as

> *Eros is up and away, away!*
> *Eros is up and away!*
> *The son of Urania born of the sea,*
> *The lover of lads and liberty.*
>
> *He is calling aloud to the men, the men!*
> *He is calling aloud to the men—*
> *'Turn away from the wench, with her powder and paint,*
> *And follow the Boy, who is fair as a saint.'*

And in *The True Aristocracy* (1923), Bradford modifies his previous view in propagandizing for the cause:

> *In future aristocracy*
> *Will not depend on pedigree. . . .*
> *But rather he whose heart is free*
> *To love and serve humanity.*

IN THE LATE nineteenth century, many Uranians sought fulfillment of their aesthetic and religious needs in the Anglican Church. Those raised in narrowly puritanical Nonconformist sects found in Anglo-Catholicism a new spiritual freedom and in its ritualism and symbolism a compelling experience associated with liturgical mysteries. (During the 1830s and 1840s, the Oxford Movement within the Anglican Church had urged adoption of substantially Roman Catholic religious practices that had been abandoned during the Reformation.) The nationally approved Church also provided a community for those struggling with their sense of isolation in a heterosexual culture. The experience of male bonding within the hierarchical clergy thus provided many Uranians (or those uncertain of their sexual orientation) with security and purpose in their lives despite the official attitude of the Church towards "unnatural vice." Such affiliations enabled clerics like Reverend Bradford to maintain an interest in homosexual themes by transmuting them into harmless poems, justifying what one observer has called "guilt-free pederasty" dissociated from paganism. In *The New Chivalry,* for example, Bradford wrote:

> *Is boy-love Greek? Far off across the seas*
> *The warm desire of Southern men may be;*
> *But passion freshened by a Northern breeze*
> *Gains in male vigour and in purity.*
> *Our yearning tenderness for boys like these.*

With the revival of religious brotherhoods, "whose members delighted in religious ceremonials and the picturesque neo-Gothic externals of monastic life," the requirement of chastity was a useful defense for those troubled by homoerotic impulses. There were, however, a number of brotherhoods in the so-called "Anglo-Catholic underworld" that had "very little of a normal religious community about its spirit or observances." One of them, the Order of St. Augustine, established a priory in South London in 1872, where Walter Pater often went to observe its colorful rituals and to visit his close friend, a lay brother named Richard Charles Jackson. For his birthday, Pater asked Jackson to write a poem, which reveals Uranian presences amid the presumed holiness of the setting:

> *. . . Your darling soul I say is enflamed with love for me;*
> *Your very eyes do move I cry with sympathy;*
> *Your darling feet and hands are blessings ruled by love,*
> *As forth was sent from out the Ark a turtle dove!*

At Oxford in the mid-1860s, Pater had tutored Gerard Manley Hopkins, who, in a paper written for him, explicated Plato's erotic content in the *Symposium* and *Phaedrus*. As his undergraduate notebooks reveal, Hopkins was already deeply troubled by homoerotic impulses: In one entry, he condemns himself, "Looking at a chorister at Magdalen [College], and evil thoughts"; in another: "Imprudent looking at organ-boy and other boys"; in still another, he alludes to the younger brother of a Balliol student: "Looking at temptations, esp. at E. Geldart naked." Indeed, he abandoned a possible career as a painter because the required drawing of nude men and women might lead to mortal sin. During his years at Oxford, in a world consisting exclusively of young men who often walked arm in arm and established close relationships, the opportunities for emotional attachments to women were restricted.

Acutely concerned with the state of his soul, he modeled some of his early verse after Coventry Patmore rather than Walt Whitman, who, remarks a recent critic, "might have encouraged a side of himself that he did not care to develop." But the ambivalence of his own fascination with Whitman continued in later years, as revealed in a letter to his friend Robert Bridges: ". . . I may as well say what I should not otherwise have said, that I always knew in my heart Walt Whitman's mind to be more like my own than any man's living. As he is a very great scoundrel this is not a pleasant confession. And this also makes me the more desirous to read him and the more determined that I will not."

In February 1865, Hopkins met Digby Dolben, a young cousin of Bridges, who described Dolben as "tall, pale, and of delicate appearance." Having met him only once, Hopkins admired Dolben for his spiritual devotion and physical beauty. Devoted to the Anglo-Catholic High Church Movement, Dolben was a member of the Anglican Brotherhood of St. Benedict in Sussex, and, donning a monk's habit, called himself "Brother Dominic of the Third Order." He was also a poet, one of his poems celebrating Christ in suggestive imagery:

> *Jesu, my Beloved,*
>   *Come to me alone;*
> *In thy sweet embraces*
>   *Make me all thine own.*

In his brief association with Dolben, Hopkins exercised discretion, having no doubt heard of John Addington Symonds's notorious indiscretions in pursuing a Magdalen chorister. In 1863, Symonds was in his final term as a fellow of Magdalen College when Hopkins entered Balliol College. Having suffered a breakdown, as he later said, because of his unfulfilled desire, Symonds left Oxford. The dangers of such homoeroticism were perhaps a major factor in Hopkins's decision to convert from his liberal Anglicanism to the more demanding Roman Catholicism. Victorians sometimes spoke of such a conversion as "perversion," a charge apparently derived from Reformation views that monasteries had been "hothouses of unhealthy friendships between males."

For Hopkins, a devotion to earthly beauty (even when its "inscape" revealed a manifestation of divine beauty) continued to hold a potential for mortal sin. In a letter to Bridges in October 1879 after being ordained a priest, Hopkins revealed the extent to which repression had become a necessity and a desire: ". . . no one can admire beauty of the body more than I do, and it is of course a comfort to find beauty in a friend or a friend in beauty. But this kind of beauty is dangerous." Poetic expression of the beauty of divinity provided him with a means of emotional release in his mystic "marriage" to Christ, as in "At the Wedding March":

> *Then let the March tread our ears:*
> *I to him turn with tears*
> *Who to wedlock, his wonder wedlock,*
> *Deals triumph and immortal years.*

Hopkins's late poem "The Bugler's First Communion" reveals how the figure of Christ resolves tensions between his love of physical beauty and his repressed homoerotic impulses: By celebrating the boy bugler, Hopkins fuses art, divinity, and chastity—the means of maintaining his own state of blessedness:

> There! and your sweetest sendings, ah divine,
> By it, heavens, befall him! as a heart Christ's darling, dauntless;
>   Tongue true, vaunt- and tauntless;
> Breathing bloom of a chastity in mansex fine.

But the circumstances of his life among the Jesuits in Dublin progressively led to depression and crisis. In January 1888, he revealed his anguish to Bridges by alluding to St. Matthew's gospel (". . . there be eunuchs, which have made themselves eunuchs for the kingdom of heaven's sake," 19:12): "I find most against poetry and production in the life I lead. . . . All impulse fails me: I can give myself no sufficient reason for going on. Nothing comes: I am a eunuch—but it is for the kingdom of heaven's sake." Yet (as in the case of the so-called "terrible sonnets" of 1885) the creative impulse thrived in the soil of despair, for early in 1889, just months before his death, Hopkins wrote "Thou Art Indeed Just, Lord," an ironic protest that he was sterile:

> . . . birds build—but not I build; no, but strain,
> Time's eunuch, and not breed one work that wakes.
> Mine, O thou lord of life, send my roots rain.

THE INFLUENTIAL FIGURE of Whitman, intriguing to many fin-de-siècle Uranians, had distressed Hopkins and puzzled Symonds. Calling himself Whitman's "disciple," Symonds wrote in 1890 to ask him about the precise nature of "comradeship" in "Calamus": ". . . do you contemplate the possible intrusion of those semi-sexual emotions and actions which no doubt do occur between men? I do not ask, whether you approve of them, or regard them as a necessary part of the relation? But I should much like to know whether *you are prepared to leave them to the inclinations and the conscience of the individuals concerned?*" He had been reading Havelock Ellis's discussion of Whitman in *The New Spirit* (1890), which voices perplexity concerning the doctrine of "manly love" and "the intimate and physical love of comrades and lovers." The question that Symonds had for many years posed in one form or another wearied Whitman, who replied that in "Calamus" there were no "morbid inferences—wh' are disavow'd by me & seem damnable." Though Symonds now had his answer—a response that deeply disappointed and puzzled him—his admiration for Whitman remained undiminished. The question of comradeship and manly love continued to absorb his attention: In Symonds's essay on Swiss sports for *Our Life in the Highlands* (1892), written with his daughter, a Swiss gymnast responds to his query why gymnasts were so "brotherly": " 'Oh,' he replied, 'that is because we come into physical contact with one another. You only learn to love men whose bodies you have touched and handled.' "

When presumed non-Uranians, such as Kipling, depicted manly love, they clarified its nature with professions of austerity acceptable to conventional Victorians. In *The Light That Failed* (1890), for example, Kipling describes the friendship between Dick Helder, the painter, and Torpenhow, who offers him the tenderness and understanding that the women in his friend's life often lack: "Torpenhow . . . looked at Dick with his eyes full of the austere love that springs up between men who have tugged at the same oar together and are yoked by custom and the intimacies of toil. This is good love, and, since it allows, and even encourages strife, recrimination, and the most brutal sincerity, does not die, but increases, and is proof against any absence and evil conduct." Torpenhow, in his manly way, often hugs and holds Dick, whereas Maisie, a characteristic New Woman, is reluctant to permit Dick to kiss her. When Dick goes blind, Torpenhow cares for him, putting him to bed with a light kiss on the forehead "as men do sometimes kiss a comrade in the hour of death to ease his departure."

In the late 1880s and 1890s, there were many popular novels that, as one critic states, "featured male trios and duos acting as collective heroes," the response to the increasing sense among men that "their prowess [was] being threatened, rather than flattered, by women," who were increasingly asserting themselves. Such male companionship and solidarity were celebrated in H. Rider Haggard's *King Solomon's Mines* (1885), Jerome K. Jerome's *Three Men in a Boat* (1885), A. Conan Doyle's *A Study in Scarlet* (1887), George Du Maurier's *Trilby* (1894), and Bram Stoker's *Dracula* (1897). Because of the Wilde trials, W. T. Stead feared that such emotional relationships between men would be suspected as homosexual. To Edward Carpenter, he wrote: "A few more cases like Oscar Wilde's and we should find the freedom of comradeship now possible to men seriously impaired to the permanent detriment of the race."

The outcome of such complex non-Uranian and Uranian attitudes, derived from Whitman and developed by Symonds and others, may be seen in the sensual wrestling scene between Gerald and Birkin in D. H. Lawrence's *Women in Love* (1920), an expression of mystical *Blutbruder-*

shaft (blood-brotherhood) with Wagnerian and chivalric allusions to "old German knights." As Birkin later tells Gerald with anti-Victorian intensity: "You've got to take down the love-and-marriage ideal from its pedestal. We want something broader. I believe in the *additional* perfect relationship between man and man—additional to marriage."

BECAUSE OF PHILISTINE attitudes, legal and religious considerations of Uranian love rarely proceeded in the nineteenth century beyond the condemnation of its criminal or sinful nature. In 1892, Symonds and Havelock Ellis undertook a more enlightened approach when they agreed to collaborate on a study of "inversion." Until he discovered that his wife, Edith Lees, was having a lesbian affair, Ellis had had little interest in homosexuality. Her startling confession, however, led him to contemplate a study of sexuality, later admitted to be "a mistake": ". . . I had found that some of my most highly esteemed friends were more or less homosexual (like Edward Carpenter, not to mention Edith), and partly I had come into touch through correspondence with John Addington Symonds, for whose work I had once had an admiration which somewhat decreased with years."

Symonds believed that Ellis's medical training would be helpful in their "impartial and really scientific survey of the matter." Their ultimate intent, however, was to bring about a change in public attitudes. (Perhaps

Edith Lees and Havelock Ellis (From Phyllis Grosskurth, *Havelock Ellis: A Biography*, 1980; courtesy of Professor François Lafitte)

fearful that his involvement might jeopardize the project, Symonds never revealed his Uranian orientation, though it became increasingly clear to Ellis.) They devised strategies by which sexual histories could be gathered and informants protected by anonymity. Most of the thirty-three case histories (a method of obtaining data that anticipated modern sociological studies of sexuality) involved members of the upper middle class, an indication of the study's limitations. Soliciting case histories from Carpenter, Ellis informed him: "We want to obtain sympathetic recognition for sexual inversion as a psychic abnormality which may be regarded as the highest ideal. . . . Nothing of the kind has yet been published, at least in England, and I cannot help feeling that the book will do much good." In submitting case histories involving himself and various lovers, Symonds pretended that such material had been sent by other people (his own case history is identifiably No. XVIII). The methodology involved in gathering such "scientific" information was, to say the least, questionable. Nevertheless, as Ellis's biographer has written, *Sexual Inversion* was "fundamentally a polemic, a plea for greater tolerance" recognized by many at the time as revolutionary.

When Symonds died in 1893 during an influenza epidemic, Ellis completed the book, which appeared in German translation in 1896. Determined to publish the work in England, Ellis encountered difficulties over Symonds's name on the title page: Mrs. Symonds and Horatio Brown, himself a Uranian, believed that the book would do little except bring injury to Symonds's reputation. When Brown bought the entire English edition from the publisher and destroyed it, Ellis prepared a new edition for publication in 1897 without Symonds's essay on Greek ethics and without his name.

Designated later as the first volume of the *Studies in the Psychology of Sex* (in 1901, renumbered as volume 2), *Sexual Inversion* begins with a statement revealing the basic influence of Ulrichs, but Ellis rejects the view that an invert has a female soul imprisoned in his male body: "Sexual inversion, as here understood, means sexual instinct turned by inborn constitutional abnormality towards persons of the same sex," though without the element of disease, a view with which Symonds had concurred. Ellis theorizes that lesbianism, treated briefly in only six case histories (Edith's is No. XXXVI), is more widespread than male inversion but not usually recognized as a social evil. Though revolutionary, *Sexual Inversion* was soon opposed by Freud's *Three Essays on the Theory of Sexuality* (1905), which regarded inversion not as a genetic but a psychological condition brought about by a disturbed sexual development involving the Oedipus complex. Rejecting such a theory, Ellis insisted that "any theory of the etiology of homosexuality which leaves out of account the hereditary factor in inversion cannot be admitted."

WHILE SYMONDS AND Ellis tried to provide a scientifically enlightened view of homosexuality by theorizing about its sources and manifestations, other writers had been publishing paeans to male beauty. Their work is populated by beautiful youths whose names—Hyacinthus, Ganymede, Narcissus, Antinous, and Adonis—derive from Greek mythology and suggest Uranian orientations. Edward Carpenter's first volume of verse was titled *Narcissus* (1873); Wilde, by employing the characteristic device of a Greek name for Dorian Gray, suggests the novel's intent, and Lord Henry Wotton emphasizes the Uranian subtext by alluding to him as "a young Adonis" and "a Narcissus."

Uranian verse rarely depicts homosexual acts besides kissing, though glowing descriptions of male physical beauty are common. Often accompanying such verse are expressions of the Whitmanesque ideal of comradeship, praised as a spiritual reality. Also, the superiority of Uranian devotion as opposed to heterosexual relationships is a persistent theme. In one poem, "Philebus" (John Leslie Barford, a doctor in the merchant marine, who took his pseudonym from one of Plato's dialogues) presents the fin-de-siècle opposition between the Philistine and Uranian view of homosexuality:

> . . . *minds more crude*
> *Judge us more harshly still and fain would prove*
> *By their smug tenets how unnatural, lewd*
> *And altogether foul is this, our love.*
>
> *Is it unnat'ral then that I should joy*
> *To join you in the heart of natural things?*
> *To run and swim and ride with you, my boy?*
> *To feel the thrill that sweating effort brings?*
> *To watch with envious love your limbs' display?*
> *Or should I chase some chocolate-chewing girl?*

In March 1894, a debate touching on such preoccupations erupted over Grant Allen's *Fortnightly Review* article, "The New Hedonism." By attacking the traditional concept of religious asceticism and self-sacrifice, Allen contended that hedonism, with its basis in the sexual instincts, was responsible for all that was noble in our nature and in the arts, "those things which raise us most of all above the ape and tiger." Christianity was a "religion of Oriental fanatics" who advocated asceticism at the time of the Roman Empire's decline. The need in modern life was for "self-development," which would make "all stronger, and saner, and wiser, and better. . . . To be healthy of body and mind; to be educated, to be emancipated, to be free, to be beautiful—these things are ends towards which all should strain, and by attaining which all are happier in themselves, and more useful to others. That is the central idea of the new hedonism."

Hedonism would introduce a "new system" to relationships between men and women, sadly lacking, Allen remarks, in modern London:

> An evening walk from Charing Cross by Leicester Square to Piccadilly Circus will serve to show the most abandoned optimist that they are not quite perfect. A system which culiminates in the divorce court, the action for breach of promise, seduction, prostitution, infanticide, abortion, desertion, cruelty, husband-poisoning, wife-kicking, contagious disease, suicide, illegitimacy, unnatural vice, the Strand by night, the London music-halls, might surely be bettered by the wit of man.

The "Strand by night" alludes to the notorious "night-houses" and female and male prostitutes; anticipating current usage, male prostitutes sometimes called themselves "gay" after their female counterparts, the "gay ladies."

Though Allen's list of evils mentions "unnatural vice," the article was attacked in the *Humanitarian* (August 1894) by the Reverend Professor T. G. Bonney, who believed that Allen had condoned rather than condemned such vice. In the September number, Allen responded that he was "a Social Purity man": "I can find no language sufficiently strong enough to say with what dislike and repulsion I regard such vices." In October, the *Humanitarian* carried a further article on the "New Hedonism Controversy," this time by the Uranian George Ives, a poet, criminologist, and friend of Wilde. Ives insists that Allen cannot demonstrate that "classical sensuality" has ever been injurious to "mental purity, refinement of love, or, strangely enough, the poetry of love." The New Morality and the New Hedonism insist that "acts that add to the sorrow of living things are evil, but if they conduce to the world's happiness they must be accounted good." In the same month, W. T. Stead's *Review of Reviews* condemned the implications of Ives's remarks: "The New Morality, which is seeking for a new heaven and a new earth might, I should have thought, have gone elsewhere for its ideal than to Sodom and Gomorrah. . . ." Having followed the controversy, Wilde wrote to Ives: "When the prurient and impotent attack you, be sure you are right."

In his diaries, Ives confided his thoughts on what he called the "Cause," the means by which "all sorts" of Uranians would "work in their particular sphere" in order to transform society so that they could live openly and freely: ". . . if only organised, which we have never been before, we shall go on to victory." In 1893, Ives organized a secret society of homosexuals, "The Order of Chaeronea,"* with rituals, insignia, and codes reminiscent of the Masons, though it is unclear from Ives's diaries how extensively the society reached into Uranian circles. Nevertheless, Ives's efforts on behalf of the "Cause" (and periodicals like the *Chameleon*) indicate that fin-de-siècle Uranians had a new sense of solidarity and purpose. The Order included the poets the Reverend Edwin Bradford, the Reverend Ellsworth Cottam, and the Reverend Montague Summers, the author of books on demonology and witchcraft, the Gothic novel, Restoration drama, and *Antinous and Other Poems* (1907), a characteristic Uranian volume that prevented his advancement in the Church.

Through Wilde, Ives met Lord Alfred Douglas, whom he found charming but reckless, noting in his diary: "I want him to change his life, for his own good, but especially for the Cause, which is sacred to us both. . . . But of course the Cause must not be injured by an individual, however charming." In 1894, Ives often entertained Wilde and Douglas, along with other Uranians, in his homosexual menage at E4, The Albany (by the early twentieth century, referred to merely as "Albany"), a London residence long reserved for bachelors. Bordering on Piccadilly next to Burlington House and the Royal Academy, The Albany consisted of two rows of chambers, lettered A to L on both sides of a paved, covered walk. In Act I of the original four-act version of *Earnest,* Wilde alludes to E4 as Jack Worthing's address, another instance of Wilde's wish to amuse his Uranian friends. In the rehearsal copy, however, he changed the address to B4, perhaps to avoid a too-obvious allusion to Ives's flat (though "B" and "E" are, appropriately, homophones). He also removed a passage from an early draft of Act II, in which Miss Prism remarks that the wicked Ernest must be "as bad as any young man who has chambers in the Albany, or indeed even in the vicinity of Piccadilly, can possibly be."

Though Wilde's cleverness impressed Ives, he wrote in his diary that advancing the "Cause" required a more committed personality: "He seems to have no purpose, I am all purpose. Apparently of an elegant refined nature and talented as few men are, brilliant as a shining jewel, yet he teaches many things which cannot be held and which are so false as not even to be dangerous. Well, I shall find out in time, no one can conceal their real nature for ever. . . . I feel it is a terrible task to fight the battle of

---

*Chaeronea, in Boeotia, is where the Thebans and Athenians were defeated by Philip II of Macedon in 338 B.C. A large stone lion was erected commemorating the victory; in the late nineteenth century, under the restored statue, workers found the remains of 254 men, apparently of the Sacred Band, an elite corps of 150 pairs of lovers bound together by loyalty to their city state. Chosen from noble families, they were pledged to defend Thebes against Sparta.

Our Truth, weighed down by weakness and all manner of littleness, yet when I look at the goal, at the wonderful future which will come to Man, then I remain loyal."

IN THE NINETIES, the poet who had the least social contact with Uranian poets but who surpassed them all in the power and pathos of his writing was A. E. Housman. As a distinguished Latin scholar at the University of London, then at Cambridge University, Housman lived the intensely sublimated life of one who was homoerotic.* Hence, the poems he published in his lifetime lack any direct expression of his Uranian orientation; unlike other poets who included glowing accounts of the physical attributes of beautiful youths, Housman depicted young men facing the bleakness of death in an inhospitable, fallen world. The imaginative landscape of *A Shropshire Lad* (1896) does not therefore contain the special pleading that often informs Uranian verse but such larger concerns as the transitory nature of life, the need for stoic endurance when faced with alienation from "the land of lost content" (No. XL), and the bitter ironies of love and desire. Of Housman's songs of innocence and experience, one of his best known, "To an Athlete Dying Young" (No. XIX), expresses a recurrent theme in the volume:

> *Smart lad, to slip betimes away*
> *From fields where glory does not stay*
> *And early though the laurel grows*
> *It withers quicker than the rose.*

Nature offers no consolation, merely the repository of the grave, Housman's break with the Romantic notion that the earth houses spiritual emanations. In No. XXVI, an indifferent aspen tree, observing the lad and his lass, envisions their inevitable destiny:

> *"Two lovers looking to be wed;*
> *And time shall put them both to bed,*
> *But she shall lie with earth above,*
> *And he beside another love."*

---

*As one of Housman's biographers remarks: "Housman never spoke of his homosexuality to [his brother] Laurence, though he would certainly have received a sympathetic hearing; but Laurence wrote [in an unpublished letter in the Library of Congress] after his brother's death: 'I have known for many years what Alfred's tendency was. He knew that I knew. . . .'" (Norman Page, *A. E. Housman: A Critical Biography* [New York, 1983], 2).

Jesus regards his sacrificial act as useless in such a world. In "The Carpenter's Son" (No. XLVII), he utters his last advice as he is about to be hanged:

> *See my neck and save your own:*
> *Comrades all, leave ill alone.*
>
> *Make some day a decent end,*
> *Shrewder fellows than your friend.*
> *Fare you well, for ill fare I:*
> *Live, lads, and I will die.*

Here Housman's tonal ironies, rather than solemn religiosity, are predominant as the traditional ritual of crucifixion is transformed.

As a student at Oxford in 1880, Housman discreetly suppressed his homoerotic urges for his close friend, Moses Jackson, an unliterary athlete who rowed for St. John's College. When Jackson married in 1887, Housman was his groomsman, but only years later did he write "Epithalamium" (Greek, "at the bedroom," a traditional song sung by young men and women on the wedding night) to celebrate the event and to remind Jackson of their former closeness:

> *He is here, Urania's son*
> *Hymen come from Helicon;*
> *God that glads the lover's heart,*
> *He is here to join and part.*
> *So the groomsman quits your side*
> *And the bridegroom seeks the bride;*
> *Friend and comrade, yield you o'er*
> *To her that hardly loves you more.*

In later years, when Laurence Housman visited his brother at Cambridge University, he inquired about a portrait hanging over the fireplace: "In a strangely moved voice he answered, 'That was my friend Jackson, the man who had more influence on my life than anybody else.' "

On a visit to Wilde in prison, Robert Ross recited some poems by heart from *A Shropshire Lad,* Wilde's first acquaintance with them. Upon Wilde's release in 1897, A. E. Housman's brother, Laurence, also a Uranian, sent him a copy of his allegorical stories *All-Fellows: Seven Legends of Lower Redemption* (1896), "hoping he would find in it something to suit his condition." When the same post brought a copy of *A Shropshire Lad* sent by the author, Wilde exclaimed to Laurence: ". . . you two brothers have between you given me that rare thing called happiness." But before experiencing that moment of "happiness" and perhaps of "lower redemption," he had encountered the dark night of his own soul.

9

Trials and Tribulations

In THE EARLY months of 1897 in his cell at Reading Prison, Wilde wrote to Lord Alfred Douglas: "All trials are trials for one's life, just as all sentences are sentences of death and three times have I been tried." This long prison letter to Douglas, filled with acrimonious recriminations but also impelled by a need for reconciliation and self-justification, reviews the history of their relationship and the inevitable disaster that befell Wilde. But its larger significance was that revelations of "unnatural vice" in the sexual life of such a renowned man of letters were unprecedented in the Victorian age. Indeed, their consequences, amounting to cultural upheaval, profoundly affected the publishing and theatrical worlds as well as the individual lives of many artists and writers. For some of Wilde's friends who had observed his behavior, the tragic plot had reached its climax. Wilde had brought on his own disaster by leading a life of indiscretion. Within ten years of the passage of the Criminal Law Amendment Act, the dandy who challenged the cherished morality of the Philistines not only in his actions but also in his literary works was finally brought before the bar of justice.

The mythic and dramatic implications of this cultural confrontation appealed to Wilde. Indeed, he cites Christ in his prison letter to suggest the equivalent sorrow of the trial and passion of martyrdom, "one of the most wonderful things in the whole of recorded time: the crucifixion of the Innocent One before the eyes of his mother and of the disciple whom he loved." By elaborating on his version of the parallel, Wilde sought to elevate the significance of his own suffering. Wilde's letter to Douglas, then, served as a catharsis in the purgatory of Reading Prison: Its eloquence and imaginative vision restored him from the symbolic death endured in two years of imprisonment for being "unnatural." In his own personal Romantic drama, Wilde now regarded society as unnatural and inhumane, a perversion of nature, to which the former disciple of artifice turned as the only true source of his salvation:

Society, as we have constituted it, will have no place for me, has none to offer; but Nature, whose sweet rains fall on unjust and just alike, will have clefts in the rocks where I may hide, and secret valleys in whose silence I may weep undisturbed. She will hang the night with stars so that I may walk abroad in the darkness without stumbling, and send the wind over my footprints so that none may track me to my hurt: she will cleanse me in great waters, and with bitter herbs make me whole.

IN JUNE 1891, Lionel Johnson brought Douglas, then twenty, to Tite Street for tea with Wilde, who was thirty-six.* Like Dorian Gray, the handsome Douglas was Wilde's visible symbol of eternal youth—another instance, Wilde insisted, of life imitating art. Later, Wilde regarded him as the "true author of the hideous tragedy" of his life, one whom he professed to love, whom he recognized as the central destructive force in his life, but whom he felt helpless to resist. From Reading Prison, he lamented to Robert Ross that the grim reality had replaced the earnest ideal: "My genius, my life as an artist, my work, and the quiet I needed for it, were nothing to him when matched with his unrestrained and coarse appetites for common profligate life: his greed for money: his incessant and violent scenes: his unimaginative selfishness. . . . I curse myself night and day for my folly in allowing him to dominate my life."

Soon, Douglas, or "Bosie," as his friends and relatives called him (a name derived from "Boysie" in his childhood), was introducing Wilde to male prostitutes who were to blackmail him, then betray him at his trials. But as the relationship deepened, Wilde discovered that it was the younger man's father, John Sholto Douglas, the Marquess of Queensberry, with whom he would have to contend. By 1894, the unstable Queensberry had become increasingly furious when he saw Wilde and Bosie together. In April, after encountering them in the Café Royal, he wrote to his son: "With my own eyes I saw you both in the most loathsome and disgusting relationship as expressed by your manner and expression. Never in my experience have I seen such a sight as that in your horrible features. No wonder people are talking as they are." In re-

---

*Within a year, Johnson wrote a sonnet titled "The Destroyer of a Soul," addressed, it is generally believed, to Wilde, whom Johnson condemned for his destructive effect on Douglas:

I hate you with a necessary hate.
Mourning for that live soul, I used to see;
Soul of a saint, whose friend I used to be:
Till you came by! a cold, corrupting, fate.

sponse, Bosie sent him the now famous telegram: "What a funny little man you are." The exasperated Queensberry continued to warn him of the consequences if he continued associating with Wilde.

In October, an event occurred that propelled Queensberry into precipitous action. His eldest son, secretary to the foreign secretary, Lord Rosebery, shot and killed himself. Rumors persisted that the son had feared exposure of his intimacy with Rosebery (whom Queensberry had suspected of being homosexual). Queensberry was now determined not only to save Bosie but also to expose Wilde as an invert. He planned to create a disturbance in the theater on the opening night of *The Importance of Being Earnest,* with Wilde in attendance, perhaps even mounting the stage to lecture the audience on the playwright's perverse sexuality. On that night, he appeared with a prize fighter* as his bodyguard and, said Wilde, "a grotesque bouquet of vegetables"—in all probability, carrots and turnips, emblems of Wilde's sexual preference. Alerted to the plan, the police prevented him from entering the theater. "He prowled about for three hours," Wilde told Bosie, "then left chattering like a monstrous ape" after leaving the vegetables. Four days later, Queensberry appeared at Wilde's club and left his calling card, on which he had written: "For Oscar Wilde posing Somdomite,"† in his haste misspelling the offensive word.

The ensuing events reveal Wilde's self-destructive course, for Bosie, seeking revenge on his hated father, urged Wilde to bring criminal charges against him for libel. Instead of ignoring the card, Wilde lied to his solicitor by claiming total innocence of any homosexual acts. However, for Wilde lying had a distinctly aesthetic rather than Philistine significance. In "The Decay of Lying" (1889/1891), he wrote that he regarded lying as "the telling of beautiful untrue things . . . the proper aim of Art." In the creation of an imaginative world divorced from and superior to the world of fact and bourgeois morality, lying was the means of distinguishing good from bad domains inhabited by dandies and Philistines respectively. Deception, secrecy, and the double life are central elements in his social comedies, and in *Earnest,* lying is the very means by which the superior dandiacal world triumphs. As he said in his prison letter summarizing his ultimate achievement: "I treated Art as the supreme reality, and life as a mere mode of fiction: I awoke the imagination of my century so that it created myth and legend around me: I summed up

*Queensberry's life-long interest in boxing resulted in the Queensberry Rules, which he endorsed but did not originate. See Brian Roberts, *The Mad Bad Line: The Family of Lord Alfred Douglas* (London, 1981), 55–57.

†Queensberry's scrawl has usually been read as "For Oscar Wilde, posing as a Somdomite," but there seems to be little justification for the addition of "as a" after "posing."

all systems in a phrase, and all existence in an epigram."

On some level of consciousness, Wilde most likely assumed that the elements that he had so brilliantly mastered in art could also be controlled in life by an act of will and imagination. Indeed, like other fin-de-siècle Aesthetes, he believed that life should be transformed into art, which existed as transcendent order and beauty. As a dandy, the living embodiment of that order, he was determined to exhibit perfect control in order to destroy Queensberry in the theatrical setting of the Old Bailey Sessions House of the Central Criminal Court.

AT THE TIME of the first trial, which began on April 3, 1895, most of the newspapers were sympathetic to the defendant, Queensberry, who was generally regarded as a concerned father protecting his young son. *Reynold's Weekly Newspaper,* one of the few papers partial to Wilde, had offered the minority opinion on March 3 that Wilde "had been the object of a most cruel persecution at the hands of Lord Queensberry." On the witness stand, Wilde gave an extraordinary performance. For one who was an overt Uranian pretending to be innocent of *posing* as a sodomite, Wilde exhibited a mask of grandiose invulnerability reinforced, undoubtedly, by the success of his two comedies, *An Ideal Husband* and *Earnest,* both playing at the time to packed houses in the West End. He could not, apparently, grasp the disparity between his dandiacal composure and his obvious guilt or the potential danger that might at any moment destroy him. As the defense attorney mentioned the names of young men who had earlier blackmailed Wilde and who would testify against him (the result of Queensberry's success, with the help of private detectives who apparently threatened or bribed these crucial witnesses), there were now urgent reasons for Wilde's counsel to drop the suit. On the same day, April 5, Wilde was arrested on the basis of documentation provided to the public prosecutor by Queensberry that Wilde was guilty of more than merely posing as a sodomite.

Wilde's arrest precipitated an extraordinary panic in London literary and social circles. Henry Harland, the literary editor of the *Yellow Book,* informed Edmund Gosse: "Do you know that on the night of Wilde's arrest 600 gentlemen crossed from Dover to Calais? The average number is 60." If this was exaggeration, local wits pressed on with rumors that every suitcase in London was packed for instant flight. More serious, in one newspaper, Wilde's arrest was emblazoned in misleading headlines: "WILDE ARRESTED: YELLOW BOOK UNDER HIS ARM." Since John Lane's Bodley Head published not only Wilde's works but also the periodical presumably alluded to and since Beardsley's illustrations for *Salome* and the *Yellow Book* were beyond respectability, some popular

Bodley Head authors—notably the poet William Watson and the journalist Wilfrid Meynell, husband of the poet Alice—insisted that if Beardsley were not dropped as art editor of the *Yellow Book,* they would withdraw their books from the firm. But when arrested, Wilde had not carried the notorious periodical with him but, it has been said, a French novel with a yellow cover.*

In New York at the time, Lane instructed his business manager, Frederick Chapman, to remove Beardsley's drawings from the April issue, which was due on the sixteenth; as for Beardsley's position as art editor, Lane "left the decision to Chapman, suggesting he take the advice of Watson and Meynell." In Paris on holiday, Harland was unaware that Chapman was sacking Beardsley. From the offices of the Bodley Head, the subeditor and contributor to the periodical, Ella D'Arcy, jocularly described how she had to contend with Chapman's "ingrained melancholy"† and the sudden changes required in the next issue just as she was growing accustomed to Beardsley's presence: ". . . and I, who for the last year, have been struggling heroically to acquire a taste for Beardsley's work—incited thereunto mostly by you, isn't it true? for have you not praised Beardsley's drawings, when I, poor, ignorant, Philistine that I am, have seen nothing in them but repellancy?" D'Arcy expresses her mock despair at the significance of the cultural crisis that she had endured: "Oh, this is a weird world, and I'm inclined to give up Art and Literature altogether (since they seem inseparable from Decadence) and go back to the comfortably prosaic circles of suburban grocers from which I so (foolishly) came."

As might be expected, the press lost few opportunities to exploit the crisis at the *Yellow Book.* Perhaps the wittiest of the satiric effusions appeared in the weekly paper the *World* under the pseudonym of "Testudo" (Mostyn Piggott), who composed "The Second Coming of Arthur: A Certain Past Adapted to a Possible Future." Echoing Lewis Carroll's

---

*In "The Arrest of Oscar Wilde at the Cadogan Hotel" (1937), John Betjeman immortalizes the moment, though Wilde is not depicted as carrying either the periodical or the French novel under his arm:

> *He rose, and he put down* The Yellow Book.
> *He staggered—and, terrible-eyed,*
> *He brushed past the palms on the staircase*
> *And was helped to a hansom outside.*

See Betjeman, *Collected Poems* (Boston, 1971), 18–19.

†In later years, D'Arcy told Katherine L. Mix: "If Harland had only been at the Bodley Head everything would have been different. He would have made Chapman wait until Lane got back. But Chapman was a little man and he didn't like Beardsley. He took this opportunity to be important" (quoted in Mix, *A Study in Yellow: The Yellow Book and Its Contributors* [Lawrence, Kansas, 1960], 145).

"jabberwocky" and recalling the prophecy that King Arthur would return to save an endangered Britain, the comic analogy depicts Arthur—representing the forces of respectability, the "Philerotes" (Philistines)—returning to confront the "Yallerbock," associated with the "Aub-Aub Bird" (Aubrey Beardsley), "the stumious Beerbomax" (Max Beerbohm), and the "Daycadongs" (Decadents):

> 'Twas rollog, and the minim potes
>   Did mime and mimble in the cafe;
> All footly were the Philerotes,
>   And Daycadongs outstrafe.
>
> Beware the Yallerbock, my son!
>   The aims that rile, the art that racks,
> Beware the Aub-Aub Bird and shun
>   The stumious Beerbomax.

Excalibur in hand, the heroic Arthur succeeds in destroying the Yallerbock that "Came piffling through the Headley Bod" (the Bodley Head).

As a result of Wilde's arrest, the worried T. Fisher Unwin, the publisher of Edward Carpenter's *Towards Democracy,* demanded that Carpenter remove the stock of his books from the firm's premises. Subsequently, Carpenter obtained a new publisher for the remaining part of his work. At the time that Lane and Unwin moved to disassociate themselves from all implications of Wildean vice, much of the London press reveled in Wilde's downfall, as though cultural health had been miraculously restored to Victorian society. The *Echo* (April 5), an evening paper, announced that Queensberry was "triumphant" and that Wilde was "damned and done for": "He appears to have illustrated in his life the beauty and truthfulness of his teachings. He said in cross-examination that he considered there was no such thing as morality, and he seems to have harmonized his practice with his theory." W. E. Henley's *National Observer* (April 6), the stronghold of anti-Decadence, was perhaps most ferocious in its condemnation not only of Wilde but also of the avant-garde:

> There is not a man or woman in the English-speaking world possessed of the treasure of a wholesome mind who is not under a deep debt of gratitude to the Marquess of Queensberry for destroying the High Priest of the Decadents. The obscene imposter, whose prominence has been a social outrage ever since he transferred from Trinity Dublin to Oxford his vices, his follies, and his vanities, has been exposed, and that thoroughly at last.

The *Daily Telegraph* (April 6, 1895) also attacked Wilde but focused upon a familiar source of what many late Victorians regarded as cultural pathology: The aestheticism from France that had imported into "healthy and honest English art and life the pagan side of bygone times, with all its cynicism, scepticism, and animalism. . . . Everybody can see and read for himself, and every honest and wholesome-minded Englishman must grieve to notice how largely this French and Pagan plague has filtered into the healthy fields of British life." As a result, French aestheticism—with the "showy paradoxes and false glitter of this school of poseurs"—had undermined "the sanctity and sweetness of the home." To the editor of one of the more virulent papers, the *Star* (April 20, 1895), Bosie protested that the press had already tried Wilde: ". . . his case has been almost hopelessly prejudiced in the eyes of the public from whom the jury who must try his case will be drawn, and that he is practically delivered over to the fury of a cowardly and brutal mob." Again, here was a Uranian pretending innocence on behalf of his lover, both of whom were guilty under the existing law.

With Wilde's arrest, two London theaters were faced with the dilemma of either continuing with *An Ideal Husband* and *Earnest* or withdrawing them. At the Theatre Royal, *An Ideal Husband,* which had been running since January, closed on April 6, the day after Wilde's arrest. Though a closing notice had already been posted to permit a new play to open, there is little doubt that the theater manager thought it prudent to end its run immediately. Without Wilde's name on either the playbill or program, it reopened at the Criterion Theatre on April 13 and closed on April 27. At the St. James's Theatre, *Earnest,* also with Wilde's name suppressed, continued running until May 8. The removal of Wilde's name prompted a protest from the playwright Sydney Grundy in a letter to the *Daily Telegraph* (April 8). That Wilde's two plays continued in production after his arrest indicates that there were many in London who went to see them despite the sensationalism surrounding the trials or who went out of curiosity. Nevertheless, the actor-manager George Alexander, who created the role of Jack Worthing in *Earnest,* insisted that Wilde's arrest had resulted in a loss of £300 on the production.

In addition to the public reaction to Wilde's arrest, the broad spectrum of responses in personal correspondence of the time ranged from a sense of the appalling waste of genius to facetiously defensive posing. On April 8, Henry James told Edmund Gosse that the case was "hideously, atrociously dramatic and really interesting," though it also had "a sickening horribility":

> But the *fall*—from nearly twenty years of a really unique kind of "brilliant" conspicuity (wit, "art," conversation—"one of our

two or three dramatists, etc.") to that sordid prison-cell and this gulf of obscenity over which the ghoulish public hangs and gloats—it is beyond any utterance of irony or any pang of compassion! He was never in the smallest degree interesting to me—but this hideous human history has made him so—in a manner.

After sealing the envelope, James, in an afterthought, wrote across the back in French that it was a pity and a blessing that John Addington Symonds was no longer in this world. Untouched by the tragic element of Wilde's fall or lacking James's complex response, Robert Bridges delighted in Wilde's disgrace, not because of "unnatural vice" but because of the Aesthete's effect on contemporary art: "I am very glad that Oscar Wilde is quite shown up. No one has done more harm to art than he in the last 20 years. I did not know he was so bad, but I confess that I have a grain of satisfaction in the collapse of the traducer of idealism." The irony of Bridges's remark is that Wilde had always thought of himself as an idealist but in the service of causes of which Bridges obviously disapproved. *Punch* (April 13, 1895), defender of the bourgeois life and opponent of the avant-garde, provided a characteristic poem echoing Bridges's attitude towards Wilde, who remains unmentioned but alluded to as one of the "aesthete-hierophants [who] fair Art betray":

> *And shall the sweet and kindly Muse be shamed*
> *By unsexed 'Poetry' that defiles your page?*
> *Has Art a mission that may not be named,*
> *With 'scarlet sins' to enervate the age?*
>
> *If such be 'Artists,' then may Philistines*
> *Arise, plain sturdy Britons as of yore,*
> *And sweep them off and purge away the signs*
> *That England e'er such noxious offspring bore!*

Still smarting, perhaps, by his firing from the *Yellow Book*, Aubrey Beardsley, whose friendship with Wilde had progressively soured since the difficulties over his illustrations for *Salome*, wrote to the satirist Ada Leverson: "I look forward eagerly to the first act of Oscar's new Tragedy. But surely the title *Douglas* has been used before" (*Douglas*, a romantic tragedy by John Home, had been a success in 1756). And in a letter to the bisexual Herbert Horne, the editor of the *Century Guild Hobby Horse*, the heterosexual Arthur Symons wrote facetiously of his own behavior to assure him that he was living an exemplary life at a time when Wilde's friends and acquaintances were all now suspect:

For me, I have carried out your wishes in living a quiet and virtuous life. I have been nowhere, seen nothing; in fact, I have stayed in so much that I have broken one of the castors of my sofa and two of the springs. If M[uriel Broadbent, a prostitute he had met at the Empire Theatre] tells you that we discussed S-d-my at the Empire, don't believe her. If [Will] Rothenstein tells you he saw me in earnest conversation with a small, but comely, person in a remote neighbourhood at a late hour, and that, with his usual fine sense of fitness, he yelled out "Arthur Symons!" don't believe him. . . . I have corrected a few proofs, had dinner every few days, and said my prayers when I didn't forget them.

THE SECOND TRIAL, now with Wilde as defendant, opened on April 26. Before it began, Wilde's counsel, Sir Edward Clarke, advised Bosie to leave London since his continued presence in the courtroom might be misconstrued by judge and jury. His name had been mentioned in the first trial in connection with various letters with erotic overtones written to him by Wilde. The trial covered much familiar ground, but the appearance of the young blackmailers associated with Wilde complicated the picture and placed him in increasing jeopardy. A bright moment occurred when Wilde gave his celebrated speech on Uranian love after the prosecutor had stated that such love was "unnatural":

> "The love that dare not speak its name" in this century is such a great affection of an elder for a younger man as there was between David and Jonathan, such as Plato made the very basis of his philosophy, and such as you find in the sonnets of Michelangelo and Shakespeare. It is that deep, spiritual affection that is as pure as it is perfect. . . . It is beautiful, it is fine, it is the noblest form of affection. There is nothing unnatural about it. . . . The world mocks at it and sometimes puts one in the pillory for it.

A burst of applause mingled with hisses filled the courtroom, requiring the judge to warn the spectators against any further disturbances. Max Beerbohm, who had spent the day at the trial, told Reginald Turner that Wilde was "simply wonderful and carried the whole court right away. . . . Here was this man, who had been for a month in prison and loaded with insults and crushed and buffeted, perfectly self-possessed, dominating the Old Bailey with his fine presence and musical voice." Wilde never modified his attitude toward homosexuality, which he implied was "Platonic" but in fact was physical. In a letter to Robert Ross, Wilde wrote after his release from prison: "To have altered my life would have been to have admitted that Uranian love is ignoble. I hold it to be noble—more noble than other forms."

Faced with possible perjury from at least one witness and with evidence provided by obvious blackmailers, the jury was deadlocked. Wilde now had to submit to another ordeal in the Old Bailey. William Archer, who had praised *Earnest,* wrote to his brother: "Really the luck is against the poor British drama—the man who has more brains in his little finger than all the rest of them in their whole body goes and commits worse than suicide in this way. However, it shows that what I hoped for in Oscar could never have come about—I thought he might get rid of his tomfoolery and affectation and do something really fine." The *Pall Mall Gazette* (May 2), regretting the hung jury, lamented: "Once again the country will be flooded with a mass of filthy details. . . . For our part, unless there are what is called fresh developments, we shall decline to report the case at all. Most men who know anything of the world have made up their minds on the moral, if not the criminal, aspect of the case. . . ." In Paris, Harland and his wife had been following the newspaper coverage of "poor Oscar" and "the story of his ruin with the keenest pain," as he wrote to Gosse:

> I suppose he *is* ruined, even though he may not be convicted. The case for the prosecution can never be stronger than it was. Yet, if a first jury disagreed, it is hardly likely that a second jury will convict. It seems to us a pity that the law should take cognizance of a man's private morals, his vices, his bad tastes. . . . But, dear me, if all the men of Oscar's sort in England were suddenly to be clapped into gaol, what miles of new prison-houses Her Majesty would have to build, and what gaps would be left in the ranks of artists, statesmen, and men o' letters!

On May 7, Wilde was released on bail, his first taste of freedom since his arrest on April 5. His sureties, each of whom provided £1250, were Bosie's elder brother and the Reverend Stewart Headlam, with whom Wilde had previously had only a passing acquaintance. For his generosity, a mob threatened Headlam outside his Bloomsbury house. In the *Church Reformer* (June 1, 1895), he defended his action by protesting that most of the press as well as the theater managers and publishers were, by their actions, prejudicial to Wilde's defense before the trial had begun: "I was a surety, not for his character, but for his appearance in Court to stand his trial. . . . My confidence in his honour and manliness has been fully justified by the fact that (if rumour be correct), notwithstanding strong inducements to the contrary, he stayed in England and faced his trial."

Once the formalities for his release were completed at the Bow Street Magistrates' Court, Wilde proceeded to the Midland Hotel, St. Pancras, where rooms had been reserved for him, probably by Headlam. As he was about to dine, the manager abruptly opened the door to the sitting-room and confronted him: "You are Oscar Wilde, I believe." When he acknowledged his identity, the manager insisted that he leave at once. This was Queensberry's doing: he had hired thugs to trail Wilde and prevent him from obtaining rooms in any hotel in town or in the suburbs. Exhausted, Wilde found his way to his mother's house in Oakley Street, Chelsea, where she was living with Oscar's elder brother, Willie. As Willie melodramatically described the scene, Oscar collapsed on the threshold "like a wounded stag," then staggered into the narrow hall and sank into a chair, pleading: "Willie, give me a shelter or I shall die in the streets."

Many of Wilde's friends urged him to jump bail and escape to the Continent. Indeed, Bosie's elder brother informed Headlam that he would willingly bear the entire amount of the bail if Wilde fled: "It will practically ruin me if I lose all that money at the present moment, but if there is a chance even of a conviction, for God's sake let him go." Wilde's wife, Constance, also pleaded with him to leave London. Yeats informed a correspondent that a yacht and "a very large sum of money" had been offered to Wilde to flee London, but he refused to go. To Bosie, Wilde expressed the Victorian ideal of moral earnestness at the ironic moment of his criminal trial: "I decided that it was nobler and more beautiful to stay. . . . A dishonoured name, a disguise, a hunted life, all that is not for me. . . ." Yeats never doubted that Wilde had made the "right decision," to which he owed "half of his renown."

THE THIRD TRIAL began on May 22 and ended with a conviction on May 25.* Immediately following the jury's verdict, the presiding judge sentenced Wilde to two years at hard labor. Yeats noted that, when the verdict was announced, "the harlots in the street outside danced upon the pavement." One of the few popular newspapers sympathetic to Wilde, the *Illustrated Police Budget* (June 1, 1895), referred to him as "a talented man, a learned scholar, and a great dramatist going to his doom. . . . No matter how one might deplore the criminal actions for which he was justly

---

*Shaw later wrote: "Oscar Wilde, being a convinced pederast, was entirely correct in his plea of Not Guilty; but he was lying when he denied the facts; and the jury, regarding pederasty as abominable, quite correctly found him Guilty" (letter to the *Times Literary Supplement,* March 2, 1940; rpt. in *Agitations: Letters to the Press, 1875–1950,* eds. Dan H. Laurence and James Rambeau [New York, 1985], 316).

found guilty, it was impossible to keep down a certain amount of pity."
The reporter, carried away by the "final scene" in the courtroom, remarked that even Queensberry could not help "in his heart pitying the
prisoner when he looked at the awful agony depicted on his face when he
heard his fate." In the *Free Review* (June 1, 1895), Ernest Newman, later
an authority on Wagner, praised Wilde's genius for paradox and asserted
that when the "stupid" and "prejudiced" British public "howls a man
down or grins him down, he is certain to be possessed of genius. . . . It is
very hard to say anything original about genius, and still harder to say
anything original about the British public." Echoing Newman's attack on
the "prejudiced" British public, Max Beerbohm remarked in the *Daily
Chronicle* (August 12, 1895) that the "tragedy and ruin of the most distinguished of the aesthetes has given the public its cue. 'Art,' it cries, 'is all
wickedness.' It dives into the pages of the genial Nordau. 'Art,' it cries, 'is
all madness. We were quite right after all. . . .' Now this, it seems to me, is
the extent of the revolution—that the public need pretend no longer."

When W. T. Stead observed that a major portion of the press was
congratulating itself on Wilde's conviction, he raised the question in the
Review of Reviews (June 1895) of society's inequity concerning punishment for sexual acts:

> If Oscar Wilde, instead of indulging in dirty tricks of indecent
> familiarity with boys and men, had ruined the lives of half a
> dozen innocent simpletons of girls, or had broken up the home
> of his friend by corrupting his friend's wife, no one could have
> laid a finger upon him. The male is sacro-sanct: the female is fair
> game. To have burdened society with a dozen bastards, to have
> destroyed a happy home by his lawless lust—of these things the
> criminal law takes no account.

Stead then pointed to a discrepancy between punishing Wilde's "vice"
and "the tacit universal acquiescence" of the same behavior in the public
schools (something no other journalist had dared to raise): "It is to be
hoped that our headmasters will pluck up a little courage from the result
of the Wilde trial, and endeavour to rid our Protestant schools of a foul
and unnatural vice which is not found in Catholic establishments, at all
events in this country."

Though it has often been said that publishers would not touch Wilde's
writings after the trials, two of his works were, in fact, reissued in 1895.
On May 30, just five days after his conviction, Arthur L. Humphreys, the
manager of Hatchard's bookshop in Piccadilly, issued fifty copies of the
essay *The Soul of Man* (omitting *under Socialism*), and Ward, Lock, &
Bowden Ltd., the publisher of the second edition of *The Picture of Dorian*

Gray, reissued it in October, presumably to capitalize on its renewed
notoriety (at the trials, the prosecution had charged that the novel was
immoral). In both works, Wilde's name appeared on the title page. However, Wilde's conviction may have led to the suppression of other writers'
works. On June 6, George Gissing recorded in his diary that "owing to
the reaction consequent on the Wilde case," two publishers had refused
to publish a book by Grant Allen, "greatly to his astonishment." Allen, to
be sure, was not associated with the Decadents, but in the previous year
he had advocated the New Hedonism, and earlier in 1895 *The Woman
Who Did* had depicted a "free union" of lovers.

In evaluating the cultural implications of the Wilde trials, Havelock
Ellis concluded that they appeared "to have generally contributed to give
definiteness and self-consciousness to the manifestations of homosexuality, and have aroused inverts to take up a definite stand." The "Cause,"
however, had already achieved an identity and a purpose, as George
Ives's diaries reveal, among those in the Uranian subculture of the fin de
siècle. Unquestionably, the trials intensified the sense of social isolation
for Uranians; what emerged, as a modern historian has suggested, was "a
sense of self rather than of oppression. But it was an essential step in the
evolution of a modern homosexual consciousness."

Still, for those troubled by homoerotic impulses, we can safely assume
that the Wilde debacle produced new anxieties. An indication of the
emotional climate may be seen in A. E. Housman's reaction to a newspaper item reporting the suicide on August 6, 1895, of a nineteen-year-old
cadet at the Royal Military Academy in Woolwich. He had left a long
letter to the coroner explaining that he was ending his life after "several
weeks of careful deliberation," citing two reasons for his decision:

> The first is utter cowardice and despair. There is only one thing
> in this world which would make me thoroughly happy; that one
> thing I have no earthly hope of obtaining. The second—which I
> wish was the only one—is that I have absolutely ruined my own
> life; but I thank God that as, so far as I know, I have not morally
> injured, or "offended," as it is called in the Bible, anyone else.
> Now I am quite certain that I could not live another five years
> without doing so, and for that reason alone, even if the first did
> not exist, I should do what I am doing. . . . At all events it is final,
> and consequently better than a long series of sorrows and dis-
> graces.

Laurence Housman recalled seeing the article on the cadet in a copy of
his brother's *A Shropshire Lad* (1896) alongside poem No. XLIV, inspired by the suicide:

Shot? so quick, so clean an ending?
  Oh that was right, lad, that was brave:
Yours was not an ill for mending,
  'Twas best to take it to the grave.

Oh soon, and better so than later
  After long disgrace and scorn,
You shot dead the household traitor,
  The soul that should not have been born.

Since the young cadet's end occurred soon after the Wilde trials, the letter to the coroner may have convinced Housman that it contained veiled allusions to the consequences of homosexuality ("Now I am quite certain that I could not live another five years without [offending others]"). If so, Housman's identification with the desperate cadet provided emotional catharsis in the wake of the recent Wilde affair:

Now to your grave shall friend and stranger
  With ruth and some with envy come:
Undishonoured, clear of danger,
  Clean of guilt, pass hence and home.

The poem, of course, restates a central theme of *A Shropshire Lad,* that an early death may be preferable to moral decline, but the time and setting of the cadet's suicide surely found resonances in Housman's own Uranian sensibility.

During the Wilde affair, Housman wrote a poem withheld from publication in his lifetime perhaps because it was too obviously topical. He draws a sardonic parallel between the incarceration of a person for the mere color of his hair and Wilde's incarceration for his sexual behavior. Clearly, Housman regards homosexuality as a God-given, guiltless element in human nature:

Oh who is that young sinner with the handcuffs on his wrists?
And what has he been after that they groan and shake their fists?
And wherefore is he wearing such a conscience-stricken air?
Oh they're taking him to prison for the colour of his hair.

In his ironic manner, Housman calls the color of the young sinner's hair "a shame to human nature," one that would have resulted "in the good old time" in a hanging. Now, however, " 'tis oakum for his fingers and the treadmill for his feet":

And between his spells of labour in the time he has to spare
He can curse the God that made him for the colour of his hair.

DURING THE YEARS of his imprisonment, the press scrupulously avoided mentioning Wilde's name. Shaw, however, cited him with praise in two drama reviews. In 1896, while discussing a minor play, he remarked on the superiority of Wilde's comedies: ". . . Mr. Wilde has creative imagination, philosophic humour, and original wit, besides being a master of language. . . ." When the *Academy* (November 6, 1897) proposed the founding of an academy of letters and published a list of forty possible nominees (including such figures as Ruskin, Gladstone, Swinburne, Meredith, Kipling, James, Henley, Gosse, Yeats, and Alice Meynell but omitting, significantly, the poet laureate, Alfred Austin, and not unexpectedly Oscar Wilde), Shaw protested in a letter to the editor (November 13) that the "only dramatist, besides Mr. Henry James, whose nomination could be justified is Mr. Oscar Wilde" (Shaw remained discreetly silent on the omission of his own name). In the same issue and in succeeding weeks, the *Academy* printed many other letters from readers on the question of the academy of letters. A letter by Wells (November 13), who called the list of proposed members a "parlour game," also took issue with the selection of names and offered alternatives: George Gissing, George Moore, Bernard Shaw, and Oscar Wilde. The proposal for an academy of letters quickly died, however, when Swinburne sent a letter to the *Times* (November 22) condemning the enterprise as "too seriously stupid for farce and too essentially vulgar for comedy."

MOST OF WILDE'S incarceration was spent in Reading Prison, the name of which he changed for his poem, *The Ballad of Reading Gaol* (1898), describing his life as convict C.3.3 (referring to Block C, the third cell on the third floor):

> *Each narrow cell in which we dwell*
>   *Is a foul and dark latrine,*
> *And the fetid breath of living Death*
>   *Chokes up each grated screen,*
> *And all, but Lust, is turned to Dust*
> *In Humanity's machine.*

By the end of 1895, Wilde's friends in England and France began circulating petitions for his early release. There were unexpected refusals to sign, one by the Pre-Raphaelite painter W. Holman Hunt (whom Wilde had earlier championed): "I must repeat my opinion that the law treated him with exceeding leniency, and state that further consideration of the facts convinces me that in justice to criminals belonging to other classes of society I should have to join in the cry for doing away with all personal responsibility for wickedness if I took any part in appealing. . . ." Henry James also refused, as did George Meredith and Zola. Gide, however, did sign. Wilde's own appeal for early release was refused. Having served the full term, he was discharged on May 19, 1897, from Pentonville Prison in the north of London (having been transferred from Reading the day before) and soon left England for France, where he lived for the remaining three and a half years of his life. At Berneval-sur-Mer, he assumed the name of Sebastian Melmoth, derived from the martyred saint (celebrated in Wilde's poem "The Grave of Keats") and the central character of the Gothic novel *Melmoth the Wanderer* (1820) by his great-uncle Charles R. Maturin.

Almost immediately, he began writing his ballad of prison life. Though ostensibly concerned with the execution of a trooper in the Royal Horse Guards who had killed his wife, the poem focuses on the refrain, "Yet each man kills the thing he loves," alluding to the mystery of Wilde's own self-destruction. By October, "the great poem," he told Reginald

Wilde's cell in Reading Prison

Turner, was finished. When he attempted to place it in America, there was much resistance: ". . . I find that I cannot get my poem . . . accepted even by the most revolting New York paper." To another friend, he wrote in November: ". . . I am depressed by the difficulty of reaching an audience; the adventures of my American poem have been a terrible blow to my ambition, my vanity, and my hopes." His name, he told Leonard Smithers, had terrified the American newspapers.

When, in February 1898, Smithers issued the *Ballad of Reading Gaol* in book form (with only Wilde's cell block number on the title page), the critical reception was generally favorable, though the *Daily Chronicle,* Wilde remarked, seemed to think that the poem was "a pamphlet on prison-reform." Only one periodical mentioned Wilde's name, but presumably everyone knew who the author was. Wilde was most pleased with Symons's review in the *Saturday Review* (March 12, 1898), which noted: "We see a great spectacular intellect, to which, at last, pity and terror have come in their own person, and no longer as puppets in a play."

The poem sold out the first printing of eight hundred copies within a few days. The demand continued for several more printings. In June, the seventh printing contained Wilde's name in square brackets under "C.3.3."* In addition, the printer also identified himself for the first time, an indication that wide public acceptance had broken—momentarily, at least—the taboo of Wilde's name. Delighted and encouraged by the critical and popular reception, Wilde told George Ives in March 1898: "Yes: I have no doubt we shall win, but the road is long, and red with monstrous martyrdoms. Nothing but the repeal of the Criminal Law Amendment Act would do any good. That is the essential. It is not so much public opinion as public officials that need educating."

AWARE OF THE sensitive nature of his book on sexual inversion in the aftermath of Wilde's disgrace, Havelock Ellis sent the manuscript to a minor publisher, Williams and Norgate, known for their list of scientific books. Dr. Hack Tuke, the publisher's reader and the editor of the *Journal of Medical Science* in which several articles by Ellis had appeared, rejected the manuscript. A close friend of Dr. Symonds, Tuke had previously refused to discuss inversion with John Addington Symonds. Possibly because his own son, the well-known painter Henry Scott Tuke, was himself a Uranian, Tuke informed Ellis that the publication of a book

---

*Smithers, however, remained cautious when he issued editions of *The Importance of Being Earnest* (1899) and *An Ideal Husband* (1899). The title pages of these plays identify the writer only by the phrase "By the Author of Lady Windermere's Fan."

at that time on such a volatile subject might go beyond specialist readers and disturb the general public. Apparently concerned that the workers at the print shop might be instrumental in disclosing the material, he said: "There are always the compositors!"

When it finally appeared in November 1897, Ellis was unprepared for the ensuing legal troubles. A young man in Liverpool ordered a copy of *Sexual Inversion,* which so alarmed his parents that they complained to the police. On May 27, 1898, Detective John Sweeney, who had been maintaining a surveillance of the Legitimation League, concerned principally with children born out of wedlock and with legislative reform in the marriage and divorce laws, entered the office of the league where the twenty-seven-year-old George Bedborough, editor of the radical paper the *Adult,* sold copies of various publications. Sweeney purchased a copy of *Sexual Inversion* for ten shillings, then secured a warrant for Bedborough's arrest—"convinced," he later wrote, "that we should at one blow kill a growing evil in the shape of a vigorous campaign of free love and Anarchism, and at the same time discover the means by which the country was being flooded with books of the 'Psychology' type."

At the preliminary hearing in the Bow Street Magistrates' Court, where Wilde had also been brought after his arrest, Bedborough was charged with having "sold and uttered a certain lewd, wicked, bawdy, scandalous, and obscene libel in the form of a book entitled *Studies in the Psychology of Sex: Sexual Inversion."* Ellis arrived in London from Cornwall to seek legal counsel while a Free Press Defense Committee was being formed, enlisting the support of such figures as Bernard Shaw, Frank Harris, George Moore, Edward Carpenter, Grant Allen, and H. M. Hyndman, leader of the Social Democratic Federation. Shaw wrote to the organizer of the committee that Bedborough's prosecution was a "masterpiece of police stupidity and magisterial ignorance. I have read the book carefully; and I have no hesitation in saying that its publication was more urgently needed in England than any other recent treatise with which I am acquainted." Appreciative of Shaw's response, Ellis was distressed by the failure of a single British physician to join the committee or to testify in court in favor of the book.

Before the trial on October 31, 1898, there was considerable disagreement and confusion between the committee and Bedborough on the strategy for the defense. Bedborough, who refused to enact the role of martyr for the committee's ideals, had reached an understanding with the prosecutor: in court, Bedborough agreed to drop all connections with the Legitimation League. He was released, his sentence deferred. The committee had lost an opportunity to test the legal limits of free speech and to assert that *Sexual Inversion* was a legitimately scientific, not an "obscene," work.

THOUGH, IN THE nineties, the two major trials that preoccupied the English press involved Wilde and Dreyfus, the connection between the two was rarely, if ever, made by journalists. Yet the destinies of both figures had a notable impact on writers (and presumably readers) as their trials unfolded, revealing striking parallels and cultural biases. Wilde the Irish homosexual and Dreyfus the Alsatian Jew, both outsiders, became outcasts in their respective societies for different reasons: Wilde, a willing victim of English homophobia and Philistinism; Dreyfus, an unwilling victim of French corruption and anti-Semitism. Both were to be celebrated as cultural heroes.

In March 1898 at a dinner party in Paris, Wilde met the "astonishing" Major Marie-Charles Ferdinand Walsin-Esterhazy, who had written the incriminating *bordereau* (a list of secret French military documents discovered by a French spy in the German embassy), the breach of security attributed to Captain Alfred Dreyfus of the French general staff. Wilde told Henry-D. Davray, the French critic and translator of *The Ballad of Reading Gaol:* "Esterhazy is much more interesting than Dreyfus, who is innocent. It is always a mistake to be innocent. To be a criminal requires imagination and courage." Though seemingly facetious, Wilde had always admired the imaginative lawbreaker as one who rebelled against society's irrational restraints, as indeed he had himself. For example, in "Pen, Pencil, and Poison: A Study" (1889/1891), he had written of the poisoner and writer Thomas Wainewright that "the fact of a man being a poisoner is nothing against his prose" and that Wainewright's crimes "seem to have had an important effect upon his art. They gave a strong personality to his style. . . ."

Initially, when Dreyfus was arrested in October 1894 on charges of espionage and high treason for offering to sell military secrets to the German military attaché in Paris, the *Times* dutifully reported the event, but there was little reason to suspect that within four years *l'affaire Dreyfus* would have a devastating effect on French society and preoccupy the English press. After his court-martial, Dreyfus was sent to Devil's Island, French Guiana, in February 1895 to serve a life sentence and was placed in solitary confinement on April 13 at the time when Wilde was under arrest and awaiting trial.

In London, the first artistic exploitation of the affair occurred in December 1895, when the Adelphi Theatre presented *One of the Best* by Seymour Hicks and George Edwardes (the manager of the Empire Theatre), a play based on the military ceremony of degradation—the stripping of insignia from his uniform—that Dreyfus had endured in the courtyard of the École Militaire in January of that year. At the end of the performance, the principal actor reassured the audience that "no English officer has ever betrayed his country." In the *Saturday Review* (December 28), Shaw protested that the subject was "much too big" for the authors and remarked that the French taste for melodrama had produced the theatrical Dreyfus case "at the expense of common sense and public policy." The English, on the other hand, get rid of their Dreyfuses "in the quietest possible manner, instead of advertising them by regimental *coups de théâtre.*" Since Esterhazy had not yet been revealed as a German spy, the question of Dreyfus's guilt did not arise in the play or in Shaw's review.

Though evidence slowly revealed that Dreyfus was innocent, the army and the government remained steadfast on the subject of his crime in order to maintain political stability and to restore confidence in the army seriously undermined by the disastrous French defeat in the Franco-Prussian War of 1870. When the chief of intelligence discovered a letter written by Esterhazy to the German attaché in the same handwriting as that in the *bordereau,* he attempted to reopen the case but was immediately transferred to Tunisia. When Esterhazy requested a trial to clear his name, he was found innocent of treason.

Outraged by such a blatant miscarriage of justice, Emile Zola, himself unfavorably disposed towards Jews, wrote his famous open letter to the president of the Republic attacking the military tribunal that had presided at the trial and various army generals and officials at the War Office for their conspiracy in imprisoning an innocent man and clearing a guilty one. With the blazing headline "J'Accuse . . . !" provided by the editor, Georges Clemenceau (later twice a premier), for the front page of *L'Aurore* (January 13, 1898), the newspaper sold an astonishing 300,000 copies before the morning ended. The resulting social and political turmoil lasted for two years, during which time there were riots, duels, heated confrontations between friends, and divisive arguments within families between those convinced of Dreyfus's innocence (the "Dreyfusards," who included intellectuals, radicals, and socialists) and those convinced of his guilt (the "anti-Dreyfusards," who included churchmen and army officers). Among French avant-garde writers and artists, the Dreyfusards included Anatole France, Proust, Monet, and Pissarro; among the anti-Dreyfusards were Cezanne, Renoir, Degas, and Rodin.

In 1898, Zola went on trial for having libeled the army. Found guilty, he was sentenced to a year in prison. Clemenceau and other friends urged him to leave France since it seemed obvious that the government would imprison him and thus stifle his voice. By fleeing, he would keep his own case—and Dreyfus's—"open." Reluctant at first, Zola acquiesced and left for England, known for its liberal policy of granting asylum to political dissidents. (By contrast, Wilde's refusal to flee England destroyed his life.) Arriving in London on July 19, Ernest Vizetelly, the translator and son of Zola's publisher Henry Vizetelly, made arrangements to ensure Zola's anonymity. Eventually, he was brought to Surrey, where he lived quietly and worked on a novel, seeing only his family and close friends.

The only writer who visited him, according to Vizetelly, was "a well-known English novelist and art critic, M. Zola's oldest English friend, and his earliest champion in this country"—that is, George Moore. Earlier, some English writers had raised the possibility of sending a telegram supporting Zola at the time of his trial. Gosse, however, believed that writers should not become involved in politics, especially the Zola affair: "English people do not seem to realize in the least that the most thoughtful and upright Frenchmen, however willing they may be to acknowledge the purity of M. Zola's motives, are convinced that his method of action was totally indefensible."

In such London periodicals as the *Fortnightly Review,* the *National Review,* and the *Spectator,* articles covering the Dreyfus scandal led to much speculation concerning the corruption in the French military and civilian judicial proceedings and their effect on the country's reputation. Inevitably, discussions comparing the legal procedures of both countries became commonplace, the Dreyfus trial providing an ideal opportunity to advance a favorable image of British justice in the course of revealing French duplicity. A writer in *Westminster Review* (January 1898), for example, evaluated the differences between British and French courts-martial: In Britain, a court-martial was public, not secret, as Dreyfus's trial was; also, the prisoner would not have been held in ignorance of the charges against him for such a long period of time as was Dreyfus; and secret "evidence" could not be used to convict a prisoner as it was in Dreyfus's case. Concludes the writer: "To any one accustomed to the fair and open procedure of English courts of justice, the whole inquiry and trial seems a most lamentable example of distorted ingenuity in the science of prisoner-baiting."

In the *Fortnightly Review* (January 1, 1898), a writer goes further by alleging that newly uncovered details of the investigation were "almost incredible, and smack[ed] of Star Chamber procedure rather than of the judicial system of a civilised nation." Also, in the *Saturday Review* (February 19, 1899), an article focusing on the cursory Esterhazy court-martial and the irregularities of the Zola and Clemenceau trials found gross breaches of the commonly accepted methods of presenting evidence and in the restrictions on the defendants' capacity to respond to the charges against them: "Is it possible to add anything to the criminal absurdity of all this cock-and-bull story that is degrading France, and rendering her ridiculous among the nations?"

As the complex unraveling of the Dreyfus affair (involving disclosures of forged documents, a suicide by the forger, and the flight of Esterhazy) proceeded, Henry James tried to remain impartial but with little success, writing from France to his brother, William, in April 1899: "I treat the 'Affaire' as none of my business (as it isn't), but *its* power to make one homesick in France and the French air, every hour and everywhere today, is not small. It *is* a country *en décadence*. Once one *feels* that, nothing—on the spot—corrects the impression." Shaw, however, was furious with the anti-Dreyfusards, as he wrote to a Fabian colleague in May: "What is it they do? Why, pick out all the general vices of humanity—all its greed and ambition and sensuality—and denounce the Jews for them, as if Christians were any less greedy, ambitious and sensual."

On June 3, Dreyfus's conviction was revoked and another court-martial ordered held in Rennes. On September 9, Dreyfus was again found guilty but with "extenuating circumstances." His sentence: ten years. But on September 20 the French president granted him a pardon. Since it implied guilt, the Dreyfusards were furious. In London, Henry Harland, having just returned from abroad, wrote to Gosse: "We were in France all through that dreadful trial, and read the *Figaro*'s verbatim reports every day. We feel as if we should never wish to go to France again." Like Zola, Harland had an unfavorable view of Jews, but his outrage over the injustice of the trial overrode all other considerations. In an ironic article for the *Academy* (October 22, 1899) titled "A Neighbourly Suggestion," he offered a modest proposal that France should be concerned with literature and art, where her genius lies, and allow the British to govern the country: ". . . we have never failed to do our work in masterly style. Look at India. Look at Egypt." However, he was convinced that the French were not likely to agree: "What is the kink, the perversity, in their intelligence, which would prevent their seeing and accepting it?"

Not until July 1906 was the Rennes verdict annulled and Dreyfus reinstated in the army. France had finally expiated its shame before the world. But it would take England longer to acknowledge its participation in what Wilde had called a "monstrous martyrdom." In October 1954, the centenary of Wilde's birth, a plaque authorized by the London County Council was unveiled at his nineties' residence in Tite Street, Chelsea, by the writer Sir Compton Mackenzie with distinguished writers and members of Parliament in attendance. Laurence Housman, now ninety, was too ill to attend, but he sent a message that was read to the gathering: "[Wilde's] unhappy fate has done the world a signal service in defeating the blind obscurantists: he has made people think. Far more people of intelligence think differently today because of him." This official recognition of Wilde's significance helped bring about the end of the Criminal Law Amendment Act, which had so disastrously changed the course of his life.

10

Defying the Commercial Periodicals

THE FAMILIAR TWENTIETH-CENTURY tactic among writers and artists of issuing manifestoes announcing the advent of a new artistic movement had few precedents in the history of English culture until the mid-Victorian period. Instead of formal manifestoes, aesthetic periodicals designed for a small elitest audience promoted avant-garde concerns and works as a radical rejection of the popular magazines. The aesthetic publications generally limited themselves to the arts, avoided articles on religious, social, and political issues, and contained no advertising other than the publishers' lists (an anticommercial gesture that inevitably raised the price—and often limited the longevity—of the periodical). In providing a voice for writers, critics, and artists who often also published in the commercial magazines to maintain a livelihood, the aesthetic periodicals were the suitable refuge for advanced ideas and works that challenged Establishment views of literature and Royal Academy strictures concerning art. Most important, the editors of such periodicals regarded the design, the typography, and the quality of the paper as an artistic expression appropriate to the contents. The total effect suggested defiance of mass-produced commercial magazines designed for an aesthetically blind public.

Such widely read publications as *Macmillan's Magazine, Cornhill Magazine,* and the *Strand Magazine* appealed to a large new readership, the result of the Education Act of 1870, which greatly extended educational opportunities for many and resulted in elevated literacy levels for a broad spectrum of the population. These magazines generally provided readers with light reading and much fiction, usually in installments, though *Macmillan's* ventured into such topics as "The Rise of British Dominion in India," "Philanthropy and the Poor Law," and "The Universities and the Counter-Reformation." Like the *Cornhill Magazine,* the *Strand Magazine,* founded in 1891, filled its pages with somewhat lighter reading than that of *Macmillan's* but also with much fiction. Within a short period of time, it attained, remarks the author of its history, "the status of a national institution. No other magazine in Great Britain ever reached that eminence of popular esteem."

At sixpence a copy, the first issue of 112 pages of articles and stories (with a free colored print from the previous year's Royal Academy show) was issued in January 1891 and sold 300,000 copies. The ugly advertising, crowded into six panels per page, became a major source of income for the magazine, whose circulation soon rose to 500,000 copies monthly and maintained that figure for many years. Such writers as Arthur Conan Doyle (whose Sherlock Holmes stories appeared regularly), Rudyard Kipling, and Grant Allen graced its pages and contributed to its success. Yet its appearance remained unattractive, and its undistinguished pen and brush illustrations, such as those for the Sherlock Holmes stories, did little for the "letterpress" (that is, the text). The fin-de-siècle aesthetic periodicals, on the other hand, often defied convention by including art for its own sake rather than as an appendage to the prose.

THE APPEARANCE IN January 1850 of the Pre-Raphaelite *Germ* inaugurated the aesthetic periodical designed for a cadre of poets, critics, and painters. After its first two numbers, the title was changed to *Art and Poetry* for its final two numbers (ending its run in April). Not all of the contributors, however, were members of the short-lived Pre-Raphaelite Brotherhood (which advocated a return to the "purity" of painting before the idealizing tendencies of Raphael and his followers in the Renaissance). Established in 1848 by Dante Gabriel Rossetti, William Holman Hunt, and John Everett Millais, the Brotherhood signed its paintings with the mystifying "PRB." Soon, four additional members joined the Brotherhood, including the only nonartist, William Michael Rossetti, a critic who edited the periodical. In addition, Swinburne, Christina Rossetti, and William Morris were associated with some members of the group when the brotherhood dissolved in 1852.

The rediscovery of William Blake's visionary poems and drawings inspired the Pre-Raphaelites, particularly the two Rossetti brothers, William Michael (the editor of Blake's works in 1874) and Dante Gabriel (the owner of Blake's manuscript notebook), as well as Swinburne (author of an influential study of Blake in 1868). Such an interest led to a major revival of Blake as evidenced in the later aesthetic periodicals and the many volumes on Blake that appeared in the late Victorian and early Edwardian periods. The dominance of Blake, as well as the late medieval and Renaissance literary tradition shaped much of the Brotherhood's literature and art, particularly in the use of Christian symbolism, myths, and dreams despite the fact that in its early years the group subscribed to the doctrine of truthfulness to nature. Indeed, the first number of the *Germ* begins with two poems by the only Brotherhood sculptor, Thomas Woolner: "My Beautiful Lady" and "Of My Lady in Death," which echo, though in more sensual terms, Dante's *La Vita Nuova,* Jacopo da Lentino's sonnet "Of His Lady in Heaven," Pugliesi's "Canzone of His Dead Lady," and other such late medieval works written in the *dolce stil nuovo,* the "sweet new style" of religious inspiration resulting from the death of the poet's adored lady.

The three Rossettis—Christina (publishing under the name of "Ellen Alleyn"), William Michael, and Dante Gabriel—contributed verse and prose to both the *Germ* and *Art and Poetry.* Among Dante Gabriel's influential works are the poem "The Blessed Damozel" and the story "Hand and Soul"—sacred texts for the fin-de-siècle Aesthetes and Decadents, who acknowledged their indebtedness to Pre-Raphaelitism. "The Blessed Damozel," with its characteristic vision of a lost ideal of Beauty, transposed the conventions of *dolce stil nuovo* to Pre-Raphaelite evocations of the mystical and erotic, which the fin-de-siècle Decadents envisioned as inseparable. In "Hand and Soul," a young medieval painter who, like Dante, reveres "his mystical lady (now hardly in her ninth year, but whose solemn smile at meeting had already lighted on his soul . . .)," discovers that his reverence, which he had mistaken for faith, "had been no more than the worship of beauty." A vision of his own soul appears, urging him to paint her as she is, the symbolic embodiment of autonomous art: "So shall thy soul stand before thee always, and perplex thee no more."

In the final issue of *Art and Poetry* (April 1850), Dante Rossetti contributed six sonnets on works of art, underlining the Pre-Raphaelite aesthetic intention: to unite literature and art, one art enriching and drawiing inspiration from the other (curiously, the periodical had only one illustration in each of the four issues). Though the Brotherhood did not uniformly accept the notion of art for art's sake, Rossetti, as visionary and Symbolist, provided a significant link between the Pre-Raphaelite devotion to art and the later Aesthetic Movement.

AFTER THE DEMISE of *Art and Poetry,* London was without such an aesthetic periodical until the appearance in April 1884 of the first number of the *Century Guild Hobby Horse,* the organ of the Century Guild of Artists, which Arthur Mackmurdo, an architect, had founded in 1882. Edited by Mackmurdo and his young partner Herbert Horne (who assumed sole responsibility for issues published between 1886 and 1891), the *Century Guild Hobby Horse* was a self-conscious periodical designed to illustrate and encourage the unity of the arts. By creating a stunning example of their basic principles, Mackmurdo and Horne established a model for the ensuing aesthetic periodicals of the fin de siècle with its handmade rag paper and untrimmed edges, aesthetically appropriate to the large Caslon typography (designed by the great eighteenth-century English typographer, William Caslon). The unusually wide margins were an innovation in periodical publication (the commercial magazines at the time were often printed in double-columns, anathema to the aesthetic periodicals). The decorated capital letters at the beginning of each selection and the tail-pieces at the end added to the exquisite layout of the page. The quality of reproductions, particularly of Pre-Raphaelite paintings and Renaissance woodcuts, was considerably enhanced by the latest photogravure methods, in color as required.

The fin-de-siècle revival of printing and its collateral development, the advent of "total book" design, owe their development to the achievements of the Hobby Horsemen and to William Morris's Kelmscott Press, founded in 1890.* In addition to being an architect, Horne designed typography and books, seeking inspiration from the severity of Renaissance publications. Morris's single greatest achievement in book design was the exquisitely decorated edition of Chaucer's *Canterbury Tales,* for which black ink, paper, and typography were created in the cottage workshop near his Hammersmith home. Over a three-year period, the Pre-Raphaelite painter Edward Burne-Jones assisted Morris in the intricate designs. When Morris saw the first page from the press, he exclaimed: "How good it is!" This great volume, Morris said, was "not only the finest book in the world, but an undertaking that was an absolutely unchecked success from beginning to end."

The *Century Guild Hobby Horse* illustrated one of the aesthetic convictions of Mackmurdo and Horne: that the outer and inner design of a building as well as its furnishings should be regarded as a unified whole, in the twentieth century a basic premise of the Bauhaus school of architecture. The idea of the unity of the arts, derived from Pre-Raphaelitism, was a prominent theme in essays published in the periodical. The Hobby Horsemen assumed that there were universal principles of design that eliminated the distinction between fine and applied art, an aesthetic approach central to the arts and crafts movement of the late nineteenth century. As a consequence, Mackmurdo and Horne regarded their furniture and book designs as significant steps in counteracting the encroach-

*James G. Nelson states that the Bodley Head books, beginning with Richard Le Gallienne's *Volumes in Folio* (1889), "were a marked departure from the tasteless, often vulgar bindings, designless title pages, and ugly typography of the books supplied by the large commercial firms. In make-up and in design they anticipated the modern book" (*The Early Nineties: A View from the Bodley Head* [Cambridge, Mass., 1971], 37).

ing industrialism of the age. Like William Morris, who influenced him, Mackmurdo believed that contemporary overdecorated machine-made products were shoddy reflections of the true artist's craft, for they showed no understanding of abstract principles governing form. In an attempt to eliminate the unimaginative imitation of nature, Horne and Macmurdo emphasized the simple curving lines associated with the later flat designs of art nouveau, which opposed the conventional realism of Victorian art. Stating the characteristic views of the Hobby Horsemen in an article titled "On Art and Nature" (January 1886), Selwyn Image contended that "Fine Art is not imitation, but invention: it is not reflection, but creation."

Image, a former cleric who had left the ministry to devote his life to the arts, had joined the Century Guild as a designer of stained-glass windows. In addition to contributing literary and art criticism to the *Century Guild Hobby Horse,* he also designed books. His cover for the periodical (anticipating Beardsley's illustrations for *Le Morte D'Arthur* ten years later) depicts two knights on prancing hobby horses adorned with Pre-Raphaelite roses, the background of rays heralding a new dawn in art; it remained on all issues through 1892. Horne, Mackmurdo, and Image, prominent in the various issues of the periodical were, like the Pre-Raphaelites, influenced by late medieval and Renaissance art, which suggested spiritual worlds in its depictions of sacred and secular myth and symbol drawn from Christian and pagan sources. Having attended Ruskin's lectures at Oxford, Mackmurdo was religiously inspired in his social and moral concerns (in the following century, he retired to write socialist tracts), whereas Horne and Image were drawn to Pater and to the doctrine of art for art's sake. In various issues of the periodical, Horne included his own essays on such great seventeenth- and eighteenth-century English architects as Inigo Jones and Christopher Wren. Concerned about the deplorable state of contemporary London architecture, he evoked the spirit of Inigo Jones in the poem "On Certain New Buildings in Covent Garden" (January 1886):

> O Inigo,
>   Could you rise again,
> Then might men know
>   What sins in stone they chain. . . .

In the first number (April 1884), Horne contributed poetry and art as "MCG" (Member, Century Guild) to imply continuity with the Pre-Raphaelite Brotherhood. Other issues suggesting such a connection contained contributions by Christina Rossetti, William M. Rossetti, William Morris, Edward Burne-Jones, and Ford Madox Brown. In addition to

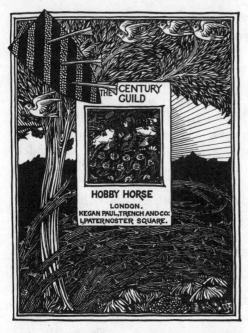

Cover of the *Century Guild Hobby Horse*

establishing its Pre-Rapahelite connections, the issue was notable in its emphasis on Blake and his work, indicating his importance in the fin de siècle. Among the essays on Dante Gabriel Rossetti, one by Horne asserts that, unlike Blake, Rossetti had no "new attitude towards religion but he brought a new temper more exalted and more sumptuous than had been known before to the passions of men." In the same issue (October 1887), Blake's "Marriage of Heaven and Hell" appears in its entirety, as does the *Book of Los* in the July 1890 issue; moreover, Blake engravings appeared sporadically—all reminders of the visionary tendencies of the periodical.

Though the artists and writers in the *Century Guild Hobby Horse* preferred, like the Pre-Raphaelites, the aesthetic achievements of the past to the ugliness of the industrial present, there were in its pages anticipations of the future. In "Art and Poetry" (January 1886),* Image offered the startling idea, perhaps derived from Whistler, that Raphael's painting of the Madonna and an unknown painter's patterns on a wall or on a water pot were equally artistic products regardless of the subject matter (a view rejected by the conservative Royal Academy, whose artists often favored noble subjects from the Bible, mythology, and history): "That one em-

---

*This issue, which appeared two years after the initial appearance of *Century Guild Hobby Horse* in 1884, was also designated "No. 1," thereby creating everlasting bibliographical confusion.

ploys himself in representing the human form and the highest human interests, while the other employs himself in representing abstract lines and masses, this, so far as the claim to being an artist goes, makes no difference"—an anticipation of the attitudes associated with Abstract Expressionism in our time. Aware of the consequences of his remark that "all kinds of invented Form, and Tone, and Colour are alike true and honourable aspects of Art," Image concludes: ". . . you see something very much like a revolution looming ahead of you."

That the *Century Guild Hobby Horse* was illustrative of the aesthetic and avant-garde trends of the period is also indicated by its contributors: renowned, notorious, and emerging writers and artists of the time who clearly regarded the periodical as the significant voice of the late 1880s, whether they adhered to a traditional view of art's moral purpose or to the more advanced view of art for art's sake. All wished to counter the stultifying effects of commercialism and industrialism in the modern world and thus found themselves within the covers of the same periodical: John Ruskin, Matthew Arnold, John Addington Symonds, Oscar Wilde, Charles Shannon, Richard Le Gallienne, Ernest Rhys, Lionel Johnson, and Ernest Dowson, whose most famous poem, "Non sum qualis eram bonae sub regno Cynarae," first appeared in the April 1891 number and reappeared in *The Second Book of the Rhymers' Club* (1894). Despite the fact that it seemed out of place in the periodical, Horne was proud to have published it. Before its appearance, Dowson told a friend after seeing the proofs of the poem: "It looks less indecent in print, but I am still nervous! though I admire Horne's audacity." In the same issue, Johnson's essay on current French verse attempted a definition of *décadence* and *symbolisme* with only faint success; in the January 1892 number, Richard Le Gallienne attacked French *décadence* in his review of Churton Collins's *Illustrations of Tennyson,* which, as we have seen, prompted Arthur Symons to write his famous 1893 essay on the Decadent Movement.

Because of illness, Horne relinquished the editorship of the periodical with the October 1891 issue, Mackmurdo undertaking the responsibility for the January, April, and July issues in 1892. When Horne resumed his editorship in 1893, he dropped the *Century Guild* portion of the title and adopted his own new cover design (again, a knight on a hobby horse). In the autumn of 1894, with the final issue in production, Selwyn Image wrote to his brother: "Yes, the Hobby-Horse comes shortly to an end. It is wise, I think, that it should. It has done its work, and has told in certain directions, so we shall bury it without tears." The "certain directions" alluded to by Image suggest, however, a division of aesthetic aims in the *Hobby Horse* (a paradigm of the Victorian dilemma regarding the function of art) between the "Utopian idealism of Morris and Ruskin and the specialized art for art's sake coterie world of the *Yellow Book* and *The Savoy.*"

AT THE SAME time that the *Century Guild Hobby Horse* was in its prime, another aesthetic magazine appeared from the youthful circle of Charles Ricketts and Charles Shannon, painters and illustrators who lived together for many years in a house once owned by Whistler in a Chelsea cul-de-sac called "The Vale," a bucolic lane leading from King's Road. There they founded the *Dial,* which they edited between 1889 and 1897, establishing its reputation quickly—in Dowson's view—as "that mad, strange art review." Although Wilde facetiously called Ricketts and Shannon "the Dialists" after he received a copy of the first issue, the introduction led to a a long friendship. As a result, Ricketts and Shannon, singly and jointly, designed and decorated most of Wilde's books. Ricketts also designed the famous *Silverpoints* (1893) by John Gray and *In the Key of Blue* (1893) by John Addington Symonds for the Bodley Head.

The largest in format of the aesthetic periodicals, the *Dial,* with its subtitle "An Occasional Publication," was occasional indeed, for only five issues of 200 copies each appeared between 1889 and 1897. Yet its importance is unquestionable since it advanced the tradition of the aesthetic periodical. Despite its pseudomedieval cover depicting a walled lush garden and sundial surrounded by bearded stone figures staring down on the scene, the *Dial* contained a new emphasis on avant-garde French writers and artists, a major shift from the *Century Guild Hobby Horse,* which, like the *Germ,* focused principally on the English and Italian traditions. Such figures as the French painter Puvis de Chavannes and the French Naturalists the Goncourt brothers were the subjects of articles in the first number; in No. 2 (1892), T. Sturge Moore published a poem in memory of Rimbaud, and John Gray (who contributed to all five numbers) published "Parsifal," a version of the Verlaine poem, and reviewed Huysmans's *En Route;* issue No. 5 (1897), contained an untranslated Verhaeren poem.

WHILE THE *Dial* had attracted talented writers to its pages, it had not startled the general public or the literary world and their protectors, the conservative critics and journalists. When, however, the periodical most often associated with the Yellow Nineties appeared in April 1894, it evoked a storm of protest by offended reviewers, who regarded it as an emblem of decadence. Yet the editors of the innovative hard-cover *Yellow Book*—Henry Harland, a successful American novelist who had emigrated to England in 1889, and Aubrey Beardsley, who, at the age of twenty-three, had already revealed his genius for illustration—had not "intended to organize the decadence," as one modern critic has asserted. Arthur Waugh, who had been present at early discussions between Harland, John Lane, and Edmund Gosse concerning the aim of the periodical, reported that the *Yellow Book* would not be the organ of Decadence or, indeed, of any "new movement." Privately, however, Beardsley informed a friend: "Our idea is that many brilliant story painters and picture writers cannot get their best stuff accepted in the conventional magazine, either because they are not topical or perhaps a little risqué." But the contributions that were "a little risqué" were only part of the broad spectrum of literary and artistic work that was representative of the nineties, at once avant garde and traditional. In their daring attempt to go public, the editors and publishers of the *Yellow Book* understood that unconventional literature and art could be included only by pacifying readers with acknowledged conservative contributors.

To insure such a balance, Harland and Beardsley included in the first number Henry James, George Saintsbury, Edmund Gosse, Richard Le Gallienne, Arthur Symons, George Moore, John Davidson, Max Beerbohm, and Arthur Waugh; the artists included Sir Frederick Leighton (president of the Royal Academy), Beardsley, Walter Sickert, Laurence Housman, Will Rothenstein, Max Beerbohm, and the American Joseph Pennell. Following the tradition of the aesthetic periodicals with respect to contributions by the editor, Harland published his own fiction and criticism, the latter inaugurated with Volume 7 (October 1895) and signed as "The Yellow Dwarf," whom Beerbohm pictured in Volume 11 (October 1896) as a rotund figure wearing a fringed black mask with bow and arrows.

The initial offense to the outraged was Beardsley's cover, with its leering, masked woman adorned with a beauty mark—suggesting a prostitute—followed by his picture within the volume wittily titled "L'Education Sentimentale," depicting an aging whore instructing a young girl in the trade. Furthermore, Beerbohm's ironic essay, "A Defence of Cosmetics," alluding to the prostitute's stock-in-trade but also associated with Decadence, defended artifice in opposition to Victorian reverence of nature and unadorned purity. Beardsley's striking "Night Piece," its streetwalker in a low-cut dress placed in the symbolic asymmetry and isolation of the surrounding darkness, precedes Arthur Symons's poem "Stella Maris," not, as the title suggests, about the Virgin Mary but, as we have seen, about the "chance romances of the streets, / The Juliet of a night":

> *I feel the perfume of your hair,*
> *And your soft breast that heaves and dips,*
> *Desiring my desirous lips . . .*

"A little risqué," Beardsley might call it, and "a little daring for an English review," Symons told Verlaine. Harland, Beardsley, and the Bodley

Cover of the *Yellow Book*

Head expected a critical reaction that might help publicize the first number, but the degree of hostility in the press was unforeseen. It would forever after brand the periodical unjustifiably as decadent and set the stage for Beardsley's firing at the time of the Wilde trials.

The inclusion in the first number of Arthur Waugh's essay "Reticence in Literature" was clearly designed to emphasize the balance between avant-garde and traditional views, for Waugh pleads that "Midway between liberty and license, in literature as in morals, stands the pivot of good taste, centre-point of art. . . . The inclination of frankness, restrained by the tutored to the limitations of art and beauty, is to speak so much as is in accordance with the moral idea." Basing his argument on the acknowledged relativity of contemporary standards, Waugh concludes that the "standard of taste in literature . . . should be regulated by the normal taste of the hale and cultured man of its age: it should steer a middle course between the prudery of the manse, which is for hiding everything vital, and the effrontery of the pot-house, which makes for ribaldry and bawdry. . . ." Citing Hogarth as an English artist undeniably coarse, Waugh regards him as nevertheless "profoundly moral" in his condemnation of the vice that he portrays: "It is only the schoolboy who searches the Bible for its indecent passages."

Also to be deplored, Waugh remarks, is the "realistic fiction abroad" that is copied in England, an allusion to Zola's Naturalism as adopted by George Moore in *A Mummer's Wife,* summarized but not named: "We will trace the life of the travelling actor, follow him into the vulgar, sordid surroundings which he chooses for the palace of his love, be it a pottery-shed or the ill-furnished lodging-room. . . . Is that the sort of literature that will survive the trouble of the ages? It cannot survive." The new frankness has resulted in "small poets and smaller novelists [who] bring out their sick into the thoroughfare, and stop the traffic while they give us a clinical lecture upon their sufferings" and poets "who know no rhyme for 'rest' but that 'breast' whose snowinesses and softnesses they are for ever describing." (In the realistic story "Modern Melodrama" by Hubert Crackanthorpe, a consumptive woman hears that she has only a short time in which to live and in "Stella Maris," Symons rhymes "breast" with "unrest." Possibly, Harland had shown Waugh these works before publication in order to have him direct his remarks accordingly.) Enduring literature, Waugh concludes, requires the writer to "assume that habit of reticence, that garb of humility by which true greatness is best known."

The reception of the *Yellow Book,* a celebrated episode in Victorian critical abuse, revealed that, regardless of the attempt by Harland and Beardsley to achieve a suitable balance between the traditional and advanced, many reviewers followed Waugh's schoolboy in searching for indecent passages. The reviewer in the *Times* (April 20, 1894), regarding the *Yellow Book* as "the organ of the New Literature and the Art," deplored it as "a combination of English rowdiness with French lubricity," though remarkably he praised Symons's "Stella Maris" as "graceful and melodious." In the *Westminster Gazette* (April 18, 1894), the reviewer called for an "Act of Parliament to make this kind of thing illegal." But the review that particularly offended Harland appeared in the *Speaker* (April 28, 1894), which imagines the publishers John Lane and Elkin Mathews instructing the "band of Bodley Head disciples": "Be mystic, be weird, be precious, be advanced, be without value." Harland contemplated a libel suit, "in which case," he told Lane, "we could make them apologize or pay damages," but no doubt Lane advised taking such abuse in stride. An attack in the press was, after all, better than stony silence. Harland, however, confided to Lane that "Aubrey must modify himself in Vol. II," an indication that the *Yellow Book* had succeeded too well for a periodical whose principal intent was not merely to shock its readers.

Beardsley, to be sure, was delighted by the furor, even if much of it was abusive. To Henry James, he wrote: "Have you heard of the storm that raged over No. 1? Most of the thunderbolts fell on my head. However, I enjoyed the excitement immensely." But James, as might be expected, regretted being associated with the periodical, though he also contributed to the July number. From Rome, he wrote to his brother, William:

I haven't sent you "The Yellow Book"—on purpose. . . . I say
on purpose because although my little tale which ushers it in

("The Death of the Lion") appears to have had, for a thing of mine, an unusual success, I hate too much the horrid aspect and company of the whole publication. And yet I am again to be intimately—conspicuously—associated with the second number. It is for gold and to oblige the worshipful Harland. . . .

No doubt "gold" (James received £75 for his story "The Coxon Fund")* as much as public exposure was the motive for most of the writers contributing to the periodical, but unlike James, who contributed to three more numbers, others retreated. Mrs. Pearl Craigie ("John Oliver Hobbes"), who, in the first number, had contributed the first act of a play, *The Fool's Hour,* told her collaborator George Moore: "[Harland] wants me to write a poem, story, an article, anything, for the next number. I fear I cannot oblige him. *The Speaker* on *The Yellow Book* is only too just. I have never seen such a vulgar production." When Katherine Bradley and Edith Cooper ("Michael Field," the "double-headed nightingale") saw the periodical displayed in the windows of the Bodley Head in Vigo Street, they were "almost blinded by the glare of hell." Though they had been listed among the forthcoming contributors to the *Yellow Book,* they submitted nothing. At Beardsley's insistence (the result no doubt of the unpleasant experience in illustrating *Salome*), Wilde had not been invited to contribute to the *Yellow Book.* When the first number appeared, he gloated in a letter to Lord Alfred Douglas that it was "dull and loathsome, a great failure. I am so glad."

The public, however, flocked to bookstores to see what had aroused the critics. At five shillings a copy (a rather expensive price for a periodical), the first number of the *Yellow Book* quickly sold a surprising 7,000 copies. In Volume 2 (July 1894), with a new front cover by Beardsley but with drawings of the same obvious prostitutes on the back who had appeared in the first number, several previous contributors reappeared along with new ones: Henry James, John Davidson, Max Beerbohm, William Watson, Walter Sickert (with familiar scenes in music halls and a striking painting of a consumptive Beardsley in dandiacal dress), John Singer Sargent (with a classic drawing of James), and Beardsley, as well as new women writers, including the "sub-editor" Ella D'Arcy (who contributed ten stories in the thirteen issues of the periodical), Dollie Radford (the wife of the Rhymer Ernest Radford), and Charlotte Mew

---

*Payments to contributors depended as much on reputation as on length of the story, article, or poem. James, of course, was handsomely paid by comparison with less well-known contributors. For example, Dowson's story "Apple-Blossom in Brittany" in the October 1894 issue yielded only £10 (in length, it is approximately a third of James's "The Coxon Fund"). Harland often included his own stories and criticism without payment to keep the periodical on a sound financial basis.

(whom Harland regarded as "a new *Y.B.* discovery"). Much of the fiction, particularly by women writers, is concerned with disastrous marriages, suggesting the influence of French Naturalism.

Seizing the opportunity to exploit controversy, Harland invited Hubert Crackanthorpe to reply in the July number to Waugh's "Reticence in Literature." Coeditor of the short-lived periodical the *Albemarle* (1892) and author of a volume of realistic prose sketches titled *Wreckages* (1893), Crackanthorpe alludes to "the gentleman [presumably Waugh] who objects to realistic fiction on moral grounds" in order to reveal his mistaken beliefs in the nature of literature and in the "weird word [that] has been invented to explain the whole business": "Decadence, decadence: you are all decadent nowadays. Ibsen, Degas, and the New English Art Club [which associated itself with French Impressionism]; Zola, Oscar Wilde, and the Second Mrs. Tanqueray." What the Philistine does not understand, Crackanthorpe argues, is that "a work of art can never be more than a corner of Nature, seen through the temperament of a single man," a view derived from Zola, and that "the business of art is, not to explain or to describe, but to suggest," a Modernist view derived from Pater and the French Symbolists: "We are each of us conscious, not of the whole world, but of our own world; not of naked reality, but of that aspect of reality which our peculiar temperament enables us to appropriate." Concluding, Crackanthorpe anticipates that "Before long the battle for literary freedom will be won."

In addition to following the method of the New Journalism by inviting Crackanthorpe to attack Waugh, Harland also asked the well-known art critic Philip Gilbert Hamerton to evaluate the first number of the *Yellow Book*—an invitation that was an "entirely novel idea," said Hamerton. Obviously, Harland had assured him that there would no attempt at suppressing adverse criticism, for Hamerton regretted the publication of Symons's "Stella Maris": "We know that the younger poets make art independent of morals, and certainly the two have no necessary connection; but why should poetic art be employed to celebrate common fornication?" In general, however, Hamerton praises the first number, noting with approval that in the *Yellow Book* "the principle seems to be that one kind of contribution should *not* be made subordinate to another. . . . The independence of the two arts is favourable to excellence in both. . . ."

Harland's inclusion of Hamerton's critique was, in essence, a form of journalistic self-congratulation, as was the inclusion of Beerbohm's "A Letter to the Editor," which facetiously protested that the "mob [that is, the reviewers of the *Yellow Book*] lost its head, and, so far as any one in literature can be lynched, I was": "If I had only signed myself D. Cadent or Parrar Docks, or appended a note to say that the MS. had been picked up not a hundred miles from Tite Street [where Wilde lived], all the pressmen would have said that I had given them a very delicate bit of satire."

In the next three volumes (October 1894, January 1895, April 1895) Harland retained many of the previous contributors, now clearly regarded by the critics as the coterie of the avant-garde. Up to the time of Wilde's trial, when the *Yellow Book* underwent its turbulent change, some of the new contributors—Lionel Johnson, Ernest Dowson, Olive Custance (later Lady Alfred Douglas), and Anatole France—reinforced the impression that the *Yellow Book* was an "advanced" periodical. In the remaining eight volumes (the final appearing in April 1897), Harland continued to publish many figures from his own circle, established and promising: Among the new writers of fiction were Arnold Bennett, George Gissing, John Buchan, H. G. Wells, and "Baron Corvo" (Frederick Rolfe); the significant new poets were W. B. Yeats and Stephen Phillips.

The common view that the *Yellow Book* "turned grey overnight" after Beardsley's dismissal—a form of cultural catharsis imposed on John Lane—is only a half truth, appropriate perhaps to the quality of the art, which became obviously weaker than the literature. That the periodical was able to survive after the Wilde debacle testifies to Harland's capacity to attract important new writers and to his loyalty to many who were with him from the beginning. The *Yellow Book* demonstrated that an expensive advanced publication could actually thrive, albeit for three years, in the commercial world of the New Journalism and that the potential audience for such a periodical was larger than perhaps anyone had expected.

AFTER BEARDSLEY'S DEPARTURE from the *Yellow Book* in April 1895, Leonard Smithers asked Arthur Symons to edit "a new kind of magazine, which was to appeal to the public equally in its letterpress and its illustrations." Symons lost no time in asking Beardsley to be his principal illustrator. After "endless changes and uncertainties" concerning a name for the periodical, Beardsley suggested the *Savoy,* presumably naming it after the area in the Strand, near Smither's flat and offices. However, the choice of such a title was also daring, perhaps foolhardy, since it evoked, whether intended or not, the fashionable hotel that had figured so prominently at the recent Wilde trials. Perhaps because of the unsavory association, Thomas Hardy did not like the title; nevertheless, he was willing to have his name listed in the prospectus as a forthcoming contributor. Despite Symons's urging, Hardy sent nothing to be published, but there may have been a further reason: Beardsley had submitted an illustration for the prospectus in which George Moore noted, to his dismay, that the figure of John Bull, entering a stage with huge pens and an announcement in his hands, had an obscene swelling in his tight breeches.

Some of the outraged prospective contributors, such as Moore, Shaw, and Selwyn Image, held a hurried meeting in the rooms shared by Edgar Jepson and Herbert Horne in King's Bench Walk, The Temple, to decide on a course of action. Since Smithers had already circulated some 80,000 copies of the prospectus, the situation was serious; moreover, the recent furor over Beardsley and the *Yellow Book* no doubt evoked visions of renewed abuse by the press. At the meeting, Shaw proposed, after he was unanimously chosen to assume the "post of fighting man in chief . . . by the scandalised contributors," that they converge on Smithers in his offices and demand the withdrawal of Beardsley's drawing. When Smithers expressed pleasure with the prospectus, the delegation urged that at least the drawing should be modified to remove what Shaw called "the subtle stroke that emphasized the virility of John." Convinced of the "poisonous" element as well as the "puerile mischievousness" in Beardsley's work, Shaw argued that it could be "exploitable by speculators in pornography." Smithers offered no resistance; a less excited image of John Bull appeared before the contents page.

The first of eight numbers of the *Savoy* (all published in 1896) appeared in January as a quarterly, larger in format than that of the *Yellow Book,* whose January issue, as though in response to its new rival, was its lengthiest—406 pages—as opposed to the *Savoy*'s mere 170 pages. In the

Prospectus for the *Savoy*
(Greater London Photograph
Library)

tradition of the aesthetic periodical, its spacious margins and attractive, widely spaced type, its absence of advertising, except for its publisher's listings, and its elegant cover by Beardsley of a stately Pre-Raphaelite woman in a classical, pastoral landscape revealed no attempt at commercialism or sensationalism. (Just before publication, however, Smithers had alertly detected that Beardsley's malicious cover illustration contained a mostly bare Cupid in the foreground seemingly about to urinate on a copy of the *Yellow Book*. He ordered the rival periodical removed from the drawing and the Cupid figure desexualized.) Symons's "Editorial Note," if not disingenuous and evasive, was at least direct: "We have no formulas, and we desire no false unity of form or matter. We have not invented a new point of view. We are not Realists, or Romanticists, or Decadents. For us, all art is good which is good art." No manifesto, to be sure, since Smithers wanted a financial success, such as he had observed in the *Yellow Book*, without public scandal or obvious contentiousness.

The contributors to this first number reveal Symons's determination to surpass the *Yellow Book* in name recognition: Shaw, Beerbohm, Dowson, Yeats, Image, Havelock Ellis, Whistler, Shannon, and, of course, Symons and Beardsley. From the contents, there is little to suggest a particular artistic ideology, except when one turns to the first three chapters of Beardsley's tale *Under the Hill,* to which he also contributed three illustrations. The world of Decadent artifice, which Beerbohm had ironically

Initial cover for the *Savoy*

welcomed in his piece for the *Yellow Book,* is here elaborately drawn, verbally and visually. However, Beardsley had radically expurgated his comic "romantic novel" to secure its publication. The original version, titled *Venus and Tannhäuser,* was a polymorphously perverse story that Beardsley never completed because of illness (Smithers privately printed ten chapters in 1907). Despite the presence of poets, such as Symons and Dowson, reputed by reviewers to be decadent, a modern critic has observed that "the reader who turns to the *Savoy* expecting to find a luscious garden of exotic and forbidden poetry will be largely disappointed." The periodical contains such an unexpected surprise as John Gray's "The Forge" (April 1896), a radically different poem from much of the Symbolist/Decadent verse of his *Silverpoints* (1893). The startling hell of industrialism is depicted with such dissonances as "Flame-flesh-shapes, sweat-swamped clinging cotton swathed"—recalling Gerard Manley Hopkins, whose verse Gray had probably not seen.

In the following numbers, the *Savoy* revealed its avant-garde intentions in its preponderance of material concerned with the French Symbolists, with the occult, and with Blakean Pre-Raphaelitism. In April, for example, Verlaine was the central figure in articles by Gosse ("A First Sight of Verlaine"), Yeats ("Verlaine in 1894"), and Verlaine himself recalling his visit to London in 1893. However, though other French writers—such as Mallarmé, Verhaeren, Zola, Edmond de Goncourt, and Jean Moréas—appear in translation or are subjects of criticism, the *Savoy* was not, as some modern critics have called it, an "Anglo-French enterprise." Associated with the French Symbolists, Yeats's occult story "Rosa Alchemica" (April 1896) involves the narrator's quest for the transformation of the self and for "the birth of that elaborate spiritual beauty which could alone uplift souls weighted down with so many dreams." Yeats recalls how Poe discovered a "mood" (an immortal, ancient reality), which "took possession of Baudelaire, and from Baudelaire passed to England and the Pre-Raphaelites," wandering still, "enlarging its power as it goes, awaiting the time when it shall be, perhaps, alone or with other moods, master over a great new religion. . . ."

Yeats's Pre-Raphaelite preoccupations and his previous editorial work on Blake's poetry in 1893 were now directed in three articles to the poet's illustrations for the *Divine Comedy* (July, August, and September). The first of the three articles unites the French Symbolists with Blake and the Pre-Raphaelites in their "recoil from scientific naturalism" and their expression of "a new and subtle inspiration." Blake, Yeats contends, "was certainly the first great *symboliste* of modern times, and the first of any time to preach the indissoluble marriage of all great art with symbol." But with the inclusion in the July issue of Blake's illustration "Antaeus Setting Virgil and Dante upon the Verge of Cocytus," the manager for W. H.

Smith, the bookseller who controlled railway book and magazine stalls, ordered the *Savoy* removed because of the nude figure of Antaeus. When Symons argued that Blake was "a very spiritual artist," the manager responded with Victorian certitude: "O, Mr. Symons, you must remember that we have an audience of young ladies as well as an audience of agnostics."

If Yeats was the principal contributor who advanced the Symbolist, occult, and Blakean cause in the *Savoy,* Havelock Ellis was the periodical's polemicist, "conducting a sustained if discreet attack on the *cant Britannique.*" In the first number, Ellis defended Zola, whose name—"a barbarous, explosive name, like an anarchist's bomb"—had been "tossed about amid hoots and yells for a quarter of a century." However, Zola (who by the mid-nineties was being widely praised) had been a pioneer in enlarging the "field of the novel" by bringing the "modern material world into fiction." Ellis next undertook a three-part article on Nietzsche (April, July, and September), who had been for some years the object of "passionate admiration or denunciation" in Germany. And, Ellis remarks, "we may expect a similar outburst in England now that a complete translation of his works has begun to appear."

Among the first in England to write an extended essay on Nietzsche, Ellis was drawn to him for his attack on centuries of received morality: Nietzsche "stood at the finest summit of modern culture, who has thence made the most determined effort ever made to destroy modern morals . . . [and who] represents, perhaps, the greatest spiritual force which has appeared since Goethe. . . ." The reason for such widespread interest in Nietzsche in the late Victorian and Edwardian periods by Yeats, Shaw, Symons, George Moore, John Davidson, and D. H. Lawrence undoubtedly lies in Ellis's revealing statement: "Modern democracy, modern utilitarianism, are largely of English manufacture, and he came at last to hate them both. During the past century, he asserted, they have reduced the whole spiritual currency of Europe to a dull plebeian level, and they are the chief causes of European vulgarity." Nietzsche "ended by asserting that the world only exists for the production of a few great men." For Ellis and others in the avant-garde—whether Socialists, Decadents, or Symbolists—Nietzsche validated their conviction that the late nineteenth century required a radical new vision to jettison old pieties.

Pursuing his interest in those who challenged "dull plebeian" culture, Ellis wrote in the October issue supporting Hardy's *Jude the Obscure* (1895), which had been attacked in the press for its sexual candour. Ellis concludes that the "austere and restrained roads of art" which Hardy has followed in his novel mark it as "the greatest novel written in England for many years": "It deals very subtly and sensitively with new and modern aspects of life, and if, in so doing, it may be said to represent Nature as often cruel to our social laws, we must remark that the strife of Nature and Society, the individual and the community, has ever been the artist's opportunity." Ellis saw "strife of Nature and Society" also operating in Casanova's life, of which he wrote in the November issue as though summing up the motivating impulses of the avant-garde: "Whatever offences against social codes he may have committed, Casanova can scarcely be said to have sinned against natural laws. He was only abnormal because so natural a person within the gates of civilization is necessarily abnormal and at war with his environment."

What Ellis called in Hardy's fiction the "new and modern aspects of life" is evident in several of the *Savoy* contributions that focus on the fin-de-siècle concern with madness. In the October issue, for example, Joseph Conrad's story "The Idiots" symbolizes the degeneration of modern life by four idiots born to Brittany peasants, the wife's murder of her husband, and her own ensuing insanity—a radical departure from the British preference for depicting the nobler aspects of human nature in fiction. The relationship between madness and creativity—prominent in earlier Romanticism and a preoccupation of the late Victorians—is suggested in Ellis's translation of Cesare Lombroso's essay "A Mad Saint" in the April issue. The Italian criminologist and physician describes one of his patients who had had auditory and visual hallucinations since childhood. After the self-sacrificial woman had seen "wonderful visions of the Madonna and the saints" as well as "evil spirits," finally of God Himself, she began writing extraordinary religious verse, an indication, says Lombroso, of "how genius often arises from a matrix of insanity": "The germ of holiness, as well as that of genius, must be sought among the insane."

A further vision of madness occurs in Beardsley's "The Ballad of a Barber" (in the July issue), a poem possibly inspired by John Gray's "The Barber" or by the popular Victorian melodrama *Sweeney Todd; or, the Demon Barber of Fleet Street.* Like Gray, Beardsley depicts the barber as a Decadent artist dealing with the instruments of artifice; abruptly, he turns into an insane slasher of a young girl whose coiffure he has failed to master—"surely intended," says a modern critic, "to convey a complete allegory of Decadence itself."

The *Savoy* came to an end with the December 1896 issue, entirely illustrated by Beardsley and written by Symons (who included his translation of the major Symbolist poem, Mallarmé's "Hérodiade"). Smithers had obviously miscalculated the size of the audience. When the first three numbers sold well, he decided to publish monthly instead of quarterly, a decision that increased his financial burden without a corresponding increase in sales. By November, Symons announced the forthcoming end in an editorial note: The *Savoy* had "conquered the prejudices of the press" but had not "conquered the general public." In the final number, Symons lamented that "we assumed that there were very many people in the world who really cared for art, and really art's sake," but "art cannot appeal to the multitude. It is wise when it does not attempt to." The major achievement of this most important aesthetic periodical of the 1890s, as Richard Ellmann has remarked, was that it was "the first and the only English magazine to expound and illustrate" the Symbolist Movement.

LIKE THE *Yellow Book* and the *Savoy,* which sought to appeal to a wide audience interested in the latest trends in literature and art, the *Pageant,* a hard-cover annual selling at the expensive price of six shillings, challenged the commercial periodicals in its appearance in December 1895 (though its title page has the date of publication as 1896). Charles Shannon and J. W. Gleeson White, the art critic and anthologist, its editors, secured the talents of Charles Ricketts, who designed the cloth cover of six birds in flight, and Selwyn Image, who designed the graceful title page. Many of the contributors, such as Verlaine, Swinburne, Yeats, and John Gray, reveal the *Pageant*'s aesthetic allegiances to French Symbolism and Pre-Raphaelitism. The 1897 issue of the *Pageant* (issued in December 1896) contained many of the same contributors to the preceding volume and some notable new ones, such as Edmund Gosse, Dante Gabriel Rossetti, Maurice Maeterlinck, Villiers de l'Isle-Adam, Ernest Dowson, and Gustave Moreau. The French Symbolist and Pre-Raphaelite influences thus remained strong. Despite an array of illustrious names, the *Pageant* was unable to survive its second number, the predictable fate of the aesthetic periodical.

When the *Yellow Book,* the *Savoy,* and the *Pageant* passed out of existence, the *Dome: A Quarterly Containing Examples of All the Arts,* appeared in March 1897—"as though," one critic has observed, "the death of one minority periodical must generate another." Edited by the former Nonconformist clergyman and now novelist and publisher Ernest J. Oldmeadow, the *Dome* was undistinguished in its typography, its covers, and its page design. Unlike many previous aesthetic periodicals, it particularly emphasized music, with prose contributions by Frederick Delius (under the name of "Fritz" Delius), Arnold Dolmetsch, and Edward Elgar; in addition, it published essays on Berlioz, Wagner, and Tchaikovsky as well as reviews of concerts featuring their works. Perhaps the most distinguished prose piece was Yeats's essay "The Symbolism of Poetry," written in response to Symons's *The Symbolist Movement in Literature* (1900) and published in the April 1900 issue of the *Dome.* Because Oldmeadow absorbed the cost of publishing the periodical (much as Mackmurdo kept the *Century Guild Hobby Horse* going by underwriting its publication), the *Dome* survived for three years. His determination to maintain it for his own amusement continued until the costs of paper rose suddenly during the Boer War and ended his self-indulgence.

Being "too highbrow" had doomed many of the aesthetic periodicals. For most of the literary and artistic elite that regarded itself as avant garde, failure was the consequence of their refusal to compromise with the petit bourgeoisie and of their determination to separate themselves from mass readership. Without outrageous manifestoes and assaults on conventional readers, such as those Wyndham Lewis and Ezra Pound launched in their own short-lived publication *Blast* (1914–15), the aesthetic periodicals developed the foundations for Modernism in their subdued rejection of many of the narrow Victorian attitudes and conventions in art and literature, enabling Lewis and Pound to emerge as self-appointed saviors of English culture. In their rejection of Aestheticism and the aesthetic periodicals as an appropriate model for their own explosive publication ("CURSE with expletive of whirlwind THE BRITANNIC AESTHETE"), Lewis and Pound were unwilling to concede that their own views of the artifice and autonomy of art had derived from the fin-de-siècle Aesthetes and Decadents. Predictably, with the second number, *Blast* went the way of preceding aesthetic periodicals, though the First World War no doubt hastened its demise by turning the public's attention away from the pretensions of high culture to the desperation of survival in the trenches.

11

Whistler, the Fantastic Butterfly

W<small>HEN</small> J<small>AMES</small> M<small>ACNEILL</small> W<small>HISTLER</small> died in 1903, Arthur Symons wrote in tribute:

> Whistler is dead, and there goes with him one of the greatest painters and one of the most original personalities of our time. . . . He deceived the public for many years; he probably deceived many of his acquaintances till the day of his death. Yet his whole life was a devotion to art, and everything that he said or wrote proclaimed that devotion, however fantastically.

As an American who subscribed to the French notion of *l'art pour l'art,* Whistler adopted a witty and combative stance against those who regarded his art as somehow amoral, associated with the writings of the Aesthetes and Decadents from Swinburne to Wilde. As Symons remarked, Whistler was serious about his art though he seemed "to be the irresponsible butterfly of his famous signature." Reluctant to align himself with any avant-garde group, Whistler deceived the public into believing that he was a frivolous dandy with monocle and walking stick when, in fact, he was intent on directing the academic art of his time to a new sense of painting's visionary possibilities.

In his lifelong insistence that a painting was a work of artifice rather than a mere imitation of external reality or the depiction of an anecdote with moral implications, Whistler challenged the approved art of his era, specifically the preferences of the Royal Academy, which catered to Victorian bourgeois taste. The paintings exhibited at the academy in Burlington House—usually depicting scenes from the Bible or from mythology as well as realistic, sentimental genre subjects and familiar landscapes—were often designed for the comfortable new homes of successful merchants and manufacturers. Such taste was, to be sure, cul-

Giovanni Boldini's *Portrait of James McNeill Whistler* (Courtesy of The Brooklyn Museum, 09.849, Gift of A. Augustus Healy)

turally determined: Underlying it was a deep need for confirmation of social and religious values, increasingly imperiled as the nineteenth century progressed.

Whistler was destined to encounter John Ruskin, Slade Professor of Art at Oxford, who espoused Establishment views on art (though he harshly criticized the use of art and architecture to advance the materialistic values of an industrial society). Art in any country, he insisted, *"is the exponent of its social and political virtues"*; to advance such values, he advocated a return to the absolute rules that the earlier Romantics had abandoned: ". . . laws of truth and right . . . just as fixed as those of harmony in music, or of affinity in chemistry." He attacked the French Impressionists for their violation of what he regarded as a basic rule in art: Objects must be painted with clarity of detail. As a supporter of Whistler, W. E. Henley wrote (with some misunderstanding) in opposition to Ruskin's urging that the Pre-Raphaelites devote themselves to the doctrine of truth to nature: "To render the facts . . . grain by grain, or hair by hair, or petal by petal, is to play a losing game with the camera. Imitation for its own sake is the basest of aims, and the pursuit of it can have but the meanest results."

Whistler was not the only artist to incur Ruskin's wrath. One unhappy painter, lamenting his fate as victim of Ruskin's authority in the art world, wrote in comic doggerel:

I paints and paints,
Hears no complaints,
    And sells before I'm dry;
Till savage Ruskin
Sticks his tusk in
    And nobody will buy.

WHISTLER IS KNOWN, though not exclusively, for his visionary paintings of the Thames. In the early Victorian period, writers and artists generally avoided depictions of the less attractive aspects of London (among major writers, Dickens was a notable exception). The bewildering vastness and sordidness of "the world's Metropolis," which grew rapidly to over six and a half million inhabitants by the end of the nineteenth century, were inhibiting factors for artists who catered to middle-class preferences for inspiring art. Indeed, as has been observed, "even the urban poor responded—or were trained to respond—more readily to art that ignored the realities of their lives than that which did not."*

In 1859, when Whistler settled in London, the Thames and its vibrant life on the river so fascinated him that he focused on a world relatively untouched by native artists. He proceeded to "re-educate the sensibilities of the public and his fellow practitioners" with a series of etchings and oil paintings depicting life on and around the river in a manner different from that of the academy artists. On occasion, these painters, in the approved academic style, celebrated and idealized the historical events associated with the Thames, such as the opening of the Houses of Parliament and the Embankment. Whistler, however, depicted the common lives of sailors and the activities on the docks and bridges; progressively, he envisioned a shadowy night world that required a new technique in applying paint to canvas.

Through the 1860s and 1870s, Whistler painted what he called "symphonies," "nocturnes,"† "harmonies," and "arrangements," the most

---

*It was not until the 1870s and 1880s that London became a common subject for artists, among them some of Whistler's followers: Walter Sickert, Walter Greaves, and Mortimer Menpes. The "most significant visual record" of the extremes of Victorian urban life is the series of 180 engravings by the French illustrator Gustave Doré for *London: A Pilgrimage* (1872), which recalls his illustrations for Dante's infernal world. See Ira Bruce Nadel, "Gustave Doré: English Art and London Life," *Victorian Artists and the City,* eds. Ira Bruce Nadel and F. S. Schwartzbach (New York, 1980), 152–53.

†Around 1872, the shipping magnate F. R. Leyland, who was an amateur pianist, suggested the use of the musical term *nocturne* for some of Whistler's paintings. Whistler informed his patron: "I say I can't thank you too much for the name Nocturne as the title for my Moonlights. You have no idea what an irritation it proves to the critics

famous of which is the geometric *Arrangement in Grey and Black* (over the years, it has acquired a subtitle—sometimes "The Artist's Mother" or "Portrait of the Painter's Mother"—which Whistler never intended). The use of musical terms suggested a harmony of elements achieved through tone and color frequently subdued (in opposition to the brilliant colors employed by the Royal Academy painters), sometimes without identifiable objects in the painting. The intent was not synaesthetic but ideological, for Whistler, insisting on art for art's sake, employed the transposition of the arts in the tradition of Gautier and Baudelaire as an affront to Victorian convention. He may also have recalled Pater's famous remark: *"All art constantly aspires towards the condition of music,"* a view suggesting that the "subject" in a work of art is—or, at least, should be—inseparable from the means of expression. Art, Whistler contended, was the result of the artist's manipulation of his medium in order to evoke aesthetic pleasure, not to instruct spectators or to confirm moral preferences. In the *World* (May 22, 1878), Whistler defended his practice of using musical terms in order to suggest the artifice and autonomy of art:

> As music is the poetry of sound, so is painting the poetry of sight, and subject-matter has nothing to do with harmony of sound or of colour. . . . Art should be independent of all clap-trap—should stand alone, and appeal to the artistic sense of eye or ear, without confounding this with emotions entirely foreign to it, as devotion, pity, love, patriotism, and the like. . . . Take the picture of my mother, exhibited at the Royal Academy as an "Arrangement in Grey and Black." Now that is what it is. To me it is interesting as a picture of my mother; but what can or ought the public to care about the identity of the portrait?

One of the notable events of the Victorian age that dramatized the conflict between the artist and the Establishment involved Whistler's suit in 1878 against the mentally unstable Ruskin, who had condemned his painting titled *Nocturne in Black and Gold: The Falling Rocket,* an impression of fireworks at the Cremorne Gardens in Chelsea (which had closed in 1877). Its daring lay in the barely discernible subject: a falling rocket suggested at a fleeting moment of perception by the layers of gold pigment cascading downwards in the dark night. Whistler had affixed his

---

and consequent pleasure to me; besides it is really charming and does so poetically say all I want to say and *no more* than I wish" (quoted in E. R. and J. Pennell, *The Life of James McNeill Whistler* [Philadelphia, 1908], 1: 116).

price for the painting when it went on view at the fashionable Grosvenor Gallery in New Bond Street. In his July 2 monthly newsletter titled *Fors Clavigera* ("Fate Bearing a Hammer"), designed to educate the working classes on a variety of subjects, Ruskin wrote: "I have seen, and heard, much of Cockney impudence before now; but never expected to hear a coxcomb ask two hundred guineas for flinging a pot of paint in the public's face."

Convinced that Ruskin's comment warranted legal redress and perhaps hopeful that a dramatic confrontation between artist and critic would provide the public with an appreciation of his own art, Whistler sued for injury to his reputation. His wit and shrewd theatricalism in responding to the inept questions posed by Ruskin's barrister won over the spectators in court. When questioned concerning his painting titled *Nocturne in Blue and Gold: Old Battersea Bridge* (1872–73),* Whistler defended it in much the same manner that he had other paintings in which traditional representation was abandoned: "I did not intend it to be a 'correct' portrait of the bridge. It is only a moonlight scene and the pier in the center of the picture may not be like the piers at Battersea Bridge as you know them in broad daylight. As to what the picture represents, that depends upon who looks at it."

The jury, apparently convinced that Whistler had suffered no great damage, awarded him a farthing (one fourth of a penny). Such a pyrrhic victory, granted by a jury presumably made up of respectable bourgeoisie, reminded him painfully that the innovative artist in Victorian society was treading on dangerous ground. Art was expected, after all, to confirm man's moral nature and—particularly for Ruskin—to reveal the beauty of a divinely ordained world. The jury's token award implied condemnation of Whistler's challenge to society's spiritual needs. The final blow was that court costs left him bankrupt.

Curiously, Ruskin, who was too ill to appear in court, had been a defender of the early nineteenth-century artist J. M. W. Turner, whose luminous images of the sea had inspired Whistler to attempt experiments with light and color to approximate the near obliteration of subject matter until the artist's impression was all that remained. Mallarmé, who became a close friend, sensed Whistler's parallel in this respect to Symbolist technique—that is, the suppression of an object's precise outlines to enable the imagination to perceive ultimate realities. French Impressionism of the 1870s and Whistler's own version of Impressionism in England (differing in their respective techniques of applying paint to canvas, the former involving "flickering brushwork" to depict the play of light on

---

*In his own account of the court trial, Whistler refers to this painting as "the nocturne in blue and silver." See *The Gentle Art of Making Enemies* (1892; New York, 1967), 7–8.

Whistler's *Nocturne in Black and Gold*

Whistler's *Nocturne in Blue and Gold*

objects, dissolved in the process, whereas Whistler thinned the paint "often to the consistency of a juice that let the canvas or the panel show through" as he strove for "pure arrangement"). Such fin-de-siècle developments were significant, for much ensuing twentieth-century art went further in abandoning subject matter and external reality entirely for the private, sometimes spiritual, visions of Abstract Expressionism.

AS HE STRUGGLED to survive financially (for years, he could not sell his painting of the falling rocket, now in the Detroit Institute of Arts, or the portrait of his mother, now in the Louvre),* Whistler persisted in provoking critics by his vitriolic flashes of wit in innumerable letters to newspapers and periodicals; indeed, he emerged as the dandy with a caustic pen and adopted, as his signature, the image of a deceptively innocent butterfly with a sting in its tail. He employs this graphic image in a variety of suggestive forms in *The Gentle Art of Making Enemies* (1890), which he himself designed in order to break with Victorian conventions. On the

*"The *Mother* purchase [in 1891] electrified artistic London and set critics in England and America to bemoaning the loss to France of a painting either nation could have had any time over the years" (Stanley Weintraub, *Whistler: A Biography* [New York, 1974], 354).

title page, he uses italics in an asymmetrical arrangement, and in the pages following, he maintains wide margins, which he often fills with comments on his own and his enemies' remarks.

In addition to articles and letters (including his combative correspondence with Oscar Wilde, who, he insisted, shamelessly plagiarized his ideas on the nature of art), the book includes his lecture titled "Ten O'Clock," which he delivered at Prince's Hall, Piccadilly, at that odd hour on the evening of February 20, 1885. In a style almost baroque in its eccentricity and energy, Whistler asserts that art is "selfishly occupied with her own perfection only—having no desire to teach—seeking and finding the beautiful in all conditions and in all times" and that "the people have acquired the habit of looking . . . not *at* a picture but *through* it, at some human fact, that shall, or shall not, from a social point of view, better their mental or moral state." Attacking Romantic and Victorian attitudes towards nature, Whistler asserts that nature is "usually wrong": It rarely presents the artist with "the condition of things that shall bring about the perfection of harmony worthy a picture." In short, the artist, rather than nature, creates harmony, as in the famous passage that suggests the transforming power of the imagination:

> And when the evening mist clothes the riverside with poetry, as with a veil, and the poor buildings lose themselves in the dim sky, and the tall chimneys become campanili, and the warehouses are palaces in the night, and the whole city hangs in the heavens, and fairy-land is before us . . . Nature, who, for once, has sung in tune, sings her exquisite song to the artist alone, her son and her master. . . .

Directing a barb at the flamboyant Wilde, Whistler remarked that "the Dilettante stalks abroad. The amateur is loosed. The voice of the aesthete is heard in the land, and catastrophe is upon us." Wilde, who, like George Moore and Walter Sickert, was among those in the fashionable audience, reviewed the lecture in the *Pall Mall Gazette* (February 21, 1885). Calling Whistler "a miniature Mephistopheles, mocking the majority," Wilde declared the lecture a "masterpiece." Alluding to Whistler's famous painting that had goaded Ruskin, Wilde remarked that Whistler had launched "some arrows barbed and brilliant, shot off, with all the speed and splendour of fireworks, at the archeologists, who spend their lives in verifying the birthplaces of nobodies, and estimate the value of a work of art by its date or its decay, and the art critics who always treat a picture as if it were a novel, and try and find out the plot." Ending his piece, Wilde included his own clever barb that deflated the high praise that preceded it, as though in retaliation for Whistler's remark concerning "the Dilettante" that stalks abroad:

Not merely for its clever satire and amusing jests will it be remembered, but for the pure and perfect beauty of many of its passages—passages delivered with an earnestness which seemed to amaze those who had looked on Mr. Whistler as a master of persiflage merely, and had not known him, as we do, as a master of painting also. For that he is indeed one of the very greatest masters of painting, is my opinion. And I may add that in this opinion Mr. Whistler himself entirely concurs.

In a letter to the *World* (February 25, 1885), Whistler alluded to Wilde's "exquisite article" and its remark that "the poet is the supreme artist . . . lord over all life and all arts." Whistler responded with the expected sting of the Butterfly: "Nothing is more delicate, in the flattery of 'the Poet' to 'the Painter' than the *naïveté* of 'the Poet'. . . ." To which, Wilde riposted: "Be warned in time, James; and remain, as I do, incomprehensible: to be great is to be misunderstood."

When the lecture was published in 1888, Whistler suggested through the poet Theodore Watts-Dunton that a review from Swinburne would be welcome. But Swinburne's piece in the *Fortnightly Review* (June 1888) ended their friendship abruptly, for though it opens with a passage filled with guarded praise for the lecture's "brilliant and pungent wit, wisdom salted with paradox and reason spiced with eccentricity," the review limps to a conclusive phrase referring to Whistler's "truths and semi-truths, admirable propositions and questionable inferences." Of two of Whistler's major portraits, that of Thomas Carlyle and of the artist's mother, Swinburne contends that they are more than the "merest 'arrangements' in colour":

> It would be quite useless for Mr. Whistler to protest—if haply he should be so disposed—that he never meant to put study of character and revelation of intellect into his portrait of Mr. Carlyle, or intense pathos of significance and tender depth of expression into the portrait of his own venerable mother. The scandalous fact remains, that he has done so; and in so doing has explicitly violated and implicitly abjured the creed and the canons, the counsels and the catechism of Japan.

Swinburne called Whistler's devotion to Japanese art "Asiatic aestheticism," with which, he said, Whistler had attempted "unhappily . . . to depreciate and degrade his genius."

Furious, Whistler dashed off a letter to the *World* (June 3, 1888): "Cannot the man who wrote *Atalanta* and the *Ballads Beautiful*—can he not be content to spend his life with *his* work, which should be his love, and has for him no misleading doubt and darkness, that he should stray about blindly in his brother's flower beds and bruise himself! ... Who are you, deserting your Muse, that you should insult my Goddess with familiarity ... ?'' In response, Swinburne turned to the more controlled and biting form of light verse:

> *Fly away, butterfly, back to Japan,*
> *Tempt not a pinch at the hand of a man,*
> *And strive not to sting ere you die away.*
> *So pert and so painted, so proud and so pretty,*
> *To brush the bright down from your wings were a pity—*
> *Fly away, butterfly, fly away!*

As his friendship with Swinburne dwindled, Whistler now sought to dispose of Wilde, who had lately been publishing art criticism. In the *World* (November 17, 1888), Whistler plunged to the heart of his adversary with mocking alliteration: "What has Oscar in common with Art? except that he dines at our tables and picks from our platters the plums for the pudding he peddles in the provinces?" The "amiable, irresponsible" Oscar, he said, had "the courage of the opinions ... of others!" Wilde replied in "The Decay of Lying" (1889), which not only brazenly echoes some of Whistler's artistic views but also extends them in his witty remark that "Life imitates Art far more than Art imitates Life."* In the revised version of the essay in *Intentions* (1891), Wilde adds that "Nature, no less than Life, is an imitation of Art" and parodies Whistler's famous fog passage in the "Ten O'Clock" lecture with an ironic allusion to the "master":

> Where, if not from the Impressionists, do we get those wonderful brown fogs that come creeping down our streets, blurring the gas-lamps and changing the houses into monstrous shadows? To whom, if not them and their master, do we owe the lovely silver mists that brood over our river, and turn to faint forms of fading grace curved bridge and swaying barge? The extraordinary change that has taken place in the climate of London during the last ten years is entirely due to a particular school of Art. ... At present, people see fogs, not because there are fogs, but because poets and painters have taught them the mysterious loveliness of such effects.

---

*Citing the original draft of *The Picture of Dorian Gray*, Richard Ellmann regards Basil Hallward, the painter, whom Dorian kills, as "clearly and libelously Whistler"— perhaps Wilde's fantasy that, in this instance, life would do well to imitate art. See Richard Ellmann, *Oscar Wilde* (New York, 1988), 278.

The Whistlerian vision also inspired George Egerton, whose story "A Lost Masterpiece" in the *Yellow Book* (April 1894) is told by a narrator who boards a river steamer at Chelsea bound for London Bridge: "The tall chimneys ceased to be giraffic throats belching soot and smoke over the blackening city. They were obelisks rearing granite heads heavenwards!" The fascination with the city was tolerable only when such imaginative transformation took place, for the Aesthetes regarded the Victorian industrialized world as truly a decadent one.

DESPITE THEIR STAGED verbal duels, Wilde had admired Whistler as one of his "heroes" and adopted his practice of combining the arts to emphasize artifice and to exclude the sentimentality of much popular verse. He was drawn to Whistler's night scenes of the Thames, which evoked the mystery of the transformed city. Before Whistler's "Ten O'-Clock" lecture, Wilde had embodied the haunting vision of Whistler's oil painting *Nocturne in Blue and Gold: Old Battersea Bridge* (1872–73) in his own "Impression du Matin" (1881):

> *The Thames nocturne of blue and gold*
> *   Changed to a Harmony in gray:*
> *   A barge with ochre-coloured hay*
> *Dropt from the wharf: and chill and cold*
>
> *The yellow fog came creeping down*
> *   The bridges, till the houses' walls*
> *   Seemed changed to shadows, and St. Paul's*
> *Loomed like a bubble o'er the town.*

The final image of the "pale woman all alone" who loiters beneath the "gas-lamp's flare, / With lips of flame, and heart of stone" is, despite the striking vision, a conventional moral condemnation of the prostitute.

Wilde's color design in "Symphony in Yellow" (1889), one of his purest poems, contains a series of clearly defined impressions (un-Whistlerian, perhaps) and an absence of moral discourse, anticipating the later Imagists, such as Pound, who advocated hard, clear images (a reaction to the cultivated indefiniteness of French Symbolism):

> *The yellow leaves begin to fade*
> *   And flutter from the Temple elms,*
> *   And at my feet the pale green Thames*
> *Lies like a rod of rippled jade.*

By the nineties, the Whistlerian influence was increasingly evident among the aesthetically inclined poets who challenged prevailing Victorian notions of acceptable artistic expression. The city became for writers of the decade, as it had not been for the mid-Victorians, the symbol of one's soul with implications of spiritual and psychological turmoil. (Baudelaire's *Les Fleurs du mal,* in its visions of Paris as analogies of the poet's psyche, had shown the way.) In a nineties' piece, G. K. Chesterton implied such a view that absorbed the early Modernists:

> A city is, properly speaking, more poetic even than a country-side, for while nature is a chaos of unconscious forces, a city is a chaos of conscious ones. . . . There is no stone in the street and no brick in the wall that is not actually a deliberate symbol—a message from some man. . . . The narrowest street possesses, in every crook and twist of its intention, the soul of the man who built it. . . .

Arthur Conan Doyle's Sherlock Holmes stories, with their nocturnal settings in the fogbound, labyrinthine streets of London, suggest such symbolic analogies in the troubled lives of its characters.

In 1893, Symons argued that, to be regarded as modern, the poet (and, by extension, the painter, such as Whistler) had to include the less attractive aspects of the city, a means of eliminating conventional nature imagery and sentiments associated with popular poetry. Of Henley, he wrote: "Here, at last, is a poet who can so enlarge the limits of his verse as to take in London. And I think that might be the test of poetry which professes to be modern . . .to represent really oneself and one's surroundings, the world as it is today, to be modern and yet poetical, is, perhaps, the most difficult, as it is certainly the most interesting, of all artistic achievements." Even Henley, who favored socially responsible literature (but who championed Whistler because painting, he believed, consisted of line and color "subject to no particular ethical connotation"), employed the device of correspondences in the arts. In *London Voluntaries* (1893), he suggests a symphony by naming the four major sections *Andante con Moto, Scherzando, Largo e Mesto,* and *Allegro maëstoso,* designed to evoke four moods of London with Whistlerian touches, as in

> *O, the mysterious distances, the glooms*
> *Romantic, the august*
> *And solemn shapes! At night this City of Trees*
> *Turns to a tryst of vague and strange*
> *And monstrous Majesties. . . .*

In "Rhymes and Rhythms: XIII" (1892), dedicated "To James MacNeill Whistler," Henley acknowledges his indebtedness to his friend who had revealed a striking new vision of London:

> *Under a stagnant sky,*
> *Gloom out of gloom uncoiling into gloom,*
> *The River, jaded and forlorn,*
> *Welters and wanders wearily—wretchedly—on.*

In appreciation, Whistler offered him a nocturne to illustrate the poem in Henley's edited volume, *A London Garland* (1895).

Always at the center of the avant-garde, Arthur Symons wrote Whist-lerian-inspired poems titled "Pastel," "Impression," and "Nocturne," the latter evoking

> *. . . the Embankment with its lights,*
> *The pavement glittering with fallen rain,*
> *The magic and mystery that are night's . . .*

Other nineties poets focus upon the same mysterious world in the most industrialized, presumably most prosaic, city on earth. Richard Le Gal-lienne's "Sunset in the City" (1891) reveals a probable reading of Whist-ler or Wilde, for the image of the transformed city is clearly derived from the famous fog passage in the "Ten O'Clock" lecture and its variation in Wilde's *Intentions:*

> *Within the town the streets grow strange and haunted,*
> *And, dark against the western lakes of green,*
> *The buildings change to temples . . .*

In Laurence Binyon's "Deptford" (1896), referring to the principal dock area in East London, the fog obscures the decay and depression of its inhabitants:

> *Alas, I welcome this dull mist, that drapes*
> *The path of the heavy sky above the street*
> *Casting a phantom dimness on these shapes*
> *That pass. . . .*

John Davidson—who, T. S. Eliot states, was a poet who "impressed me deeply in my formative years between the ages of sixteen and twenty"— wrote a Whistlerian "Nocturne" (1891) and "Fog" (1909), with its irony "That Doomsday somewhere dawns among / The systems and the galaxies" while we are "simply swallowed up / In London fog for ever-more." And in "Railway Stations: London Bridge" (1895), he depicts the unfeeling "human tide" that flows across the bridge:

> *And yet this human tide,*
> *As callous as the glaciers that glide*
> *A foot a day, but as a torrent swift,*
> *Sweeps unobservant save of time—*

Such impressionistic images of London as presented by Wilde, Henley, Symons, Binyon, and Davidson, with Whistlerian touches of fog, mist, and gloom, prepared the way in the fin de siècle for the symbolic vision of the modern city's sterility and death, particularly in Eliot's *The Waste Land* (1922), a depiction of a fragmented, spiritually dead civilization:

> *Unreal City,*
> *Under the brown fog of a winter dawn,*
> *A crowd flowed over London Bridge, so many,*
> *I had not thought death had undone so many.*

Eliot's description of the Thames also draws upon Whistler's painterly effects and their echoes in the fin-de-siècle poets:

> *The river sweats*
> *Oil and tar*
> *The barges drift*
> *With the turning tide*

BEGINNING IN 1862, Whistler completed four paintings later titled *Symphony in White,* the first two later given the the subtitles *The White Girl* and *The Little White Girl*—a series of haunting images that intrigued fin-de-siècle writers.* One of Whistler's critics complained that *Symphony in White* was a misnomer since there were various other colors in the paintings—at which the painter growled: *"Bon Dieu!* did this wise person expect white hair and chalked faces? And does he then, in his astounding consequence, believe that a symphony in F contains no other note, but

---

*In an instance of life imitating art, Max Beerbohm was entranced by a seventeen-year-old music hall mime and singer, Cissy Loftus, to whom he referred in his letters as "the White Girl." See *Max and Will: Max Beerbohm and William Rothenstein: Their Friendship and Letters, 1893–1945,* eds. Mary M. Lago and Karl Beckson (Cambridge, Mass., 1975), 18–19. Wilde's Dorian Gray is so in love with Sibyl Vane that his "soul had turned to this white girl and bowed in worship before her."

shall be a continued repetition of F, F, F.? . . . . . . Fool!"

The White Girl in its many variations is one of the motifs that identify Whistler's influence among the fin-de-siècle poets. In the Decadent context of "Morbidezza" (1892), Symons suggests the figure's "virginal" quality as disturbingly remote as that of Mallarmé's Hérodiade:

> *White girl, your flesh is lilies,*
> *Under a frozen moon. . . .*

In one of his "Colour Studies" (1895), Symons suggests a Whistler setting with an appropriate figure no doubt inspired by one of his symphonies in white:

> *White-robed against the three-fold white*
> *Of shutter, glass, and curtains' lace,*
> *She flashed into the evening light.*

And Richard Le Gallienne's "prose fancy" titled "White Soul" (1895) begins with several lines of poetry also suggestive of Whistlerian sources:

> *What is so white in the world, my love,*
> *As thy maiden soul—*

AT THE SAME time that Whistler transposed the arts, if only to reinforce the concept of artifice, he was instrumental in stimulating an interest in Oriental art, principally blue and white porcelain and Japanese prints, which had been the craze in France in the 1850s soon after Commodore Perry brought pressure upon Japan to open her ports to foreign trade. In the 1860s, Whistler established a reputation as an avid collector of Oriental art and artifacts, competing with Rossetti for supremacy, but more important, Whistler "revealed the artistic significance of the Japanese print to his English colleagues." Indeed, he was often called "the Japanese artist."

In a number of Whistler's paintings, oriental settings are prominent, though his interest in *Japonaiserie* did not exclude his fascination with local scenes. In *Variations in Flesh Colour and Green: The Balcony* (1867–68), the view of the south bank of the Thames, with its smoky factories in the mist, is from Whistler's balcony in Chelsea while the contrasting foreground depicts kimono-clad English women in elegant poses. The *Symphony in White, No. 2: Little White Girl* (1864) contains such Oriental accessories as a Japanese fan, a blue and white vase, and the characteristic decorations of flowers. The figure (Whistler's model and mistress, Joanna

Heffernan), standing at an Occidental mantelpiece in a white dress, gazes sideways towards the mirror reflecting the startling other side of her face, melancholy and troubled. Twenty-four years before Swinburne taunted Whistler on his "Ten O'Clock" lecture, *Symphony in White, No. 2* had intrigued him, perhaps because it depicted a divided self. When Swinburne wrote "The Little White Girl" (1865), incorporated into "Before the Mirror" (1866), based on the painting, Whistler was so pleased that he had stanzas four to six printed on gold paper and affixed to the frame of the painting. Part of stanza five reads:

> *Art thou the ghost, my sister,*
> > *White sister there,*
> *Am I the ghost, who knows?*
> *My hand, a fallen rose,*
> > *Lies snow-white on white snows, and takes no care.*

The nineties poets who were attracted to Whistler's transposition of the arts were likewise drawn to his *Japonaiserie,* as in Henley's "Ballade of a Toyokuni Colour-Print" (1888), which, in depicting an Oriental girl standing beneath a blossoming plum tree, concludes a description of her "flowing-gowned / And hugely sashed" with the wistful "I loved you once in old Japan." Wilde's "Fantaisies Decoratives: I. Le Panneau" (1887), originally titled "Impression Japonais: Rose et Ivoire," describes an Oriental panel in which "a little ivory girl" stands under a rose tree (standing under trees was apparently a sign of Oriental respectability). In an incomplete manuscript version, the title of the poem is "Symphonie en Rose," thereby reinforcing the sense of color harmony.

WRITING ON WHISTLER at the time of his death, Symons noted that it was the "rarity of beauty, always, that he seeks, never a strange thing for the sake of strangeness." The Butterfly had rediscovered "one of the first truths of art . . . in these times, though it has been put into practice by every great artist, and has only been seriously denied by scientific persons and the inept . . . that art must never be a statement, always an evocation." In *The Symbolist Movement in Literature* (1900), Symons quotes the latter observation by Mallarmé as a central doctrine of the Symbolists, also subscribed to by the poets who followed Whistler into the mists of London.

Whistler's prominence in the fin de siècle, not only in London but also in Paris, is attested to by the French portrait painter and memoirist Jacques-Émile Blanche, who wrote that at the end of the 1880s "the Whistler cult became entangled in people's minds with Symbolism, the

Mallarmé and . . . the Wagner cults." Blanche cites these cults as "formulas that enchanted our youth; they were preciosities suitable for affectedly superior persons like us. . . ." But such enthusiasms of the nineties as Aestheticism, Impressionism, Symbolism, Wagnerism, and Decadence—though regarded by many as affectations or subversions—were indications of a need for artistic and spiritual transcendence that periodically erupted as protests against an increasingly industrialized world. Though Whistler had refused to ally himself with any movement, he established himself in the 1860s and 1870s as a major figure in the avant-garde, one who was decidedly *"fin-de-siècle* before the end of the century."

12

Perfect and Imperfect Wagnerites

IN WILDE'S *The Picture of Dorian Gray,* Lady Henry Wotton informs Dorian: "I like Wagner's music better than anybody's. It is so loud that one can talk the whole time without other people hearing what one says." Wilde's wit captures the nature of much nineteenth-century criticism of Wagner: that his music was overbearing and pretentious. Yet there was, Shaw said, "an inner ring of superior persons" (including a number of Anglo-Germans in London) who not only studied Wagner's music for its "most urgent and searching philosophic and social significance" but also responded to its spiritual reverberations. Wilde describes Dorian Gray (the fictional equivalent of many such Wagnerites) sitting in his box at the opera and listening, like a Symbolist sensing analogies, "in rapt pleasure to 'Tannhäuser' and seeing in the prelude to that great work of art a presentation of the tragedy of his own soul."

The heroic figure of Tannhäuser attracted fin-de-siècle Decadents, who, like Dorian Gray, regarded Wagner's depiction of the legendary thirteenth-century poet and singer of courtly love as a reflection of their own despair over the abandonment of religious ideals for pagan pleasures. Tannhäuser's final redemption by love in the opera thus provided many with the solace of "Wagnerism," an aesthetic and religious evocation of transcendent realities that stimulated an international movement with the passion of an ideological crusade. The many forms that Wagnerism took—artistic, social, and political—indicated that a dazzling new visionary had come into the world.

Wagner's impact on avant-garde circles in London, on the Continent, and in the United States was vast and far-reaching, "arguably," a modern critic remarks, "the greatest single fact to be reckoned with in the arts during the past century." In his resurrection of medieval Germanic and Celtic myth, Wagner provided new versions of a heroic, imaginative past that opposed the deadening industrialism and scientific materialism of the nineteenth-century. Moreover, the solemn religiosity of Wagner's art attracted many who sought an alternative to discredited Christian dogma. At the same time, the redemptive eroticism of *Tristan and Isolde* especially beguiled Aesthetes and Decadents, as though justifying their personal visions. In short, for fin-de-siècle England, "Wagner was drafted for the task of overthrowing Victorianism."*

Wagner's most notable self-proclaimed defender in late nineteenth-century London was Bernard Shaw, who had no formal musical training (though his mother gave him lessons on the piano and taught him the technique of vocal production). His early love of opera and his attraction to the utopian aspects of Wagnerism inevitably led him into controversy over Wagner's politics, anti-Semitism, and theatrical innovations. A member of the Wagner Society, Shaw later exaggerated his role when he said that he had undertaken a defense of Wagner, who was "the furiously abused coming man of London." The "wars of religion," Shaw said, "were not more bloodthirsty than the discussions of the Wagnerites and the Anti-Wagnerites." However, when Shaw began writing music criticism in the late 1870s, the virulent attacks on Wagner had waned considerably, and when Shaw called him "the greatest of modern composers," his judgment aroused little opposition. Wagner's acclaim during this time distressed the exiled Karl Marx in London, who, in 1876, wrote: "No matter where one goes, one is plagued with the question 'What do you think of Richard Wagner?' " Marx had the answer: Wagner was a charlatan, and Bayreuth, Germany, was a "fools' festival." Wagner's attempt in the *Ring of the Nibelungs* to restore the power and magic of myth to a decadent industrial world had probably vexed Marx, whose own writings advocated radical socialism as a solution to social problems. In the late nineties, Shaw established a Marxist interpretation in his own brilliant analysis of the *Ring* cycle.

The major figure among the early Wagnerites who had effected the major change in Wagner's reputation was Dr. Francis Hueffer (the father of Ford Madox Ford). Hueffer's death in 1889, wrote Shaw, was "a loss to the best interests of music in London. Fortunately, his warfare was accomplished before he fell.† The critics who formerly opposed him on

---

*The diplomat, author, and translator Maurice Baring dramatizes such an impulse in his autobiographical novel titled *C.* (New York, 1924), which portrays the young hero's first hearing of *Tannhäuser* in the late nineteenth century: "Never did he receive a more violent electric shock. . . . He did not follow all of it, but he was swept away. . . . He would like, he thought, a crashing, thunderous Venusberg song to be sung before all his aunts, which would cause their conventions, creeds, prejudices, morals and ideals to come crashing to the ground" (195).

†In the early 1870s, Hueffer had published a series of articles on Wagner in the *Fortnightly Review,* collected as *Richard Wagner and the Music of the Future* (1874), the

the grounds that Wagner's music had no form and no melody, that it was noisy and wrong, and never ought to have been written, and could never be popular, came at last to be only too grateful to Hueffer for his willingness to forget their folly."

On Shaw's first journey to the Wagner festival in Bayreuth in late July 1889, he was initially unimpressed by the Festspielhaus, "a dim freestone-colored auditorium, reminding you strongly of a lecture theatre by the steepness of the bank of seats and the absence of a gallery." When the lights went out, preparatory to the *Parsifal* prelude, the "angry hushing and hissing from overstrained Wagnerians" who resented noises from unnecessary movements in the audience suddenly faded as the music began, and "you at once recognize that you are in the most perfect theatre in the world for comfort, effect, and concentration of attention." *Tristan and Isolde* impressed Shaw as "an ocean of sentiment, immensely German, and yet universal in its appeal to human sympathy": ". . . all the merely romantic love scenes ever turned into music are pallid beside the second act of Tristan." *Die Meistersinger* overwhelmed him with the "flood of melody throughout the work," which would astonish the "few survivors of the sceptics who originated the brilliant theory that Wagner devoted his existence to avoiding anything of a musical nature in his compositions." And a performance of *Parsifal* convinced Shaw that another hearing was "a necessity of life."

By October, however, he believed that the productions that he had seen in Bayreuth just two months before were following the traditional law: "Do what was done last time." The "law of all living and fruitful performance," on the other hand, is "obey the innermost impulse which the music gives, and obey it to the most exhaustive satisfaction." Since London orchestras had demonstrated their superiority to the Bayreuth "band," he suggested that the London branch of the Wagner Society reconsider its enthusiastic support of the Festspielhaus: "It would be too much to declare that the true Wagner Theatre will arise in England; but it is certain that the true English Wagner Theatre will arise there. The sooner we devote our money and energy to making Wagner's music live in England instead of expensively embalming its corpse in Bavaria, the better for English art in all its branches."

BEFORE THE fin de siècle, interest in Wagner among British writers and artists developed not only from their close relationship with avant-garde

---

first major commentary in English on Wagner's prose works. Another Anglo-German pioneer in the serious study of Wagner was Edward Dannreuther, a prominent musician and critic who published *Wagner and the Reform of the Opera* (1872) and *Wagner: His Tendencies and Theories* (1873).

French intellectuals but also from Wagner enthusiasts in London who apparently discovered his importance simultaneously with the French. "Wagner mania," however, had an inauspicious beginning. Unknown and virtually penniless, Wagner first visited London in 1839, when he made little impression on those musicians whom he met. But on his return early in 1855 to conduct a series of concerts that included excerpts from *Tannhäuser* and *Lohengrin,* he provoked controversy during his four-month stay. Most critics, who regarded Wagner as principally a conductor, reacted to him unfavorably—some for his anti-Semitism, others for his revolutionary politics. In the *Athenaeum* (January 27, 1855), one writer objected to the appointment of Wagner because his "avowed and public creed" was contemptuous of "all such music as the English love" (the Queen was particularly fond of Mendelssohn's music, which Wagner had condemned in his 1850 tract, *Judaism in Music*); his presence on the podium before the philharmonic orchestra would therefore be "a wholesale offence to the native and foreign conductors resident in England." The audiences, however, were pleased, as was Victoria, for whom Wagner gave a command performance.

Since only excerpts from Wagner's music could be heard in London, many went abroad to see his operas performed. In the spring of 1863, Swinburne was in Paris with Whistler, who took him to the studio of the artist Henri Fantin-Latour, at work on a painting of a scene from *Tannhäuser.* Later, Fantin-Latour produced a series of lithographs depicting various scenes from Wagner's *Ring* cycle and contributed pastels and drawings on Wagnerian subjects to the *Revue wagnérienne.* From French acquaintances, Swinburne undoubtedly heard of the furor over the 1861 production of *Tannhäuser:* Young aristocrats from the Jockey Club engaged in incessant whistling at some performances ("Wagner whistles" were subsequently hawked on the boulevards) because of the omission of the traditional "grand ballet" in the second act, which deprived them of a glimpse of the pretty dancers.

Baudelaire later sent Swinburne a signed copy of his pamphlet *Richard Wagner et "Tannhäuser" à Paris* (1861), an essay that developed Symbolist correspondences while discussing an opera he had never heard in its entirety. He had been in the Paris audience when Wagner conducted excerpts from such operas as *Tannhäuser* and *Lohengrin,* which overwhelmed him with "a bizarre sensation . . . a truly sensual voluptuousness." After the disruption at the opera performance of *Tannhäuser,* Baudelaire wrote his pamphlet defending Wagner's drama of

> Languishings, delights, blended with fevers shot through with anguish, incessant returnings to voluptuousness, almost promising to quench one's thirst for it, but never doing so, raging palpitations of the heart and sense, imperious commands of the

flesh, the entire dictionary of onomatopoeias identified with love is heard here. Finally, the religious theme slowly regains its empire, gradually absorbing the other in a peaceful and glorious victory, as an irresistible being does over a sickly, disorderly one. . . .

Such a view, expressed in the characteristic language of Decadence, helped to establish Wagner as a visionary for later Symbolists.

Swinburne's immersion in Germanic myth had already prepared him for his interest in Wagner's music. He had known of the old German ballad of Tannhäuser since the early 1860s, when more than one translation had appeared in London, and he had already begun writing his shocking poem in praise of Venus, "Laus Veneris" (1866), before his journey to France. In his characteristic manner, Swinburne emphasized Tannhäuser's erotic fascination with Venus, clearly inspired by Baudelaire's vision of the opera, which foreshadowed the fin-de-siècle obsession with the femme fatale. Instead of Wagner's penitent hero, Swinburne's Tannhäuser, regarding heaven as "barren," embraces sin: "Ah love, there is no better life than this."

In the *Academy* (March 15, 1871), Dr. Francis Hueffer published what is "commonly considered the first important public declaration of the English Wagnerites." Reviewing Wagner's pamphlet on Beethoven, Hueffer asserted that in Wagner "we must recognise the reformer who reunites the two arts of drama and music, which seemed to be separated by a profound chasm, and in reality are one." With the first Bayreuth production in 1876 of the entire *Ring* cycle, the English Wagnerites regarded a pilgrimage to the Festspielhaus as obligatory, but the ritual occasion was soon marred (except for the already converted) by the degrading aura of commercialism and the startling attire of some in the audience. A prominent critic in *Daily Telegraph* found the Bayreuth festival dull, but he was amused by some of the attendees: "Why, then, is it, that faith in the Art-Work of the Future [Wagner's prose work, 1849; English trans., 1892] goes in company with spectacles, long hair, and funny head-gear?"

Wagner was in London in 1877 for his third and final visit to conduct eight concerts of his own music at the Royal Albert Hall. The success of these performances indicated, as one critic has written, that for the "British musical public, Wagner had at last 'arrived.' " In London artistic circles, Wagner was lionized by such figures as Robert Browning, the Pre-Raphaelite painter Edward Burne-Jones, and the novelist George Eliot. She and the critic G. H. Lewes, with whom she lived, were Germanophiles who had translated German poetry and philosophy and who were well acquainted with Wagner's works. In May and June of 1882, several of Wagner's music dramas hitherto unproduced in London were presented for the first time. The entire *Ring* cycle was given at Her Majesty's Theatre in the Haymarket and several other operas at the Theatre Royal, including *Die Meistersinger*. Ruskin, who saw the latter production, ranted to Mrs. Burne-Jones:

> Of all the . . . clumsy, blundering, boggling, baboon-blooded stuff I ever saw on a human stage . . . of all the affected, sapless, soulless, beginningless, endless, topless, bottomless, topsiturviest, tuneless . . . doggerel of sounds I ever endured the deadliness of, that eternity of nothing was the deadliest, as far as the sound went. I never was so relieved, so far as I can remember, in my life, by the stopping of any sound—not excepting railway whistles—as I was by the cessation of the cobbler's bellowing.

When Wagner died in February 1883, the *Times* (February 14) called him "the greatest musician of our time." For the devoted Wagnerites, the loss of the "messiah of a new age" produced shock. Swinburne composed "The Death of Richard Wagner" for the *Musical Review* (February 24, 1883), which regards the master's music as emanating from a divine source: ". . . we heard as a prophet that hears God's message against him, and may not flee." And even *Punch* (February 24, 1883) was reduced to solemn versifying:

> *He outstripped the gewgaw'd shams of Opera,*
> *Lord of two spheres, he wedded Art with Art,*
> *And Music, sunned in brighter, larger fame,*
> *May date its nobler dawn from WAGNER'S mighty name.*

THE FRENCH SYMBOLISTS and Naturalists were among the first to explore the possibilities of employing Wagner's innovations in music drama in their own literary works. The *Revue wagnérienne* (1885–88) was edited by Edouard Dujardin, whose 1888 novel, *Les Lauriers sont coupées (The Laurels Are Cut Down)*, fusing Wagnerism and Symbolism in a newly devised stream-of-consciousness technique, later provided Joyce with a method for fiction. Dujardin's circle of contributors to the journal included such Symbolist poets as Mallarmé, Verlaine, Huysmans, and Villiers de l'Isle-Adam, some of whom had regularly undertaken pilgrimages to Bayreuth in the belief that Wagner's views on music and drama held promise and perhaps confirmation of mystical realms that the Symbolists sought to express in their verse. The power of music, Wagner had suggested, could reveal the relationship between conscious and unconscious worlds, as in *Tristan and Isolde:* "Life and death, the whole import and existence of the outer world here hang on nothing but the innermost movements of the soul."

For the Naturalists, as Zola (a member of the Wagner Society in Marseilles) made clear, the use of the Wagnerian leitmotif in fiction was a means of organizing and unifying narratives: "What you call repetitions occurs in all my books. This is a literary device that I began by using with some timidity, but have since pushed perhaps to excess. In my view it gives more body to a work, and strengthens its unity. The device is somewhat akin to the motifs of Wagner, and if you will ask some musical friends of yours to explain his use of these, you will understand pretty well my use of the device in literature."

Wagner's influence on Shaw was far-reaching and pervasive. As a modern critic has observed, "the material of the Wagnerian poems . . . would be transformed into the glittering stuff of Shavian drama." In *Candida* (1897), for example, the "almost unearthly" eighteen-year-old poet Eugene Marchbanks challenges Candida to choose between him and her dull husband, the Reverend Mr. Morell. Shaw revealed to the American critic James Gibbons Huneker that when Marchbanks, having been rejected by Candida, exclaims, "Out, then, into the night with me," he is going out into "Tristan's holy night" (an ironic echo of the "heil'ge Nacht," enfolding Tristan and Isolde in erotic ecstasy). In Act IV of *The Doctor's Dilemma* (1906), a more direct Wagnerian borrowing occurs when Shaw's amoral artist Louis Dubedat exclaims on his deathbed the creed of the Religion of Art with its dogma of art for art's sake: "I believe in Michael Angelo, Velasquez, and Rembrandt, in the might of design, the mystery of colour, the redemption of all things by Beauty everlasting, and the message of Art that has made these hands blessed. Amen. Amen." Dubedat's dying speech closely follows that of the dying German musician in Wagner's story "Death in Paris" (1841), which offers another version of artistic martyrdom associated with the Religion of Art:

> I believe in God, Mozart, and Beethoven, and likewise their disciples and apostles; I believe in the Holy Spirit and the truth of the one, indivisible Art; I believe that this Art proceeds from God, and lives within the hearts of all illumined men. . . . I believe that through this Art all men are saved, and therefore each may die for Her of hunger. . . . I believe that true disciples to high Art will be transfigured in a heavenly fabric of sun-drenched fragrance of sweet sounds, and united for eternity with the divine fount of all Harmony. . . . Amen!

Shaw's major critical statement concerning Wagner that has influenced productions in our own time is, of course, *The Perfect Wagnerite* (1898), which transforms the four operas of the *Ring* cycle into a witty socialist parable. Since his admiration for Wagner was that "he fought with the wild beasts all his life," both as a political revolutionary and theatrical innovator (not to mention his preference for vegetarianism), Shaw was able to identify with the composer and interpret his music dramas as splendid instances of the need for Fabianism.* As a "preliminary encouragement" to the "ordinary citizen visiting the theatre to satisfy his curiosity," Shaw insists that the *Ring*, "with all its gods and giants and dwarfs, its water-maidens and Valkyries, its wishing-cap, magic ring, enchanted sword, and miraculous treasure, is a drama of today, and not of a remote and fabulous antiquity." In the first scene of *Das Rheingold*, the period of the golden age, Alberic the dwarf comes "stealing along the slippery rocks of the river bed," one who is "fierce of passion, but with a brutish narrowness of intelligence and selfishness of imagination. . . . Such dwarfs are quite common in London." Here, then, is the beginning of Shaw's socialist allegory: when Alberic renounces love for the Rhine gold, he establishes a primitive capitalistic system that has continued into the modern world:

> For his gain, hordes of his fellow-creatures are thenceforth condemned to slave miserably, overground and underground, lashed to their work by the invisible whip of starvation. They never see him, any more than the victims of our "dangerous trades" ever see the shareholders whose power is nevertheless everywhere, driving them to destruction. The very wealth they create with their labor becomes an additional force to impoverish them. . . . You can see the process for yourself in every civilized country today, where millions of people toil in want and disease to heap up more wealth for our Alberics. . . .

Fortunately, there is, says Shaw, a "higher power in the world to work against Alberic"; otherwise, there would be "utter destruction." This power is "Godhead," which Shaw was soon to call the "Life Force," embodied in "wonderfully . . . rare persons who may by comparison be called gods [presumably members of the Fabian Society], creatures capa-

---

*By December 1851, however, when writing the poems for the *Ring* cycle, Wagner had altered his view of revolution as the key to society's redemption. In a letter to the critic and composer Theodore Uhlig, he revealed that he had "completely abandoned every attempt to combat the prevailing mood of stupidity, dulness of mind and utter wretchedness. . . . I intend to let what is rotten continue to rot and not waste my remaining powers of production and enjoyment on a painful and utterly futile effort to galvanize the corpse of European civilization" (*Selected Letters of Richard Wagner*, translated and edited by Stewart Spencer and Barry Millington [New York, 1987], 241).

ble of thought, whose aims extend far beyond the satisfaction of their bodily appetites and personal affections, since they perceive that it is only by the establishment of a social order founded on common bonds of moral faith that the world can rise from mere savagery." But, Shaw asks, how can the godhead establish such an order in "a world of stupid giants"? The only answer is that, "face to face with Stupidity," godhead must compromise—in short, the method of Fabian gradualism and permeation. Throughout his discussion, Shaw stresses the fact that the world "is waiting for Man to redeem it from the lame and cramped government of the gods. Once grasp that; and the allegory becomes simple enough." Siegfried is Wagner's hero, but not Shaw's, since in the *Ring,* love (which Shaw regarded as mere eroticism) is "the remedy for all evils." For Shaw, such a hero lacks a sense of human destiny and a moral imperative—that is, to create a new order.

Shaw's hero (influenced by Nietzsche's belief in the superman's heroic will to power) is the product of an evolutionary development in which "life continues thrusting towards higher and higher organizations." The hero, then, is the product of godhead ("he feels that in his own Godhead is the germ of such Heroism, and that from himself the Hero must spring"), and his "first exploit must be to sweep the gods and their ordinances from the path of the heroic will." In *Major Barbara* (1905), Shaw depicts such a seemingly anarchic hero, the munitions manufacturer Undershaft, who, aware that he embodies the Life Force, responds to the question about what drives his utopian community of Perivale St. Andrews: "A will of which I am a part." But in *Die Götterdämmerung,* a music drama burdened with the conventional trappings of Romantic grand opera complete with stage villains, Siegfried dies without fulfilling his destiny as a true hero. Hence, states Eric Bentley, Shaw ridicules Wagner's "happy ending" (involving renunciation, love, and redemption) "perhaps because he could not see how a man can affirm and deny the life-force in the same work. Shaw himself was to be a 'perfect Wagnerite,' a Wagner without negation or nihilism. . . . But Wagner remained an imperfect one."

AS THE MYTHIC world of Wagner's music dramas provided Shaw with yet another means of advancing the socialist cause, other fin-de-siècle writers and artists with alternative ideologies also turned to Wagner for inspiration. In his quest for order amidst the chaos of modern life, Aubrey Beardsley found in Wagner a new Religion of Art. Some of his early illustrations depicted scenes from *Tannhäuser* and *Die Götterdämmerung.* In 1893–94, he fulfilled a commission to complete dozens of drawings for Thomas Malory's *Morte D'Arthur* (1485), based on the ancient Celtic legends used by Wagner. Several illustrations depict the Tristan and Iseult relationship, the most celebrated moment involving the drinking of the love potion. Notably absent from this drawing, however, is any suggestion of transcendent passion. Beardsley's design is theatrical, with stage boards and wings, the statuesque, posturing lovers dressed in stylized *Japonesque* dress with extensive swirling designs associated with art nouveau.

For the first number of the new art periodical the *Studio* (April 1893), Beardsley's *Siegfried, Act II* depicts the climactic moment in the opera after Siegfried has slain Fafner the Dragon, who had guarded the Nibelungs' gold. In Wagner's text, Siegfried peers at his arm where drops of Fafner's blood have touched it: "The hot blood burns like fire!" But Beardsley's drawing contains such an abundance of decorative details in his early hairline style that the androgynous Siegfried is merely another elaborate design rather than Wagner's mythic hero depicted at a crucially dramatic moment.

Beardsley's *The Wagnerites,* which appeared in the *Yellow Book* (October 1894), reveals a new attitude towards his own Wagnerian preoccupations in his satirical view of the master's apparently devoted disciples. Obviously aware of the long-standing charge of anti-Semitism against Wagner, Beardsley places in the stalls a single middle-aged male, obviously Jewish, entirely surrounded by unescorted hulking amazons, who are there for a performance, the drawing indicates, of *Tristan and Isolde.* The drawing thus implies a comic incongruity: The presence of apparently New Women indifferent to Romantic passion witnessing the tragic death of Wagner's lovers.

Beardsley's variations on Wagnerian themes are also evident in his contributions to the *Savoy.* Three chapters of his unfinished prose tale appeared in No. 1 (January 1896) with the title *Under the Hill,* a bowdlerized version of *The Story of Venus and Tannhäuser,* based, like Wagner's opera, on the medieval legend. From the beginning, when he began writing *Venus and Tannhäuser* in 1894, his intent was to shock readers with a frankly sexual and witty depiction of Venus's domain of elegant depravity under the hill (the Venusberg, or *mons veneris,* of her body, an obscene emblem of the earthly paradise). In *Under the Hill,* the names are changed, and the world of artifice, with only a touch of amorous dalliance between Helen/Venus's attendants, is designed to amuse with its unusual attention to matters of dress. Clearly, the original version could not have been published without risk of prosecution. At the opening of the first chapter of *Under the Hill,* the venereal image is thus muted: "The Abbé Fanfreluche,* having lighted off his horse, stood doubtfully for a moment

---

*In French, a *fanfreluche* is a bauble; here, presumably, the Abbé is Venus's indecent ornament or plaything. In an earlier draft, the hero was the Abbé Aubrey, implying autobiographical possibilities. In *Venus and Tannhäuser,* the hero is called the "Chevalier Tannhäuser." The shift to "Abbé" in *Under the Hill* underscores the theme of sacred and profane love from Wagner's opera.

Beardsley's "How Sir Tristram . . ."

Beardsley's "The Wagnerites"

beneath the ombre gateway of the mysterious Hill. . . ." In the fourth chapter in the *Savoy* (April 1896), Fanfreluche studies the score of Wagner's *Das Rheingold:*

> Once more he was ravished with the beauty and wit of the opening scene; the mystery of its prelude that seems to come up from the very mud of the Rhine, and to be as ancient, the abominable primitive wantonness of the music that follows the talk and movements of the Rhine-maidens, the black, hateful sounds of Alberic's love-making, and the flowing melody of the river of legends.

In the accompanying drawings for *Under the Hill,* Beardsley included one titled *For the Third Tableau of Das Rheingold. Under the Hill* did not proceed beyond the four published chapters, the result of Beardsley's terminal illness.

In September 1896, Beardsley asked his publisher Leonard Smithers to secure Wagner's prose works, translated by William Ashton Ellis (one of the master's most devoted disciples who, in 1888, founded and edited the *Meister,* devoted to Wagnerism and theosophy.) During this period when

Beardsley's "Fanfreluche"

Beardsley suffered devastating hemorrhaging from tuberculosis, he told Smithers: "Wagner alone consoles me somewhat." He was then writing *The Comedy of the Rheingold,* an "elaborate version," he called it, of Wagner's *Das Rheingold,* four illustrations of which appeared in the final number of the *Savoy* (December 1896). The manuscript of the unfinished *Rheingold* comedy has not survived.

As "WAGNER MANIA" grew in the late nineteenth century, the composer's name began to appear in popular novels, for it seemed to evoke a magical reality in fictive worlds. Wagnerian allusions, however, were generally fleeting, as in such novels as Grant Allen's *Philistia* (1884), Mrs. Humphrey Ward's *Robert Elsmere* (1888), and Stanley Makower's *The Mirror of Music* (1895). When George Moore first discovered Wagner's music, his account of its emotional power was characteristic of similar descriptions by devoted Wagnerites drawn to the vast drama of cosmic conflict, an indication of troubling reverberations underlying the seemingly placid nature of daily Victorian life: "The fanfare of the Rhine told me something undreamed of had come into my life, and I listened as a child listens, understanding nothing, for my poor ears could not follow the intricate weaving and interweaving; my reason tottered like one in a virgin forest, for there seemed to be no path to even a partial understand-

Beardsley's "Fourth Tableau . . ."

ing of this fulgurant orchestra, predicting at every moment wars and rumors of wars, giants against gods."

Though Moore included allusions to Wagner in many of his works, his novel *Evelyn Innes* (1898) is the first major attempt in British fiction to use parallels drawn from the operas to create a unified narrative. (The ironic contrasts between the imaginative myths of the past and the sordid facts of contemporary life anticipate Joyce's technique in *Ulysses* [1922], but the latter's Homeric parallels are more systematically employed.) Having eloped with Sir Owen Asher, owner of the *Wagnerian Review,* to study voice in Paris, Evelyn becomes a noted opera singer. Moore employs numerous allusions to *Tristan and Isolde* to suggest the parallel passion of Evelyn and Sir Owen's romance. A devout Roman Catholic, Evelyn is obsessed by the sinfulness of their affair and of her "entirely sensual life," for not only is she Sir Owen's mistress but Ulick Dean's as well. Dean, whose "dark lock of hair" falls over his forehead, is clearly modeled after Yeats. Devoted to Celtic myths and mysteries, Dean talks to Evelyn about the College of Adepts and about the Rosicrucians: In the twilight, "his strange figure grew symbolic, and his words . . . seemed to bring the unseen world nearer."

APPROPRIATELY, MOORE DEDICATED *Evelyn Innes* to Yeats and Symons, "two contemporary writers with whom I am in sympathy." In Yeats, Moore admired his devotion to Celtic myths, the ultimate source of ancient tales upon which Wagner had drawn. In Symons, Moore saw reflected his own sense of beauty and artistic autonomy as well as a shared enthusiasm for Wagner. In 1883, at the age of eighteen, Symons began studying Wagner's music as a devoted Wagnerite. When Wagner died in that year, Symons wrote to his former schoolmaster: "What a calamity is the death of Wagner!" In August 1897, he made the pilgrimage to Bayreuth with Havelock Ellis to see *Parsifal.* Later, Ellis wrote that the opera was a "superb echo of the romance of the early Christian world" and that the Festspielhaus was a "Temple on the hillside calculated, in a degree unparalleled in the modern world, to evoke an inspiring enthusiasm of art." Symons interpreted *Parsifal* as Wagner's attempt "to render mysticism through the senses," whereby "pure ideas take visible form, humanise themselves in a new kind of ecstasy." He commemorated the experience at Bayreuth in a poem suggesting the attitudes and imagery of artistic Decadence:

> *Parsifal has out-blushed the roses: dead*
> *Is all the garden of the world's delight,*

And every rose of joy has drooped its head,
And for sweet shame is dead.

In August 1899, he was again in Bayreuth, this time to see the *Ring* cycle for the first time. Symons (who had abandoned the Nonconformist faith of his youth and, like many Wagnerites, sought a spiritual alternative) asserted that "like the few supreme artists, Wagner has found the unity of the cosmos."

In his major work, *The Symbolist Movement in Literature* (1900), Symons not only made clear to the British the importance and complexity of Symbolism but also its relationship to Wagnerism. In describing the loneliness of Villiers de l'Isle-Adam ("for he had been living, in his own lifetime, the life of the next generation"), Symons observed that one man among Villiers's contemporaries gave him "perfect sympathy": "That man was Wagner." Villiers regarded Wagner as "a genius such as appears on earth once every thousand years." In his essay on Mallarmé, Symons suggested connections between Symbolism and Wagner's theories, particularly the concept of *Gesamtkunstwerk,* or the total work of art, combining music, drama, dance, acting, painting, and sculpture—derived from ancient Greek tragedy: "Carry the theories of Mallarmé to a practical conclusion, multiply his powers in a direct ratio, and you have Wagner. It is his failure not to be Wagner. And, Wagner having existed, it was for him to be something more, to complete Wagner." Moreover, Symons states, Mallarmé achieved Wagner's "ideal"—that " 'the most complete work of the poet should be that which, in its final achievement, becomes a perfect music': every word is a jewel, scattering and recapturing sudden fire, every image is a symbol, and the whole poem is visible music." Wagner also inspired Yeats, who hoped to establish a theater in Dublin as an equivalent of that in Bayreuth. Like Wagner, Yeats believed that "the arts are but one Art," and that a unified verse drama of dance and music could express through symbol and mask the unity of being revealed to him by his occult studies. By recreating Celtic mysteries in mythic drama, Yeats sought to revive a sense of the past and to unite the Irish—in short, like Wagner, Yeats envisioned himself as a cultural hero.

The Victorians were notable for their hero worship in myth and literature, the legacy of Romantic individualism rebelling against repressive authority yet striving for an ideal. In the 1830s and 1840s, Carlyle's *Sartor Resartus* and *On Heroes and Hero-Worship* were responses to an increasing awareness in the nineteenth century that a progressively democratic society required extraordinary individuals in times of social stress and crisis. For Carlyle, the hero had the creative vision to advance social progress. The Wagnerites found their hero in one whose mythic, transcendent art delivered them from the mundane realities of the industrial age. Though devoted to Wagner, Shaw was influenced by Nietzsche's *The Case of Wagner* and *Nietzsche Contra Wagner* (both published in English translation in 1896), which attacked the composer for transforming Schopenhauer's Will into redemptive love in such music dramas as *Tristan and Isolde* and the *Ring* cycle. Shaw increasingly regarded such love as antithetical to the evolving Life Force and its manifestation in the superman, one whose wisdom, nobility, and will to power could regenerate the world.

In 1900 Yeats published his Wagnerian play, *The Shadowy Waters,* which echoes *The Flying Dutchman,* but he did not see it produced by the Irish National Theatre Society until January 1904. The hero is the captain of a pirate ship driven by spirits inhabiting the bodies of birds. Fated to wander in search of an ideal woman, he must contend with a mutinous crew that later deserts him. Having captured a ship transporting a queen, the captain is saved from her sword by the melodious strains of his magical, dream-inducing harp (at the end of the Dublin production, the harp stubbornly refused to burst into flames on cue). The passion between the captain and queen parallels that of *Tristan and Isolde,* but their drifting into the unknown on a mysterious ship (ecstatically, in a symbolic consummation in death) also recalls Villiers de l'Isle-Adam's Symbolist drama *Axël* (1890), which had entranced Yeats by its antinaturalism.

In 1904, Yeats told the Irish critic and actor Frank Fay that *The Shadowy Waters* was "almost religious, it is more a ritual than a human story. It is deliberately without human characters." Such drama as Yeats had developed in the nineties and in the early twentieth century, drawing upon Symbolist/occult sources and inspired by Wagnerian suggestions of mythic worlds, of cadenced verbal music alternating with silences and associated with symbolic stage imagery, looked forward to the Modernist "theater of the interior" as exemplified by such playwrights as T. S. Eliot, Beckett, and Pinter.

Also stirred by Wagner's *Tristan and Isolde,* Symons began writing his own *Tristan and Iseult,* a four-act play in verse that he was never to see staged. In March 1902, the revival of verse drama (which Tennyson had laid to rest) was achieved by Stephen Phillips, whose *Paolo and Francesca* ran for 164 performances at the St. James's Theatre. The success of the play was undoubtedly a factor in Symons's wish to dramatize the Tristan legend in verse. However, in the *Academy* (March 15, 1902), Symons was critical of Phillips, who had written some picturesque scenes but without "real life . . . in the fatal sense, 'literature.' " But Symons faced a formidable task in his *Tristan and Iseult,* for the story, after all, had already been set to music by an acknowledged operatic composer of genius, the work widely judged to be a masterpiece. What, then, could Symons do to distinguish his play from Wagner's *Tristan?* He returned to the original legend and sought to exploit differences. For example, Symons used two characters named Iseult—Iseult of Ireland and Iseult of Brittany—whereas Wagner had used only the former. But in most respects, the play follows the same plot as Wagner's opera.

In order to avoid the "literary" qualities of Phillips's play, Symons employed a more colloquial style within his varied blank verse. At moments of Iseult of Ireland's passion, however, Symons slips into familiar Symbolist/Decadent echoes of Wilde's *Salome* and Swinburne's "Dolores" in *Poems and Ballads:*

> *Tristan, it is my life*
> *Your lips drink up: I cannot bear your lips:*
> *I feel them to the marrow of my bones.*
> *O I would be a fire and burn your lips,*
> *O I would be a beast and eat your lips,*
> *I would annihilate their sweetness. Now*
> *My blood is all an anguish of desire.*
> *Speak, slay me, do not kiss me. Kiss me now!*

The death blow to Symons's hope for a production of his play undoubtedly occurred when, in September 1906, J. Comyns Carr's *Tristram and Iseult* took the stage for 46 performances, a modest run, but sufficient perhaps to make theater managers wonder whether the dramatized legend could attract audiences without Wagner's music (the opera was now in the standard repertory at Covent Garden). In 1917, the discouraged Symons entombed his play in book form.

In 1905, Symons published his major critical essay on the composer, "The Ideas of Wagner," which focuses, as Wagner does in *The Art-Work of the Future,* on the unconscious element in all great creative work. Symons regarded Wagner as a "unique . . . man of genius," a musician, poet, playwright, thinker, and administrator who "worked to a single end" in building up "a single structure." His music dramas brought music and drama "more intimately into union than they have ever before been brought"—the idea of total theater that Symons had long advocated. Yeats, who at this time was revising *The Shadowy Waters,* told Symons that his Wagner essay touched his "own theories at several points, and enlarges them at one or two . . .": "A certain passage had always seemed wrong to me, and after I had rewritten it several times it was still wrong. I then came on that paragraph where Wagner insists that a play must not appeal to the intelligence, but by being . . . a piece of self-consistent life directly to the emotions. . . . Your essay is a substitute for more volumes than anything of the kind I have seen. . . ."

———

IN THE EARLY twentieth century, Wagnerism remained a potent idea among twentieth-century Modernists. As one critic has observed, "Anybody who considered himself at all intellectual had to know something about Wagner." Though not the characteristic Wagnerite, Joseph Conrad was nevertheless influenced by Wagnerism. In *Nostromo* (1904), for example, the curse of the silver mine echoes that of the stolen gold in *Das Rheingold*, avarice providing the principal motive for self-destruction in both novel and opera. These epic tales depict the loss of love and ensuing death, and both works express, though in different ways, the grand theme of redemption through restored love.

Wagnerism was also a major enthusiasm among those in the Bloomsbury group. In the *Times* (April 24, 1909), Virginia Woolf hailed the new opera season with a passage suggesting that the cult of Wagnerism existed even among those far removed from privileged Bloomsbury:

> Strange men and women are to be found in the cheap seats on a Wagner night; there is something primitive in the look of them, as though they did their best to live in forests, upon the elemental emotions, and were quick to suspect their fellows of a lack of "reality," as they call it. They find a philosophy of life in the operas, hum "motives" to symbolise stages in their thought, and walk off their fervour on the Embankment, wrapped in great black cloaks.

Later that year, Woolf was in Bayreuth (her customary ritual) for a performance of *Parsifal*, which she described as having an "overwhelming unity." But in 1913, her reaction to Wagner's *Ring* in London reveals a startling reaction to this music drama (an indication, perhaps, of emotional instability preceding her mental breakdown): "My eyes are bruised, my ears dulled, my brain a mere pudding of pulp—O the noise and the heat, and the bawling sentimentality, which used once to carry me away, and now leaves me sitting perfectly still. Everyone seems to have come to this opinion, though some pretend to believe still." Nevertheless, the Wagnerian magic touches several of her novels, beginning with her first work, *The Voyage Out* (1915), in the allusions to Wagner and in the use of the leitmotif as an organizing principle to intensify the narrative.

Among those in the Bloomsbury circle, E. M. Forster was a more devoted Wagnerite than Woolf, making pilgrimages to Bayreuth through most of his life. His novels make extensive use of Wagnerian allusions in order to heighten narrative and develop character. He was also aware of the lingering misconceptions among the liberally educated concerning Wagner's achievement. In *Howards End* (1910), for example, his central character Margaret Schlegel strenuously objects to what she apparently believes is Wagner's theatrical concept of *Gesamtkunstwerk:*

> "But, of course, the real villain is Wagner. He has done more than any man in the nineteenth century towards the muddling of the arts. . . . Every now and then in history there do come these terrible geniuses, like Wagner, who stir up all the wells of thought at once. For a moment it's splendid. Such a splash as never was. But afterwards—such a lot of mud; and the wells—as it were, they communicate with each other too easily now, and not one of them will run quite clean. That's what Wagner's done."

In fact, she is alluding to the nineteenth-century interest in the transposition of the arts with distant suggestions of synaesthesia, as in Gautier's poem "Symphony in White Major," Whistler's "nocturnes" and "symphonies," and Wilde's "Symphony in Yellow"—obviously different from Wagner's concept of total theater.

During this period, D. H. Lawrence had developed an interest in Wagner, but it never became a passion. His early novel, *The Trespasser* (1912), originally titled *The Saga of Siegmund,* attempts, perhaps, to follow Moore's *Evelyn Innes* in constructing Wagnerian parallels. Lawrence's greater work, *Women in Love* (completed in 1916; published in 1920), employs, like Conrad's *Nostromo,* the central symbol of a mine (coal rather than silver) and a character who owns it with such single-minded devotion that it paralyzes his capacity for love. The parallel to the *Ring* cycle is further emphasized by descriptions of the miners, enslaved like the Nibelungs in the darkness of the earth. Two further works should be mentioned, both employing allusions to Wagner's works as ironic commentaries on the vacuous nature of daily existence by enlarging settings with mythic dimensions: T. S. Eliot's *The Waste Land* (1922), which quotes from *Tristan* and *Die Götterdämmerung,* with singing Thames-maidens replacing Rhine-maidens; and Joyce's *Ulysses* (1922), in which Stephen Dedalus shatters the Nighttown brothel chandelier *("ruin of all space, shattered glass, and toppling masonry")* with his ashplant, which he hails as *"Nothung!"*—the sacred sword fashioned by Wotan and embedded in an ashtree for the heroic Siegfried, whom Wagner called "the man of the future."

ON FEBRUARY 2, 1914, the first performance in England of Wagner's last music drama *Parsifal* was given at the Royal Opera House, Covent Garden. Until this time, London Wagnerites had heard only excerpts of the opera at concerts or had had to journey to Bayreuth or Munich to see it. The production was designed to approximate a Bayreuth performance (J. Comyns Carr was recruited to supervise the creation of costumes and sets similar to those at the Festspielhaus). For the opening performance, a queue began forming on the night before for the unreserved gallery. Most observers agreed that "nothing as magnificent as the Grail scene had ever been seen at Covent Garden." In less than six weeks of the special winter season, fourteen performances of *Parsifal* were presented. After August 4, when Britain declared war on Germany, Wagner (like other German composers) was soon omitted from many concert and opera programs as resistance increased to "enemy music." Though new developments in music were beginning to make Wagner seem like a quaint, outmoded Romantic who wrote in a conventionally chromatic style, it took a world war to bring nineteenth-century "Wagner mania" to an abrupt but only momentary end.*

*Aside from the familiar story of the Nazi expropriation of Wagnerism in the 1930s, Bryan Magee reports an extraordinary manifestation of "Wagner mania" that erupted thirty years later in London, an echo of the Victorian discovery of Wagner's grandeur in depicting the "dusk of the gods": "After a Promenade Concert in the mid-sixties which concluded with the third act of *Götterdämmerung* the young audience cheered for half an hour and then, when the performers finally went home and the lights of the Albert Hall were switched off, carried on cheering in the dark" (*Aspects of Wagner* [New York, 1969], 61).

13

In the Troughs of Zolaism

IN THE EARLY nineteenth century, British critics attacked Balzac as evidence of the shocking immorality imported from France in the dubious form of fiction. A critic in the *Quarterly Review* (April 1836) wrote in rage: "... a baser, meaner, filthier scoundrel never polluted society." By the fin de siècle, however, Balzac was the honored "father of French Realism, the chief precursor of Naturalism," and in 1898 the Establishment critic George Saintsbury edited translations of forty novels of *La Comédie humaine,* an indication that Balzac's reputation was now secure. Since the mid-nineteenth century, the increasing prominence of such daring writers as Baudelaire, Flaubert, Maupassant, and Zola made Balzac less offensive to British sensibilities. Convinced that, among recent French writers, Zola and his followers were befouling literature and corrupting readers, Tennyson expressed his anxiety through his aging speaker in "Locksley Hall Sixty Years After" (1886):

> *Authors—essayist, atheist, novelist, realist, rhymester, play your part,*
> *Paint the mortal shame of nature with the living hues of art.*
>
> *Rip your brothers' vices open, strip your own foul passions bare;*
> *Down with Reticence, down with Reverence—forward—naked—let*
> * them stare.*
>
> *Feed the budding rose of boyhood with the drainage of your sewer;*
> *Send the drain into the fountain, lest the stream should issue pure.*
>
> *Set the maiden fancies wallowing in the troughs of Zolaism,*
> *Forward, forward, ay and backward, downward too into the abysm!*

Cultural pollution had resulted, Tennyson suggested, from the shamelessness of writers who had forsaken traditional British reticence. At its worst, Zolaism—a term of contempt, suggesting a lack of reverence for Victorian proprieties—could "set the maiden fancies," otherwise pure and virginal, wallowing in images at once shamefully animalistic and morally degrading. Within two years after the appearance of Tennyson's poem, the publisher of Zola's novels in translation would be prosecuted for violation of the Obscene Publications Act of 1857.

British reactions to Zola in the 1870s had established the French novelist's reputation before translations of the major novels appeared. In 1877 Swinburne, who, as we have seen, had been the object of attacks for his verbal fleshliness in *Poems and Ballads* (1866), vented his own offended aesthetic sensibilities over Zola's untranslated 1877 novel, *L'Assommoir* (often translated as *The Dram Shop*), whose passages dealing with physical matters "might have almost turned the stomach of Dean Swift . . . [and] details of brutality and atrocity practiced on a little girl, as would necessitate the interpolation of such a line as follows in the police report of any and every newspaper in London: 'The further details given in support of the charge of cruelty were too revolting for publication in our columns.'" In the following year, as *L'Assommoir* went into its forty-eighth printing in France, a critic in *Gentleman's Magazine* (December 1878) delineated the cultural and moral differences between French and English authors that accounted for Victorian critical resistance to French literature:

> M. Zola frequently revolts us by his unvarnished allusions to things which lie outside the pale of modest decency. There is, however, it must be remembered, in justice to him, a vast difference in their treatment of man as an animal between French and English writers. English authors will not leave a celestial bed to prey on garbage. French writers sometimes do not shun even ordure. French literature knows but little reticence in the mention of such things. English writers avoid, with the reticence of fine shame, all allusion to the ignobler needs and functions of the body.

In such comparisons between the two nations, the Victorian insistence on cultural superiority to the French is a persistent theme, as in Charles Kingsley's *Sanitary and Social Lectures and Essays* (1880), which condemns French "ruinous self-conceit": ". . . we . . . have been trained at once in a sounder school of morals, and in a greater respect for facts."

In the *Fortnightly Review* (April 1882), Andrew Lang provided a further reason for British resistance to Zola's novels, which were widely popular on the Continent: "The cause of our isolation is only too obvious. Our unfortunate Puritanism, alas! prevents us from understanding M. Zola and the joys of *naturalisme.*" Though, said Lang, Zola had the capacity to create scenes of beauty, his impersonality and humorlessness would alienate most English readers, particularly in such a work as *Thérèse Raquin* (1867) in which Zola "has deliberately chosen the meanest characters, the most repulsive environment which his memory or his imagination could suggest." Moreover, Zola had "almost exhausted the dictionary in the effort to find words unpleasant enough for the unpleasant place he has to describe." Zola remarked that he and his school were like surgeons who preferred "unhealthy subjects." This admission, said Lang, "shows the true value of *naturalisme.*" A characteristic Victorian in his concern with a balanced view, Lang questions why "the scientific knowledge of man" should "dwell so much on man's corruption, and so little on the nobler aspects of humanity."

Zola had not invented the term *naturalism.* It had long been used in nineteenth-century Europe to refer to scientific investigation of natural phenomena, and the term *naturalist* was used to describe such a scientist. Long before Zola achieved fame, he had written that the positivist Hippolyte Taine was "a naturalist philosopher" who declared that the "intellectual world is subject to laws in the same way as the material world." Balzac had developed methods of composing novels, Taine said, that resembled those of the scientific naturalists. In articles published as early as 1866, Zola was using the term *naturalist* to refer to the creative process as well as to Balzac's works, and in his preface to the second edition of *Thérèse Raquin* (1868), Zola defended his method of analytical presentation by stating that his "aim was above all a scientific one," each chapter designed as "a curious physiological case."

Zola issued his Naturalist manifesto in a volume of essays, *The Experimental Novel* (1880), which influenced writers on the Continent, in Britain, and in America. In Claude Bernard's *Introduction to the Study of Experimental Medicine* (1878), Zola found confirmation of his theories, particularly in such scientific procedures as observation and experimentation as well as the view that "absolute determinism" was inherent in natural phenomena. As Zola describes the Naturalistic novelist's methodology, ". . . the whole operation consists in taking facts in nature, then in studying the mechanism of these facts, acting upon them, by the modification of circumstances and surrounds, without deviating from the laws of nature. Finally, you possess knowledge of the man, scientific knowledge of him, in both his individual and social relations." The "experimental novel," then, reveals the "machinery of [a character's] intellectual and sensory manifestations, under the influences of heredity and environment, such as physiology shall give them to us. . . ."*

---

*The term *realism,* often associated with *Naturalism,* implies not the scientific determinism and methodology of the latter but a general fidelity to commonplace experi-

Though Zola insisted that the methods in the creation of a Naturalistic novel could be applied to any level of society, his novels generally focused on the working classes and dramatized the effects of depravity and vice, particularly sex and alcoholism, as in his greatest work, *L'Assommoir.* Victorian critics attacked such preoccupations as morbid and immoral despite the fact that, in his essay "The Experimental Novel," Zola described Naturalistic novelists as "experimental moralists," whose aim was "to master certain phenomena of an intellectual and personal order, to be able to direct them." Nevertheless, the melioristic aspect of Naturalism was strangely ignored by many Victorians, who responded one-dimensionally to Zola's plots and characters without grasping the moral vision of his essay: "The day in which we gain control of the mechanism of this passion we can treat it and reduce it, or at least make it as inoffensive as possible." Moreover, Zola never insisted that his own manifesto calling for a scientific approach to the novel was inviolable; in fact, he regarded himself as an imaginative writer who made use of documents and notes based on observation in order to shape a more profound sociological vision of reality than had previously existed in fiction. In a letter written on December 28, 1882, he called himself a "poet" whose works "are built like musical symphonies. . . . I am steeped in romanticism up to my waist."

Zola's manifesto had its widespread impact on writers not usually regarded as Naturalists. Henry James, for example, often expressed ambivalence towards Naturalism, but in 1884 he told the American novelist William Dean Howells that Zola and his followers were doing "the only kind of work, to-day, that I respect; and in spite of their ferocious pessimism and their handling of unclean things, they are at least serious and honest." At the end of that year, James wrote to a friend that he was gathering information for the prison scene in his novel *The Princess Casamassima* (1886): "I have been all the morning at Millbank prison (horrible place) collecting notes for a fiction scene. You see I am quite the Naturalist." His hero, with the aesthetic name of Hyacinth, is the illegitimate son of a French working girl and (it is suggested) an English aristocrat—an unstable mix of hereditary factors. Environment also plays its crucial part in this "experimental novel" insofar as the young man is beset by conflicting republican sympathies and aristocratic allegiances in a setting of revolutionary activity. Naturalism's bent for factual accuracy also affected Joyce while writing *Ulysses* (1922) on the Continent. In his wish

---

ence—in settings, characters, and dialogue—to evoke a sense of the real world as opposed to romantic fantasy. Late Victorian critics often used the terms *realism* and *Naturalism* interchangeably because of their frequent association with similar subject matter in fiction and drama, often the sordid lives of lower-class characters and their involvement in crime, sex, and vice.

to reconstruct Dublin, the setting of the novel, he wrote constantly to friends and relatives for detailed information concerning streets and places as they had existed in 1904, the time of the story, an instance of Naturalistic methodology in the service of Symbolist vision.

IN FIN-DE-SIÈCLE ENGLAND, Zola's principal disciple was George Moore, who had known the "master" (as well as such other Naturalists as Goncourt and Huysmans) since the 1870s, when he was in Paris. In his fictionalized *Confessions of a Young Man* (1888), he recalled that Zola's articles in the periodical *Le Voltaire* on the experimental novel had stunned him with their new doctrine:

> *Naturalisme, la vérité, la science,* were repeated some half-a-dozen times. Hardly able to believe my eyes, I read that you should write, with as little imagination as possible, that plot in a novel or in a play was illiterate and puerile, and that the art of M. Scribe was an art of strings and wires, etc. I rose up from break-fast, ordered my coffee, and stirred the sugar, a little dizzy, like one who has received a violent blow on the head.

The "new art," based upon science, "in opposition to the art of the old world that was based on imagination, an art that should explain all things and embrace modern life in its entirety . . . a new creed in a new civilisation, filled me with wonder, and I stood dumb before the vastness of the conception, and the towering height of the ambition." As we have seen, Moore's satirical depiction of his autobiographical hero was designed to mirror his own naïveté as well as that of the British public. Clearly, his second novel, *A Mummer's Wife* (1884), revealed his grasp of Naturalistic fiction, specifically how heredity and environment produced their disastrous effects on the central character (desertion of her ill husband, alcoholism, and prostitution)—a deterministic vision of reality enhanced by Moore's imaginative symbol-making capacity.

Aside from the fact that Moore's novel was the first significant Naturalistic work published by a British writer under the direct influence of Zola, it signaled the ultimate transformation of how fiction was published in the nineteenth century. Following Zola's suggestion, Moore urged Henry Vizetelly to issue a one-volume edition of *A Mummer's Wife* instead of the customary three volumes. The "three-decker novel" had been the commercial godsend of the circulating libraries in Britain since Sir Walter Scott's success with his first novel, the three-volume *Waverley* (1814). The arrangement between publishers and circulating libraries was that three-volume novels, published at one and a half guineas (exceeding a week's wages for the average working man), were sold to the libraries for half that price.

For the two largest circulating libraries founded in the mid-nineteenth century by Charles Mudie and W. H. Smith, novels published at the announced price yielded a large number of subscribers in various cities, since most readers could not afford to purchase the staggering three-deckers. At the time of Mudie's death in 1890, there were 25,000 subscribers to Mudie's Select Library and 15,000 to W. H. Smith's library. By this time, however, the impact of the one-volume novel had taken its toll of Mudie's subscribers. When the company went out of business, the *Times* (July 12, 1937) estimated that "at one time" Mudie's had over 50,000 subscribers. An anonymous rhyme in the nineteenth century testified to the reliance of readers on the library:

> *As children must have Punch and Judy,*
> *So I can't do without my Mudie.*

For an annual subscription of a guinea (a pound and a shilling), a reader could borrow the latest fiction unavailable in the public libraries. On occasion, however, the circulating libraries threatened to withold their purchases of novels from publishers when moral questions arose, as they did in Moore's first two novels. In wishing to protect their readers from what they regarded as corrupting influences, thus establishing a reputation for respectability from which profits accrued, the libraries assumed unofficial positions as censors and arbiters of literary taste. Hence, they selected inoffensive works deemed suitable to middle-class subscribers, principally women with the leisure to read lengthy fiction.*

Inspired by the French Naturalists' devotion to truth, Moore's first novel, *A Modern Lover* (1883), met with resistance from Mudie's when the library refused to circulate fifty copies despite generally good reviews from leading literary papers. Two women readers in the country had complained of a scene in which the female character poses as Venus for a painter. Moore's riposte, an attack titled "A New Censorship of Literature" for the radically inclined *Pall Mall Gazette* (December 10, 1884), complained that "nothing beyond the value of a sentimental tale is to be found in the circulating libraries." While accepting Henry James's "canon of art" to "go to nature and study it," Moore responded: "What is

---

*Edmund Gosse contended that "middle-aged people in the country, who are cut off from much society, and elderly ladies, whose activities are past, and who like to resume the illusions of youth, are far more assiduous novel-readers than girls." But, he added, "men read novels a great deal more than is supposed, and it is probably from men that the first-class novel receives its *imprimatur*" (*Questions at Issue* [London, 1893], 13–14).

nature but religion and morals? and the circulating library forbids discussion on such subjects. The subtraction of these two important elements of life throws the reading of fiction into the hands of young girls and widows of sedentary habits." Worse still, "at the head of English literature sits a tradesman [Mudie, alluded to elsewhere in the essay as "Mr. X——"], who considers himself qualified to decide the most delicate artistic question that may be raised, and who crushes out of sight any artistic aspiration he may deem pernicious." With such a "vulture gnawing at their hearts," said Moore, writers despaired of doing good work.

As a result of his confrontation with Mudie in his private office ("I can accept no opinion except that of my customers," the tradesman responded), Moore urged Vizetelly to publish *A Mummer's Wife* in one volume: "Whether others will follow my example, whether others will see as I see that the literary battle of our time lies not between the romantic and realistic schools of fiction, but for freedom from the illiterate censorship of a librarian, the next few years will most assuredly decide." In the ensuing days, the *Pall Mall Gazette* received letters to the editor from authors who had endured comparable indignities from circulating libraries, but some readers defended the libraries, one woman reader asking on December 15: "Why must we have thrust on us the mere dishwater from the banquets of MM. les Realistes, of whom even their own compatriots, it is rumoured, are beginning to grow weary?" Moore, she insisted, had chosen "to write books which ordinary English readers do not care to read." In another letter published in the same issue, George Gissing wondered whether Moore had "lost a little by directing his indignation in the wrong quarter." Abolishing the circulating libraries would not improve matters, he suggested: ". . . you are no nearer improving the state of things, unless you can find literary men with power and courage to produce original books. English novels are miserable stuff for a very miserable reason, simply because English novelists fear to do their best lest they should damage their popularity, and consequently their income."

Determined to undermine what he called the "odious tyranny" of the circulating libraries, Moore wrote a pamphlet satirically titled *Literature at Nurse; or Circulating Morals,* which Vizetelly published in 1885. He again related his encounter with Mudie and delighted in the success of the recently published *A Mummer's Wife* in one volume at six shillings: "The result exceeded my expectations, for the book is now in its fourth edition." Now, "with a firm heart," he was determined to "return to the fight—a fight which it is my incurable belief must be won if we are again to possess a literature worthy of the name." Moore examined three novels from Mudie's Select Library, quoting some passages from each to demonstrate that these books were decidedly prurient in plot and character as opposed to the one passage in *A Modern Lover* objected to by the "ladies in the country" or to the passage in *A Mummer's Wife,* in which Kate Ede, living a life of boredom and despair as a draper's wife, yields to the advances of Dick Lennox, the manager of a traveling opera company. All that is shown is Kate entering his room. Then, passing beyond the satirical tone of his exegesis, Moore launches into a tirade directed at Mudie:

> I hate you because you dare question the sacred right of the artist to obey the impulses of his temperament; I hate you because you are the great purveyor of the worthless, the false and the commonplace; I hate you because you are a fetter about the ankles of those who would press forward towards the light of truth; I hate you because you feel not the spirit of scientific inquiry that is bearing our age along. . . .

Concluding, Moore insists that "no unfortunate results" are likely to occur by reading a novel written "by a member of the school to which I have the honour to belong." It is the "romantic story, the action of which is laid outside the limits of her experience . . . independent of the struggle for life," that is more likely to seduce a young girl and lead her to sin. Moore's pamphlet and Vizetelly's one-volume novels did not instantly administer the death blow to the circulating libraries; it took years before major publishers began abandoning their traditional practice with respect to fiction. In 1894, Heinemann accelerated the process when he began publicizing and publishing one-volume novels. Kipling satirized the old popular form of romantic fiction in his poem "The Three-Decker" (1894), using the metaphor of an aging ship heading for its well-deserved rest in the "Islands of the Blest" with "stolen wills for ballast and a crew of missing heirs," the subcaption reading: "The three-volume novel is extinct." The passing of the elephantine novel, for much of the nineteenth century associated with loose, episodic plotting for long-running serials in the popular magazines, resulted in a progressive concern among serious writers with the craft of fiction.

IN THE 1880S, attacks on Zola and his art continued unabated. A characteristic misunderstanding of the "most popular school of contemporary French fiction" appeared as "The New Naturalism" in the conservative *Fortnightly Review* (August 1885). The misconceptions reveal the endemic Victorian anxiety over cultural invasions from across the Channel, recalling British reactions to French *décadence,* often identified with Zolaism. The author, W. S. Lilly, summarizes with some accuracy Zola's manifesto in *The Experimental Novel* but ignores Zola's views concerning morality, the imagination, and the creative process. For example, he never alludes to the Naturalists as moralists and meliorists, as Zola had. Indeed, unlike Flaubert, the Goncourts, and Maupassant, who were often associated by British critics with Naturalism, Zola had greater faith than his fellow writers in the possibility of moral progress by exposing the truth. In granting that the New Naturalism followed scientific protocols concerning observation and experimentation, Lilly reveals his misjudgment concerning the role of the imagination: "Formerly the greatest compliment you could pay a novelist or playwright was to say, 'He has a great deal of imagination.' If such a speech were addressed to M. Zola he would regard himself as a very ill-used gentleman."

Moreover, Lilly asserts that the New Naturalism means "the banishment of sentiment" and of "poetic idealism." The result is that Zola "never rises" above the mud: ". . . it is his native element." When the Naturalist follows the "latest methods adopted by the student of experimental medicine," art "must disappear from the novel and the drama." And just as claims for vivisection have proved to be hollow and untenable, the "results obtainable by [Zola's] researches in the latrine and brothel are of precisely the same value as those which the vivisector derives from the torture trough" (could this be the source of Tennyson's "in the troughs of Zolaism," which appeared in the following year?). Lilly sees no human dignity in Zola's characters, only "the instincts of the *bétè humaine.*" British critics had as little difficulty in misinterpreting Zola's novels as they had Ibsen's plays.

At the time of Lilly's article, Henry Vizetelly, who had engaged Havelock Ellis to undertake "unexpurgated editions" of the Elizabethan dramatists in the Mermaid Series, was in the process of issuing English translations of Zola's major novels and thus embarking on a collision course between himself and the government. Descended from an Italian family that had settled in Elizabethan London as artisans in glass and by the eighteenth century had achieved renown as printers, Vizetelly established a reputation as an enterprising publisher with an unerring eye for the unusual, issuing such works as Poe's tales and *Uncle Tom's Cabin* to English readers as well as translations of works by such French authors as Daudet, Flaubert, George Sand, and Merimée. While publishing translations of Zola's *Nana* and *L'Assommoir* in 1884 and 1885, Vizetelly also issued translations of Tolstoy and Dostoevsky. As readers responded favorably to the first two Zola novels, he proceeded with other translations despite hostility from reviewers.

By 1888, Vizetelly & Co. had issued eighteen translations of Zola's novels, usually expurgated to suit an English audience (though Vizetelly later claimed that the novels were "absolutely unmutilated"). The National Vigilance Association, a resurrected version of the Society for the Suppression of Vice (having expired for lack of funds in the 1870s), inaugurated a campaign against the publisher by issuing a booklet titled *Pernicious Literature* (1889), which included characteristic remarks from the *Methodist Times:* "We have never been able to believe in the moral intentions of Zola, and it has always been a marvel to us that such a critic as Mr. James should seriously contend for them. Zolaism is a disease. It is a study of the putrid. Even France has shown signs that she has had enough of it. No one can read Zola without moral contamination." Many in the association were clerics undoubtedly incensed by Zola's views of churchmen and their efforts at social regeneration:

> You claim to reform the world, you preach and you prate; but although your endeavours may be honest you do little or no good. Evil exists on all sides, society is rotten at the core; but you merely cover up abominations, you even feign at times to ignore their existence, though they lie little below the surface and poison all around them. . . . Well, I am resolved to tear the veil asunder, to set forth everything, to conceal nothing. I shall shock the world undoubtedly, but it is only by bringing things to light, by disgusting people with themselves and their surroundings, that there will be a possibility of remedying the many evils which prey on the community at large.

Ernest Vizetelly, the publisher's son who translated Zola's novels and wrote the earliest English biography of the novelist, remarked that Zola was reluctant to preach in his novels, contenting himself with "picturing vice as vile, and the viler he made it appear, the more was he abused, the more was he accused of wallowing in it, of giving full rein to filthy libidinous propensities for the express purpose of corrupting all who read him!" Similar charges, said Ernest Vizetelly, were published in hundreds of reviews and articles in London and provincial papers.

The National Vigilance Association moved with such evidence towards a confrontation with Vizetelly & Co., "accused of having deliberately chosen 'the very worst' of Zola's books for translation." The eighteen volumes by Zola had been selling well in Britain when a motion was brought before the House of Commons on May 8, 1888: "That this House deplores the rapid spread of demoralising literature in this country, and is of opinion that the law against obscene publications and indecent pictures and prints should be vigorously enforced and, if necessary, strengthened." The M.P. responsible for the motion, the evangelical Samuel Smith, remarked that lately there had been "an immense increase of vile literature in London and throughout the country, and that this literature was working terrible effects upon the morals of the young" (an assertion often assumed but rarely proved, then and now). Indeed, he questioned "whether at the present time the people of this country were suffering more from the effect of an excessive use of strong drink than they were from the more subtle poison of vile and obscene literature."

Smith singled out Henry Vizetelly as "the chief culprit in the spread of pernicious literature" (an indication that the National Vigilance Association may have urged the motion). Of Zola's works, he said, "nothing more diabolical had ever been written by the pen of man; these novels were only fit for swine, and their constant perusal must turn the mind into something akin to a sty." He read a passage from the weekly paper *Society* (April 21, 1888), which confirmed his view of Zola's "realism": ". . . dirt and horror pure and simple; and the good-humoured Englishman . . . will be disgusted and tired with the inartistic garbage which is to be found in Zola's *La Terre*. Yet Messrs. Vizetelly, of Catherine Street, Strand, are allowed with impunity to publish an almost word for word translation of Zola's bestial *chef d'oeuvre.*" The House unanimously voted in favor of the motion, but the government decided not to initiate prosecutions, believing that private individuals should undertake measures to suppress obscene literature.

Through much of the Victorian age, the most significant form of moral censorship—exercised chiefly by publishers, booksellers, and circulating libraries—had occurred outside of the existing law. The novelist William Makepeace Thackeray, as editor of the first number of *Cornhill Magazine* (November 1859), enunciated a guiding principle: "At our social table, we shall suppose the ladies and children always present." The custom of reading the Bible, instructive books, and inspiring fiction aloud by various family members in the Victorian drawing room forbade any potentially offensive material from being published for general distribution (pornography, of course, was printed privately and sold surreptitiously by booksellers of dubious respectability). The major Victorian authors, with their sense of social responsibility, acknowledged the conventions of middle-class propriety, though Hardy, for example, increasingly challenged such restrictions in the fin de siècle.

In August 1888, a firm of solicitors retained by the National Vigilance Association applied at Bow Street Magistrates' Court for a summons against Henry Vizetelly for issuing three obscene novels by Zola: *Nana, The Soil (La Terre)*, and *Piping Hot (Pot-Bouille)*. At the hearing, the magistrate suggested to the prosecutor, Herbert Asquith, later prime minister, that he single out the worst of the three novels, *The Soil*. (Just three weeks before, Zola was nominated in France as a Chevalier to the Legion of Honor!) Vizetelly's solicitor argued that the publisher was not in violation of obscenity laws since the three novels, in French, had previously circulated in Britain without objection. The magistrate, ruling that a jury trial was called for, committed Vizetelly for trial at the Central Criminal Court but released him on bail.

Before the trial, Vizetelly issued a privately printed pamphlet that contained extracts from the greatest English authors from Shakespeare to Byron, who, at one time or another, had been singled out for suppression. In an open letter to the solicitor to the treasury, accompanying the pamphlet that was sent to the London papers, Vizetelly observed that "books burnt by the common hangman in one age come to be honoured in the next." Zola's works "will take rank as classics among the productions of the great writers of the past." At the trial on October 31, 1888, the prosecutor was the solicitor-general Sir Edward Clarke (later, Wilde's counsel in his trials), who attacked *The Soil* as full of "bestial obscenity, without a spark of literary genius or the expression of an elevated thought." To prove his point, Clarke read some twenty-five isolated passages to the jury (a strategy now generally discredited). The foreman of the jury interrupted Clarke: "We think we have heard enough of them." Clarke then asked, "If you think the passages I have read are obscene of course I will stop." Several jurymen responded, "We think so." Vizetelly's counsel withdrew the plea of not guilty for one of guilty. The court fined Vizetelly £100 and placed him on probation for one year.

Signing a letter as "A Novelist," Shaw wrote to the editor of the *Star* (November 2, 1888) to clarify the "question at issue" in the Vizetelly case: ". . . whether a writer may or may not expose to society its own wickedness." Two views had been put forward, Shaw went on: "First, the British Pharisee's view, which is that it is M. Zola's duty to hide the evil and pretend that there is no such thing. Second, M. Zola's own view that it is his duty to drag it into the light and have it seen to." Agreeing with Zola, Shaw defied the radical paper "to declare publicly" whether it disagreed with him. The editor agreed with Shaw, adding: "We stated that it was not the business of the law to interfere in such cases."

In 1889, the National Vigilance Association had additional summonses issued against Vizetelly for again selling newly expurgated translations of Zola's works (which the solicitor-general deemed inadequate) as well as Flaubert's *Madame Bovary* and Maupassant's *A Woman's Life.* Vizetelly now found that as a result of declining sales and adverse publicity (the London papers did not come to his defense) he faced bankruptcy. His health failing, Vizetelly followed his counsel's advice and pleaded guilty again. While Vizetelly was serving a three-month sentence in Holloway Prison, over one hundred writers, artists, and members of Parliament signed a petition published in the *Star* (July 30, 1889), urging his release and including the names of such figures as George Moore, Edmund Gosse, Arthur Symons, John Addington Symonds, Havelock Ellis, Olive

Schreiner, H. Rider Haggard, Arthur Wing Pinero, William Archer, Ernest Rhys, and Thomas Hardy. The home secretary replied that he could not advise her majesty to intercede in the case.

As a signatory urging Vizetelly's release, Hardy was increasingly preoccupied with restrictions—imposed by circulating libraries and by family magazines—that "in general do not foster the growth of the novel which reflects and reveals life." He had been having difficulties with Tillotson & Son, whose newspaper syndicate had requested drastic revisions and deletions in the manuscript of *Tess of the d'Urbervilles,* which Hardy had submitted for serialization; the contract was eventually cancelled. In November 1889, *Murray's Magazine* rejected *Tess* because of its portrayal of "immoral situations," and in the same month *Macmillan's Magazine* also rejected the manuscript because of certain "things that might give offense."

Incensed, Hardy contributed an essay titled "Candour in English Fiction" to a symposium in the *New Review* (January 1890), in which he advanced the idea that French Naturalistic novels were examples of the "conscientious fiction" that "can excite a reflective and abiding interest in the minds of thoughtful readers of mature age, who are weary of puerile inventions and famishing for accuracy." And employing the Naturalists' view that life was "a physiological fact," Hardy insisted that "its honest portrayal must be largely concerned with, for one thing, the relations of the sexes," not the "false colouring" of the happy ending but the "catastrophes based upon sexual relations. . . ." Despite his favorable remarks about French Naturalism, expressed in order to attack unwarranted control of artistic freedom, he nevertheless maintained a traditional British view regarding fiction, as he told a friend: "You mistake in supposing I admire Zola. It is just what I don't do. I think him no artist, & too material. I feel that the animal side of human nature should never be dwelt on except as a contrast or foil to its spiritual side."

THE SECOND VIZETELLY trial, which rallied both Establishment and avant-garde figures to his support, provided a turning point in Zola's reputation, for they insisted that the novelist was not a pornographer or a corrupter of youth. As a result, critical articles began to appear in the early nineties that departed from the conventional attacks on Zola's works as merely unredeemed "bestiality." In the *Eclectic* (May 1890), the widely published critic D. F. Hannigan insisted that in England "the artist is either afraid to tell the whole truth, or else he is intellectually incapable of revealing the complicated mechanism [a term associated with scientific naturalism] of the human heart. . . . Whenever he attempts a bold piece of realism, he mars the effect of it by introducing some irrelevant bit of didacticism. . . ." In the *National Review* (April 1892), Edmund Gosse pointed to Zola as "the one living novelist who has striven to give a large, competent, and profound view of the movement of life." And in the *Contemporary Review* (February 1893), the historian, critic, and novelist "Vernon Lee" (the pseudonym of Violet Paget) acknowledged in her article, "The Moral Teachings of Zola": "It is universally admitted that Zola's books are full of horrors and indecencies, that the reading thereof must be attended by some disgust and perhaps some danger; also that they are not really scientific nor thoroughly realistic. . . ." However, she adds, "It is salutary to be horrified and sickened when the horror and the sickness make one look around, pause, and reflect."

As such articles progressively gave credence to Zola's art, the British Institute of Journalists invited Zola, as the president of the Société des Gens de Lettres, to lecture on French journalism. Despite the honor, he was understandably reluctant, he told Ernest Vizetelly, to accept the invitation: "You know my position in London; my work is still very much questioned there, almost denied." Vizetelly urged him to accept. On September 20, 1893, Zola arrived in London with an entourage of a dozen French journalists. He received much adulation (including huge receptions and fireworks displays), despite the fact that his books were more poorly reviewed in England than in any other major European country. On September 22 at Lincoln's Inn Hall, he spoke on "Anonymity in the Press," urging that articles in literary and dramatic criticism be signed, and he aroused the audience by his insistence that anonymous authors should share in the publisher's income in the form of pensions. On September 28, Zola was the guest of honor at a dinner at the Authors' Club, attended by some eighty writers, including George Moore, Jerome K. Jerome, and Frank Harris.

After his departure from London, however, Zola was distressed at criticism directed at him by the bishop of Worcester, who wrote: "Zola has spent his life corrupting the morals and souls not only of thousands of his fellow-countrymen and especially of the young, but also by the translation of his works, thousands and hundreds of thousands of young souls elsewhere." The bishop of Truro and the headmaster of Harrow School expressed similar views. Yet there was also favorable comment, as in the *Westminster Review* (December 1893): "[Zola's] visit has of itself directed renewed attention to the works of the best abused novelist of the day. . . . Zola! Why the very name sounds like a challenge, a cry of attack, a shout of victory—clear and resonant like the notes of a clarion." But, said the writer, the reception given to Zola was also "a magnificent example of inconsistency": "One day we have a publisher severely punished for offending public morals by issuing extremely diluted translations of the works of a celebrated foreign writer, the next that he himself is feted and

M. ZOLA READING A PAPER BEFORE THE INSTITUTE OF JOURNALISTS IN THE HALL OF LINCOLN'S INN.

Emile Zola in London (*Illustrated London News*, September 30, 1893)

toasted and flattered *ad nauseum* by the very people who have just been emptying the vials of their wrath on his unfortunate representative." The metaphor of the clarion appears again in a later article as the *Westminster Review* (January 1895) continued to advance Zola's cause: "This, the end of the nineteenth century, is a time of awakening, and Zola's is a trumpet voice to arouse men from sleep. He calls to us to see on the brink of what bottomless pit we are standing." As a "prophet," he shows us not only "the very lowest depths of human depravity" but also the capacity for "saintly enthusiasm and beautiful, untiring human affection."

IN *Esther Waters* (1894), George Moore, who had come under the influence of Pater's aestheticism after reading *Marius the Epicurean* (1885), disassociated himself from his previous discipleship to Zola. Indeed, Moore had already turned from the notion of objective observation after *A Mummer's Wife* in an essay on Turgenev in the *Fortnightly Review* (February 1888), which reproached Zola for being "at his worst" when recording "mere facts" (a complaint echoed later by Symons and Yeats when they publicized the Symbolist Movement). Also, in an 1892 review of a Royal Academy exhibition, Moore was highly critical of one painter, Stanhope Forbes, who "copied the trousers seam by seam, patch by patch and the ugliness of the garment bores you in the picture, exactly as it would in nature. . . . A handful of dry facts instead of a passionate impression of life in the envelope of mystery and suggestion. Realism, that is to say, the desire to compete with nature, to be nature, is the disease from which art has suffered most in the last twenty years."

Despite such an attitude, Moore remained faithful to realism in *Esther Waters,* though he rejected the determinism implicit in Naturalism. The novel contains conventions common to both modes of presentation: That is, it depicts an uneducated, poor kitchen maid who is seduced and who struggles through her life to raise her son—at times faced by starvation and homelessness or surrounded by drinking and betting. Yet her determination is such that, despite hardship and disappointment, she triumphs in the end, whereas many around her sink into moral and economic squalor. In the final symbolic scene, Esther introduces her son, a handsome young soldier, to her employer rather abruptly without Moore offering a clear delineation of the son's character, an ending unlike those in many Naturalistic novels in which the central character is defeated by life. *Esther Waters,* then, provided readers with an inspiring moral tale that bourgeois Victorians expected in fiction. Ironically, the novel descends into the very sentimentality that Moore had wished to stab with "a dagger in the heart."

Within the year, *Esther Waters* sold 24,000 copies, a considerable success despite the fact that W. H. Smith's circulating library had refused to purchase copies because of a scene describing childbirth. Moore called in an accountant who estimated that the library had lost £1500 by refusing to circulate the book. Later, Moore recalled the "satisfaction of hearing that the partners of the firm sent word to their librarian that it would be well in the future to avoid heavy losses by banning books, especially books that Mr. Gladstone was likely to read and to express his approval of in the *Westminster Gazette.*"

IN THE fin de siècle, "slum fiction," associated with the conventions of Naturalism, emerged as a subgenre of the British novel through a variety of historical influences. Dickens had shown the way in such novels as *Oliver Twist* (1837–38) and *Our Mutual Friend* (1864), though his depictions of the poor were often eccentric or picturesque rather than representative of a distinct social class. From the mid-Victorian years onwards, the appearance of a new form of reportage, including personal anecdotes, offered new possibilities of subject matter for fiction. Henry Mayhew's four-volume *London Labour and the London Poor* (1861–65) was a landmark in sociological investigation that may have prompted, in 1865, the establishment of the first Salvation Army shelter in the East End (Act II of Shaw's *Major Barbara* takes place in such a setting). Other such surveys and exposés in the 1880s and 1890s directed further attention to East End desperation, the dramatic possibilities of which attracted such novelists as George Gissing and Arthur Morrison (both of whom had lived for a while in the slums).

For novelists and social critics, the East End was variously regarded as a symbol of degraded humanity, of revolutionary ferment, of spiritual and psychological dislocation, and of social paralysis as industrial Manchester had been in the 1840s. The Industrial Revolution had brought about mass migration to the cities from villages and farms, where families had lived for generations and where agricultural depression had been widespread since the 1870s. Suffering from disease and hunger, the displaced poorest classes in the crowded slums had little sense of community, as Beatrice Webb discovered: "no roots in neighbourhood, in vocation, in creed, or for that matter in race." In Walter Besant's *All Sorts and Conditions of Men* (1882), a novel that helped shape the image of the East End in the imaginations of late Victorians, "meanness" and "monotony" dominated descriptions of the desolation and isolation of the area:

> Two millions of people, or thereabouts, live in the East End of London. That seems a good-sized population for an utterly unknown town. They have no institutions of their own to speak of, no public buildings of any importance, no municipality, no gentry, no carriages, no soldiers, no picture-galleries, no theatres, no opera—they have nothing. . . . Nobody goes east, no one wants to see the place; no one is curious about the way of life in the east.

Throughout the nineteenth century, the isolation among the lower classes concerned politicians and social critics fearful of social unrest, particularly in the later hard-pressed decades. After Besant's novel, two publications appeared in 1883 that did much to direct further attention to the plight of those in East and South London: The journalist and novelist George Sims reprinted a series of newspaper articles in book form titled *How the Poor Live,* and an anonymous pamphlet appeared (now believed to be principally written by Andrew Mearns, secretary of the London

Congregational Union), titled *The Bitter Cry of Outcast London: An Enquiry into the Condition of the Abject Poor,* which created a sensation. Publications such as these and the worsening economic conditions in the early 1880s produced widespread anxiety over the possibility of civil disorder despite the fact that the trade unions were basically conservative, if not reactionary.

Nevertheless, in the mid-1880s, radical socialists and anarchists held demonstrations in Trafalgar Square to protest unemployment and other issues, culminating in the riot on Bloody Sunday. Characteristic of the concern at this time was the Earl of Pembroke's contention in an address to the Liberty and Property Defence League: "Radicalism necessarily ventures ground of doubtful morality, and inevitably attracts to its ranks the unprincipled, the rebellious, and the predatory elements of society." In his novel *The Old Order Changes* (1886), W. H. Mallock, who, like Henry James, was apprehensive that such social anarchy might endanger an older, privileged culture, alludes in a speech by one of the characters to the French Revolution (often cited by the Victorians as a warning of what could also occur in England): "Have you ever looked into the faces of an East End mob? Have you ever realized what an appalling sight they are? The French Ambassador has several times said to me that he thinks things in England in a most critical and dangerous condition, and that the savage and sullen spirit fermenting through the country now is just what there was in Paris before the Great Revolution."

In 1889, the appearance of the most comprehensive survey of poverty in the East End, Charles Booth's first volume of his seventeen-volume *Life and Labour of the People in London,* could only have increased the anxiety of those like James and Mallock who sensed a rising tide of chaos. Booth's object was to show "the numerical relation which poverty, misery, and depravity bear to regular earnings and comparative comfort, and to describe the general conditions under which each class lives." His survey estimated that almost half of the population in the East End was living below subsistence level, the highest proportion in London. Works such as Booth's resulted in a new influx of social reformers and salvationists to the area in an attempt to end its isolation. At the same time, the images of desperate humanity in the novels of the French Naturalists provided yet further incentives for slum novelists.

Yet even as some British writers seemed to be "wallowing in the troughs of Zolaism," they often introduced variations in fictional technique and vision to modify the audacities of French Naturalism. In his grimmest and grimiest descriptions of the slums—*Workers in the Dawn* (1880), *Demos* (1886), *Thyrza* (1887), and *The Nether World* (1889)— George Gissing progressively resisted Zola's scientific observation and determinism in his scorn toward those who submit to entrapment in the lower depths (as a modern critic remarks, Gissing was "an egoist masquerading as a fatalist"). Despite an initial impulse to depict a social problem in his fiction, Gissing ultimately relegated it to the background while focusing on plot and character. Such divided intentions prompted George Orwell to observe that Gissing (characteristic of the Modernists) "wanted to speak not for the multitude, but for the exceptional man, the sensitive man, isolated among barbarians." Drawn to the Aestheticism of the 1880s, Gissing believed that the wrongs one suffered from society's indifference might be eased by exposure to art and beauty, a theme that occurs often in his letters, as in the following to his brother:

> When I am able to summon any enthusiasm at all, it is only for ART—how I laughed the other day on recalling your amazement at my theories of Art for Art's sake! Well, I cannot get beyond it. Human life has little interest to me, on the whole— save as material for artistic presentation. I can get savage over social iniquities, but even then my rage at once takes the direction of planning revenge in artistic work.

In the Anglican weekly the *Guardian* (May 29, 1889), the reviewer of *The Nether World* perceived in Gissing a disdain for the "want of refinement" in the poor. In the bank holiday scene at the Crystal Palace, which the reviewer calls "unnecessarily crude and painful," the description of the people "has in it more of cynical contempt than of sympathy and insight." Though not a committed Naturalist, Gissing was a reader of Zola and Schopenhauer; in his determination to reveal the sordid truth of slum existence, Gissing revealed a deep-seated Schopenhauerian pessimism redeemed by his aesthetic devotion to art.

Though a number of slum novels dwell on the "meanness" and "monotony" in the East End, Rudyard Kipling's only story of the slums, "The Record of Badalia Herodsfoot" (1890), describes with convincing precision the brutal domestic violence among the residents of Gunnison Street. Badalia, charged with maintaining a record of charitable funds allotted by the local curate, dies from vicious kicks by her husband, whom she pretends was an intruder, insisting that no harm came to her record or to the money entrusted to her. The degree of brutality in the story is unusual even in slum fiction. Nevertheless, this striking vision of cockney life—with its accuracy of speech and its private morality—was a major influence on later slum novelists, for unlike Gissing, Kipling depicted the inhabitants of the East End in their own bleak image rather than through middle-class moral preconceptions.

The most striking anomaly, perhaps, among the slum novels of the nineties, one that departed radically from French Naturalism, occurred in

Israel Zangwill's *Children of the Ghetto* (1892). Zangwill's rejection of the scientific presumptions of Zola's grim objectivity is echoed by his East End heroine Esther Ansell, who has published a novel titled *Mordecai Josephs:* "I am a curious mixture. In art, I have discovered in myself two conflicting tastes, and neither is for modern realism, which I yet admire in literature. I like pictures impregnated with vague romantic melancholy, and I like the white lucidity of white statuary." Zola, said Zangwill, was the "apostle of insufficient insight": "The realistic novel, we know from Zola, is based on 'human documents' and 'human documents' are made up of facts. *But in human life there are no facts.* This is not a paradox but 'a fact.' Life is in the eye of the observer. The humour or pity of it belongs entirely to the spectator, and depends upon the gift of vision he brings." To his vision of the Jewish ghetto, Zangwill brought nostalgia and pathos (he lived there for a while); in the process, he knowingly decended into sentimentality, as in Esther's "morbid impulse to identify herself with poverty" after she had been a servant in a wealthy West End home. In her decision to return to the East End to embrace her heritage and serve others,

> The race instinct awoke to consciousness of itself. Dulled by contact with cultured Jews, transformed almost to repulsion by the spectacle of the coarsely prosperous, it leaped into life at the appeal of squalor and misery. In the morning the Ghetto had simply chilled her. . . . Now that the first ugliness had worn off, she felt her heart warming. . . . She thrilled from head to foot with a sense of a mission—of a niche in the temple of human service which she had been predestined to fill.

Unlike other slum novelists, Zangwill portrays No. 1 Royal Street in the East End not as a proving ground for vice and debauchery but as the spiritual center for "children of the ghetto," where thrice daily they pray in the synagogue on the ground floor, the earnest congregants romantically described by the author as "strange exotics in a land of prose carrying with them through the paven highways of London the odor of continental ghettos and bearing in their eyes through all the shrewdness of their glances the eternal mysticism of the Orient." At a time when large numbers of Jews from Eastern Europe had settled in the East End and tensions (and even violence) between them and the native English arose from limited employment opportunities and housing shortages, Zangwill strove for a favorable image of the new immigrants.

Less concerned with romanticizing the East End, Arthur Morrison's *Tales of Mean Streets* (1894) and *A Child of the Jago* (1896) are Zolaesque in their uncompromising portrayals of depravity and crime. When he began writing short stories, Morrison decided that "they must be done with austerity and frankness and there must be no sentimentalism, no glossing over." The "Jago district" around Old Nichol Street, Bethnal Green, was particularly noted for its crime and poverty—a situation, Morrison said, that "added to existence a terror not to be guessed by the unafflicted."* For his first novel, he decided to use such a dramatic setting when, after publishing his *Tales,* he received a letter of appreciation from the Reverend A. Osborne Jay, vicar of Holy Trinity, Shoreditch, bordering on the Jago district. On being invited by the clergyman to visit the parish, Morrison spent eighteen months, perhaps with notebook in hand, haunting the barren streets and alleys, drinking with local residents in pubs, and learning how to make matchboxes (still a widespread occupation among the indigent). Reverend Jay was not only a religious activist but also the gifted author of *Life in Darkest London* (1891), which describes his parish duties and striking scenes of life in the Jago, as in the following, after which Morrison modeled some of his own prose: "Women, sodden with drink, fighting and struggling like wild creatures; men, bruised and battered, with all the marks and none of the pleasures of vice upon them; outcasts, abject and despairing, without food or shelter; the very children, with coarse oaths and obscene jests, watching, like wild beasts, for anything, dishonest or otherwise, which might come their way."

In the introduction to *Tales,* Morrison depicts the East End as "an evil plexus of slums that hide human creeping things; where filthy men and women live on penn'orths of gin, where collars and clean shirts are decencies unknown, where every citizen wears a black eye, and none ever combs his hair." In *A Child of the Jago,* Dicky Perrott, who has been guided to the path of decency by a priest, dies in a street fight after a brief life as a petty thief in a tale of murder and drunkenness involving his own father, who is executed. Death, suggested Morrison and other slum novelists, was one of the few means of escape from the lower depths, a Naturalistic truism that environment and heredity determined one's destiny: "[Dicky Perrott] was of the Jago, and he must prey on the outer world as all the Jago did. . . . Who was he that he should break away from the Jago habit and strain after another nature! What could come of it but defeat and bitterness? Why should he fight against the inevitable, and bruise himself. The ways out of Jago . . . [are] Gaol, the gallows, and the High Mob." The degraded, doomed life in the East End convinced Morrison

*"Bethnal Green has been completely transformed during the present century by slum clearance, the building of large council estates, the loss of most of its industries and the decline of its population from the peak of about 130,000 in 1901 to about one-third of this number by the 1960s." (*The London Encyclopaedia,* eds. Ben Weinreb and Christopher Hibbert [London, 1983], 61).

that survival was barely possible. Even the fittest, the social Darwinists would have said, faced a destiny equally grievous.

In W. Somerset Maugham's first novel, *Liza of Lambeth* (1897), south-east London is less a world of the depraved than one where its inhabitants reveal their capacity for humor and boisterousness. The young, vibrant Liza, a factory worker, first appears singing Albert Chevalier's latest music-hall song, "Knocked 'em in the Old Kent Road," and eventually has everyone in Vere Street dancing around a barrel-organ. When she carries on an affair with a married man, she becomes embroiled in a street fight with the enraged wife, while those in the crowd, in a festive mood, circle about them and act as referees. Beaten, rejected by other women, Liza takes to drink. As she lies dying from a miscarriage, her mother and a midwife amuse themselves with idle, bragging conversation about "respectable" funerals and the "respectability" of their late husbands, seemingly with little concern over Liza's condition. Maugham's departure from Naturalism is strikingly evident in a section titled "The Idyll of Corydon and Phyllis," which depicts a "faithful swain" and his "amorous shepherdess," both Cockneys, transported to a pastoral setting where, among other things, they engage in an "idyllic contest" of spitting—an example of what William Empson has called "the pastoral process of putting the complex into the simple." Here, Maugham's satirical view of the poor suggests parody of the slum novel.

The reluctance by many English novelists to follow Zola's prescriptions slavishly is also apparent in Arnold Bennett's first novel, *A Man from the North* (1898), a tale of lower middle-class existence. The young aspiring writer from the north, a lowly clerk who works in a solicitor's office and who reads Zola in French, attributes his failure in London, "the natural home of the author," to his heredity and environment: "Why had nature deprived him of strength of purpose? He sought for a reason, and he found it in his father, that mysterious, dead transmitter of traits, of whom he knew so little, and on whose name lay a blot of some kind which was hidden from him. He had been born in the shadow, and after a fitful struggle towards emergence, into the shadow he must again retire." The passage, with its deferential bow to Zola, lacks conviction since Bennett provides little evidence that circumstances have conspired against the clerk. And though sexuality draws him to women below his intellectual and aesthetic standards, he settles on one ("A woman . . . his, his own!") who will end his loneliness and lead him to a commonplace, respectable life. Here at the end of the nineties, Bennett employs Zola as a convenient peg on which to hang an explanation for failure and ends the novel with the hero's dubious prospect for happiness.

———

Fore Street, Lambeth (Victoria & Albert Museum)

BY THE MID-NINETIES, *Zolaism* was no longer a term of abuse, for French Naturalism ceased to be a significant influence on the English novel or perceived as a threat to Victorian sensibilities. The association of Naturalism with positivistic, mechanistic science—limited by its nature to sensory experience and by convention to depictions of the degraded poor—may have hastened the eclipse of such fiction, for its unrelieved pessimism ran counter to Victorian tastes and the tradition of the English novel. For the Aesthetes, realism was no better than Naturalism in its mirroring of the world's ugliness, for as Wilde said in his preface to *The Picture of Dorian Gray* (1891): "The nineteenth-century dislike of Realism is the rage of Caliban seeing his own face in a glass."

By the end of the nineties, Bennett's *A Man from the North* signaled a shift by writers from Naturalistic preference for fin-de-siècle slum settings to one in the suburbs with characters drawn from a broad spectrum of the middle classes—clerks, teachers, civil servants, novelists, and professionals. The extension of railway lines and the growing use of motor cars resulted in considerable development in West and North London, and such Edwardian novelists as Bennett, Galsworthy, and Forster began the exploration of the new suburban resident, safe from the depravity and violence of life in East and South London, as suggested by a writer at the time: "Every day, swung high upon embankments or buried deep in tubes underground, [suburban man] hurries through the area where the creature lives [in the slums]. He gazes darkly from his pleasant hill villa upon the huge and smoky area of tumbled tenements which stretches at his feet."

More important, other reactions to realism and Naturalism, both rooted in the assumptions of scientific materialism, were in motion during the last decades of the nineteenth century. Earlier Victorian utopian thinkers were confident that science would usher in a new world, as expressed in an 1860 lecture by the biologist and social critic T. H. Huxley, who hailed the beneficial influence of science in the intellectual and cultural life of the age:

> The whole of modern thought is steeped in science; it has made its way into the works of our best poets, and even the mere man of letters, who affects to ignore and despise science, is unconsciously impregnated with her spirit and indebted for his best products to her methods. I believe that the greatest intellectual revolution mankind has yet seen is now slowly taking place by her agency. . . . She is creating a firm and living faith in the existence of immutable moral and physical laws, perfect obedience to which is the highest aim of an intelligent being.

Walter Pater had challenged the conviction that only in the vast mechanistic cosmos were "immutable moral and physical laws" to be discovered. In the famous "Conclusion" to *Studies in the History of the Renaissance* (1873), he asserted the primacy of subjectivism by insisting that we can only know our own impressions of external reality—a philosophical skepticism undermining the confidence and reliability of scientific knowledge. As a result of such uncertainty not only in science but also in religion, many intellectuals developed an interest during the 1880s and 1890s in the irrational and the mystical. In 1882, for example, the Society for Psychical Research, founded to explore mental telepathy, extrasensory perception, and the possible existence of a spirit world, attracted noted scientists and artists who wished to affirm the existence of a nonmaterial world by investigating unexplained phenomena with controlled experiments.

A more demanding route to the spirit, perhaps, was through occult initiation and the transcendent symbol—or so Yeats, the most eloquent advocate for a new direction in the arts, believed as he and his colleagues among the Aesthetes and Symbolists sought escape from immersion in the dead externalities of realism and Naturalism:

> The scientific movement brought with it a literature which was always tending to lose itself in externalities of all kinds, in opinion, in declamation, in picturesque writing, in word-painting, or in what Mr. [Arthur] Symons has called an attempt "to build in brick and mortar inside the covers of a book." . . . How can the arts overcome the slow dying of men's hearts that we call the

progress of the world, and lay their hands upon men's heart-
strings again, without becoming the garment of religion as in
old times?

This was Yeats's review of Symons's *The Symbolist Movement in Literature*
(1900), the introduction to which described a determined fin-de-siècle
reaction to positivistic science: ". . . after the world has starved its soul
long enough in the contemplation and re-arrangement of material things,
comes the turn of the soul; and with it comes the literature of which I
write in this volume, a literature in which the visible world is no longer a
reality and the unseen world no longer a dream." As for "material
things," Symons used the metaphor of "brick and mortar inside the covers" of a Zola novel to suggest the earthbound constriction of the imagination and the spirit. For "the slow-dying of men's hearts," liberation lay
in the occult and the symbol through such means as solemn ritual and the
evocative dance.

14

The Dance of the
Occult Mysteries

As SCIENTIFIC AND positivist attitudes, associated with the Industrial Revolution, continued to undermine Christian doctrine in the late nineteenth century, the traditional Victorian belief that reason enriched life rather than constricted it likewise underwent a decline. As a result of the "new science," the world increasingly appeared to be a mechanism of impersonal forces beyond man's control. Scientists like the physicist John Tyndall, however, had absolute confidence in the capacity of scientific method to discover the ultimate truths of nature. In his famous Belfast Address (1874), Tyndall presented what he believed to be an "impregnable position": "We claim, and we shall wrest from theology, the entire domain of cosmological theory. All schemes and systems which thus infringe upon the domain of science must, in so far as they do this, submit to its control, and relinquish all thought of controlling it."

Such attitudes by scientists prompted Browning, in 1887 to express an anxiety shared by many who sensed the devastating cultural crisis that had beset the Victorian age:

> *Which was it of the links*
> *Snapt first, from out the chain which used to bind*
> *Our earth to heaven . . . ?*

The extent of such anxiety may also be gauged by the nearly 2,000 letters sent to the editor of the London *Daily Chronicle* between January 14 and early February 1893, responding to the question "Is Christianity Played Out?" The issue had arisen following Richard Le Gallienne's review (published in the paper on January 11) of Robert Buchanan's *The Wandering Jew: A Christmas Carol,* a lengthy narrative on Christ as man rather than the son of God. A vigorous exchange of lengthy letters between Buchanan and Le Gallienne on various literary and religious attitudes soon turned to the question directed at Buchanan by Le Gallienne: ". . . is Christianity played out . . . ?" Taking up the query as though it were "a war-cry," the editor began publishing letters to the paper for the next few weeks. Many argued on theological grounds in an attempt to define Christianity and to attack or defend Le Gallienne, who separated Christ from the narrow dogmatism of Christianity, and Buchanan, who maintained that Christ had no divine origins and that his reputed mission to save mankind had failed. In the midst of such theoretical discussions, sometimes by the clergy, one letter signed by "A Working Man," provides a striking view of the writer's conviction that the lower classes needed the comfort of Christ for survival:

> . . . I represent the thoughts and feelings of thousands, nay millions, of their [that is, Buchanan's and Le Gallienne's] fellow-men who are suffering to-day on account of man's inhumanity to man. I wish I could write and speak like them, to prove that Christ is indeed not a failure: I mean, not to the poor—the rich I cannot say much about; perhaps they want to get rid of him, as it may interfere with their delightfully intellectual pleasures and pursuits.

Without Christ, he continued, "the world would be a hell to me." The writer had been friendless, an outcast in London, "but I know that Christ has been a power to me." As another example of Christ's beneficent influence, he cites a man in some back street in London with a wife and two or three children, working twelve or fourteen hours a day, often including Sundays, for twenty shillings a week: "Without hope, without Christ, what is this world to them but hell . . . ?" Addressing himself again to Buchanan and Le Gallienne, the writer concludes: ". . . tell them, Mr. Editor, if they don't want [Christ], to leave him alone, and let their grand minds talk about something else; leave him to the poor, the wretched, not to try to unsettle some poor one's mind with doubts." On January 26, a letter from "A Bricklayer" confessed to his having been a "slave to drink" but expressed gratitude to "the mighty power of the Living Christ, who can save all the drunkards in the world."

For other late Victorians, however, the impact of science on faith generated a sense of alienation and isolation, which Havelock Ellis recalls as a young man in the 1880s: ". . . I had the feeling that the universe was represented as a sort of factory filled by an inextricable web of wheels and looms and flying shuttles, in a deafening din. That, it seemed, was the world as the most competent scientific authorities declared it to be made. It was a world I was prepared to accept and yet a world in which, I felt, I could only wander restlessly, an ignorant and homeless child." In a letter to the writer and socialist R. B. Cunninghame Graham, Conrad used a similar metaphor for his Darwinian nightmare of a material world without ultimate meaning for humanity:

> There is a—let us say—a machine. It evolved itself (I am severely scientific) out of a chaos of scraps of iron and behold!— it knits. I am horrified at the horrible work and stand appalled. I feel it ought to embroider—but it goes on knitting. You come and say: "this is all right; it's only a question of the right kind of oil. Let us use this—for instance—celestial oil and the machine shall embroider a most beautiful design in purple and gold." Will it? Alas no. . . . And the most withering thought is that the infamous thing has made itself . . . without thought, without conscience, without foresight, without eyes, without heart. . . . You can't interfere with it. . . . It knits us in and it knits us out. It has knitted time, space, pain, death, corruption, despair and all the illusions—and nothing matters.

Such a conviction propelled Hardy to depict the lugubrious twelve-year-old little Father Time in *Jude the Obscure* (1895), who kills his siblings and himself after he hears that still another child is expected in the troubled Fawley family. Informed of what Freud would later call "Thanatos," the death instinct, Jude tells his wife: "The doctor says there are such boys springing up amongst us—boys of a sort unknown in the last generation—the outcome of new views of life. They seem to see all its terrors before they are old enough to have staying power to resist them. He says it is the beginning of the coming universal wish not to live."

In response to such bleak views of the universe, writers and artists unable to accept narrow ecclesiatical doctrine increasingly sought other means in their quest for a meaningful reality. Yeats recalled that, having been "deprived . . . of the simple-minded religion" of his childhood by such Victorian scientists as T. H. Huxley and John Tyndall, whom he detested, he turned to a more rewarding vision of the world: "I had made a new religion, almost an infallible church of poetic tradition. . . ." In the fin de siècle, the Religion of Art central to Aestheticism and Decadence became for many Modernists a means of coping with their alien world. Joyce's *A Portrait of the Artist as a Young Man* (1916) strikes one as the last great Victorian novel, as the climax of nineteenth-century Aestheticism as well as a brilliant harbinger of Modernism. The embryonic artist, Stephen Dedalus (his first name recalling the first Christian martyr), envisions himself as "a priest of eternal imagination, transmuting the daily bread of experience into the radiant body of everliving life."

Other artists, like the Pre-Raphaelite painter Edward Burne-Jones, concentrated on the spiritual qualities of art, those that were ineffable and visionary: "The more materialistic Science becomes," he announced, "the more angels shall I paint." Conrad himself developed an aesthetic to introduce the visionary experience into a fiction rooted in the sensuous world. In the preface to *The Nigger of the "Narcissus"* (1897), he argued a point drawn from the French *symbolistes,* Wagner, Pater, and Schopenhauer that "all art . . . appeals primarily to the senses. . . . It must strenuously aspire to the plasticity of sculpture, to the colour of painting, and to the magic suggestiveness of music—which is the art of arts." And following the *symbolistes,* Conrad spoke of the "light of magic suggestiveness [that] may be brought to play for an evanescent instant over the commonplace surface of words. . . ."

Also, in the final two decades of the century, a reaction to the increasing materialism of the age arose in the widespread interest in the occult—secret knowledge that had ancient and mysterious sources—which provided "Adepts" with confirmation that the cosmos consisted of an eternal order beyond the world of the senses. If scientists and positivists had usurped the latter world and subjected it to rational inquiry, the eternal world remained beyond their reach. For occultists, it was the source of truth. Poets such as Yeats and George Russell who were attracted to the study of the occult saw possibilities of new subject matter and aesthetic theory in the doctrines established over the centuries, for they sensed analogies between the occult magician and the visionary poet: Both were possessed with the power to summon transcendent images. In his essay titled "Magic" (1901), Yeats echoed what had become in the late nineteenth century a central attitude of writers fascinated by the occult: "I cannot now think symbols less than the greatest of all powers whether they are used consciously by the masters of magic, or half unconsciously by their successors, the poet, the musician, and the artist. . . ."

In 1884 at the Metropolitan Art School in Dublin, Yeats made the acquaintance of Russell, who wrote and painted as AE, a pseudonym derived from the "most primieval thought" that he could think of—"Aön"—which he later associated with "Aeon," the name given to the "earliest beings separated from the Deity." On June 16, 1885, with AE in the audience, Yeats presided at the founding of the Dublin Hermetic Society, named after the legendary ancient seer, Hermes Trismegistis, the Hellenized version of the Egyptian god Thoth, inventor of speech and writing. *The Emerald Tablet,* attributed to Hermes and published in 1541, revealed that the transcendental world had its corresponding reality in the earthly world—"As above, so below"—essentially a Platonic notion of correspondences at the root of virtually all occult interpretations of the universe. Hermeticism, a means of reconciling paganism and Christianity

in the Renaissance, was substantially ignored by eighteenth-century ratio-
nalism but rediscovered by the Romantics. Now, the promise of unity in
all things attracted many late Victorian intellectuals and particularly
poets, who, uncertain of their faith in Christianity, sought to reestablish a
sense of coherence in their lives and to discover a secret method for their
art.

At the first meeting of the Hermetic Society, Yeats announced that the
members had gathered to study the "wonders of Eastern philosophy." In
subsequent meetings, they discussed such topics as the fourth dimension
and *Esoteric Buddhism* (1883), a popular work by A. P. Sinnett, the author
of *The Occult World* (1881), which had absorbed Yeats. Such study by
Yeats and AE of Eastern and occult doctrines that offered a new vision of
cosmic unity later struck W. H. Auden as a futile gesture. Perhaps because he failed to understand that for Yeats the occult provided not only a
means of escape from spiritual despair but also the promise of material for
a new poetic, Auden dismissed—in no uncertain terms—Yeats's lifelong
study of magic and mysticism in "all those absurd books": ". . . but
mediums, spells, the Mysterious Orient—*how* embarrassing."

Yeats proposed to his fellow members of the Dublin Hermetic Society
"that whatever the great poets had affirmed in their finest moments was
the nearest we could come to an authoritative religion, and that their
mythology, their spirits of water and wind were but literal truth." Yeats's
extraordinary capacity to believe (or, more significantly, to embody) the
"ancient doctrine" provided him with a vast new array of interrelated
images for his poems and plays freed from commonplace logic and rea-

Yeats cartoon by W. T. Horton (Collection of Professor George Mills Harper)

son. The occult was thus his "secret fanaticism," a means of confounding the literal minded. In an early poem, "The Song of the Happy Shepherd," Yeats expresses such a rejection of scientific truth by affirming Romantic subjectivism:

> *There is no truth,*
> *Saving in thine own heart.*
> *Seek, then,*
> *No learning from the starry men,*
> *Who follow with the optic glass*
> *The whirling ways of stars that pass. . . .*

The writings of such mystics as Swedenborg and Boehme opened his eyes to the presence of universal symbols, an indication of how secret knowledge lay in imaginative interpretation; he read about magicians who claimed that they could summon and control unseen realities by employing magic just as poets could evoke hitherto unknown experiences by employing symbols.

THE DUBLIN HERMETIC SOCIETY took its name from the London chapter (the Hermetic Lodge) of the Theosophical Society, founded by Madame Helena Petrovna Blavatsky, a Russian emigré whose extraordinary combination of scholarly, spiritual, and entrepreneurial energies approached mythic dimensions. At the age of eighteen, she had married a general twice her age who was the vice-governor of a southern Russian province. Within three months, she left with his name and, she insisted, with her chastity undefiled. Throughout a second marriage and in various other liaisons, she continued this claim.

While traveling restlessly around the world and reading voluminously, she developed a sense of mission. In 1873, she was in New York, conducting seances at 16 Irving Place and sharing her spiritual vision with devoted disciples. As a medium and magician, she demonstrated her powers by instigating table-rappings, levitations, materializations, and the mysterious ringings of astral bells. In 1875, at forty-four, she was a founder of the Theosophical Society, devoted to the study of the cabala, spiritualism, and the occult. She was also the author of *Isis Unveiled* (1877), the subtitle revealing its ambitious scope: "A Master-Key to the Mysteries of Ancient and Modern Science and Theology." This work sought to reveal, by means of a secret doctrine, the fundamental similarities of all religions (comparable to modern anthropological and comparative studies of religion). The doctrine had been revealed to her, she said, by the guardians of an oral tradition, her "Masters" in the higher elevations of Tibet; on occasion, they also communicated with her telepathically. As she worked on the two volumes, she told her sister that she was the medium by which the ancient wisdom was revealing itself to the world: "I am writing *Isis;* not writing, rather copying out and drawing that which She personally shows to me. Upon my word, sometimes it seems to me that the ancient Goddess of Beauty in person leads me through all the countries of past centuries which I have to describe."

In 1878, she traveled to India, where, in Adyar, near Madras, she founded the international headquarters of the Theosophical Society and won many adherents throughout that country and in Ceylon. By the mid-1880s, she was at work on *The Secret Doctrine,* which traced the origin and development not only of the universe but of man as well, a work often condemned, like *Isis Unveiled,* for its shoddy scholarship and evident plagiarism, though the revelation of hitherto unsuspected unity in the cosmos provided new visions to those, like Yeats, in need of such confirmation.

While she was in Europe, Madame Blavatsky's handyman and housekeeper at the headquarters of the society in Adyar came forward with disturbing accusations concerning her integrity: They accused her of producing "marvellous phenomena" by using sliding panels and other devices. In England, the Society for Psychical Research dispatched an investigator, a Cambridge-educated lawyer named Richard Hodgson, to determine the truth of such allegations. In London at the time, Madame Blavatsky devised a desperate plan to vanish; such a mysterious disappearance, she believed, might arouse sympathy for her and restore theosophy's influence. Eventually, she made her way to Ceylon and India. In the midst of plots against her, one of which involved an accusation that she had been a Russian spy, she left India for the last time in March 1885.

Upon his return from India after three months of intensive research, Hodgson reported in December 1885 that Madame Blavatsky was "one of the most accomplished, ingenious, and interesting imposters in history." Despite such a damaging judgment, she continued to attract new adherents with astonishing success, for her visionary powers (no matter how undermined by Hodgson) enthralled her followers, one of whom, the versatile Annie Besant, was attracted to the Theosophical Society in 1889. After turning to atheism, she became an officer in the National Secular Society, then a member of the executive committee of the Fabian Society. She could not believe that Madame Blavatsky was capable of "trickery and hypocrisy" or that theosophical truths had been discredited. On the death of Madame Blavatsky in 1891, she became president of the Theosophical Society.

After a period of ill health on the Continent, Madame Blavatsky returned to London in May of 1887 and lived in Upper Norwood, in the southeastern part of the city. Yeats, who had come to London in the preceding month, visited her on hearing of her arrival: ". . . I was admitted and found an old woman in a plain loose dark dress: a sort of old Irish peasant woman with an air of humour and audacious power." He admired her for those qualities that he had also found in William Morris: "They had more human nature than anybody else; they at least were unforeseen, illogical, incomprehensible." With her "vast and shapeless body, and perpetually rolling cigarettes," she talked to whoever called on her. Yeats, who had carefully read Hodgman's damaging report to the Society for Psychical Research, recalled W. E. Henley's remark: "Of course she gets up fraudulent miracles, but a person of genius must do something; Sarah Bernhardt sleeps in her coffin."

In August, Madame Blavatsky moved to Holland Park, where Yeats often visited her. Yearning for experiences of the unknown, he noticed one night as he sat silently amidst a group of conversationalists that in an adjoining room a "curious red light" had fallen on a painting, but as he approached it, the light vanished. She told him that it was his clairvoyance: "If it were mediumship, it would stay in spite of you. Beware of that—it is a kind of madness, I have been through it." Despite her tarnished reputation, Yeats joined the Blavatsky Lodge of the Theosophical Society and urged Ernest Rhys to accompany him to see its high priestess—an invitation that Rhys believed was designed to draw him "into the same mystic circle." Though Rhys found her "almost hypnotic," she was "not likely to tempt one into becoming a convert."

In 1888, Madame Blavatsky published *The Secret Doctrine,* which attracted Yeats by its discussions of reincarnation and by its assertion that Hinduism and Hermetic philosophy were identical. In that year, she established, at the request of some of her disciples, the Esoteric Section of the Society, which Yeats joined in December. However, he had difficulty in signing two of its pledges, which he alludes to in his esoteric journal: " . . . promise to work for Theosophy and promise of obedience to HPB in all Theosophical matters." A year later, when he wanted a group to undertake occult research, he doubted that Madame Blavatsky, who condemned black magic, would approve; to his surprise, she welcomed his suggestion. One of his experiments involved raising the ghost of a burned flower, an attempt that failed; another involved sleeping with symbols under his pillow to influence his dreams. His wish to test his power as a magician led to disaffection among the esoteric members, who were intent on spreading the society's teachings rather than on experimenting with magic. Yeats, who disdained abstraction, resigned from the Blavatsky Lodge in August 1890, probably at Madame's request.

———

ON MARCH 7, 1890, several months before his resignation from the Theosophical Society, Yeats had been initiated into the secret Hermetic Order of the Golden Dawn. Between 1887 and 1890, Yeats had been associated with a group called "The Hermetic Students," some of whom probably included "several prominent members of the Golden Dawn." The order's initiation ceremony occurred in the Fitzroy Street studio of the artist Mina (later Moina) Bergson, the sister of the French philosopher Henri Bergson. In June 1890, she married MacGregor Mathers, a prominent member of the circle. By September 1893, the order had initiated 170 members, and by 1896 there were 315. Many were also Rosicrucians, devoted to the occult symbol combining the mystical rose of love blossoming from the sacrificial cross. The traditional Christian symbols of the rose and the lily (suggesting love, death, and resurrection) had been widely used, sometimes in a startlingly secular manner, by such mid-century Pre-Raphaelite artists and poets as Dante Rossetti and Swinburne. By the 1890s, these symbols were increasingly associated with the occult in such works as Wilde's "Rosa Mystica," Yeats's "Rosa Alchemica" in *The Secret Rose* (1897), Symons's "Rosa Mundi," and John Davidson's "The Last Rose."

The Hermetic Order of the Golden Dawn was one of many such cults in Britain and France inspired by the French cleric Abbé Constant, who, as Eliphas Levi, wrote books on the mystical Hebrew writings known as the cabala. Interpretations of words, letters, and numbers in the Hebrew Scriptures were believed to contain hidden mysteries and magical powers. Pursuing analogies, Mathers pressed colored geometrical symbols on cardboard to his forehead, presumably to evoke visions. In one of his own experiments, Yeats wrote, "mental images" arose that he could not control: "a desert and black Titan raising himself up by his two hands from the middle of a heap of ancient ruins" (he used a similar vision in his 1921 poem "The Second Coming"). To Yeats, Mathers was an accomplished magician, whom he depicted as "Maclagan" in his unfinished novel, *The Speckled Bird* (begun in 1896) and on whom he based his character Michael Robartes in various stories and poems.

MacGregor Mathers, who had published *Kabbala Unveiled* (1887), a mystical interpretation of the Pentateuch, dominated the group. Yeats had first seen him in the British Museum: "a man of thirty-six, or thirty-seven, in a brown velveteen coat, with a gaunt resolute face, and an athletic body, who seemed . . . a figure of romance." Mathers had been copying manuscripts on magic and would copy more on the Continent. "It was through him mainly," says Yeats, "that I began certain studies and experiences, that were to convince me that images well up before the mind's eye from a deeper source than conscious or subconscious memory." On the strength of his learning, Mathers, who had been initiated into the order as one of three "Chiefs," devised with Yeats's assistance most of the group's secret rituals, drawn from Freemasonry and ancient Egyptian religions.

The order, which often conducted ceremonies in various members' drawing-rooms, encouraged adherents to experiment with ritual magic; by a series of initiations, which involved progressive purification of the soul through symbolic death and resurrection, an Adept achieved greater power over the external world as he or she moved from the Outer Order to the Inner Order. Of particular interest to Yeats was the study of alchemical and astrological symbolism as well as the cabalistic Tree of Life in his continuing quest for unity of being. Among the other members in the order's Isis-Urania Temple (as the London group was mystically called) were John Todhunter, Florence Farr, and, briefly, Mrs. Oscar Wilde and Maude Gonne. In her memoirs, Gonne, who advanced through four initiations before resigning, recalls being "oppressed by the drab appearance and mediocrity of my fellow-mystics . . . the very essence of British middle-class dullness. They looked so incongruous in their cloaks and badges at initiation ceremonies."

McGregor Mathers

In 1892, Mathers and his wife settled in Paris, where he established the Ahathoor Temple of the Golden Dawn. He continued, however, to exert influence on the London temple. In 1898, the eccentric Aleister Crowley joined the Ahathoor Temple and became Mathers's rival and later his enemy as a struggle for power arose within the order. Like Maud Gonne, Crowley regarded his fellow occultists as "muddled middle-class mediocrities," with the exception of Yeats, whom he viewed as "a lank disheveled demonologist who might have taken more pains with his personal appearance without incurring the reproach of dandyism." Like Yeats, Crowley admired Mathers as "unquestionably a Magician of extraordinary attainments." Despite his alleged magical powers, Mathers was losing control over himself. He transformed his home into an ancient temple and gave performances of his presumably secret rite of Isis in public theaters. Mathers's mind, Yeats wrote, "became unhinged, as Don Quixote's was unhinged—for he kept a proud head amid great poverty." He developed delusions that Europe would be transformed and Egypt's former glories restored while he himself would rise to extraordinary heights; in a petty quarrel, he fired a gun at another occultist.

By early 1900, he was charging that certain letters authorizing the bestowal of degrees of attainment within the London temple were forged; the result was an internal struggle that culminated in a confrontation between members of the order and Crowley ("a mad person," said Yeats), whom Mathers had sent to seize the meeting rooms at 36 Blythe Road; on April 20, Crowley appeared "in Highland dress, a black mask over his face, and a plaid thrown over his head and shoulders, an enormous gold or gilt cross on his breast, and a dagger at his side." (The Highland dress was inspired by Mathers, who, believing that he was a descendant of a titled Scots family, had adopted the name MacGregor and transformed himself into the Comte de Glenstrae.) Yeats and a constable confronted Crowley, who immediately retreated. On the following day, Mathers was expelled from the order. Such seriocomic episodes within the Golden Dawn reveal the deep-seated anxieties on the part of the members who, in their search for spiritual transcendence, found themselves struggling in the mire of this world.

IN HIS ESSAY "Magic" (1901), Yeats distinguished his use of magic from that of Mathers. The imagination, Yeats states, has the power to summon transcendent images (rather than spirits, as Mathers had wished): ". . . at whatever risk, we must cry out that imagination is always seeking to remake the world according to the impulses and the patterns in that Great Mind, and that great Memory. . . ." This "great mind and great memory can be evoked by symbols," Yeats believes, because "the borders of our mind are shifting, and . . . many minds can flow into one another, as it were, and create or reveal a single mind, a single energy." The poet, possessing such magical power, embodies his visions in symbols revealing analogies, or correspondences, hitherto unknown. The Romantics, convinced that the imagination possessed such potency, had anticipated the Symbolists of the late nineteenth century. Blake's famous tiger burning bright in the forests of the night, while a concrete image, evokes the other half of the analogy: God's creative power. Yeats was inspired by Blake's belief in the holiness of the imagination, which had the capacity to transform our vision of reality.* However, Yeats believed that the "very intensity" of his vision made Blake "a too literal realist of the imagination."

In the late 1880s and early 1890s, Yeats had been at work with his fellow Rhymer Edwin J. Ellis on a three-volume edition and commentary of Blake's work in an attempt to establish coherence in the Romantic poet's mythology and symbolism. In the chapter, "The Necessity of Symbolism," written with Ellis's assistance, Yeats employs his knowledge of the occult in asserting the interpenetration of the earthly and transcendent realms embodied in "moods," a concept he developed in the nineties: "Sometimes the mystical student, bewildered by the different systems, forgets for a moment that the history of moods is the history of the universe, and asks where is the final statement—the complete doctrine. The universe itself is itself that doctrine and statement. All others are partial, for it alone is the symbol of the infinite thought which is in turn symbolic of the universal mood we name God." The imagination, which unites the visible with the invisible, permits poets "to become vehicles for the universal thought and merge in the universal mood." Arthur Symons, though he admired Yeats as a poet, maintained a discreet distance from his occult enthusiasms. In 1896, while in Paris with Yeats, Symons wrote "Haschisch," a poem purporting to record the effect of the drug that both poets had taken. It concludes with Symons's witty comment on Yeats's concept of moods:

> *Who said the world is but a mood*
> *In the eternal thought of God?*

*The Modernist view of the creative imagination, adapted from such Romantics as Blake and Coleridge as well as from traditional occult ideas concerning correspondences, is expressed succinctly in T. S. Eliot's essay "The Metaphysical Poets" (1921): "When a poet's mind is perfectly equipped for its work, it is constantly amalgamating disparate experience; the ordinary man's experience is chaotic, irregular, fragmentary. The latter falls in love, or reads Spinoza, and these two experiences have nothing to do with each other, or with the noise of the typewriter or the smell of cooking; in the mind of the poet these experiences are always forming new wholes" (rpt. in *Homage to John Dryden* [London, 1924], 219).

I know it, real though it seem,
The phantom of a haschisch dream
In that insomnia which is God.

For Yeats, symbols revealed spiritual essences by means of material or intellectual forms. He admired Blake as a true Symbolist, who had the visionary capacity

To see a World in a Grain of Sand
And a Heaven in a Wild Flower,
Hold Infinity in the palm of your hand
And Eternity in an hour.

Blake drew his symbolism from the great Western tradition, medieval in its mystical and magical origins. By the seventeenth and eighteenth centuries, Yeats said, culture "began to break into fragments" under the impact of science and reason. In response, Blake was "the first of any time to preach the indissoluble marriage of all great art with symbol"—in short, a means of restoring unity of being to the world.

Yeats's attraction to systematic thought that confirmed spiritual realities in the universe led him to attempt a fusion of such elements as Blake's occult, symbolic vision with the heroic Celtic myths. He yearned for a workable system of his own that would provide him with universal vision summoned by symbols from "the Great Memory," another name for the Neoplatonic *Anima Mundi.* By evoking the "great memory" of the past, Yeats envisioned the revitalization and unity of Ireland's cultural life. With his uncertain spelling, he wrote to John O'Leary defending himself against his mentor's apparent charge that the study of magic might distract him from the crucial work of advancing the Irish literary renaissance:

> If I had not made magic my constant study I could not have written a single word of my Blake book nor would "The Countess Kathleen" have ever come to exist. The mystical life is the centre of all that I do & all that I think and all that I write. . . . I have all-ways considered my self a voice of what I believe to be a greater renaisance [than Shelley's]—the revolt of the soul against the intellect—now begining in the world.

In short, Yeats regarded his mystical interests as serving a nationalist cause, a symbolic merging of the Golden Dawn with the Celtic Twilight. In September 1888, he wrote with Blakean rhetoric: "To the greater poets everything they see has its relation to the national life, and through that to the universal and divine life: nothing is an isolated artistic moment;

there is a unity everywhere; everything fulfills a purpose that is not its own; the hailstone is a journeyman of God; the grass blade carries the universe upon its point." The movement towards a higher spiritual consciousness occurs in his play *The Countess Kathleen* (1892), which depicts the self-sacrifice of the Countess, who sells her soul to the devil to save the peasants from starvation, and in his "Apologia addressed to Ireland in the coming days," which appeared in the same volume with the play:

> *Know that I would accounted be*
> *True brother of that company*
> *Who sang to sweeten Ireland's wrong. . . .*
> *For round about my table go*
> *The magical powers to and fro.*

Such a merging of mystical and nationalist impulses in the nineties achieved further expression, though brief, when Yeats and Maud Gonne envisioned a "Castle of Heroes" on an island containing the ruins of the Abbey of the Trinity in the middle of Lough Key, County Roscommon, Ireland. The spiritual indoctrination of gifted young Irish men and women would unite occult and nationalist ideals. With the assistance of MacGregor Mathers, Yeats and Gonne worked on magical rituals as expressions of the Celtic mysteries. However, this Wagnerian enterprise, characteristic of much late nineteenth-century apocalyptic thought, came to nothing.

In 1893, when Yeats and Ellis's edition of Blake appeared, Yeats also published his volume of stories, *The Celtic Twilight,* which advanced his view that to the Irish peasant "everything is a symbol," for, unaffected by scientific materialism, he perceives invisible presences in nature: Fairies and ghosts endow the material world with spiritual realities that affirm a divinely sanctioned universe, albeit mysterious and haunted. In search of a mythology, Yeats found it in his own land among those who had inherited traditional beliefs and stories. His study of Christian mystics and occult magicians revealed the nature of a universal symbolism that transcended the circumscribed world of fact; now, principally through his friendship with Arthur Symons, he learned of the French Symbolists, who would illuminate and confirm those subjective realms of the mind that he regarded as manifestations of the divine imagination.

IN HIS 1862 review of *Les Fleurs du mal,* Swinburne had apprised the British public of the notorious Baudelaire; it was not until 1888 that George Moore, in his *Confessions of a Young Man,* made the same public aware that a Symbolist Movement had already developed in France.* But Moore lacked clarity concerning its significance and its basic doctrines. Though he had visited Mallarmé on his Tuesday evening gatherings of poets in the rue de Rome and had read his *L'Après-midi d'un faune,* he thought it "absurdly obscure" and wrote that Symbolism was "vulgarly speaking, saying the opposite to what you mean." Probably facetious, Moore nevertheless acquainted readers across the channel with the term "Symbolist" as a designation of the "modern school" of French poetry. In the *Hawk* (September 23, 1890), Moore published the first discussion of Rimbaud and Laforgue in England (Rimbaud is merely mentioned in the *Confessions*), but the focus is principally on the Romantic elements of their lives, particularly on Rimbaud's relationship with Verlaine, rather than on their artistic achievements.

In 1890, Moore moved into rooms in King's Bench Walk in the Temple, and in January 1891, Arthur Symons, who had first met Moore in Paris, took rooms there overlooking Fountain Court. The two became instant friends, for they both had an abiding interest in French culture, and they had met many of the same writers and artists on the Continent. As the principal conduits for information on continental developments in the arts, Moore and Symons produced a body of significant criticism revealing the transition from Victorianism to Modernism. And like Moore, Symons traveled incessantly to France. In 1890, he and Havelock Ellis spent three months in Paris, where they met, among others, Verlaine, Huysmans, and Mallarmé.

Symons found the fashionable Parisian literary labels difficult to untangle. In a review of Verlaine's *Bonheur* (1891), he deplored the fact that Verlaine had been claimed as "master" by the "noisy little school of *Décadents,* the brainsick little school of *Symbolistes";* they had, Symons complained, carried Verlaine's innovations in form and rhythm "to the furthest limits of unconscious caricature." With respect to style, Symons praised Verlaine's verse for its "exquisite simplicity, a limpid clearness, a strenuous rejection of every sort of artistic 'dandyism.' " Moore also preferred Verlaine for precisely these reasons and particularly for his musical cadences: ". . . Verlaine hears a song in French verse that no French poet has ever heard before, a song ranging from the ecstasy of the nightingale to the robin's little homily." Both Symons and Moore wrote on Verlaine more often than on any other French poet in preference to Mallarmé's "frozen impenetrability."

---

*The movement had officially been given a name with the publication of Jean Moréas's Symbolist manifesto in *Le Figaro* (September 18, 1886). By 1891, however, Moréas rejected the obscurities of Symbolism and turned to a neoclassical interest in traditional forms and mythologies.

In his own attempts at imitation, Symons generally avoided the effects of strangeness and mystery associated with much Symbolist verse, nor did he customarily challenge the reader with an enigma. Characteristically British, he preferred Verlaine's simplicity and directness. One of Symons's most notable lyrics, "La Mélinite: Moulin Rouge" (written in 1892), involves Symbolist technique with suggestions of a Decadent sensibility in the image of the dream-like dancer, yet the poem does not employ arcane diction or an impenetrable surface that mystifies the reader. The rhythms, employing run-on lines, approximate the movements of the dancer in her narcissistic transcendence, symbolic of the artist's need to create a mirrored image of the isolated self for art's sake:

> Alone, apart, one dancer watches
> Her mirrored, morbid grace;
> Before the mirror, face to face,
> Alone she watches
> Her morbid, vague ambiguous grace.
>
> And, enigmatically smiling,
> In the mysterious night,
> She dances for her own delight,
> A shadow smiling
> Back to a shadow in the night.

Yeats later called "La Mélinite" one of the "most perfect lyrics of our time."

Because of its emblematic suggestion of artistic autonomy, the ubiquitous image of the dancer in late nineteenth-century French and British literature and art was a persistent Symbolist preoccupation. The Decadent version occurs in the many depictions of Salome dancing as a femme fatale, most notably in Wilde's play and Aubrey Beardsley's drawings. As a modern critic has written, "A fusion of the erotic, spiritual and aesthetic elements, the ultimate aim of symbolist mysticism, is the motivation behind many of the depictions of the dance in the period." In the nineties, the most eloquent statement concerning the dance, with its "intellectual as well as senuous appeal of a living symbol," occurs in Symons's essay "The World as Ballet" (1898): "Nothing is stated, there is no intrusion of words used for the irrelevant purpose of describing; a world rises before one . . . and the dancer, with her gesture, all pure symbol, evokes, from her mere beautiful motion, idea, sensation, all that one need ever know of [the] event. There, before you, she exists, in harmonious life; and her rhythm reveals to you the soul of her imagined being." There is little doubt of this essay's effect on Yeats, whose dancers embody mysteries of being, particularly his most famous dancer, a symbol of final unity—motion and stillness, body and soul, form and matter—in "Among School Children" (1928), which concludes:

> *O body swayed to music, O brightening glance,*
> *How can we know the dancer from the dance?*

IN BRITAIN, only a small number of writers were attracted to the French Symbolists perhaps because they were associated with Decadence, which, as we have seen in the case of Richard Le Gallienne, blinded many to the importance of the new movement abroad.* The *Fortnightly Review* (March 1891), for example, contained a study of Verlaine that employed the pejorative connotations of Decadence with the critical terminology of the nineties: ". . . if carnality pure and simple repels him, depravity in its more refined forms exercises a quite morbid attraction for his spirit. . . . No great poet, no world-poet, is Paul Verlaine. But the exquisite, delightful, diseased, lacerated poet of a morbid elite." The "morbid elite," a characteristic view of the Decadence by the British Establishment, includes many writers who may or may not have regarded themselves as "morbid" but certainly regarded themselves as the "elite." In his preface to the expanded version of *The Picture of Dorian Gray* (1891), Wilde acknowledged, as we have seen, the significance of Symbolism by announcing: "All art is at once surface and symbol." His new direction was probably suggested by his "cher maître" Mallarmé, whom he visited in February 1891; later, Wilde sent him a copy of his novel as a gesture of admiration for Mallarmé's "noble and severe art."

AS THE NINETIES progressed, the most prestigious literary periodicals and papers published in London took greater note of the French Symbolists. Between 1890 and 1900, twenty-five articles appeared on their work; of these, ten were on Verlaine, most of them published before 1896, an indication that the British were particularly receptive to his work; seven were written on Mallarmé, several by Edmund Gosse. In a review in the *Academy* (January 7, 1893), he describes Mallarmé as one "who is at the present time more talked about, more ferociously attacked, more passion-

---

*On the association of Decadence with Symbolism, Anna Balakian has remarked: "If at a certain point in the development of the movement, critics were justified in separating 'symbolist' from 'decadent,' everything points to the fact that in the last ten years of the century the two become so intertwined that without the 'decadent' spirit there would be little left to distinguish symbolism from Romanticism" (*The Symbolist Movement: A Critical Appraisal* [New York, 1967], 115).

ately beloved and defended, and at the same time less understood, than perhaps any other man of his intellectual rank in Europe." And though Mallarmé "marches at the head of very noisy rabble, exceedingly little seems to be clearly known about him in this country."

In 1875, Gosse had seen Mallarmé in the streets of London, a "little brown gentle person with an elephant folio under his arm, trying to find Mr. Swinburne by the unassisted light of instinct." The folio contained his version of Poe's *The Raven* with Manet's illustrations. Now, almost twenty years later, Gosse confessed that he had read *Le Tombeau d'Edgar Poe* "over and over and over. I am very stupid, but I cannot tell what it *says."* Nevertheless, Mallarmé was "a true man of letters" despite confusion over his literary identity: "M. Mallarmé has been wrapped up in the general fog which enfolds our British notions of symbolists and impressionists. If the school has had a single friend in England, it has been Mr. Arthur Symons, one of the most brilliant of our younger poets; and even he has been interested, I think, more in M. Verlaine than in the Symbolists and Décadents proper."

Admitting that he did not pretend in the "formal and minute sense" to comprehend Mallarmé's poems, Gosse compounds the difficulty by associating him with the Decadents at one point, with the Symbolists at another. In suggesting why Symbolist poems were difficult to read, Gosse states that Mallarmé uses "words in such harmonious combinations as will suggest to the reader a mood or a condition which is not mentioned in the text, but is nevertheless paramount in the poet's mind at the moment of composition." Gosse calls *L'Après-midi d'un faune* a "famous miracle of unintelligibility" but a "delicious experience" nonetheless. He fears that the Symbolists, having been read with "so great an effort by their own generation . . . may, by the next, not be read at all, and what is pure and genuine in their artistic impulses be lost."*

Like other British critics who crossed the Channel to maintain their contacts with French developments in the arts, Gosse went to Paris in April 1893 to visit Henry Harland, who was busily writing short stories. Gosse, who said that he was "much interested—not wholly converted, certainly, but considerably impressed" by the French Symbolists and Decadents whom he had read, asked Harland to lead him on a tour of Symbolist cafés along the Boulevard Saint-Michel: "I determined to

---

*In 1913, Gosse defended Symbolism in his presidential address to the English Association: "I cannot help believing that the immense importance of this idea is . . . perhaps the greatest discovery with regard to poetry which was made in the last generation" (*The Future of English Poetry* [Oxford, 1913]; rpt. in *Some Diversions of a Man of Letters* [London, 1919]). However, by 1916, he was convinced that "Mallarmé's influence in England was disastrous" (Ann Thwaite, *Edmund Gosse: A Literary Landscape, 1849–1928* [Chicago, 1984], 370).

haunt that neighbourhood with a butterfly-net, and see what delicate creatures with powdery wings I could catch." Though, said Gosse, Harland had little interest in the "Symbolo-decadent movement," he seized upon the "sport of the idea" with enthusiasm. For the next few days, they captured several butterflies in their natural habitats, including "that really substantial moth, Verlaine." In the process, Gosse reported, "I had heard a great many verses recited which I did not understand because I was a foreigner, and could not have understood if I had been a Frenchman." The entire expedition, Gosse concluded, was a "great success."

IN FEBRUARY 1894, Yeats was in Paris not only to see Maud Gonne but also to meet some French poets (Symons had given him an introduction to Verlaine). To a friend, he wrote: "I am staying with the Mathers— my occult friends & have introductions to a good many French men of letters. . . ." Unfortunately, Mallarmé had already left for England to deliver lectures at Oxford, but Verlaine invited Yeats to have coffee and cigarettes in his little room atop a tenement in the rue St. Jacques. Their conversation ranged from Shakespeare to Villiers de l'Isle-Adam, whose play *Axël* was interpreted (Yeats believed "somewhat narrowly") as "meaning that love was the only important thing in the world." Yeats sensed that Verlaine, "a great temperament," was the "servant of a great daimon," one who "had been made uncontrollable that he might live the life needful for its perfect expression in art, and yet escape the bonfire."

On February 26, Yeats went to see Villiers de l'Isle-Adam's Symbolist play *Axël* at the Théâtre de la Gaîté with Maud Gonne, who presumably provided the translation since Yeats's command of French was slight. Dazzled by this "symbolical" Rosicrucian play, which had a significant influence on his verse,* he was fond of repeating one of its famous lines— "As for living, our servants will do that for us"—spoken by Axël before he and Sara take poison to renounce the world and seek the infinite. *Axël* was the sacred book for which Yeats had longed. In its turning away from realism in the theater, he wrote in a review, it rejected the intrusion of the "scientific movement which has swept away so many religious and philosophical misunderstandings of ancient truth. . . ." But those among the younger generation, receptive to the "new current, the new force, have

---

*In the play, Sara says to Axël, who has threatened to kill her: "Oh, to veil you with my hair, where you will breathe the spirit of dead roses." Struck by the suggestive imagery, Yeats employed variations of the image of the hair that veils, frequently in association with the mystical rose; moreover, allusions to the play and to Villiers de l'Isle-Adam recur in his essays and letters. See Lloyd Parks, "The Influence of Villiers de l'Isle-Adam on W. B. Yeats," *Nineteenth-Century French Studies* 6 (Spring–Summer 1978):258–76.

grown tired of the photographing of life, and have returned by the path of symbolism to imagination and poetry, the only things which are ever permanent."

In October 1895, Yeats sublet two of Symons's four rooms in Fountain Court, where he lived until March of the following year. During these months, when Symons was first planning, then editing the *Savoy*, their discussions were undoubtedly on the French Symbolists, for, as we have seen, the periodical was to include articles, poems, and stories by and about such leading French and Belgian writers as Verlaine, Mallarmé, Moréas, and Verhaeren as well as Symons's translation of Mallarmé and reviews of works by Edmond de Goncourt and Verlaine. Yeats recalled the experience of hearing Symons read aloud his translation of a portion of "Hérodiade" (subsequently included in the final number of the *Savoy* in December 1896). Symons's translations of Mallarmé, he said, "may have given elaborate form to my verses of those years." Echoes from the translation later occurred in Yeats's poems and plays.

On December 10, 1896, Symons and Yeats were again in Paris, when they attended a performance of Alfred Jarry's "Symbolist farce" *Ubu Roi* at the avant-garde Théâtre de l'Oeuvre. Before the curtain rose, two workmen brought on stage a cane-bottomed chair and a little wooden table, at which Jarry ("a small, very young man, with a hard, clever face") seated himself and read a lecture on his play. In his review, Symons remarked on the "insolence with which a young writer mocks at civilization itself, sweeping all art, along with all humanity, into the same inglorious slop-pail." Jarry satirizes humanity by "setting human beings to play the part of marionettes, hiding their faces behind cardboard masks, tuning their voices to the howl and squeak . . . , and mimicking the rigid inflexibility and spasmodic life of puppets by a hopping and reeling gait." Meanwhile, an orchestra of piano, cymbals, and drums played intermittantly behind the curtain, and the scenery was painted to represent indoors and outdoors as well as the torrid, temperate, and arctic zones simultaneously. To the side were palm trees, around one of which a boa constrictor coiled itself.

Yeats recalled that those in the audience were shaking fists at one another, presumably to approve or disapprove. Symons whispered to him, "There are often duels after these performances." But Symons later saw little merit in "the gesticulation of a young savage of the woods" who had "somehow forgotten his intention before writing. . . .": "In our search for sensation we have exhausted sensation. . . . *Ubu Roi* is the brutality out of which we have achieved civilisation. . . ." Yeats agreed. Despite the fact that he and Symons had shouted their approval in the theater, Yeats was sad on their return to the hotel that "objectivity" had displayed "its growing power once more": "After Stéphane Mallarmé, after Paul Verlaine, after Gustave Moreau . . . after our own verse, after all our subtle colour and nervous rhythm . . . what more is possible? After us the Savage God." Yeats had seen the gathering darkness in Western civilization.

THE INCREASING PERCEPTION by British writers of a convergence between occult and Symbolist realms led them to Baudelaire's sonnet in *Les Fleurs du mal* titled "Correspondances," with its image of a shadowy and mysterious "forest of symbols" awaiting interpretation by the visionary. A sacred text for Symbolists and for later Surrealists seeking realities beyond mere matter, the poem implies that between images and ideas, between colors, odors, and sounds, or between spirit and matter, there are undisclosed correspondences (either horizontal, among the objects or sensory experiences of this world;* or vertical, between this world and a transcendental reality). As Baudelaire wrote in *Journaux intimes* (published posthumously in 1887), "In certain almost supernatural states of soul, the depth of life is revealed in ordinary everyday happenings. Ordinary life then becomes the Symbol." At the beginning of the third chapter of Joyce's *Ulysses* (1922), which draws upon occult concepts and Symbolist method, Stephen Dedalus walks along Sandymount beach in Dublin, contemplating possible correspondences between the random objects that he sees (such as pebbles and shells: "signatures") in the material world and a spiritual reality beyond: "Ineluctable modality of the visible: at least that if no more, thought through my eyes. Signatures of all things I am here to read. . . ." (*The Signature of all Things* is the title of a work by the seventeenth-century German mystic Jacob Boehme, an inspiration to the Symbolists.) In *Les Fleurs du mal,* Baudelaire implied, the sordid images of Paris were analogies of his own anguished inner life, simultaneously concealed and revealed. Symbols, as Blake had also shown, provided the artist with the means of escape from the destructive world of time into a world of the timeless imagination. In the high Modernist mode, Yeats's "Sailing to Byzantium" (1927) expresses such late nineteenth-century Decadent/Symbolist attitudes towards art and nature:

> *Once out of nature I shall never take*
> *My bodily form from any natural thing,*
> *But such a form as Grecian goldsmiths make*
> *Of hammered gold and gold enamelling. . . .*

---

*In his novel *A Drama in Muslin* (1886), George Moore was among the first in England to employ Symbolist synesthesia: a description of women whose dance suggests an "allegro movement of odours . . . interrupted suddenly by the garlicky andante, deep as the pedal notes of an organ, that the perspiring armpits of a fat chaperon exhaled slowly."

The Paterian urge to transform one's life into art (here, a golden bird) and thus escape from the meaningless flux of time and matter achieves its ultimate consummation in the "artifice of eternity," a rejection of the bourgeois, Romantic devotion to nature.

Symons's close association with the French Symbolists and with Yeats progressively led to an awareness that the occult was a principal means of understanding Symbolism. Having published his notable essay "The Decadent Movement in Literature" in 1893, in which he characterized Symbolism as a "branch" of Decadence, Symons had intended to write a book with the same title. Indeed, it was announced as "In Preparation" in an advertisement of Leonard Smithers's forthcoming publications in the final number of the *Savoy* (December 1896): The book would contain essays on Verlaine, the Goncourts, Huysmans, Villiers de l'Isle-Adam, and Maeterlinck. In time, not only would he change the title to *The Symbolist Movement in Literature,* but he would change its philosophical orientation as well, and other figures would be added to make it the most important critical work of the fin de siècle.

By 1898 Symons had composed most of the essays for his Symbolist study, which now included (in addition to those figures initially announced) Mallarmé, Rimbaud, Laforgue, and Gérard de Nerval. The omission of Baudelaire from the book is odd in view of his reputation and influence as a Symbolist, but Symons regarded him as more Decadent than Symbolist. In the introduction to *The Symbolist Movement in Literature,* Symons expresses the belief that Baudelaire has a "certain theory of Realism which tortures many of his poems into strange, metallic shapes, and fills them with imitative odours, and disturbs them with a too deliberate rhetoric of the flesh."

Yeats was also pondering the significance of Decadence, to which he assigned not only literary but also cultural significance. If the late nineteenth century implied the end of an age and if that age was one of "decadence," had an illusion misled the imagination because of the symbolic correspondence between decline and death? In his apocalyptic essay "The Autumn of the Flesh" (1898), later retitled "The Autumn of the Body," Yeats believes that a new age is at hand, one that augurs a new spirituality in contrast to the bankrupt materialism of the nineteenth century:

> I see, indeed, in the arts of every country those faint lights and faint colours and faints outlines and faint energies which many call "the decadence," and which I, because I believe that the arts lie dreaming of things to come, prefer to call the autumn of the body. . . . Its importance is the greater because it comes to us at the moment when we are beginning to be interested in many things which positive science, the interpreter of exterior law, has always denied. . . .

We may be, Yeats suggests, "at the crowning crisis of the world, at the moment when man is about to ascend, with the wealth he has been so long gathering upon his shoulders, the stairway he has been decending from the first days." Because "man had wooed and won the world, and has fallen weary" from his devotion to materialism, "he can only return the way he came, and so escape from weariness, by philosophy." The way is presumably through the occult, and those who can guide us to forgotten spiritual realities are the artists: "The arts are, I believe, about to take upon their shoulders the burdens that have fallen from the shoulders of priests, and to lead us back upon our journey by filling our thoughts with the essences of things, and not with things." Earlier, Matthew Arnold, concerned as Yeats was with the increasing skepticism of the age, suggested in a famous passage in his essay "The Study of Poetry" (1880) that poetry might assume a new role in replacing religion as the principal interpreter of life; in 1893, Yeats and Edwin J. Ellis, embracing the Religion of Art, asserted in their edition of Blake that the "priests and missionaries . . . are,—or should be,—artists and poets."

In 1899, Yeats's finest examples of his early style appeared in *The Wind among the Reeds,* which contains much of his best-known work, a summation of his mystical and Celtic preoccupations in such poems as "Into the Twilight," "The Song of Wandering Aengus," "The Cap and Bells," "He Remembers Forgotten Beauty," "The Secret Rose," and "He Wishes for the Cloths of Heaven." Reviewing the volume, Symons noted the predominant motive: "Here is a poet who has realised, as no one else, just now, seems to realise, that the only excuse for writing a poem is the making of a beautiful thing. But he has come finally to realise that, among all kinds of beauty, the beauty which rises out of human passion is the one most proper to the lyric." In its "embodied ecstasy," Symons suggests, the lyric poem "becomes a part of the universal consciousness" (an indication that Yeats's influence has touched his friend), and the symbolism drawn from Irish mythology gives Yeats "the advantage of an elaborate poetic background, new to modern poetry." Later Modernists, such as Pound, Joyce, D. H. Lawrence, and T. S. Eliot, similarly employed various mythologies as structural devices to express personal visions.

WHILE COMPLETING HIS Symbolist book,* Symons consulted with Yeats and asked him to suggest revisions of the introduction and the dedication (the latter in the form of a letter). Calling Yeats the "chief

---

*Though its scheduled publication date was 1899, *The Symbolist Movement in Literature* was not released until March 5, 1900, because the publisher, William Heinemann, had been attempting to arrange publication in the United States. The Boer War may have been an additional factor in the book's delayed release.

representative of [the Symbolist] movement in our country" and the Irish literary renaissance "one of its expressions," Symons acknowledges his friend's help in shaping his vision of Symbolism: "How often have you and I discussed all these questions, rarely arguing about them, for we rarely had an essential difference of opinion, but bringing them more and more clearly into light, turning our instincts into logic, digging until we reached the bases of our convictions."

In his introduction, Symons cites Carlyle's *Sartor Resartus* (1838) as an English source of insight into the nature of Symbolism: "In a Symbol [Carlyle states], there is concealment and yet revelation: hence therefore, by Silence and by Speech acting together, comes a double significance." Moreover, Carlyle attributes to the symbol the "revelation of the Infinite." Symons's interpretation of the French Symbolist Movement as an expression of mysticism mutes the fact that most Symbolists were agnostics and that many Symbolist poets in the late nineteenth century were obsessed by such Decadent obsessions as the abyss, inaction, death, and strangeness. These elements in Symbolist poetry are quietly disposed of by Symons, who states that Decadence, which he now limits to any "ingenious deformation of language," had been a "mock-interlude" that "diverted the attention of the critics while something more serious was in preparation."

Symbolists wish, says Symons, to "spiritualize literature, to evade the old bondage of rhetoric, the old bondage of exteriority. Description is banished that beautiful things may be evoked, magically; the regular beat of verse is broken in order that words may fly upon subtler wings." But since responsibility lies in this new freedom, Symons speaks gravely of the "heavier burden" that literature now accepts, "for in speaking to us so intimately, so solemnly, as only religion had hitherto spoken to us, it becomes itself a kind of religion, with all the duties and responsibilities of the sacred ritual." Indeed, *The Symbolist Movement in Literature* reiterates this notion of the Religion of Art in a variety of ways to emphasize the avant-garde position that the artist is Victorian culture's inevitable enemy and only hope. In his essay on Verlaine, Symons expresses the familiar idea that he had derived from Gautier: "It is the poet against society, society against the poet, a direct antagonism." And in his essay on Mallarmé, Symons alludes to the "aristocracy of letters," those artists who, like ancient oracles, "hide their secrets in the obscurity of many meanings. . . . Might it not, after all, be the finest epitaph for a self-respecting man of letters to be able to say, even after the writing of many books: I have kept my secret, I have not betrayed myself to the multitude?"

Entrusted to the elite, the creation of art becomes arcane, private: ". . . the whole mystery of beauty can never become comprehended by the crowd," Symons states in his essay on Gérard de Nerval. *L'art pour l'art* thus asserts its autonomy and isolation. Such an anti-democratic view of art and the artist in protest against an egalitarian culture emerged, we again note, as a central theme of Modernism. In Paris in the 1920s, for example, the work of such writers as James Joyce, Dylan Thomas, Samuel Beckett, and Gertrude Stein appeared in the avant-garde periodical *transition,* which established continuity with fin-de-siècle Decadent/Symbolist attitudes in its manifesto, "The Revolution of the Word": "The writer expresses. He does not communicate. The plain reader be damned."

Never deeply involved in the occult, Symons probably derived inspiration from Yeats in the following passage from the *Symbolist Movement* essay on Huysmans: "What is Symbolism if not an establishing of the links which hold the world together, the affirmation of an eternal, minute, intricate, almost invisible life, which runs through the whole universe?" If such was the case, the word, as a magical force, forged the "links which hold the world together," as in the Symbolist poem, which fused rhythm, image, and color (the subtle shading of meaning in language) to achieve a self-contained subjective vision that mysteriously mirrored transcendent realities: "To evoke, by some elaborate, instantaneous magic of language . . . to be, rather than to express:* that is what Mallarmé has consistently, and from the first, sought, in verse and prose. . . . Remember his principle: that to name is to destroy, to suggest is to create."

Symons's apocalyptic "Conclusion," alluding to our entrapment "in smiling and many-coloured appearances," echoes Pater's in *The Renaissance,* which talks of experience "reduced to a swarm of impressions . . . ringed round for each one of us by that thick wall of personality. . . ." However, Symons asserts that mysticism, with which Symbolism is concerned, enables us to escape from the "great bondage" of death. And "because it has so much the air of a dream," the ancient doctrine is the "more likely to be true. . . ." Yet Symons was ambivalent towards such a doctrine, which, he states, may "slay as well as save, because the freedom of its captivity might so easily become deadly to the fool." One wonders whether he was cautioning Yeats not to immerse himself so deeply in his occult studies.

The critical reaction to *The Symbolist Movement in Literature* revealed that what was meant by Symbolism was subject to continuing confusion. Reviewers in such literary papers as the *Academy* and the *Saturday Review* contended that there was no Symbolist Movement. Edmund Gosse, however, wrote to Symons that *The Symbolist Movement in Literature* was "quite a wonderful book." Hailing him as "the best English critic since Pater," he confessed that with all his "lifelong passion for literature" he was

---

*Archibald MacLeish echoes this ontological view in his poem "Ars Poetica" (1926): "A poem should not mean / But be."

incapable of writing such a work. Yeats referred to *The Symbolist Movement in Literature* as "a subtle book which I cannot praise as I would, because it has been dedicated to me. . . ." In "The Symbolism of Poetry" he clarified what he found unclear in Symons's study—that is, poetic symbols express themselves through "all sounds, all colours, all forms, either because of their preordained energies or because of long association, evoke indefinable and yet precise emotions, or, as I prefer to think, call down among us certain disembodied powers. . . ." And in a suggestive passage, he accounts for the method by which rhythm and symbol have their uncanny effect on our psyches: "The purpose of rhythm, it has always seemed to me, is to prolong the moment of contemplation, the moment when we are both asleep and awake, which is the one moment of creation, by hushing us with an alluring monotony, while it holds us waking by variety, to keep us in that state of perhaps real trance, in which the mind liberated from the pressure of the will is unfolded in symbols." Yeats's essay and Symons's book—in part, inspired by occult thought—are unquestionably the two most important discussions regarding Symbolism in fin-de-siècle Britain.

Soon after its appearance, *The Symbolist Movement in Literature* was widely regarded as a sacred book, especially by the young. The Irish writer Mary Colum recalled that it was avidly read by undergraduates in Ireland who regarded Symons as "a sort of god." (The English, as might be expected, were generally less receptive because of the Symbolist association with French Decadence.) At University College in Dublin, Yeats attended a debate on the book (which may have seemed to many more pagan than spiritual). One of Joyce's friends recalls that in 1900 Joyce was talking enthusiastically about Baudelaire, Verlaine, and other Symbolist poets. When T. S. Eliot, as an undergraduate, came across the book at Harvard, he regarded it as a "revelation" because it was "an introduction to wholly new feelings." He later acknowledged: "I myself owe Mr. Symons a great debt: but for having read his book, I should not, in the year 1908, have heard of Laforgue or Rimbaud; I should probably not have begun to read Verlaine; and but for reading Verlaine, I should not have heard of Corbière. So the Symons book is one of those which have affected the course of my life." And in 1917, the eighteen-year-old Hart Crane read *The Symbolist Movement in Literature* at the New York Public Library after hearing that the mad Nerval had led a lobster by a blue ribbon in the Palais-Royal because, he said, "it does not bark and knows the secrets of the sea." Crane then questioned Mary and Padraic Colum enthusiastically about "Rimbodd" and "Boddelaire."

THE CONVERGENCE OF Aestheticism and Symbolism in Britain gave rise to the Modernist poetic, which, in its stress on autonomy, its new conception of language, and its view of the writer as occult magician, extended the artist's range of expression and provided new vision. Less than a month before *The Symbolist Movement in Literature* appeared, Symons revealed the impact of his study in "The Loom of Dreams," in which the poet, "in a little lonely room," commands the world by the power of his imagination:

> *I am master of earth and sea,*
> *And the planets come to me.*
>
> *And the only world is the world of my dreams,*
> *And my weaving the only happiness.*

Symons's "weaving" is not the labor of the productive worker in a dreadful factory but that of the "useless" poet, like Yeats, embroidering the cloths of heaven. The radicalization of aesthetic theory in the fin de siècle thus transformed the prevailing conviction that the role of the artist, like that of Tennyson, was to provide enlightenment and guidance in matters of religion, science, and morality. As Frank Kermode has suggested, the "Romantic Image," strikingly represented in the figure of the dancer, symbolized the Modernists' attempt to eliminate intellectual discourse as the raison d'être of art and to reject bourgeois society's wish to control and restrict the imaginative vision that the artist summons magically from his own private world. In the early twentieth century, such poets and artists as the Imagists and Vorticists focused on the nondiscursive image, and by the 1930s the New Critics affirmed and legitimized the Modernists' insistence on the autonomy of art.

15

Empire Builders and Destroyers

WHEN ALEC MACKENZIE, the hero of Somerset Maugham's novel *The Explorer* (1907), reads of "the marvellous records of African exploration," his "blood tingle[s] at the magic of those pages." Inspired, he becomes an explorer who, in the tradition of British expansionism on the "Dark Continent" that had begun in the 1850s, is determined, "single handed, to crush the [Arab] slave traffic in a district larger than England, to wage war, unassisted, with a dozen local chieftains and against twenty thousand fighting men." (Slavery had been outlawed in all British territories in 1833.) He admired such notable African explorers as the Scottish missionary Dr. Livingstone, "men who've built up the empire piece by piece." Like his predecessors, MacKenzie takes pride in the fact that he will add "another fair jewel to her crown." Maugham's celebration of a distant age suggests a decline in the Edwardian period of the call to heroism and adventure that had animated many Victorians.

In addition to the call that had stirred patriotic fervor, most Victorians believed that colonialism had a significant civilizing influence on primitive or "savage" peoples. In 1850, the statesman Charles Adderley argued in the House of Commons that the establishment of new colonies was motivated by the benevolent "desire of spreading throughout the habitable globe all the characteristics of Englishmen—their energy, their civilization, their religion and their freedom." This imperial ideology, widespread among the educated classes and generally endorsed by both Liberals and Conservatives, inflamed John Ruskin, who, in his 1870 inaugural address as Slade Professor of Art, urged Oxford undergraduates to pursue the ideal of expansionism:

> A destiny is now possible to us, the highest ever set before a
> nation to be accepted or refused. Will you youths of England
> make your country again a royal throne of kings, a sceptered

isle, for all the world a source of light, a centre of peace? This is what England must do or perish. She must found colonies as fast and as far as she is able, formed of the most energetic and worthiest of men; seizing any piece of fruitful waste ground she can set her foot on, and then teaching her colonists that their chief virtue is to be fidelity to their country, and that their first aim is to advance the power of England by land and sea.

Though evangelical and materialistic motives differed in degree as the British devoted themselves to "civilizing the world," a basic principle provided the driving force, as a recent British historian has observed: "God in harness with Mammon."

As the empire expanded dramatically in the nineteenth century, it embraced territories from Canada to India—indeed, one-quarter of the earth's land surface—to make it the most powerful in the world. By the late nineteenth century, its relative stability (despite such uprisings as the bloody Indian Mutiny of 1857, the Jamaica Rebellion of 1865, territorial unrest in Africa, and the seemingly endless difficulties with Ireland) gave the impression that the empire was destined to endure indefinitely. In John Davidson's ironic closet drama "Fleet Street Eclogue: St. George's Day," published in the *Yellow Book* (April 1895), a chauvinist sings the praises of the empire in the well-worn clichés of late nineteenth-century New Imperialism:

> *And England still grows great,*
> *And never shall grow old;*
> *Within our hands we hold*
> *The world's fate.*
>
> *The Sphinx that watches by the Nile*
> *Has seen great empires pass away:*
> *The mightiest lasted but a while;*
> *Yet ours shall not decay.*

As an "ideology or political faith," British imperialism was in part a substitute for the decline of Christianity and an expression of confidence in Britain's economic and political future. In effect, the empire provided a stunning example of the social Darwinists' conviction that, among the various nations, Britain was the fittest to survive. Such an interpretation of history informed J. A. Cramb's *The Origins and Destiny of Imperial Britain* (1900), which pronounced that "empires are successive incarnations of the Divine idea," an imprimatur justifying expansionist policies. However, the anxiety expressed by many late Victorians over the political and economic wisdom of expansionism revealed an emotional crisis concerning the legitimacy of the enterprise. Politicians themselves were often "reluctant imperialists," such as Gladstone, who unwillingly consented to the invasion of Egypt in 1882. In the eighties, Gladstone was convinced that expansionism would bring few benefits to England.* Free trade, he believed, had a greater commercial potential as well as a beneficial moral effect in international relations.

Aware that the empire had been the principal source for the nation's economic and political power, Davidson also recognized it as a source of widespread despair when colonies were affected by their own economic and political turmoil or when Britain's overseas markets suffered from intense international rivalry—hence, the possibility of civil disorder at home, as his disgruntled character, Menzies, laments:

> I hear the idle workmen's sighs;
> I hear their children's hungry cries;
> I hear the burden of the years;
> I hear the drop of women's tears;
> I hear despair, whose tongue is dumb,
> Speak thunder in the ruthless bomb.

To his friend's hollow insistence that all in Britain are "All Englishmen, all Englishmen!" Menzies responds:

> . . . and either pole
> We reach with sprawling colonies—
> Unwieldy limbs that lack a soul.

Despite his dismissal of "the hackneyed brag / About the famous English flag," Menzies concludes that the British, in the expansion of the empire,

> . . . wander far astray,
> And oft in utter darkness grope,
> Fearless we face the roughest day,
> For we are the world's forlorn hope.

The empire builder Cecil Rhodes, member of Parliament in the Cape Colony in the 1880s and prime minister in 1890, envisioned imperialism

---

*A modern historian has confirmed Gladstone's views: "The actual increase in British overseas trade derived from the vast territories annexed after 1880 was negligible: by 1901 it only amounted to 2½ per cent of the total, 75 per cent of which was still with foreign countries; a fact which made the imperialist argument based on commercial opportunities look ridiculous" (C. J. Lowe, *The Reluctant Imperialists: British Foreign Policy, 1878–1902* [London, 1967], 4).

THE RHODES COLOSSUS
STRIDING FROM CAPE TOWN TO CAIRO.

Punch on Cecil Rhodes (*Punch*, December 10, 1892)

as the means of avoiding civil disturbances at home, a narrowed alternative that implied the inevitability of foreign domination "from the Cape to Cairo." After attending a meeting of the unemployed in London's East End, he remarked to his friend, the journalist W. T. Stead:

> I listened to the wild speeches, which were just a cry for "bread! bread!" and on my way home I pondered over the scene and I became more than ever convinced of the importance of imperialism. . . . My cherished idea is a solution for the social problem, i.e., in order to save the 40,000,000 inhabitants of the United Kingdom from a bloody civil war, we colonial statesmen must acquire new lands to settle the surplus population, to provide new markets for the goods produced by them in the factories and mines. The Empire, as I have always said, is a bread and butter question. If you want to avoid civil war, you must become imperialists.

In July 1895, the former Liberal politician Joseph Chamberlain (the father of later Prime Minister Neville Chamberlain) had recently joined the Conservative government as the colonial secretary. In a speech which echoed Rhodes's remarks to Stead, Chamberlain advanced the idea of imperialism as the solution to social problems and ensuing unrest:

> ... to my mind the cause of bad trade, of want of employment, is clear. It is the continual growth of our population at the same time that our trade and industry does not grow in proportion, and if we want our trade and industry to grow we must find new markets for it. Old markets are getting exhausted, some of them are being closed to us by hostile tariffs, and unless we can find new countries which will be free to take our goods you may be quite satisfied that lack of employment will continue to be one of the greatest of social evils.

(Chamberlain was later regarded as having plunged Britain into the Boer War, or "Chamberlain's War," as his enemies called it.)

In his influential work titled *Imperialism: A Study* (1902), the radical economist J. A. Hobson remarks of such arguments as those by Rhodes and Chamberlain: "It has become a commonplace of history how Governments use national animosities, foreign wars and the glamour of empire-making, in order to bemuse the popular mind and divert rising resentment against domestic abuses." The British masses were particularly susceptible to such a strategy, for, says Hobson, "Popular education, instead of serving as a defence, is an incitement towards Imperialism: it has opened up a panorama of vulgar pride and crude sensationalism to a great inert mass who see current history and the tangled maze of world movements with dim, bewildered eyes." By means of imperial strategies, "the vested interests at the same time protect their economic and political supremacy at home against movements of popular reform." Hobson's interpretation has met with wide agreement among modern cultural historians, one of whom suggests: ". . . imperialism functioned as an ideological safety valve, deflecting both working-class radicalism and middle-class reformism into non-critical paths while preserving fantasies of aristocratic authority at home and abroad."

IN THE MID-VICTORIAN period, books by and about British explorers were best sellers, which Britons avidly read with pride in their country-men's pioneering discoveries, particularly in Africa. David Livingstone's *Missionary Travels* (1857), which sold 70,000 copies in its first few months, described his attempt to establish missionary stations and to open Africa to commerce, a characteristic Victorian fusion of evangelical passion to spread the gospel, to end the slave trade, and to establish British spheres of economic and political influence. By so doing, missionaries could convert the benighted "savages" to Christianity and thereby lead them to the light of civilization, synonymous with "the British Empire." Such attitudes, tinged with racism, were the justifications for missionary intrusions into the "Dark Continent" and for appeals for financial aid from religious organizations at home. Indeed, in their writings, missionaries sometimes exceeded the facts in describing African "savagery" in order to dramatize the difficult conditions under which they had labored in the service of Christ.

By 1866, when Livingstone undertook his last African expedition to discover the source of the Nile, he was widely regarded as a saint.* The process of apotheosis reached its climax when the Anglo-American journalist Henry Morton Stanley published his best seller *How I Found Livingstone* (1872), which describes his mythic encounter with the ill missionary-explorer at Lake Tanganyika, both maintaining British decorum by raising their hats to each other as though meeting on a London street while Stanley uttered what became the most famous—and perhaps, considering the setting, the most comic—query of the age: "Dr. Livingstone, I presume?"† Later an explorer himself, Stanley took up the search for sources of the Nile and discovered the Congo River, along which he established stations. Under the auspices of King Leopold II of Belgium, later accused of fomenting unspeakable barbarism against the Congo natives, Stanley was instrumental in establishing the Congo Free State. His extraordinary experiences in contending with barbarous tribes in the vast tangled jungle, with malaria, and with the intolerable heat while charting hitherto unknown features of the landscape were described in his bestselling *Through the Dark Continent* (1878) and in *In Darkest Africa* (1890).

THE POPULARITY OF romance fiction exploiting the "Dark Continent" and raising questions concerning the beneficial effects of expansionism

---

*One of Livingstone's biographers writes that on April 18, 1874, the day of the explorer's burial in Westminster Abbey, "those who wept in the streets . . . did not know that the Lualaba was not the Nile—had they done so, it is doubtful whether they would have cared. Knowledge of Livingstone's mistake would only have deepened for them the pathos of his death. Very few found it necessary to examine his aims or to ask whether a search for the Nile's source had anything to do with missionary work or the spreading of Christianity" (Tim Jea, *Livingstone* [London, 1973], 371).
†In Maugham's short story "The Outstation" (1924), the Resident at an Indian post greets his new assistant:

"Mr. Cooper, I presume?"
"That's right. Were you expecting anyone else?"
The question had a facetious intent, but the Resident did not smile.

began with H. Rider Haggard's spectacular success, *King Solomon's Mines* (1885). Written as a challenge to Robert Louis Stevenson's widely read *Treasure Island* (1883), indeed even borrowing the device of an old map that guides the three main figures to the diamond mines, the novel was initially conceived as a boy's adventure story. Aware of the book's potential as a best seller, Cassell's Publishing Co. made Haggard famous overnight by the unprecedented device of hoisting banners throughout London hailing "KING SOLOMON'S MINES—THE MOST AMAZING BOOK EVER WRITTEN." Such innovative advertising resulted in a sale of over 30,000 copies within a year in the recently inaugurated format of the one-volume novel. Haggard, whose two previous novels had sold poorly, found a formula for popular success by drawing upon his knowledge of the Zulus from his four years in South Africa as private secretary to the Natal Colony governor and assistant to the Transvaal administrator, even helping to raise the British flag at Pretoria during ceremonies annexing the territory.

Yet *King Solomon's Mines* is not a paean to imperialism. Rather, it exploits the current interest in the scramble among the European nations for control of various portions of Africa. In 1884–85, the Berlin West Africa Conference, at which some fourteen major powers carved up the African continent for imperial domination, had received much attention in the British press. In such periodicals as *Black and White* and the *Illustrated London News,* the strange new worlds that were being written about— accompanied by photographs and drawings of bare-bosomed native women and tribal chieftains—prepared readers for Haggard's narratives of heroic adventurers facing constant danger in the deserts and jungles of Africa.

When the three Englishmen in *King Solomon's Mines* intervene to save a doomed native girl at a pagan ceremony, Victorian readers undoubtedly congratulated themselves on the beneficent effect of civilization, yet Haggard reveals a society of noble savages who have no need of the white man's world. After discovering that their African servant is the rightful king, the Englishmen participate bravely in the armed struggle against the ruling tyrant. In bidding his English friends farewell, the new king, having lived among white men, expresses firm antiimperialist convictions: "No other white man shall cross the mountains. . . . I will see no traders with their guns and gin. . . . I will have no praying-men to put a fear of death into men's hearts, to stir them up against the law of the king, and make a path for the white folk who follow to run on."

Despite such passages in his novels, Haggard was devoted to the traditional view of British imperialism, which he outlined as honorary president of the Anglo-African Writers' Club in London, arguing that "for our good, for the good of the Empire, and of the world at large, Englishmen with English traditions and ideas should dominate in Africa." Haggard's antiimperialistic sentiments in the fictive world of mythic struggle and his staunchly imperialistic views on public platforms suggest a divided self concerning the idea of empire. His imaginative world enabled him to indulge in intriguing fantasies, daringly confronting British respectability with his own "savage" longing, while his public persona maintained its Victorian propriety. In *Allan Quatermain* (1887), the aging hero, Haggard's own fictive mask, declares, "Civilisation is only savagery silver-gilt." Drawn to the Zulus, who lived nobly without the "civilized" constraints of Victorian culture, Haggard made them a principal subject in his novels and delivered formal lectures revealing his attraction to their primitive world: As guest speaker at the Zululand Mission Congress in Westminster, for example, he once spoke on the merits of polygamy. When he read Stevenson's *The Strange Case of Dr. Jekyll and Mr. Hyde* (1886), he discovered a duality similar to his own, a striking revelation of a primitive, savage other self inhabiting the mind of the respectable Dr. Jekyll—"enough," Haggard wrote in his memoirs, "to cause the hair to rise."

With the publication of *She* (1887) and *Allan Quatermain* (1887), Haggard solidified his reputation as the supreme writer of popular adventure fiction in the late nineteenth century. Despite a long career as a writer of some sixty-five other books, he remains known for his three best-selling novels of the late 1880s. Like *King Solomon's Mines,* his two other famous stories of high adventure follow the established formula of describing imminent danger and narrow escapes. In what appears to be a jest directed at Haggard's own solemn conception of the British Empire, the beautiful 2,000-year-old white demigoddess, She-who-must-be-obeyed, suggests to her beloved Leo Vincey that they go to England, overthrow Victoria, and reign over Britain. Holly, the narrator, observes wryly of this potential African conqueror: "In the end she would, I had little doubt, assume absolute rule over the British dominions, and probably over the whole earth, and, though I was sure that she would speedily make ours the most glorious and prosperous empire that the world has ever seen, it would be at the cost of a terrible sacrifice of life."

A social Darwinist, She reveals her ruthlessness, as though a New Woman run wild: "Those who are weak must perish; the earth is to the strong, and the fruits thereof. For every tree that grows a score shall wither, that the strong one may take their share. We run to place and power over the dead bodies of those who fail and fall. . . ." Her destruction by the very pillar of fire that gave her seeming immortality is Haggard's convenient means of disposing of the threat to England and empire (though he restored life to her in *Ayesha, The Return of She,* 1905). Freud described *She* as "a *strange* book, but full of hidden meaning . . . the eternal feminine, the immortality of our emotions," and alluded to imagery from the novel that appeared in one of his dreams. Likewise fascinated by *She,* Carl Jung characterized Haggard as one in whom "the motif of the anima [the feminine soul in a masculine man] is developed in its purest and most naïve form. . . ."

AT THE ANGLO-AFRICAN Writers' Club dinner in the Grand Hotel on May 16, 1898, Haggard as chairman proposed the toast to his friend Rudyard Kipling, who had just returned from South Africa: ". . . such men as he are the watchmen of our Empire." In Rhodesia, Haggard remarked, Kipling had "found a land which but a few years ago was a home of savagery, but which is to-day a flourishing British colony, and, as I believe, will within a few years become a great country. (Cheers.) . . . He has looked out on the great beyond of Africa, which will become the seat of empires in the future, or, as most of us hope, the sea of an empire flying one flag, the flag we know. (Cheers.)" Haggard reaffirmed his own imperial belief "in the divine right of a great civilising people—that is, in their divine mission." That mission, he said, was nowhere better expressed than in his friend's poems "The Flag of England" (1891) and

Rudyard Kipling

"The Song of the English" (1893), the author of which "has communed with the very Spirit of our race": "In heart he has gone out with the forgotten thousands who step by step and stone by stone have built up this great Empire of ours, not for the most part with the help of Governments, but rather in the teeth of Governments. The whole earth is white with the bones of those men, the wide road of our rule is paved with them."

Kipling began by praising the "strong men who are building up our Empire" in South Africa. It was they "who needed our help and sympathy and understanding" because the local population "objected acutely to those things which we understood as the elementary rudiments of civilisation":

> We must try by example and precept to coax them along the road to the material development of the land. It was no use getting angry with the unprogressive settlers. Our people have to live with these people. The Colonials and Dutch had married and inter-married until you could hardly tell the one from the other. There was room in the land for both, and it was time to stop jabbering about "anti-Dutch," "anti-British," and so on.

As for the Transvaal, he could see no way to resolve the difficulties, for "we are dealing with a people who have considered themselves our masters and our bosses." If the Boers rose and gave trouble, he said, that would be "the time to 'scoop' them out. (Cheers.)"*

In "The Song of the English," which embodied, said Haggard, the sense of mission, Kipling appeals for a renewal of faith in England's sacred calling ("He hath smote for us a pathway to the ends of all the Earth!"), admits to the sins of the past ("We were led by evil counsellors"), and concludes with religious homily:

> *Keep ye the Law—be swift in all obedience—*
> *Clear the land of evil, drive the road and bridge the ford.*

*Following the report of the meeting of the Anglo-African Writers' Club, the *African Review* (May 21, 1898) published an anonymous poem in Cockney dialect titled "A Humble Tribute," in which the " 'umble" waiter who served Kipling at the banquet responds as a true patriot to his speech:

". . . I listened to yer speakin' (I was 'id behind the screen)
An' I said, 'Well, this 'ere Kiplin', 'e's a man, an' no mistake;'
An' I said, 'Oh—this waitin', chuck it, let's go out an' fight,
I should like to punch some fellow's 'ead for good old England's sake!'

Now the Chairman, Mr. 'Aggard, 'e's a hauthor I admires,
I 'ave read 'is stories many times, I fairly dotes on 'She,'
All the same—and Mr. 'Aggard, 'e'll agree with this, I know—
For a general good all-rounder you're a greater man than 'e.'

Make ye sure to each his own
That he reap where he hath sown;
By the peace among Our peoples let men know we serve the Lord!

The "Law" is not, as Kipling suggests, man-made but in nature itself, as he uses the concept in the opening of the story "How Fear Came" in *The Jungle Books* (1894): "The Law of the Jungle—which is by far the oldest law in the world—has arranged for almost every kind of accident that may befall the Jungle-People, till now its code is as perfect as custom can make it." In the final story, "The Spring Running," the law is the "burden of self-accomplishment," a concept eminently suitable for an imperial view of the world.

In "The White Man's Burden" (1899), written after the United States acquired the Philippines in the Spanish-American War, Kipling urged that Americans assume the "burden" of governing a race unable or unwilling to govern itself by sending "forth the best ye breed":

Take up the White Man's burden—
The savage wars of peace—
Fill full the mouth of Famine
And bid the sickness cease;
And when your goal is nearest
The end for others sought,
Watch Sloth and heathen Folly
Bring all your hope to nought.

The capacity to persevere in bringing enlightenment to the "heathens" despite their possible ingratitude ("The hate of those ye guard") is the true test, Kipling suggests, of the conquering nation's "manhood / Through all the thankless years." Almost immediately, the phrase "white man's burden," with its image of self-sacrifice under adverse conditions, became a central icon of British imperialism and confirmed Kipling, for good or ill, as the "Laureate of the Empire."

But in the *Contemporary Review* (December 1899), he encountered the wrath of Robert Buchanan, of "Fleshly School" notoriety, who now attacked Kipling as "the voice of the Hooligan." Focusing on Kipling's *Barrack-Room Ballads and Other Verses* (1892), Buchanan condemned it as "descriptive of whatever is basest and most brutal in the character of the British mercenary . . . a cruel libel on the British soldier." He was distressed that many readers accepted such verse as "a perfect and splendid representation of the red-coated patriot on whom our national security chiefly depended, and who was spreading abroad in every country the glory of our Imperial Flag!" Instead of presenting a noble image of the British soldier, as Buchanan believed preferable, Kipling depicted the lonely Tommy Atkins, who, in various poems, brawls with other soldiers and steals from civilians.

When *Barrack-Room Ballads* first appeared, the Rhymer Lionel Johnson remarked in the *Academy* (May 28, 1892) that they gave "a picture of life and character more estimable and praiseworthy for many rugged virtues of generosity, endurance, heartiness, and simplicity, than are the lives and characters of many 'gentlemen of England, who stay at home at ease.' " In the *Contemporary Review* (January 1900), Walter Besant responded to Buchanan's attack by defending Kipling as "the Poet with the deepest reverence for those who have built up the Empire: the deepest respect for the Empire" and quoted Henry James, who, in his introduction to Kipling's volume of stories *Mine Own People* (1891), expressed surprise that Kipling, "being so much the sort of figure that the hardened critic likes to meet, he should also be the sort of figure that inspires the multitude with confidence. . . ."

Kipling's stories are likely to be his enduring achievement, in addition to his major novel *Kim* (1901), which depicts India as a wondrous, chaotic land where neither the British nor the Indians alone are capable of effective rule, an indication that Kipling sensed the failure of the colonial adventure. The past is evoked by an old soldier who recalls the Indian Mutiny, when "the land from Delhi south [was] awash with blood." Kipling presents British soldiers as dominated by racial supremacy, a sergeant regarding India as "a wild land for a God-fearin' man"; and at the military school, the brutal drummer boy assigned to Kim, an Irish boy raised as an Indian, has little regard for Indians, whom he calls "niggers." The secret police, however, in which Kim is recruited, consist of generally humane Britons and honest Indians who work well together in maintaining some semblance of order, a vision of a united India achieved by a small group of dedicated civil servants.

In his short stories, Kipling depicts British administrators in India who must cope with such difficulties as a debilitating climate, deadly black cholera, and a disheartening distance from home. In "Without Benefit of Clergy" (1890), the institution of the club compensates for their loneliness and initiates a proper sense of British decorum by focusing on formal dress for dinner. But the central character, secretly married to a beautiful young Indian girl who gives birth and later dies of cholera, must live a divided life because of British protocol and the unstated presumption of racial superiority. In "At the End of the Passage" (1890), four British civil servants meet weekly to play whist in order to ward off their isolated existence and the hardships of Indian life. One of them reads a cutting from a home paper reporting a speech by an M.P. ignorant of life in India:

"And I assert unhesitatingly that the Civil Service in India is the preserve—the pet preserve—of the aristocracy of England.

What does the democracy—what do the masses—get from that country, which we have step by step fraudulently annexed? I answer, nothing whatever. It is farmed with a single eye to their own interests by the scions of the aristocracy. They take good care to maintain their lavish scale of incomes, to avoid or stifle any inquiries into the nature and conduct of their administration. . . ."

Bitterly amused by the speech, the others respond with a sardonic " 'Ear! 'Ear!'' They speak of the immediate threat of black cholera and the suspected suicide of a colleague. The climate, another disagreeable aspect of life in India, combines with various odors to send "the heart of many a strong man down to his boots, for it is the smell of the Great Indian Empire when she turns herself for six months into a house of torment." One of them, having reached the ultimate breaking point when rationality can no longer contend with the uncontrollable forces of a subjected land, reveals the horror of his last moments in his lifeless eyes.

WHEN KIPLING CAME to London from India in 1889, James wrote to Robert Louis Stevenson, then in Samoa, that his "nascent rival" had "killed one immortal—Rider Haggard. . . ." Hoping that Stevenson would return to London, James sent a volume published by the "Rising Star" in order to "goad" him "all hither with jealousy." Ill health, however, kept Stevenson in the South Seas, the setting for some of his best fiction in his last years. Throughout his career, his tales of adventure were analogous to what he regarded as an ideal day-to-day existence described by a recent critic: "Participation in a hazardous enterprise—climbing a mountain, fighting a duel, exploring an island—is a way of simplifying reality and therefore a way of pretending." The Victorians regarded such an activist impulse as an important means of contending with anguish, whether caused by social or personal adversity. Tennyson's "Ulysses" (1842) had expressed the need "to strive, to seek, to find, and not to yield," and his speaker in "Locksley Hall" (1842) asserted: "I myself must mix with action, lest I wither by despair." In *Nostromo* (1904), Conrad, who struggled with his own depression, declared, "Action is consolatory. Only in the conduct of our action can we find the sense of mastery over the Fates"—a view affirmed by modern psychiatry.

In the 1880s, the revival of the adventure novel by Stevenson and Haggard was a challenge to the mid-Victorian domestic realism of Trollope and George Eliot and to the New Naturalism, which, said Zola, was "the intellectual movement of the century." Though all fiction is, to be sure, a form of "pretending," readers agreed with Andrew Lang, a champion of the adventure novels of Sir Walter Scott, Alexandre Dumas, Stevenson, and Haggard, that in the late nineteenth century, deliverance from scientific knowledge and from the world's squalor required a writer possessed of a singular imagination: "As the visible world is measured, mapped, tested, weighed, we seem to hope more and more that a world of invisible romance may not be far from us. . . . I can believe that an impossible romance . . . might still win us from the newspapers, and the stories of shabby love, and cheap remorses, and commonplace failures."

As a semi-invalid, Stevenson regarded pretending as having more significance than a momentary sense of being alive: In his late novels, he progressively revealed a deeper sense of human depravity and anxiety through "pretending" than he had customarily written about in his earlier stories designed for young readers. In *The Beach of Falesá* (1892/1893), for example, Stevenson presents a view of British traders in the far-flung islands of the South Seas, their distance providing opportunities for scoundrels to exploit the natives. Hoping to return someday to Britain to open a pub, the unlettered Wiltshire is convinced of his fundamental beneficence in the spirit of imperialism's sacred mission: "I'm a white man, and a British Subject, and no end of a big chief at home; and I've come here to do [the natives] good and bring them civilisation. . . ." Eventually he cleanses the island of villainy by killing the "splendidly educated" Case, who had monopolized the copra trade by terrorizing the natives. Though Wiltshire has a strong dislike of the local inhabitants, he "goes native" in a mock marriage. The devotion of his native wife helps him in his final confrontation with Case, who exemplifies the conventions of Romantic myth in his moral corruption by civilization, whereas Wiltshire retains something of his natural goodness.

Stevenson's *Ebb-Tide* (1893/1894), written in collaboration with his stepson Lloyd Osbourne, was the last work published before his death. Stevenson called this extraordinary novel of three beachcombers in one of the outstations of the British Empire "a black, ugly, trampling, violent story" and "about as grim a tale as was ever written, and as grimy, and as hateful." Images of debris on the beach reflect the despair and moral nihilism of the "three most miserable English-speaking creatures in Tahiti" who have become scavangers and thieves. In the second half of this tale, the three embark on a quest for a suitable refuge after the theft of a ship and its cargo, arriving at an island with a flourishing trade in pearls over which rules the Cambridge-educated Attwater, an imperial figure who mouths Christian doctrine, a missionary turned sinister in his evangelical Puritanism. When the three plot to kill him, Attwater reads their degenerate natures accurately, for they mirror his own fallen state, and he survives brilliantly—thanks, in part, to one of the three plotters, the Oxford-educated Herrick, who, in choosing to warn Attwater, not unexpect-

edly aligns himself with one of his own social class, for some Victorians
the sign of a true gentleman.

ALONG WITH THE works of Kipling and Haggard, Stevenson's late novels, combining such conventions of the adventure story as exotic, unexpected incidents with characters who are the human debris of empire
building, had created a considerable audience for such fiction. The possibility of achieving success with such material encouraged Joseph Conrad
to exploit the settings that he had experienced in his years as a seaman. In
his first novel, *Almayer's Folly* (1895), the setting is the Malayan archipelago, but Conrad modifies the popular tale of high adventure by
employing the motif of buried treasure without the customary quest. The
focus in the tale is the Dutch colonialist Almayer's profound disappointment in his half-caste daughter, Nina, who loves and eventually departs
with the Malay chief Dain. Almayer's "folly" is not only his dream that he
and Nina will someday be rich and live a splendid life in Europe but also
his assurance that a London trading company will be establishing a new
post in Sambir. In preparation for the English, "who knew how to develop a rich country," he had built a splendid new house for them, now
empty, for the company has decided against the plan. In the absence of
the English, the Dutch have sent in their navy to secure the territory for
themselves. The image of the luxuriant but potentially destructive jungle,
"hiding fever, rottenness, and evil under its level and glazed surface,"
dominates the story, acquiring symbolic reverberations associated with
local and European greed. In a later essay, Conrad contended that by the
end of the nineteenth century the imperialistic enterprise had had such a
devastating impact on Europe that it had become "only an armed and
trading continent, the home of slowly maturing economical contests for
life and death, and of loudly proclaimed world-wide ambitions."

Like Haggard and Stevenson, Conrad regarded the "savages" as potentially noble in their opposition against degenerate whites who had in-
vaded their land, as when Almayer's Malay wife urges Nina to inspire
Dain with the courage to defeat his enemies: " 'Let him slay the white
men that come to us to trade, with prayers on their lips and loaded guns in
their hands. Ah'—she ended with a sigh—'they are on every sea, and on
every shore; and they are very many!' " The secret love affair between
Dain and Nina reveals their determination to rise above the materialism
of the West as well as Almayer's hatred of what he regards as her degrading relationship with Dain, the setting for their tryst expressing their
intense passion and their ultimate triumph:

> All around them in a ring of luxuriant vegetation bathed in the
> warm air charged with strong and harsh perfumes, the intense

work of tropical nature went on: plants shooting upward, entwined, interlaced in inextricable confusion, climbing madly
and brutally over each other in the terrible silence of a desperate
struggle towards the life-giving sunshine above—as if struck
with sudden horror at the seething mass of corruption below, at
the death and decay from which they spring.

Conrad's negative view of European imperialism continued in many of
his late nineteenth-century stories and novels, as in *An Outcast of the Islands*
(1896), again set in the Malay archipelago some twenty years before that
of *Almayer's Folly* with many of the same characters, including Almayer.
The most striking short story that Conrad published before his masterpiece *Heart of Darkness* (1899/1902) was "An Outpost of Progress"
(1897/1898), which, in its concentrated form, expressed his outrage towards imperialistic domination of the Congo, where Conrad had spent six
months in 1890. The Congo Free State had fallen prey to the ambitions of
Leopold II, who, in seeking to enlarge his kingdom, urged the establishment in 1876 of the International Association for the Suppression of
Slavery and the Opening Up of Central Africa.

At its initial conference in Brussels, he proposed the association's intent: "To open to civilization the only area of our globe to which it has
not yet penetrated, to pierce the gloom which hangs over entire races,
constitutes, if I may dare to put it in this way, a Crusade worthy of this
century of progress." Leopold's rhetoric, his use of Stanley in establishing
stations along the Congo River, and his political skill in maneuvering
among the major powers in the scramble for Africa enabled him to win
their acknowledgment of his dominion over the Congo Free State. In
1885, the Berlin West Africa Conference ratified his status, which
granted him sole possession of a vast territory of nearly 900,000 square
miles.

Within three years, British critics of the Congo Free State were condemning Stanley for his ruthless destruction of villages, the shooting of
men, and the massacre of their wives and children. In 1888, only one
brief query was directed to the undersecretary of state, Sir James Fergus-
son, by a member of Parliament, who cited a report in the *Scotsman* that
such atrocities had been committed in the Congo Free State. Sir James
responded that the administration of the territory had "formally and in-
dignantly denied the truth of the statement; asserting that in the few
instances in which it has been found necessary to punish Natives at the
instance of traders in the region referred to, for hostile acts to caravans or
theft, the greatest moderation has been shown, and bloodshed has generally been avoided." The curt reply ended, for a while, any official concern
with the inhuman treatment of the Congolese.

Concerned about British subjects and interests in that part of Africa, the Foreign Office maintained cordial relations with Leopold II in the late 1880s and early 1890s despite the rising tide of reports by missionaries and travelers that native soldiers, under orders from Belgian officials concerned with the rubber crop, were brutalizing the Congolese in order to increase production. When such reports persisted, the Congo government founded the Commission for the Protection of the Natives in September 1896 and appointed a state inspector to enforce its powers, though evidence suggests that this move was designed to pacify critics rather than to institute reforms. However, the founding of the commission apparently satisfied the British Foreign Office, which remained reluctant to intervene. In the late 1890s, the British press began reporting extensively on charges of brutality towards the Congolese. The *Times* (May 25, 1899), for example, printed excerpts from a diary kept by an Englishman who had held various posts in the territory. One passage describes the pressures on army officers who "are told how much rubber is expected from each village. If that amount does not come in . . . war is made against that village, and natives are killed, the black soldiers, in order to justify their statements as to the number dead, afterwards cutting off hands and ears."

In "An Outpost of Progress," Conrad avoids direct allusions to the worst brutalities reported in the Congo; instead, he depicts the parasitical existence of the two white men—one a former bureaucrat, the other a former noncommissioned officer in the cavalry—who depend on Makola from Sierra Leone to run the isolated trading compound in the "vast and dark country." The ironic title of the story and the unsuitability of the two men to such conditions are preludes to their eventual disaster: ". . . the contact with pure unmitigated savagery, with primitive nature and primitive man, brings sudden and profound trouble into the heart." These two, who "understood nothing, cared for nothing but for the passage of days that separated them from the steamer's return," find an old newspaper discussing " 'Our Colonial Expansion' in high-flown language": "It spoke much of the rights and duties of civilization, of the sacredness of the civilizing work, and extolled the merits of those who went about bringing light, and faith and commerce to the dark places of the earth. Carlier and Kayerts read, wondered, and began to think better of themselves."

Their moral deterioration begins when they accede to an exchange of ivory for the company hands, who are enslaved by ivory hunters. When food begins to run low, Carlier and Kayerts's homocidal frenzy over some remaining sugar signals their reversion to savagery. After killing Carlier, Kayerts awaits the arrival of the steamer, which makes its way through the mist "white and deadly, immaculate and poisonous," its whistle shrieking: "Progress was calling to Kayerts from the river. Progress and civilization and all the virtues. Society was calling to its accomplished child to come, to be taken care of, to be instructed, to be judged, to be condemned." Kayerts hangs himself from the cross marking Carlier's grave, and his corpse is discovered "irreverently . . . putting out a swollen tongue" at the managing director of the "Great Civilizing Company (since we know that civilization follows trade)."

In 1898, as he was composing *Heart of Darkness,* Conrad told his publisher that "the subject is of our time distinc[t]ly—though not topically treated." This short novel begins with Conrad's ominous vision of London, the dark heart of Britain's imperial empire, the "mournful gloom, brooding motionless over the biggest, and the greatest, town on earth." In contemplating the history of the Thames, the narrator recalls those "great knights-errant of the sea," such as Sir Francis Drake, who set out to explore and colonize: "Hunters for gold or pursuers of fame, they all had gone out on that stream, bearing the word, and often the torch, messengers of the might within the land, bearers of a spark from the sacred fire." In Marlow's ruminations about highly civilized Romans living "in the midst of the incomprehensible" in primitive Britain ("darkness was here yesterday"), Conrad suggests parallels between two empires: one long since gone, the other facing a Darwinian return of "darkness."

The principal setting of the story is again the Congo Free State, and the dramatic focus is on the effect of the primitive jungle on two characters: Marlow, whose determined quest is to find Kurtz, an ivory trader described by an associate as "an emissary of pity, and science, and progress, and devil knows what else." Marlow's discovery that Kurtz has yielded to the savagery of his own heart of darkness is a shattering experience, for the Africans reveal little of the "savagery" traditionally attributed to them by Europeans. Rather, Marlow senses a kinship between himself and the natives he encounters in his journey; at one point, when he observes them in a frenzy on the bank of the river, he muses: ". . . what thrilled you was just the thought of their humanity—like yours—the thought of your remote kinship with this wild and passionate uproar." Marlow discovers a primeval world, atavistic in its barbaric splendor and destructive in its "unspeakable rites"—those "subtle horrors" performed for and presumably by Kurtz. The decapitated heads on poles around his outpost of progress are thus his symbols of omnipotence over those who serve him at the inner station; turned inwards, the heads also reveal his narcissistic need for adoration. Such moral retrogression, Conrad suggested, had resulted from a spiritually exhausted Europe, which "contributed to the making of Kurtz."

Having written a report for the International Society for the Suppression of Savage Customs, Kurtz reveals his transformation from noble visionary to self-proclaimed savage god on the final page of the document, which becomes his confessional. Astonished, Marlow relates that "at the end of that moving appeal to every altruistic sentiment it blazed at you, luminous and terrifying, like a flash of lightning in a serene sky: 'Exterminate all the brutes!' " Kurtz's final words as he dies—"The horror! The horror!"—provide the central unresolved ambiguity. Marlow, whose Victorian values of self-restraint and devotion to duty have saved him from depravity, regards Kurtz's judgment as "an affirmation, a moral victory," Marlow's desperate attempt to minimize Kurtz's degradation. In *The Explorer,* Maugham's hero echoes Marlow's views concerning the precarious existence that whites face in Africa when morally isolated in the vast jungle, a remarkable gloss on Conrad's *Heart of Darkness:*

> ... The effect of Africa was too strong. Alec had seen many men lose their heads under the influence of that climate. The feeling of an authority that seemed so little limited, over a race that was manifestly inferior, the subtle magic of the hot sunshine, the vastness, the remoteness from civilisation, were very apt to throw a man off his balance. The French had coined a name for the distemper and called it *folie d'Afrique.* Men seemed to go mad from a sense of power, to lose all the restraints which had kept them in the way of righteousness. It needed a strong head or a strong morality to avoid the danger. . . .

When *Heart of Darkness* was being serialized in February 1899, Conrad, apparently in a depressed state, sensed that nineteenth-century culture, beyond redemption, would be succeeded by a dangerous new age. In a letter to R. B. Cunninghame Graham, he was pessimistically blunt: "Man is a vicious animal. His viciousness must be organised. Crime is a necessary condition of organised existence. Society is fundamentally criminal—or it would not exist. . . . For myself, I look at the future from the depths of a very dark past, and I find I am allowed nothing but fidelity to an absolutely lost cause, to an idea without a future." Kurtz's final words shatter such prevailing illusions as the Romantic belief in humanity's essential goodness, in a rationally ordered civilization, and in the promise of social progress. Lionel Trilling regarded Kurtz as a foreshadowing of the future, for "nothing is more characteristic of modern literature than its discovery and canonization of the primal, non-ethical energies."

WHILE HAGGARD, KIPLING, Stevenson, and Conrad were depicting the lives of explorers, traders, and colonists in hazardous settings, a popular literary form called "invasion scare novels" had been developing since the appearance in *Blackwood's Magazine* (May 1871) of Lieutenant-Colonel Sir George Chesney's story titled *The Battle of Dorking.* * When published by public demand in a sixpenny pamphlet, it sold 80,000 copies. In the story, the narrator tells how, some fifty years earlier, a superior German army had landed on the coast at Brighton while the Royal Navy was on the high seas protecting the far-flung empire. Designed to warn the British of the dangers of ill-preparedness, the story concludes with the admonition: "A nation too selfish to defend its liberty could not have been fit to retain it"—a vision of social Darwinism in the struggle between nations. At stake is the empire itself, doomed to extinction because of German penetration. (When Germany was planning to invade England in 1940, a new translation of *The Battle of Dorking* was issued under the title *Was England erwartet* [What England Can Expect].)

In the months following the appearance of *The Battle of Dorking,* publishers rushed nine works into print, most of them pamphlets written anonymously by British Army and Royal Navy officers to calm the fears of the public (and perhaps their own anxieties) by showing how the Royal Navy would, in fact, destroy an invading German army before it reached shore or how the British Army would be victorious in land battles. These narratives, all appearing in 1871, had such eye-catching titles as *After the Battle of Dorking; or, What Became of the Invaders?* and *The Suggested Invasion of England by the Germans.* Though Germany and France were the principal villains in the invasion literature of the late nineteenth and early twentieth century, other countries such as Russia, China, Japan, and the United States were also depicted as invaders or would-be invaders of Britain. Generally, the hostile invaders in such works were from a nation currently undergoing censure by the Foreign Office and by the press.

Invasion stories and novels after Chesney's doomsday tale involved the onslaught of foreign armies on Britain with the inevitable defeat of the enemy. Such fantasies were generated by the fear that the great success of the empire, inspiring envy and hostility from other European countries, left Britain vulnerable to attack because of alleged neglect of military preparedness. Between 1860 and 1900, British expenditures for arms had trebled, whereas German expenditures increased fivefold, and with the stunning Prussian victory over France in 1870, Germany was widely regarded as a potentially malevolent power as well as a formidable economic competitor in empire-building. The response among the British was the New Imperialism, a more frenetic vision of expansionism and

---

*In *Voices Prophesying War, 1763–1984* (London, 1966), I. F. Clarke has listed hundreds of works depicting "imaginary wars" published between 1763 and 1965 in English, French, and German. In 1803, for example, an anonymous "farce" in three acts, *The Invasion of England,* provided a title often used, sometimes with variations, by later novelists.

militancy that intensified through the fin de siècle and acquired the name of "jingoism." In 1878, the term was associated with a popular song "By Jingo" by G. W. Hunt, sung during the Russo-Turkish War (1877–78) in the music halls, known as the "fount of patriotism." "Jingoes" were those politicians who were intent on bringing Britain into the conflict on the side of the Turks. The chorus of Hunt's song went as follows: "We don't want to fight, but, by jingo, if we do, / We've got the ships, we've got the men, we've got the money, too." The New Imperialism thus underlay the popular literature that simultaneously produced anxiety at the thought of invasion and confidence in England's capacity to defeat an enemy.

In the *National Review* (May 1885), a writer offered an apology for jingoism by emphasizing the fact that "aggression is carefully excluded from the Jingo manifesto. The very first article [from the music hall song] is '*We don't want to fight.*' England, during the last two centuries, has never been an aggressive Power." However, he reminds his readers, "The aggressive Powers *were* France and Spain, and *are* now France and Russia." The great national heroes of Britain, such as Wellington and Nelson, were "Jingoes to a man, and shaped all their measures on Jingo principles . . . penetrated by the belief that an Englishman was more than a match for the citizen of any other nation. . . . The history of a thousand years taught them, as it should teach us, that we *are* superior to any other nation." An indication of how the darker side of jingoism and the New Imperialism permeated Victorian sensibilities in the fin de siècle occurs in Gissing's *The Whirlpool* (1897). When Carnaby jokingly recommends "nigger-hunting" as "a superior big-game," his friend Rolfe responds with a prophetic vision of Britain's imperial destiny:

> There's more than that to do in South Africa. . . . Who believes for a moment that England will remain satisfied with bits here and there? We have to swallow the whole, of course. We shall go on fighting and annexing until—until the decline and fall of the British Empire. That hasn't begun yet. Some of us are so over-civilised that it makes a reaction of wholesome barbarism in the rest. We shall fight like blazes in the twentieth century. It's the only thing that keeps Englishmen sound; commercialism is their curse.

The arguments over jingoism, as a term of honor or of abuse, became increasingly vitriolic as the century came to an end with the outbreak of the Boer War. In *The Psychology of Jingoism* (1901), J. A. Hobson assailed the concept in his striking definition of its social pathology:

> A coarse patriotism, fed by the wildest rumours and the most violent appeals to hate and the animal lust of blood, passes by

quick contagion through the crowded life of cities and recommends itself everywhere by the satisfaction it affords to sensational cravings. It is less the savage yearning for personal participation in the fray than the feeding of a neurotic imagination that marks Jingoism.

For those, however, who subscribed to jingoist propaganda in the fin de siècle, the myth of Britain's essentially defensive policy and its determination to survive any assault at home provided a measure of comfort. Earlier, the endemic fear of invasion among Britons reached a stage of acute anxiety when the French developed steam-powered ships able to cross the Channel within a few hours and built a port at Cherbourg, a potential staging area for invasion. Convinced that the nation must be aroused, Tennyson published "The War" in the *Times* (May 9, 1859), the title subsequently changed to "Rifleman, Form!" which urged a reordering of national priorities:

> *Let your Reforms for a moment go,*
> *Look to your butts and take good aims.*
> *Better a rotten borough or so,*
> *Than a rotten fleet and a city in flames!*
> *Form! form! Riflemen form!*
> *Ready, be ready to meet the storm!*

As a result of the poem, a volunteer force was organized three days later.

Between Chesney's *The Battle of Dorking* (1871) and the outbreak of the First World War, more than sixty pamphlets and books appeared in which an invasion of Britain is fictively described. As the literature of invasion was churned out to meet a seemingly insatiable demand for such fantasies, a new cause for anxiety arose over the proposal for an English Channel tunnel, which Parliament debated in 1882 and which resulted in the smashed windows of the Channel Tunnel Company by a London mob. The potential threat from France through the tunnel was felt not only by the man in the street but also by such figures as Tennyson, Browning, Cardinal Newman, the Archbishop of Canterbury, as well as by fifty-nine generals and seventeen admirals, who all signed a petition opposing its construction. Adjutant-General Wolseley composed a memorandum expressing the fear that "a couple of thousand armed men might easily come through the tunnel in a train at night, avoiding all suspicion by being dressed as ordinary passengers, or . . . with the blinds down, in their uniforms and fully armed." With the seizure of the English terminus, "England would be at the mercy of the invader."

Such an event is depicted in the profusion of popular novels feeding on these new invasion fears with such titles as *The Channel Tunnel; or En-*

gland's Ruin (1876), *The Capture of the Channel Tunnel* (1882), and *The Capture of London* (1887). The fear generated by the possibility of a French invasion brought Mrs. Thomas Hardy to such an emotional state that she kept a packed suitcase handy in order to escape to the countryside.

In the midst of such alarmist fiction, the *Pall Mall Gazette* (September 15, 1884) implied in a leading article that the Royal Navy was in an inadequate state, and there appeared on September 18 a six-page exposé, "The Truth about the Navy" as revealed "By One Who Knows the Facts." The anonymous author of both articles was W. T. Stead, who had recently become the editor. In the first article, he sounded the alarm: "Not only our Imperial position, but the daily bread of twenty millions out of thirty millions of our population depends entirely upon our dominion of the sea. If that is lost, or even endangered, our existence is at stake." From an informant who was a navy captain, he had learned (and subsequently confirmed) that for the previous fifteen years, expenditures for the fleet had been steadily declining. Though Britain exceeded other navies in large ironclads, France, for example, was rapidly building smaller vessels with more effective armaments. The "truth about the Navy," Stead insisted, was that "our naval supremacy has almost ceased to exist."

Stead's articles created a cause célèbre, the *Daily Telegraph* acknowledging "a cry of patriotic anxiety rising in the country to which no Ministry could close its ears." Stead's demands for first-class battleships, cruisers for the protection of merchant shipping, torpedo boats, and improvements in the defense of coaling stations were widely approved by the press and by navy officials. In succeeding issues of the *Pall Mall Gazette,* signed articles by naval officers and government officials, as well as letters to the editor, generally supported Stead's position. The first lord of the admiralty Lord Northbrook, who did not fully agree with those agitating for more expenditures, nevertheless announced that £5,500,000 would be spent over the next five years in the construction of naval vessels, naval ordnance, and coaling stations. However, Northbrook's critics believed that the program was inadequate (the *Pall Mall Gazette* insisted that an additional £4,000,000 was essential as an annual expenditure for the navy). Again caught up in the nation's preoccupation with an inadequate defense against the possibility of foreign aggression, Tennyson addressed a poem to Lord Northbrook in the *Times* (April 23, 1885) titled "The Fleet (On its reported Insufficiency)":

> You—you—if you have fail'd to understand—
> The Fleet of England is her all in all—
> On you will come the curse of all the land,

If that Old England fall,
  Which Nelson left so great—

You—you—who had the ordering of her Fleet,
If you have only compass'd her disgrace,
When all men starve, the wild mob's million feet
  Will kick you from your place—
  But then—too late, too late.

Despite the fact that expenditures fell short of such demands, the "scare" ended, but it provided writers of invasion literature with new opportunities to capitalize on old anxieties.

By the early 1890s, however, the earlier invasion literature that had embodied solemn warnings to Britons was seized upon by writers interested principally in commercial exploitation. One of these prolific writers, William Le Queux, "an opportunistic panicmonger," depicts an onslaught on England by Russian and French forces in his immensely popular novel *The Great War in England in 1897* (1893/1894). The French come ashore on the South Coast while the Russians charge through the Midlands as England falls into chaos when anarchists lead mobs in looting and murder from the East End to Trafalgar Square. At the National Gallery, the cry goes up: "What do we want with Art? Burn it!" The "denizens of the slums" fling paintings into a bonfire and engage in "wild reckless orgies." Meanwhile, stories circulate that Russians are impaling babies on bayonets (similar reports involving German soldiers in Belgium later circulated as propaganda during the First World War).

In Le Queux's tale, the Germans attack France, and among Britons "a feeling of thankfulness spread through the land." Also, Italy invades southern France, and 25,000 Irishmen abandon their political antagonisms to join their English compatriots—a rescue fantasy, indeed! The complicated plot involves the destruction of Westminster Abbey and other London landmarks by the French and the defeat of the Russians in Glasgow and Manchester. After the war ends and prosperity flourishes, the Royal Navy and Imperial German Army conduct joint operations. Up through the First World War, Le Queux continued grinding out potboilers about spies, international intrigue, and invasions (his success providing the stimulus for such later spy novelists as John Buchan and Ian Fleming), after 1900 usually involving Germany as economic competition with England intensified. Indeed, as a result of the scare, in part induced by the invasion writers, German nationals in Britain were imprisoned during the Great War.

The most notable of the fin-de-siècle writers depicting the immanent destruction of Britain was H. G. Wells, whose *The War of the Worlds*

(1897/1898), superior in its imaginative conception to the hordes of novels following the prescribed plots of the invasion genre, suggested an ironic antiimperialist perspective. Instead of British troops dominating "savages" in a demonstration of Darwinian superiority, Martians with more advanced intelligence and technology invade England, presumably regarding the English "as alien and lowly as are the monkeys and lemurs to us." Indeed, the novel begins with such a view:

> No one would have believed in the last years of the nineteenth century that human affairs were being watched keenly and closely by intelligences greater than man's and yet as mortal as his own; that as men busied themselves about their affairs they were scrutinised and studied perhaps almost as closely as a man with a microscope might scrutinise the transient creatures that swarm and multiply in a drop of water.

The English, "dreaming themselves the highest creatures in the whole vast universe, and serene in their assurance of their empire over matter," face total annihilation from one hundred–foot mechanical monsters guided by Martians whose bodies have evolved into huge heads and tentacles and whose weapons are the deadly heat ray and black smoke.

Wells's narrator, who is writing a "series of papers discussing the probable developments of moral ideas as civilisation progressed," is in the middle of a sentence at the time of the Martians' first appearance: "In about two hundred years we may expect—," which is never completed. In revealing not only the destructive nature of the invaders but also his own terror and helplessness, the narrator concludes that moral progress is an illusion. A portion of his narrative includes the events experienced by his brother in London, where the terrified population has abandoned rationality and civilized behavior as they flee from the Martians in "a stampede gigantic and terrible, without order and without a goal, six million people unarmed and unprovisioned, driving headlong. It was the beginning of the rout of civilisation, of the massacre of mankind." Since Wells's intent was not to point a moral concerning the lack of preparedness against such a powerful enemy, he employed an ironic method of disposing of the Martians: They are "slain by the putrefactive and disease bacteria, against which their systems were unprepared."

London having recovered, the narrator is astonished when he visits Fleet Street and the Strand, observing "the busy multitudes": ". . . it comes across my mind that they are but the ghosts of the past haunting the streets that I have seen silent and wretched, going to and fro, phantasms in a dead city, the mockery of life in a galvanised body." This final vision, increasingly common among pessimistic intellectuals and artists in the fin de siècle, suggests not only the final exhaustion but also the unreality of civilization itself, of Kurtz's parallel horror in the Congo, and of the poet Francis Thompson's chilling evocation in 1900 of London having fallen into Darwinian retrogression:

> The very streets weigh upon me. These horrible streets, with their gangrenous multitudes, blackening ever into lower mortifications of humanity! The brute men; these lads who have almost lost the faculty of human speech, who howl & growl like animals, or use a tongue which is itself a cancerous disintegration of speech: these girls whose practice is a putrid ulceration of love. . . . Nothing but the vocabulary of the hospital, images of corruption and fleshly ruin, can express the objects offered to eye and ear in these loathsome streets. The air is fulsome with its surcharge of tainted humanity. We lament the smoke of London:—it were nothing without the fumes of congregated evil, the herded effluence from millions of festering souls. At times I am merely sick with it.

The climactic expression of such a vision occurs in the "Unreal City" and death-in-life of T. S. Eliot's *The Waste Land* (1922), where "A crowd flowed over London Bridge, so many, / I had not thought death had undone so many." It was precisely this dead civilization that Wells wished to discard, as he wrote facetiously to a friend from his home in Woking, Surrey, while at work on *The War of the Worlds:* "I'm doing the dearest little serial for Pearson's new magazine, in which I completely wreck and destroy Woking—killing my neighbours in painful and eccentric ways, then proceed . . . to London, which I sack, selecting South Kensington for feats of peculiar atrocity." Four years before in the *Pall Mall Gazette* (September 23, 1894), Wells had written on "The Extinction of Man," arguing that while "man is undisputed master at the present time . . . so it has been before with other animals": ". . . man's complacent assumption of the future is too confident. . . . Even now, for all we can tell, the coming terror may be crouching for its spring and the fall of humanity be at hand. But if some poor story-writing man ventures to figure this in a tale, not a reviewer in London but will tell him his theme is the utterly impossible."

IN 1897, AS Wells's apocalyptic *War of the Worlds* was being serialized between April and December in *Pearson's Magazine,* the empire began its celebration in June of the Diamond Jubilee of Queen Victoria's sixty-year reign, unprecedented among British monarchs. Foreign guests were limited principally but not exclusively to splendidly attired colonial premiers and Indian princes from the empire in an attempt to minimize the burdens of the aging Queen, now seventy-eight, half blind and lame (she could not kneel in church). On June 22, a decreed bank holiday, the grand celebration was to be held throughout the city. After breakfast, the Queen dispatched a message by telegraph to all parts of the empire: "From my heart I thank my beloved people. God bless them!" By eleven fifteen, the six-mile procession of the Queen's carriage with the mounted Life Guards as escorts proceeded at a slow pace through the sunny decorated streets as crowds cheered and waved. At St. Paul's, the colorful colonial troops were at the ready as the "Mother of the Empire" entered for the Thanksgiving service. This "never-to-be-forgotten-day" confirmed for many the inescapable truth that the sun could not—indeed, dare not—set on the British Empire. The later prime minister Clement Attlee recalled that, at the time of the jubilee, "most of us boys were imperialists."

To honor Queen and Empire, Kipling composed the famous "Recessional" for publication in the *Times* (July 17, 1897), but the poem is an ominous warning wrapped within a tentative celebration of power:

> *God of our fathers, known of old,*
> *Lord of our far-flung battle-line,*
> *Beneath whose awful Hand we hold*
> *Dominion over palm and pine—*
> *Lord God of Hosts, be with us yet,*
> *Lest we forget—lest we forget!*

The allusion in the third stanza to Nineveh and Tyre, ancient cities that have passed into dust, warns readers that the empire could someday meet the same fate:

> *Far-called, our navies melt away;*
> *On dune and headland sinks the fire:*
> *Lo, all our pomp of yesterday*
> *Is one with Nineveh and Tyre!*
> *Judge of the Nations, spare us yet,*
> *Lest we forget—lest we forget!*

Four stanzas repeat the increasingly foreboding refrain "Lest we forget" with the final stanza ending: "Thy mercy on Thy People, Lord!"—a conclusion that deflates British pride in empire, a curious sentiment in a poem of celebration. Nevertheless, the oracular expression of the poem created a sensation: In *Blackwood's Magazine* (October 1898), a critic recalled that "Recessional," which "took England by storm," seemed "to

Queen Victoria's Diamond Jubilee (Library of Congress)

concentrate in itself the glowing patriotism of a Shakespeare, the solemn piety of a Milton, and the measured stateliness of a Dryden." Walter Besant later reminded readers that Kipling, "alone of poets or preachers, saw, as in a vision of inspiration, the one thing that needed to be said: We were drunk with the pageant of power and of glory."

Within two years, the test of power and the decline of glory were to take place in the Transvaal, first settled by the Boers (the Dutch word for "farmers," now known as "Afrikaners"). With the discovery of gold and diamonds in the last third of the nineteenth century, British settlers from the adjacent British Cape Colony (whom the Boers called "Uitlanders," or "Outlanders") flocked to the Transvaal, resulting in increasing tensions between the two territories. The disastrous attempt to overthrow the Transvaal, engineered by Dr. L. Storr Jameson of the British South Africa Company in his infamous raid of the territory, had prepared the way for war. When the Boers denied the franchise to the Uitlanders, the British high commissioner for South Africa from 1897, Sir Alfred Milner, believed that "a show of force" would convince the Transvaal president S. J. P. Kruger that the issue of the Uitlanders could not be ignored. The Boers reacted by attacking the Cape Colony on October 11, 1899. In the first months, the British suffered a series of humiliating defeats requiring the replacement of soldiers from Canada, Australia, and New Zealand.

Almost immediately after the outbreak of war, patriotic verse attacking the Boers appeared with a vengeance. In the *Times* (October 12, 1899), on the day following the Boers' initial attack, Swinburne's "The Transvaal" lashed out with an intemperate allusion to the Boers as "dogs, agape with jaws afoam" and its urging: "Strike, England, and strike home!" Alfred Austin also appeared in the *Times* (November 2, 1899) with "Inflexible as Fate," its lines reminding Britons of the Roman Empire beset by barbarians (a nightmare image, as we have seen, that haunted the late Victorians and Edwardians): "Not less resolved than Rome, now England stands, / Facing foul fortune with unfaltering hands." A writer in the *South African News* (November 25, 1899) called Austin's lines "The dismal twaddle of [England's] Laureate." As the Boer victories continued through the end of the year, poetic inspiration rose to confront them. Sir Lewis Morris, who, after Tennyson's death, had been seriously considered as the next poet laureate, offered rhythmic consolation:

> *Though her generals may blunder, though her bravest sons are slain,*
> *Though her best blood flows like water, and the sacrifice seems vain—*
> *Chorus: Still cheer for noble Britain. . . .*

In December 1899, W. E. Henley offered "Remonstrance" with its central question: "Where is our ancient pride of heart?" And urging "Rise, England, rise!," he borrowed Swinburne's line from "The Transvaal," presumably regarding it as the last word: "Strike, England, and strike home!"

In Europe, the Boers were hailed as heroic defenders, and in Britain there was a strong pro-Boer movement. With no unanimity at home concerning the validity of the war and its accompanying jingoism, there was an outpouring of antiwar verse both by those who were noncombatants as well as by those involved in the fighting. Prior to this time, Tennyson's acclaimed poem "The Charge of the Light Brigade" (1854) had been a major influence upon poets celebrating military heroism and upholding the ideal of a glorious sacrificial death in the service of the Queen. Indeed, during the period of the New Imperialism, the young were inculcated with such ideals associated with the empire, which by its very existence demonstrated British superiority. The curricula of the most prestigious public schools and more than eighty boys' adventure novels by G. A. Henty, which sold an astounding 25 million copies, celebrated the glory of empire. Henley contributed to the proper education of the young by compiling selections dealing with patriotism, military heroism, and self-sacrifice drawn from the works of great English writers from Shakespeare to Kipling. The anthology, titled *Lyra Heroica: A Choice of Verse for Boys* (1892), which achieved six printings by the time of the war, begins with a brief preface that all too clearly establishes its point of view: "To set forth, as only art can, the beauty of the joy of living, the beauty and the blessedness of death, the glory of battle and adventure, the nobility of devotion—to a cause, an ideal, a passion even—the dignity of resistance, the sacred quality of patriotism, that is my ambition here."

When the Boer War erupted, however, a large body of verse—much of it now forgotten—presented the unheroic aspects of war, its degradation of the spirit and its waste of life, an anticipation of the poetry written during the First World War by such poets as Wilfred Owen and Isaac Rosenberg. The changes in attitude arose from some thirty years of universal education and a more democratic society, as manifested in an organized and articulate "radical, socialist, and humanitarian opposition to war." Perhaps the most famous of the antiwar poems, Hardy's "Drummer Hodge," which first appeared in *Literature* (November 25, 1899) under the title "The Dead Drummer," alludes to a young farm boy thrown "to rest / Uncoffined—just as found," never understanding why he was in South Africa:

> *Young Hodge the Drummer never knew—*
> *Fresh from his Wessex home—*
> *The meaning of the broad Karoo,*
> *The Bush, the dusty loam,*
> *And why uprose to nightly view*
> *Strange stars amid the gloam.*

Like Hardy, Austin Dobson in "Rank and File," published in the *Sphere: An Illustrated Newspaper for the Home* (February 3, 1900), mourns the "Undistinguished Dead," their identities and the significance of their sacrifice now obliterated:

> *. . . for you I mourn—I weep,*
> *O Undistinguished Dead!*
>
> *None knows your name,*
> *Blackened and blurred in the wild battle's brunt,*
> *Hotly you fell . . . with all your wounds in front:—*
> *This is your fame!*

In the *Nineteenth Century* (January 1901), Stephen Phillips's "Midnight—The 31st of December, 1900," a poem in which the Lord pronounces judgment on events of the past century, attacks the jingoist vision of patriotism: "I will make of your warfare a terrible thing, / A thing impossible, vain. . . ."

The divisions over the war were felt deeply among the socialists, who found themselves supporting diametrically opposed positions concerning imperialistic policies in South Africa. Shaw and Webb increasingly opposed the Liberals, pacifists, and free traders known as "Little Englanders," who were passionately against the war. Such views were complicated by the fact that many Liberals and Fabians regarded the Boers as distasteful religious fundamentalists impeding progress; indeed, Beatrice Webb called the Transvaal Republic "that remnant of seventeenth-century puritanism." The Fabian Hubert Bland argued in the *Labour Leader* (December 10, 1898) that if Britain "did not make use of her opportunities in [expanding the empire], other countries would oust her" and that Britain was "the only country fit to pioneer the blessings of civilisation."

With the exasperation of those who found themselves divided over the war, the socialist and journalist Robert Blatchford wrote in his publication, the *Clarion* (October 1899): "I cannot go with those Socialists whose sympathies are with the enemy. My whole heart is with the British troops. . . . Until the war is over I am for the Government." On October 30, 1899, Beatrice Webb noted in her diary that Shaw and others among the Fabians were "almost in favour of the war, J. R[amsay] MacDonald and Sydney Olivier desperately against it, while Sidney [Webb] occupies a middle position, thinks that better management might have prevented it but that now that it has begun recrimination is useless and that we must face the fact that henceforth the Transvaal and the Orange Free State must be within the British Empire."

In late 1899, there was increasing pressure within the Fabian Society to take a stand against the war. In debates held in November and December, Shaw argued that the society should urge that, after the war was won, the mines in the Transvaal should be nationalized to provide suitable working conditions. If the government refused, it would be responsible for "having spent the nation's blood and treasure, and outraged humanity by a cruel war, to serve the most sordid interests under the cloak of a lofty and public-spirited Imperialism." The antiimperialist Fabians defeated such a suggestion by a vote of more than two to one. A general vote by mail was called for early in 1900 to decide whether the society should condemn the war, but Shaw and Webb, among others, continued to argue that the issue was "outside the special province of the Society," which could be damaged by such a declaration. Out of more than 800 Fabians eligible to vote, only about half did so: In a close vote of 259 to 217, Shaw, Webb, and Bland (the "Old Gang") defeated the motion that the society issue a formal statement on the war. As a result, Ramsay MacDonald, Walter Crane, Mrs. Emmeline Pankhurst, and fifteen other Fabians resigned. Like his colleagues, MacDonald believed that economic motives were impelling Britain to undertake foreign adventures.

Following this episode, Shaw undertook the editing of a pamphlet for the society titled *Fabianism and the Empire: A Manifesto* (1900). To achieve a consensus of opinion within the society, he shaped the opinions expressed in the pamphlet by making corrections offered by his colleagues on proofs sent out to the membership (only 134 responded with suggestions for revision). The manifesto takes no position on the war, nor is there a call for the dissolution of or withdrawal from any parts of the empire. With respect to "Imperial Policy," what was needed was a "definite constitutional policy to be pursued by the Empire towards its provinces":

> The real danger against which such a policy must be directed is not the danger of attack on the Empire from without, but of mismanagement and disruption from within. The British Empire, wisely governed, is invincible. The British Empire, handled as we handled Ireland and the American colonies, and as we may handle South Africa, if we are not careful, will fall to pieces without the firing of a foreign shot.

Acknowledging that the empire was multiracial and religious, the society pointed to two faulty imperial policies: One was democratic for provinces in which the white colonists were in a large majority; the other was a bureaucratic policy where the majority consisted of "coloured natives." Therefore, "the Empire cannot be governed either on Liberal or Conservative, democratic or aristocratic principles exclusively; and cannot be governed on Church of England or Nonconformist principles at all." In the "moral of it all," one senses the obvious stylistic hand of Shaw himself: ". . . what the British Empire wants most urgently in its government is not Conservatism, not Liberalism, not Imperialism, but brains and political science. Most of our Cabinet Ministers at present are like captains of penny steamers put in command of a modern battleship."

To be sure, the conclusion for the Fabians was that there was "only one way forward. That way is our way: the way of International Socialism." In supporting the empire, the Fabians believed that more flexible means were essential in order to govern such a diverse group of peoples and societies. The abandonment of the empire, the Fabians argued, was impracticable, even foolhardy. Ironically, they were in agreement with the imperialists that Britain's power and wealth were the potential agents of good in an imperfect world. Clearly, the divisions among the socialists on the fortunes of the empire were symptomatic of the deep fissures within Victorian society at large; as a result, the new century found Britain in a bitterly divided state over both the war and the empire.

WITH THE DEATH of the Queen on January 22, 1901,* the age named
after her finally ended. The lame Queen, final symbol of the decline of
Victorianism in the fin de siècle, was, said Wells, like "a great paper-
weight that for half a century sat upon men's minds, and when she was
removed their ideas began to blow all over the place haphazardly."
Though an attractive hyperbole, Wells's metaphor does not take into
account the many cultural and intellectual developments preceding the
Queen's demise that continued rather than began in the new century. For
most of her subjects, however, Victoria's passing was a glorious end to a
great period in British history. In his funeral oration in the House of
Lords, Lord Salisbury, the Queen's last prime minister, summed up the
significance of her reign and the importance of her achievements by
stressing that she had "bridged over that great interval which separates
old England from new England":

> Other nations may have had to pass through similar trials, but
> have seldom passed through them so peaceably, so easily, and
> with so much prosperity and success as we have. I think that
> future historians will look to the Queen's reign as the boundary
> which separates the two states of England—England which has
> changed so much—and recognise that we have undergone the
> change with constant increase of public prosperity, without any
> friction to endanger the peace or stability of our civil life and at
> the same time with a constant expansion of an Empire which
> every year grows more and more powerful.

In the House of Commons, Arthur Balfour expressed the "grief [that]
affects us not merely because we have lost a great personality, but because
we feel that the end of a great epoch has come upon us."

With Victoria gone and her son Edward VII on the throne, the Boer
War finally ended in May 1902. The overwhelming odds against the
Boers (the British eventually assembling half a million soldiers as opposed to some 50,000 of the enemy) had resulted in the occupation by
the British of the Boer capital, Pretoria, in June 1900. For two more
frustrating years, General Kitchener reduced guerrilla resistance by employing a burnt-earth policy. Wells later wrote that the "acute disillusion-
ments" arising from three years of conflict haunted the Edwardians, who

---

*Within a month of her death, some 3,000 elegies appeared in the local British press
and in the colonies, a selection of which was published in *The Passing of Victoria,* ed. J.
A. Hammerton (London, 1901).

suffered through "a decade of badly strained optimism. Our Empire was nearly beaten by a handful of farmers amidst the jeering contempt of the whole world—and we felt it acutely for several years." The sense of decline that had obsessed the Victorians in the fin de siècle was confirmed by some startling revelations concerning British youth during the Boer War. When a British Army general reported in the *Contemporary Review* (January 1902) that 60 percent of the recruits were physically unfit for military duties, widespread soul-searching began, accompanied by numerous government reports, concerning the substandard living conditions of the poor that had contributed to such a deplorable state of affairs.

Not only the indigent but also the privileged were contributing to the perception that Britain, a great nation that had presided over a glorious empire, was in the process of degeneration. In "The Islanders," which appeared in the *Times* (January 4, 1902), Kipling insisted on such a view in his brutal denunciation of British sloth and pleasure-seeking at the expense of those from the empire who were sacrificed in the Boer War:

> *Ye set your leisure before their toil and your lusts above their need.*
> *Because of your witless learning and your beasts of warren and chase,*
> *Ye grudged your sons to their service and your fields for their camping-*
> *place . . .*

Published in the final months of the war, when the British were already demoralized, the poem struck with wounding alliteration and rhyme into the very heart of complacency:

> *And ye vaunted your fathomless power, and ye flaunted your iron pride,*
> *Ere—ye fawned on the Younger Nations for the men who could shoot*
> *and ride!*
> *Then ye returned to your trinkets; then ye contented your souls*
> *With the flanneled fools at the wicket or the muddied oafs at the goals.*

The poem created an instant response from readers of the *Times,* which received letters for days, a number of them expressing indignation at Kipling's bruising references to cricket and football. Most of the readers, however, agreed with Kipling that relying on ill-prepared soldiers from the "Younger Nations" of the empire was a grievous error in conducting the war.

In "The Islanders," Kipling's focus on moral decline in British culture had also been a preoccupation among the Victorians, but with the revelations during and after the Boer War, the Edwardians now lamented the physical decline of young British men. In 1905, the appearance of an anonymous pamphlet (written by Elliott E. Mills) with the title *The De-*

cline and Fall of the British Empire recalled Gibbon's great work on the similar fate of the Roman Empire. The implied parallels between the two empires captured the imaginations of reviewers in the conservative papers and particularly of the inspector-general of cavalry Robert Baden-Powell, who had served in the Boer War and who was now planning a Boy Scout movement. In a speech, he urged the audience to demonstrate its patriotism by buying the pamphlet: "If you will carefully study it personally, each one of you, no matter what his line of life may be, will see what should be his share in saving his country from the possibility of disaster." In his *Scouting for Boys* (1908), he drew familiar parallels between Rome and Britain, and he quoted from a speech "by one of our best known democratic politicans": "Our great Empire is to-day to the rest of the world very much what the Roman Empire was two thousand years ago. But the Roman Empire, great as it was, fell. 'The same causes which brought about the fall of the great Roman Empire are working to-day in Great Britain.' "

Elsewhere in his handbook, Baden-Powell echoed the alarm following reports during the Boer War that most of the army recruits were rejected for military service because of their poor physical condition—one cause, said Baden-Powell, "which contributed to the downfall of the Roman Empire: "Recent reports on the deterioration of our race ought to act as a warning to be taken in time before it goes too far." Inspired by Baden-Powell, the Boy Scouts resolved, in its original motto: "Be prepared to defend your country." But prudence prevailed, for it was soon shortened to "Be prepared." The coming Great War would test their valor.

Epilogue

To those who regarded the 1890s as the "Decadent Nineties," (a misnomer, as we have seen), Oscar Wilde's death on November 30, 1900 seemed to have officially ended the nineteenth century. In *De Profundis*, he avowed: "I was a man who stood in symbolic relations to the art and culture of my age." As public symbol and secret cipher by which the age can be read, he converted to Roman Catholicism on his death bed while in a semi-comatose state, an admirer of the beauty and pageantry of its rituals. Modernist in his aesthetic criticism and attitudes though essentially traditional in his use of literary forms (with the exceptions of *Salome* and *The Importance of Being Earnest,* proto-Modernist triumphs of innovative artifice), Wilde sought to transform Victorian culture. A serious dandy who performed before a trivial audience, he remains the decade's tragic figure who sensed the underlying rot of civilization. If he found himself narcissistically entrapped in his own theatricality and in his self-destructive sexual impulses, he nevertheless helped to establish the 1890s as the decade of the unforgettable.

After the nineties ended, the Edwardian era provided fertile soil for developing Modernism: James Joyce, Virginia Woolf, D. H. Lawrence, and T. S. Eliot, all born in the 1880s, were destined to join such older Victorians as Conrad and Yeats within the pantheon of Modernism. As late Victorians, they carried the emotional and spiritual baggage of the perplexing fin de siècle with them into the more turbulent twentieth century, when cultural transformations, adumbrated earlier, resulted in literature and art that embodied private visions and developed enigmatic forms for a new age. Like Yeats, Shaw, Symons, Moore, and Wilde—some of the most eloquent critical voices of the 1890s—Conrad knew the consequences of rejecting cherished, guarded conventions. In a letter to his publisher in 1902, Conrad implied his immersion into the "destructive element" of the creative process, inspired by the thought that great avant-garde artists eventually achieve acceptance in an initially hostile culture: "I am *modern,* and I would rather recall Wagner the musician and Rodin the sculptor who both had to starve a little in their day—and Whistler the painter who made Ruskin the critic foam at the mouth with scorn and indignation. They too have arrived. They had to suffer for being 'new.' "

Such a Romantic mythology of the modern artist derived from the growth of the industrial state with its accompanying growth of the middle classes. As Frank Kermode has suggested, central to Modernism is the serious artist's isolation in the creation of private vision destined to be rejected by an uncomprehending public. Modernist assaults on conventional conceptions of art recall Symons's fin-de-siècle view: ". . . might it not, after all, be the finest epitaph for a self-respecting man of letters to be able to say, even after the writing of many books: I have kept my secret, I have not betrayed myself to the multitude?" A challenge more than a description, such attitudes undermined the Victorian belief in the agreed-upon artistic and moral standards of the artist and public. The artist's cultivation of his own alienation, a common theme of fin-de-siècle Aestheticism, Decadence, and Symbolism, prompted a continuing rejection of bourgeois taste and morality: The result was the Modernists' increasing preference for a more problematic art.

In the 1870s, Whistler's avant-garde "nocturnes" and, in the 1890s, Beardsley's startling illustrations for the *Yellow Book* produced violent reactions that left one without a penny and the other without a job. Despite their artistic innovations, neither artist had abandoned identifiable representations of nature, but both anticipated some forms of later Modernist art, notably Abstract Expressionism and Surrealism. In 1907, Picasso produced a major upheaval in the art world with his radical distortions of human forms in the epoch-making *Les Demoiselles d'Avignon,* which led to international Cubism and—Ortega y Gasset later pronounced—to a progressive "dehumanization of art" as recognizable subject matter gave way to perplexing visions of reality bearing little or no resemblance to common experience. The ultimate Modernist work designed for an intellectual elite, Joyce's *Finnegans Wake* (1939), implied indifference, even hostility, to the common reader.

By the time of King Edward VII's death in 1910, when Modernism had begun to achieve an identity, Virginia Woolf hailed its arrival in her droll remark that "on or about December 1910 human nature changed." She no doubt had in mind the acclaim accorded the first post-Impressionist exhibition, which opened at the Grafton Galleries on November 8, 1910. Organized by her friend, the critic Roger Fry, whose biography she would later write, the exhibition revealed to the British the paintings of such artists as Van Gogh, Cezanne, Gauguin, and Manet. In the second post-Impressionist exhibition (1912), Fry exhibited paintings by Picasso and Braque. In the preface to the exhibition catalogue, Fry wrote that the modern artist did not wish to imitate nature but to create new forms, a view expounded, as we have seen, by the Hobby Horsemen of the 1880s.

In the *Yellow Book* (July 1894), Hubert Crackanthorpe had also voiced such an aesthetic conviction, anticipating Roger Fry and Clive Bell's concept of "significant and expressive form," the obliteration of "subject matter" in the new abstract art of the post-Impressionists. Wrote Crackanthorpe: "Art is not invested with the futile function of perpetually striving after imitation or reproduction of Nature; she endeavours to produce, through the adaptation of a restricted number of natural facts, an harmonious and satisfactory whole." In the denunciation of realism, which the Aesthetes often regarded as the triumph of the unimaginative, George Moore had proclaimed in the early nineties: "Realism, that is to say the desire to compete with nature, to be nature, is the disease from which art has suffered most in the last twenty years."

The Modernists' characteristic turning away from nature in favor of a new and startling artifice had been prepared in the last decades of the nineteenth century by Aestheticism, Decadence, and Symbolism—attempts to negate the effects of scientific materialism and utilitarian imperatives on fin-de-siècle culture and to affirm the integrity of private vision, new artistic forms, and transcendent, spiritual realities. Unfortunately, satires of the Aesthetes and Decadents in *Punch* and in Gilbert and Sullivan's *Patience* ("A pallid and thin young man, / A haggard and lank young man, / A greenery-yallery, Grosvenor Gallery, / Foot in the grave young man") have obscured the crucial role that Aestheticism and Decadence played in the development of Modernism.

The technology and industrialism of the age—often condemned by the Aesthetes as a depressing achievement of bourgeois culture—nevertheless informed their verse and prose as urban imagery, a celebration of artifice's triumph over nature. In reaction to what many late Victorians regarded as science's view of the world—a "pitiless mechanism"—avant-garde artists and writers focused on aesthetic form, which improved on nature's lack of feeling and design. Virginia Woolf's pronouncement that human nature changed in 1910 expresses her awareness that the artist was empowered by the imagination to create new realities beyond the world of fact. The physicist John Tyndall had long before contended in "The Scientific Use of the Imagination" (1870) that the imagination was "the architect of physical theory. . . . Scientific men fight shy of the word because of its ultra-scientific connotations; but the fact is that without the exercise of this power, our knowledge of nature would be a mere tabulation of co-existences and sequences; . . . the concept of Force would vanish from our universe; causal relations would disappear. . . ." In 1874,

Frederic Harrison concluded that "our sciences are *verified* poems," and the mathematician Karl Pearson suggested in *The Grammar of Science* (1892), the "outside world is a *construct*" of our minds. As a recent critic has remarked: "Newton did not discover gravity, he created it." The "laws of nature," then, were creations of the human imagination—that extraordinary, mysterious instrument described by such Romantics as Wordsworth and Coleridge, later by T. S. Eliot, as the source of the artist's unique, unified vision of reality.

The radical view of the mind's enclosure had appeared, of course, in Pater, who spoke of "that thick wall of personality through which no real voice has ever pierced on its way to us," each mind "keeping as a solitary prisoner its own dream of a world." The sense of human isolation in an unknowable world had been previously posited by the German idealist philosophers, particularly Kant and Schopenhauer, who regarded ultimate reality (*noumenon,* the thing-in-itself) as transcendent. The influence of Kantian philosophy on Tyndall is apparent in his remark that our "states of consciousness are mere *symbols* of an outside entity which produces them and determines the order of their succession, but the real nature of which we can never know." In reaction to such philosophical views, various forms of empiricist psychology in the late nineteenth century proclaimed that the only evidence for that which existed outside of ourselves lay in our senses and that consciousness was the key to reality. In his *Principles of Psychology* (1890), William James advanced his radical empiricism, modifying eighteenth-century British empiricist philosophy, by advocating introspection for an understanding of the individual perceiver's "stream of consciousness." The self was dynamic, not static, and the act of perceiving dissolved the rigid distinction between subject and object.

Such theories implied that a consistent point of view was no longer a reliable method of constructing narratives in fiction. To capture the essence of subjective experience, Conrad in *Lord Jim* (1900) and Ford Madox Ford in *The Good Soldier* (1914) redesigned the novel. Stream of consciousness subsequently developed as a fictional technique in such later writers as Dorothy Richardson, James Joyce, and Virginia Woolf. In 1919, Woolf, employing Paterian metaphor and empiricist psychology to reject the "objectivity" of such writers as Arnold Bennett and John Galsworthy, envisioned the interior world of sense impressions as the proper domain for the artist: ". . . life is a luminous halo, a semi-transparent envelope surrounding us from the beginning of consciousness to the end." The extreme existential expression of such a view occurs in *Murphy* (1948), in which Samuel Beckett portrays human isolation as the symbol of spiritual alienation: "Murphy's mind pictured itself as a large hollow sphere, hermetically closed to the universe without."

Scientists acknowledge John Tyndall's contention that their "laws" of nature can only be expressed by the same human imagination that enables artists to create "unverified" works of art (lying, Wilde said, that reveals truth). Early Modernist thought in the late nineteenth century thus helped to inaugurate radical transformations of cultural attitudes towards both the arts and the sciences, transformations that have altered our very vision of self and reality.

Notes

Prologue

xi   "taken up to Heaven": Grant Richards, *Memories of a Misspent Youth, 1872–1896* (London, 1932), 112.

xi   "striving after better things": Frederic Harrison, "A Few Words about the Nineteenth Century," *The Choice of Books and Other Literary Pieces* (London, 1896), 425.

xii   "absorbed or emitted": John Marks, *Science and the Making of the Modern World* (London, 1983), 264.

xii   "at present constituted": William Thomson (Lord Kelvin), *Mathematical and Physical Papers* (Cambridge, Eng., 1882), 1: 514.

xiv   "our wretched hypocrisies": Letter to Georgiana Burne-Jones, dated May 13, 1885, in *The Collected Letters of William Morris*, ed. Norman Kelvin (Princeton, 1987), 2: 436.

xiv   "the end of the world": From the opening of Shaw's letter to the editor of *Liberty* (July 27, 1895), "A Degenerate's View of Nordau"; rpt., revised as *The Sanity of Art* (1908) in *Major Critical Essays*, intro. by Michael Holroyd (Middlesex, Eng., 1986), 319.

xv   "care/To name": Quotations on fin de siècle in Eugen Weber, *France: Fin de Siècle* (Cambridge, Mass., 1986), 9.

xv   "the coarse, the barbarous": Letter to Leo Marxe [c. 1894], in *More Letters of Oscar Wilde*, ed. Rupert Hart-Davis (New York, 1985), 123.

xvi   "purest painted ill": Quoted in Jerome Hamilton Buckley, *Tennyson: The Growth of a Poet* (Boston, 1965), 164.

xvi   "an integrated culture": Buckley, 165.

xvii   "young men": *The Autobiography of William Butler Yeats* (New York, 1965), 86.

xvii   "intellectual suffering": Yeats, *Autobiography*, 95.

xviii   "cities of Modernism": Malcolm Bradbury, "The Cities of Modernism," in *Modernism, 1890–1930*, eds. Malcolm Bradbury and James McFarlane (New York, 1976), 96–104.

xviii   "sweeping away the Victorian tradition": Evelyn Sharp, *Unfinished Adventure* (London, 1933), 56.

xviii "their purest energy": Walter Pater, "Conclusion," *The Renaissance* (1873; New York, 1959), 158.

xviii "no part in modern life": Max Beerbohm, "Be It Cosiness," *Pageant* (1896); rpt., title changed to "Diminuendo" in *The Works of Max Beerbohm* (London, 1896), 158.

xviii "compendium of the world": *The Notebooks of Henry James,* eds. F. O. Matthiessen and K. B. Murdock (New York, 1947), 28.

xviii "opens but at night": Richard Le Gallienne, *Robert Louis Stevenson: An Elegy, and Other Poems* (New York, 1895), 26.

xviii "miraculous April weather": Arthur Symons, "April Midnight," *Silhouettes* (1892); rpt. in *The Collected Works of Arthur Symons* (1924; New York, 1973), 1: 140.

1: Socialist Utopias and Anarchist Bombs

5 "banner of Socialism militant": G. Bernard Shaw, *Essays in Fabian Socialism* (London, 1932), 126.

5 "service of man": Quoted in Norman and Jeanne MacKenzie, *The Fabians* (New York, 1977), 124.

6 "the inhabitants of Great Britain": Beatrice Webb, *My Apprenticeship* (London, 1926), 154, 155.

7 "an East End slum": Beatrice Potter, "The Jews of London," *Charles Booth's London,* eds. Albert Fried and Richard M. Elman (New York, 1968), 138–39.

8 " 'unendowed' little socialist": Entry for May 24, 1895, *The Diary of Beatrice Webb,* eds. Norman and Jeanne MacKenzie (Cambridge, Mass., 1982), 2: 76.

8–9 "alas! both names": Entry for July 23, 1892, *The Diary of Beatrice Webb,* 1: 371.

9 "mission in life": Quoted in Michael Holroyd, *Bernard Shaw* (New York, 1988), 1: 130.

9 "acknowledged Great Man": *Shaw: An Autobiography, 1856–1898,* ed. Stanley Weintraub (New York, 1969), 155.

10 "the cash nexus": "Preface to *Major Barbara*" (1905), *Prefaces by Bernard Shaw* (London, 1934), 121.

11 "men into mere machines": "A Factory as It Might Be," *William Morris,* ed. G. D. H. Cole, Centenary Edition (New York, 1934), 646–54.

11 "in the prompter's box": *Shaw: An Autobiography, 1856–1898,* 122.

11 "theoretically or from me": Quoted in *The Webbs and Their Work,* ed. Margaret Cole (London, 1949), 628.

11–12 "extinction of the human race": Quoted in Holroyd, 1: 175.

12 "extreme in his utterances": MacKenzie and MacKenzie, 19.

12 "purser of a Dutch brig": MacKenzie and MacKenzie, 20.

12 "prisoners is quite another": Quoted in MacKenzie and MacKenzie, 109.

12 "classically educated men": Shaw, *Autobiography,* 131.

12 "working classes of this country": Quoted in Holroyd, 1: 189.

13 "as did Plato": H. G. Wells, *Experiment in Autobiography* (New York, 1934), 201.

13   "might otherwise lack": Quoted in MacKenzie and MacKenzie, 28.

14   "disgrace to the capital": Quoted in MacKenzie and MacKenzie, 80.

14   "tens of thousands": Shaw *Autobiography,* 150.

14   "turned tail and fled": Quoted in Holroyd, 1: 186.

14   "a thousand to one": G. Bernard Shaw, *Collected Letters, 1874–1897,* ed. Dan H. Laurence (New York, 1965), 177.

16   "audience of 20": Letter to Archibald Henderson, dated September 11, 1905, in Shaw, *Collected Letters, 1898–1910,* ed. Dan H. Laurence (London, 1972), 556–57.

16   "beyond pleasure": See Lionel Trilling, "Aggression and Utopia: A Note on William Morris's 'News from Nowhere,' " *Psychoanalytic Quarterly* 42 (1973): 214–25.

17–18   "The Soul of Man under Socialism": Robert Ross, Wilde's literary executor, told Shaw, after Wilde's death, how the essay had come to be written. See Shaw, *Autobiography,* 248. For a slightly different account, see *The Playwright and the Pirate: Bernard Shaw and Frank Harris, a Correspondence,* ed. Stanley Weintraub (University Park, Pa., 1982), 30–31.

18   "day of the dynamitards": See Barbara Arnett Melchiori, *Terrorism in the Late Victorian Novel* (London, 1985), 21–28.

19   "beard and lovable expression": Quoted in James W. Hulse, *Revolutionists in London* (Oxford, 1970), 53.

19   "finally to *nil"*: Pëtr Alekseevich Kropotkin, "The Coming Anarchy," *Nineteenth Century* 22 (August 1887): 152–54.

21   "failed as yet to attain": G. Bernard Shaw, "A Refutation of Anarchism," *Our Corner* (May 1891); rpt., rev. as *The Impossibilities of Anarchism,* Fabian Tract No. 45 (London, 1893), 4, 15.

21   "live our own lives": Quoted in Holroyd, 1: 173.

21   "an intense Individualist": Quoted in Holroyd, 1: 125.

22   "side of the police": Shaw, *Autobiography,* 139.

22   "contact with real life": Letter to William Archer, dated October 4, 1887, in Shaw, *Collected Letters, 1874–1897,* 176.

23   "on the same ground": Shaw, *Autobiography,* 268.

24–25   "resolved to try again": Shaw, *Autobiography,* 277.

25   "sexual and domestic morals": Shaw, *Autobiography,* 165.

25   "all poets and dramatists": Quoted in Holroyd, 1: 297.

26   "Shakespear or Euripides?": G. Bernard Shaw, *Sixteen Self Sketches* (London, 1949), 143.

26   "a state of damnation": Shaw, *Platform and Pulpit,* ed. Dan H. Laurence (New York, 1961), 44.

27   "smiled, smiled perpetually": *The Autobiography of William Butler Yeats* (New York, 1965), 187–88.

27   "doing original work": Entry for September 21, 1894, *The Diary of Beatrice Webb,* 2: 57.

27   "matter-of-fact side of marriage": Entry for September 16, 1896, *The Diary of Beatrice Webb,* 2: 100.

27   "she ever met": Letter to Ellen Terry, dated May 27, 1897, in Shaw, *Collected Letters,* 767–68.

28   "was much startled": Letter to Ellen Terry, dated August 5, 1897, in Shaw, *Collected Letters, 1874–1897,* 792.

28 "cowardly infamy": Shaw, *Prefaces,* 120.

29 "the unmoral purpose": Entry for November 29, 1905, *The Diary of Beatrice Webb,* 3:12–13.

30 "my dear Wells!": Letter to Wells, dated November 19, 1905, in *Henry James and H. G. Wells: A Record of Their Friendship,* eds. Leon Edel and Gordon Ray (Urbana, Ill., 1958), 80.

30 "party of paralysis": See H. G. Wells, "The Faults of the Fabian," in Samuel Hynes, *The Edwardian Turn of Mind* (Princeton, 1968), Appendix C.

30–31 "we don't know": Letter to Wells, dated March 24, 1906, in Shaw, *Collected Letters, 1898–1910,* 613–14.

2: The Damnation of Decadence

32 "a decadent indeed": Andrew Lang, "Decadence," *Critic* 37 (August 1900): 172. Arthur Symons's obituary had appeared in the *Fortnightly Review* (June 1900); rpt. in *Studies in Prose and Verse* (London, 1904).

32 "most horrible decadence": Quoted in Eugen Weber, *France: Fin de Siècle* (Cambridge, Mass., 1986), 14.

33 "Bible of the Decadence": Mario Praz, *The Romantic Agony,* trans. Angus Davidson (1933; London, 1970), 332.

35 "confound the bourgeois": Ellen Moers, *The Dandy* (London, 1960), 288.

36 "the degenerate capital": A. E. Carter, *The Idea of Decadence in French Literature, 1830–1920* (Toronto, 1958), 14–15.

36 "the Decadent Movement turns": Praz, 322.

37 "and remould society": Swinburne review of *Les Fleurs du mal* in the *Spectator* (September 6, 1862); rpt. in *Swinburne as Critic,* ed. Clyde K. Hyder (London, 1972), 28, 29, 32.

37 "admired him as a god": Edmund Gosse, *Portraits and Sketches* (London, 1912), 4.

38 "biting's no use": Quoted in Philip Henderson, *Swinburne: The Portrait of a Poet* (London, 1974), 131.

39 "as mangy as his own": *The Swinburne Letters,* ed. Cecil Y. Lang (New Haven, 1959), 2: 161–62.

39 "untidy lives: T. S. Eliot, *Selected Essays* (New York, 1950), 392.

39–40 "face of one's friend": Quotations from Walter Pater, "Conclusion" to *Studies in the History of the Renaissance* (1873), in *Walter Pater: Three Major Texts,* ed. William E. Buckler (New York, 1986), 217–20.

40–41 "secrets of the grave": Quotations from Pater, "Leonardo da Vinci," 142, 149–50.

41 "so-called 'aesthetic' school": Arthur Symons, "Walter Pater, 'Imaginary Portraits,' " *Time* (Aug 1887); portion rpt. in "Walter Pater," *Studies in Prose and Verse,* 64.

41 "moment it was written": *The Autobiography of William Butler Yeats* (New York, 1965), 87.

41 "broods over these pages": Symons, *Studies in Prose and Verse,* 65.

42 "a dead tongue": Linda Dowling, *Language and Decadence in the Victorian Fin de Siècle* (Princeton, 1986), 5.

43 "organization which preceded ours": T. H. Huxley, *Social Diseases and Worse Remedies* (London, 1891), 53.

43 "pre-eminence in infamy": Charles Merivale, *A History of the Romans under the Empire* (London, 1858), 6: 160.

43 "amazed" by it: Letter to Robert H. Sherard [postmarked May 17, 1883], *The Letters of Oscar Wilde,* ed. Rupert Hart-Davis (New York, 1962), 148.

44 "a final epigram": George Ross Ridge, *The Hero in French Decadent Literature* (Athens, Georgia, 1961), 11.

44 "temple in my soul": George Moore, *Confessions of a Young Man,* ed. Susan Dick (1888; Montreal, 1972), 165.

44 "copies as waste paper": Joseph Hone, *The Life of George Moore* (New York, 1936), 88.

44 "stand aloof and disdainfully": Letter to Nancy Cunard [1922], in Cunard, *G. M.: Memories of George Moore* (London, 1956), 137.

45 "device for multiplying inferiority": See Arthur Symons, "In Praise of Gypsies," *Journal of the Gypsy Lore Society* (April 1908); rpt. in *Bookman's Journal* 4 (July 22, 1921): 205–06.

45 "sincerity and seriousness": Richard Ellmann, "The Uses of Decadence," *a long the riverrun: Selected Essays* (London, 1988), 13–14.

46 "Still—!": Letter to George Moore, dated March 4 [1888], in *Letters of Walter Pater,* ed. Lawrence Evans (Oxford, 1970), 81.

46 "education in public": Quoted in Frank Harris, *Oscar Wilde* (1916; New York, 1960), 295.

47 "our inartistic age": Letter to E. W. Pratt [postmarked April 15, 1892], in Wilde, *Letters,* 313.

47 "magic-picture mania": See Kerry Powell, "Tom, Dick, and Dorian Gray: Magic-Picture Mania in Late Victorian Fiction," *Philological Quarterly* 62 (1983): 147–70.

47 "consult your mirror": Masao Miyoshi, *The Divided Self: A Perspective on the Literature of the Victorians* (New York, 1969), 311.

48 "destroyed by one": Robert Viscusi, *Max Beerbohm, or The Dandy Dante: Rereading with Mirrors* (Baltimore, 1986), 83.

48 "in other ages, perhaps": Letter to Ralph Payne, [postmarked February 12, 1894], in Wilde, *Letters,* 352.

48 artistic "error" in the book: Wilde, *Letters,* 259.

49 "in love with him": Letter to Arthur Galton, dated February 18, 1890, quoted in Wilde, *Letters,* 254–55n.4.

49 "sweet sins": The poem, translated by Ian Fletcher, appears in *Aesthetes and Decadents of the 1890's,* ed. Karl Beckson (Chicago, 1981), 116–17.

49–50 "The Cultured Faun": First appeared anonymously in the *Anti-Jacobin* (March 14, 1891); rpt. in *Aesthetes and Decadents of the 1890's,* 110–13.

51 "quite another thing": "The Censure and *Salomé, Pall Mall Budget* (June 30, 1892); rpt. in *Oscar Wilde: Interviews and Recollections,* ed. E. H. Mikhail (New York, 1979), 1: 186–89.

51 "boil a tea-kettle": Quoted in Percival W. H. Almy, "New Views of Mr. Oscar Wilde," *Theatre* (March 1894); rpt. in *Oscar Wilde: Interviews and Recollections,* 1: 230.

51 "farce and vulgar melodrama": Wilde, *Letters,* 316.

51 "peace for the moment": Wilde, *Letters,* 335.

53 "beautiful and quite irrelevant": *The Letters of Aubrey Beardsley,* eds. Henry Maas, J. L. Duncan, and W. G. Good (Rutherford, NJ, 1970), 58.

55 dinner party in London: An unpublished memoir by Frank Liebich men-

tions the presence of Wilde and Gray (No. 1418 in *Oscar Wilde and His Literary Circle,* comp. John Charles Finzi [Univerity of California Press, 1957], William Andrews Clark Memorial Library, UCLA).

58   "Boom in Yellow": Richard Le Gallienne, *Prose Fancies: Second Series* (London, 1896), 79–89; rpt. in *Aesthetes and Decadents of the 1890s,* 128–33.

59   "independence of the word": Quoted in R. K. R. Thornton, *The Decadent Dilemma* (London, 1983), 39.

59–60   "often insane thinking": Richard Le Gallienne, review of Churton Collins's *Illustrations of Tennyson,* in *Retrospective Reviews: A Literary Log* (London, 1896), 1: 24–25.

60–62   "The Decadent Movement in Literature": First published in *Harper's New Monthly Magazine* (November 1893); rpt. with omissions (the sections on Pater and Henley removed) in Arthur Symons's *Dramatis Personae* (1923) and in its original version in *Aesthetes and Decadents of the 1890's,* 134–51.

62   "the Henley Regatta": Quoted in *Men and Memories: Recollections of William Rothenstein, 1872–1900* (New York, 1931), 1: 285.

63   "a false gospel": Letter to Ada Leverson, dated September 22, 1894, in Wilde, *Letters,* 373.

63   "The book is not": Wilde, *Letters,* 373.

63   "gallant protest against Art": Jerome Hamilton Buckley, *William Ernest Henley: A Study in the "Counter-Decadence" of the 'Nineties* (Princeton, 1945), 148.

64   "to submerge civilization": Eugen Weber, "Blemishes in the Breed?," *Times Literary Supplement* (London) March 30–April 5, 1990: 335 (a review of Daniel Pick's *Faces of Degeneration*).

64   "most improbable parents": Joseph Anthony Mazzeo, *The Design of Life* (New York, 1967), 128.

65   "dark side of progress": See *Degeneration: The Dark Side of Progress,* eds. J. Edward Chamberlin and Sander L. Gilman (New York, 1985).

67   "others are afraid of": Quoted in Vincent O'Sullivan, *Aspects of Wilde* (New York, 1936), 102.

67   "with the diabolical monocle": *The Memoirs of Arthur Symons: Life and Art in the 1890s,* ed. Karl Beckson (University Park, Pa., 1977), 183.

67   "flow of the ages": Arthur Symons, "Preface," *London Nights* 2d ed. (1897); rpt. in *Aesthetes and Decadents of the 1890's,* 164–66.

69   "fifteen years out of date": Linda Dowling, "Introduction," *Aestheticism and Decadence: A Selective Annotated Bibliography* (New York, 1977), x.

70   "Sons of Fame": Robert Service, *Ballads of a Bohemian* (New York, 1921), 84–85.

3: Tragic Rhymers and Mythic Celts

71   "cliffs, or going mad": William York Tindall, *Forces in Modern British Literature: 1885–1956* (New York, 1956), 9–10.

71   "men in their triumph": Yeats, "Modern Poetry: A Broadcast," *Essays and Introductions* (New York, 1961), 493.

72   "one of them still alive": Yeats's lecture reported in *Path* 1 (1910): 105.

72   "than you am typical": Letter to Ernest Rhys, dated November 17 [1910?], in *Letters from Limbo,* ed. Ernest Rhys (London, 1936) 159.

73   "this dreadful London": Letter to Katharine Tynan, dated February 12 [1888], in *The Collected Letters of W. B. Yeats,* eds. John Kelly and Eric Domville (Oxford, 1986), 1: 50.

73   "characterize their tribe": Letter to Katharine Tynan, dated May 18, 1887, in Yeats, *Collected Letters,* 1: 15.

73   "young litterary men": Letter to Katharine Tynan, dated June 25, 1887, in Yeats, *Collected Letters,* 1: 22.

73   "but very earnest": Letter to Katharine Tynan, dated May 31 [1887], in Yeats, *Collected Letters,* 1: 17.

73   "nor even an umbrella": Ernest Rhys, *Everyman Remembers* (London, 1931), 21.

73   "much socialistic conversation": Letter to Katharine Tynan, dated July 1, 1887, in Yeats, *Collected Letters,* 1: 23.

73   "cities and countries abroad": Rhys, *Everyman Remembers,* 161.

74   "it is my work": Letter to Katharine Tynan, dated June 25, 1887, in Yeats, *Collected Letters,* 1: 23.

74   "altogather alien": Letter to Katharine Tynan [July 11, 1887], in Yeats, *Collected Letters,* 1: 26.

74   "my kind of poetry": Quoted in W. B. Yeats, *Memoirs,* ed. Denis Donoghue (New York, 1972), 21.

74   "an influence, a glory": Victor Plarr, *Ernest Dowson, 1888–1897* (London, 1914), 68. Plarr lived in the house at one time.

75   "in each other's triumph": *The Autobiography of William Butler Yeats* (New York, 1965) 111.

75   "the pure work": Yeats, *Autobiography,* 112.

75   "turn up later": Letter to Katharine Tynan, dated [c. 18] May [1890], in Yeats, *Collected Letters,* 1: 217.

76   "came once but never joined": Yeats, *Autobiography,* 111.

76   "literature without nationality": Yeats, *Letters to the New Island,* eds. George Bornstein and Hugh Witemeyer, vol. 7 of the *Collected Works of W. B. Yeats,* (New York, 1989), 59.

76   found his "theme": Yeats, *Essays and Introductions* (New York, 1961), 510.

77   "a Celtic renaissance": Edgar Jepson, *Memories of a Victorian* (London, 1933) 237.

77   "of the club for criticism": Rhys, *Everyman Remembers,* 105.

77   "nothing but impressions": Yeats, *Autobiography,* 112.

77   "came into their heads": Yeats, *Autobiography,* 112.

77–78   "climbed about upon it": Plarr, 64.

78   "all their lives": John Davidson, *Sentences and Paragraphs* (London, 1893), 119.

78   "in *Star* and *Chronicle*": Quoted in J. Benjamin Townsend, *John Davidson: Poet of Armageddon* (New Haven, 1961), 151.

78   "preserve of the Bodley Head": Arthur Waugh, *One Man's Road* (London, 1931), 242–43.

78–79   "the faery world": W. P. Ryan, *The Irish Literary Revival* (London, 1894), 29.

79   "many times over": Yeats, *Autobiography,* 133.

79–80   the fall of Charles Stewart Parnell: See F. S. L. Lyons, "The O'Shea Affair," Chapter 2 in *The Fall of Parnell, 1890–91* (Toronto, 1960).

80   "some noble stag": Yeats, *Autobiography,* 211.

81   "meeting of the 'Irish Literary' ": Rhys, *Letters,* 103.

81   "to make me Irish": Letter to T. W. Rolleston, dated April 29, 1892, in Raymond Roseliep, "Some Letters of Lionel Johnson," Ph.D. diss. (Univ. of Notre Dame, 1954), 122.

81–82   "cause of Irish letters": Letter to T. W. Rolleston [May 10, 1892], in Yeats, *Collected Letters,* 1: 294–95.

82   "almost at once": Letter to Katherine Tynan, [late June 1891], in Yeats, *Collected Letters,* 1: 253.

82   "very uncivil indeed": Letter to John Butler Yeats, dated July 21 [1906], in *The Letters of W. B. Yeats,* ed. Allan Wade (London, 1954) 474.

83   "scum does no good": Letter from Lionel Johnson to George Greene, dated September 6, 1893 (G. C. R. Greene Collection). This collection, once owned by George A. Greene's son, is now apparently lost. I am indebted to Dr. Desmond Flower for permitting me to see his transcriptions.

85   "The dark of Death": *The Poetical Works of Ernest Christopher Dowson,* ed. Desmond Flower (London, 1934), 133.

85   "dealing with London": Arthur Symons, "Mr. Henley's Poetry," *Fortnightly Review* (August 1892); rpt., revised as "Modernity in Verse," *Studies in Two Literatures* (1897).

85   "condition of human life": Raymond Williams, *The Country and the City* (New York, 1973), 236.

87   "has still full tables": See "The Rhymers' Club" in Yeats, *Letters to the New Island,* 57–60.

87   "poetry of insight and knowledge": Letter to Katharine Tynan, dated March 14 [1888], in Yeats, *Collected Letters,* 1: 54–55.

87   "literature of energy and youth": *Uncollected Prose by W. B. Yeats: First Reviews and Articles,* vol. 1, ed. John P. Frayne (New York, 1970), 248–49. *United Ireland* had printed "Decadents," which is here corrected to "Decadence."

88   "London with Rimbaud": *Men and Memories: Recollections of William Rothenstein, 1872–1900* (New York, 1931), 127.

88   "words of the street!": Arthur Symons, *Colour Studies in Paris* (London, 1918), 200.

88   "supporter in this country": Arthur Waugh, "London Letter," *Critic* [New York] (December 9, 1893): 383.

88   "greatly love and admire": See Verlaine, "My Visit to London," *Savoy,* No. 2 (April 1896): 119–35.

89   "of the elect": Quoted in R.K.R. Thornton, *The Decadent Dilemma* (London, 1983) 141. First published in the *Dublin Review* (October 1907).

89   "Johnson & Le Galliene": Yeats, *Collected Letters,* 1: 391.

89   "melancholy lyric poetry": Richard Ellmann, *Yeats: The Man and the Masks* (New York, 1958) 141.

90   "shift of rhythm": Eliot, "Preface" to *John Davidson: A Selection of His Poems* (London, 1961) xi.

90   "poem of its decade": Bloom, *Yeats* (New York, 1970) 46.

91   "some of my old authors": Unpublished letter in Mrs. G. Dugdale's collection, London.

91–92   "Celtic anvil henceforward": Ryan, *Irish Literary Revival,* 119.

92   "of movements or of societies": Symons, *Studies in Prose and Verse,* 263.

92   "rhythm of heroic failure": Ian Fletcher, "Rhythm and Pattern in 'Autobiographies,' " in *An Honoured Guest: New Essays on W. B. Yeats,* eds. Denis Donoghue and J. R. Mulryne (London, 1965), 169.

93   "but pursue antithesis?": Yeats, *Autobiography,* 202.

93   "rope in a storm": Yeats, *Autobiography,* 201.

93   "in small, dry things": Quoted in Glenn Hughes, *Imagism and the Imagists* (London, 1960), 16–17.

94   "difference only of precision": René Taupin, *The Influence of French Symbolism on Modern American Poetry* (1929; New York, 1985), 29.

94   "priestess intoning a litany": Rhys, *Everyman Remembers,* 252, 255.

94   "for an aural paradigm": See Ronald Schuchard, " 'As Regarding Rhythm': Yeats and the Imagists," *Yeats: An Annual of Critical and Textual Studies* 2 (1984): 209–26.

94   "fell dead": Charles Norman, *Ezra Pound* (New York, 1960), 115.

4: The Quest for a Poet Laureate

95   "actual man's life": Robert Bernard Martin, *Tennyson: The Unquiet Heart* (Oxford, 1980), 580.

96   "all decent expression": Letter to Edward Burne-Jones, dated October 15, 1892, in *The Swinburne Letters,* ed. Cecil Y. Lang (New Haven, 1962), 6: 36.

96   "death loves best": Algernon Charles Swinburne, "Threnody: Alfred, Lord Tennyson, October 6, 1892," *Nineteenth Century* (January 1893); rpt. in *Complete Works,* eds. Edmund Gosse and Thomas James Wise (London, 1925), 6: 153–54.

96   "the pure work": *The Autobiography of William Butler Yeats* (New York, 1965), 112.

96–97   "unwholesome and obscene": *Letters of Ernest Dowson,* eds. Desmond Flower and Henry Maas (Rutherford, NJ, 1967), 243.

97   "prince of song": *Poetical Works of Ernest Christopher Dowson,* ed. Desmond Flower (London, 1934), 169.

97   "entry into immortality": *The Romantic '90s* (London, 1951), 67, 69.

97   "soul hath passed": *Robert Louis Stevenson: An Elegy, and Other Poems* (London, 1895), 33.

99   "monger of platitudes": Letter to the editor of the *Bookman,* is reprinted in *The Collected Letters of W. B. Yeats,* eds. John Kelly and Eric Domville (Oxford, 1986) 1: 324–26.

100–1   "no vote unweighed": Quoted in George Lafourcade, *Swinburne: A Literary Biography* (London, 1932), 287.

101   "in my dominions": Quoted in Edmund Gosse, *The Life of Algernon Charles Swinburne* (London, 1917), 277.

101   "look of the affair": Quoted in Alan Bell, "Gladstone Looks for a Poet Laureate," *Times Literary Supplement* (London) July 21, 1972: 847. Hereafter, quotations from letters exchanged between Gladstone, Lord Action, Sir Henry Ponsonby, and James Bryce are taken from Bell.

102   "immediate intention" to do so: *The Parliamentary Debates,* 4th ser. (London, 1893), 8: 255.

103   "making the appointment": *Parliamentary Debates,* 4th ser. (London, 1893), 15: 210.

103   "and his partner": *Parliamentary Debates,* 4th ser. (London, 1894), 27: 178–79.

103–4   "unknown poets of the day": Edward Valentine, "William Watson," *Conservative Review* 1 (May 1899): 348.

104   "crown of my head!": Owen Seaman, *The Battle of the Bays* (London, 1896), 4.

105   "as it would be just": Coventry Patmore, "The Proposed Compliment to Journalism," *Saturday Review* (October 26, 1895); rpt. in *Courage in Politics and Other Essays, 1885–1896* (1921; Freeport, NY, 1968), 200–2.

106   "was certainly welcomed": Lady Gwendolen Cecil, *The Life of Robert Marquis of Salisbury* (London, 1932), 4: 55.

106   "small beer as a poet": "Robert Graves on John Masefield," *Times Literary Supplement* (London) June 22, 1967: 568.

107   "came into the room": Quoted in Ann Thwaite, *Edmund Gosse: A Literary Landscape* (Chicago, 1984), 329.

107   "day of the year": Letter to Austin Dobson, dated January 4, 1896, in Alban Dobson, *Austin Dobson, Some Notes* (London, 1928), 155.

107   "head of English literature": Letter from Wilfred Blunt to Sydney Cockerell, dated July 9, 1913, in *Friends of a Lifetime: Letters to Sydney Carlyle Cockerell,* ed. Viola Meynell (London, 1940), 183.

107   "England's appointed bards": Norton B. Crowell, *Alfred Austin: Victorian* (London, 1955), 20–21.

109   "sing it with vehemence": Quoted in *The Letters of Queen Victoria,* 3d ser., ed. George Earle Buckle (New York, 1932), 3: 24.

109   "ought to be cashiered": Quoted in A. G. Gardiner, *The Life of Sir William Harcourt* (London, 1923), 2: 385.

109   "its death-blow": *The Letters of Francis Thompson,* ed. John Evangelist Walsh (New York, 1969), 44.

109   "grin and bear it": William Archer, "Quousque Tandem?" *Critic* 37 (August 1900): 145.

109   "his fellow countryman": Alfred Austin, "The Poet Laureate Defends Himself," *Critic* 37 (November 1900): 404.

109   "Poet Laureate and Mrs. Austin": Crowell, *Alfred Austin,* 27n. 56.

5: Prostitutes on the Promenade

110   "a few years back": *Charles Booth's London,* eds. Albert Fried and Richard M. Elman (New York, 1968), 124–33.

110   figure was obviously unreliable: See E. M. Sigsworth and T. J. Wyke, "A Study of Victorian Prostitution and Veneral Disease," in *Suffer and Be Still: Women in the Victorian Age,* ed. Martha Vicinus (Bloomington, Ind., 1972), 78–80.

110   "habitually by prostitution": William Booth, *In Darkest England and the Way Out* (London, 1890), 56.

111   " 'upper crust' ": Charles D. Stuart and A. J. Park, *The Variety Stage* (London, 1895), 191.

111 "only—ladies present": Max Beerbohm, "Music Halls of My Youth," *Mainly on the Air* (New York, 1947), 43.

112 "hunger for the commonplace": W. B. Yeats, "The Rhymers' Club," *Letters to the New Island,* eds. George Bornstein and Hugh Witemeyer, vol. 7 of *The Collected Works of W. B. Yeats* (New York, 1989), 59.

113 "their new art": Max Beerbohm, "A Blight on the Music Halls," *More* (London, 1899), 122.

113 "scholar in music halls": Yeats, "The Rhymers' Club," *Letters to the New Island,* 58.

113 "secured the Laureateship": Beerbohm, "A Blight on the Music Halls," 121.

113 "sort of symbolic corruption": Arthur Symons, "At the Alhambra: Impressions and Sensations," *Savoy,* No. 5 (September 1896): 77.

114–15 "over his artistic life": Wendy Baron, *Sickert* (London, 1973), 22.

115 "secret underground passageway": Kellow Chesney, *The Anti-Society: An Account of the Victorian Underworld* (Boston, 1970), 311.

116 "attractive features": Tracy C. Davis, "Actresses and Prostitutes in Victorian London," *Theatre Research International* 13 (Autumn 1988): 228.

116 "only rather illegal": Quoted in Margaret Steen, *A Pride of Terrys* (London, 1962), 204.

116 "temple of the Holy Ghost": Stewart Headlam, *The Function of the Stage: A Lecture* (London, 1889), 22.

116 "man conscientiously pursued": Quoted in T. H. Gibbons, "The Reverend Stewart Headlam and the Emblematic Dancer: 1877–1894," in the *British Journal of Aesthetics* 5 (October 1965): 333.

116–17 "possible for the people": Quoted in Gibbons, 334.

117 "and outside criticism": Letter to Stewart Headlam, dated December 26, 1922, in Shaw, *Collected Letters, 1911–1925,* ed. Dan H. Laurence (London, 1985), 802.

117 "jokes of the Church and Stage Guild": Quoted in Karl Beckson, *Arthur Symons: A Life* (Oxford, 1987), 78.

117 trying to dissociate themselves: See F. G. Bettany, *Stewart Headlam: A Biography* (London, 1926), 100–3.

117–18 "discomfort and even disgust": Letter to Katherine Willard, dated December 21, 1891, in *Arthur Symons: Selected Letters, 1880–1935,* eds. Karl Beckson and John M. Munro (London, 1989), 91.

118 "unsatisfied erotic needs": Peter Gay, *The Bourgeois Experience: Victoria to Freud* (Oxford, 1986), 2: 259.

119 "impure thought and passion": Quoted in "Pudibundery," *Pall Mall Gazette* (October 11, 1894): 1.

119 "at conspicuous points": John Stokes, *In the Nineties* (Chicago, 1989), 60.

120 "of London, of England": Mrs. Ormiston Chant, *Why We Attacked the Empire* (London, [1895]), 16.

120 "voluntary and gradual": Judith R. Walkowitz, *Prostitution and Victorian Society: Women, Class, and the State* (Cambridge, Eng., 1980), 80.

120 "admission to the Empire": Chant, 4.

120 "if need be turned out": Chant, 4. Italics are Chant's.

121 "only be regulated": Arthur Symons letter to the *Pall Mall Gazette:* Rpt. in *Arthur Symons: Selected Letters,* 106–8.

121–22   "should not believe her": G. Bernard Shaw, letter to the *Pall Mall Gazette:* Rpt. in G. Bernard Shaw, *Agitations: Letters to the Press, 1875–1950,* eds. Dan H. Laurence and James Rambeau (New York, 1985), 30–34.

123   "thus directed to me": Chant, 19.

123   "on streets is supplied": Chant, 16.

123   "be reduced thereby?": Quoted in Chant, 18.

124   "Public Amusements": Chant, 11.

124   "woman on the County Council": Chant, 5.

125   "a cheerful countenance": "The License of the Empire," *Pall Mall Gazette* (October 27, 1894): 7.

126   "charges and insinuations": Winston Churchill, *My Life: A Roving Commission* (London, 1930), 65.

127   "what it was": Sir Compton Mackenzie, *Figure of Eight* (London, 1936), 8.

128   "responsible for this!": Quoted in John Cowen, "Music Halls and Morals," *Contemporary Review* 90 (November 1916): 614.

128   "offered in music halls": Cowen, 612.

128   "purposes of prostitution": Quoted in Cowen, 612.

6: The New Woman

130   "duty, not love": George Egerton, "Virgin Soul," *Discords* (London, 1895), 155.

130   "anarchism and decay": Linda Dowling, "The Decadent and the New Woman in the 1890s," *Nineteenth-Century Fiction* 33 (1979): 440–41.

130   "do nothing for them": Gail Cunningham, *The New Woman and the Victorian Novel* (London, 1978), 11.

130   "All else confusion": Tennyson, *The Princess,* part v, ll. 437–41 (1847).

130–31   "taught you this?": *The Princess,* part vii, ll. 280–91.

131   "the necessities of Nature": T. H. Huxley, "Emancipation—Black and White," *Collected Essays* (London, 1905), 3: 66.

132   "named after her": Elizabeth K. Helsinger, Robin L. Sheets, and William Veeder, "Queen Victoria and 'The Shadow Side,'" *The Woman Question: Defining Voices, 1837–1883* (New York, 1983), 1: 63.

132   "willed it so": Letter dated February 15, 1858, in *Dearest Child: Letters between Queen Victoria and the Princess Royal, 1858–1861,* ed. Roger Fulford (New York, 1964), 44.

132   "give the weaker sex": Quoted in Sir Theodore Martin, *Queen Victoria as I Knew Her* (Edinburgh, 1908), 69–70.

132   "of course, *intensely*": Letter to King Leopold of Belgium, dated February 3, 1852, in *Letters of Queen Victoria,* eds. Arthur C. Benson and Viscount Esher (London, 1904), 2: 362.

133   "a suspicious world": Rita McWilliams-Tullberg, "Women and Degrees at Cambridge University, 1862–1897," in *A Widening Sphere: Changing Roles of Victorian Woman,* ed. Martha Vicinus (Bloomington, Ind., 1977), 117.

133–34   "with a sort of passion": Quoted in Lee Holcombe, "Victorian Wives and Property: Reform of the Married Woman's Property Law, 1857–1882," in *A Widening Sphere,* 27.

136   "arise from my sex": Beatrice Webb, *My Apprenticeship* (London, 1926), 341–43.

136   "forced into public work": Entry dated August 29, 1887, *The Diary of*

Beatrice Webb, eds. Norman and Jeanne MacKenzie (Cambridge, Mass., 1982), 1: 214.

136 "apparition in their midst": Entry dated March 25, 1889, *The Diary of Beatrice Webb,* 1: 280.

137 "to be no children": Phyllis Grosskurth, *Havelock Ellis: A Biography* (New York, 1980), 153.

137 "one man with one woman": Letter to Mary Roberts, [January–March 1889], in *Olive Schreiner Letters,* ed. Richard Rive (Oxford, 1988) 1: 145.

137–38 *"ourselves* within ourselves": Letter to Mary Roberts [January–March 1889], in *Olive Schreiner Letters,* 1: 145.

138 "would convince no one": Ruth First and Ann Scott, *Olive Schreiner* (New York, 1980), 288.

138 "three hundred years' time": Letter to Karl Pearson [May 12, 1886], *Olive Schreiner Letters,* 1: 78.

138–39 "the new revelation": Mrs. Havelock Ellis, "Olive Schreiner and Her Relation to the Woman Movement," *Book News Monthly* 33 (February 1915): 266.

139 "reason to fear": Ernest Rhys, *Everyman Remembers* (London, 1931), 47–48.

139 "instrument of that attack": Elliot L. Gilbert, " 'Tumult of Images': Wilde, Beardsley, and *Salome,*" *Victorian Studies* 26 (Winter 1983): 133–34.

139 "an oriental Hedda Gabler": William Archer, "Mr. Wilde's New Play," *Black and White* (May 11, 1893); rpt. in *Oscar Wilde: The Critical Heritage,* ed. Karl Beckson (London, 1970), 142.

141 "acts of self-mortification": Jacob Korg, *George Gissing: A Critical Biography* (London, 1965), 153.

141 "always be the ideal state": "A Chat with Mme Sarah Grand," *Woman,* "Literary Supplement," May 2, 1894: i–ii.

142 "sex has yet produced": Eliza Lynn Linton, "The Wild Women as Social Insurgents," *Nineteenth Century* 30 (October 1891): 604.

142 "lies before us now": Mary Haweis, *Words to Women: Addresses and Essays,* ed. Rev. H. R. Haweis (London, 1900), 70.

143 *"the ought to be":* Katherine Bradley [Michael Field], *Works and Days,* eds. T. Sturge Moore and D. C. Sturge Moore (London, 1933), 8.

144 "by men for men": G. Bernard Shaw, "An Aside," preface to Lillah McCarthy, *Myself and My Friends* (1933); rpt. in Shaw, *An Autobiography, 1856–1898,* ed. Stanley Weintraub (New York, 1969), 267.

144 "absurd and ridiculous things": Richard Le Gallienne, "The Arbitrary Classification of Sex," *Prose Fancies: Second Series* (London, 1896), 139.

145 "exercise of their minds": Letter to Miss Price, November 2, 1888, in *The Collected Letters of George Meredith,* ed. C. L. Cline (Oxford, 1970) 2: 936.

145 "New Woman novels": Cunningham, 59.

146 "its logical conclusion": H. G. Wells, *Experiment in Autobiography* (London, 1934), 2: 549–50.

147 *A Woman with Ideas:* Michael Millgate, *Thomas Hardy: His Career as a Novelist* (New York, 1971), 312.

147 "many years ago": Letter to Millicent Fawcett, dated November 30, 1906, in *The Collected Letters of Thomas Hardy,* eds. Richard Little Purdy and Michael Millgate (Oxford, 1982), 3: 238.

147 "on every side": Margaret Oliphant, "The Anti-Marriage League," *Black-*

wood's Magazine (January 1896); rpt. in *Thomas Hardy: The Critical Heritage,* ed. R. G. Cox (London, 1970), 256–62.

148   "and the Time-Spirit": Richard Le Gallienne, "The Revolt of the Daughters," *Sphinx* 2 (January 20, 1895): 1.

149   "the heads of saints": Ian Fletcher, *Aubrey Beardsley* (Boston, 1987), 168.

151   "society restricts her": Nina Auerbach, *Woman and the Demon: The Life of a Victorian Myth* (Cambridge, Mass., 1982), 1.

152   "deliberately preposterous": Bruce R. McElderry, Jr., "Max Beerbohm: Essayist, Caricaturist, Novelist," *The Surprise of Excellence: Modern Essays on Max Beerbohm,* ed. J. G. Riewald (Hamden, Conn., 1975), 224.

154   before the First World War: A. E. Metcalfe, *Woman's Effort* (Oxford, 1917), 306–17.

155   "Women's Social and Political Union?": Sandra Stanley Holton, "In Sorrowful Wrath: Suffrage, Militancy, and the Romantic Feminism of Emmeline Pankhurst," in *British Feminism in the Twentieth Century,* ed. Harold L. Smith (Amherst, Mass., 1990), 7.

155   "representative parliamentary government": Holton, 11.

155   fifty-nine arrests were made: E. Sylvia Pankhurst, *The Suffragette* (London, 1911), 138–42.

156   "deeper into the mire": Arthur Symons, *The Knave of Hearts, 1894–1908* (London, 1913), 50; rpt. in *The Collected Works of Arthur Symons* (1924; New York, 1973), 3: 56.

156   *The Superwomen:* The typescript of this unproduced, unpublished play is in the Ransom Humanities Research Center, University of Texas, Austin.

156   "lectures and manifestoes": Sidney Webb, *Fabian Essays* (1920; London, 1962), 279.

156   "to make pronouncements": Margaret Cole, *The Story of Fabian Socialism* (London, 1961), 128.

156   "between men and women": Quoted in Constance Rover, *Women's Suffrage and Party Politics in Britain, 1866–1914* (London, 1967), 159.

157   "community as a whole": *Letters of Sidney and Beatrice Webb,* ed. Norman MacKenzie (Cambridge, Eng., 1978), 2: 241–42.

157   "by this question": Shaw's lecture reprinted as "Why All Women Are Peculiarly Fitted to Be Good Voters," *Fabian Socialist: Bernard Shaw and Woman,* ed. Rodelle Weintraub (University Park, Pa., 1977), 248–54.

158   "to look into it": H. G. Wells, Letter to the editor, *Spectator,* December 4, 1909: 945.

159   "the old values": Cunningham, 155.

159   early twentieth century: Cunningham, 3.

7: The New Drama

161–62   "especially in the provinces": Letter to Charles Charrington, dated January 28, 1890, in G. Bernard Shaw, *Collected Letters, 1874–1897,* ed. Dan H. Laurence (New York, 1965), 239.

162   "it is first rate": Shaw, *Collected Letters,* 239.

162   "Still after the Doll's House": Reprinted in G. Bernard Shaw, *Short Stories, Scraps, and Shavings* (1932).

162   of the successful Théâtre Libre: Part one of Moore's article was reprinted

as "Théâtre Libre" and part three as "On the Necessity of an English Théâtre Libre" in *Impressions and Opinions* (London, 1891).

164   "take its place?": Henry Arthur, Jones, "The Future of the English Drama," *New Review* (August 1893); rpt. in *The Renascence of the English Drama* (London, 1895), 130–1.

164   "than in his plays": James Woodfield, *English Theatre in Transition, 1881–1914* (London, 1984), 26.

164   "unwholesomely realistic nature": See J. T. Grein and C. W. Jarvis, "A British 'Théâtre Libre' " in Woodfield, Appendix A.

165   "history of our stage": Quoted in Samuel M. Waxman, *Antoine and the Théâtre Libre* (Cambridge, Mass., 1926) 216.

165   "Ghosts and Gibberings": Rpt. in *William Archer on Ibsen: Major Essays, 1889–1919,* ed. Thomas Postlewait (Westport, Conn., 1984), 23–27.

166   "some hope in it": Quoted in *Shaw and Ibsen: Bernard Shaw's "The Quintessence of Ibsenism" and Related Writings,* ed. J. L. Wisenthal (Toronto, 1979), 81.

166   "distresses me": Quoted in Michael Holroyd, *Bernard Shaw* (New York, 1988), 1: 197–98.

167   an open letter to Shaw: Archer's letter is reprinted in *William Archer on Ibsen,* 29–34.

167   "prophet" of the New Drama: Thomas Postlewait, *Prophet of the New Drama: William Archer and the Ibsen Campaign* (Westport, Conn., 1986), xiv.

168   "and all his works": Shaw, *Collected Letters,* 288.

169   "systematic body of doctrine": Quoted in Norman MacKenzie and Jeanne MacKenzie, *The Fabians* (New York, 1977), 170.

169   "Old Man has been gratified": Letter to Edmund Gosse, dated March 29, 1898, quoted in Joseph O. Baylen, "Edmund Gosse, William Archer, and Ibsen in Late Victorian Britain," *Tennessee Studies in Literature* 20 (1975): 133.

171   "irrepressibly witty personality": William Archer, *World* (February 20, 1895); rpt. in *Oscar Wilde: The Critical Heritage,* ed. Karl Beckson (New York, 1970), 189–91.

171   "bustled into it": G. Bernard Shaw, *Saturday Review* (February 23, 1895); rpt. in Shaw, *Our Theatres of the Nineties* (London, 1932), 1: 41–44; and in *Oscar Wilde: The Critical Heritage,* 194–95.

172   "long been awaiting": Harold Fromm, *Bernard Shaw and the Theater in the Nineties* (Lawrence, Kansas, 1967), 97.

173   Pinero (thirty), Jones (thirty-two), and Grundy (thirty-six): See J. P. Wearing, "The London West End Theatres in the 1890s," *Educational Theatre Journal* 29 (October 1977): 328.

173   "becoming wretchedly respectable": G. Bernard Shaw, "The Independent Theatre Repents," *Saturday Review* (March 23, 1895); rpt. in *Our Theatres,* 1: 66.

174   "lost wills and mysterious murders": William Archer, *About the Theatre* (London, 1886), 19.

174   "disease, ugliness and vice": Quoted in John Russell Taylor, *The Rise and Fall of the Well-Made Play* (New York, 1967), 40.

174   "its parochial aims": Jones, *The Renascence of the English Drama,* ix.

174   " 'healthy' or pathological": A. B. Walkley, *Playhouse Impressions* (London, 1892), 114.

174   "termination of my story": Letter to Clement Scott, dated May 7, 1889, in *The Collected Letters of Sir Arthur Wing Pinero,* ed. J. P. Wearing (Minneapolis, 1974), 106.

176   "theatre to overflowing": H. Barton-Baker, *History of the London Stage and Its Famous Players, 1596–1903* (London, 1904), 470.

176   "on his real level": G. Bernard Shaw, "A New Play and a New Old One," *Saturday Review* (February 23, 1895); rpt. in *Our Theatres,* 1: 45, 47.

176   "culture and intellectual acuteness": G. Bernard Shaw, "Mr. Pinero's New Play," *Saturday Review* (March 16, 1895); rpt. in *Our Theatres,* 1: 60.

176   "Meredith, or Sarah Grand": Shaw, *Our Theatres,* 1: 45.

177   "away from the consequences": Shaw, *Our Theatres,* 1: 61–63.

177   "Michael and his Lost Angel": Shaw, *Saturday Review* (January 18, 1896); rpt. in *Our Theatres,* 2: 19.

178   "of European dramatic art": G. Bernard Shaw, "John Gabriel Borkman," *Saturday Review* (May 8, 1897); rpt. in *Our Theatres,* 3: 122.

179   "influence of the Censor": Incorporated Stage Society, *Ten Years, 1899 to 1909* (London, 1909), viii–ix.

179   "first Symbolist farce": Arthur Symons, "A Symbolist Farce," *Saturday Review* (December 19, 1896); rpt. in *The Memoirs of Arthur Symons: Life and Art in the 1890s,* ed. Karl Beckson (University Park, Pa., 1977), 200.

179   "classical gravity of speech": W. B. Yeats, *Essays and Introductions* (New York, 1961), 199, 201.

180   "new sort of Stage Society": Quoted in Ronald Schuchard, "W. B. Yeats and the London Theatre Societies, 1901–1904," *Review of English Studies* 29 (November 1978): 433.

180   "on the Committee": Quoted in Schuchard, 433.

180   "at any rate harmless": Quoted in Schuchard, 434.

181   "tumult that is drama": W. B. Yeats, "The Freedom of the Drama," *United Irishman* (November 1, 1902); rpt. in *Uncollected Prose by W. B. Yeats,* eds. John P. Frayne and Colton Johnson (New York, 1975), 2: 298.

181   "the same enemies": Quoted in Katharine Worth, "Ibsen and the Irish Theatre," *Theatre Research International* 15 (Spring 1990): 24.

181   "played in London": W. B. Yeats, "The Freedom of the Drama," *Uncollected Prose,* 2: 297.

182   "almost miraculous renascence": William Archer, *The Old Drama and the New* (New York, 1929) 25.

183   "police if necessary": Quoted in Stanley Weintraub, "The Royal Court and the New Drama," *Modern British Dramatists, 1900–1945,* part 2, ed. Weintraub (Detroit, 1982), 300.

183   "entered upon his greatness": Maurice Valency, *The Cart and the Trumpet: The Plays of George Bernard Shaw* (New York, 1973), 200.

183   "the same central idea": Entry dated January 16, 1903, *The Diary of Beatrice Webb,* eds. Norman MacKenzie and Jeanne MacKenzie (Cambridge, Mass., 1983), 2: 267.

183   "autobiographical and apologetic": Valency, *The Cart and the Trumpet,* 213.

185   "indistinguishable from life": Max Beerbohm, " 'Justice,' " *Saturday Review* (March 5, 1910); rpt. in Beerbohm, *Around Theatres* (London, 1953), 565–68.

8: Love in Earnest: The Importance of Being Uranian

187 "homosexual pickup, 'bunbury' ": Linda Gertner Zatlin, *Aubrey Beardsley and Victorian Sexual Politics* (Oxford, 1990), 151.

187 "he was writing it": Auden, "An Improbable Life" (a review of *The Letters of Oscar Wilde,* ed. Rupert Hart-Davis), in the *New Yorker* (March 9, 1963); rpt. in *Oscar Wilde: A Collection of Critical Essays,* ed. Richard Ellmann (Englewood Cliffs, NJ, 1969), 136.

188 "a boy called Ernest": Letter to Henry Graham Dakyns, dated July 2, 1892, in *The Letters of John Addington Symonds,* eds. Herbert M. Schueller and Robert L. Peters (Detroit, 1969) 3: 704.

189 "of strange beauty": Letter to Ada Leverson [early December 1894], in *The Letters of Oscar Wilde,* ed. Rupert Hart-Davis (New York, 1962) 379.

190 "a little obscure": Letter to Ada Leverson [early December 1894], in Wilde, *Letters,* 379.

191 Criminal Law Amendment Act: See F. B. Smith, "Labouchere's Amendment to the Criminal Amendment Bill," *Historical Studies* 17 (October 1976): 165–73.

192 " 'between the Acts' ": Jeffrey Weeks, "Inverts, Perverts, and Mary-Annes: Male Prostitution and the Regulation of Homosexuality in England in the Nineteenth and Early Twentieth Centuries," *Journal of Homosexuality* 6 (Fall/Winter 1980–81): 118.

192 "unnatural tastes in private": Quoted in Weeks, 119.

193 "abnormal propensities": Frank Harris, *My Life and Loves,* ed. John F. Gallagher (New York, 1963), 336.

193 "point by prostitution": G. Bernard Shaw, *Collected Letters, 1874–1897,* ed. Dan H. Laurence (New York, 1965), 230–32.

193 "the public morals": *Scots Observer* (July 5, 1890); rpt. in *Oscar Wilde: The Critical Heritage,* ed. Karl Beckson (London, 1970), 74–75.

194 the *Scots Observer* letters: See Wilde, *Letters,* 265–72.

194 "one's own class": Jeffrey Weeks, *Sex, Politics, and Society: The Regulation of Sexuality since 1800* (London, 1981), 113.

194 "half the excitement": Letter to Lord Alfred Douglas [January and March, 1897], in Wilde, *Letters,* 492. This prison letter has frequently been published separately as *De Profundis.*

194 "loved by him": E. M. Forster, *The Life to Come and Other Stories* (Harmondsworth, Eng., 1975), 16.

194 "pure Carpenter" and "pure Whitman": Robert K. Martin, "Edward Carpenter and the Double Structure of *Maurice,* " in *Literary Visions of Homosexuality,* ed. Stuart Kellogg (New York, 1983), 44.

195 "unlike other men": Phyllis Grosskurth, *The Woeful Victorian: A Biography of John Addington Symonds* (New York, 1964), 279.

195 "disgust and loathing": For a detailed account of Symonds's experiences at Harrow, see *The Memoirs of John Addington Symonds,* ed. Phyllis Grosskurth (New York, 1984).

196 "public school system": Robert Graves, *Goodbye to All That* (1929; New York, 1957), 19.

196 "its hidden strength": George Grote, *Plato, and Other Companions of Socrates* (London, 1865), 3: 460.

197   "the transposition himself": Benjamin Jowett, *The Dialogues of Plato*, vol. III (1875; Oxford, 1953), 120.

197   merely metaphorical: Grosskurth, *The Woeful Victorian*, 268.

197   "conventional morality": Quoted in A. L. Rowse, *Homosexuals in History: A Study of Ambivalence in Society, Literature, and the Arts* (New York, 1977), 149.

197   "immoral, pagan": *The Notebooks of Henry James*, eds. F. O. Matthiessen and Kenneth B. Murdock (New York, 1947), 71.

198   "too-indiscreet—H.J.": Quoted in Grosskurth, *The Woeful Victorian*, 270.

198   "I have never seen": Letter to William James, dated February 15 [1885], in *Henry James Letters*, ed. Leon Edel (Cambridge, Mass., 1980), 3: 71.

198   "normally constituted individuals": John Addington Symonds, *A Problem in Modern Ethics* (London, 1896), 85.

198   "discreet about it": Quoted in Grosskurth, *The Woeful Victorian*, 272.

198   "on moral problems": Letter to Horatio Brown, dated July 22 [1890], in Symonds, *Letters*, 3: 477.

200   "The New Chivalry": Rpt. in *Sexual Heretics: Male Homosexuality in English Literature from 1850 to 1900*, ed. Brian Reade (New York, 1970), 313–19.

200   " 'sort of spiritual myopia' ": Miriam J. Benkovitz, *Frederick Rolfe: Baron Corvo: A Biography* (New York, 1977), 35.

201   "guilt-free pederasty": See Brian Taylor, "Motives for Guilt-Free Pederasty: Some Literary Considerations," *Sociological Review* 24 (1976): 97–114.

202   "externals of monastic life": See David Hilliard, "UnEnglish and Unmanly: Anglo-Catholicism and Homosexuality," *Victorian Studies* 25 (Winter 1982): 181–210.

202   "a turtle dove!": Quoted in Thomas Wright, *The Life of Walter Pater* (London, 1907), 2: 22.

202   "at E. Geldart naked": Norman H. MacKenzie, *The Early Poetic Manuscripts and Note-books of Gerard Manley Hopkins* (New York, 1989), 195, 174.

202   "did not care to develop": MacKenzie, 26.

202–3 "I will not": Letter to Robert Bridges, dated October 18, 1882, in *Gerard Manley Hopkins: Selected Letters*, ed. Catherine Phillips (Oxford, 1990), 170–71.

203   "of delicate appearance": *The Poems of Digby Mackworth Dolben*, ed. Robert Bridges (London, 1911), viii–ix.

203   "all thine own": "Homo Factus Est," in *The Poems of Digby Mackworth Dolben*, 2.

203   conversion as "perversion": Paddy Kitchen, *Gerard Manley Hopkins* (London, 1978), 95, 78.

203   "friendships between males": MacKenzie, 26.

203   "beauty is dangerous": Letter dated October 22, 1879, in *The Letters of Gerard Manley Hopkins to Robert Bridges*, ed. Claude Colleer Abbott (London, 1935), 95.

203   "At the Wedding March": *The Poems of Gerard Manley Hopkins*, 4th edition, eds. W. H. Gardner and N. H. MacKenzie (London, 1967), 86.

204   "The Bugler's First Communion": *Poems of Gerard Manley Hopkins*, 82.

204   *"the individuals concerned?":* Letter to Walt Whitman, dated August 3, 1890, in Symonds, *Letters*, 3: 482. (Symonds's emphasis)

204–5   "& seem damnable": Walt Whitman, *The Correspondence,* ed. Edwin Havi-
land Miller (New York, 1969), 5: 72–73.

205   "flattered, by women": Fraser Harrison, *The Dark Angel: Aspects of Victorian Sexuality* (New York, 1977), 129.

205   "detriment of the race": Quoted in Jeffrey Weeks, *Coming Out: Homosexual Politics in Britain, from the Nineteenth Century to the Present* (London, 1977), 21.

206   "decreased with years": Havelock Ellis, *My Life* (London, 1940), 295.

206   "survey of the matter": Quoted in Phyllis Grosskurth, *Havelock Ellis: A Biography* (New York, 1980), 175.

207   "will do much good": Quoted in Grosskurth, *Havelock Ellis,* 177–78.

207   "plea for greater tolerance": Grosskurth, *Havelock Ellis,* 186.

207   "cannot be admitted": Quoted in Grosskurth, *Havelock Ellis,* 189.

208   "chocolate-chewing girl": "Philebus" (John Leslie Barford), *Young Things* (Edinburgh, 1921), 8.

209   "you are right": Letter to George Ives, postmarked October 22, 1894, in Wilde, *Letters,* 375.

210   "on to victory": See John Stokes, "Wilde at Bay: The Diaries of George Ives," *English Literature in Transition* 26 (1983): 175–86.

210   E4, The Albany: *The Definitive Four-Act Version of "The Importance of Being Earnest",* ed. Ruth Berggren (New York, 1987) 72.

210   "can possibly be": Quoted in *The Importance of Being Earnest,* ed. Russell Jackson, (London, 1980), 117.

212   "loves you more": A. E. Housman, *Last Poems* (New York, 1923), 47.

212   "than anybody else": Laurence Housman, *My Brother, A. E. Housman* (New York, 1938), 61.

212   On a visit to Wilde: The exchange between Ross and Wilde is described in a letter to Seymour Adelman, dated June 21, 1928, in *The Letters of A. E. Housman,* ed. Henry Maas (Cambridge, Mass., 1971), 267.

212   "thing called happiness": Letter to Laurence Housman, dated August 9 [1897], in *More Letters of Oscar Wilde,* ed. Rupert Hart-Davis (New York, 1985), 152.

9: Trials and Tribulations

213   "have I been tried": *The Letters of Oscar Wilde,* ed. Rupert Hart-Davis (New York, 1962), 509–10 (the prison letter later titled *De Profundis*).

213   "disciple whom he loved": Wilde, *Letters,* 478.

214   "herbs make me whole": Wilde, *Letters,* 510.

214   "dominate my life": Letter to Robert Ross [November 1896], in Wilde, *Letters,* 413–14.

215   "little man you are": Quotations in Brian Roberts, *The Mad Bad Line: The Family of Lord Alfred Douglas* (London, 1981), 187.

215   "like a monstrous ape": Wilde, *Letters,* 383.

215–16   "existence in an epigram": Wilde, *Letters,* 466.

216   "number is 60": Letter to Edmund Gosse [May 5, 1895], in *Transatlantic Dialogue: Selected American Correspondence of Edmund Gosse,* eds. Paul F. Matthiesen and Michael Millgate (Austin, Texas, 1965), 231.

216   "UNDER HIS ARM": Quoted in J. Lewis May, *John Lane and the Nineties* (London, 1936), 80.

217   "Watson and Meynell": Katherine L. Mix, *A Study in Yellow: The Yellow Book and Its Contributors* (Lawrence, Kansas, 1960), 144.

217   "so (foolishly) came": See Karl Beckson, "Ella D'Arcy, Aubrey Beardsley, and the Crisis at 'The Yellow Book': A New Letter," *Notes and Queries* 26 (August 1979): 331–33.

217–18   "The Second Coming of Arthur": First appeared in the *World* (May 8, 1895); rpt. in *Aesthetes and Decadents of the 1890's,* ed. Karl Beckson (Chicago, 1981), 316–17.

219–20   "in a manner": Letter to Edmund Gosse, dated [April 8] 1895, in *Henry James Letters,* ed. Leon Edel (Cambridge, Mass., 1984), 4: 9–10.

220   "traducer of idealism": Letter to Lionel Muirhead [April 1895], in *The Selected Letters of Robert Bridges,* ed. Donald E. Stanford (Newark, Delaware, 1983), 1: 288.

220   "has been used before": Letter to Ada Leverson [April–May 1895], *The Letters of Aubrey Beardsley,* eds. Henry Maas, J. L. Duncan, and W. G. Good (Rutherford, NJ, 1970), 82.

221   "I didn't forget them": Letter to Herbert Horne, dated April 29, 1895, in *Arthur Symons: Selected Letters, 1880–1935,* eds. Karl Beckson and John M. Munro (Iowa City, 1989), 110.

221   "the pillory for it": Quoted in H. Montgomery Hyde, *The Trials of Oscar Wilde* (1962; New York, 1973), 201.

221   "presence and musical voice": Letter postmarked May 3, 1895, in *Max Beerbohm's Letters to Reggie Turner,* ed. Rupert Hart-Davis (Philadelphia, 1965), 102.

222   "noble than other forms": Wilde, *Letters,* 705.

222   "do something really fine": Quoted in Charles Archer, *William Archer: Life, Work, and Friendships* (New Haven, 1931), 215–16.

222   "men o' letters!": Letter to Edmund Gosse [May 5, 1895], in *Transatlantic Dialogue,* 231.

223   "Oscar Wilde, I believe": Quoted in Richard Ellmann, *Oscar Wilde* (New York, 1988), 467.

223   "a wounded stag": Quoted in Robert H. Sherard, *The Life of Oscar Wilde* (New York, 1906), 358.

223   "die in the streets": Quoted in Sherard, 358.

223   "let him go": Quoted in Hyde, 224.

223   "large sum of money": Letter to Edward Dowden, May 19 [1895], in *The Collected Letters of W. B. Yeats,* eds. John Kelly and Eric Domville (Oxford, 1986), 1: 466.

223   "is not for me: Wilde, *Letters,* 398.

223   "half of his renown": *The Autobiography of William Butler Yeats* (New York, 1965), 192.

223   "danced upon the pavement": Yeats, *Autobiography,* 193.

225   "to his astonishment": George Gissing, *London and the Life of Literature in Late Victorian England: The Diary of George Gissing,* ed. Pierre Coustillas (Lewisburg, Pa., 1978), 375.

225   "a definite stand": Havelock Ellis, *Sexual Inversion* (1897; New York, 1936), 352.

225   "modern homosexual consciousness": Jeffrey Weeks, *Coming Out: Homosex-*

ual Politics in Britain, from the Nineteenth Century to the Present (London, 1977), 98.

225 "sorrows and disgraces": Quoted in Laurence Housman, *My Brother, A. E. Housman: Personal Recollections* (New York, 1938), 104. See J. M. Nosworthy, "A. E. Housman and the Woolwich Cadet," *Notes and Queries* 17 (September 1970), 351–53.

226–27 "the colour of his hair": Quoted in Laurence Housman, 226.

227 "a master of language": G. Bernard Shaw, *Our Theatres in the Nineties* (London, 1932), 2: 217.

228 "any part in appealing": Quoted in Ellmann, 493.

228 "the great poem": Wilde, *Letters,* 656.

229 "revolting New York paper": Letter to Ada Leverson, dated November 16, 1897, in Wilde, *Letters,* 674.

229 "and my hopes": Letter to More Adey [November 28, 1897], in Wilde, *Letters,* 687.

229 "pamphlet on prison-reform": Letter to Leonard Smithers [February 18, 1898], Wilde, *Letters,* 704.

229 "officials that need educating": Wilde, *Letters,* 721.

230 "always the compositors!": Quoted in Phyllis Grosskurth, *Havelock Ellis: A Biography* (New York, 1980), 180.

230 "the 'Psychology' type": John Sweeney, *At Scotland Yard* (London, 1905), 184.

230 "with which I am acquainted": Letter to Henry Seymour [August 1898], in G. Bernard Shaw, *Collected Letters, 1898–1910,* ed. Dan H. Laurence (London, 1972), 57.

231 "imagination and courage": Quoted in French in Wilde, *Letters,* 727 n.1.

232 "regimental *coups de théâtre*": Shaw's review was reprinted in *Our Theatres,* 1: 282–88.

233 "champion in this country": Ernest Alfred Vizetelly, *With Zola in England* (Leipzig, 1899), 252.

233 "totally indefensible": Quoted in Ann Thwaite, *Edmund Gosse: A Literary Landscape, 1849–1928* (Chicago, 1984), 387.

234 "corrects the impression": Letter to William James, dated April 2, 1899, in *Henry James Letters,* 4: 101.

234 "greedy, ambitious and sensual": Letter to A. J. Marriott, dated May 1, 1899, in Shaw, *Letters,* 88.

234 "to go to France again": Letter to Edmund Gosse, dated September 30 [1899], quoted in Karl Beckson, *Henry Harland: His Life and Work* (London, 1978), 113.

234 "because of him": Quoted in H. Montgomery Hyde, *The Love That Dared Not Speak Its Name* (Boston, 1970), 31.

10: Defying the Commercial Periodicals

236 "eminence of popular esteem": Reginald Pound, *Mirror of the Century: The Strand Magazine, 1891–1950* (New York, 1966), 7.

238 "from beginning to end": Quoted in E. P. Thompson, *William Morris: Romantic to Revolutionary* (1955; New York, 1977), 625–26.

241 "I admire Horne's audacity": Letter to Samuel Smith [March 1891], in *The Letters of Ernest Dowson,* eds. Desmond Flower and Henry Maas (Rutherford, NJ, 1967), 190.

241 "bury it without tears": Letter to John Image, dated October 19, 1894, in *Selwyn Image Letters,* ed. A. H. Mackmurdo (1932; New York, 1977), 86.

241 "coterie world . . . of *The Savoy*": Julie F. Codell, "The Century Guild Hobby Horse, 1884–1894," *Victorian Periodicals Review* 16 (1983): 51.

242 "strange art review": Letter to Arthur Moore [October 9, 1890], in Dowson, *Letters,* 169.

242 "organize the decadence": William York Tindall, *Forces in Modern British Literature, 1885–1956* (New York, 1956), 24.

243 "perhaps a little risqué": Letter to Robert Ross [ca. January 3, 1894], in *The Letters of Aubrey Beardsley,* eds. Henry Maas, J. L. Duncan, and W. G. Good (Rutherford, NJ, 1970), 61.

243 "an English review": Letter to Paul Verlaine, dated February 12, 1894, in *Arthur Symons: Selected Letters, 1880–1935,* eds. Karl Beckson and John M. Munro (Iowa City, 1989), 105.

245 "apologise or pay damages": Quoted in Karl Beckson, *Henry Harland: His Life and Work* (London, 1978), 71.

245 "himself in Vol. II": Quoted in Beckson, *Henry Harland,* 71.

245 "enjoyed the excitement immensely": Letter to Henry James, dated April 30 [1894], in Beardsley, *Letters,* 68.

245–46 "the worshipful Harland": Letter to William James, dated May 28, 1894, *Henry James Letters,* ed. Leon Edel (Cambridge, Mass., 1980), 3: 482.

246 "a vulgar production": Quoted in John M. Richards, *The Life of John Oliver Hobbes* (London, 1911), 86.

246 "glare of hell": Michael Field, "Days and Years," entry for April 17, 1894, partly unpublished diary in the British Library.

246 "I am so glad": Letter to Lord Alfred Douglas [ca. April 16, 1894], in *The Letters of Oscar Wilde,* ed. Rupert Hart-Davis (New York, 1962), 354.

248 "letterpress and its illustrations": *The Memoirs of Arthur Symons: Life and Art in the 1890s,* ed. Karl Beckson (University Park, Pa., 1977), 170.

249 "by the scandalised contributors": Letter to Charles Charrington, November 28, 1895, in G. Bernard Shaw, *Collected Letters, 1874–1897,* ed. Dan H. Laurence (London, 1965), 572.

249 "speculators in pornography": Shaw quotations in Stanley Weintraub, *Aubrey Beardsley: Imp of the Perverse* (University Park, Pa., 1976), 156.

251 "will be largely disappointed": See Wendell V. Harris, "Innocent Decadence: The Poetry of the *Savoy,*" *PMLA* 77 (1962): 629–36.

252 "audience of agnostics": Quoted in *The Autobiography of William Butler Yeats* (New York, 1965), 216.

252 "attack on the *cant Britannique*": Ian Fletcher, "Decadence and the Little Magazines," *Decadence and the 1890s,* ed. Ian Fletcher (London, 1979), 199.

253 "allegory of Decadence itself": Jerome H. Buckley, *The Victorian Temper: A Study in Literary Culture* (1951; New York, 1964), 236.

254 "illustrate" the Symbolist Movement: Richard Ellmann, "Back Number," *New York Review of Books* (April 28, 1966): 20–21 (a review of *The Savoy: Nineties Experiment,* ed. Stanley Weintraub).

254   "must generate another": Fletcher, "Decadence and the Little Magazines," 200.

11: **Whistler, the Fantastic Butterfly**

256   "however fantastically": Arthur Symons, "Whistler," *Weekly Critical Review* (July 30, 1903); rpt. in *The Memoirs of Arthur Symons: Life and Art in the
1890s,* ed. Karl Beckson (University Park, Pa., 1977), 211.

257   *"social and political virtues":* Lectures on Art in *The Works of John Ruskin,* eds.
E. T. Cook and Alexander Wedderburn (London, 1904), 20: 39.

257   "affinity in chemistry": "Preface," *Modern Painters,* III, in *The Works of John
Ruskin,* 5: 5.

257   "the meanest results": Quoted in Jerome H. Buckley, *William Ernest Henley: A Study in the "Counter-Decadence" of the 'Nineties* (Princeton, 1945),
115.

258   "nobody will buy": Quoted in G. M. Trevelyan, *English Social History,* 2d
ed. (London, 1946), 525.

258   "the world's Metropolis": Mr. Podsnap's description in Dickens's *Our Mutual Friend* (1864–65).

258   "that which did not": "Preface," *Victorian Artists and the City,* eds. Ira
Bruce Nadel and F. S. Schwartzback (New York, 1980), xiv.

258   "his fellow practitioners": Nadel and Schwartzback, xiv.

259   *"towards the condition of music":* Walter Pater, "The School of Giorgione,"
Studies in the History of the Renaissance (1873); rpt in *Walter Pater: Three
Major Texts,* ed. William E. Buckler (New York, 1986), 156.

259   "identity of the portrait": Reprinted in J. A. M. Whistler, *The Gentle Art of
Making Enemies,* 2d ed. (1892; New York, 1967), 127–28.

261   strove for "pure arrangement": Roy McMullen, *Victorian Outsider: A Biography of J. A. M. Whistler* (New York, 1973), 216.

262   "her son and her master": Whistler, "Ten O'Clock," in *The Gentle Art,*
144.

263   "is to be misunderstood": Letter to Whistler, [ca. February 23, 1885], in
The Letters of Oscar Wilde, ed. Rupert Hart-Davis (New York, 1962), 171.
The final seven words in the passage are a quotation from Emerson's essay
"Self-Reliance."

264   "butterfly, fly away!": Quoted in Stanley Weintraub, *Whistler: A Biography*
(New York, 1974), 332.

264   "opinions . . . of others!": Reprinted in Whistler, 164.

264   "loveliness of such effects": "The Decay of Lying" in *Oscar Wilde,* ed.
Isobel Murray (Oxford, 1989), 232–33.

266   "man who built it": Chesterton, "A Defense of Detective Stories," *The
Defendant* (London, 1901), 119–20.

266   "all artistic achievements": See Arthur Symons, "Mr. Henley's Poetry,"
Fortnightly Review (August 1892); rpt., revised as "Modernity in Verse" in
The Collected Works of Arthur Symons (1924; New York, 1973), 8: 46.

266   "particular ethical connotation": Buckley, 115.

267   "ages of sixteen and twenty": T. S. Eliot, "Preface," *John Davidson: A
Selection of His Poems,* ed. Maurice Lindsay (London, 1961), xi.

268–69 "Fool!": Whistler, 45.

269 "his English colleagues": Denys Sutton, *Nocturne: The Art of James McNeill Whistler* (Philadelphia, 1964), 46.

271 "superior persons like us": Quoted in McMullen, 252–53.

271 "the end of the century": McMullen, 253.

12: Perfect and Imperfect Wagnernites

272 "what one says": *Oscar Wilde,* ed. Isobel Murray (Oxford, 1989), 81.

272 "philosophic and social significance": G. Bernard Shaw, "Preliminary Encouragements," *The Perfect Wagnerite* (1898); rpt. in Shaw, *Major Critical Essays,* intro. by Michael Holroyd (Middlesex, Eng., 1986), 193.

272 "his own soul": *Oscar Wilde,* 148.

272 "during the past century": William Blissett, "Wagnerian Fiction in English," *Criticism* 5 (1963): 239.

273 "overthrowing Victorianism": Ann Dzamba Sessa, *Richard Wagner and the English* (Rutherford, NJ, 1979), 87.

273 "Wagnerites and Anti-Wagnerites": G. Bernard Shaw, *London Music in 1888–1890* (London, 1937), 29–30.

273 "greatest of modern composers": "Cathedral Reforms," *Hornet* (April 11, 1877); rpt. in *Shaw's Music,* ed. Dan H. Laurence (London, 1981), 1: 111.

273 "fools' festival": Quoted in Gordon Craig, *The Germans* (New York, 1982), 198.

273–74 "to forget their folly": "Dr Francis Hueffer," *Star* (January 23, 1889); rpt. in Shaw, *London Music,* 55–56.

274 "concentration of attention": "Bassetto at Bayreuth," *Star* (August 1, 1889); rpt. in Shaw, *London Music,* 183.

274 "in his compositions": "Die Meistersinger," *Star* (August 6, 1889); rpt. in *Shaw's Music,* 1: 728.

274 "all its branches": "Wagner in Bayreuth," *English Illustrated Magazine* (October 1889); rpt. in *Shaw's Music,* 1: 791, 795.

275–76 "sickly, disorderly one": Quoted in Bettina L. Knapp, "Baudelaire and Wagner's Archetypal Operas," *Nineteenth-Century French Studies* 17 (Fall–Winter, 1988–89): 66–67.

276 "declaration of the English Wagnerites": Sessa, 27.

276 "funny head-gear": Joseph Bennett, *Letters from Bayreuth* (London, 1877), 23.

276 "at last 'arrived' ": Percy A. Scholes, *The Mirror of Music, 1844–1944: A Century of Musical Life in Britain* (London, 1947), 1: 250.

277 "the cobbler's bellowing": Quoted in E. T. Cook, *The Life of John Ruskin* (London, 1911), 2: 457.

277 "messiah of a new age": J. F. Rowbotham, "The Wagner Bubble," *Nineteenth Century* 24 (October 1888): 501.

278 "movements of the soul": Quoted in Raymond Furness, *Wagner and Literature* (New York, 1982), 142.

278 "device in literature": Quoted in E. K. Brown, *Rhythm in the Novel* (Toronto, 1950), 28.

278 "stuff of Shavian drama": Arthur Ganz, "The Playwright as Perfect Wag-

nerite: Motifs from the Music Dramas in the Theatre of Bernard Shaw," *Comparative Drama* 13 (1979): 189.

278 "Tristan's holy night": Letter to James Gibbons Huneker, dated April 6, 1904, in Shaw, *Collected Letters, 1898–1910,* ed. Dan H. Laurence (London, 1972), 415.

278 "Harmony. . . . Amen!": Quoted in *Richard Wagner's Prose Works,* trans. William Ashton Ellis (London, 1898), 7: 66–67.

280 "an imperfect one": Bentley, *A Century of Hero-Worship,* 2d ed. (Boston, 1957), 181.

284 "consoles me somewhat": *The Letters of Aubrey Beardsley,* eds. Henry Maas, J. L. Duncan, and W. G. Good (Rutherford, NJ, 1970), 171.

284 "elaborate version": *The Letters of Aubrey Beardsley,* 164.

284–85 "giants against gods": George Moore, "Nineness in the Oneness," *Chesterian* 1 ns (September 1919); and *Century Magazine* 99 (November 1919), 65.

285 "the death of Wagner": Letter to Churchill Osborne, dated March 1, 1883, in *Arthur Symons: Selected Letters, 1880–1935,* eds. Karl Beckson and John M. Munro (Iowa City, 1989), 11.

285 "inspiring enthusiasm of art": Havelock Ellis, *Impressions and Comments, Second Series* (Boston, 1923) 6–8.

285 "a new kind of ecstasy": Arthur Symons, "Bayreuth: Notes on Wagner," *Dome* (September 1899); rpt. in part II of "Notes on Wagner at Bayreuth," *Plays, Acting and Music,* 2d ed. (London, 1909), 300–1.

285–86 "sweet shame is dead": "Parsifal," *Images of Good and Evil* (1900); rpt. in *The Collected Works of Arthur Symons* (1924; New York, 1973), 2: 108.

286 "arts are but one Art": W. B. Yeats, "The Theatre," *Ideas of Good and Evil* (1903); rpt. in *Essays and Introductions* (New York, 1961), 167.

287 "without human characters": *The Letters of W. B. Yeats,* ed. Allan Wade (London, 1954), 425.

288 "before been brought": Arthur Symons, "The Ideas of Richard Wagner," *Quarterly Review* (July 1905); rpt. in *Studies in Seven Arts* (London, 1906), 297.

288 "I have seen": Letter to Arthur Symons, dated September 10 [1905], in *Yeats Letters,* ed. Allan Wade, 460.

289 "know something about Wagner": John DiGaetani, *Richard Wagner and the Modern British Novel* (Rutherford, NJ, 1978), 110.

289 "great black cloaks": "The Opera," *Times* (April 24, 1909); rpt. in *The Essays of Virginia Woolf,* ed. Andrew McNeillie (San Diego, 1986), 1: 271.

289 "overwhelming unity": "The Impressions at Bayreuth," *Times* (August 21, 1909); rpt. in *The Essays of Virginia Woolf,* 1: 289.

289 "pretend to believe still": Letter to Katherine Cox, dated May 16 [1913], in *The Letters of Virginia Woolf,* ed. Nigel Nicholson (New York 1976), 2: 26.

291 "seen at Covent Garden": Harold Rosenthal, *Two Centuries of Opera at Covent Garden* (London, 1958), 381.

13: In the Troughs of Zolaism

292   "chief precursor of Naturalism": Clarence R. Decker, *The Victorian Conscience* (New York, 1952), 49.

293   "publication in our columns": Swinburne, "Note on a Question of the Hour," *Athenaeum,* June 16, 1877: 767–68.

294   the term *naturalism:* See Haskell Block, "Introduction: The Problem of Naturalism," *Naturalistic Triptych: The Fictive and the Real in Zola, Mann, and Dreiser* (New York, 1970), 3–15.

294   "give them to us": Zola, *The Experimental Novel* (1880; New York, 1964), 9, 20–21.

295   "up to my waist": Quoted in Block, 10.

295   "serious and honest": Letter to William Dean Howells, dated February 21, 1884, in *Henry James Letters,* ed. Leon Edel (Cambridge, Mass., 1980), 3: 28.

295   "quite the Naturalist": Letter to Thomas Sergeant Perry, dated December 12 [1884], in James, *Letters,* 3: 61.

296   "blow on the head": Moore, *Confessions of a Young Man,* ed. Susan Dick (1888; Montreal, 1972), 94.

296   "height of the ambition": Moore, 95.

297   "without my Mudie": Quoted in Guinevere L. Griest, *Mudie's Circulating Library and the Victorian Novel* (Bloomington, Indiana, 1970), xiv.

297   "A New Censorship of Literature": Reprinted, with letters to the editor, in Moore, *Literature at Nurse, or Circulating Morals: A Polemic on Victorian Censorship,* ed. Pierre Coustillas (Hassocks, Surrey, 1976), 27–32.

301   *Pernicious Literature:* Reprinted in *Documents of Modern Literary Realism,* ed. George Becker (Princeton, 1963), 351–82.

301   "community at large": Quoted in Ernest Alfred Vizetelly, *Emile Zola: Novelist and Reformer, An Account of His Life and Work* (London, 1904), 258–59.

301   "corrupting all who read him!": Vizetelly, 258.

301   "books for translation": Quoted in Vizetelly, 261.

302   "something akin to a sty": *Hansard Parliamentary Debates,* 3d. ser. (London, 1888), 325: 708–09.

303   "writers of the past": Quoted in Vizetelly, 273.

303   "an elevated thought": As reported by Vizetelly, 279.

303   "We think so": Quoted in Graham King, *Garden of Zola: Emile Zola and his Novels for English Readers* (London, 1978), 242.

304   "Candour in English Fiction": Reprinted in *Thomas Hardy's Personal Writings,* ed. Harold Orel (Lawrence, Kansas, 1966), 125–33.

304   "to its spiritual side": Letter to Florence Henniker, dated March 31, 1897, in *The Collected Letters of Thomas Hardy,* eds. Richard Little Purdy and Michael Millgate (Oxford, 1980), 2: 157.

305   "questioned there, almost denied": Quoted in Vizetelly, 324.

305   "thousands of young souls elsewhere": Quoted in Vizetelly, 337.

307   "in the last twenty years": George Moore, "The Royal Academy Exhibition," *Fortnightly Review* (June 1892); incorporated in Moore, "Our Academicians," *Modern Painting* (London, 1893), 116–17.

307   "in the *Westminster Gazette*": George Moore, *A Communication to My Friends* (London, 1933), 77.

308 "for that matter in race": Beatrice Webb, *My Apprenticeship* (1926; London 1950), 35–36.

309 "predatory elements of society": Earl of Pembroke, "An Address to the Liberty and Property Defence League," *National Review* 5 (August 1885): 800.

310 "masquerading as a fatalist": Michael Collie, "George Gissing, Cosmopolitan," *English Studies in Canada* 7 (Summer 1981): 157.

310 "isolated among barbarians": George Orwell, "George Gissing," *London Magazine* (June 1960); rpt. in *Collected Articles on George Gissing,* ed. Pierre Coustillas (London, 1968). 50–57.

310 "revenge in artistic work": Letter to Algernon Gissing dated June 12, 1884, in *Letters of George Gissing to Members of His Family* (London, 1927), 138–39.

311 "vision he brings": Israel Zangwill, *Without Prejudice* (London, 1896), 83.

312 "no glossing over": Quoted from a *Daily News* (London) interview in Peter Keating, *The Working Classes in Victorian Fiction* (London, 1971), 172.

313 "into the simple": William Empson, *Some Versions of Pastoral* (London, 1935), 23.

314 "stretches at his feet": C. F. G. Masterman, *The Condition of England* (London, 1909), 72.

315 "an intelligent being": Quoted in Decker, 19.

315–16 "as in old times: W. B. Yeats, "The Symbolism of Poetry," *Dome* (April 1900); rpt. in *Essays and Introductions* (New York, 1968), 155, 162.

14: The Dance of the Occult Mysteries

317 "thought of controlling it": See John Tyndall, *Fragments of Science* (London, 1892) 2: 197.

317 "earth to heaven": Robert Browning, "Parleyings with Gerard de Lairesse," *Parleyings with Certain People of Importance in Their Day* (London, 1887), 121.

318 "a war-cry": Richard Whittington-Egan and Geoffrey Smerdon, *The Quest of the Golden Boy: The Life and Letters of Richard Le Gallienne* (Barre, Mass., 1962), 209.

318 "ignorant and homeless child": Havelock Ellis, *The Dance of Life* (London, 1923), 199.

319 "and nothing matters": Letter to R. B. Cunninghame Graham, dated December 20, 1897, in *The Collected Letters of Joseph Conrad,* eds. Frederick R. Karl and Laurence Davies (Cambridge, Eng., 1983), 2: 425.

319 "church of poetic tradition": *The Autobiography of William Butler Yeats* (New York, 1965), 77.

320 "shall I paint": Quoted in Rita Wellmann, *Victoria Royal* (New York, 1939), 296.

320 "musician, and the artist": W. B. Yeats, "Magic," *Essays and Introductions* (New York, 1961), 49.

321 *"how* embarrassing": W. H. Auden, "Yeats as an Example," *Kenyon Review* (Spring 1948); rpt. in *The Permanence of Yeats,* eds. James Hall and Martin Steinman (New York, 1950), 311.

321   "were but literal truth": Yeats, *Autobiography*, 60.

322   "secret fanaticism": Quoted in Richard Ellmann, *Yeats: The Man and the Masks* (New York, 1958), 44.

322   "stars that pass": Yeats, *Crossways* (1889); rpt. in *The Poems*, ed. Richard Finneran, vol. 1 of *The Collected Works of W. B. Yeats* (New York, 1989), 7–8.

323   "I have to describe": Quoted in Geoffrey A. Barborka, *H. P. Blavatsky, Tibet and Tulku* (Adyar, 1966), 204.

323   "imposters in history": Quoted in John Symonds, *Madame Blavatsky: Medium and Magician* (London, 1959), 222.

323   "trickery and hypocrisy": Arthur H. Nethercot, *The First Five Lives of Annie Besant* (Chicago, 1960), 286.

324   "humour and audacious power": Yeats, *Autobiography*, 117.

324   "perpetually rolling cigarettes": Yeats, *Memoirs*, ed. Denis Donoghue (New York, 1973), 24.

324   "sleeps in her coffin": Yeats, *Autobiography*, 117.

324   "I have been through it": Quoted in Yeats, *Memoirs*, 25.

324   "becoming a convert": Ernest Rhys, *Wales England Wed* (London, 1940), 105–06.

324   "all Theosophical matters": Quoted in Mary Catherine Flannery, *Yeats and Magic: The Earlier Works* (New York, 1978), 24.

325   "members of the Golden Dawn": George Mills Harper, *Yeats's Golden Dawn* (New York, 1974), 8.

325   the occult rose: See Lothar Hönnighausen, *The Symbolist Tradition in English Literature: A Study of Pre-Raphaelitism and Fin de Siècle* (1971; English trans., Cambridge, Eng., 1988), 242–45.

325   "heap of ancient ruins": Yeats, *Autobiography*, 125.

325   "a figure of romance": Yeats, *Autobiography*, 123.

325   "subconscious memory": Yeats, *Autobiography*, 124.

326   "badges at initiation ceremonies": Maud Gonne MacBride, *A Servant of the Queen*, 2d ed. (Dublin, 1950), 247–48.

327   "Magician of extraordinary attainments": *The Confessions of Aleister Crowley*, eds. John Symonds and Kenneth Grant (London, 1969), 188.

327   "amid great poverty": Yeats, *Autobiography*, 124.

327   "a mad person": Letter to Lady Gregory, dated April 25, [1900], *The Letters of W. B. Yeats*, ed. Allan Wade (London, 1954), 340.

327   "dagger at his side": From a Golden Dawn document in Harper, 213.

328   "realist of the imagination": W. B. Yeats, Part I, "William Blake and His Illustrations to the *Divine Comedy*," *Savoy* (July 1896) rpt. in *Essays and Introductions*, 119.

328   "we name God": *The Works of William Blake*, eds. W. B. Yeats and Edwin J. Ellis (London, 1893), 1: 24.

328   "the universal mood": *The Works of William Blake*, 1: 242–43.

328–29 "insomnia which is God": *Images of Good and Evil* (1899); rpt. in *The Collected Works of Arthur Symons* (1924; New York, 1973), 2: 106.

329   "Eternity in an hour": William Blake, "Auguries of Innocence" (ca. 1807); rpt. in *The Complete Writings of William Blake*, ed. Geoffrey Keynes (Oxford, 1966), 431.

329   "break into fragments": Yeats, *Autobiography*, 129.

329   "great art with symbol": Yeats, *Essays and Introductions,* 116.
329   "begining in the world": Letter to John O'Leary [ca. late July 1892], in *The Collected Letters of W. B. Yeats,* eds. John Kelly and Eric Domville (Oxford, 1986), 1: 303.
329–30   "universe upon its point": W. B. Yeats, "The Poet of Ballyshannon," *Letters to the New Island,* eds. George Bornstein and Hugh Witemeyer, vol. 7 of *The Collected Works of W. B. Yeats* (New York, 1989), 78.
330   "everything is a symbol": *Fairy and Folk Tales of the Irish Peasantry,* ed. W. B. Yeats (London, 1888), xii.
331   "opposite of what you mean": George Moore, *Confessions of a Young Man,* ed. Susan Dick (1888; Montreal, 1972), 85.
331   "sort of artistic 'dandyism' ": Arthur Symons, "Bonheur," *Academy* (April 18, 1891); rpt. in *Colour Studies in Paris* (London, 1918), 206.
331   "robin's little homily": George Moore, *Memoirs of My Dead Life* (London, 1921), 86.
332   "shadow in the night": Arthur Symons, *London Nights* (1895); rpt. in *The Collected Works,* 1: 190–91.
332   "lyrics of our time": *Uncollected Prose of W. B. Yeats, 1897–1939,* eds. John P. Frayne and Colton Johnson (New York, 1976), 2: 40.
332   "dance in the period": Hönnighausen, *The Symbolist Tradition in English Literature,* 240.
332   "her imagined being": Arthur Symons, "The World as Ballet," *Studies in Seven Arts* (New York, 1907) 391; rpt. in *The Collected Works,* 9: 24–26.
333   "noble and severe art": Letter to Stephane Mallarmé [early November 1891], in *The Letters of Oscar Wilde,* ed. Rupert Hart-Davis (New York, 1962), 297.
334   "artistic impulses be lost": Gosse's review was reprinted as "Symbolism and M. Stéphane Mallarmé" in his *Questions at Issue* (London, 1893), 219–34.
335   "great success": Edmund Gosse, "A First Sight of Verlaine," *The Savoy,* No. 2 (April 1896): 113–16.
335   "French men of letters": Letter to John Quinn, dated February 9, [1894], in Yeats, *Collected Letters,* 1: 379.
335   "yet escape the bonfire": "Verlaine in 1894," *Savoy* (April 1896); rpt. in *Uncollected Prose by W. B. Yeats, 1886–1896,* ed. John P. Frayne (New York, 1970), 1: 398–99.
335–36   "which are ever permanent": Yeats, "A Symbolical Drama in Paris," *Bookman* (April 1894); rpt. in *Uncollected Prose,* 1: 322–23.
336   "verses of those years": Yeats, *Autobiography,* 214. See Bruce Morris, "Elaborate Form: Symons, Yeats, and Mallarmé," *Yeats: An Annual of Critical and Textual Studies* 4 (1986): 99–119.
336   "achieved civilisation": Arthur Symons, "A Symbolist Farce," *Saturday Review* (December 16, 1896); rpt., rev. in *The Memoirs of Arthur Symons: Life and Art in the 1890s,* ed. Karl Beckson (University Park, Pa., 1977), 200–2.
336–37   "Savage God": Yeats, *Autobiography,* 233–34.
339   "not with things": W. B. Yeats, "The Autumn of the Flesh," *Daily Express* (December 3, 1898); rpt. as "The Autumn of the Body" in *Essays and Introductions,* 191–93.

339   "new to modern poetry": Arthur Symons, "Mr. Yeats as a Lyric Poet,"
       Saturday Review (May 6, 1899); rpt., rev. as "Mr. W. B. Yeats," Part I,
       Studies in Prose and Verse (London, 1904) and in *W. B. Yeats: The Critical
       Heritage*, ed. A. Norman Jeffares (London, 1977), 112.

341   "plain reader be damned": Quoted in Renato Poggioli, *The Theory of the
       Avant-Garde* (Cambridge, Mass., 1968), 38.

341   "deadly to the fool": For an account of Symons's ambivalence towards
       Symbolist poetry, see Karl Beckson, "Symons, Yeats, and the Symbolist
       Movement," *Victorian Poetry* 28 (Autumn/Winter 1990): 125–33.

341   "lifelong passion for literature": Letter from Edmund Gosse to Arthur
       Symons, dated March 7, 1900, in *Arthur Symons: Selected Letters, 1880–1935*,
       eds. Karl Beckson and John M. Munro (Iowa City, 1989), 147.

342   "unfolded in symbols": W. B. Yeats, "The Symbolism of Poetry," *Dome*
       (April 1900); rpt. in *Essays and Introductions*, 156–57.

342   "a sort of god": Mary Colum, *Life and the Dream* (London, 1947), 258.

342   other Symbolist poets: C. P. Curren, *James Joyce Remembered* (New York,
       1968), 31.

342   "wholly new feelings": T. S. Eliot, *The Sacred Wood* (London, 1920) 5.

342   "course of my life": [Review by T. S. Eliot of Peter Quennell's *Baudelaire
       and the Symbolists*] *Criterion* 9 (1930): 357.

342   "Rimbodd" and "Boddelaire": Colum, *Life and the Dream*, 258.

343   "Loom of Dreams": First published in the *Saturday Review* (August 25,
       1900); rpt. in *The Collected Works of Arthur Symons* (1924; New York,
       1973), 2: 123.

15: Empire Builders and Destroyers

344   "religion and their freedom": Quoted in Elie Halevy, *A History of the En-
       glish People in the Nineteenth Century: Victorian Years, 1841–1895* (New
       York, 1951), 4: 411.

344–45   "England by land and sea": Quoted in John Marlowe, *Cecil Rhodes: The
       Anatomy of Empire* (London, 1972), 9.

345   "in harness with Mammon": Bernard Porter, *The Lion's Share: A Short
       History of British Imperialism, 1850–1983* (London, 1984), 6.

345   "ideology or political faith": Patrick Brantlinger, *Rule of Darkness: British
       Literature and Imperialism, 1830–1914* (Ithaca, NY, 1988), 228.

347   "you must become imperialists": Quoted in Brantlinger, 34.

347   "authority at home and abroad": Brantlinger, 35.

350–51   "should dominate in Africa": H. Rider Haggard quoted in the *Pall Mall
       Gazette*, (April 24, 1894): 8.

351   "the hair to rise": H. Rider Haggard, *Days of My Life* (London, 1926), 1:
       241.

351–52   "immortality of our emotions": Sigmund Freud, *The Interpretation of
       Dreams*, trans. and ed., James Strachey (1900; New York, n.d.), 453.

352   "and most naïve form": Carl Jung, *The Symbolic Life*, trans. R. F. C. Hull
       (Princeton, 1980), 545.

353   "paved with them": Quoted in "Rudyard Kipling," *African Review*, May
       21, 1898: 311–12.

353   " 'scoop' them out": *African Review,* May 21, 1898: 312.

356   "hither with jealousy": Letter to Robert Louis Stevenson, dated March 21, 1890, in *Henry James Letters,* ed. Leon Edel (Cambridge, Mass., 1980), 3: 272–73.

356   "way of pretending": Robert Kiely, *Robert Louis Stevenson and the Fiction of Adventure* (Cambridge, Mass., 1965), 38.

357   "and commonplace failures": Andrew Lang, "The Supernatural in Fiction," *Adventures among Books* (London, 1905), 279–80.

357   "trampling, violent story": Letter to Marcel Schwob, dated August 19, 1890, in *The Letters of Robert Louis Stevenson,* ed. Sidney Colvin (New York, 1911), 3: 208.

357   "grimy, and as hateful": Stevenson, *Letters,* 4: 184.

358   "world-wide ambitions": Conrad, "Autocracy and War" (1905), in *Notes on Life and Letters* (London, 1921), 106.

359   "this century of progress": Quoted in Neal Ascherson, *The King Incorporated: Leopold II in the Age of Trusts* (London, 1963), 94.

359   "has generally been avoided": *Hansard Parliamentary Debates,* 3d. ser. (London, 1888), 324: 1709.

361   "not topically treated": Letter to William Blackwood, dated December 31, 1898, in *The Collected Letters of Joseph Conrad,* eds. Frederick R. Karl and Laurence Davies (Cambridge, Eng., 1986), 2: 140.

362   "idea without a future": Letter to R. B. Cunninghame Graham, dated February 8, 1899, in Conrad, *Collected Letters,* 2: 160–61.

362   "non-ethical energies": Lionel Trilling, *Beyond Culture* (New York, 1965), 19.

365   "mercy of the invader": Quoted in I. F. Clarke, *Voices Prophesying War, 1763–1984* (London, 1966), 112.

366   "could close its ears": Quoted in Arthur J. Marder, *The Anatomy of British Sea Power: A History of British Naval Policy in the Pre-Dreadnought Era, 1880–1905* (1940; Hamden, Conn., 1964), 121.

367   "an opportunistic panicmonger": Cecil D. Eby, *The Road to Armageddon: The Martial Spirit in English Popular Literature, 1870–1914* (Durham, NC, 1987), 26.

369   "merely sick with it": Letter to Wilfrid Meynell [July 25, 1900?], in *The Letters of Francis Thompson,* ed. John Evangelist Walsh (New York, 1969), 210.

369   "feats of peculiar atrocity": Quoted in Norman MacKenzie and Jeanne MacKenzie, *The Time Traveler: The Life of H. G. Wells* (London, 1973), 113.

370   "God Bless them!": Quoted in Stanley Weintraub, *Victoria: An Intimate Biography* (New York, 1987), 581.

370   "boys were imperialists": Quoted in John M. MacKenzie, *Propaganda and Empire: The Manipulation of British Public Opinion, 1880–1960* (Manchester, Eng., 1984), 194.

371   "power and of glory": Walter Besant, "Is it the Voice of the Hooligan?" *Contemporary Review* (January 1900); rpt. in *Kipling: The Critical Heritage,* ed. Roger Lancelyn Green (New York, 1971), 257.

372   "for noble Britain": Sir Lewis Morris, "For Britain: A Soldier's Song," *Harvest Tide* (London, 1901), 138.

372   "pride of heart": W. E. Henley, *For England's Sake: Verses and Songs in Time of War* (London, 1900), 3.

373   "humanitarian opposition to war": M. Van Wyk Smith, *Drummer Hodge: The Poetry of the Anglo-Boer War (1899–1902)* (Oxford, 1978), 3.

374   "seventeenth-century puritanism": Entry for September 10, 1899, *The Diary of Beatrice Webb,* eds. Norman MacKenzie and Jeanne MacKenzie (Cambridge, Mass., 1983), 2: 165.

374   "within the British Empire": Entry for October 30, 1899, *The Diary of Beatrice Webb,* 2: 166.

374   "public-spirited Imperialism": Quoted in Norman MacKenzie and Jeanne MacKenzie, *The Fabians* (New York, 1977), 272.

376   "over the place haphazardly": Quoted in MacKenzie and MacKenzie, *The Time Traveler,* 101.

376   "more and more powerful": *Parliamentary Debates* 4th ser., 89 (January 25, 1901): 10.

376   "come upon us": *Parliamentary Debates* 4th ser., 89: 19–20.

377   "acutely for several years": H. G. Wells, *The Wife of Sir Isaac Harman* (London, 1914), 259.

378   "possibility of disaster": Quoted in Samuel Hynes, *The Edwardian Turn of Mind* (Princeton, 1968), 26.

Epilogue

380   "suffer for being 'new' ": Letter to William Blackwood, dated May 31, 1902, in *The Collected Letters of Joseph Conrad,* vol. 2, eds. Frederick R. Karl and Laurence Davies (Cambridge, Eng., 1986), 418.

380   "myself to the multitude?": Arthur Symons, "Stéphane Mallarmé," *The Symbolist Movement in Literature* (1900); rpt. in *The Collected Works of Arthur Symons* (1924; New York, 1973), 8: 173.

380   "human nature changed": "Character in Fiction," *Criterion* (July 1924); rpt. in *The Essays of Virginia Woolf,* ed. Andrew McNeillie (New York, 1988), 3: 421.

381   "in the last twenty years": George Moore, *Modern Painting* (London, 1893), 116–17.

381   "causal relations would disappear": John Tyndall, *Fragments of Science* (London, 1892), 2: 104.

382   "sciences are *verified* poems": Quoted in Tess Cosslett, *The "Scientific Movement" and Victorian Literature* (New York, 1982), 26.

382   "he created it": Carl Woodring, *Nature into Art: Cultural Transformations in Nineteenth-Century Britain* (Cambridge, Mass., 1989), 189.

382   "dream of a world": Walter Pater, "Conclusion," *Studies in the History of the Renaissance* (1873); rpt. in *Walter Pater: Three Major Texts,* ed. William F. Buckler (New York, 1986), 156.

382   "we can never know": Tyndall, 2: 193.

382   "consciousness to the end": Virginia Woolf, "Modern Novels," *Times Literary Supplement* (London, April 10, 1919); rpt., rev. as "Modern Fiction," *The Common Reader* (London, 1925) and *Collected Essays* (London, 1967), 2: 106.

Selective Chronology

[Note: Plays listed under date of first performance or first printing, whichever occurred first.]

Biography	The Arts	History/Science
1880		
George Eliot dies	George Gissing, *Workers in the Dawn*	Gladstone becomes prime minister
Lytton Strachey is born	Wilde, *Vera; or, the Nihilists*	Transvaal declares its independence of Britain
		Elementary education made compulsory
1881		
Carlyle dies	Gilbert and Sullivan, *Patience*	First Boer War begins
Disraeli dies	D'Oyly Carte builds Savoy Theatre, the first lit by electricity	Social Democratic Federation founded
Picasso is born	Moore, *Pagan Poems*	
	Stevenson, *Treasure Island* (serialized; book 1883)	
	Wilde, *Poems*	
	Rossetti, *Ballads and Sonnets*	
1882		
Virginia Woolf is born	Wilde lectures in USA and Canada on the Aesthetic Movement	Married Women's Property Act passed
James Joyce is born	Swinburne, *Tristram of Lyonesse and Other Poems*	Society of Psychical Research founded
Rossetti dies		British occupy Egypt and Sudan
Darwin dies		Channel tunnel proposed
Trollope dies		

Biography	The Arts	History/Science
1883		
Wagner dies	Carpenter, *Towards*	
Marx dies	*Democracy* (–1902)	
	Meredith, *Poems and*	
	Lyrics of the Joy of Earth	
	Schreiner, *The Story of an*	
	African Farm	
	Nietzsche, *Thus Spake*	
	Zarathustra (trans.)	
	Moore, *A Modern Lover*	
1884		
	Carpenter, *Towards*	Fabian Society founded
	Democracy (Part 1)	Socialist League
	Moore, *A Mummer's*	founded
	Wife	First steam turbine to
	Huysmans, *A Rebours*	make electricity
	Jones, *Saints and Sinners*	Third Reform Bill
	Century Guild Hobby	passed
	Horse (–1894)	
1885		
D. H. Lawrence is born	Whistler, "Ten	Congo Free State
Dictionary of National	O'Clock"	becomes Leopold II's
Biography is begun by	Pater, *Marius the*	possession
Leslie Stephen	*Epicurean*	Gladstone resigns
Pound is born	Haggard, *King Solomon's*	Lord Salisbury succeeds
	Mines	as prime minister
	Gilbert and Sullivan,	Gold discovered in
	Mikado	Transvaal
	Moore, *Literature at*	Internal combustion
	Nurse	engine invented
	Burton, *Arabian Nights*	Hodgson reports on
	Stevenson, *The*	Madame Blavatsky
	Dynamiter	
	Revue wagnérienne	
	(–1888)	

Biography	The Arts	History/Science
1886		
	Morris, *A Dream of John Ball* (serialized; book 1888)	Gladstone again becomes prime minister (Feb.)
	New English Art Club founded by Whistler, Sickert, and others	Salisbury again becomes prime minister (Aug.)
	Gissing, *Demos*	Marx, *Capital* (first English trans., vol. 1)
	Stevenson, *Dr Jekyll and Mr Hyde*	Gladstone's Home Rule Bill for Ireland loses
	James, *The Princess Casamassima*	
1887		
	Antoine founds Théâtre Libre in Paris	Victoria's Golden Jubilee occurs
	Haggard, *Allan Quatermain*	Bloody Sunday takes place in Trafalgar Square
	Haggard, *She*	
	Doyle, *A Study in Scarlet*	
	Pater, *Imaginary Portraits*	
1888		
Matthew Arnold dies	Moore, *Confessions of a Young Man*	Rhodes amalgamates Kimberley diamond companies
T. S. Eliot is born	Zola, *La Terre* (trans.)	Vizetelly trial occurs
	Hardy, *Wessex Tales*	Blavatsky, *The Secret Doctrine*
1889		
Browning dies	Moore, *Mike Fletcher*	London Dock Strike occurs
Hopkins dies	Yeats, *The Wanderings of Oisin*	Charles Booth, *Life and Labour of the People in London* (–1903)
	Gissing, *The Nether World*	Vizetelly goes to prison
	James, *The Tragic Muse* (serialized; book 1890)	
	Jerome, *Three Men in a Boat*	
	Ibsen, *A Doll's House* (in London)	

Biography	The Arts	History/Science
	Pater, *Appreciations* Wilde, "Decay of Lying" (rpt. in *Intentions,* 1891) Pinero, *The Profligate Dial* (–1897)	
1890 Newman dies Rimbaud dies	Rhymers' Club founded Morris founds Kelmscott Press Morris, *News from Nowhere* (serialized; book 1891) Wilde, *The Picture of Dorian Gray* (enlarged 1891) Ellis, *The New Spirit* Kipling, *The Light That Failed* (rev. 1891) Ibsen, *Hedda Gabler* Whistler, *The Gentle Art of Making Enemies*	Rhodes becomes premier of Cape Colony Parnell/O'Shea divorce case is tried William Booth, *In Darkest England and the Way Out* Frazer, *The Golden Bough* (–1914)
1891	Wilde, "The Soul of Man under Socialism" (book 1895) Doyle, *Adventures of Sherlock Holmes* begins in *Strand Magazine* (book 1892) Grein founds Independent Theatre Society Ibsen, *Ghosts* (in London) Shaw, *The Quintessence of Ibsenism* Wilde, *Intentions* Gissing, *New Grub Street* Hardy, *Tess of the d'Urbervilles*	Lombroso, *The Man of Genius* (trans.)

Biography	The Arts	History/Science
1892		
Whitman dies	Kipling, *Barrack-Room Ballads*	Gladstone again becomes prime minister
Tennyson dies	Wilde, *Lady Windermere's Fan*	Irish Literary Society founded in London
	The Book of the Rhymers' Club	
	Shaw, *Widowers' Houses*	
	Zangwill, *Children of the Ghetto*	
	Yeats, *The Countess Kathleen*	
	Le Gallienne, *English Poems*	
	Nicholson, *Love in Earnest*	
	Stevenson, *The Beach of Falesá* (serialized; book 1893)	
1893		
Wilfred Owen is born	Pinero, *The Second Mrs. Tanqueray*	Independent Labour Party founded in Manchester
Symonds dies	Wilde, *A Woman of No Importance*	
	Wilde, *Salomé* (in French)	
	Gray, *Silverpoints*	
	Yeats, *The Celtic Twilight*	
	Gissing, *The Odd Women*	
	Symonds, *In the Key of Blue*	
	The Works of William Blake (Yeats and Edwin Ellis, editors)	
	Verlaine lectures in London	
	Teleny; or the Reverse of the Medal (anon.)	
	Stevenson, *The Ebb-Tide* (serialized; book 1894)	

Biography	The Arts	History/Science
1894		
Pater dies	Shaw, *Arms and the Man*	Gladstone resigns;
Stevenson dies	*Yellow Book* (−1897)	Rosebery becomes
	The Second Book of the Rhymers' Club	new prime minister
	Wilde, *Salome* (trans.)	Dreyfus arrested,
	Moore, *Esther Waters*	charged with treason
	Kipling, *The Jungle Book*	
	Hichens, *The Green Carnation*	
	Morrison, *Tales of Mean Streets*	
	Gissing, *In the Year of Jubilee*	
	Grundy, *The New Woman*	
	Meredith, *Lord Ormond and His Aminta*	
	Chameleon (periodical)	
	Du Maurier, *Trilby*	
	Villiers de l'Isle-Adam, *Axël* (in Paris)	
1895		
T. H. Huxley dies	Wilde, *An Ideal Husband*	Wilde's three trials and
	Wilde, *The Importance of Being Earnest*	conviction take place
	Symons, *London Nights*	London School of Economics founded
	Hardy, *Jude the Obscure*	Röentgen discovers
	Conrad, *Almayer's Folly*	X-rays
	Nordau, *Degeneration* (trans.)	Marconi invents wireless telegraphy
	Wells, *The Time Machine*	Lumière brothers devise
	Pageant (−1896)	the cinematograph
	Allen, *The Woman Who Did*	Jameson raids the Transvaal
	Davidson, *Earl Lavender*	
	Pinero, *The Notorious Mrs. Ebbsmith*	
	Shaw, "A Degenerate's View of Nordau" (book, rev. as *The Sanity of Art,* 1908)	
	Carpenter, *Homogenic Love*	

Biography	The Arts	History/Science
1896		
Verlaine dies	*Savoy* (periodical)	Austin named poet
Morris dies	Jones, *Michael and His*	laureate
Crackanthorpe dies	*Angel*	London School of
Patmore dies	Housman, *A Shropshire*	Economics opens
	Lad	A. H. Becquerel
	Beerbohm, *The Works of*	discovers radioactivity
	Max Beerbohm	
	Morrison, *A Child of the*	
	Jago	
	Morris and Burne-Jones	
	design the Kelmscott	
	Chaucer	
	Dowson, *Verses*	
	Nietzsche, *Thus Spake*	
	Zarathustra (trans.)	
	Seaman, *The Battle of the*	
	Bays	
	Jarry, *Ubu Roi* (in Paris)	
	Beardsley, *Venus and*	
	Tannhäuser	
1897		
	Yeats, *The Secret Rose*	Victoria's Diamond
	Maugham, *Liza of*	Jubilee takes place
	Lambeth	Ellis, *Sexual Inversion*
	Stoker, *Dracula*	J. J. Thompson discovers
	Tate Gallery opens	the electron
	Shaw, *Candida*	
	Wells, *The Invisible Man*	
	New Century Theatre	
	Company founded	
	Dome (–1900)	
	Gissing, *The Whirlpool*	
	Wells, *The War of the*	
	Worlds (serialized;	
	book 1898)	
	Conrad, *The Nigger of the*	
	"Narcissus"	

Biography	The Arts	History/Science
1898		
Mallarmé dies	Shaw, *Mrs. Warren's Profession*	Zola's open letter, "J'Accuse ..." is
Beardsley dies	Shaw, *The Philanderer*	published.
Lewis Carroll dies	Shaw, *Plays Pleasant and Unpleasant*	Forgery admitted in Dreyfus case
	Shaw, *The Perfect Wagnerite*	
	Moore, *Evelyn Innes*	
	Wilde, *The Ballad of Reading Gaol*	
	Bennett, *A Man from the North*	
	Hardy, *Wessex Poems*	
1899		
Grant Allen dies	Kipling, *Stalky and Co.*	Boer War (−1902)
	Conrad, *Heart of Darkness* (serialized; book 1902)	Dreyfus pardoned
	Yeats, *The Wind among the Reeds*	
	Stage Society founded	
1900		
Ruskin dies	Symons, *The Symbolist Movement in Literature*	Max Planck devises quantum theory.
Dowson dies	Conrad, *Lord Jim*	British Labour Party
Nietzsche dies	Yeats, *The Shadowy Waters*	founded
Wilde dies		Freud, *The Interpretation of Dreams*
		Fabianism and the Empire (Shaw, editor)
		Transvaal annexed by Britain
1901		
Victoria dies	Moore, *Sister Teresa*	Edward VII enthroned
Besant dies	Kipling, *Kim*	

Biography	The Arts	History/Science
1902 Rhodes dies Lord Acton dies Samuel Butler dies Lionel Johnson dies Zola dies G. A. Henty dies		Boer War ends
1903 Whistler dies Spencer dies Gissing dies Henley dies	Butler, *The Way of All Flesh* James, *The Ambassadors*	Mrs. Pankhurst founds Women's Social and Political Union
1904 Stanley dies	Shaw, *John Bull's Other Island* Conrad, *Nostromo* Barrie, *Peter Pan* First Vedrenne-Barker season at Court Theatre Abbey Theatre founded	Ernest Rutherford discovers radioactivity in radium
1905 Harland dies William Sharp dies Henry Irving dies	Shaw, *Man and Superman* Shaw, *Major Barbara* Wilde, *De Profundis* (expurgated) Wells, *A Modern Utopia*	Einstein devises special theory of relativity Freud, *Three Essays on the Theory of Sexuality*
1906 Beckett born Ibsen dies	Shaw, *The Doctor's Dilemma* Galsworthy, *The Man of Property* Galsworthy, *The Silver Box*	Self-government granted to the Transvaal and Orange River colonies

Biography	The Arts	History/Science
1907		
Auden is born	Conrad, *The Secret Agent*	Baden-Powell founds
Huysmans dies	Maugham, *The Explorer*	the Boy Scouts
Francis Thompson dies	Picasso, *Les Demoiselles d'Avignon* exhibited at Cubist exhibition, Paris	
	Synge, *The Playboy of the Western World*	
1908		
"Ouida" dies	Bennett, *The Old Wives' Tale*	
	Chesterton, *The Man Who Was Thursday*	
	The Book of the Poets' Club	
	Wells, *Tono-Bungay* (serialized; book 1909)	
1909		
Swinburne dies	Wells, *Ann Veronica*	Trade Boards Act ends
Meredith dies	Shaw, *Press Cuttings*	"sweating" in
Davidson dies		industry
Synge dies		
1910		
Edward VII dies	Galsworthy, *Justice*	George V enthroned
	Fry's post-Impressionist exhibition in London	Union of South Africa becomes a dominion
	Forster, *Howards End*	

Acknowledgments

THE PLEASURE OF completing a book includes the additional pleasure of publicly acknowledging those to whose generosity and encouragement I am greatly indebted. My greatest debt is to my editor Hilary Hinzmann, who not only suggested initially that I write a book on the British 1890s but who also guided me gently and persuasively through more than three-and-a-half years of its composition. His perceptive judgments as he read successive drafts of the book contributed mightily to whatever success it may enjoy. I am indeed grateful for his patience, confidence, and friendship.

To those friends and colleagues (in this case, happily synonymous) who willingly read early drafts of various chapters, who sent me valuable material that I would not have discovered for myself, or who suggested fruitful lines of investigation, I wish to acknowledge my appreciation: G. A. Cevasco, Gloria and Harold Fromm, Edwin Gilcher, George Mills Harper, Norman Kelvin, Clinton Krauss, Bruce Morris, James G. Nelson, Pierre Coustillas, Peter Raby, Morton Seiden, John Stokes, and Martha and Albert Vogeler. I also wish to acknowledge the kindness of Carl Woodring, who had a hand in the genesis of this book.

Without such institutions as the New York Public Library and the Columbia University Library, I could not have conducted the necessary research for this book. They provided not only the necessary volumes and periodicals but also a number of illustrations contained herein. Other institutions that I wish to acknowledge for kindly providing me with photographs and permission to publish are the Library of Congress, Pierpont Morgan Library (New York), University of Bristol Library, Ashmoleon Museum of Oxford University, Greater London Photograph Library, International Museum of Photography (Rochester), Brooklyn Museum, Museum of London, Princeton University Library, Victoria and Albert Museum (London), and the Beinecke Rare Book and Manuscript Library of Yale University.

For Max Beerbohm's classic drawing, "Some Persons of 'the Nineties,' " I am grateful to Mrs. Eva Reichmann for permission to reproduce it here. I am also grateful to George Mills Harper for permission to reproduce W. T. Horton's drawing of Yeats as effete occultist, which is in his collection.

I wish, also, to express my gratitude to Robert Langenfeld, editor of *English Literature in Transition, 1880–1920,* for permission to reprint, in somewhat different form, my article originally titled "After Tennyson: The Quest for a Poet Laureate," which appeared in the Special Series, No. 4 (1990), an issue dedicated to the memory of our late colleague, Ian Fletcher, noted scholar of the 1890s.

Index